The dynamics of treason:
Boer collaboration in the South African War of 1899–1902

The dynamics of treason:
Boer collaboration in the South African War of 1899–1902

Albert Grundlingh
Translated by Bridget Theron

PROTEA BOOK HOUSE
PRETORIA
2006

The dynamics of treason:
Boer collaboration in the South African War of 1899–1902
First edition, first impression, 2006
Originally published as *Die "hendsoppers" en "joiners":*
Die rasionaal en verskynsel van verraad, 1979.
Second edition, 1999, by Protea Boekhuis

Protea Book House
PO Box 35110, Menlo Park, 0102
1067 Burnett Street, Hatfield, 0083
protea@intekom.co.za

Typography and design by Hond CC
Printed and bound by Paarl Print

ISBN 1-86919-079-3

© 1979, 1999 Afrikaans edition Albert Grundlingh
© 2006 English translation Protea Book House
© All rights reserved. No part of this book may be reproduced in any way without the permission of the publisher.

Foreword to the English edition, 2006

The original Afrikaans edition of this book, which appeared in 1979 under the title, *Die 'Hendsoppers' en 'Joiners': Die rasionaal en verskynsel van verraad*, dealt with the phenomenon of Boer collaboration during the Anglo-Boer War of 1899–1902, and addressed an issue which, over the years, has been a most controversial one in Afrikaner ranks. Allegations of treason, real or imagined, always rankle and so much more when a life-and-death struggle of a nation is perceived to be at stake. Yet treason is common in warfare and accusations of sedition abound in any war. While this book focuses specifically on the intricacies of alleged Afrikaner treason during a particularly volatile period, the analysis is also informed by an awareness of the wider context of treason.

At the time of its original publication, this book was seen to challenge the prevailing Afrikaner nationalist historiography on the war which emphasised the heroic nature of Boer resistance to rampaging British imperialism. Personally I did not regard the book as an overt challenge, but merely an attempt to provide a more rounded and multi-dimensional perspective on Boer participation (or non-participation) in the war. Afrikaner nationalist historiography has since then run its course and has lost much of its earlier purchase. Particularly after the seismographic political changes in the country, earlier Afrikaner history of the nationalist kind has been thoroughly rejected. In more extreme cases Afrikaner history, of whatever variety, has virtually been excised from the South African past, or Afrikaners are paraded as one-dimensional villains in interpretations which flatten nuance and complexity. There is a renewed need to guard against an overarching master narrative which leaves little room for the many vagaries of history and the counter narratives which seek to highlight discrepancies and anomalies, contributing ultimately to a more heterogeneous whole. Afrikaner history in particular needs to be 'normalised' and treated as the travails of a group of people whose experiences were unique in many ways, but in other ways also carry a more universal message. As in any other society Afrikaners had their heroes and dissidents; moreover, at times it is not always that simple in telling them apart. It is in such a spirit that I have attempted to investigate the phenomenon of treason.

The recent centenary of the war witnessed a renewed interest in the manifold dimensions of the most devastating conflict experienced on South African soil during the 20th century. Sparked by the centenary, new forays followed into previously neglected aspects of the war. The question of treason, however, remained untouched. This translation of the Afrikaans text makes the absorbing topic of Boer collaboration also available to a broader audience.

This book has indebted me to many people. Professionally I would like to single out Burridge Spies, former Professor of History at the University of South Africa, who guided my first tentative research into this topic. Dr Bridget Theron undertook the arduous task of translation. On a personal level Annamari Grundlingh has been an unwavering supporter of my work. I dedicate this book to her.

Albert Grundlingh
Stellenbosch
2006

Contents

List of abbreviations in notes — *page 9*
Introduction — *page 11*

Chapter 1 — page 19
The formation of a group of surrendered burghers who voluntarily laid down their arms in 1900
1. Background: the republican forces – mobilisation, discipline and demoralisation
2. The first British proclamations in the Free State and Transvaal and the annexation of the two republics
3. Surrender in the Free State and the Transvaal

Chapter 2 — page 51
Vicissitudes of the surrendered burghers and their ilk, March – December 1900
1. Republican re-commandeering
2. British treatment of the surrendered burghers and further British proclamations
3. Some surrendered burghers cross the republican borders
4. British measures to protect the surrendered burghers
5. Sporadic peace-making initiatives by the surrendered burghers and their ilk

Chapter 3 — page 117
The burgher peace committees, December 1900 – September 1901
1. Establishment of burgher peace committees
2. Work of the burgher peace committees and renewed peace initiatives in the Transvaal
3. Work of the burgher peace committees and other peace initiatives in the Free State
4. Activities of the burgher peace committees in the Cape Colony
5. Results and significance of the peace movement

Chapter 4 — page 183
The surrendered burghers from January 1901 – May 1902
1. Reasons why burghers continued to lay down their arms
2. Surrendered burghers in the concentration camps and towns
3. The oath of allegiance and the impact of the surrendered burghers on the war

Chapter 5 — page 221
In British military service: local burgher corps, guides and scouts
1. British enrolment of burghers and the question of treason
2. Local burgher corps in the Free State
3. The guides and scouts
4. Local burgher corps in the Transvaal

Chapter 6 — page 267
In British military service (continued): the National Scouts and Orange River Colony Volunteers
1 Establishment, recruitment and organisation of the National Scouts and Orange River Colony Volunteers
2 Participation and its impact

Chapter 7 — page 311
The rationale of treason and the implications of the final peace negotiations at Vereeniging
1 Motives of the rank and file
2 Motives of the leaders: the Orange River Colony Volunteers and the National Scouts
3 The Peace of Vereeniging

Chapter 8 — page 365
British assistance in South Africa after the war
1 Repatriation
2 Land settlement
3 Compensation

Chapter 9 — page 409
Afrikaner disunity after the war and the attitude of the British authority
1 Interpersonal relations within Afrikaner ranks
2 Friction in religious circles and the formation of a new church
3 The attitude of the British authority and the demise of the Scout Church

Chapter 10 — page 446
Reconciliation in Afrikaner ranks
1 Afrikaner politics as a unifying factor
2 Other factors that contributed to reconciliation

A final word – page 469

Annexure 1 — *page 472*
List of Ex-Burghers of the late O.V.S. who have served the British Army
Annexure 2 — *page 479*
Return of Ex-Burghers employed in the Field Intelligence Department, O.R. Colony District
Annexure 3 — *page 498*
Names of National Scouts No. 5 Klerksdorp Wing
Sources — *page 502*
Index — *page 518*

List of abbreviations in notes

Africa (South)	Confidential Print.
Cd.	British Parliamentary Papers published by command of the British Government.
Chamberlain Papers	Papers of Joseph Chamberlain.
CO	Colonial Office Records. (The original CO number is given first, followed by the FK number and page of the photocopy series in the National Archives, Pretoria.)
CS	Archives of the Colonial Secretary, Transvaal.
CSO	Archives of the Colonial Secretary, Orange River Colony.
CT	Archives of the Colonial Treasurer, Transvaal.
DSAB	*Dictionary of South African Biography.*
EC	Archives of the Executive Council, Transvaal.
FO	Foreign Office Records. (The original FO number is given first, followed by the microfilm number of the microfiche series in the National Archives, Pretoria.)
GOV	Archives of the Private Secretary of the Governor.
GRD	Archives of the Government Relief Department, Orange River Colony.
HC	Archives of the High Commissioner for South Africa.
IOP	Archives of the Intelligence Officer to the Military Governor, Pretoria.
KG	Archives of the *Kommandant-Generaal, Zuid-Afrikaansche Republiek* (Commandant-general of the South African Republic).
Kitchener Letters	Letters of General Lord Kitchener. (The original series number is given first, followed by the FK number and page of the photocopy series in the National Archives, Pretoria.)
KK	*Konsentrasiekampstukke* (Concentration camp items).
LAJ	Archives of the Legal Assistant to the Military Governor, Johannesburg.
Leyds Archive	W.J. Leyds Archive.
Lt. Gov.	Archives of the Lieutenant-governor of the Transvaal Colony.
MGB	Archives of the Military Governor, Bloemfontein.
MGP	Archives of the Military Governor, Pretoria.
Milner Papers	Papers of Lord Milner. (The original series number is given first, followed by the FK number and page of the photocopy series in the National Archives, Pretoria.)

N.G. Kerk	*Nederduitse Gereformeerde Kerk* (Dutch Reformed Church).
N.H. of G. Kerk	*Nederduitse Hervormde of Gereformeerde Kerk* (Dutch Reformed Church).
Official history	History of the War in South Africa 1899–1902, compiled by the direction of His Majesty's Government. Vols I & II by F. Maurice. Vol III compiled by the direction of His Majesty's Government. Vol IV by M.H. Grant.
PMO	Archives of the Provost Marshal's Office, Army Headquarters, South Africa.
PMP	Archives of the Provisional Mounted Police.
Potch	Potchefstroom University.
PSY	Archives of the Political Secretary.
RAU	Rand Afrikaans University, Johannesburg.
Roberts Papers	Papers of Field-marshal Lord Roberts. (The original WO number is given first, followed by the microfilm number of the microfiche series in the National Archives, Pretoria. In the case of a manuscript accession, the original number precedes the archival number.)
SAC Papers	South African Constabulary Papers.
SNA	Archives of the Secretary for Native Affairs, Transvaal.
SO/POW	Archives of the Staff Officer Prisoners of War, Cape Town.
SOP/Natal	Archives of the Staff Officer Prisoners of War, Natal.
Times History	L.S. Amery (ed), *The Times History of the War in South Africa 1899–1902*.
UK	University of Cape Town.
Unisa	University of South Africa, Pretoria.
UOVS	University of the Orange Free State, Bloemfontein.
UP	University of Pretoria.
US	University of Stellenbosch.
UW	University of the Witwatersrand, Johannesburg.
WO	War Office Records. (The original WO number is given first, followed by the number and the microfilm series in the National Archives, Pretoria.)
WO	Confidential Telegrams South African War, 1899–1902; Confidential Telegrams, October 1899 – October 1902.
ZAR	Zuid-Afrikaansch Republiek (South African Republic, SAR).
ZTPD	*Hooggeregshofstukke* (Supreme court items).

Introduction

This work, which covers the period from 1900 to 1907, focuses primarily on two groups of Orange Free State and Transvaal burghers: groups which, in the Boer vernacular and general usage, were known as the *hendsoppers* (burghers who surrendered voluntarily) and the *joiners* (those who fought on the British side).

For the purposes of this study a bona fide surrendered Boer can be defined as a conscripted male burgher from either of the two Boer republics, who first fought on the Boer side, after which he voluntarily withdrew from the conflict and handed over his weapons to the British military authorities. He usually signed an oath of neutrality, and did not subsequently break this oath by rejoining the Boer commandos or by later fighting on the British side. Also under scrutiny are the republican burghers who were not liable for military service, but identified themselves with those who had surrendered. Because they had not at any stage taken up arms during the war, it would be inaccurate to group them with the surrendered burghers. In instances where these people aligned themselves with the stance of the surrendered burghers, they are referred to as "their ilk", their fellow men who shared their convictions. Mention is also made of burghers liable for military service, but who, right from the outset, refused to take up arms, as well as those who throughout the entire war did not join the commandos at all. The republican burghers who, under varying degrees of military pressure on the battlefield, were taken prisoner and held in the South African or overseas prisoner-of-war camps, fall outside the scope of this study. Reference is made to them only when the historical context makes this necessary. The same applies to the *uitlanders* (foreigners) in the South African Republic and the Africans in the two Boer republics.

In time, some of the surrendered burghers went over to the British side in an active military capacity. By fighting for the British they went a step further than the surrendered burghers, who were no longer militarily active in the war after their withdrawal. There is thus a clear distinction between those who surrendered and those who entered the service of the British, and this makes closer examination of the latter group unnecessary at this stage. Because of this sharp demarcation, each group is discussed, for the period spanning the war, in a separate chapter.

Both groups did, however, have one important factor in common: they both abandoned the republican war effort. The surrendered burghers gave notice of their dissociation by withdrawing from the war from 1900 onwards, while the burghers in British military service did so in a more dramatic manner by actually fighting against their own countrymen. These two groups were in direct contrast with the bitterenders who persevered, upholding the republican ideals and continuing the struggle until 31 May 1902. Shortly before the end of the Anglo-Boer War a war correspondent for *The Times* of London predicted: "When the Anglo-Boer war has been consigned to the limbo of history and becomes subjected to the dispassionate criticism of posterity, one feature that will always command attention ... will be the active support afforded us, especially in the latter half of the campaign, by a large body of the Boers themselves."

The historiography on the Anglo-Boer War does not, however, bear this out. There are only a few documented historical works dealing specifically with the period of the Anglo-Boer War that refer in passing to this particular issue. For example, the work by M.H. Buys makes limited reference to the Transvaal burghers who deserted the republican war effort from 1900 onwards. Of more significance here is the work by S.B. Spies. In a wide-ranging study he analyses the policy of the British army command towards civilians in the two Boer republics. Under his definition of civilians he does in fact include the burghers who laid down their arms, but because of the scope of his research he does not cover all aspects which have a bearing on this group. Then too, because of the specific emphasis of his study, he gives little attention to the burghers who actually entered the service of the British military. Nevertheless his work does provide important new dimensions to the history of the Anglo-Boer War, and the author found it particularly useful. The publication by J.P. Brits is also relevant to the subject of Boer collaboration. It is an unusual diary, written by a burgher who fought on both the Boer and British sides, but although it provided a few valuable insights, it is not necessarily representative of the joiners in general.

There are some appropriately documented works that do in fact give relevant information on this aspect of the Anglo-Boer War, but these deal primarily with the post-war period. A.P.J. van Rensburg concentrates on the economic recovery of the bitterenders in the Orange River Colony and sheds light on important issues such as compensation and repatriation. He also mentions those who were not bitterenders, but naturally they are not central to his investigation. In a work which deals mainly with the reasons for the failure of the British policy in the Transvaal after the war, D.J.N. Denoon makes several challenging remarks on the topic under debate here, but otherwise it falls outside his specific field of research. The same is true of G.H.L. le May's study on British hegemony in South Africa. It was also necessary to refer to certain documented church histories because there were a few burghers who fought on the British side and who subsequently formed their own church after the war. J.A.S. Oberholster, G.D. Scholtz and C.P.H. Olivier all discuss aspects of surrender and collaboration, but as will be shown in this study, they did not fully utilise the available sources and a reinterpretation of certain issues was therefore necessary.

As far as articles are concerned, there is a short piece by V.E. Solomon based on a few secondary sources, which addresses the matter under discussion, but it is very superficial. Likewise, in a popular article A.P.J. van Rensburg touches in passing on the surrendered Boers as well as the burghers who rendered military service, while in another article he provides some interesting insight about a burgher who is particularly important in this investigation. J.L. Hattingh also throws some light on a controversial burgher who decided to surrender.

This brief overview of the historiography is evidence that, while a few authors have referred in passing to burghers who forsook the republican war effort from 1900, no comprehensive and specialised investigation on the subject has yet appeared. This study was therefore undertaken to fill this specific gap. It attempts to explore the exact nature of the circumstances in which these particular burghers found themselves during the Anglo-Boer War and in the post-war period until 1907, as well as the role they played during this time. Furthermore, the aim was to investigate why they took the action they did and the extent to which this influenced the republican war effort. In a wider perspective, this study can therefore also be seen as an investigation of the polarisation which occurred in republican ranks during the war and the impact this had on Afrikaner society in the post-war period. Despite concerted attempts to analyse the issue in detail and to provide conclusive explanations, the lack of sources on specific aspects sometimes made this difficult. Nevertheless, it is hoped that the veil obscuring the conduct of burghers who deserted the republican war effort from 1900 onwards has been lifted to some extent, thus revealing something of the dynamics of treason.

Certain criteria applied in this work demand closer attention. It is of course essential that the historian, without compromising insight, should evaluate the topic as impartially as possible for the specific period. The existence of a set of generally valid, appropriate and contemporary norms can facilitate this process and this basic blueprint was particularly useful in scrutinising events that took place during the war.

In July 1899 the representatives of 24 states, including Great Britain, signed the provisions of the first Hague Convention. The purpose of this convention was *inter alia* to lay down general rules to serve as a set of norms for the conduct of "civilised" warfare. The two Boer republics were not signatories. Non-signatories were, however, free to regard the terms of the Hague Convention as binding provided that they made a formal statement of their intention to do so to the other signatories, through the mediation of the government of the Netherlands. However, the Boer republics gave no such formal notice that they had decided to abide by these norms. Because Britain had indeed agreed to the Hague Convention and the Boers had not, this immediately begs the question whether or not the Convention was applicable to the Anglo-Boer War. The answer is that, although the provisions of the Hague Convention were not formally or technically applicable to the two warring parties, they can nevertheless be used as historical norms, because the Convention did in fact reflect the generally accepted standards of the time regarding the manner in which warfare on land should be conducted. In a letter of protest dated August 1900 the republican delegation in Europe reminded the British government of this aspect of the Hague Convention: "Although the South African republics are not party to the Convention agreement signed by other Powers, we nevertheless call upon you to adhere to the principles ... as laid down therein ... because this merely formalises what for centuries has been generally accepted in the conduct of warfare between civilised people." Although the officials in the British Colonial Office, in a somewhat high-handed manner, recommended that the protest letter should not be answered, they did not dispute the republics' right to appeal to this aspect of the Hague Convention. Sir John Ardagh, the director of the British military information service in London, also made it known that although the provisions of the Hague Convention were not formally binding on the combatants, they could indeed serve as a norm for both parties. Significantly, the British refrained from denying the validity of this informal aspect of the Hague Convention. On the grounds of the above argument, it was regarded as justifiable to accept the provisions of the Hague Convention that embodied the contemporarily acceptable practices of warfare waged on land as the norm where this was appropriate.

In this study some instances emerged which the compilers of the Hague Convention had not foreseen, and for which there was thus no provision. In such cases the works of authoritative jurists were used and the principles which they had laid down in that context, were applied to evaluate specific situations with due consideration for the particular circumstances. As far as possible, but not exclusively, the works of contemporary jurists were used.

It could be argued that the logical commencement of this study should perhaps be the pre-war republican disposition to the possibility of war. Where it was essential to establish the pre-war stance of certain burghers who later surrendered, this has been done, but it was not found necessary to make an earlier starting date for the study. Only unconfirmed rumours could be traced that certain Free State and Transvaal burghers had allegedly made it known that they were not prepared to defend the republican independence. In the South African Republic's First *Volksraad* (parliament), despite shades of opinion, there was wide agreement that the Transvaal would have to defend its independence in a war which had been forced upon it by imperial Britain. In the Free State the members of the *volksraad* were not all convinced to the same extent of the expediency of supporting the Transvaal in the event of war, but on 27 September 1899 a proposal to do so was unanimously accepted. In the *volksraad* minutes of the South African Republic and Orange Free State the researcher seeks in vain for direct evidence of the existence of a group of dissident Boers in 1900. It would appear that the external threat of war strengthened internal solidarity and that it was only in the harsh reality, the melting-pot of war, that a group of burghers openly showed their misgivings about the continuation of the conflict.

Notes

1   With the outbreak of the Anglo-Boer War and the official declaration of martial law in the *Buitengewone Staatscourant der Zuid-Afrikaansche Republiek* (the South African Republic's government gazette) on 11 October 1899, all male burghers between the ages of 16 and 60 years were liable for military service. Concessions which gave certain people exemption from military service expired on this date. See Act 20 of 1898, *Voor den Krijgdienst in De Zuid-Afrikaansche Republiek*, articles 28, 42 and 44, for these provisions. In the Free State the same age stipulations applied as those in the Transvaal. See Act 10 of 1899, *De Krijgs- en Commandowet*, article 28. In terms of article 32 of this act, the following people were exempted from military service: members of the *volksraad* and the executive council, salaried civil service officials, ministers of religion, theology students, people who were physically disabled, and men who managed the farms belonging to members of the *volksraad* or the executive council while the latter were absent to attend council meetings. Free State law did not, however, stipulate that these people were liable for military service when martial law was declared. It can arguably be accepted that with the declaration of martial law eligible burghers would be expected to give their full support to the armed forces in times of war. See J.H. Breytenbach, *Die Geskiedenis van die Tweede Vryheidsoorlog in Suid-Afrika, 1899–1902*, I, p. 32.
2   See Chapters 2 and 3 below.
3   For a study on the Boer prisoners of war see S.P.R. Oosthuizen. "Die Beheer, Behandeling en Lewe van die Krygsgevangenes gedurende die Anglo-Boereoorlog, 1899–1902" (Unpublished D.Phil thesis, UOVS), 1975.
4   *The Times*, 21 May 1902 (news report).
5   M.H. Buys, "Militêre Regering in Transvaal, 1900–1902" (Unpublished D.Phil. thesis, UP), 1972.

6   S.B. Spies, "Roberts and Kitchener and Civilians in the Boer Republics, January 1900 – May 1902" (Unpublished Ph.D. thesis, UW), 1973. This study has since been published as *Methods of Barbarism? Roberts and Kitchener and Civilians in the Boer Republics: January 1900–May 1902*, 1978. A second edition was published in 2001.

7   J.P. Brits (ed), *Diary of a National Scout P.J. du Toit 1900–1902*, 1974.

8   A.P.J. van Rensburg, "Die Ekonomiese Herstel van die Afrikaner in die Oranjerivierkolonie, 1902–1907" in *Archives Yearbook for South African History*, 30(II), 1967.

9   D.J.N. Denoon, *A Grand Illusion: The failure of imperial policy in the Transvaal Colony during the period of reconstruction, 1900–1905*, 1973.

10 G.H.L. le May, *British Supremacy in South Africa, 1899–1907*, 1965.

11 J.A.S. Oberholster, *Die Gereformeerde Kerke onder die Kruis in Suid-Afrika: hul ontstaan en ontwikkeling*, 1956.

12 G.D. Scholtz, *Die Geskiedenis van die Nederduitse Hervormde of Gereformeerde Kerk van Suid-Afrika, 1885–1910*, II, 1960.

13 C.P.H. Olivier, "Die Geskiedenis van die Scoutkerk in Transvaal" (Unpublished proponent thesis, UP), 1969.

14 See Chapter 9, section 3 below.

15 V.E. Solomon, "The Hands-Uppers" in *Krygshistoriese Tydskrif*, 3(1), June 1974.

16 A.P.J. van Rensburg, "Die skandkol wat nie wou toegroei nie" in *Die Huisgenoot*, 8 August 1969.

17 A.P.J. van Rensburg, "Pieter Daniël de Wet" in *DSAB*, II, 1970.

18 J.L. Hattingh, "Die geval van Meyer de Kock en die ontstaan van die Konsentrasiekampe tydens die Anglo-Boereoorlog, 1899–1902" in *Historia*, 17(3), September 1973.

19 S.B. Spies, "The Hague Convention of 1899 and the Boer Republics" in *Historia*, 15(1), March 1970, pp. 43, 46.

20 Spies, "Civilians", pp. 7–8.

21 Translated from the Dutch. W.J. Leyds, *Derde Verzameling (Correspondentie 1900)* II, Annexure EE, p. 98, W.J. Leyds, A. Fischer, C.H. Wessels and A.D.W. Wolmarans – British prime minister (Salisbury), 18 August 1900.

22 CO 417/302/27895 (FK 385, pp. 789–93), margin notes by H. Lambert and H.B. Cox, officials in the Colonial Office, with reference to the letter, 28 August 1900.

23 Spies, "Civilians", p. 8.

24 In the Free State there was talk that certain burghers in the Smithfield district were not prepared to support the Transvaal if war broke out. According to J.M. Wessels, who was the *volksraad* (parliament) member for the district, the rumour was unfounded. He assured the *volksraad* that the burghers in that part of the Free State "were every bit as patriotic as those in other parts of the State and would conduct themselves just as bravely as the others". (Translated from the Dutch.) *OVS Volksraadsnotules* (OFS parliamentary minutes), p. 40, 22 September 1899. In the Transvaal there were also rumours that Lieutenant-colonel S.P.E. Trichard, commanding officer of the State Artillery, would leave the republic in the lurch in the event of a war. Trichard dismissed these rumours as "ridiculous untruths". *De Volksstem*, 2 September 1899 (letter from S.P.E. Trichard). See also O.J.O. Ferreira (ed), *Geschiedenis Werken en Streven van S.P.E. Trichard Luitenant Kolonel der vroegere Staats-Artillerie Z.A.R. door hemzelve beschreven*, pp. 113, 223–4.

25 *ZAR Eerste Volksraadsnotules* (SAR, minutes of the First Parliament), 8 and 14 September 1899, articles 1171 and 857; J.H. Barnard, "Die Politieke Strominge in die Volksraad van die Suid-Afrikaanse Republiek van 1881–1899" (Unpublished MA dissertation, UP), 1944, pp. 108–12.

26 *OVS Volksraadsnotules* (OFS parliamentary minutes), pp. 68–80, 138; 23, 24, 25 and 27 September 1899.

Chapter 1
The formation of a group of surrendered burghers who voluntarily laid down their arms in 1900

1 Background: the republican forces – mobilisation, discipline and demoralisation

The war between Great Britain and the Boer republics became a reality on 11 October 1899 and by this date the mobilisation of the republican force was already in full swing. On 27 September 1899 Commandant-general Piet Joubert, who was commander of the burgher forces in the Transvaal, ordered the commandants of the various districts to call up their burghers for military service, and five days later (2 October 1899) the mobilisation of the Free Staters also began.[1]

At the time of the outbreak of the war there were about 54 667 Transvaal burghers who were liable for compulsory military service. Of these it appears that between 32 000 and 35 000 men – at the very most 56% to 65% of the combined republican military force – were initially mobilised.[2] Between 35% and 44% of the total number who were liable for conscription did not, therefore, leave for the front at the beginning of the war. According to state historian J.H. Breytenbach the archival sources do not shed much light on the reasons why the republics did not mobilise on a larger scale, but he does offer two possible explanations. Firstly, there was a large number of burghers who had to remain on the home front to maintain essential services and promote the smooth running of the republican war effort. Many officials fell into this category. The second reason can be found in the Boers' military strategy of preferring not to attack a powerful enemy with a large army, electing instead to use a smaller force to inflict maximum damage on the opposing army.[3] This would appear to explain why all the available burghers were not mobilised immediately.[4]

It would be incorrect to assume on these grounds that all the burghers who were called up obeyed the mobilisation orders. To be sure, most of the republican burghers took up arms with great enthusiasm. According to the authors of the official British history of the war, "at the order to mobilize the manhood of the Boer Republics sprang to arms as quickly, as well prepared, and with incomparably more zeal than the best trained conscripts of Europe." But significantly, the same authors add that "[it was] a call which ... was easy for the laggard to disobey, and almost uncared for by the forethought of anyone but themselves".[5]

In Johannesburg, Commandant (later General) Ben Viljoen, who was responsible for the commandeering of local burghers, found that many of them engineered all manner of excuses to avoid military service.[6] On 29 September 1899 Viljoen was able to leave for the front with only 400 burghers instead of the 750 which he had envisaged.[7] It was not only Johannesburg burghers who tried to evade their military duties. The magistrate at Nylstroom reported that some burghers had flatly refused to perform military service of any kind,[8] and 18 women from Carolina raised objections that "healthy burghers who were not sick or incapacitated had contributed nothing by way of their services or anything else for the commandos".[9] Similar instances occurred in the Free State. In the Winburg district about 13% of the burghers who were liable for military service at the beginning of the war evaded commando service.[10] There were also burghers in the Philippolis district who remained behind on their farms without good reason for doing so.[11] According to General Philip Botha of Vrede, by the end of January 1900 there were still various burghers who tried to use all sorts of illegal tactics to avoid commando service.[12]

The number of burghers who ignored the initial mobilisation orders without valid reasons for doing so is unknown,[13] but it is significant that even at the time of the initial mobilisation of the republican forces, there were certain reluctant burghers who did not feel obliged to do their duty by way of military service. Although these burghers may subsequently have been forced to join the commandos, it can readily be assumed that given any opportunity at all to stop fighting they would probably not have hesitated to lay down their arms.

As the war progressed the republican authorities called up additional burghers for military service. On 20 March 1900 Louis Botha, who was the assistant commandant-general, reported from Glencoe: "Every burgher is now being called up and is obliged to take up his rifle to defend his country, the future of his people, his home and his possessions."[14] By the beginning of May 1900 the Transvaal government appointed a special Commandeer Commission to "root out the burghers who were in hiding …".[15] This commission was comprised of five influential people from each district. They had to move from farm to farm to round up tardy burghers and bring them before the district magistrate. The magistrate could, if he deemed it necessary, punish the reluctant burghers with a few days hard labour before sending them off to the commandos.[16]

Despite all this, there were still burghers who were liable for military duty who did not take up arms at all, at any stage of the war.[17] Because of the lack of information on this issue, it is difficult to make any sort of accurate assessment on the number of burghers in this category. However, in 1905 H. Goold-Adams, the lieutenant-governor of the Orange River Colony after the war, mentioned that 138 burghers who had not served in the commandos at all had corresponded with him in connection with the payment of their compensation claims.[18]

In view of the fact that Goold-Adams mentioned only those who had written to him, it is clear that his figure of 138 did not include all those Free State burghers who were eligible to serve but evaded commando duty. However, this number can be seen as an indication that only a very small percentage of the total number of republican burghers who were liable for military service did not at any time during the war find themselves on commando. This was also the opinion of the Netherlands military attachés with the Boer forces, Captain J.H. Ram and Lieutenant L.W.J.K. Thomson: "There were indeed burghers who did not do any commando service … but the large majority did in fact do so."[19]

Legally, burghers who defied the mobilisation orders in the two republics were liable for punishment in the form of fines from £5

(£10 in the Free State) to £37 10s, or to imprisonment for anything from three days to three months.[20] These legal provisions were clearly not enforced very strictly and in June 1900, for example, J.N. van Rensburg, a burgher from the Pietersburg (now Polokwane) district, was given the minimum fine of £5 because he flatly refused from the very outset to go on commando.[21]

It is not surprising that a slack burgher was punished comparatively lightly. In the republican forces there was initially little question of strict military discipline. In times of peace the Boer held undisputed sway over his farm and was unaccustomed to interference about what he could and could not do. As a result, when he was on commando he initially found it difficult to submit to others. Orders that did not particularly appeal to him, in the words of a contemporary Hollander, meant "that the Boer, used to having his own way and not being ordered around by others, became stubborn. If he no longer wished to fight, no one could restrain him".[22] Whereas the British had a professionally trained army, the defence force of the two republics (other than their very small permanent force) was virtually reliant on a peoples' army. In civilian life officers were the burghers' equals. Commandants and field-cornets were chosen as officers in a democratic manner by the burghers themselves and were thus to a large extent dependent on the burghers for the rank which they held. The measure of obedience that an officer could expect from his burghers depended largely on the strength of his personality and not on the rank that he held.[23]

The informal discipline in the republican forces had both positive and negative implications. On the one hand, it ensured that the Boers' natural military flair and individualism was not smothered by a rigid and often soul-destroying military discipline. Particularly in the later mobile phase of the war, under outstanding leaders such as Generals J.H. de la Rey, C.R. de Wet and Louis Botha, a burgher's personal initiative would often be the decisive element in a battle. These same generals, by virtue of their personal influence and charisma, also managed to secure the cooperation of most republican burghers. Under their guidance particular attention would also be paid to sharpening commando discipline.[24] On the other hand, an initial lack of discipline led to self-willed, headstrong action. Military councils were sometimes unable to punish military offenders simply because offenders dodged the hearings. As the *Official History* so aptly puts it, "the burgher of the close of the nineteenth century knew as many methods of evading the stroke of justice as did his father of escaping the stalk of a lion or the rush of a Zulu spearman."[25] At the beginning of the war, when an officer of the Soutpansberg commando, Field-cornet A.Z.A. Briel, was summoned to a military hearing because of remiss behaviour, he simply disappeared without a trace.[26] It is perhaps significant that after he had voluntarily laid down his arms, Briel fought in 1902 as a National Scout on the British side.[27] Because of the slack discipline in the republican forces, many burghers left the commandos without leave of absence. This particular misdemeanour caused many a headache for commanding officers. Although they tried to implement an ordered system of leave, burghers often simply ignored this and took leave without the permission of their officers.[28]

As a result of the dearth of proper control there were very few obstacles in the path of the slack burgher who wanted to stop fighting. Indeed, the ease with which he could leave the commando gave him ample opportunity to surrender. This is clearly shown in the case of the Jacobsdal commando. In March 1900 they were expressly forbidden to go on leave, but despite this, many burghers took leave and used the opportunity to take the British oath of neutrality.[29]

Overseas military attachés and professional soldiers often passed harsh criticism on the republican forces. Although they did not always see things from the perspective of the entire war and were also inclined to judge the Boer forces according to European standards, their impressions are nevertheless of value because of the impartial way in which they throw light on certain issues. In the view of Captain J. Allum, the Norwegian military attaché with the Boers, rigid military discipline in times of crisis might well have had a positive effect on the republican forces. Indeed, it was the lack of such discipline that led him to form the following impression of the Boer forces on 20 May 1900: "There is an old saying that in an army there are at most 20% courageous soldiers, 40% cowards and 40% who are neither courageous nor cowardly – a saying which has been fully confirmed in this war."[30] Colonel G. de Villebois-Mareuil, a French mercenary who voluntarily joined the Boer forces, also differentiated between three groups in a Boer army: "the elite, those who fight because of their temperament or conscience; the dead weight, those who always remain at the laager and count at meal-times only; and those ... whose time is spent on leave, and who become more jingo the further they are from the front. But why be astonished? Such things are inevitable in any social and political state if military bonds are not drawn tighter around a people, even to the point of cutting to the flesh in the hour of its crisis."[31]

Lodi Krause, a lawyer from Pietersburg who later became a commandant in the Soutpansberg commando, also expressed a similar view on the poor military discipline and tardy burghers in the Boer laagers. He calls these men "layabouts" or "camp loafers" and significantly also mentions that most of these loafers, if the opportunity arose, handed over their weapons to the British military authorities.[32]

Next it is necessary to assess the prevailing morale in the republican forces in the period during which a group of burghers began surrendering. From the end of February 1900 onwards the military tide turned against the Boers. Whereas at the beginning of the war they had gained some spectacular victories over the British, notably at Stormberg (10 December 1899) and Magersfontein (11 December 1899) as well as at Colenso and Spioenkop (15 December 1899 and 24 January 1900 respectively), in the longer term they were unable to check the British army with its ever-increasing numerical superiority on the southern, western and Natal fronts.

On the Natal front the British broke through on 27 February 1900 at Pietershoogte, with demoralising implications for the Boer commandos.[33] That same day General P.A. Cronjé surrendered with 3919 men (excluding the 150 who were wounded) at Paardeberg on the western front.[34] Cronjé's surrender had a particularly devastating effect on the military morale of the republican forces. Many burghers reasoned that if an eminent general like Piet Cronjé and nearly 4000 of his men had been forced to surrender, there was no glimmer of hope left for the republican cause. A wave of despair and helplessness engulfed many burghers and the feeling took root that any further resistance would be useless.[35] Some burghers simply left the commandos and refused to return.[36] General Christiaan de Wet was witness to this demoralisation: "No pen can describe ... the effect [of Cronjé's surrender] ... on the burghers. On every face there was dejection and despair to be seen. The demoralisation – I cannot reiterate it enough – prevailed right through until the end of the war."[37]

The republican leaders realised the gravity of the situation. On the insistence of the elderly President S.J.P. Kruger of the Transvaal, his Free State counterpart, President M.T. Steyn, agreed that on 5 March 1900 they would approach the British prime minister, Lord Salisbury, with an offer of peace. The crux of the offer was that the two presidents were prepared to initiate peace negotiations, but only on the express condition that the republican independence was fully acknowledged, failing which the republics would persevere with the struggle. When Salisbury rejected this offer on 11 March, Steyn resolved that he would never again solicit Britain for peace.[38]

Meanwhile Lord Roberts, commander of the British forces, had begun his planned march towards Bloemfontein. On 7 March 1900 the Boers offered token resistance at Poplar Grove, but many of the demoralised burghers abandoned the battle in the early stages.[39] At Abraham's Kraal (10 March 1900) the Boers offered more determined resistance, but were unable to prevent Roberts from occupying the Free State capital on 13 March 1900 without striking a blow.[40] In Bloemfontein certain eminent residents immediately aligned themselves with the British. Among these were J.G. Fraser, an English-speaking member of the *volksraad* who had been a presidential candidate in 1896, Dr B.O. Kellner, the mayor of Bloemfontein as well as the magistrate, H.F.D. Papenfus. Together with Raaff, the sheriff, these men rode out on horseback to meet Roberts and hand him the keys of the town hall as a gesture of full surrender.[41] As a member of the burgher peace committee movement, Fraser was later to work closely with the British.[42] According to Fraser's biographer there were a number of reasons why Fraser decided to subject himself to British authority: his cultural and political disposition as an English speaker; the fact that he regarded himself as representative of the residents of Bloemfontein; his standpoint that from the very beginning the republics had taken on a hopeless task; and finally – apparently the most important reason – his belief that to continue the struggle would be useless.[43]

By 27 February 1900 there was already one of the *volksraad* members in the Free State, quite possibly Fraser, who was of the opinion that "If [the] British take Bloemfontein ... our army will melt away like snow; ninety per cent will be only too glad of an excuse to go home to plough."[44] This prediction proved not unduly far-fetched. The British occupation of the Free State capital, so soon after Cronjé's surrender, disrupted the republican forces even more. A great number of burghers were war-weary and looked forward to a speedy end to hostilities.[45] President Kruger was gravely concerned about the implications of the fall of Bloemfontein for the republican forces, while Steyn was later to bemoan the demoralising impact of this setback.[46] General de Wet also emphasised the paralysis it had caused: "Not only was it that the English had occupied our capital, but what was of more concern was what happened to the burghers. They were utterly dejected and it seemed as if they did not have the heart to offer the least resistance any more."[47] Under the dynamic leadership of General de Wet the war was soon to be continued with renewed vigour, but not before many Free State burghers had voluntarily laid down their arms.

Less than three months after the occupation of Bloemfontein, Roberts's overwhelming army crossed the Vaal River and entered the Transvaal. At Doornkop on 29 May 1900 a section of the Transvaal force made a futile attempt to resist the British. The following day the burghers retreated in disorderly fashion in the direction of Pretoria, and on 31 May Roberts occupied Johannesburg.[48]

Just as in the Free State, many Transvalers were now war-weary after the military setbacks which had befallen the republican troops from February 1900 onwards. It was a dejected President Kruger who telegraphed his Free State counterpart on 31 May: "It appears from reports by our officers that there is a small number of our burghers who are unwilling to continue the struggle and are returning home."[49] By 2 June 1900 Roberts began to make arrangements to reach his ultimate goal: Pretoria. The nearer the British troops moved towards the seat of the Transvaal government, the clearer it became that there were people who would opt out of the war and distance themselves from the republican cause. An old Transvaal resident remarked: "Our eyes are being opened where the enemy is invading our country, and we now discover who is the false ones, cowards and dishonest members among us are. They were the first to sit together and sing psalms with us and now they are howling with the [English] dogs."[50] By 29 May the Transvaal government had decided that Pretoria would not be defended. This confused the ordinary burghers even more. "If Pretoria was not worth fighting for, what was? And what was the object of continuing the war?" According to J.C. Smuts this was the reasoning of many war-weary burghers.[51]

On 5 June 1900 Roberts occupied Pretoria. The military morale of the Transvaal forces had now plummeted to an all-time low and many burghers turned dispiritedly homewards.[52] General Smuts even claimed that some of the telegraph clerks in Pretoria went over to the British and kept Roberts informed on the Boers' official war correspondence.[53] Apart from Smuts's evidence, no other known source makes specific reference to this, but the fact that the British were in possession of an almost complete set of war telegrams reflecting the demoralisation and lack of order in Boer ranks during the period from 29 May to 5 June 1900[54] seems to bear out Smuts's claim. In the light of the general dejection that prevailed in the Transvaal at the time, it is not surprising that at the beginning of June 1900 Lieutenant-colonel V.I. Gurko, a Russian military attaché with the Boers, expressed the following opinion on the continuation of the war: "If one observes the demoralisation of the Transvaal forces, one sees every day that there are burghers who assuredly do not wish to continue to expose themselves to danger. One comes to the conclusion that the matter is finally and irredeemably lost, and that the war cannot continue because of the loss of those who are not prepared to go on fighting."[55]

The origin of a group of burghers in the Free State and Transvaal who voluntarily laid down their arms must therefore be seen against this background. Despite the fact that the war was by no means over, an increasing number of burghers realised that Britain could call upon an almost inexhaustible number of military reinforcements and that any chance the republics had of winning had begun to fade rapidly from about March 1900.[56] A spirit of defeatism began to overwhelm many of the ordinary burghers and even some of the officers. For the Boer who was not a professional soldier, but a civilian with farming and family concerns, it was very difficult under such circumstances to relate to his military role. And the slack discipline in the Boer forces indirectly and unconsciously created fertile ground for defection. Exercising the proper authority in the republican forces was done so informally that it could simply not deter the ordinary burgher from laying down his arms and taking the British oath of neutrality.[57]

Whether or not the lacklustre discipline and large scale demoralisation of the republican forces predisposed the inception of a dissident group of men who wished to lay down their arms, it is clear that the policy introduced by the British military command from February 1900 was directly instrumental in giving them the opportunity to do exactly that.

2 The first British proclamations in the Free State and Transvaal and the annexation of the two republics

At just about the time when there was widespread demoralisation of the Boer forces in the Free State and the Transvaal, Roberts issued the first in a series of proclamations. In February 1900, shortly after the British army had entered the Free State, Roberts announced the first of these. After a lengthy introduction he declared that the British government would have honoured the independence of the Free State had the republic remained neutral when war broke out. He went on to accuse the Free State government of unnecessary, aggressive action in invading British territory (the Cape Colony and Natal), but said that he did not hold the people responsible for the conduct of their government. Because the British government, according to Roberts, wanted to protect the Free Staters from the injudicious guidance of their leaders, he warned all burghers "to desist from any further hostility towards Her Majesty's Government and the troops under my command", and undertook "that any of them, who may so desist and who are found staying in their homes and quietly pursuing their ordinary occupations, will not be made to suffer in their persons or property on account of their having taken up arms in obedience to the order of their Government".[58]

Although Roberts signed the proclamation, it was compiled in consultation with Sir Alfred Milner, the British high commissioner.[59] Milner was responsible for the long introduction, and the idea of driving a wedge between the people and their government was his. "I think that it would be politically useful to have a little more preamble," he wrote to Roberts. "The Dutch are influenced by that sort of thing. Like all uneducated people, they do not understand a purely businesslike statement and *almost expect* a little bunkum. Moreover there is a likelihood that some of the Free State people may break away from the President, being angry with him for having got them into this mess. I want to make a distinction between the Government and the people, and to throw all the blame on the former ... ."[60] Milner then informed Joseph Chamberlain, the secretary of state for the colonies, that "every phrase of [the] proclamation has been carefully considered with a view to what was most likely to influence the Dutch population. The phraseology is Dutch in character".[61] This proclamation was thus drawn up with the express purpose of sowing discord in Boer ranks and encouraging defection. Milner was convinced that the proclamation would meet his objective, "namely to encourage any tendency there may be to throw up the sponge amongst the Orange Free State burghers without unduly tying the hands of Her Majesty's Government in the political arrangements necessary when the war is over".[62]

After the demoralising defeat that the Boers had suffered at Paardeberg (27 February 1900) and the occupation of Bloemfontein on 13 March 1900, the British made use of the right psychological moment to issue a further proclamation, similar to the February one, on 15 March. In the March proclamation, also signed by Roberts, the promise of protection was repeated. In addition, the following tempting offer was also made: "All burghers who have not taken a prominent part in the policy which has led to the war between Her Majesty and the Orange Free State, or commanded any forces of the Republic, or commandeered or used violence to any British subjects, and who are willing to lay down their arms at once, and to bind themselves by an oath to abstain from further participation in the war, will be given passes to allow them to return to their homes and will not be made prisoners of war, nor will their property be taken from them."[63]

The purpose of this proclamation was the same as the February one, but the details differed slightly. In February any burgher, regardless of his status and rank, could withdraw from the war without the danger of being sent away as a prisoner of war. In terms of the March proclamation the concession did not apply to burghers who had played a prominent political or military role. In addition, in February it was not expected of a burgher to give any formal notification that he would not take any further part in the war, while the March proclamation required that he take an oath to confirm his surrender as a combatant and make it official and binding. This oath became known as the oath of neutrality.[64]

Milner drew up the March proclamation in consultation with Chamberlain, and Roberts was merely responsible for its promulgation.[65] In February 1901, when it became clear that the war was far from over, Milner reluctantly admitted that "I am, I say it with shame, the inventor and sole patentee of the original policy of leniency. When the Boers were first decisively beaten, I advocated the policy of making it easy for them to come in. I suggested myself the plan of allowing them to go back to their farms at once on taking the oath of neutrality."[66]

It is highly doubtful whether these proclamations, which were designed to entice away members of the republican forces, violated the current war practices or laws of warfare in any specific way. J.M. Spaight, a contemporary jurist in the field, held the following well-considered opinion on these particular proclamations: "A belligerent has an admitted right to receive deserters from his enemy's army ... No army which is well disciplined ... has anything to fear from incitement to disloyalty. The etiquette of war may be against such incitements, but they do not appear a whit more dishonourable or underhand than the employment of mercenary spies, which is admitted by usage."[67] L. Oppenheim, a jurist of more recent times, agrees that there can be no objection raised against the use of such methods of persuasion.[68] A further related issue is whether or not the British had the legal right to demand an oath of neutrality. Article 45 of the Hague Convention lays down that the invader may not exercise any pressure on the population of an occupied region to take an oath, but this stipulation refers to an oath of allegiance and not to an oath of neutrality.[69] An oath of neutrality is therefore not in violation of the existing practices of warfare. It must be noted, however, that the British would certainly not have permitted their own soldiers to take a similar oath. A private could not simply walk out of the British army, and soldiers who deserted risked the death sentence.[70]

Theoretically, these first British proclamations can be seen as very indulgent. Most of the male republican citizens who came into contact with the British on republican soil were members of the republican forces. The British were perfectly within their rights to treat these people indiscriminately as prisoners of war, but instead they gave them the opportunity, by taking an oath, to avoid this fate. The military attachés from the Netherlands who were with the Boer forces were also of the opinion that "one can only with difficulty describe these measures as anything but conciliatory".[71] In practice, however, Roberts was not really as accommodating as might appear. The reality was that he regarded the people who took the oath simply as prisoners of war on parole. Even if they did not formally take the oath they could not, according to Roberts's reckoning, take part in the war again.[72]

Once Roberts had crossed the Vaal River he saw in the pervading demoralisation of the Transvaal forces a good opportunity to direct a proclamation to the residents of the South African Republic on 31 May 1900. In as far as current military operations allowed, Roberts promised firstly to respect the personal freedom and property of the civilian population. In article 2 he then made the following promise: "All burghers who have not taken a prominent part in the policy which has led to the war between Her Majesty and the South African Republic, or commandeered or used violence to any British subjects, or committed any acts contrary to the usages of civilized warfare, and who are willing to lay down their arms at once, to bind themselves by an oath to abstain from further participation in the war, will be given passes to allow them to return to their homes, and will not be made prisoners of war."[73] This proclamation differs in one particularly important respect from the proclamation which Roberts issued in the Free State on 15 March 1900. The clause, "nor will their property be taken from them" which comes after "prisoner of war" was omitted. This was presumably done because by this time it had become clear in the Free State that military proceedings prevented the British army from meeting this provision.[74]

On 6 June 1900, when the morale of the Transvaal forces reached an all-time low with the occupation of Pretoria the previous day, Roberts once again, in exchange for the oath of neutrality, promised the Transvaal burghers that they could go and live unhindered on their farms and retain all their cattle. Passes would be issued to the burghers who, because of winter grazing, moved periodically to the Bushveld with their cattle.[75] A contemporary Dutch author emphasises the underhand nature of this proclamation. According to him " by offering these conditions Lord Roberts is undoubtedly taking advantage of the Boers' susceptibility. Do they not see cattle as the most precious of their possessions? And now that the winter is here they have been offered this unexpected, special advantage: to be able to take their cattle unhindered, despite all the ravages of war, to the ... veld. In this way the trust and patriotic spirit of the burghers is being tested fearfully again, and certainly many will fall for this tempting offer made by the English commander ...".[76] Roberts's promises were thus also designed to make the dejected Boers even more convinced that for all practical purposes the war was over and they could go ahead uninterrupted with their farming interests. In reality it was simply a continuation of the policy which Roberts followed in the Free State. The first proclamations which Roberts issued in the Free State and Transvaal were thus directly responsible for the origin of a group of Boers who decided to lay down their arms. They were the framework within which republican burghers were given the opportunity to withdraw from the war and return to their homes. In direct contrast to these burghers there were two other distinct groups. Firstly, there were the prisoners of war, who after capture on the battlefield were sent away to camps, and secondly, those who persevered with the struggle even after the proclamations had been issued. With these proclamations Britain thus set the scene for the inception of a separate group of burghers – those who during the period of demoralisation in republican ranks did not wish to go on fighting any longer. Later, when there was a revival of the Boer spirit, many men from this group were to take up arms again, but others chose to retain their status as surrendered Boers and to desert the Boer cause completely.[77] These proclamations can thus also be seen as marking the beginning of the polarisation within Afrikaner society. Significantly, in 1904 General Christiaan de Wet referred to the proclamations as "the murderous Lyddite bombs ... that shattered Afrikanerdom".[78]

The burghers who laid down their arms as a result of Roberts's proclamations then became part of the non-combatant population in the two republics. According to contemporary laws of warfare there were mutual obligations between the occupying force of a particular region and the non-combatant population in that area,[79] so this issue merits closer examination in order to determine the situation of those who responded to Roberts's proclamation. What were the obligations of the occupying force towards a person who had signed the oath of neutrality, and on the other hand, to what extent had such a person made himself subject to the authority of the occupying force? According to article 46 of the Hague Convention, the non-combatant residents of an occupied region could legally expect that the sanctity of the family, religion, private property and personal freedom be respected.[80] This is then also implicit in the promises which Roberts made to those who took the oath of neutrality.[81] On the other hand a person who took the oath of neutrality subjected himself, to a significant extent, to the authority of the occupying force. In a discussion of articles 23, 44 and 52 of the Hague Convention, L. Oppenheim points out that when an individual took the oath of neutrality, he placed himself in a position that allowed the occupying force to expect a great many services, with the exception of military activities, from him.[82]

The mutual fulfilment of these obligations is closely linked to the effectiveness of the occupation. In terms of article 42 of the Hague Convention there are two basic tenets which underpin the juridical meaning of effective occupation. Firstly, "the invader must have established his authority", and secondly "he must be in a position to enforce it".[83] According to J.M. Spaight these ideas, legally formulated, are "to limit the rights of a belligerent in respect to a hostile province through which he has swept hurriedly on his way to a more distant province ...".[84] Roberts's ultimate objective was the subjugation of the South African Republic and he did not wait until the Free State was effectively occupied before he pushed on to the Transvaal.[85] In the early stage when Roberts issued his first proclamations in the Free State (February and 15 March 1900), he was by no means able to exercise full authority there. He was in possession only of the capital and a few towns, and by far the greatest portion of the Free State was still in Boer hands. This was also the case in the Transvaal when Roberts issued his first proclamations on 31 May and 6 June 1900.[86] Under such circumstances, his course of action in calling for a neutrality oath is also questionable.[87]

Just as significant is the fact that the republican governments did not recognise the neutrality oath.[88] This meant that a burgher who, in terms of Roberts's proclamations, decided to lay down his arms exposed himself to prosecution by his own government because he was still subject to republican law and was thereby still liable for active military service.

Right from the start, then, a person who took the oath of neutrality found himself in a parlous situation. Firstly, the unstable nature of the British occupation meant that he had no absolute guarantee that the British army was in a position to protect him and his property as outlined by Roberts's proclamations and by article 46 of the Hague Convention. And secondly, the British, despite the ineffectiveness of their occupation, would expect the surrendered burgher as a non-combatant member of the population to keep his part of the contract, namely to provide certain services.[89] Thirdly, his actions did not meet with the approval of his government. Demoralised and in good faith, many burghers were to step into the British trap. After the war the Boer side claimed with justification that Roberts bought the surrender of many burghers with promises which he was unable to keep.[90] For some of these burghers Roberts's proclamations also held unpleasant and far-reaching implications. According to General J.C. Smuts, "[M]any ... poor deluded people lived to curse the day that they believed in the honest words of the proclamations and started on that smiling but treacherous road which was to lead them to the fate of National Scouts and to the scorn and contempt of their fellows."[91]

In addition to Roberts's first proclamations, the early annexations of the republics as British colonies also strengthened the impression that by 1900 the Boers had already irretrievably lost the war. The annexation of the Free State took place in terms of a proclamation dated 24 May 1900 and was announced officially on 28 May at a military parade on the market square in Bloemfontein.[92] In the Transvaal the same policy was followed when the annexation took place on 1 September 1900.[93]

Milner was of the opinion that by an early annexation "we would encourage the party in [the] Free State favourable to British rule to declare themselves as soon as possible".[94] According to Roberts an early annexation would remove all doubt about the permanent nature of the British occupation. It would give a feeling of security to the burghers who had already decided to heed his first proclamations and "the majority ... would ... settle down if they were satisfied that we were not going to leave the country".[95]

The British annexations of the Free State and the Transvaal theoretically implied that the republics did not exist any more and that the burghers therefore no longer had a government. That Roberts subscribed to this line of thought is also clear from a proclamation that he issued on 14 September 1900, subsequent to President Kruger's departure from the Transvaal. In this proclamation Roberts erroneously announced: "Mr. Kruger has formally resigned the position he held as President of the South African Republic, thus severing his official connection with the Transvaal ... and his desertion of the Boer cause should make it clear to his fellow burghers that it is useless for them to continue the struggle any longer." He also emphasised the annexations of the republics as if a new constitutional dispensation was already an accomplished fact: "If any further doubts remain in the minds of the burghers as to Her Britannic Majesty's intentions, they should be dispelled by ... the Proclamations signed by me on the 24th May and 1st September 1900, annexing the Orange Free State and the South African Republic respectively, in the name of Her Majesty."[96]

Both republican governments issued counter-proclamations in which they declared the annexations to be null and void.[97] President Steyn was of the opinion that the annexation of the Free State was in violation of international law because, subsequent to the revival in Boer ranks, the war was again in full swing.[98] There can be no doubt that these annexations were indeed invalid. In an unequivocal manner the official British historians on the war regard the annexations of the Boer republics during the Anglo-Boer War as being "in flagrant defiance of the well-established provision of international law that the outright assumption of sovereignty, as opposed to its temporary exercise by a military occupant in place of the lawful government, must await the conclusion of a treaty of peace or the complete subjugation of the enemy".[99] L. Oppenheim is also of the opinion that in terms of international law "The British government ought not ... to have proclaimed their annexation."[100]

The invalidity of these proclamations is further underlined by the fact that Britain was obliged to regard the Boer delegates to the peace negotiations in May 1902 as the legal representatives of the republics. Roberts's "paper" annexations and his distorted portrayal of President Kruger's departure from the Transvaal nevertheless had an impact on the mental attitude of some burghers. From Olifantsnek on 22 September 1900 General Smuts reported that "Such proclamations are naturally not without influence among our ordinary people."[101] In October 1900 A. Pohl, a burgher from Pietersburg who had laid down his arms, said to his fellow burghers who were still fighting: "Where is your government, your government has fled with eight million pounds sterling [sic] and no longer exists. You burghers are cowardly and you are fighting for a government that is no longer legal."[102] In October 1900 L.J. le Grange of Piet Potgietersrus made a similar remark to some fighting burghers: "Your president has run away and you have no right to fight. Your whole government is nothing other than a bunch of robbers and therefore I do not want to remain with you. I do not see why the English cannot rule here because their government is better than our government."[103]

After their occupation of the republics the British began their administration of these regions. In Bloemfontein Major General G.T. Pretyman was the military governor, the hub around whom the administration turned, while Colonel C. Mackenzie and Major General J.G. Maxwell respectively undertook similar duties in Johannesburg and Pretoria. The administration of occupied rural areas was done by British district commissioners.[104] This management was not always efficient, but along with the annexations of the Free State and the

Transvaal it served to reinforce the impression that the burghers should henceforth submit themselves to this new "legal" government.[105]

The outcome of Roberts's policy in the two republics and the number of burghers who withdrew from the struggle to form a group of surrendered burghers as a result of his proclamations will be examined next.

3 Surrender in the Free State and the Transvaal

Roberts made certain that the proclamation of 15 March 1900, which gave the Free State burghers the opportunity to lay down their arms, was distributed as widely as possible. In the Edenburg and Reddersburg districts this task was undertaken by the Scots Guards under Lieutenant-general R. Pole-Carew and in the Philippolis and Fauresmith districts by General R.A.P. Clements and his troops. Lieutenant-general W. Gatacre's men covered the area south of Springfontein, while Major-general J.D.P. French's column distributed the proclamation in the district to the east of Bloemfontein.[106] According to Lieutenant-general Gatacre, small patrols were sent out to deliver the proclamation to as many farms as possible[107] – a task that the British troops described as "bill-sticking".[108] The local magistrates, who held their posts temporarily under the British government, also had to bring the proclamation to the attention of the population. African people were also used for this purpose.[109] Sir Godfrey Lagden, the resident commissioner in Basutoland (Lesotho), undertook to distribute the proclamation along the boundary between the Free State and Basutoland.[110] According to President Steyn, the censors who scrutinised the correspondence of the prisoners of war in Cape Town also helped by including copies of the proclamation in the letters that the prisoners sent to their family members in the Free State.[111]

Shortly after the occupation of the Free State capital (13 March 1900), Roberts wrote optimistically to Queen Victoria that "the Orange Free State south of this ... is rapidly settling down. The proclamations I have issued are having the desired effect, and men are daily laying down their arms and returning to their usual occupations."[112] Roberts had reason to be optimistic.

According to General Smuts, the southern and western districts of the Free State were at this stage "in undisturbed occupation of the enemy, and the great majority of the burghers of those districts surrendered at leisure and were living quietly on their farms as if no war existed any more".[113] General Christiaan de Wet indicated that by the end of May 1900 there were barely 439 men from the districts of Boshof, Jacobsdal, Fauresmith, Bethulie and Bloemfontein who were still fighting, while the ranks of the Rouxville, Smithfield, Wepener and Ladybrand commandos were also badly depleted. At Philippolis and Hoopstad very nearly all the burghers had laid down their arms.[114] There were even some officers who took the lead there. The commandant of the Edenburg commando, F. Cloete, as well as the field-cornets concerned, made a special appointment to discuss the question of surrender with Pole-Carew. In the discussions they promised to go along with Roberts's proclamation and to inform the burghers in their commando accordingly. On the orders of Cloete most of the Edenburg burghers duly laid down their arms on 25 March 1900.[115]

The available evidence provides additional information on the number of burghers who withdrew from the struggle. According to British war correspondents there were 400 men in the vicinity of Bloemfontein who laid down their arms immediately after Roberts issued the March proclamation.[116] British records show that the number of burghers who surrendered in the other regions of the Free State from 15 March to 5 June 1900 were as follows: Boshof 300; Jacobsdal 264; Bethulie 596; Edenburg 389; Fauresmith 589; Jagersfontein 331; Luckhoff 99; Koffiefontein 102; Philippolis 463; Smithfield 460; Trompsburg 306; Thaba Nchu 53; Dewetsdorp 32 and Ficksburg 170.[117] Together with those from Bloemfontein this comes to a total of 4554 men in the given period who laid down their arms in the southern, western, and eastern Free State.

These figures do not, however, take into consideration the number of burghers who surrendered in the northern parts of the Free State. As Roberts began marching from Bloemfontein early in May 1900, small groups of Boers regularly came to surrender but not in the same numbers as had been the case directly after the occupation of the Free State capital.[118] On 12 May Roberts reached Kroonstad and delayed there for ten days. According to British records, up until 5 June 1900 about 450 men in the Kroonstad district, approximately 385 in the Hoopstad-Bultfontein vicinity and 150 men in the Senekal vicinity handed in their arms.[119] Roberts then sent out divisions to Heilbron, Vredefort and Parys.[120] To the commanding officer, Lieutenant-general I.S.M. Hamilton, Roberts gave the following orders: "On your line of march encourage the people generally to surrender their arms and to behave peacefully, assuring them, that we have no wish to injure them, and as long as they remain on their farms no harm will happen to them."[121] The burghers in this region did not however surrender their arms on a large scale. Old rifles rather than their Mausers were often handed in.[122] From the beginning of June to the end of July 1900, according to British reports, there were no more than 400 burghers in the Heilbron, Vredefort and Parys districts who laid down their arms.[123] On the basis of this information, the number of burghers in the northern districts of the Free State who surrendered up until the end of July 1900 can thus be put at about 1385.

Together with the 4554 burghers from the southern, western and eastern Free State who withdrew from the struggle, the British records indicate that an estimated consolidated total of 5939 Free State burghers surrendered from 15 March until about the end of July 1900. It must be emphasised that this number did not remain constant. Some men decided later to rejoin the commandos, while there were also burghers who did not lay down their arms immediately, but did so after July 1900.[124] The statistics provided here also only cover the period from 15 March until about the end of July 1900. For the period from July 1900 to December 1900 there are, as far as can be established, no statistics available for the Free State.

It is significant that so many more burghers in the southern and western Free State surrendered than in the northern Free State. Milner was of the opinion that "the bulk of them [the burghers] in the south of the [Free] State … has always been less anti-British … than the north",[125] but even if there is an element of truth in what he says, it cannot be regarded as a conclusive statement under these specific circumstances. Of more importance is the fact that, with the occupation of Bloemfontein on 13 March 1900, the burghers in the southern and western Free State were cut off from the main army and the huge number of British soldiers in that region gave the impression of a permanent occupation.[126] The burghers in these areas thus had far more reason than their northerly compatriots to think that the war was practically over. Even more significant is the spirit of revival which was experienced in Boer ranks in the Free State during April, May and June 1900. Under the inspiring influence of President Steyn and General Christiaan de Wet, many of those in the northern regions who were wavering took new heart and decided to continue the struggle.[127]

Because of the dearth of comprehensive evidence it is not possible to establish the full extent of surrender in the Transvaal from June to December 1900 with absolute accuracy. General Smuts nevertheless claimed that thousands of burghers laid down their weapons after the occupation of Pretoria (5 June 1900).[128] Judging from the available evidence, his statement is not exaggerated. According to the British estimates, between 4000 and 5000 burghers laid down their arms in the Pretoria vicinity up until 14 June 1900. When Colonel R.S.S. Baden-Powell occupied Rustenburg on 14 June 1900, a further 1000 rifles were immediately handed in. At Wolmaransstad, taken on 15 June, 460 burghers withdrew from the struggle.[129] Lieutenant-general A. Hunter occupied Krugersdorp on 18 June 1900 and according to General Smuts between 900 and 1200 burghers surrendered their weapons in this region.[130] It would thus appear that the number of those who surrendered in the specified areas subsequent to the occupation of Pretoria can be put at between 6360 and 7960 men. These figures do not include the burghers who went home without handing in their weapons. Numbers for the other regions in the Transvaal which were occupied by the British at a later stage are unknown.

Based on the available evidence the combined total of Free State and Transvaal burghers who surrendered their weapons in the period from March 1900 to about July 1900 can be estimated at between 12 000 and 14 000 men (in round numbers). This means that the initial number of surrendered burghers in the republics was between 22% and 26% of the total number of men who were liable for military service.¹³¹ This is perhaps a slightly conservative estimate, particularly on account of the lack of evidence for the Transvaal, but nevertheless it provides a reasonable indication of the number of burghers in the two republics at the time who withdrew from the war in reaction to Roberts's first proclamations.

The large-scale surrender that took place in the two republics can be ascribed primarily to the demoralisation that pervaded the Boer forces at the time of the British breakthrough at Paardeberg (27 February 1900), the occupation of Bloemfontein (13 March 1900), and the occupation of Pretoria (5 June 1900). Reference has already been made to the crippling effects of these setbacks. At the same time Roberts's proclamations, which also gave the dejected burghers the chance to avoid possible capture as prisoners of war, provided an opportunity to lay down arms. Apparently some of the burghers had a particular fear of overseas captivity¹³² and this gave them all the more reason to surrender.

A contemporary author from Holland, F. Rompel, graphically describes the general state of mind of many a war-weary burgher at the time: "When Lord Roberts issued his misleading proclamation last month, the Boer, who was very close to his wife and children and was very attached to the property which he had developed to its present state by dint of his own hard work, ... would be able to return to it all if he laid down his rifle. No more privation, no more danger of death, no more separation from wife and child. The offer was so tempting that his general or commandant could barely hope to restrain him. He himself had been in the veld for months and knew little of how things were going back home on his land. The retreating commandos took him very close to his property, and if he went home he could keep everything, at least this is what he believed; if he went on fighting he would lose it all, everything which had cost him and his fathers so many years of hard labour."¹³³ For some burghers it was also a difficult decision to have to choose between their personal interests and those of the state. In September 1900, Philip Pienaar, a Transvaal telegraphist, who was an eyewitness to the inner conflict that the British protection promises caused for a number of burghers in the vicinity of Greylingstad, said: "I saw the changing expressions on their faces while they struggled with their own personal interests against the love of their fatherland. In the conflict between courage and the fear that they would lose the fruits of their years of hard work, the men gathered there had a strong inclination to accept the offer made by the enemy. But nobody dared to express his feelings. Their eyes moved from one to another and then they looked downwards. It was easy to see what the result would be. I felt that my duty was to protest against this but what ... could I say to these men ... they recoiled from making the heaviest sacrifice of all – that of their home and hearth."[134]

For other burghers there was no such inner conflict. They simply saw no sense in continuing the fight. "The call of 'let's go home' which arose after the occupation of Bloemfontein was certainly not a way out for cowardliness, but simply the result of reasoning by each individual burgher: 'The enemy is now so overwhelming that to fight any more is foolish; there is no longer any chance that we can still win, why then must we subject ourselves to the dangers of war?'" wrote an anonymous contemporary Hollander.[135] Similarly, the member of the *Volksraad* for Bethulie, N.J.J.J. van Rensburg, was of the opinion in April 1900 that many surrendered burghers in that district honestly felt that to continue the struggle was futile.[136] On the other hand, in the ranks of those who laid down their arms there were also faint-hearted men who were only too pleased that Roberts's proclamations had given them the opportunity to surrender. Because of the proclamations and the British annexations these men could begin to follow what seemed to be a new dispensation. Even Milner admitted in October 1900 that the "cowardly" behaviour of some surrendered burghers in the southern Free State had meant that the British were initially able to occupy the region very easily.[137]

Then there were also burghers who withdrew from the struggle for material gain. "They love their property more than they hate the British ..." remarked Milner dryly.[138] The wealthy Boers in particular apparently gave up the struggle without suffering too many pangs of conscience. In Ermelo on 11 June 1900 a German, Oskar Hintrager, wrote in his diary: "It is specially the richer Boers that are quietly sitting in their homes, because after all they have something to lose!"[139] In an official Free State wartime newspaper a similar opinion was expressed in April 1901: "There was a time when some OFS burghers must have been afraid, *specially the rich ones; they were afraid to lose their material goods*, and they even went so far as to hand over their weapons to the English."[140] Major-general Pretyman, the military governor in Bloemfontein, made the following unequivocal statement in January 1901 about certain burghers who had surrendered: "The fact is the larger proprietors of whom there are many in the South-eastern districts [of the Free State] are anxious to see the end of the war, if from no other motive than self-interest."[141] On the basis of the quoted evidence it can be accepted that there were many wealthy landowners among those who surrendered, burghers who had a special interest in retaining their property and thus chose to accept Roberts's proclamations instead of fighting on and thereby possibly risking everything they owned.[142] It would, however, be incorrect to assume that only those who were large landowners laid down their arms. Boers who were not as well-to-do and owned less land certainly also had interests involving their property. In addition there is evidence that even burghers who owned no property at all were just as prepared to surrender their arms. In December 1900, when the British were seriously concerned about the way the surrendered burghers were rejoining the commandos, the district commissioner of Smithfield, Major K.P. Apthorp, remarked after retuning from a visit to the various districts that "we found very many bijwoners on farms ... [and] ... there was nothing against these men".[143] Among the *bywoners* (from the Dutch *bijwoners*, meaning farmers who did not own the land but were given use of it in exchange for service), who were by and large the less developed, lower class of burghers in the two republics, there were also apparently those who did not have the ability to recognise the deeper moral issues of the war. Therefore, the ideological aspect of the republican independence ideal presumably had little impact on them.[144] Among the first burghers to withdraw from the struggle in response to Roberts's proclamations there were also those who were not convinced that they had taken the correct step. A burgher from the Rustenburg district who had taken the oath of neutrality subsequently said: "my hand has signed the accursed thing, but God knows my heart is pure and that I intend tearing it up as soon as the first commando appears."[145]

In conclusion it can be said that a group of surrendered burghers in the two republics arose at a time when the military morale of the Boer forces had plunged to a very low level and it appeared to all intents and purposes that Britain had already won the war. Added to this, to a greater or lesser extent, these burghers all had their own personal reasons for responding to Roberts's proclamations. Attempting to gauge the relative importance of these reasons can only lead to speculation. Nevertheless it is highly questionable whether the surrendering would have occurred on such a large scale had it not been for the widespread demoralisation in republican ranks after the defeat at Paardeberg and the British occupations of Bloemfontein and Pretoria.[146] It also appears that these first burghers who laid down their arms had not distanced themselves uniformly from the republican war effort. Certain surrendered burghers promptly rejoined the struggle, but for others, who thought that Roberts's proclamations would grant them immunity, there was to be cruel disillusionment.

Notes

1 J.H. Breytenbach, *Die Geskiedenis van die Tweede Vryheidsoorlog in Suid-Afrika, 1899–1902*, I, pp. 132–3.
2 Breytenbach, *Geskiedenis*, I, pp. 36, 153. The estimates given by the *Times History* and *Official History* on the number of burghers who were originally mobilised differ from those of Breytenbach. The *Times History*, II, p. 88 puts this number at between 37 000 and 40 000 men, while the *Official History*, I, pp. 457–8, annexure 4, gives an even higher figure of 48 216 burghers. According to G. Preller, *Kaptein Hindon: Oorlogsavonture van 'n Baasverkenner*, p. 49 initially 33 500 men were mobilised. Because two authors (Breytenbach and Preller) have arrived independently at more or less the same number (between 32 000 and 35 000 men), it can reasonably be accepted that this estimate is the most likely to be correct.
3 Breytenbach, *Geskiedenis*, I, p. 154.
4 See also Hancock and Van der Poel, *Selections*, I, p. 319 for Smuts's memorandum of 4 September 1899 to the Transvaal government, in which he stresses the necessity that there be enough burghers on the home front for the maintenance of essential services.
5 *Official History*, I, p. 76.
6 Viljoen, *Mijne Herinneringen*, p. 19.
7 *The Standard and Diggers' News*, 29 September 1899 (news report).
8 Leyds Archive, 709(i) p. 59, Magistrate Nylstroom – State secretary, 26 October 1899.
9 Translated from the Dutch. *De Volksstem*, 20 April 1900 (letter from Mrs J.H.W. de Clerq and 17 other women of Carolina, dated 29 March 1900).

10 See W.H. Venter, "Die Geskiedenis van Winburg tot 1902" (Unpublished MA dissertation, UOVS), 1974, p. 176.
11 Steyn Collection, 156/1/122, pp. 177–83, Mrs F. van Rensburg – Steyn, 15 January 1900.
12 Steyn Collection, 156/1/122, pp. 499–503, General Philip Botha – Steyn, 27 January 1900; Spies, "Civilians", p. 16.
13 The writers of the *Times History*, III, p. 73 give the impression that between 15 000 and 20 000 "laggards" originally refused to go to the front. These figures have no real value because the writers did not take into account the fact that many burghers, although liable for military service, had valid reasons to remain on the home front for the maintenance of essential services. No indication could be obtained of the number of burghers who refused to respond to the initial mobilisation orders.
14 Translated from the Dutch. Leyds Archive, 719(e), Telegram 16 of 20 March 1900, Botha – Magistrate Vryheid. See also Leyds Archive, 719(e), Telegram 41 of 20 March 1900, F.W. Reitz – Botha.
15 Translated from the Dutch. SS 8437/R.7823, circular to all magistrates, 4 May 1900.
16 SS 8437/R.7824, Reitz – Kruger, 1 May 1900.
17 Spies, "Civilians", p. 17.
18 HC 120/165, Goold-Adams – Selborne, 17 July and 9 August 1905. Goold-Adams gave a figure of 153 men, but of these 15 were not liable for military service because of illness, physical disability or age. On the handling of the compensation claims of burghers who had not done any commando service at all, see Chapter 8 section 3 below.
19 Translated from the Dutch. Leyds Archive, 781(ii), report of Ram and Thomson, p. 546.
20 Act 20 of 1898, *Voor den Krijgsdienst in De Zuid-Afrikaansche Republiek*, article 36; Act 10 of 1899, *De Krijgs- en Commandowet*, article 36.
21 Archive Landdros (magistrate) Zoutpansberg, 122, "State vs. J.N. van Rensburg re infringement of Martial Law", 20 June 1900.
22 Translated from the Dutch. F. Rompel, *Uit den Tweeden Vrijheidsoorlog: Schetsen en Portretten*, p. 5.
23 See Breytenbach, *Geskiedenis*, I, p. 49; H.C. Hillegas, *With the Boer Forces*, pp. 89–91; *Times History*, II, p. 77; G.D. Scholtz, "Die Tweede Vryheidsoorlog in Wêreldverband", III in *Historia*, 20(2), September 1975, pp. 122–3.
24 See Breytenbach, *Geskiedenis*, I, p. 50; Hillegas, pp. 114–7, *Times History*, III, p. 72.
25 *Official History*, I, pp. 77–8.
26 A787, Preller Collection, 80, L.E. Krause, "Anglo-Boer War", p. 95.
27 HC 65/121, Records on numbers of National Scouts and officers, 24 June 1902; see Chapter 6, section 1 below.
28 See Leyds Archive, 709(ii), p. 176, Commandant-general – General L. Meyer, 21 October 1899; KG 333 (10), p. 947, Acting commandant Vryheid – Acting commandant-general, 31 October 1899; KG 334(1), p. 53, Magistrate Rustenburg – Acting commandant-general, 1 November 1899; Steyn Collection, 156/1/122, p. 933, Commandant W. Theunissen – Steyn, 9 February 1900; *Times History*, III, p. 74.
29 A787, Preller Collection, 81, "Geskiedenis Jacobsdal Kommando", p. 80. The disposition of the burghers and the personal influence of the officers naturally also contributed to the extent to which leave was used and misused. See, for example,

the case in which General Christiaan de Wet granted his burghers leave shortly before the occupation of Bloemfontein (13 March 1900), and 12 days later they were all back at their posts. C.R. de Wet, *De Strijd tusschen Boer en Brit*, pp. 51–3.

30 Translated from the Afrikaans. C. de Jongh and J. Ploeger, "Verslae van Neutrale Militêre Waarnemers tydens die Anglo-Boereoorlog (Kapt. J. Allum)" in *Militaria*, 4(1), 1973, p. 33.

31 [G.] de Villebois-Mareuil, *War Notes*, p. 289, 4 March 1900.

32 A787, Preller Collection, 80, L.E. Krause, "Anglo-Boer War", p. 44.

33 For the events on the Natal front and their impact on the republican burghers see C.J. Barnard, *Generaal Louis Botha op die Natalse Front 1899–1900*, pp. 119–47; Breytenbach, *Geskiedenis*, III, pp. 526–67; C.M. Bakkes, *Die Britse deurbraak aan die Benede-Tugela op Majubadag 1900*, pp. 56–8.

34 *Times History*, III, p. 484; Spies, "Civilians", p. 44.

35 J.L. Basson, "Die Slag van Paardeberg" (Unpublished MA dissertation, UP), 1971, p. 153; F.D. Conradie, *Met Cronjé aan die Wesfront (1899–1900)*, p. 194.

36 De Villebois-Mareuil, pp. 285, 288, 3 and 4 March 1900; N. Hofmeyr, *Zes Maanden bij de Commando's*, p. 325.

37 Translated from the Dutch. De Wet, *Boer en Brit*, p. 42.

38 Cd. 35, p. 2, Steyn and Kruger – Salisbury, 5 March 1900; N.J. van der Merwe, *M.T. Steyn. 'n Lewensbeskrywing*, II, pp. 8, 53–7; *Times History*, VI, p. 3.

39 Cd. 457, pp. 18–22, Roberts's report, 15 March 1900; Leyds Archive, 718(f), telegram 18 of 9 March 1900, A. Fischer – P. Grobler; *Times History*, III, p. 562; De Wet, *Boer en Brit*, pp. 44–9.

40 *Times History*, III, pp. 574–90.

41 S.F. Malan, "Die Rol van J. Geo. Fraser in die Vrystaat, 1863–1927" (Unpublished MA dissertation, UOVS), 1971, p. 224; S.F. Malan, "Die Britse Besetting van Bloemfontein, 13 Maart 1900" in *Historia*, 20(1), May 1975, p. 40; Spies, "Civilians", p. 48.

42 Malan, "Fraser", p. 236; see Chapter 3, section 1 below.

43 Malan, "Fraser", pp. 225–6.

44 CO 417/2B7/9582 (FK 313, p. 28), Milner – Chamberlain, 3 March 1900 and enclosures, Resident commissioner Maseru – High commissioner, 1 March 1900 and member of *volksraad* of Scottish origin – Resident commissioner, 27 February 1900. See also Malan, "Die Britse Besetting van Bloemfontein, 13 Maart 1900", p. 36.

45 Malan, "Die Britse Besetting van Bloemfontein, 13 Maart 1900", p. 41.

46 Leyds Archive, 718(f), telegram 15 of 18 March 1900, Kruger – Commandantgeneral; Leyds Archive, 749(a), telegram 28 of 1 June 1900, Steyn – Kruger.

47 Translated from the Dutch. De Wet, *Boer en Brit*, p. 50.

48 J.C. Roos, "Johannesburg en die Tweede Vryheidsoorlog, Oktober 1899 – Mei 1900" (Unpublished D.Litt. thesis, Unisa), 1949, pp. 381–2; *Times History*, IV, pp. 143–8; *Official History*, III, pp. 77–89; D. Reitz, *Kommando: 'n Boere-dagboek uit die Engelse oorlog*, pp. 105–6.

49 Translated from the Dutch. Leyds Archive, 781(i), report from Ram and Thomson, p. 541 (copy).

50 Translated from the Dutch. *De Volksstem*, 2 June 1900 (Letter from an "Old Burgher").

51 Hancock and Van der Poel, *Selections*, I, pp. 543–4, "Memoirs".

52 *Official History*, III, pp. 226–7; J.F. Naudé, *Vechten en Vluchten van Beyers en Kemp 'bôkant' de Wet*, p. 110; A787, Preller Collection, 80, L.E. Krause, "Anglo-Boer War", p. 128; Hancock and Van der Poel, *Selections*, I, p. 547, "Memoirs".
53 Hancock and Van der Poel, *Selections*, I, p. 551, "Memoirs".
54 CO 417/291/23673 (FK 333, pp. 636–47), "Telegrams found [sic] at Pretoria", 29 May to 5 June 1900.
55 Translated from the Afrikaans. E. Williams-Foxcroft and M.C.E. van Schoor (eds), "Die dépêches van die Russiese attachés, kol. Stakhovitch en lt.kol. Gurko" in *Christiaan de Wet-annale*, 3, 1975, p. 197.
56 Breytenbach, *Geskiedenis*, III, p. 570; *Times History*, III, p. 595.
57 Breytenbach, *Geskiedenis*, I, pp. 50–1.
58 Cd. 426, p. 2, Proclamation I. The proclamation is only dated "February 1900". Apparently it was issued on 17 February 1900. See Spies, "Civilians", p. 37 note 10.
59 WO *Confidential Telegrams*, 154a, Roberts – British secretary of state for war, 10 February 1900.
60 C. Headlam, *The Milner Papers*, 1899–1905, II, p. 52, Milner – Roberts, 21 January 1900. Headlam claims incorrectly that this letter refers to a later proclamation which Roberts issued on 15 March 1900, after the occupation of Bloemfontein (13 March 1900). The date and the content of the letter show that the letter refers to the February proclamation. See also Spies, "Civilians", p. 38 note 13.
61 CO 417/286/4864 (FK 310, p. 194), Milner – Chamberlain, 13 February 1900.
62 CO 417/286/5158 (FK 311, p. 271), Milner – Chamberlain, 16 February 1900.
63 Cd. 426, p. 3, Proclamation III, 15 March 1900.
64 Cd. 426, p. 23, XLI, "Oath of Neutrality".
65 Spies, "Civilians", pp. 50–1.
66 *Milner Papers*, 32, (FK 1168, p. 517), Milner – P. Lyttelton Gell, 19 February 1901.
67 J.M. Spaight, *War Rights on Land*, pp. 148–9.
68 L. Oppenheim, *International Law. A Treatise*, (edited by H. Lauterpacht), II, *Disputes, War and Neutrality*, p. 427.
69 Cd. 800, p. 26; Spies, "Civilians", p. 49; Buys, p. 20.
70 MGP 263, "Army Order" 487, 27 January 1901; M.C. Jackson, *A Soldier's Diary, 1899–1901*, p. 347. See Chapter 2, section 1 below.
71 Translated from the Dutch. Leyds Archive, 781(ii), report of Ram and Thomson, p. 526.
72 *Telegrams and Letters sent by Field-marshal Lord Roberts*, i, p. 83, Military Secretary – Revds H.C.J. Becker and W. Postma, Bethulie, 1 April 1900.
73 Cd. 426, p. 7, XII, Proclamation 1 of 1900, 31 May 1900.
74 Spies, "Civilians", p. 72.
75 Cd. 426, pp. 8–9, XVI, Proclamation 2 of 1900, 6 June 1900.
76 Translated from the Dutch. W. van Everdingen, *De Oorlog in Zuid-Afrika, Tweede Tijdvak*, I, p. 310.
77 See Chapter 2, section 1 below.
78 Translated from the Dutch. *Officieel Verslag van de Verrichten van het Nasionaal Kongres gehouden te Brandfort, 1 en 2 Desember 1904*, (Official report of the proceedings of the National Convention held at Brandfort ...) p. 34.

79 Cd. 800, pp. 26–9, section III of the Hague Convention; Spaight, pp. 335, 372.
80 Cd. 800, p. 26.
81 Cd. 426, p. 3, Proclamation III, 15 March 1900.
82 Oppenheim, II, pp. 439–40.
83 Cd. 800, p. 26; Spaight, p. 327.
84 Spaight, p. 327.
85 *Times History*, IV, pp. 6–7, 82.
86 See Hancock and Van der Poel, *Selections*, I, p. 577, "Memoirs"; Chapter 2, section 1 below.
87 Spaight, p. 373 shows that although an oath of neutrality was not in violation of the existing practices of war, demanding an oath of neutrality without the reality of an effective occupation can be seen as grounds for censure.
88 See Van der Merwe, II, pp. 13–4; *Buitengewone Staatscourant der Z.A.R.* (Government Gazette, SAR), 14 June 1900; Chapter 2, section 1 below.
89 In some cases the surrendered burghers, for example, had to provide food for the British troops and care for their horses. Cattle belonging to the surrendered burghers were also commandeered on a large scale by the British army. Leyds Archive, 734(16), Republican circular, 15 June 1900; M.G.P. 28/4031/00, P.J. Bornmann – Military governor, 28 September 1900; Chapter 2, section 2 below.
90 *The Friend*, 7 October 1904 (editorial).
91 Hancock and Van der Poel, *Selections*, I, p. 547, "Memoirs".
92 Cd. 426, p. 6, XI, 24 May 1900; Leyds Archive, 771(b), (1 1), P.A. Nierstrasz, "Der Süd-Afrikanische Krieg", p. 921.
93 Cd. 426, p. 16, XXIX, 1 September 1900.
94 CO 417/287/10966 (FK 315, p. 557), Milner – Roberts, 16 March 1900.
95 *Telegrams and Letters ... Roberts*, ii, p. 32, telegram C1532, Roberts – Milner, 9 May 1900.
96 Cd. 426, XXXI, Proclamation 17 of 1900, 14 September 1900. Contrary to what Roberts claimed in this proclamation, the executive council of the SAR in fact granted the ageing President Kruger leave on 28 August 1900 to go to Europe to further the republican cause. Government Gazette SAR, 14 September 1900.
97 Cd. 261, p. 155, English version of President Steyn's counter-proclamation, 11 June 1900; Government Gazette SAR, 3 September 1900.
98 Cd. 261, p. 155.
99 Quoted by Spies, "Civilians", p. 91.
100 Oppenheim, II, pp. 435–6 n. 4.
101 Translated from the Dutch. Hancock and Van der Poel, *Selections*, I, p. 340, Smuts – Botha.
102 Translated from the Dutch. Archive Landdros (magistrate) Zoutpansberg, 122, "The Government vs A. Pohl", 20 October 1900. The case was not heard.
103 Translated from the Dutch. Archive Landdros (magistrate) Zoutpansberg, 122, "The Government vs L.J. le Grange", 20 October 1900. Le Grange was sentenced to three months imprisonment with hard labour.
104 For the establishment and functioning of the military administration see Buys, pp. 309–42 and *passim*; Spies, "Civilians", pp. 80–135.
105 *Times History*, VI, p. 4; Hancock and Van der Poel, *Selections*, I, p. 577, "Memoirs".

106 Spies, "Civilians", p. 51.
107 Roberts Papers, WO 105/26/191 (A392), Gatacre – Roberts, 15 March 1900.
108 L.M. Phillipps, *With Rimington*, p. 93.
109 Spies, "Civilians", p. 52.
110 CO 417/287/10953 (FK 315, p. 619), Lagden – Milner, 18 March 1900 (copy).
111 WO 32/878/8721 (A379), "Translation of the Proceedings of the Volksraad of the OFS", Kroonstad, 2 April 1900 (copy).
112 Quoted by D. James, *Lord Roberts*, p. 305.
113 Hancock and Van der Poel, *Selections*, I, p. 568, "Memoirs".
114 De Wet, *Boer en Brit*, pp. 84–5.
115 A787, Preller Collection 81, "Geskiedenis Edenburg Kommando", p. 50; *Times History*, III, p. 591.
116 *The Cape Argus*, 17 March 1900 (news report); *The Times*, 19 March 1900 (news report).
117 These statistics are complied from the following sources: PMO 77/P.77, "Return of Arms handed in by the Free State", 15 March 1900 to 5 June 1900; MGB 4, District commissioners Smithfield – Military governor, 24 May 1900; MGB 5, District commissioners Boshof and Jacobsdal – Military governor, 7 June 1900. As far as is known this is the only set of records which can be regarded as anywhere near complete. The version which appears in the Transvaal colonial blue book, *List of burghers who surrendered their arms in the Transvaal and Orange River Colony, 1900*, is very unreliable indeed. For Fauresmith for example, only four surrendered burghers are listed. This is known to be inaccurate. According to De Wet, *Boer en Brit*, p. 85 the Fauresmith commando was thinned out to such an extent that only 28 burghers remained. On the Boer side there are apparently no full records.
118 CO 417/290/18248 (FK 327, p. 213), Milner – Chamberlain, 23 May 1900; *The Times*, 21 May 1900 (news report).
119 PMO 77/P77, "Return of Arms handed in by the Free State", 15 March 1900 to 5 June 1900; *Official History*, III, p. 107.
120 *Times History*, IV, p. 127; *Official History*, III, p. 63; De Wet, *Boer en Brit*, p. 79.
121 *Telegrams and Letters ... Roberts*, II, pp. 39–40, telegram C. 1602, Roberts – Hamilton, 14 May 1900.
122 *Times History*, IV, p. 127.
123 See Chapter 2, section 1 below and Chapter 4, section 1 below.
124 See Chapter 2, section 1 below and Chapter 4, section 1 below.
125 Milner Papers, 45, (FK 1205, p. 1044), Milner – Kitchener, 31 October 1900.
126 A787, Preller Collection, 81, "Geskiedenis Jacobsdal Kommando", p. 79.
127 See *Times History*, IV, pp. 23–5, 264–8; De Wet, *Boer en Brit*, pp. 55–68, 86–102; Chapter 2, section 1 below.
128 Hancock and Van der Poel, *Selections*, I, p. 547, "Memoirs".
129 MGP 287, "Official Bulletin", no 1 and 2, respectively 14 and 15 June 1900.
130 Hancock and Van der Poel, *Selections*, I, p. 566, "Memoirs".
131 According to Breytenbach, *Geskiedenis*, I, p. 36 there were about 54 667 burghers in the two republics who were liable for military service when the war broke out. See also Chapter 1, section 1 above.

132 Oosthuizen, "Krygsgevangenes", pp. 89, 486.
133 Translated from the Dutch. Rompel, pp. 13–4.
134 Translated from the Dutch. P. Pienaar, *Met Steyn en De Wet*, p. 130.
135 Translated from the Dutch. A1149, "Het Volkskarakter der Zuid-Afrikaansche Boeren door eigen ervaring en aanschouwing gegeven", anonymous and undated piece (apparently 1901).
136 WO 32/878/8721 (A379), "Translations of the Proceedings of the Volksraad of the OFS", Kroonstad, 2 April 1900 (copy).
137 *Milner Papers*, 45, (FK 1205, p. 1044), Milner – Kitchener, 31 October 1900.
138 *Milner Papers*, 45, (FK 1205, p. 1044), Milner – Kitchener, 31 October 1900.
139 Translated from the Afrikaans. J.J. Oberholster (ed), "Dagboek van Oskar Hintrager: Saam met Christiaan de Wet, Mei tot September 1900" in *Christiaan de Wet-annale*, 2, October 1973, p. 31.
140 Translated from the Dutch. *De Brandwacht*, 25 April 1901 (editorial). Italics: A.G.
141 *Milner Papers*, 46, (FK 1135, pp. 193–4), Pretyman – Milner, 2 January 1901.
142 Undisciplined behaviour in the period March – April by British troops had already led *inter alia* to the plundering of farmsteads and the theft of cattle on farms where the owners were absent. See Spies "Civilians", pp. 61–4.
143 MGB 4, District commissioner Smithfield – Military governor Bloemfontein, 3 December 1900.
144 See Solomon, p. 14 who is of the opinion that there were burghers "who were not sufficiently endowed to grasp the deeper issues involved in the war itself". For the disposition of some *bywoners* see Chapter 7, section 1 below.
145 Hancock and Van der Poel, *Selections*, I, p. 578, "Memoirs".
146 As the war progressed there were naturally also burghers who withdrew from the war on their own initiative. For a discussion of this during the period January 1901 to May 1902, see Chapter 4, section 1 below.

Chapter 2
Vicissitudes of the surrendered burghers and their ilk, March – December 1900

1 Republican re-commandeering

The republican leaders reacted sharply to the British proclamations that had given rise to this group of surrendered burghers. On the eve of the occupation of Bloemfontein by Roberts, the seat of the Free State government was hurriedly moved to Kroonstad. As he departed, President Steyn addressed the remaining members of the commandos at Brandfort and Smaldeel and appealed to them not to heed Roberts's proclamations.[1] On 17 March 1900 a general meeting of the war council was held at Kroonstad where it was decided to continue the war with renewed vigour.[2] Two days later (19 March 1900) Steyn issued two counter-proclamations in reply to Roberts's proclamations.[3]

In the first of these proclamations Steyn assured the Free State burghers that the government was still functional and that Roberts's proclamations were therefore null and void within the boundaries of the republic. Burghers who took the oath of neutrality were thus still liable for military service and those who gave assistance to the British or who simply laid down their arms rendered themselves guilty of high treason and were punishable to the full extent of the law.

In the second proclamation Steyn adopted a more informal tone and appealed to the patriotism of each burgher. He made the point that if Roberts succeeded in dividing the Free State people, it would make his task of defeating the republics so much easier. He hotly denied Roberts's claim that the republican leaders had misled the people,[4] their *volk*, and pointed to the fact that the war was being

51

waged with their full consent, freely given. Steyn then went on to express his misgivings about whether the British would leave the burghers in peace once they had laid down their arms, and warned them not to be misled by the trickery of a wily enemy. "He who attempts to win over another to falsehood," he said, "is himself not to be trusted."[5] On 9 June 1900 President Kruger made a similar attempt to neutralise the effects of Roberts's proclamation by issuing another counter-proclamation. He warned the burghers that if they were swayed by the "fine promises" Roberts had made, they would not only be neglecting their national duty, but would make themselves guilty of high treason.[6] Shortly after Kruger's proclamation, the state secretary of the Transvaal, F.W. Reitz, directed a similar warning to the burghers, pointing out to them that the government of the Z.A.R. did not recognise the oath of neutrality and that it certainly did not exempt any burgher from further military duty.[7]

The stance of the republican leaders that the surrendered burghers were liable to be re-commandeered was fully justified. No army can close its eyes to the fact that its soldiers simply discharge themselves on their own initiative – least of all while fighting a war. The British army authorities would also certainly not have allowed their soldiers to resign arbitrarily. Indeed, the British *Manual of Military Law* expressly stated: "A soldier cannot, according to the English practice give his parole except through a commissioned officer."[8] It would thus be unreasonable to expect the republican leaders to tamely accept such behaviour.[9] In the light of this it is understandable that the republican authorities made a concerted effort to bring those who had fallen prey to Roberts's proclamations back under arms. By the end of March 1900 the protection permits issued by the British to surrendered burghers in the vicinity of Ficksburg were summarily destroyed, and these people were sent to the front again.[10] The Free State government also sent out mounted police to re-commandeer burghers. This measure met with only limited success because the police were not able to operate efficiently in the areas that had been occupied by the British.[11]

The mobile General De Wet also encountered this problem, but nevertheless managed by the beginning of April 1900 to re-commandeer 110 men in the Reddersburg and Dewetsdorp area. On 4 April he came to blows with Gatacre at Mostertshoek and captured 470 British soldiers – a victory that had a favourable impact on his recruitment campaign. Roberts, who was under the impression that De Wet would move further south to destroy the railway network, temporarily withdrew the garrisons from Smithfield, Rouxville and Zastron in order to guard the railways and bridges. This made it possible, shortly afterwards, for General C.C. Froneman, on instructions from De Wet, to re-commandeer about 500 men in the southern Free State.[12] In April 1900 P.J. Fourie was also able to do some recruitment in the vicinity of Bloemfontein.[13]

The victories gained by the Free State forces by the middle of 1900 – particularly that by De Wet at Rooiwal on 7 June – were evidence that the British occupations were far from effective and this gave the republican forces new courage.[14] In the second half of 1900 concerted efforts were initiated to re-commandeer surrendered burghers in the Free State.

De Wet was the driving force behind the recruitment campaign and he had an almost magnetic influence over the burghers. At the end of July 1900, when he was encamped near the Vaal River, many surrendered burghers came forward of their own accord to rejoin the commandos.[15] On 25 July, De Wet was able to inform the Transvaal government that the "disloyal burghers" were joining up in "great numbers" and appeared to be determined to fight on with renewed courage.[16] By 8 August about 400 surrendered burghers had rejoined De Wet's commando.[17]

After De Wet's march into the Transvaal (that is to say the first British drive against De Wet), at the beginning of September 1900 he set his sights on "putting all the burghers who had laid down their arms and sworn an oath of neutrality, under arms once more".[18] Commandant P.J. Fourie was made responsible for the re-commandeering of the surrendered burghers in the districts of Bloemfontein, Bethulie, Smithfield, Rouxville and Wepener, while General J.B.M. Hertzog was in charge in the Fauresmith, Philippolis and Jacobsdal districts. Commandant (later General) C.C.J. Badenhorst covered the districts of Boshof and Hoopstad. The method usually followed was to send ahead a number of officers, each accompanied by a few men, to inform the burghers and warn them to prepare themselves for military service. This commandeering campaign was largely successful and during September and the first part of November 1900, Fourie commandeered 750 men, Hertzog 1200 and Badenhorst 1000 burghers.[19] In the northern Free State General P. Botha and Commandant A. Ross called up surrendered burghers in the vicinity of Frankfort and Vrede,[20] but the exact number recruited is unknown.

In the Transvaal, action was also taken against those who had surrendered, particularly after General de la Rey's decisive victory at Silkaatsnek on 11 July 1900. According to Smuts this was "a blow the effects of which were almost immediately to be felt all over the Western Transvaal".[21] De la Rey himself realised that he could capitalise on this victory and without delay he took steps to put all inactive burghers under arms again. That he was absolutely correct in his assessment is demonstrated by the fact that barely ten days later he had persuaded 1200 men to re-arm.[22] His hard-hitting military tactics and dramatic successes clearly underlined the ineffectiveness of the British occupation in the western Transvaal. The aftermath of victory spread far and wide and many of the demoralised burghers who had laid down arms came to the realisation that the republican cause was not yet lost. There were many burghers who now rejoined the commandos on their own initiative.[23]

In the northern Transvaal General C.F. Beyers was equally uncompromising in his actions against burghers who had surrendered. He regarded these people as traitors, because in his opinion their absence from the commandos had strengthened the hand of the enemy. In September 1900 he sent out patrols to re-commandeer them and at the same time he had their names published in the local newspaper, *De Zoutpansberg Wachter*. Within a week of the publication of the list of names, the burghers concerned had to report to their commandos.[24] The editor of *De Zoutpansberg Wachter* assisted with this recruiting campaign, and in a leading article he addressed the surrendered burghers as follows: "For what reason are you so indecisive; why do you turn your back towards the enemy; why do you withdraw from the struggle? Where now is your faith; where are the people who were so imbued with heroism; where is the spirit of the Voortrekkers? ... Fellow burghers, you must change your attitude immediately. Otherwise we shall lose our country and our freedom will be gone forever."[25] This wake-up call, coming at the same time as the actions of Beyers, had the desired effect, and many burghers rejoined the commandos.[26]

From October 1900 measures were taken in the eastern Transvaal to commandeer the surrendered burghers. By 12 October 1900 various Boer patrols in the Utrecht district made a concerted effort to place these men under arms again.[27] By the end of October patrols were sent out for the same purpose in the Heidelberg and Bethal districts.[28] Approximately a month later Commandant-general Louis Botha issued orders from Ermelo that the field-cornets in the various wards should draw up lists of the names of burghers who had surrendered and should see to it that these people were enlisted again.[29] It is clear that some of these initiatives bore fruit because even the reports drawn up by the British military intelligence service make mention of the fact that the re-commandeering of surrendered burghers in the eastern Transvaal met with considerable success.[30]

The success of the republican campaign to re-commandeer those who had surrendered can be ascribed to several factors. The Boer military victories and the influence of dynamic leaders like De Wet, De la Rey and Botha served as strong encouragement to the men to join up again.[31] Another important aspect that boosted the republican recruitment campaign was the ineffectiveness of the British occupation and Roberts's inability to protect the men who had surrendered from those Boers who were still fighting. Had Roberts been able to keep the districts in which the surrendered burghers were living effectively separated from the commandos, it would have been almost impossible for the surrendered Boers to rejoin the commandos and thus break the oath of neutrality.[32] An equally important reason was the poor treatment the surrendered burghers received at the hands of the British. Many of those who were bitterly disillusioned by their experiences decided voluntarily to rejoin the commandos.[33] It is estimated that about 3960 Free Staters took up arms again.[34] Comparative numbers are not available for the Transvaal.

How did the republican authorities treat the burghers who surrendered? Those who voluntarily rejoined the commandos were almost without exception welcomed with open arms. De Wet was more than prepared to be indulgent towards them if they were committed to remaining loyal in the future. However, some of the burghers in the field were of the opinion that these burghers should be punished.[35] De Wet was not in favour of this and warned: "You know, my brothers, that we all have a conscience and that this conscience often dozes off to sleep. Many of these fell asleep when Lord Roberts occupied Bloemfontein, but I was confident that the consciences of these people would awaken again. Now I think, brothers, that they have enough to bear, because when their consciences awakened they caused dreadful pangs of remorse."[36] As a matter of form these burghers were each fined £5.[37] Because the integrity of some of the burghers was still in doubt, it was decided that those who had surrendered should be required to make a new commitment to the republican cause by taking an oath of loyalty and renouncing the British oath of neutrality which they had signed.[38] By voluntarily rejoining the Boer forces these men withdrew from the ranks of surrendered burghers and thus cannot for practical purposes still be seen as *hendsoppers*.

But there were also many surrendered burghers who used every possible means to evade the attempts to make them commit to the republican war effort again. Some hid under the floorboards of their homes or in caves.[39] According to a war correspondent from *De Zuid-Afrikaan*, "There were reports coming in from everywhere that republicans were hiding out on their farms, spending the days in the hills and ravines and returning to their homes at night when it became bitterly cold … It is amazing that the Boer force can maintain its strength if there are so many deserters."[40] Many of the surrendered burghers in the Free State fled to the Fouriesburg district where they sought shelter in the mountains.[41]

On the question of whether the authorities at any stage forced surrendered burghers to go on commando again there is conflicting evidence. General de Wet and Commandant C.C.J. Badenhorst claimed that reluctant burghers were never forced to rejoin the commandos.[42] On the other hand, Colonel A. Western, a British officer, alleged that the surrendered burghers in the Boshof district "are being tied with reins and in one instance [a] farmer was brought away handcuffed".[43] This evidence is corroborated to some extent by Captain Danie Theron, the renowned Boer scout. Theron had very little patience with deserters and declared that "those who do not obey must be forced by means of loaded rifles to do their duty".[44] According to P.S. Lombard, a heliographer under De Wet, they were told that burghers who refused to join up should be arrested.[45] Other available evidence also shows that the Boers did indeed use force against dissident Boers on commando.[46] In the light of other evidence, the statement by De Wet and Badenhorst should perhaps not be seen as generally valid, but it cannot be alleged that the republican actions in this regard were in any way irregular. As previously mentioned, they had every right to demand military service from the surrendered burghers. Deserters who rejoined the commandos were not simply re-issued with arms. This applied particularly to those who joined only after being subjected to pressure from the authorities. It is understandable that there would be a measure of distrust as far as these men were concerned. In such cases they were grouped together apart from the other men. Despite the fact that they were also guarded to prevent them from leaving the commando and taking information about the Boer movements to the British, a number did manage to escape.[47] There are historians who claim that the Boers burned down the homes of some surrendered burghers when they refused to return to the commandos.[48] Kitchener also held this opinion and in June 1902 he gave it as one of the reasons for the establishment of the concentration camps.[49] It appears that this deduction is based primarily on a letter which Commandant-general Botha wrote to the magistrate at Bethal, in which he made mention of his intention to confiscate the possessions of the surrendered burghers. He also threatened that their houses could be burned down.[50] This is the only evidence that Botha did in fact consider such measures against the surrendered burghers. Although he made it clear in a circular issued on the same day that "from now on action will be taken: all the property of surrendered burghers is at risk", he makes no mention that their homes would be burned down.[51] The issue is put into clearer perspective in his circular of 3 December 1900 that provided instructions on the treatment of surrendered burghers. In this circular he insisted that, in cases where a gaol term had been imposed upon a deserter and his movable property confiscated, sufficient provisions, and by implication also the house, had to be left for the family members who remained on the farm. Furthermore, in this circular there is no mention at all of the burning of homes.[52] It is clear that Botha only mentioned the possibility of destroying deserters' houses in passing and as a threat; he had no intention of implementing it as a form of punishment. Botha was not a man with a destructive disposition[53] and he would not lightly have resorted to such measures. Furthermore, burning down the homes of these dissident compatriots was not part of the official Boer policy.[54]

This is not to deny that there were a few cases where the homes belonging to surrendered burghers were burned down by Boers who were still fighting.[55] But these were isolated incidents and are fully understandable in the light of the war and the emotional state of mind of some of the burghers. Where it did in fact occur, it was contrary to the wishes of the republican high command. It also happened that the Boers sometimes purposely cut a telegraph line near the home of a surrendered burgher so that the British military authorities might suspect that he was perhaps still secretly cooperating with the Boers. This being the case, the British troops would then burn down the burgher's house because they were under the impression that the Boers would not have cut the telegraph line without the connivance of the home owner.[56]

On 19 July 1900 Steyn issued a proclamation in which he held out the prospect of the death penalty for surrendered burghers. The relevant article of the proclamation reads as follows: "Any conscript who leaves his commando without lawful reason will immediately be arrested and brought before the Commandant-general, and may, after investigation by the Commandant-general or a person appointed by him, be condemned to death."[57] As far as can be ascertained there were no bona fide surrendered burghers – who in other words remained fully committed to the oath of neutrality and thus did not join the commandos or provide information to the British – who were convicted under this proclamation. In some circles the republican forces were accused of shooting some of these people. A war correspondent of *The Bloemfontein Post*, for example, alleged that in December 1900 De Wet shot a certain J. Rademan of the Harrismith district: "He refused to break his oath of neutrality and was thereupon shot in the presence of his aged mother and the rest of the family."[58] Revd S.J. du Toit, one of the founder members in 1875 of the

Genootskap van Regte Afrikaners (an early Afrikaner language and cultural organisation) and an eminent figure in religious circles, alleged after the Anglo-Boer War that "Thousands [of surrendered burghers] were forced to break the oath they had sworn and there are instances where some of them were actually shot dead because they remained true to their oath."[59] No confirmation could be found for these allegations. *The Bloemfontein Post* was a self-confessed enemy of the republican cause and it is a well-known fact that after 1890, when he grew friendly with Cecil John Rhodes, Revd du Toit became estranged from the political ideals of the Afrikaners.

As a consequence of Steyn's proclamation Commandant Badenhorst, who was now in charge of the re-commandeering of surrendered burghers, said that only after a thorough investigation and then "only in very serious cases" were these men shot[60] – in other words only when they had broken the neutrality oath and had supported the British war effort in one way or another. Generally speaking the dissidents who made a concerted effort to remain neutral were given one or more of the following punishments: a fine, a prison sentence, corporal punishment – usually 25 lashes with a stirrup leather – or the confiscation of their movable assets.[61]

In cases where the surrendered burghers did in fact provide the British with information and thereby broke their oath of neutrality, the Boers showed less clemency. The district commissioner of Boshof, Captain R.J. Ross reported: "The Boers have shot several men who have attempted to get away with information ...".[62] According to Commandant Badenhorst these burghers were executed by firing squad, but only after a proper military hearing.[63] In accordance with military law the republicans were fully entitled to execute these persons because they were not simply deserters from the republican forces, but in addition were guilty of spying as they had secretly passed information about Boer movements to the British.[64]

Only one incident could be traced where a surrendered burgher provided the British with information and was executed by the Boers without first being granted a legal hearing. According to a statement by Mrs L.F. Krynauw of Ladybrand, her husband A.C. Krynauw, who regularly provided information to the British, was shot dead on his farm, Woodlands, in the Ladybrand district by Barend Scheepers on

26 November 1900. She claims that Scheepers and 11 other Boers of the Ficksburg commando came to the farm to take her husband to the Boer laager. Krynauw adopted a defiant attitude and flatly refused to budge, whereupon Scheepers shot him.[65] There is little reason to doubt Mrs Krynauw's version of the incident.[66]

Although it should be taken into consideration that in addition to acting as a spy for the British, Krynauw was also a deserter from the republican forces, nevertheless the fact that he was shot without a military hearing is a contravention of article 30 of the Hague Convention.[67] People who prejudiced the republican cause by their disloyalty, often aroused vehement emotions on the Boer side. A fiery patriot such as De Wet said at the end of June 1900 that he "… would be the first to shoot such a man down in cold blood".[68] There is no evidence that De Wet in fact ever carried out his threat and the vast majority of surrendered burghers who provided information to the British were tried by properly constituted military courts. In many of the cases where the death penalty was imposed, it was not carried out.[69]

When the republican authorities in fact carried out the death penalty, the burghers who were still fighting sometimes found it very difficult to reconcile themselves to the execution of their compatriots. Prior to the execution by firing squad of R. McLachlan, J.P.D. Theunissen, H. Ahrens, R. Boyd and C.J. Matthysen on charges of high treason on 23 February 1901 in the district of Wolmaransstad, 218 burghers signed a petition pleading unsuccessfully that mercy be shown to those who were sentenced to die.[70] When the war was over, H.M. Guest, who was the editor of the *Klerksdorp Mining Record* wrote of this incident: "The executions were undoubtedly legal, but the fact that the judges, executioners, and condemned were all friends and of one race, made the circumstances peculiarly painful, and it is one of the lamentable results of the late struggle that it has aroused personal animosities and feuds which will survive a long time … ."[71] For some of the fighting Boers the execution of their renegade compatriots was one of the most distasteful aspects of the war. Years later in 1938, I. van W. Raubenheimer, who was attached to De la Rey's commando during the war, wrote in his memoirs: "The worst memory of the Second War of Independence was witnessing the execution of a few republican renegades. The four men had been sentenced to death by a Boer council of war. A number of young Cape rebels were ordered to be at a specific place at a predetermined time ... The young men experienced the same emotional anguish as those who had been sentenced. Among the four who were spending their last moments on earth was an old man with a beard hanging well down his chest; the other three were members of his family. As the prisoners were led to the place of execution they began to sing 'Yea, though I walk through the valley of the shadow of death'. This made the firing squad almost insane with emotion ... That evening when the commando as usual held its prayer hour, it was the young men who uncharacteristically led the prayers. When the one was too choked with emotion after a few words, the next one took over."[72]

In spite of the fact that the republican forces treated the surrendered burghers justly under the circumstances,[73] some members of this group did not see it this way. After the war a number of them alleged that the re-commandeering of surrendered burghers meant that they were forced to break a holy vow – "in contravention of all godly and earthly laws" – and that this compelled them "to place ourselves under the protection of the British military forces".[74] An anonymous surrendered burgher also expressed his dissatisfaction about the Wolmaransstad executions. In a wildly emotional outburst after the war he wrote: "They [the executed] had to be blind-folded and were shot down like murderers to fall into their graves, and those who did not die at once were again shot through the head down in the grave! Do they call this legal? We know that there are thousands who may to-day still rejoice in the death of those dear ones, but fortunately not all."[75] Some of the family members of surrendered burghers who had been sentenced to imprisonment also wrote anonymous letters to General Ben Viljoen, threatening him with death because of his actions in this regard.[76]

2 British treatment of the surrendered burghers and further British proclamations

The manner in which the surrendered burghers were treated by the British must be seen against the background of the inability of the

British army to put an end to the mobile warfare tactics which the Boers had adopted. From about the middle of 1900 the Boers turned increasingly, and with great success, to this type of warfare. In the Free State, De Wet was the real epicentre around whom these military tactics revolved, and in the Transvaal it was De la Rey, Botha and Beyers who distinguished themselves. The struggle changed from a conventional war, with the emphasis on set-piece battles, to one which was far more mobile. In practice, this meant that the republicans would entice the British into smaller clashes and damage their lines of communication by blowing up railway and telegraph lines. Roberts was unable to restrict these activities by employing purely military measures. The counter-tactics that he decided to use were to impact significantly on the surrendered burghers.[77] The fact that Roberts was unable to prevent the Boer commandos from entering the districts under British control meant that he could also not stop the surrendered burghers from being re-commandeered. Because of the lack of British protection, many of the surrendered burghers virtually had no other choice than to break their oath of neutrality and rejoin the Boer forces. Captain R.J. Ross, the district commissioner of Boshof, confirms this contention: "… the burghers in this district are not for war, but being between the devil and the deep sea, they are so flurried that we have not much chance of holding them, except by a display of force."[78] Despite the fact that he was unable to afford the surrendered burghers any protection, Roberts insisted that they had to remain true to their oath of neutrality.[79] This placed them in a highly invidious position. According to Le May, "Many an individual was faced with the grim alternative of being treated by the British as an oath-breaker or by his own people as a renegade; and usually it was his own people who presented the immediate alternative more compellingly."[80] Roberts made it abundantly clear that he would act harshly against burghers who broke the oath,[81] but by May 1900 he was still prepared to allow such people to return to their homes provided that they could prove that they had been forced into joining the commandos.[82] This concession presumably arose because Roberts felt that an increase in the number of surrendered burghers would bring a speedy end to the war. He explained this to Lieutenant-general Buller as follows: "It is much to be regretted that we cannot give protection to all burghers who surrender; nevertheless I think, we must do all we can to get them to surrender. The more they do so, the sooner the war will be over."[83] Roberts thus saw the surrendered Boers as a possible instrument to end the war, but this vain hope was soon dashed by among other things the indifferent treatment which the surrendered burghers received at the hands of the British army.

Even as early as April 1900 there was talk that the homesteads of those who broke their oath would be burned down by the British army, and by September it was the general practice.[84] Roberts was not acting in contravention of the terms of the Hague Convention by punishing these people, but this does not mean that burning down their homes can be regarded as a justifiable method of exacting punishment.[85] Although the policy of farm burning was originally aimed at surrendered burghers who voluntarily rejoined the commandos, it also had grave implications for bona fide surrendered Boers. The problem was that Roberts was not always able to exercise full control over his subordinate officers and there were times when even he himself sanctioned the burning of farms.[86] At a word, the British columns acted indiscriminately, and sometimes also destroyed the homes of burghers who had remained true to the oath. The British army made no concerted effort to differentiate between those who had broken the oath, the bona fide surrendered burghers and the bitterenders who were still fighting. The mere fact that a person was absent from his farm was regarded as reason enough to burn down his home.[87] Because of the lack of protection from the British and the desire to avoid being commandeered by the republican forces, some of the surrendered burghers decided to vacate their farms and flee to the cities and towns that were under British control. When the British troops came upon these deserted farms, they simply burned down the homesteads.[88]

There were also allegations from republican quarters that those who honoured the oath of neutrality were humiliated and treated in an arrogant manner by the British troops. A republican circular dated 15 June 1900 cited the following description of the handling of the surrendered burghers: "To give an impression of the abuse to which our brothers who have surrendered and those who have since rejoined us have been subjected, one example of many can be cited. If troops or policemen arrive on a farm where a burgher (or rather, an ex-burgher) with a British permit resides, the unfortunate ex-burgher is obliged to tend their horses, take the animals to the water and see to it that they are stabled; all this must be done personally by our burgher while our 'friends' the soldiers or policemen go into the house. Here they sit and enjoy the coffee and cake they have demanded, which has to be served personally by the farmer's wife."[89] Although this portrayal may have been somewhat exaggerated in order to discourage other burghers from surrendering,[90] there is no doubt that the behaviour of the British troops was prejudicial towards the surrendered burghers. In addition it provided the republican forces with some very useful propaganda material.

Surrendered burghers also discovered to their dismay that their boundary fences were damaged, livestock taken, hoses commandeered and crops burned.[91] On 4 November 1900 a group of surrendered burghers south of Bloemfontein was notified that all livestock, provisions and wagons would be removed from their farms.[92] These measures were taken to prevent any provisions from falling into the hands of the Boers and to provide the necessary supplies for the British troops.[93]

In terms of the Hague Convention the British were indeed entitled to expect certain services (exclusive of active military service) and requisitions from the surrendered burghers.[94] However, these could not be demanded arbitrarily and were qualified as follows: "Requisitions and services shall only be demanded on the authority of the commander in the locality occupied. The contributions in kind shall, as far as possible, be paid for in ready money; if not, their receipt shall be acknowledged."[95] The British columns took very little notice of these restrictions. In the Jacobsdal district where Brigadier-general H.H. Settle was in command in November 1900, "the order of the day appeared to be capturing those farmers who had remained true to their oath, and rounding up all their stock without giving receipts".[96] In the Transvaal too, the British army commandeered the provisions belonging to surrendered burghers without paying for the supplies or providing receipts.[97] Thus not only was this particular stipulation of the Hague Convention contravened, but the promise that the property of surrendered burghers would be protected –

as laid down in Roberts's first proclamations, namely Proclamation 3 of 15 March 1900 and Proclamations 1 and 2 of 31 May and 6 June respectively[98] – was also broken. It was therefore hardly surprising that H.C. Marais, a surrendered burgher from Pretoria wrote after the war: "We gulled fools ... have been ruined and demoralised by a kind of protection to which Dante's *Inferno* is a common garden party."[99]

The guarantee of personal freedom that was promised in Roberts's first proclamations was also not honoured. Despite the fact that they had laid down their arms voluntarily, some of the surrendered burghers found themselves in concentration camps. Admittedly the British columns had a difficult situation on their hands because some surrendered Boers who gave the appearance of remaining true to their oaths were in fact giving shelter to fighting burghers and passed on information to the Boer forces.[100] On the other hand, the British officers did not go to much trouble to ascertain whether a person was in fact guilty of this practice or not. J.G. Fraser, who acted as a spokesman for the surrendered burghers, reported to the Military Governor of Bloemfontein, Major-general G.T. Pretyman, that "not the slightest discrimination was exercised by officers ... between the burghers who were quietly occupying their farms, loyally complying with the terms of the Proclamations and those who by suspicious conduct contrary to their neutrality had laid themselves open to penalty". The result was that "burghers ... who surrendered under the proclamation of Lord Roberts and who were acting fairly up to their undertaking are now Prisoners of War, taken from their homes without warning, hurried to the nearest Railway Station and sent down without so much as a chance of making any provision for their affairs or even taking farewell of their wives and children ...".[101]

The exact number of surrendered burghers who were taken prisoner in this manner in the republics is difficult to establish because it was not until early in September 1900 that the British officers who controlled the prisoner-of-war camps in Cape Town began to collect information on surrendered burghers and to classify them as such.[102] Later in the war 3194 of these prisoners of war – the majority of whom had been wrongly arrested – were taken to concentration camps in the Transvaal and Free State.[103] These surrendered burghers had been in Cape prisoner-of-war camps, but others were also sent to overseas camps.[104] The surrendered burghers were naturally highly dissatisfied with the treatment that had been meted out to them. A.S. Wessels, who had been unjustly arrested, perhaps put it too mildly when he wrote to the provost marshal in Pretoria: "Sir you can imagine that being in the veld for ... months, and being very tired, you are offered by a British General a home and a rest, and then go and take his word and expecting to find that; you are taken and sent away from that home you love more than the world; that Sir is not very pleasant."[105]

The fact that the British army was unable to crack down effectively on the republican forces meant that its actual occupation of republican territory was restricted to the towns and the railways. And even the towns were not always effectively occupied. At times, because of military pressure, the British were compelled to evacuate places such as Potchefstroom, Klerksdorp, Rustenburg and Zeerust in the Transvaal and Heilbron, Wepener, Boshof, Jacobsdal, Smithfield, Bethlehem, Rouxville and Dewetsdorp in the Free State.[106] This placed surrendered burghers who were in these towns in a difficult position. After the evacuation of Rustenburg and Zeerust, Milner wrote: "We have had the unpleasant experience of seeing men, who have once accepted British authority and relied upon the power of British arms to protect them, handed back to the enemy, and it involves ... much material damage to our friends or to those who are prepared to become reconciled to our rule."[107] The British had made no provision for the protection of the surrendered burghers who were living in the towns that had been evacuated and they sometimes had to join the commandos whether they liked it or not.[108]

The method of warfare employed by the republican forces meant that the Boers made frequent attacks on the British rail and telegraph connections. In the period from June to November 1900 the Boers launched 110 successful raids on railway and telegraph communications, and 21 attacks were made on trains.[109] Roberts attached great importance to the railway lines for the transportation of troops and food supplies so he had to take drastic counter-measures. On 16 June 1900 he issued a proclamation in which he laid down the proposed punitive measures for the destruction of railway bridges, culverts and the cutting of telegraph lines.[110] The proclamation was directed at the residents of the Transvaal and the Free State. Roberts was of the opinion that this kind of damage could not occur without the knowledge of the residents in the immediate vicinity, so he warned the local people that he would hold them co-responsible for damaging public property in their region. The nearby houses would be burned down and the prominent local residents would be treated as prisoners of war.

Three days later, on 19 June 1900, Roberts issued another proclamation in which he held out the prospect of even stricter measures.[111]

1 The prominent residents of the town and the district would be held both jointly and individually responsible for an amount equal to the damage suffered in the district concerned.

2 In addition to payment of compensation for the damages, each burgher was also liable for a fine in accordance to the circumstances of each incident, but the fine would not be less than an amount calculated on 2s 6d per morgen of the property owned by that particular burgher. Furthermore, in the districts where property or lines of communication were damaged, there would be no more payments made for supplies which were claimed by the British army.

3 As an additional precaution and deterrent, the director of the military railways was empowered to select, periodically, as many residents from each district as he saw fit, and these people would then have to travel on the trains which moved through these districts.

4 The houses and farms in the vicinity where the damage had occurred would be destroyed and the residents in the immediate surroundings would be treated in accordance with martial law.

5 The military authorities would also afford the prominent residents of each district the opportunity to communicate the contents of the proclamation to the other members of the community so that everyone was fully aware of the responsibility that rested upon them.

These proclamations which Roberts had issued were in contravention of articles 25 and 50 of the Hague Convention.[112] They also placed the surrendered burghers in an unfavourable position. Although they were not as such implicated by articles 1 and 2 of the proclamation of 19 June 1900 – namely the levies which had been proposed[113] – they were indeed prejudiced by article 3. In terms of this particular article there were at least three residents of Heilbron, Field-cornet F. Els, Revd D.J. Minnaar and the former magistrate, P. Roos, as well as two residents of Winburg, D. Roux, a local attorney, and T.C.L. Bergstedt, a general dealer and member of the Free State *Volksraad*, all of whom were forced to accompany the trains. The British hoped that this would stop the Boers from attacking the trains or blowing up the railway line.[114] In Pretoria the same was demanded of a local attorney, Edward Rooth. Rooth, who had signed the oath of neutrality, pointed out to Roberts that this was in fact in contravention of Proclamation 1 of 31 May 1900. Furthermore he emphasised the extremely parlous position in which he had been placed: "I am, without any fault of my own ... in a worse position than I would have been had I been under arms and fighting, as then, if captured I could only have been treated as a Prisoner of War, whilst now, after having ... surrendered my arms and taken the Oath of Neutrality I receive notice that if certain acts which I cannot possibly prevent or be aware of, are committed by men I know nothing of, at places I cannot be present at, I will be made a Prisoner of War, may be taken from my home and compelled to personally accompany Railway Trains – and in addition thereto will have to pay a heavy fine as well as compensation for the damage caused."[115] After submitting this objection Rooth was apparently exempted from having to accompany trains.[116]

G.V. Fiddes, Roberts's political secretary, was very critical of this particular measure. According to Fiddes, the people who had to accompany trains should, in practice, only have been selected from among those who had already laid down their arms or those who had not at any stage ever taken up arms. But this would have been tantamount to breaking the contract Roberts had made with the surrendered burghers in Proclamation 1 of 31 May 1900. Fiddes also made mention of the futility of the proclamation of 19 June 1900. He thought that the presence of the surrendered burghers on a train would in many cases be a motivation for the Boers to attack the train rather than to deter them from doing so.[117] Due largely to pressure from Fiddes, Roberts was obliged to withdraw the controversial article 3 at the end of July 1900.[118] The other retaliatory measures which Roberts had laid down for the blowing up of railways and cutting of telegraph lines (the destruction of homes in terms of article 4) also impacted heavily on the surrendered burghers. The burning of houses in the vicinity where the British lines of communication had been damaged was a punishment that was applied indiscriminately. In most cases, according to S.B. Spies, there was "no direct link between the men who attacked British communications and the non-combatants whose houses were burnt".[119] In one such case, J.J.J. van Rensburg, who had taken the oath of neutrality and was resident in the Heidelberg district, had his house burned and his livestock removed in September 1900 – this despite the fact that he was in no way involved in the blowing up of the railway line and had actually even alerted the British military authorities that the Boers were in the area.[120]

Roberts's inability either to protect the surrendered burghers or to force the republicans into submission made it necessary for him to issue yet another proclamation (Proclamation 12 of 1900) on 14 August 1900.[121] This proclamation was directed at the residents of the South African Republic and radically changed the position of the surrendered burghers. In terms of articles 1 and 2 of Proclamation 12 of 14 August 1900, the concessions that had been granted to surrendered burghers in Proclamations 1 and 2 (of 31 May and 6 June 1900 respectively) were now revoked. In terms of article 3 the breaking of the oath of neutrality – by burghers who voluntarily rejoined the commandos – was punishable by a prison term, a fine or the death penalty. As far as the bona fide surrendered burghers and those who might surrender in the future were concerned, the most important stipulations were articles 4 and 6. Boers who might surrender in the future were affected by article 4, which laid down that all burghers in the occupied regions except those who had already taken the oath of neutrality would in future be regarded as prisoners of war or be treated as Roberts saw fit. Bona fide surrendered burghers, and by implication also those who might surrender in the future, were affected by the terms of article 6 that "persons are hereby warned to acquaint Her Majesty's Forces with the presence of the enemy upon their farms and failing to do so, they will be regarded as aiding and abetting the enemy".[122] In the Free State the concessions laid down in Proclamation 3 of 15 March 1900 were not formally revoked, but article 7 of Roberts's proclamation of 1 September 1900 to the residents of this territory also compelled them to pass on information to the British.[123]

Article 4 of Proclamation 12 of 1900 meant that people who voluntarily laid down their arms after 14 August 1900 would be regarded as prisoners of war and would be treated in the same manner as people who were taken prisoner on the battlefield. In the Middelburg district a group of burghers surrendered after 14 August 1900, not knowing about the terms of the new proclamation.[124] The British regarded them, for all practical purposes, as prisoners of war and they and many others who had also withdrawn from the war after that date, were sent off to prisoner-of-war camps overseas. Indeed, Major T.H.B. Forster, the British staff officer in charge of the concentration camp in Durban reported that "it was the rule to send all prisoners of war who arrived at Durban, to Ceylon at this period [14 August to 22 September] irrespective of the conditions under which they surrendered".[125] In view of the fact that many of these burghers surrendered under the impression that they were doing so under the old dispensation (Proclamations 1 and 2 of 31 May and 6 June respectively), the treatment that was meted out to them can be regarded as extremely unjust.

Roberts must have realised that this was unreasonable, because on 20 September 1900 he informed Pretyman that although in future surrendered Boers would still be regarded as prisoners of war, they should no longer be sent out of South Africa.[126] A government notice to this effect was sent out two days later, followed by another notice on 28 September 1900.[127]

This modification restored the status quo somewhat. Although after 22 September 1900 surrendered burghers were still to be technically regarded as prisoners of war, in practice they would be treated as prisoners of war on parole.[128] As a result of this inconsistent and erratic policy a contemporary writer remarked with some justification: "Bewildered and embarrassed, Lord Roberts began to wage war by proclamations ... Many in number and inconsistent in policy, the proclamations proceeded from clemency to sternness and from sternness to clemency."[129]

Although article 4 was neutralised by the government notices of 22 and 28 September 1900, the far-reaching article 6 of proclamation 12 of 1900 – by which the surrendered burghers in the Transvaal were compelled to provide information to the British – was never revoked. The same stipulation (article 7) also applied in the Free State.[130] These articles contradicted Roberts's first proclamations (Proclamation 3 of March 1900, as well as Proclamations 1 and 2 of 31 May, and 6 June respectively) in terms of which it was demanded that surrendered burghers remain neutral. To help one side and not the other is certainly not remaining neutral. Furthermore this was a contravention of article 44 of the Hague Convention.[131]

Maxwell was of the opinion that "Proclamation 12 has put a wholesome dread in the Transvaalers", and Milner's only comment was that it was "a very sensible proclamation".[132] L.A. Tancred, the British Crown's legal adviser in the Free State, was not as complacent about the implications and legality of this proclamation. He expressed the following well-considered view: "In my opinion the oath of neutrality taken before the proclamations mentioned [Proclamation 12 of August 1900 in the Transvaal and proclamation 14 of 1 September 1900 in the Orange River Colony] converted the deponent into a man *non hostis* or a person who c[ou]ld not side with either party in the war and all that can be claimed from him is entire abstinence from any assistance to either party. He stands in the passive relation of a *non-interferum*. The Proclamations subsequently issued cannot in my opinion alter this position. Further I think an oath signed either before or after the Proclamations containing an undertaking that the deponent will report the presence of his belligerent countrymen, cannot strictly be called an oath of *neutrality*. Neutrality does not consist in the mere impartial treatment of opposing belligerents but it is also *entire* abstinence from any assistance to either party in this warfare. To report the presence of one belligerent to the other is *assistance* and such an act is totally inconsistent with the meaning of the word. Moreover I think, to attempt to impose or enforce such conditions w[ou]ld not be considered the act of a civilized state."[133]

Tancred's logical exposition did not however make much impression on the British authorities. H.F. Wilson, secretary of the Orange River Colony administration, merely reacted by saying: "As Miss Hobhouse has gone home can't this be put by?"[134]

The British implementation of these proclamations led to flagrant juridical discrepancies and it was the surrendered burghers who became the victims. For example, on 11 December 1900 a British court martial sentenced Gideon de Wet, a prominent resident of Rouxville, to two years imprisonment because he refused, on the grounds of his oath of neutrality, to provide information to the British forces.[135]

In addition to the legal contradictions of article 6 of Proclamation 12 of 14 August 1900 in the Transvaal and article 7 of Proclamation 14 of 1 September 1900 in the Free State, in practice the implementation of these articles – by which the surrendered burghers were compelled to provide information to the British – also placed considerable pressure on these burghers to resort to active support of the British war effort. With reference to these particular articles Goold-Adams, the assistant administrator of the Orange River Colony, said in April 1901: "I have come upon case after case where men who have taken the oath of neutrality are by us expected to report to us, work for us and even been asked to fight in our ranks."[136] In the light of Goold-Adams's statement there seems to be a great deal of truth in Smuts's assertion that "[the] handsuppers, ground to despair between the upper and nether millstone of British proclamations, [were] forced in their progressive demoralization first to give information to the enemy, then to collect loot on the profit sharing system, and finally to take up arms against their people ...".[137]

When the treatment of the surrendered burghers by the British is put under scrutiny, it appears that these burghers were often put in an invidious position by Roberts's military policy. Because he was simply unable to come up with an answer to the Boer guerrilla-type warfare, Roberts sought refuge in drastic compensatory measures without really keeping in mind the promises of protection that he had made to the surrendered burghers. As a result these burghers were placed in an almost untenable position.

3 Some surrendered burghers cross the republican borders

Because of the lack of British protection and under pressure from the republican forces, some of those who had surrendered came to the realisation that it would be very difficult for them to maintain their neutrality and come through the war unscathed. Under these circumstances they thought it would be advisable to seek refuge outside the theatre of the war.

For the surrendered burghers in the Free State the neighbouring Basutoland (Lesotho) was a convenient and popular refuge. Although Basutoland was formally neutral during the war, the resident commissioner, Sir Godfrey Lagden, was prepared to receive and harbour refugees of any nationality.[138]

Among the first people who made their way to Basutoland were a number of English-speaking Free State burghers who refused to render military service to the republican forces. By 6 February 1900 there were 12 of these people in Maseru.[139]

When, at the end of March 1900, the republicans began to re-commandeer surrendered burghers in the vicinity of Ladybrand and Ficksburg, Lagden claimed that the Boers prosecuted them, confiscated their property, and put them in gaol. Lagden sympathised with the surrendered burghers and guaranteed protection and care to everyone who fled into Basutoland.[140] Many burghers must have availed themselves of this offer because two months later (May 1900), Lagden reported that "surrendered burghers … regularly cast themselves upon us …".[141]

During July 1900 more republican burghers handed in their weapons at the various British border posts daily and then crossed the border into Basutoland.[142] The stream of refugees to Basutoland continued and in August there were so many surrendered burghers trying to take their cattle by train into Basutoland that considerable railway congestion resulted.[143] When, as a temporary measure, the British army was forced to evacuate the border districts of Ladybrand and Ficksburg in September 1900 owing to pressure from the republican forces, the surrendered burghers were left unprotected and they fled in even greater numbers into Basutoland. It is alleged that there were two former republican commandants, two field-cornets and a general among these refugees.[144]

Basutoland was a place of refuge throughout the war for Free Staters "who did not have clear consciences".[145] By the end of the war in May 1902 there were more than 2000 refugees in this protectorate.[146]

Although this influx of a large number of white refugees increased the white population in Basutoland threefold,[147] there was very little friction between the new arrivals and the Basotho people. J.C. Macgregor, assistant commissioner of the Leribe district, was of the opinion that "they [the refugees] have as a whole behaved well, though their presence and necessary supervision entails much labour and some embarrassment and anxiety ...".

As far as Macgregor was concerned the added work was worthwhile in the light of the fact "that the protection afforded, has been the means of keeping a large number of able-bodied men and horses from the enemy's commandos".[148] However, indirectly the refugees caused friction between the combatant Boers and the Basotho people. On 18 October 1901 a Boer patrol crossed the Basutoland border at Letsikas and tried to force back the Free State refugees and their livestock. The Basotho police intervened and in the scuffle which ensued one of the Boers was wounded.[149]

Generally speaking, the refugees in Basutoland were well treated. They were allowed to keep their livestock and were provided with the necessary grazing.[150] This made it possible for them to return with their livestock to their various farms once the war was over and in comparison with the bitterenders, they were able to continue their faming activities with very little material loss.[151] According to C.J. Uys, some refugees cunningly left their livestock in Basutoland after the war and lodged bogus claims, which were later paid out, for compensation for the livestock they had supposedly lost.[152]

In the social sphere too, the refugees were well provided for. In February 1902 the refugees at Tsietasnek received monetary support for the education of their children. To this end the British authorities in Bloemfontein also agreed to pay the salary of a teacher who was one of the refugees.[153]

That the refugees themselves were satisfied with the treatment they received is borne out by the petition which was submitted to

Milner after the war by J. Robertson and T. Robertson of Bloemfontein (presumably surrendered burghers who were English speaking): "We desire to place on record our high appreciation of the many privileges the inhabitants of the O.R.C. have enjoyed in Basutoland during the continuance of the war, and that His Excellency, the Administrator, be requested to convey our deep sense of the many obligations under which we have been placed by ... the Resident Commissioner and through him his officers, the people of Basutoland and Lerothodi, the paramount chief."[154]

By July 1900 there were many burghers in the Transvaal who had deserted from the commandos and had moved in an easterly direction to seek refuge in the adjacent Swaziland, Gazaland and Mozambique. By 13 July 1900 there were more than 100 burghers in Mozambique.[155]

In September 1900, after the battle of Bergendal on 27 August, there were many more burghers who crossed the Portuguese border. The British victory at Bergendal had two important results. Firstly, it meant that Roberts could occupy the entire Delagoa Bay railway line and secondly, after this defeat the republican forces in the Transvaal decided to change over to mobile warfare.[156] In this new type of guerrilla warfare it would become essential for every burgher to possess a reliable horse and those burghers who did not have one would simply not be able to keep up the pace on foot. The commandos were reorganised and by the middle of September 1900 Botha and Viljoen moved northwards from Hectorspruit, while the burghers on foot were sent to Komatipoort to act as border guards.[157]

By 16 September 1900 a very demoralised force of about 3000 men was stationed at Komatipoort. This force was made up of a number of heterogeneous elements. According to the *Times History*, "The Komati Poort force was composed of all the *'voetgangers'* [pedestrians], men whose inability to secure a horse indicated a cooling of enthusiasm, most of the foreign volunteers and of the Cape rebels, besides fugitives and deserters who had hitherto been skulking in the bush."[158] Among them were also burghers who were very keen to continue fighting, but because they did not have access to horses were obliged, from sheer necessity, to go to Komatipoort.[159] The force at Komatipoort was thus not entirely composed of shirkers, but on the other hand there were certainly many men who would have been readily inclined to lay down their arms.

The Portuguese authorities were afraid that the republican force at Komatipoort would blow up the bridge over the Komati River, which would put a spoke in the wheel of the profitable Portuguese trade with the Transvaal. Because Mozambique was supposed to be neutral ground, the Portuguese were anxious to prevent any possibility of a confrontation between the Boers and the British in Portuguese territory.[160] J. Machado, the governor-general of Mozambique, was particularly concerned about the possibility of the violation of the Portuguese border. On 16 September 1900 he sent four secret agents – "men ... of influence who had themselves been fighting with the Boers throughout the campaign" – to Komatipoort in order to persuade the burghers to come over to Mozambique and voluntarily lay down their arms. These negotiations had the desired effect and by midnight on 18 September 700 burghers had crossed the border.[161] Meanwhile the British under Lieutenant-general Pole-Carew had marched to Komatipoort and on 21 September Machado again sent secret agents to negotiate with General F.J. Pienaar,[162] who, together with General J. Coetzer, was in command of the Boer force. The burghers were promised that they would be well received and cared for in Mozambique and Pienaar thereupon agreed that they would hand over their weapons voluntarily to the Portuguese authorities. That same evening the burghers crossed the border – first in small groups and then in their hundreds – and surrendered their arms. On 22 September a further 500 burghers crossed the border with Pienaar, bringing the total number of men who were now in Mozambique to 2500.[163] On 24 September Pole-Carew occupied Komatipoort, but General Coetzer, who had been against Pienaar's actions from the very beginning, succeeded in escaping with between 200 and 300 burghers and managed to rejoin the Boer forces.[164]

Once in Mozambique the various groups among the refugees crystallised more clearly. Members of the different foreign volunteer corps, who were often drunk and caused the Portuguese authorities a great deal of trouble, were sent back to their home countries.[165] The burghers who through force of circumstances now found themselves in Mozambique, but were still loyal to the republican cause, were under the supervision of a Refugee Commission with W.J. Geerling as secretary. They were in close contact with Dr W.J. Leyds, the Transvaal minister plenipotentiary in Europe, and also requested financial assistance from him.[166]

A third group, those burghers who had forsaken their loyalty to the republic, were keen to swear an oath of allegiance to the British crown so that they could return to their homes. Milner was not prepared to go along with this idea and notified Roberts accordingly: "I think that it is impossible to agree to this. We might promise not to send them out of South Africa but to allow them simply to return to their homes would be treating them better than Britishers who are still prevented from doing so; besides the risk that some of them might rise again." Roberts thought that they should all be regarded as prisoners of war.[167] Pienaar meanwhile continued his campaign to persuade the refugees in Mozambique to give themselves over to the British authorities. On 21 November 1900 F. Crowe, the British consul general in Lourenço Marques, informed Milner that "General Pienaar has persuaded many Boers ... to ... surrender, if assured that their families now in the Transvaal would be allowed [to] rejoin them at place interned ... [I] consider such a surrender would have [a] good moral effect and probably cause the rest to follow." But Milner reiterated his objections to this step.[168]

After protracted diplomatic negotiations between the British and Portuguese governments it was finally decided to send all the refugees as prisoners of war to Portugal in February, March and April of 1901. Here they were held in the towns, among others, of Peniche, Tomar, Caldas da Reinha and Alcobaça.[169] In Alcobaça there were also some burghers who by August 1901 wanted to take the oath of allegiance to the British crown in the hope that they would be allowed to return to South Africa.[170] Milner was, however, of the opinion that "it is undesirable to allow any of the Boer refugees in Portugal to take the oath of allegiance at present".[171]

To the north of the Transvaal, Rhodesia (Zimbabwe) offered a place of refuge to surrendered burghers. Jan du Plessis de Beer, a member of the First *Volksraad* for Waterberg from 1883 to 1900, was among the people who went to Rhodesia. During the first few months of the war he was responsible for the safe custody of some government-owned livestock. He also controlled the finances of a fund which assisted the families of the fighting burghers, and it was alleged that he had put a great deal of this money into his own pocket. He managed to smuggle the government livestock into Rhodesia and sold it there to local butchers for £25 a head.[172] During October and November 1900 Du Plessis de Beer clashed with General Beyers, who was busy at the time with the re-organisation and encouragement of the commandos in the Soutpansberg district. After this quarrel Du Plessis de Beer left for Rhodesia where he remained on parole. He also had a short stay in Bechuanaland (Botswana).[173]

By the end of December 1900 four republican burghers from the Soutpansberg district had handed over their weapons to the Rhodesian Field Force at Pontdrif – on the border between Rhodesia and the Transvaal – with the request that they be allowed to remain with their livestock in Rhodesia for the duration of the war. They were promised good treatment and protection from the republican forces and it was decided to settle them near Bulawayo. The police in Bulawayo would keep a careful eye on them. M. Clarke, the resident commissioner in Salisbury, hoped that if these surrendered burghers were well treated, more burghers in northern Transvaal might follow their example.[174]

Clarke's endeavours were soon rewarded and in the course of 1901 various other surrendered burghers fled to Rhodesia. On 6 June 1901 a certain Labuschagne with 20 wagons and 50 men (accompanied by their families and in possession of protection passes issued by Colonel H.M. Grenfell) crossed the border at Rhodes Drift. They also took a great deal of livestock with them – 500 head of cattle and 71 mules, donkeys and horses.[175] Even more burghers were soon to cross the border. A week later R.H. Everett, an acting staff officer of the British South Africa Police, reported: "Several more families have come over and are now at Tuli. Details as follows: 15 men, 12 women, 22 children, 194 cattle and 10 wagons."[176]

By the end of June 1901 a great many surrendered burghers with their wagons and oxen had gathered near the Rhodesian border. They wanted to settle permanently in Rhodesia if they could be assured of work as transport riders in that country. During the war there was an urgent need for transport riders in Rhodesia because large numbers of oxen and wagons were sent to the front to be of service there. The Rhodesian authorities were thus prepared to accept the offer made by the surrendered burghers. Even after the war there would still be enough work opportunities for them as transport riders.[177] Some of the surrendered burghers who were in concentration camps in the Transvaal during 1902 also requested that they be allowed to go to Rhodesia. Milner was not in favour of letting them leave the concentration camps for this purpose.[178]

The burghers and their families who had fled to Rhodesia were housed in a "refugee camp for surrendered burghers". The camp was 13 kilometres from Bulawayo, on a portion of Cecil John Rhodes's farm, and was about two kilometres in size, with good pastures and sufficient water nearby. In the winter months the Boers were allowed to trek to Manzingama so that their livestock could graze beside the Rumenyi and Umchabezi Rivers. Initially, members of the Kings's Own Scottish Borders were in charge of the camp, but later the British South Africa Police took over and a police station under Lieutenant Spain was built in the vicinity. The surrendered burghers were not permitted to leave the camp at will and no one was allowed to visit the camp without the written permission of R.H. Everett, who was the superintendent.

Some of the burghers received a permit and remuneration for providing transport between Bulawayo and the Criterion mine. The manager of the Globe and the Phoenix mines also wanted to avail himself of their services and the burghers were made responsible for transporting wood to these mines. Because most of them had money, livestock and tented wagons, they did not receive rations, but special provision was made for those who were not self-sufficient. The refugees were apparently well satisfied with the treatment they received in Rhodesia, and in the words of Everett: "I have received no complaints from any one of them and they have stated to Lieut. Spain and myself that the treatment accorded to them is better than they expected."[179] In an article on the Afrikaners in Rhodesia, R. Hodder-Williams makes no mention of these surrendered Boers who fled to Rhodesia and were housed near Bulawayo. He does, however, make passing reference to 24 Free State refugees who were welcomed by the Rhodesian officials in Salisbury in August 1901.[180]

In February 1902, S.N. de Kock and 50 other surrendered burghers from the concentration camps at Balmoral even considered moving to Uganda in the hope that they would be able to buy cheap farms there. In the letter they sent to the British authorities they requested answers to 27 queries, most of them about agricultural prospects and labour issues. They asked for example: "When a farm is leased where Kaffirs are living on, supposing that these Kaffirs won't *work*, or pay something for living on said farm, will lessor have the right to turn them off if they won't *work* or pay something for living on said farm?" They were also interested to know: "When we are there [in Uganda] will you allow our doctors to doctor? By doctors we mean of experience, that are really good doctors; but have no diploma." The superintendent of the concentration camp at Balmoral began to doubt whether the burghers had the faintest idea where Uganda was. According to him they were "alright [sic] in the camp, but I don't think that the Boer will ever like the camp as they don't like living together".[181]

Then there were also surrendered burghers who took refuge in Bechuanaland (Botswana). On 7 January 1901 Commandant S.P. Grobler of the Waterberg commando arrived at Palapye and reported to the assistant commissioner, Ashburnham, and requested protection from the republican forces. Grobler claimed that he had withdrawn from the war in the light of Roberts's proclamation of 1 September 1900 (in terms of which the Transvaal was annexed as British territory). Shortly afterwards he was captured by the Boers and sentenced to death by a court martial for "incitement, questionable loyalty, fraud and desertion". The sentence still had to be ratified, but Grobler, who was out on bail, had decided to flee to Palapye before the final decision was made known.[182] Grobler told Ashburnham that more than 100 burghers from his former commando planned to surrender if there was the possibility of protection in Bechuanaland, and with this in mind he wrote to the Waterberg commando advising the burghers concerned to abandon the struggle and move with their livestock to Bechuanaland. Ashburnham planned to set up a camp at Palapye to house the burghers who reacted to Grobler's letter.[183] Milner, who had been kept abreast of these developments, was in favour of a camp for surrendered burghers in Bechuanaland, but had his doubts about the suitability of Palapye. He was of the opinion that it was undesirable "to place the families, cattle and stock of such persons [surrendered Boers] in the centre of a large native population such as Palapye". According to him, Nwapa would be a suitable place for the camp.[184] Although very few people reacted to Grobler's letter,[185] a number of surrendered burghers did in fact make their way to Bechuanaland where they were housed in a camp at Nwapa. By 12 June 1901 there were 150 refugees there.[186] During the winter months there was insufficient water and grazing for their livestock in the Nwapa area and the camp was moved to San's Post, beside the Crocodile River on land which was part of the protectorate.

Because the surrendered burghers now found themselves on the border between the Transvaal and Bechuanaland, they were afraid that the commandos under General Beyers would try to re-commandeer them or take their cattle. They requested protection and 50 followers of Khama, the local chieftain, were armed, paid 2s 0d a day, and sent to San's Post to guard the burghers. This step was taken because the British military authorities were hesitant to arm the surrendered burghers to any great extent – the 150 men were given only 15 rifles for self-protection.[187]

The British military authorities also allowed the republican burghers to remain on parole in the Cape Colony and Natal. According to British records, by the end of December 1900 there were 546 Boers on parole in the Cape Colony and 126 in Natal.[188] A few burghers who forsook the republican cause went to Britain and Europe during the war.[189]

British attempts to afford the surrendered burghers greater security within the borders of the republics will now be investigated.

4 British measures to protect the surrendered burghers

The discussion in the preceding sections of this chapter has shown that the surrendered burghers were placed under considerable pressure by both the republican forces and the British army. They reacted to this pressure in various ways: some rejoined the commandos, others passed on information to the British, while some moved beyond the republican borders. Because of the arbitrary action of the British army, certain surrendered burghers also found themselves in prisoner-of-war camps. Nevertheless there were still many surrendered burghers who remained true to the oath of neutrality despite the difficult circumstances.[190] As the war progressed, their numbers were increased by a steady flow of fighting burghers who decided to lay down their arms.[191]

To give the surrendered Boers their due, the British authorities at the very least should have introduced constructive protection measures. As early as 13 May 1900 General E.Y. Brabant (commander of Brabant's Horse, a Cape colonial regiment) came to this realisation and he suggested that the surrendered burghers in the Free State should be sent for protection to a place near the Free State border. Brabant was of the opinion that Aliwal North, situated on the Cape side of the Orange River, would be a suitable place.[192] In principle, Milner was in favour of Brabant's suggestion, but he seriously doubted whether there would be enough British troops available there to protect the surrendered burghers. Roberts entertained the same misgivings and also added, "Such a policy would, in my opinion, strengthen the hands of Steyn and the Transvaalers, who keep on warning the Burghers that if they surrender to us, they will be sent down country as prisoners."[193]

Brabant's suggestion had a great deal to recommend it, particularly in the light of the fact that in the country districts the British were unable to protect the surrendered burghers from the commandos. "We must bear in mind," wrote Maxwell, "that we give little or no protection in outlying districts to those who have surrendered, and if a Boer commando comes their way, it is often a case of 'Force Majeure'".[194] The only practical solution was to remove the surrendered burghers from the theatre of war. Milner felt that if this was not done the war could continue more or less indefinitely.[195]

Lieutenant-general Buller thought along the same lines. He considered sending the surrendered burghers, with their livestock, to Natal and placing them there on the vacated farms of Natal rebels. By 25 July 1900 one person had been settled in this way, but before the policy could be fully implemented Buller thought it advisable to ask the approval of the Natal government.[196] The Natal government raised basic objections against the introduction of such a policy and argued that "The government has no power to deal with land of persons suspected of treason ... When the Commission Court sits, it is probable that many rebels will be released from gaol on bail and allowed to return to their farms. If they find them occupied by Transvaal refugee burghers, there will be difficulties." The Natal government also had doubts about the military authorities' ability to implement such a policy without any blunders: "It is always on the cards that mistakes will be made and refugee burghers placed on farms belonging to loyalists, which have been temporarily deserted owing to the fear of the enemy; this would cause great trouble."[197]

By August 1900 the British military authorities had still not made any proper provision for the protection of the surrendered burghers. On the contrary, British action was marked by particularly futile retaliatory measures.[198] Because of the lack of British protection, some of the burghers fled to the towns and cities under British control. The district commissioners encouraged this because it was the only way they were able to protect the surrendered burghers.[199] In Pretoria these people were settled in empty houses and they received rations to the value of 2s 6d per day.[200] The military authorities also introduced a scheme to take the burghers into municipal service, on the one hand to offset the rations they were receiving and on the other to enable them to earn money so that they could buy food. But there was a very poor response to this scheme from the surrendered burghers. Despite the fact that 2000 notices were distributed, only 12 people came forward and of these, six wanted to be foremen.[201]

In practice, the British authorities found it impossible to settle all the surrendered burghers in the towns and cities. In the first place, housing for all these people became a problem,[202] and secondly they could not bring their livestock with them. The district commissioner of Boshof, Captain R.J. Ross, reported that "I have been obliged to reply to burghers seeking protection that they can only obtain it in Boshof, under the guns of the fortress, so to speak. This alternative spells ruin for the average Boer, if he treks with his stock the latter on arrival here must starve, if he leaves his stock, it is stolen or driven away or dies from want of water."[203] To get around this obstacle Ross sent out the following notice to the surrendered burghers in the Boshof district: "Reports have reached the Military authorities of small bodies of lawless men [sic] ... who ... have formed themselves into small commandos. These men are now threatening the lives of loyal Burghers and commandeering from them ... The British Government desires to protect the loyal Burghers who are true to their oaths, and for this purpose, and for no other, I call upon you to bring into Boshof all the cattle, trained horses, geldings and mares in your possession, immediately on receipt of this notice. I will allow to each farmer two cart horses to enable him to supply himself with the necessaries of life, and to use for looking after his stock. You must inspan oxen to work your pumps or use mules. Your horses will be run on a farm near Boshof ... Your horses will not be commandeered, but if any are required by the government as remounts they will be paid for at a fair price in ready cash ... I shall give you a receipt for all horses handed over to my care. For horses that die, or are lost, fair compensation will be given. This order must be obeyed at once, ... [and] the District Commissioner trusts that he will have no trouble in the matter."[204]

Some of the surrendered burghers did indeed react to this circular from Ross and by November 1900 his assistant, Lieutenant Locke, mentioned burghers who came "to my camp for protection at Modderriver".[205] The camp was on the farm owned by Hennie Roux and the surrendered burghers also helped the military authorities to bring some of the women and children of the district into the camp. Apparently the camp was closed by February 1901 and the inmates – of whom there were 21 surrendered burghers – were transferred to Bloemfontein.[206]

Major K.P. Apthorp, the district commissioner of Smithfield, also tried to protect the surrendered burghers in a similar manner. At night they were housed in a camp near the town and during the day the people who lived in the vicinity of the camp were allowed to go to their farms at certain times to attend to their farming interests.[207] In the Fauresmith district the British were only able to protect the burghers by putting them up in the gaol each night.[208]

In the Transvaal the position of the surrendered burghers also gave the district commissioners food for thought. Colonel A.H.M.

Edwards of Krugersdorp declared at the beginning of August 1900: "At present the peaceful and peacefully inclined, and there are many of them, are being punished for the misdeed of those who are determined to carry on the war. Punished not only by us – ... confiscations, burnings etc. – but also by their own people, threatened, dragged away from their homes and forced to accompany any commando whether they like it or not." According to Edwards, the only solution was to guarantee these people protection by means of "Refugee camps for those anxious to avail themselves of it".[209] Major H. Sykes of Potchefstroom produced a similar suggestion,[210] while H.R. Abercrombie, a British information officer, was of the opinion that "There is only one remedy ... i.e. to make all surrendered farmers with their families go into laagers at various points ...".[211]

The British high command did not take immediate steps to implement any of these suggestions,[212] but Captain J.M. Vallentin, district commissioner of Heidelberg, meanwhile tried to set up a protection camp for surrendered burghers on his own initiative. On 30 July 1900 he considered the possibility and two days later he discussed it with surrendered burghers in his district. The next day he sent out notices in which he encouraged the burghers to go to his proposed camp near the Perseverance mine. This scheme was not, however, a success. The surrendered burghers were reluctant to go to the camp unless they would be protected by British troops, and Vallentin was not inclined to arm the burghers for self-protection.[213]

Despite Vallentin's fruitless efforts, the idea of protection camps began to gain more support. If they could be successfully implemented they would go a long way to solving the problems the British authorities were experiencing with the surrendered burghers. On 23 August 1900 Milner informed Roberts: "I think, if once we can make up our minds to a camp or camps in South Africa, we shall find it an absolute advantage in this respect ... My idea is that many of the more pacific of them [the burghers] would be protected against being again commandeered and, at the same time, would not be sent out of the country. Both of these objects would be secured by keeping them in custody in South Africa."[214] Roberts did not react immediately, but two weeks later General T. Kelly-Kenny, one of his senior officers, asked for permission to set up protection camps at

Bloemfontein and Kroonstad.[215] According to Kelly-Kenny the military authorities would provide the tents and rations. A British military officer, in cooperation with the police, would be in control of the camp and the inmates would be expected to help with its erection. The inmates would not be regarded as prisoners of war but they would be obliged to abide by British disciplinary and sanitary measures.[216]

Roberts approved Kelly-Kenny's suggestions and he even considered establishing similar camps in the Transvaal.[217] The camp at Bloemfontein was opened shortly after 9 September 1900 and on 22 September it was officially announced that camps for surrendered burghers would be set up at Bloemfontein and Pretoria.[218] In Pretoria these burghers were housed in the so-called "Rest Camp"[219] which was a transit camp for Boer prisoners of war. From here they were sent out to other prisoner-of-war camps outside the theatre of war. The surrendered burghers who were originally sent to the "Rest Camp" were later transferred to the Irene concentration camp near Pretoria.[220]

The establishment of these camps did in fact ensure that some of the surrendered burghers could be protected from harm, but then it was also necessary that the British government make provision for their livestock. Roberts laid down that where livestock belonging to the burghers was needed by the military authorities, valid proof to this effect had to be issued to the owner, and in cases where the animals were not needed, one or two members of a family or a group of surrendered burghers would be issued with a protection pass and would then look after the livestock.[221] In practice, some burghers were reluctant to remain on farms because they were afraid that they would either be re-commandeered or that their livestock would be taken away by the British columns without compensation.[222] Some of the surrendered burghers therefore decided to take a few sheep and cattle to the camps and to tend the animals in the immediate vicinity.[223]

Officially the camps were set up exclusively for surrendered burghers and their families.[224] However, women and children who had been rendered homeless by the British scorched earth policy, or had been forced by circumstances to make their way to the camps to seek refuge were also housed there.²²⁵ As early as 30 September 1900 Kelly-Kenny informed Roberts that he had been obliged to use his own judgement in the accommodation of people in the camp at Bloemfontein and that the camp did not necessarily house only surrendered burghers.²²⁶ During October many of the women and children of loyal republican burghers were forced to go to Bloemfontein and by 15 November there was a total of 519 people in the camp.²²⁷ It seems clear that the people in the camps were not all surrendered burghers or their families and that there was no real difference between protection camps (for surrendered burghers) and concentration camps (for women and children who were compelled to go there because of dire necessity). It has already been alleged that the origin of Britain's widespread concentration camp policy of later months can be traced back to the attempts to protect the surrendered burghers.²²⁸ Indirectly and involuntarily these burghers certainly contributed to the rise of the concentration camp policy because the British government had to set up camps for the protection of surrendered burghers and these were used simultaneously for the homeless women and children of loyal republicans.²²⁹ It is, however, important not to overemphasise the role of the surrendered burghers here. The problem of homeless women and children as a result of the British scorched earth policy was just as important, if not more so, in the British plans for setting up camps.²³⁰

5 Sporadic peace-making initiatives by the surrendered burghers and their ilk

From March to December 1900 certain surrendered burghers and their ilk – republican burghers who were not liable for military service but identified with the views of the surrendered burghers – made a number of attempts to persuade the fighting burghers and their leaders to abandon the struggle. Even before the British occupation of Bloemfontein (13 March 1900), a former presidential candidate Revd A.A. van der Lingen of Harrismith was of the opinion, apparently without any real grounds, that Steyn had embroiled the Free State burghers in a war which was really of no concern to them. Through the medium of a Dutch newspaper published in Natal he wrote the following open letter to the Free State burghers: "Fellow countrymen and burghers, it is in your interest and it is your holy duty as burghers of this state and members likewise of the Christian church, as well as your responsibility to God, for you to show humanity and to reject the actions of our leaders who are each day leading us ever nearer to the brink of total decline. Turn back from this wicked path of destruction and let your patriotism, heroism and piety encourage you to again become yourselves." Van der Lingen closed his appeal by expressing the hope that at the earliest opportunity the Free State burghers would persuade their leaders to accept any peace which might be offered by Britain – "the greatest civilised power the world has ever seen".[231]

Because Van der Lingen published his open letter in a Natal newspaper, he presumably hoped that it would come to the notice of the Boer forces in that colony. There is no evidence to confirm that it did indeed do so. Van der Lingen could in any case hardly claim to enjoy any real support in the Free State. Prior to the war he admittedly stood three times for the presidency (1888, 1893 and 1896), but each time he had suffered a crushing defeat. In the 1896 election against M.T. Steyn and J.G. Fraser he polled only 6 out of a total of 9071 votes. As far as the Free Staters were concerned his participation in the presidential elections was regarded as something of a joke rather than a serious candidature.[232] Even Milner had his doubts about Van der Lingen and considered him "rather weak-minded and a muddler".[233]

Of greater significance was the attempt made by a few Transvaal jurists to persuade President Kruger to change his way of thinking. On 15 March 1900 when the news of the British occupation of Bloemfontein was announced in Pretoria, Chief Justice R. Gregorowski, lawyers J. Esser and J.A. van Leeuwen and Adv. W.E. Hollard decided to go and talk to Kruger to convince him that the war should be stopped. According to H.J. Batts, an English minister of the Baptist Church in Pretoria, they pointed out to Kruger that the republican commandos had been forced to fall back on each of the various war fronts and that the time had come to approach the British about peace so as to prevent any further bloodshed. Kruger disagreed with them, and said that it was not the Almighty's intention that the republics should lose the war. To this Hollard retorted: "You talk of God's hand, President, look at Ladysmith, look at Cronjé, at Kimberley; and now Bloemfontein is taken." The deeply devout president was unmoved by this argument and he ended the interview abruptly by saying to Hollard: "Your God is not my God."[234] Two months later, in the middle of May 1900, Kruger was again approached by a number of influential Pretorians. The group included Sammy Marks, a wealthy Jewish industrialist and personal friend of Kruger, Marks's partner, Isaac Lewis, F. Eloff (Kruger's son-in-law) and C.J. Joubert (the head of the Department of Mines). They suggested that the republics withdraw under protest – presumably without a formal surrender. In contrast to Kruger's stance in March 1900, the president now paid close attention to Marks's plan and agreed that this could prevent further loss of human life and destruction of property.[235] Kruger was presumably more receptive to Marks's proposal than the appeal made by Hollard and the other jurists in March, because Marks had not insisted that the republics approach the British for peace, but rather that they lay down arms under protest.[236] The British scorched earth policy, which had already started in the Free State, could also have influenced his attitude. In the event, it was President Steyn, who had been summoned to Pretoria by Reitz, who nipped this peace initiative in the bud. Steyn made the point that if the republics planned to surrender in order to prevent further devastation, "then we should have done so before there were so many properties destroyed, thousands of lives already lost, and before so many colonials had joined up with us. In that case it would have been better if we had not even tried to defend our independence."[237]

Shortly after the British occupation of Pretoria (5 June 1900) another prominent Transvaal burgher made an attempt to persuade the republican leaders to stop the war. On 7 June 1900 Commandant-general Botha received a letter – in which there were proposals for peace – from L.F. de Souza, former head secretary in the office of the commandant-general. Botha regarded the letter as an insult, particularly the alleged message from Roberts that if he were to lay down arms he would not only be granted parole to live in a safe place in South Africa, but both he and General de la Rey would each receive and annual allowance of £10 000.[238] De Souza apparently acted on his own initiative because there is no evidence at all that Roberts gave his consent to this message, or that he was even aware of it.[239] Even Botha himself had doubts about the validity of these proposals and informed Roberts: "The nature of these propositions was so entirely unknown to me personally ... that I could not believe that they came from your Excellency." [240]

The peace initiatives which have been discussed thus far all took place without any cooperation or interference from the British authorities. Henceforth the surrendered burghers and their fellows would, however, have to work together with the British army authorities or at least be given their approval before any peace mission could hope to run smoothly. The British did not hesitate to make use of the services of these people and in fact encouraged them to make every effort to change the outlook of those Boers who were still fighting. By working with the British, the surrendered burghers placed themselves in an extremely tenuous position. The fighting burghers now had every justification to accuse them of overt treason, because in conveying their peace initiatives to the bitterenders the surrendered burghers were all to some extent dependent on cooperation with the British military command.[241]

Two republican burghers, J.F. de Beer, chief inspector of offices, and J.S. Smit, the commissioner of railways, negotiated with Roberts after the occupation of Pretoria and gained his approval to go to the Boer lines on 11 June 1900 with Dr W.C. Scholtz, a Cape medical practitioner and friend of the Kruger family, in an attempt to win Kruger over to the idea of concluding peace.[242] Smit in particular was an influential figure in the Transvaal. In the years from 1890 to 1899 he had played an important role in uncovering financial fraud in the construction of the Selati railway line from Komati Drift to the Soutpansberg district. Through his efforts the republic had been saved a great deal of money.[243] Furthermore Smit was also one of Kruger's confidants[244] and his voice would presumably have carried considerable weight with the president.

These three people obtained authority from Roberts to inform Kruger that if he agreed to surrender unconditionally before 20 June he would not be banned to St Helena. They left Pretoria and came upon Botha while the battle of Diamond Hill (Donkerhoek) was still in progress. According to Scholtz, Botha told them that their proposed interview with Kruger would serve no useful purpose, but that he (Botha) would inform the president about the nature of their visit. Initially Botha was not prepared to allow them to return to Pretoria, but after a heated argument lasting two hours they were permitted to leave.[245] General Ben Viljoen, who was the first to speak to these burghers, had little sympathy for them. He regarded their actions and their cooperation with Roberts as blatant high treason – an opinion which according to Viljoen was also shared by many of the fighting burghers.[246]

Milner had his doubts about these negotiations and described them as "a very extraordinary performance".[247] There is no doubt that at this point the Boer forces were not yet prepared to conclude peace without the maintenance of their independence.[248] Nevertheless there were some of the fighting burghers who in retrospect regretted that the struggle was continued after 11 June 1900. Thirty five years after Smit's visit to the Boer lines a bitterender, B.J. Botha of Carolina, posed the following question to vindicate Smit's action: "If we had made peace then, would it have been so wrong? Would our twenty-six thousand women and children's children and grandchildren not now [1953] have placed our people far in the majority?"[249] This type of question is obviously pure speculation. Neither Botha nor Smit could have known in June 1900 which direction the war would subsequently take, or what the total number of deaths in the concentration camps would be.

In June 1900 surrendered burghers in the Free State also tried to change the thinking of the burghers who were still fighting. On 9 June W.J. Butler and J.P. van Aswegen departed from Smithfield for Senekal hoping "to try and induce the Caledon River Burghers to surrender their arms".

They reached Senekal but did not succeed in making contact with the burghers. "In consequence of what we heard from influential men," they explained, "we had to abandon our intention. We were informed that no proclamations from the British Authorities were allowed to be seen or read by the Burghers, being all destroyed by their officers and all persons with any proclamations were caught by their Scouts and sent away."[250]

Then there were certain district commissioners in the Transvaal and the Free State who sent out surrendered burghers to ply the fighting burghers with arguments about surrendering. Through the mediation of a man called Honiball, Captain J.M. Vallentin of Heidelberg succeeded in persuading Field-cornet P. Groesbeek and part of his commando to surrender on 25 August 1900.[251] Vallentin followed up this success by sending three anonymous burghers to the Boer forces in the Heidelberg district at the end of September. They were to provide the Boers with information about Roberts's new proclamation. Vallentin was convinced that most of the Boers would surrender if they knew about the proclamation, but the surrendered burghers failed to get further than the Boer outposts and were not able to speak to any of the burghers at all.[252] In the Free State, Captain F.R. de Bertodano, district commissioner of Kroonstad, made use of P.M. Botha, former member of the Free State *Volksraad* for Kroonstad, to get an interview on 17 September with General De Wet. But the interview came to nothing.[253]

In collaboration with the British, former Boer officers were also prepared to make an effort to get the fighting burghers to change their attitude. One such person was Commandant A.J. Dercksen. Dercksen was a popular officer,[254] but one who was inclined to be headstrong – sometimes to the cost of his country. At the beginning of the war he was a field-cornet in the Boksburg commando. When the government, at the request of a number of burghers, decided to split the Boksburg unit and make Elandsfontein a separate field-cornetcy, Dercksen protested vehemently against the decision. He also incited his men against the idea – so much so that Commandant-general P.J. Joubert even spoke of a "revolution" among the burghers. Dercksen got his own way eventually, but the men from Elandsfontein were dissatisfied and the upshot was that Elandsfontein did not become part of Boksburg again, nor was it recognised as a separate field-cornetcy. There was a great deal of confusion about the whole affair and for five months the arguing went back and forth because Dercksen, a junior officer, was not satisfied with official state policy.[255]

During the first few months of the war Dercksen was on the Natal front. Although he was a courageous fighter, he was unreliable and Botha could not depend on him.[256] His role in the war thereafter also indicates an inability to apply himself with real commitment to his task. On 3 August 1900 he sent an open letter in his capacity as commandant of the Boksburg commando to all the burghers, regardless of whether they had surrendered or not. He urged those who were still fighting not to lose heart and to the surrendered burghers he said: "The day will come when you will say to yourselves: let the mountains fall upon me and the hills cover my shame, because I have been guilty of shedding the blood of my fellow republicans."[257] Less than two months after writing this he would undergo a complete change of heart.

By about 22 September 1900 Dercksen was in favour of a local ceasefire of eight days in the vicinity of Sybrandskraal and Witnek, about 64 kilometres north-west of Pretoria.[258] On 25 September he negotiated with Major-general A.H. Paget and declared that he was prepared to surrender, but first he wanted to ascertain the true state of the war in the Transvaal. According to Paget, Dercksen himself then suggested that "he [Dercksen] should go ... and see Botha and tell him of the hopelessness of continuing the war and ascertain for himself the true state of affairs". If, after his visit, Dercksen was then satisfied that "things are as bad as they are reported to be", he would surrender voluntarily.[259] That same day (25 September) Dercksen set off for Komatipoort with Captain Smitherman (one of Paget's staff officers) to negotiate with Botha. Paget suggested that while Dercksen was there he could also make use of the opportunity to inspect the cannons at Hectorspruit that Botha had been forced to destroy in the middle of September.[260] The purpose of this was presumably to convince Dercksen that to continue fighting the war was useless. But the journey by Dercksen and Smitherman was unproductive; they did not succeed in making contact with Botha, who had already moved off in a northerly direction to Leydsdorp.[261] On his return on 1 October Dercksen said that he was prepared to withdraw from the struggle, but that he would first have to fetch his personal belongings from the Boer laager.[262] Back in the camp he called the burghers together and told them about the cannons he had seen. There had been no sign of "our people" and he was convinced that "our cause" was hopeless and that "we have no chance".[263] On 4 October he again negotiated with Paget and on 7 October 1900 he formally laid down his arms.[264] Four days later (11 October) Dercksen once again held talks with the British. Roberts wanted him to visit Botha and General Schalk Burger to inform them of the dreadful circumstances throughout the country and to influence them to ask for peace.[265] Dercksen was however hesitant to oblige and was apparently afraid that the Boer leaders would arrest him.[266]

Although Dercksen did not dare to visit the Boers in the veld, on 16 October he was prepared to leave for Cape Town "to get up a petition among the Boer prisoner of war to be sent to Cmdt. Gen. Botha for the purpose of putting an end to the present hostilities".[267] In Cape Town during November 1900 Dercksen explained in an interview with a reporter of *The Cape Argus* why he felt that it was useless for the republican forces to continue fighting. Dercksen claimed that the only thing that could save the republics was foreign intervention and that "he had no faith in any intervention on the part of the other Powers. He had always held that view. The Boers were now helpless and his opinion was that people were only helped as long as they were in a position to help themselves. In addition to that, no nation would interfere unless it had something to gain, and so he thought there was no likelihood of France, Germany or America moving in the matter."[268] In contrast to this declaration, it seems that Dercksen had not always felt so pessimistic about foreign assistance. On 24 May 1900, brimming with confidence, he had informed President Kruger that if they were only able to keep fighting, they would surely be helped by outside powers.[269] To promote his cause while on his Cape trip, Dercksen also announced that he, "as a son of the Transvaal, had done his duty to his country and people in seven wars, and ... in the present war fought incessantly for one year and ten days in defence of his country ... I have always acted in the best interests of my people and country and hope never to act otherwise or from any other motive".[270] Whether or not Dercksen was indeed as concerned about the interests of his people and his country as he claimed to be must be seriously questioned in the light of his wilfulness and unreliable behaviour earlier in the war. Nor did his opinions have a great impact on the prisoners of war in Cape Town. They retained their loyalty to the republican cause and Dercksen was unable to get the necessary signatures for his proposed petition.[271]

In addition to Dercksen, General Hendrik Schoeman, a former Boer officer, undertook a peace mission in October 1900. As a confidant of Kruger, Schoeman was in command of the republican forces on the southern front in the first few months of the war.[272] According to his son and biographer, he acquitted himself very well in this capacity under the circumstances.[273] Breytenbach is of the opinion that this was not the case, while Smuts labelled his conduct as "gross incompetence".[274] In February 1900, on the grounds of incompetence, he was replaced by General H. Lemmer, and was sent to Bloemfontein where he carried out administrative tasks. He considered this type of work beneath his dignity and by March he was back in Pretoria where he gave himself up to the British in June 1900.[275] His biographer claims that the British did not trust him, but Maxwell was convinced that Schoeman was not playing a double role.[276] Schoeman was certainly prepared to take up arms again, but only if he was given an officer's rank.[277] General de la Rey for his part saw Schoeman as an ordinary burgher and on 31 July 1900 he was arrested on his farm near Pretoria after refusing to accompany some supply wagons.[278] On 11 September he was tried at Barberton and was acquitted on a charge of treason. On 15 September, two days after he occupied Barberton, General J.D.P. French sent Schoeman back to Pretoria.[279]

Back in Pretoria, Schoeman decided on his own initiative to get Roberts's approval to visit De la Rey in order "to see whether there was any possibility of having peace".[280] On 7 October, accompanied by Captain W.P. Anderson of the Transvaal Constabulary, he left for the Boer lines. Before he could get to De la Rey he was arrested and tried at Nylstroom, but was acquitted of high treason by a special military court. The court was divided in its verdict. Commandant J.C.G. Kemp thought that Schoeman was guilty, but because two other members, namely Commandant L.E. Krause (Chairman) and Assistant Field-cornet J.R. Bester did not concur in this, he was not given the death penalty.[281] Schoeman was kept in safe custody and had to stay in gaol in Pietersburg until 13 December 1900. Thereafter he was allowed out on bail of £1000 during the day on the understanding that he had to sleep in prison each night. From 6 February 1901 he was allowed out on bail during the day and night and on 8

April, after the British occupation of Pietersburg by Brigadier-general H.C.O. Plumer, Schoeman returned to Pretoria.[282]

On 26 May 1901 Schoeman died when a lyddite bomb – a souvenir which he used as an ashtray – exploded when he accidentally dropped a burning match into it.[283] According to Maxwell the Boers regarded the manner of his death as "the judgement of the Almighty for having surrendered".[284]

It is clearly difficult to determine the real reasons that motivated Schoeman to make his peace initiative. Buys feels that "it is unfortunate that one cannot determine what made him [Schoeman] take this stance [to promote peace], namely whether he thought that the struggle was lost after the occupation of Pretoria, or whether he was inspired by personal and material motives". According to this particular view "material gain might have played a role because of the fact that he lived prosperously under the British military government".[285] It must however be kept in mind that although Schoeman had been a prosperous farmer prior to the war,[286] his farm was accidentally burned by the British before 15 September 1900.[287] Under these circumstances he could hardly have lived in great comfort. In addition, it must be remembered that he left on his peace mission on 7 October 1900 – in other words after his farm had already been destroyed. As he had apparently not been given any assurances of compensation, it is difficult to argue that material motives were his only consideration. He naturally owned other property in Pretoria, but it nevertheless seems more likely that Schoeman was genuinely convinced that it would be better to abandon the struggle. He had planned to give De la Rey the following note (which was not delivered because Schoeman was arrested before he could reach De la Rey): "I constantly hear of new destruction to property ... and often of the death, injury and capture of our brothers. For these reasons I have decided to appeal to you, Your Excellency ...".[288] In the court hearing at Nylstroom, Schoeman testified that "I was driven by love for my people and my fellow sufferers."[289] Schoeman's evidence in court should however be treated with caution, because he naturally tried to present his case in as positive a light as possible. His biographer is convinced that he was sincere in his efforts for peace.[290] H.J. Batts, who had apparently spoken to Schoeman about the war, also claims that "I am sure Schoeman was quite genuine in his desire to assure De la Rey of the utter wrong of his persistence in the guerrilla fighting ...".[291] Although neither Schoeman's biographer nor Batts can be considered impartial observers, it does seem that their evidence in this matter can be accepted – particularly because there was apparently no personal material gain for Schoeman in such a peace mission. He must also have realised that the Boers would not be sympathetically inclined towards him because, as has already been mentioned, he had appeared before a court martial in Barberton the previous September. Despite this he persisted with his plan.

But neither Schoeman himself nor his conviction that the struggle was over made any impression at all on the Boers in the veld. Buttery (author of *Why Kruger made War or Behind the Boer Scenes* and former editor of *The Standard and Diggers' News*) wrote: "The '*taal*' [Afrikaans language] is most expressive, but I doubt whether it would be equal to the measure of contempt with which Botha and men of his class regard Schoemann [sic] and that gang."[292] Taking everything into consideration, the republican leaders had every right to take strong action against Schoeman, regardless of his motives. In the first place, in terms of military law he was a deserter from the republican army, a man who had failed to carry out his duty as a citizen. According to a renowned jurist, "A deserter may be detained, courtmartialled and punished ...".[293] Secondly, Schoeman had gone to the Boer lines in collaboration with the British, with the aim of undermining the republics' legitimate war effort. Juridically speaking, this placed Schoeman in an even weaker position and he was lucky to have come out of it alive. Because he had been arrested before he had come into contact with De la Rey, the military court could not prove whether he was indeed guilty. This was the only thing that saved him. Commandant Lodi Krause, a qualified advocate and the chairman of the court, said: "No evidence was produced that Schoeman ... had induced others to surrender ... I acquitted Schoeman because there was no *legal* evidence against him, although I was morally certain of his guilt and that he was an unmitigated scoundrel."[294]

Although the surrendered burghers placed themselves in a dangerous position by attempting to persuade some of the fighting burghers to abandon the struggle, this did not prevent the British authorities from making use of their services in this way. At the beginning of October 1900 all surrendered burghers in the vicinity of Pretoria were expected to distribute Roberts's proclamation in the district. If they had moral objections against this, they would not be forced to do so, but if the proclamation was brought to their farms, they had to make sure that it remained there. The purpose of this was to make Roberts's official policy towards surrendered burghers known as widely as possible in the hope that the fighting burghers would hear about it and might then decide to lay down their arms.[295] In October J. Maartins, a former magistrate of Lichtenburg, was also sent by Major-general C.W.H. Douglas to De la Rey. Maartins was told to try, on behalf of Douglas, to get an interview with De la Rey, but De la Rey was not prepared to negotiate with mediators.[296]

Towards the end of October, H.G. Junius of Heidelberg – according to Vallentin (the district commissioner) "an intimate friend of Commandant Louis Botha and … a very well educated man"[297] – also tried, with Roberts's approval, to make Botha change his stance. On 28 March Junius wrote to Botha and pleaded with him to halt the war. Junius claimed that he was not unsympathetic to the republican cause, but that it was his genuine conviction that the termination of the struggle was necessary to rescue the people from "total destruction and ruin".[298] Roberts identified himself with the contents of Junius's letter[299] and on 4 November it was delivered to Botha by a British officer under the protection of a white flag. On 6 November Botha sent his unequivocal reply: "Junius is one of our burghers who has not at any stage during the course of this war carried out his duties as a burgher properly, and I cannot believe that this despicable letter from such an insignificant deserter has been sent to me with Your Excellency's knowledge and under the guise of an official despatch."[300]

On the one hand Botha's reaction was typical of all the republican leaders who made it very clear that they were not prepared at that stage to accept peace without the maintenance of independence. On the other hand, by the beginning of November 1900 there were 24 prominent residents of Pretoria who were convinced that it would be expedient to end the war at all costs. They drew up a petition to this effect and sent it on 2 November to Revd H.S. Bosman of the N.H. of G. Kerk (Dutch Reformed Church) with the request that he hand it over to Botha.³⁰¹ Some of the signatories of the petition, namely J.S. Smit, the government's commissioner of railways; C.J. Joubert, the head of the Department of Mines; Sammy Marks, the well-known industrialist; the chief justice, R. Gregorowski and Adv. W.E. Hollard had all been involved in peace initiatives since March and May 1900, while Field-cornet P.F. Zeederberg and Karel Rood, a Pretoria businessman, were to become involved in the burgher peace committee in December 1900 and January 1901.³⁰²

According to the signatories, who called themselves "Afrikaner Residents" of Pretoria, the death of so many of their compatriots, the helpless widows and orphans, and the destruction of property meant that it was "hopeless and futile to continue the war with Great Britain because her strength is too overwhelming". Botha was asked to request an interview with Roberts to talk about the possibility of peace.³⁰³

According to Marks and Edward Rooth, Revd Bosman, who had reportedly been in favour of a peace mission to the republican leaders since September 1900,³⁰⁴ approved the content of the petition and said that he was prepared to deliver it to Botha.³⁰⁵ However, he then discussed the matter with his church council and they advised him very strongly against undertaking the proposed mission. Bosman notified Rooth that he unfortunately had to withdraw his offer because he was not prepared to "override the expressed wishes of my Kerkeraad for fear of schism and all other kinds of unpleasantness in the congregation".³⁰⁶ In addition to the opposition of his church council, Bosman was also uncertain that "the leaders of our fighting burghers" would be prepared to receive him and he also had no guarantee of "returning home safely".³⁰⁷ After Bosman's refusal, Marks cooperated with Roberts to recruit the services of Mrs H. Joubert (the widow of Commandant-general P.J. Joubert) who was to leave for the Boer lines on 5 November 1900 accompanied by her daughter, Mrs A. Malan (wife of Commandant A.H. Malan).³⁰⁸ They took a personal letter from Marks and the petition to deliver to Botha. In his letter Marks expressed the hope that his proposals would be laid before Steyn, Reitz and the other leaders of the people and that they might all consent to negotiate with Roberts so that the war could be brought to an end. According to Marks the republican forces could not expect any help from the European powers and the country was simply being ruined by the continuation of the war. Furthermore the Boer ranks had been decimated to such an extent that they no longer had any realistic chance of victory. "Now my dear Louis", he asked, "can 10 000 men [sic] still fondly believe ... that they are able to take on the mighty England ... who has almost unlimited sums of money and countless men at her disposal ...?"[309]

As far as can be established, Botha did not respond in writing to this letter and petition.[310] Under the circumstances it can however be presumed that he would have identified with the opinion of Commandant A.H. Malan,[311] Mrs Joubert's son-in-law, who wrote: "We are desirous of peace but are not prepared to accept it through the intervention of ... people who ... turned traitor, like Hendrik Schoeman, P. Potgieter, K. Rood, F. Eloff and so many others ... We would respect and sooner consider any communication from our enemies direct ... we are desirous of peace, but not peace at any price. If we are to lose our independence, which is still a matter of doubt, we are not prepared to sacrifice our honour as well by coming as dogs to sue for peace ... We feel more insulted than anything else by the means that have up to the present been made use of to approach us in the cause of peace."[312] Together with Marks's letter there was also one, more than likely sent without the knowledge of the military authorities, from Mrs C.F. Honey, a Pretoria widow. In her letter she told Botha that the "so-called patriots" were not representative of Afrikaner opinion and that "[they] are only doing this out of selfish motives to save their ... pockets".[313]

Mrs Honey was perfectly correct to assert that the signatories of the petition were not representative of Afrikaner opinion – the large majority of the Transvaal and Free State burghers were indeed still loyal to the republican cause. But it is doubtful whether the signatories launched the peace mission for selfish material reasons. Marks expected that this allegation might well be made against him and warned Botha: "I know that I ... have enemies and hope that none of them will say, or even think, that old Marks will make a vast amount of money out of the British Government, and that this is the reason why I have written this letter to our General." Besides the fact that the republican cause, according to Marks, was already lost, he also wrote to relieve the burden of "a great many widows and orphans".[314]

Throughout the war (both before and after the peace mission) Marks had taken pity on the needy women who had men on commando and had spent a great deal of money to provide them with food.[315] The fact that he was prepared to maintain some of the wives and children of the fighting burghers shows that humanitarian considerations were important to him. Then too, although Commandant Malan had expressed himself strongly against Marks's peace initiative, he had no illusions about its sincerity. He regarded Marks as "a friend who has ... greatly interested himself on our behalf".[316] In the light of this evidence there is little reason to suspect that Marks had ulterior motives in this peace initiative.

During November 1900, burghers who were against the continuation of the struggle made two more attempts (as far as can be established) to win the bitterenders over to their way of thinking. In the Free State, T.C.L. Bergstedt, who was a member of the *volksraad*, D. Roux and a certain Swanepoel, all three of whom were prominent residents of Winburg, persuaded Margaret Marquard (the wife of Revd J.J.T. Marquard, moderator of the N.G. Kerk) to depart with them on 8 November 1900 for Commandant Sarel Haasbroek's commando. The purpose of this visit was to persuade Haasbroek to enter into peace negotiations with the British. But Haasbroek would hear nothing of it at all, and one of his lieutenants, Tewie Wessels, said that "a voluntary surrender ... would be too palpable an act of *'ongeloof'*",[317] it would be unthinkable. In the Transvaal J.A. Neser, an attorney and prominent resident of Klerksdorp, sent a letter to General P.J. Liebenberg through the mediation of a Mrs B.D. Pienaar (presumably the wife of B.D. Pienaar, the commissioner of mines in Potchefstroom). In the letter, received by Liebenberg on 22 November 1900, Neser claimed that the Boer cause was futile and that although their patriotism and determination was to be admired, they had no chance of winning such an unequal struggle. As far as can be ascertained, Liebenberg did not even reply to the letter.[318] Although most of these sporadic attempts to promote peace met with failure, they were not without significance. Indirectly they paved the way for a more organised peace initiative, namely the burgher peace committees, and they were also symptomatic of a growing feeling among the surrendered burghers that peace would have to be made whatever the price.

Notes

1. Van der Merwe, II, p. 12; *Times History*, IV, p. 28; Leyds Archive, 771(b), (11), Nierstrasz, p. 546a.
2. KG 353 (1) War Council Minutes, 17 March 1900; Van der Merwe, II, pp. 12–3. De Wet, *Boer en Brit*, pp. 52–3 gives the date incorrectly as 20 March 1900.
3. For copies of the proclamations see Leyds Archive, 781 (ii), report of Ram and Thomson, pp. 527–30; Van der Merwe, II, pp. 13–5.
4. Cd. 426, p. 2, I, February 1900; Chapter 1, section 2 above.
5. Translated from the Dutch. Van der Merwe, II, p. 14.
6. *Buitengewone Staatscourant der Z.A.R.*, 9 June 1900. In the proclamation Kruger refers incorrectly to the oath of allegiance instead of the oath of neutrality.
7. *Buitengewone Staatscourant der Z.A.R.*, 14 June 1900.
8. *Manual of Military Law*, p. 290 as quoted in Spies, "Civilians", p. 223. See also Chapter 1, section 2 above.
9. See also Leyds Archive, 781 (ii), report of Ram and Thomson, p. 527; W.T. Stead, *How not to make Peace*, p. 82; B. Duff, *What is now being done in South Africa*, pp. 9–10.
10. Roberts Papers, WO 105 T31 (vol. 30/58/225), Lagden – Roberts, 31 March 1900.
11. Leyds Archive, 722(a), telegram 25 of 22 April 1900, Steyn – Kruger.
12. De Wet, *Boer en Brit*, pp. 54, 63–4, 67, 71; *Times History*, IV, pp. 51–5; M.C.E. van Schoor, "Christiaan Rudolph de Wet" in *DSAB*, I; J.J. Oberholster, "Die Stryd in die Vrystaat" in J.H. Breytenbach (ed.), *Gedenkalbum van die Tweede Vryheidsoorlog*, p. 209.
13. A239, Maj. A.L. la C. Bartrop Accession (British information officer), "Notice to the Burghers of the Ward Upper Modderrivier, Dist. Bloemfontein", April 1900 (translated copy of a notice by Commandant P.J. Fourie).
14. C.J. Barnard, "Grepe uit die Krygskuns van die Boeregeneraals" in *Historia*, 19(1), May 1974, pp. 9–10; *Official History*, III, pp. 114–25, 130–3; *Times History*, IV, pp. 239–68; De Wet, *Boer en Brit*, pp. 86–94.
15. Oberholster (ed.), "Dagboek van Oskar Hintrager", pp. 91–2, 27 July 1900; M.J. Grobler, *Met die Vrystaters onder die Wapen*, p. 65.
16. Translated from the Dutch. Leyds Archive, 730(e), telegram 46(a), undated, C. de Wet – Transvaal government. According to F. Pretorius, "Die Eerste Dryfjag op Hoofkmdt. C.R. de Wet" (Unpublished MA dissertation, UP), 1975, p. 172 the date of the telegram should be 25 July 1900. See also CO 417/307/35549 (FK 409, pp. 343–4), "Translated extracts from Boer circular war telegrams", for a translated copy of the same telegram.
17. Pretorius, p. 174.
18. Translated from the Dutch. De Wet, *Boer en Brit*, p. 138.
19. De Wet, *Boer en Brit*, pp. 139–40; C.C.J. Badenhorst, *Uit den Boeren-oorlog*, pp. 55–8, 67–8, 78–9; *Times History*, V, p. 3.
20. A787, Preller Collection, 81, "Geskiedenis van die Frankfort-kommando", p. 55.
21. Hancock and Van der Poel, *Selections*, I, p. 582, "Memoirs".
22. A313, De la Rey Collection, 17, p. 49, De la Rey – Kruger, 21 July 1900.
23. Hancock and Van der Poel, *Selections*, I, p. 594, "Memoirs"; J. Oosthuizen, "Jacobus Herculas de la Rey en die Tweede Vryheidsoorlog", (Unpublished D.Litt. thesis, Potch), 1950, pp. 336–7; J.S. du Plessis, "Jacobus Hercules de la Rey" in *DSAB*, I.

24 *De Zoutpansberg Wachter*, 28 September 1900 (notice dated 19 September 1900). See also Naudé, *Vechten en Vluchten*, pp. 172–3.
25 Translated from the Dutch. *De Zoutpansberg Wachter*, 28 September 1900 (leading article).
26 Leyds Archive, 722(b), (13), Nierstrasz, p. 1073.
27 PSY 57/DC 50, notice issued by district commissioner, 12 October 1900.
28 PMO 41/2801, H.Y. Buller – Provost marshal, 28 October 1900.
29 Cd. 663, p. 7, Commandant-general to all officers and magistrates, 3 December 1900 (translated published copy).
30 MGP 55/8078/00, "Summary of Intelligence", 23 December 1900. See also A787, Preller Collection, 1, p. 210, General C. Spruyt – Botha, 9 December 1900.
31 Van Schoor, "Christiaan Rudolph de Wet" in *DSAB*, I; Hancock and Van der Poel, *Selections*, I, pp. 595–6, "Memoirs"; D.S. van Warmelo, *Mijn Commando en Guerilla Commando-Leven*, pp. 70–2.
32 Spies, "Civilians", p. 224.
33 Milner Papers, 32, (FK 1168, p. 438), J. Fraser – O. Walrond, 12 December 1900; De Wet, *Boer en Brit*, pp. 71–2; I.J.C. de Wet, *Met Generaal De Wet op Kommando*, p. 56. For a discussion on the manner in which the surrendered burghers were treated by the British, see Chapter 2, section 2 below.
34 According to General de Wet 2950 men joined from September to November 1900. De Wet, *Boer en Brit*, p. 140. To this should be added the 110 men whom De Wet, as already mentioned, had commandeered at the beginning of April 1900, as well as the 500 men who joined after the battle of Mostertshoek (4 April) and the 400 men who joined at the end of July 1900 while De Wet delayed his march for a few days on the Vaal River.
35 Oberholster (ed.), "Dagboek van Oskar Hintrager", p. 92, 28 July 1900.
36 Oberholster (ed.), "Dagboek van Oskar Hintrager", p. 92, 28 July 1900. See also M.C.E. van Schoor, *De Wet en sy Verkenners*, p. 18.
37 Oberholster (ed.), "Dagboek van Oskar Hintrager", p. 95, 30 July 1900.
38 Leyds Archive, 721(d), telegram 5 of 12 April 1900, Kruger – Steyn; Badenhorst, pp. 57–8.
39 MGB 7, H.O. Pugh (assistant district commissioner Heilbron) – Pretyman, 5 September 1900; PMO 5/362, Information service Krugersdorp – Provost marshal of Pretoria, 28 October 1900.
40 Translated from the Dutch. *De Zuid-Afrikaan*, 12 May 1900 (news report).
41 P.S. Lombard, *Uit die Dagboek van 'n Wildeboer*, p. 60.
42 De Wet, *Boer en Brit*, p. 139; Badenhorst, pp. 56–7.
43 Roberts Papers, WO 105/23 (Vol. 58/271/174), Colonel Western – Roberts, 23 November 1900.
44 Translated from the Dutch. H. ver Loren van Themaat, *Twee Jaren in den Boerenoorlog*, p. 181.
45 Lombard, p. 62.
46 Van Warmelo, pp. 70–2; Spies, "Civilians", pp. 203, 222; PMO 5/368, sworn statement by J.H. Steenkamp, 31 December 1900 and Roberts Papers, WO 105 T28/5 (Vol. 42/152/69), Hunter – Roberts, 12 August 1900.

47 MGB 2, Commanding officer, Hoopstad – Information officer, Bloemfontein, 26 September 1900; PMO 23/1608, A. Venter, J. Coetzee and H. Venter – Provost marshal, Pretoria, 20 June 1901; G. Boldingh, *Een Hollandsch Officier in Zuid-Afrika*, pp. 54–5; Hancock and Van der Poel, *Selections*, pp. 594–5, I, "Memoirs".
48 James, p. 357; Headlam, II, p. 79; R. Kruger, *Good-bye Dolly Gray*, p. 381.
49 WO Confidential Telegrams, 558A and 559A, Kitchener – Brodrick, 24 and 25 June 1901.
50 Cd. 663, p. 5; WO 32/876/6300 (A377) (translated copies).
51 Translated from the Dutch. A1148, "Circulaire aan Hoofd en andere Officieren der Z.A.R." (Circular to Head and other Officers of the S.A.R.), dated 6 October 1900 at Roossenekal.
52 Cd. 663, p. 7, Commandant-general – All officers and magistrates, 3 December 1900 (translated published copies).
53 Barnard, *Botha*, p. 151.
54 Spies, "Civilians", p. 287; E. Hobhouse, *The Brunt of the War and Where it Fell*, pp. 35–7.
55 MGP 34/5332/00, Commandant Volksrust – Military governor Pretoria, 27 October 1900; PMO 6/424, J.C. Breytenbach, D.J. Erasmus and S.J. Grobler – Provost marshal Pretoria, 3 December 1900; Hobhouse, *Brunt of the War*, pp. 101–2.
56 Roberts Papers, WO 105 T 78/2 (Vol 55/227/139), Commanding officer communication lines Natal – Kitchener, 17 October 1900; Van Everdingen, *Tweede Tijdvak*, II, p. 15; Spies, "Civilians", p. 173.
57 Translated from the Dutch. A published copy of the proclamation is in Badenhorst, pp. 53–4.
58 *The Bloemfontein Post*, 26 February 1901 (news report). See also *The Bloemfontein Post*, 7 May 1901 (news report), in which the death of Rademan is ascribed to De Wet.
59 Translated from the Dutch. *De Getuige*, October 1903, p. 304 (article by S.J. du Toit).
60 Badenhorst, pp. 55–6.
61 See KG 353/2/, pp. 13–7, "Verslag van Crimineele en Andere zaken behandeld door het Militaire Hof voor de Westelijke Districten der Z.A.R." (Report of Criminal and Other matters handled by the Military Court for the Western districts of the S.A.R.), January, February and March 1901; MGB 3, Apthorp – Pretyman, 18 October 1900; MGB 3, Assistant district commissioner Wepener – Military governor Bloemfontein, 1 December 1900; C.H. Muller, *Oorlogsherinneringe*, p. 89 and B.J. Viljoen, *My Reminiscences of the Anglo-Boer War*, p. 155.
62 MGB 5, Ross – Military governor, 12 October 1900.
63 Badenhorst, pp. 55–6. Commandant Badenhorst re-commandeered surrendered burghers in the vicinity of Boshof.
64 Oppenheim, a renowned jurist, writes as follows in this regard: "The usual punishment for spying is hanging or shooting; though less severe punishments are of course admissible and are sometimes inflicted ... No regard is paid to the status, rank, position, or motive of a spy ... He may be following instructions of superiors, or acting on his own initiative from patriotic motives." Oppenheim, II, pp. 424–5. See also Spaight, pp. 210–1.
65 PMO 17/1229, sworn statement by Mrs L.F. Krynauw, 18 March 1901 (copy).
66 Mrs Krynauw's evidence was accepted by Major F. White, the commanding officer at Ladybrand, and A.J. Brand, the local magistrate. Her sister-in-law, Mrs

G. de Bruyn, also made a similar statement. PMO 17/1229, White – Knox, 5 April 1901; A.J. Brand – H. Wilson, 19 March 1901 and statement by Mrs de Bruyn, 10 April 1901 (copies).

67   Cd. 800, p. 26. The Hague Convention makes no provision for deserters who act as spies, but article 30 does specify as follows in the case of spies: "A spy taken in the act cannot be punished without previous trial." See also Oppenheim, II, p. 424, and Spaight, pp. 210–1.

68   Van Schoor, *De Wet en sy Verkenners*, pp. 18–9.

69   See Archive Landdros (magistrate) Zoutpansberg, 122, "The State vs. F.S. Grobler and C. Potgieter on charges of High Treason", 18 October 1900 (They were each given a fine of £500.); Archive Landdros (magistrate) Middelburg, Special Military Court, Minutes, 75, "The State vs. W.T. Richards on charges of High Treason", 20 December 1900 (Richards was originally sentenced to death, but this was commuted to life imprisonment with hard labour.); KG 353/21, pp. 13–7, "Verslag van Crimineele en andere zaken behandeld door het Militaire Hof voor de Westelijke Districten der Z.A.R.", January, February and March 1901; Viljoen, *Reminiscences*, p. 154; Naudé, *Vechten en Vluchten*, p. 172.

70   KG 353/21, pp. 20–87. "The State vs. H. Savage, R. McLachlan, C. Theunissen, J.P.D. Theunissen, W.J. Ahrens, H. Ahrens, C.J. Matthysen and R. Boyd on charges of High Treason", 12 January to 23 February 1901. Petition, pp. 1–4 dated 17 January 1901, signed by A. van Heerden and 217 other people. The men who were executed (R. McLachlan, J.P.D. Theunissen, H. Ahrens, R. Boyd en C.J. Matthysen) passed information to the British and also tried to persuade some of the fighting burghers to lay down their arms. C. Theunissen, who was guilty of the same offence, was reprieved because of his youth and was sentenced to five years imprisonment with hard labour. H. Savage and W. Ahrens were also shown mercy and were given five years imprisonment with hard labour because it could not be proved beyond doubt that they too had given information to the British. See also J.P. Brits, *Diary of a National Scout P.J. du Toit, 1900–1902*, pp. 35, 39 and 40; January, 23 February and 1 March 1901 and *The Bloemfontein Post*, 16 March 1900 (news report) on the same trial.

71   *Klerksdorp Mining Record*, 3 November 1903 (news report on the reburial of those who were executed).

72   Quoted by P.W. Grobbelaar (ed), *Die Afrikaner en Sy Kultuur*, II, Spieëlbeeld Oorlog 1899–1902, (compiled by C.J. Scheepers Strydom), pp. 102–3.

73   Under the heading "Deserters and Traitors", Oppenheim writes as follows: "The privileges of members of armed forces cannot be claimed by members of the armed forces of a belligerent who go over to the forces of the enemy and are afterwards captured by the former. They may be, and always are, treated as criminals ... Even if they appear under the protection of a flag of truce, deserters and traitors may be seized and punished." Oppenheim, II, p. 268.

74   Translated from the Dutch. *Stemmen des Tijds*, March 1906, p. 6 (an open letter signed by C.S. Grobler, J.C. Breytenbach, A. Smith, G. Holzinger, D.J. Taljaard, P.J.S. van Vuuren, R.J. Labuschagne, J.J. Swart, E.H. van den Berg, J.A. Cothill and P.J. Fourie).

75   *Klerksdorp Mining Record*, 20 November 1903 (letter from "Your Correspondent").

76   Viljoen, *Reminiscences*, p. 155.

77   For the military activity during the second half of 1900 and the nature of the guerrilla-type war see *Times History*, IV, pp. 344–63, 380–95, 414–83; *Times History*, V,

pp. 1–28, 94–110; *Official History*, III, pp. 104–40, 226–49, 286–357, 422–97; De Wet, *Boer en Brit*, pp. 55–62, 108–26, 151–7, 127–37, 196–8; A. Campbell, *Guerrillas: A History and Analysis*, pp. 29–41.

78 MGB 5, Ross – Pretyman, 16 September 1900.

79 *Telegrams and Letters ... Roberts*, i, p. 111, telegram C1089, Military secretary – Magistrate Jacobsdal, 13 April 1900.

80 Le May, p. 85.

81 *Telegrams and Letters ... Roberts*, i, p. 112, memorandum, Roberts – Chermside and Rundle, 13 April 1900.

82 *Telegrams and Letters ... Roberts*, ii, p. 28, telegram C1491, Roberts – Chermside, 7 May 1900.

83 *Telegrams and Letters ... Roberts*, iii, p. 31, telegram C2401, Roberts – Buller, 30 June 1900.

84 Spies "Civilians", pp. 65–6; A.C. Martin, *The Concentration Camps 1900–1902: Facts, Figures and Fables*, p. 2.

85 See Spies, "Civilians", p. 66; Cd. 800 pp. 22–3 article 12.

86 Spies, "Civilians", pp. 66, 179–80, 186; Buys, p. 107.

87 Cd. 524, *passim*.

88 Milner Papers, 47, (FK 1209, pp. 514–15), G. Fiddes – Milner, 8 June 1900; CO 417/292/27317 (FK 337, pp. 748–50), O. Jensen – Milner, 27 May 1900; MGP 16/2197/00, sworn statement by M. Jordaan, 18 August 1900.

89 Translated from the Dutch. Leyds Archive, 734, (16), republican circular, 15 June 1900.

90 See Spies, "Civilians", p. 223.

91 Milner Papers, 47, (FK 1209, pp. 539–40), J.G. Fraser – Military Governor Bloemfontein, 13 June 1900; Roberts Papers, WO 105 T1 1/25 (vol 55/225/129), Methuen – Roberts, 31 October 1900; MGP 28/4031/00, P.J. Bornmann – Maxwell, 28 September 1900.

92 MGB 26, circular to district commissioners, 4 November 1900.

93 *Telegrams and Letters ... Roberts*, vi, p. 6, telegram C5944, Roberts – Kitchener, 2 November 1900; WO Confidential telegrams, 364, Roberts – British secretary for war, 5 November 1900.

94 Cd. 800, p. 27, article 52. See also Chapter 1, section 3 above; Oppenheim, II, pp. 409–10.

95 Cd. 800, p. 27, article 52.

96 Milner Papers, 45, (FK 1134, pp. 176–7), Pretyman – Milner, 29 January 1901, enclosed report by Lieutenant Locke, assistant district commissioner Jacobsdal, November 1900.

97 PSY 56/DC 185, District commissioner Zeerust – Political secretary, 3 August 1900; Hancock and Van der Poel, *Selections*, I, p. 579, "Memoirs".

98 Cd. 426, p. 3, Proclamation 3, 15 March 1900; Cd. 426, p. 7, Proclamation 1 of 1900, 31 May 1900; Cd. 426, p. 8, Proclamation 2 of 1900, 6 June 1900; Chapter 1, section 2 above.

99 *Transvaal Advertiser*, 8 January 1903 (letter from H.C. Marais).

100 Headlam, II, pp. 80–1, Milner – T. Kerr Anderson, 12 September 1900; J. Brandt, *Kappie Kommando*, pp. 152, 193.

101 CO 224/3/7061 (FK 1032, pp. 149–50, 150–1), J.G. Fraser – Pretyman, 26 January 1901.
102 SO/POW 15/1270, Officer in command of prisoners of war – Provost marshal Pretoria, 8 April 1901.
103 *Official History*, IV, p. 704, Annexure 20. See also Chapter 3, section 4 below.
104 Milner Papers, 19, (FK 1137, pp. 666–7), Milner – Hely-Hutchinson, 23 February 1901.
105 PMO 32/2215, A.S. Wessels – Provost marshal Pretoria, 29 October 1900.
106 Spies, "Civilians", p. 121.
107 CO 417/293/29015 (FK 339, p. 460), Milner – Chamberlain, 15 August 1900.
108 Roberts Papers, WO 105 T31/5 (Vol. 46/172/116 and 117), Lagden – Roberts, 2 September 1900; CO 417/307/37817 (FK 410, p. 561), Captain E. Warwick – Altham, 23 October 1900; Milner Papers, 45, (FK 1134, p. 183), Pretyman – Milner, 13 January 1901.
109 See Spies, "Civilians", p. 172.
110 Cd. 426 p. 10, XIX, Proclamation 5 of 1900, 16 June 1900.
111 Cd. 426, p. 11, XX, Proclamation 6 of 1900, 19 June 1900.
112 Cd. 800, p. 27; Spies, "Civilians", p. 159; Buys, p. 103.
113 G.B. Beak, *The Aftermath of War. An Account of Repatriation of the Boers and Natives in the Orange River Colony, 1902–1904*, p. 3, note; Spies, "Civilians", pp. 170–1.
114 Spies, "Civilians", pp. 159, 161.
115 MGP 57/8265/00, Rooth – Roberts, 26 June 1900.
116 Spies, "Civilians", p. 160.
117 PSY 41/M3, Fiddes – Roberts, 23 July 1900.
118 Milner Papers, 47, (FK 1210, p. 10), Fiddes – Milner, 29 July 1900; Cd. 426, p. 12, XXIII, Proclamation 9 of 1900, 27 July 1900.
119 Spies, "Civilians", p. 169.
120 PSY 56/DC 130, sworn statements of J.J.J. van Rensburg and Mrs C.J.J. van Rensburg, 14 September 1900; Spies, "Civilians", pp. 165–6.
121 Cd. 426, p. 14, XXVI, Proclamation 12 of 1900, 14 August 1900.
122 Cd. 426, p. 14, XXVI, Proclamation 12 of 1900, 14 August 1900.
123 Cd. 426, pp. 15–16, XXVIII, Proclamation 14 of 1900, 1 September 1900.
124 PSY 56/DC 158, District commissioner Middelburg – Political secretary, 21 August 1900.
125 PMO 16/1141, Forster – Provost marshal Pretoria, 8 January 1901. See also PMO 30/2089, Forster – Provost marshal Pretoria, 14 September 1901.
126 *Telegrams and Letters … Roberts*, v, p. 23, telegram C4822.
127 Cd. 426, p. 18, XXXII, Government notice 111 of 1900, article 1, 22 September 1900; Cd. 426, p. 19, XXXV, Government notice 15 of 1900, article 1, 28 September 1900.
128 MGP 24/3401/00, Provost marshal – Maxwell, 18 February 1901; PMO 1/85, W. Bonham (assistant provost marshal Pretoria) – Assistant provost marshal Krugersdorp, 8 March 1901. Immediately after Roberts's proclamation of 15 March 1900 in the Free State, the surrendered burghers were in the same position. See Chapter 1, section 2 above.
129 A.M.S. Methuen, *Peace or War in South Africa*, p. 51.

130 Cd. 426, pp. 15–6, XXVII, Proclamation 14 of 1900, September 1900.
131 Cd. 800, p. 26. "Any compulsion of the population of occupied territory to take part in military operations against its own country is prohibited."
132 Roberts Papers, WO 105/29 (A395), Maxwell – Cowan, 7 September 1900; HC 80/132, Milner's undated margin note on the proclamation, presumably made on 25 August 1900. On 24 August Roberts informed Milner by telegram about the proclamation, PSY 38/12 (copy).
133 CSO 25/1230/01, L.A. Tancred – Wilson, 24 April 1901.
134 CSO 25/1230/01, Wilson's note written in the margin of Tancred's explanation, 24 April 1901. This reference is to Emily Hobhouse's visit to Bloemfontein (24 January 1901 to 10 March 1901) during which she exposed the inconsistencies in the British concentration camp system. See J.D. Kriel, "Emily Hobhouse en die Naweë van die Anglo-Boereoorlog", (Unpublished D.Phil. thesis, UOVS), 1956, pp. 67–76.
135 CSO 41/2230, G. de Wet – Assistant administrator of the Orange River Colony, 3 June 1901; Hobhouse, *Brunt of the War*, pp. 9–10.
136 CSO 25/1230/01, H. Goold-Adams – Tancred, 22 April 1901.
137 Hancock and Van der Poel, *Selections*, I, p. 547, "Memoirs". On the burghers in British military service see Chapters 5, 6 and 7.
138 G. Lagden, *The Basutos*, II, p. 609.
139 *Natal Mercury*, 6 February 1900 (news report); *Natal Witness*, 6 February 1900 (news report).
140 Roberts Papers, WO 105/T31/1 (Vol. 30/58/222), Resident commissioner Basutoland – Roberts, 29 March 1900.
141 Roberts Papers, WO 105 T31/2 (Vol. 32/73/20), Resident commissioner Basutoland – Roberts, 16 May 1900. See also *De Zuid-Afrikaan*, 24 and 29 May 1900 (news reports).
142 Roberts Papers, WO 105 T31/4 (Vol. 38/122/71), Resident commissioner Basutoland – Roberts, 29 July 1900; *African (South)*, 662, p. 71, Milner – Chamberlain, 31 July 1900.
143 Roberts Papers, WO 105 T40/2 (Vol. 44/157/175), Kelly-Kenny – Roberts, 31 August 1900; *Telegrams and Letters ... Roberts*, iv, p. 97, telegram C4141, Roberts – Kelly-Kenny, 31 August 1900.
144 CO 417/328/38436 (FK 512, p. 405), "Annual Report Leribe District", 1900–1901. In the report the officers were not identified. However, Boldingh, p. 42 mentions a Commandant De Villiers and S.G. Vilonel who fled to Basutoland at about this time. It can be presumed that they were indeed two of the officers involved. On Vilonel's movements see also Chapter 7, section 2 below.
145 Boldingh, p. 53.
146 Lagden, II, p. 614. In order to present a meaningful discussion in this section it was necessary to go beyond the chronological demarcation of the chapter (March – December 1900). Note that there were surrendered burghers who crossed the republican borders throughout the war.
147 CO 417/328/38436 (FK 512, p. 403), Milner – Chamberlain, 11 October 1901, enclosed report by the resident commissioner, 1900–1901.
148 CO 417/328/38436 (FK 512, p. 405), "Annual Report Leribe District", 1900–1901.
149 CO 417/328/37991 (FK 512, p. 459), Milner – Chamberlain, 28 October 1901, and enclosed letter, Resident commissioner Basutoland – Milner, 18 October 1901.
150 CO 417/328/38436 (FK 512, p. 415), "Annual Report Leribe District", 1900–1901.

151 A.P.J. van Rensburg, "Die Skandkol wat nie wou toegroei nie" in *Die Huisgenoot*, 8 August 1969.
152 C.J. Uys, *Rouxville (1863–1963)*, p. 92.
153 CSO 89/546/02, Resident commissioner Basutoland – Government secretary, Bloemfontein, 18 February 1901 and Wilson's margin note of 28 February 1902.
154 GOV. 250/20, J. Robertson and T. Robertson – Milner, 26 July 1902.
155 FO 365/2, (A82), "Intelligence Diary at Lourenzo Marques", 4, 6, 12 and 13 July 1900.
156 B.G. Schultz, "Die Slag van Bergendal (Dalmanutha)" (Unpublished MA dissertation, UP), 1974, p. 205.
157 Viljoen, *Reminiscences*, pp. 130–1; *Times History*, IV, pp. 476–7; *Official History*, III, p. 418.
158 *Times History*, IV, p. 476. According to British records, which are more than likely too high, there were 1500 deserters and men in this force who went into hiding. FO 365/2, (A282), "Chronological review of events attending the retreat of a portion of the Boer army to Komatipoort and thence across the Portuguese Border; Consul-General F. Crowe", 16–26 September 1900.
159 Viljoen, *Reminiscences*, pp. 130–1.
160 *Times History*, IV, pp. 481–2.
161 FO 365/2, (A282), "Chronological review …".
162 According to General Ben Viljoen, Pienaar gave himself the rank of general. Viljoen, *Reminiscences*, p. 130. See also *Times History*, IV, p. 476 n.
163 FO 365/2, (A282), "Chronological review …".
164 FO 365/2, (A282), "Chronological review …"; *Times History*, IV, p. 482; Viljoen, *Reminiscences*, p. 132.
165 FO 367/2, (A284), Crowe – Roberts and Milner, 18 September 1900; L.E. van Niekerk, "Dr. W.J. Leyds as Gesant van die Zuid-Afrikaansche Republiek" (Unpublished D.Phil. thesis, UOVS), 1972, p. 242.
166 W5/2, (ii), W.J. Geerling Accession, Letterbook of interned Boers in Lourenço Marques and Portugal, p. 6, Geerling – Leyds, 7 December 1900; Van Niekerk, p. 243.
167 CO 417/296/41018 (FK 354, pp. 158, 161, 162), Crowe – Milner, 27 September 1900, Milner – Roberts, 28 September 1900 and Roberts – Milner, 28 September 1900. See also *Africa (South)*, 663, pp. 351–2.
168 CO 417/296/41018 (FK 354, pp. 176, 178), Crowe – Milner, 21 November 1900 and Milner – Roberts, 22 November 1900.
169 FO 684 (A3211), Crowe – Milner, 17 February 1901; Van Niekerk, p. 243; Viljoen, *Reminiscences*, p. 130.
170 *Africa (South)*, 668, pp. 15–6, F. de Wet – F. Cowper (British consul in Portugal) August 1901. (The exact date is not given in the letter.)
171 *Africa (South)*, 669, p. 125, Milner – Chamberlain, 15 November 1901.
172 MGP 139/16756/01, M.R. Greenlees – Commissioner of police, 12 December 1901, report on Du Plessis de Beer's conduct during the war.
173 MGP 139/16756/01, M.R. Greenlees – Commissioner of police, 12 December 1901; Naudé, *Vechten en Vluchten*, pp. 172, 183.
174 CO 417/322/4388 (FK 479, pp. 302–3), Chief of staff, Rhodesian Field Force – Resident commissioner Salisbury, 27 December 1900 and Resident commissioner Salisbury – Chief of staff, 28 December 1900 (copies).

175　CO 417/320/23270 (FK 470, p. 465), Resident commissioner Salisbury – Acting high commissioner, 6 June 1901 (copy).
176　CO 417/320/23270 (FK 470, p. 646), R.H. Everett – M. Clarke, 13 June, 1901 (copy).
177　CO 417/320/25194 (FK 471, p. 708), Administrator Salisbury – High commissioner, 25 June 1901 and High commissioner – Administrator, 25 June 1901 (copies).
178　MGP 174/13987/01, Maxwell – Milner, 26 October 1901 and Milner – Maxwell, 29 October 1901.
179　CO 417/320/31708 (FK 472, pp. 1055, 1058–9), Everett – Resident commissioner Salisbury, 17 June 1901 and Resident commissioner – High commissioner, 24 July 1901. Report on the camp at Bulawayo (copy).
180　R. Hodder-Williams, "Afrikaners in Rhodesia" in *African Social Research*, 18, December 1974.
181　GOV 494/129, Superintendent Balmoral – Maxwell, 13 February 1902 enclosed petition from S.N. de Kock and 50 others.
182　CO 417/320/4410 (FK 479, pp. 408–9), Assistant commissioner Palapye – Acting resident commissioner Mafeking, 7 January 1901; Naudé, *Vechten en Vluchten*, p. 184.
183　CO 417/322/4410 (FK 479, p. 409), Assistant commissioner Palapye – Acting resident commissioner Mafeking, 7 January 1901 (copy).
184　CO 417/322/4410 (FK 479, p. 420), High commissioner – Acting resident commissioner Mafeking, 16 January 1901 (copy).
185　CO 417/323/9116 (FK 485, pp. 258–9), Acting resident commissioner Mafeking – High commissioner, 19 February 1901 (copy).
186　CO 417/320/24213 (FK 470, p. 649), Acting resident commissioner Mafeking – High commissioner, 12 June 1901.
187　See GOV 327/39, Acting resident commissioner Mafeking – High commissioner, 1 June 1901; CO 417/320/23270 (FK 470, pp. 522, 530), Acting resident commissioner Mafeking – High commissioner, 10 June 1901 and High commissioner – Acting resident commissioner Mafeking, 11 June 1901 (copies); CO 417/320/24213 (FK 470, pp. 649, 650) Acting resident commissioner Mafeking – High commissioner, 12 June 1901 and 17 June (copy); *The Bloemfontein Post*, 28 June 1901 (news report).
188　*Official History*, IV, Annexure 20, p. 704.
189　*Telegrams and Letters ... Roberts*, v, p. 135, telegram C5821, Roberts – High commissioner, 29 October 1900; Chapter 3, section 1 below; CO 417/370/14072 (FK 669, pp. 28–30), P.J. Potgieter (former mayor of Pretoria, who took the oath of neutrality) from Dresden, Germany – Chamberlain, 8 April 1902.
190　Cd. 547, p. 53, Roberts's report, 10 October 1900.
191　On 12 August 1900, 182 burghers from the Standerton commando voluntarily surrendered; on 25 August 94 burghers laid down their arms at Nigel and on 24 September 1900, 50 burghers withdrew from the war at Nelspruit. Leyds Archive, 722 (b), 13, Nierstrasz, p. 1020; PSY 57/DC 246, "Vallentin's Diary", 16 August 1900; MGP 30/4509/00, "Precis of Intelligence", 24 September 1900.
192　Roberts Papers, WO 105 T26 (vol 31/65/185), Rundle – Roberts, 13 May 1900; Spies, "Civilians", pp. 67–8.
193　CO 417/290/17416 (FK 226, p. 58), Milner – Roberts, 14 May 1900 (copy); *Telegrams and Letters ... Roberts*, ii, pp. 42–3, telegram C1622, Roberts – Milner, 16 May 1900.
194　MGP 27/3867/00, Maxwell – Colonel W.E.D. Ward (director of supplies), 25 September 1900.

195 CO 417/290/21000 (FK 330, p. 126), Milner – Chamberlain, 10 June 1900.
196 *Africa (South)*, 662, p. 102, Commanding officer communication lines Newcastle – Governor Natal, 25 July 1900.
197 *Africa (South)*, 662, p. 103, Governor Natal – Commanding officer communication lines Newcastle, 27 July 1900.
198 See Chapter 2, section 2 above.
199 PSY 57/DC 249, District commissioner Zeerust – Political secretary, 3 August 1900; MGP 34/5258/00 District commissioner Rustenburg – Military governor, 25 August 1900.
200 MGP 18/2584/00, Director of supplies – Military governor Pretoria, 27 August 1900.
201 MGP 32/4918/00, A. Karley – Deputy mayor Pretoria, 16 October, 1900; Spies, "Civilians", p. 218; Buys, pp. 200–1.
202 J.L. Hattingh, "Die Irenekonsentrasiekamp" in *Archives Yearbook for South African History*, 30 (i), 1967, p. 89.
203 MGB 5, Ross – Pretyman, 7 November 1900, report for October 1900.
204 MGB 5, "To the Burghers of the Boshof District", 10 September 1900 (public notice).
205 Milner Papers, 45, (FK 1134, p. 178), Pretyman – Milner, 29 January 1901, enclosed report by Lieutenant Locke (assistant district commissioner Jacobsdal under Captain Ross), November 1900.
206 E. Neethling, *Vergeten?*, pp. 36–7, evidence of Mrs A.S. Louw, undated. Mrs Louw mentions only the surrendered burghers who left the camp. The total number of inmates could not be ascertained.
207 MGB 4, K.P. Apthorp – Pretyman, 3 December 1900.
208 *Officieel Verslag ... Brandfort*, p. 44, evidence of a certain Olivier, a surrendered burgher from Fauresmith.
209 PSY 57/DC 248, Edwards – Fiddes, 1 August 1900.
210 J.C. Otto, *Die Konsentrasiekampe*, pp. 43–4; Kriel, p. 34; Spies, "Civilians", p. 224.
211 PSY 64/MC 201, Abercrombie – Fiddes, 2 August 1900.
212 Spies, "Civilians", pp. 224–5.
213 PSY 57/DC 246 "Vallentin's Diary", 30 and 31 July, 1, 2, 3 and 9 August 1900.
214 Milner Papers, 45, (FK 1205, p. 1002); Headlam, II, p. 86.
215 Roberts Papers, WO 105 T40/30 (vol 48/180/100), Kelly-Kenny – Roberts, 7 September 1900.
216 Roberts Papers, WO 105 T40/30 (vol 48/180/114) Kelly-Kenny – Roberts, 9 September 1900.
217 *Telegrams and Letters ... Roberts*, iv, p. 132, telegram C4466, Roberts – Kelly-Kenny, 9 September 1900.
218 Spies, "Civilians", p. 228; Cd. 426, p. 18, XXXII, Government notice 14 of 1900, article 4, 22 September 1900. The camp at Kroonstad was opened before the end of 1900, but was in effect a concentration camp rather than a protection camp for surrendered burghers. Hobhouse, *Brunt of the War*, Annexure E; Otto, p. 55; L. Marquard (ed), *Letters from a Boer Parsonage. Letters of Margaret Marquard during the Boer War*, p. 111, 6 November 1900.
219 Hattingh, *Irenekonsentrasiekamp*, pp. 94–5; Spies, "Civilians", p. 228.

220 Hattingh, *Irenekonsentrasiekamp*, p. 120.
221 *Telegrams and Letters ... Roberts*, v, p. 34, telegram C4909, Roberts – Paget, 24 September 1900; Cd. 426, p. 18, XXXIII, Government notice III of 1900, article 2, 22 September 1900.
222 See Chapter 2, sections 1 and 2 above.
223 Otto, p. 44; Hobhouse, *Brunt of the War*, p. 34.
224 Spies, "Civilians", p. 230; Otto, p. 44.
225 Spies, "Civilians", p. 230.
226 *Telegrams and Letters ... Roberts*, v, p. 57, telegram C5113.
227 Spies, "Civilians", p. 231.
228 Otto, pp. 42, 53; Kriel, pp. 35–6. Hattingh, *Irenekonsentrasiekamp* (p. 89) claims that this was not the case, but loses sight of the fact that the protection camps housed not only surrendered burghers but also the women and children of loyal burghers.
229 On the question of whether the surrendered burghers contributed directly to the further development of the concentration camp policy under Kitchener, see Chapter 3, section 1 below. On the relationship between the surrendered burghers and the other inmates of the concentration camps, see Chapter 4, section 3 below.
230 See Spies, "Civilians", pp. 217–9, 228.
231 Translated from the Dutch. *De Natal Afrikaner*, 13 March 1900 (open letter dated 2 February 1900 from Revd A.A. van der Lingen). An English version of this letter appears in Cd. 261, pp. 42–3.
232 On Van der Lingen's status among the inhabitants of the Free State and his participation in the presidential elections see J.C. Moll, "Francis William Reitz en die Republiek van die Oranje-Vrystaat" (Unpublished D.Litt. thesis, UOVS), 1968, pp. 144, 159, 415, 425; Malan, "Fraser", p. 136.
233 Milner Papers, 35, (FK 1174, p. 626), Milner – Central judicial commission, 25 June 1903 (copy).
234 H.J. Batts, *Pretoria from within during the War, 1899–1900*, pp. 107–8.
235 See W.L. von R. Scholtz, "Die Betrekkinge tussen die Zuid-Afrikaansche Republiek en die Oranje Vrijstaat, 1899–1902" (Unpublished MA dissertation, RAU), 1971, pp. 41–2; Van der Merwe, II, pp. 59–60 and D.W. Krüger, *Paul Kruger, 1883–1904*, II, p. 255. The exact date of Marks's interview with Kruger could not be established. It must, however, have been shortly before 16 May 1900. On this date President Steyn left for Pretoria to discuss the matter with President Kruger. Leyds Archive, 724(e) telegram 72 of 16 May 1900, Steyn – Kruger.
236 See Scholtz, "Betrekkinge", p. 42.
237 Translated from the Dutch. Van der Merwe, II, p. 59.
238 Leyds Archive, 739, telegram 39 of 17 June 1900, Botha – Kruger; Leyds Archive, 739, pp. 127–8, Telephone conversation, 7 Junie 1900, Botha & Kruger.
239 See Spies, "Civilians", p. 140; Hancock and Van der Poel, *Selections*, I, p. 552, "Memoirs".
240 HC 78/29, "Correspondence with Commandant-general L. Botha, 4–15 June 1900", Botha – Roberts, 8 June 1900. This is a typed manuscript of the correspondence between Botha and Roberts, bearing Roberts's signature (18 June 1900). A published copy of this appears in *Telegrams and Letters ... Roberts*, ii, pp. 117–24.
241 See Marquard, p. 115 n.

242 HC 78/29/31, "Correspondence ..." "Memorandum as to interview with Dr Scholtz, M.D.", 15 June 1900.
243 J.H. Meintjes, "Die Selati-Spoorwegskandaal met Besondere Verwysing na Regeringskommissaris van Spoorweë J.S. Smit" (Unpublished MA dissertation, UP), 1953, pp. 55–130, 156.
244 *Pretoria News*, 5 April 1904, (live report); B.J. Botha, "Mnr. Koos Smit se rol in die Oorlog" in *Die Huisgenoot*, 6 November 1953.
245 HC 78/29, "Correspondence ..." "Memorandum as to interview with Dr Scholtz, M.D.", 15 June 1900; Spies, "Civilians", pp. 140–1. After this visit Roberts corresponded directly with Botha over a possible cease-fire. The correspondence was however stopped on 15 June without anything having been achieved.
246 Viljoen, *Reminiscences*, pp. 98–100.
247 HC 78/29, "Correspondence ..." Milner's undated margin notes on the relevant manuscript.
248 W.J. Leyds, *Vierde Verzameling*, II, Annexure U, III, p. 95, Kruger – Erasmus, 8 June 1900; Spies, "Civilians", p. 142.
249 B.J. Botha, "Mnr. Koos Smit se rol in die Oorlog" in *Die Huisgenoot*, 6 November 1953.
250 MGB 4, W.J. Butler – K.P. Apthorp (district commissioner Smithfield), 21 June 1900.
251 PSY 57/DC 246, "Vallentin's Diary", 16 August 1900; MGP 55/7967/00, Vallentin – Maxwell, undated; Spies, "Civilians", p. 144.
252 MGP 28/4020/00, District commissioner Heidelberg – Military governor, 25 September 1900. The proclamations which the surrendered burghers had to take out were presumably those outlining Roberts's new conditions for burghers who wanted to surrender voluntarily. On 22 September 1900 Roberts had laid down that surrendered burghers would not be regarded as prisoners of war and that protection camps would be set up for them at Pretoria and Bloemfontein. Cd. 426, p. 18, XXXII, Government notice 11 of 1900; Chapter 2, sections 2 and 4 above.
253 A.J. Pienaar, "Christiaan Roedolf de Wet in die Anglo-Boereoorlog" (Unpublished MA dissertation, Potch), 1974, p. 246.
254 Muller, p. 71.
255 Roos, p. 296.
256 Barnard, *Botha*, pp. 54–5, p. 173 note 54.
257 Translated from the Dutch. A787, Preller Collection, 38, p. 255. "Een open brief aan den nog vechtenden en niet meer vechtenden Burgers in Zuid-Afrika".
258 Muller, pp. 83–7; *Official History*, III, p. 501.
259 Roberts Papers, WO 105 T42/10 (vol 50/202/214), Paget – Roberts, 25 September 1900.
260 *Telegrams and Letters ... Roberts*, v, p. 42, telegram C4985, H.V. Cowan (military secretary) – Commanding officer Bronkhorstspruit and Kitchener, 25 September 1900. With the change from conventional to mobile warfare the Boers destroyed many cannons and a great deal of ammunition at Hectorspruit so that they would not fall into the hands of the British. Viljoen, *Reminiscences*, p. 131.
261 Roberts Papers, WO 1051 T42/10 (vol 50/202/227), Paget – Roberts, 28 September 1900.
262 Roberts Papers, WO 105 T42/11 (vol 53/215/130), Paget – Roberts, 1 October 1900.
263 Muller, p. 87.

264 Roberts Papers, WO 105 T42/1 1 (vol S3/215/132), Paget – Roberts, 4 October 1900; MGP 30/4497/00, Maxwell – Military Governor Johannesburg, 8 October 1900.
265 Spies, "Civilians", p. 147.
266 Spies, "Civilians", p. 148. On 17 October 1900 Captain Smitherman was sent in Dercksen's place to take letters from Roberts to Botha. Botha was asked to call a halt to the war so as to prevent further devastation. He replied that it was not the Boers who were guilty of destruction but indeed Roberts himself. Roberts Papers, WO 105 T42/11, (vol. 53/21 S/149 and 152), Paget – Roberts, 17 and 19 October; Naudé, *Vechten en Vluchten*, pp. 181–2. Naudé does not mention Smitherman's name but the date that he provides coincides with Smitherman's visit.
267 SO/POW 6/636, R. Poore – Commanding officer Cape Town, 16 October 1900.
268 *The Cape Argus*, 23 November 1900 (news report).
269 Leyds Archive, 725(g), telegram 18 of 24 May 1900; Dercksen – Kruger.
270 *The South African News*, 6 December 1900 (quoted letter from Dercksen).
271 MGP 50/7421/00, Roberts – Maxwell, 9 December 1900; Spies, "Civilians", p. 148. Dercksen's peace initiatives did not end here. He later served on the burgher peace committee in December 1900 and January 1901. See Chapter 3, section 1 below.
272 Hancock and Van der Poel, *Selections*, I, p. 575, "Memoirs"; A 787, Preller Collection, 80, L.E. Krause, "Anglo-Boer War", p. 169; Spies, "Civilians", p. 144.
273 J.S. Schoeman, *Generaal Hendrik Schoeman. Was hy 'n Verraaier?*, pp. 184, 217, 218.
274 Breytenbach, *Geskiedenis*, II, pp. 194–5; Hancock and Van der Poel, *Selections*, I, p. 575, "Memoirs".
275 Spies, "Civilians", p. 145. On the circumstances which led to Schoeman's recall, his stay in Bloemfontein and his arrival in Pretoria, see Scholtz, "Betrekkinge", pp. 102–3; Schoeman, pp. 175–86.
276 Schoeman, p. 187; MGP 69/1641/01, Maxwell – Hughes, 6 January 1901.
277 A313, De la Rey Collection, 17, p. 52, De la Rey – Kruger, 21 July 1900.
278 A313, De la Rey Collection, 17, p. 52, De la Rey – Kruger, 21 July 1900; Schoeman, pp. 188–9.
279 Schoeman, p. 194; Spies "Civilians", p. 145.
280 MGP 86/3905/01, Schoeman – Maxwell, 16 April 1901. Schoeman's report on his mission.
281 Archive Landdros (magistrate) Zoutpansberg, 122, "The State vs. H.J. Schoeman on charges of High Treason", 29 November 1900; Schoeman, pp. 196–99, 204; Naudé, *Vechten en Vluchten*, pp. 184–5; Spies, "Civilians", pp. 145–6; A787, Preller Collection, 80, L.E. Krause, "Anglo-Boer War", p. 170.
282 MGP 86/3905/01, Schoeman – Maxwell, 16 April 1901; Spies, "Civilians", p. 146.
283 Schoeman, pp. 214–5; Spies, "Civilians", p. 146.
284 G. Arthur, *General Sir John Maxwell*, p. 92.
285 Buys, pp. 285–6. No source is given for this allegation.
286 Schoeman, pp. 83–115. There were misgivings about the manner in which he attempted to enrich himself through government concessions. Hancock and Van der Poel, *Selections*, I, p. 575, "Memoirs".
287 *Telegrams and Letters … Roberts*, v, p. 7, telegram C4656, Roberts – French, 15 September 1900.

288 Translated from the Dutch. Archive Landdros (magistrate) Zoutpansberg, 122, "The State vs. H.J. Schoeman on charges of High Treason", 29 November 1900, Schoeman – De la Rey, 6 October 1900. Schoeman made a similar statement in August 1900. Leyds Archive, 781 (i), report by Ram and Thomson, pp. 309–10, magistrate Lydenburg – State attorney, 16 August 1900 (copy).

289 Translated from the Dutch. Archive Landdros (magistrate) Zoutpansberg, 122, "The State vs. H.J. Schoeman on charges of High Treason", 29 November 1900, sworn statement by H.J. Schoeman, 29 November 1900.

290 Schoeman, p. 196.

291 Batts, p. 224.

292 CO 417/307/377SSA (FK 410, p. 570), Ardagh – Ommaney, 20 November 1900, enclosed letter from Buttery, 17 November 1900.

293 Oppenheim, ii, p. 222.

294 A787, Preller Collection, 80, L.E. Krause, "Anglo-Boer War", p. 170.

295 MGP 29/4202/00, Commanding officer post office – Maxwell, 1 October 1900.

296 Spies, "Civilians", p. 153; Oosthuizen, "De la Rey", p. 381.

297 Roberts Papers, WO 105/28 (A394), Vallentin – Roberts, 30 October 1900.

298 A787, Preller Collection, 1, Junius – Botha, 28 October 1900 (original); Roberts Papers, WO 105/28 (A394) (copy).

299 Spies, "Civilians", p. 152.

300 Roberts Papers, WO 105/29 (A395), Botha – Roberts, 6 November 1900.

301 Roberts Papers, WO 105/26 (A392) (copy). The signatories of this petition were J.S. Smit, Karel Rood, C.J. Joubert, J.F. Joubert, R. Gregorowski, B.J. Kleynhans, P.J. Potgieter, J.J. Marais, W.E. Hollard, H. Bosch, J. Grunberger, T.W. Beckett, J.C. Minnaar, J. de Braal, Carl Ueckermann, P.F. Zeederberg, S.W. Pienaar, Edw. Rooth, J. Dyer, I.J. Haarhoff, S. Marks, George J. Morice, J.P.J. van N. Kuyper and P.H. Faure.

302 See Chapter 2, section 5 above; Chapter 3, section 1 below; Spies, "Civilians", p. 150.

303 Translated from the Dutch. Roberts Papers, WO 105/26 (A392), J.S. Smit and others – Bosman, 2 November 1900.

304 Schoeman, p. 196.

305 Roberts Papers, WO 105/26 (A392), Marks and Rooth – Bosman, 3 November 1900 (copy).

306 Roberts Papers, WO 105/26 (A392), Bosman – Rooth, 3 November 1900.

307 Translated from the Dutch. Roberts Papers, WO 105/26 (A392), Bosman – Marks, Rooth, Smit and others, 5 November 1900.

308 On obtaining the services of Mrs Joubert see Spies, "Civilians", p. 149; MGP 205/C/31X/00, Loveday – Maxwell, 18 October 1900.

309 Translated from the Dutch. See A787, Preller Collection, 1, pp. 146–50 for the original letter, Marks – Botha, 31 October 1900 and Roberts Papers, WO 105/26 (A392) for a copy.

310 Botha told Mrs Joubert, who had fallen ill while on her visit, that he did not want to burden her with a letter to Marks and that he would reply to Marks's letter and petition later. (Roberts Papers, WO 105/26 (A392), Malan – Marks, 10 November 1900; Spies, "Civilians", p. 152). This letter could not be traced and it is to be doubted whether Botha did in fact write it. Marks had led Botha to

understand that "if you do not wish to write, then send me a verbal message". (A787, Preller Collection 1, p. 150, Marks – Botha, 31 October 1900). Marks could thus quite possibly have learned verbally from either Mrs Joubert or Mrs Malan on their return that Botha was strongly opposed to the mission. Botha had previously refrained from answering letters in which he was advised to give up the struggle. Letters of 5 and 10 October 1900 from Roberts, for example, were left unanswered. See A787, Preller Collection 16, pp. 5–6, 12–3, 16 and Roberts Papers, WO 105/27 (A393), H.V. Cowan – Mrs Botha, 16 October 1900.

311 See Spies, "Civilians", p. 152.
312 Roberts Papers, WO 105/26 (A392), Malan – Marks, 10 November 1900.
313 This letter (anonymous and dated 4 November 1900, Pretoria) is in A787, Preller Collection, 1, pp. 155–60. For the identity of the writer, see Spies, "Civilians", p. 151.
314 Translated from the Dutch. A787, Preller Collection, 1, pp. 146, 150, Marks – Botha, 31 October 1900.
315 MGP 15/2012/00, H. Crawford on behalf of S. Marks – Military governor, 14 August 1900; T. Gutsche, *'n Spoggerige Medalje. Die verhaal van die Witwatersrandse Landbougenootskap*, p. 72; M. Arkin, "Samuel Marks" in *DSAB*, I.
316 Roberts Papers, WO 105/26 (A392), Malan – Marks, 10 November 1900.
317 Marquard, pp. 112–15, 7 and 8 November 1900. See also Spies, "Civilians", p. 153.
318 Brits, *Diary*, p. 26, 18 November 1900 to 25 November 1900.

Chapter 3
The burgher peace committees, December 1900 – September 1901

1 Establishment of burgher peace committees

The origin of organised peace committees can be traced to developments both outside and within the republics, but in cooperation with the British authorities the surrendered burghers were certainly destined to play a leading role in this movement.

Two Transvaal burghers, J.B. Wolmarans and J.W. Erasmus, had an influence on developments outside the republics. Wolmarans was the nephew of A.D.W. Wolmarans, a member of the executive council of the South African Republic, and according to John Buttery, the author of *Why Kruger made War or Behind the Boer Scenes* and a former editorial member of *The Standard and Diggers' News*, J.B. Wolmarans was an influential figure in Pretoria.[1] In 1898 he was apparently a member of Pretoria's health committee,[2] but other than that it seems that he did not feature very prominently in public life. A reporter from *The South African News* dubbed him "not anyone in particular" and added disparagingly "he is just a dog and that's all, as the little boy said of his pup when someone asked him of what breed he was".[3] J.W. Erasmus came from Zeerust and from 1895 to 1899 he was a member of the Second *Volksraad* (parliament) of the South African Republic.[4] After the occupation of Pretoria on 5 June 1900, Wolmarans and Erasmus decided to lay down their arms and they fled to Delagoa Bay, presumably to avoid any further involvement in the war. From Delagoa Bay they sailed for England and went to the Colonial Office in London.[5]

By the end of October 1900 they had made it known that they wanted to take the oath of allegiance to the British crown and planned to return to the Transvaal where they would persuade other burghers that they, too, should abandon the war. In the wake of a number of sporadic peace initiatives which had all ended in failure, Roberts was not in favour of their idea. He felt that the word of these two surrendered burghers would carry very little weight with the Boers in the veld and that Wolmarans and Erasmus should instead be regarded as prisoners of war.[6] But Sir John Ardagh, director of the British military information service in London, disagreed with Roberts. "Lord Roberts' last telegram proposing that Wolmarans and Erasmus shall be made prisoners of war was", according to Ardagh, "rather embarrassing. These gentlemen have been quite straightforward in their conduct, have formally reported themselves to C.O. [Colonial Office] and are much anxious to take oath of allegiance and help in persuading their fellow countrymen to cease resistance."[7]

In order to obtain more information on Wolmarans and Erasmus, John Buttery was asked to conduct an interview with them so that he could then advise Ardagh on their suitability as peace delegates. On 16 and 17 November Buttery held lengthy discussions with them and he later reported that Erasmus was a member of the so-called "progressive" group in the Second *Volksraad* and prior to the war, together with men like Louis Botha in the First *Volksraad*, they had been political adversaries of President Kruger. Erasmus told Buttery that it was laughable to think that Botha and the other Boers in the veld would listen to people like General Hendrik Schoeman, "or any one of the old gang ..., inasmuch as Schoemann [sic] is suspected and reprobated by the fighting Boer as part and parcel of the Krugerian regime". According to Erasmus, "progressive" people would have to be the ones to initiate a peace movement in the Transvaal. Buttery agreed with Erasmus that Botha could only be influenced by "men of his own way of thinking". Wolmarans and Erasmus impressed Buttery so much that he informed Ardagh: "If I had any weight with the Colonial or the War Offices I would ship Erasmus and Wolmarans off to South Africa by the next steamer, help them to call round them responsible men [Boers] in the Orange River Colony and then depute that body to open up negotiations with the guerilla chiefs."[8]

Ardagh sent Buttery's recommendation to the Colonial Office where it was favourably received. In the margin of Buttery's report Chamberlain noted: "I should unhesitatingly let them [Wolmarans and Erasmus] go out ...".[9] The two Boers were back at the Colonial Office for another interview on 28 November and three days later Chamberlain urged Milner to agree that they be sent as peace emissaries to the Transvaal.[10] However, Milner was against taking this step. He felt that the influence of the two refugee Transvaal burghers had been exaggerated and that they should remain in Britain.[11] Despite Milner's objections, Chamberlain still favoured the idea that Wolmarans and Erasmus should start a peace movement in the Transvaal. "I think Milner is wrong in objecting," noted Chamberlain, "but I cannot overrule him."[12]

Chamberlain was obliged to drop the plan to send Wolmarans and Erasmus to the Transvaal, but he nevertheless tried to advance the idea of a peace movement and peace emissaries. On 7 December he gave Milner instructions to attempt, in cooperation with Kitchener (who had taken over the high command from Roberts on 29 November 1900), to persuade the Boers to accept the inevitable and end hostilities as soon as possible. "It is suggested," Chamberlain added, "that a very important effect might be produced by the issue of a Proclamation, if it is widely distributed in the Taal as well as in English, announcing in the name of the Queen that, while annexation is irrevocable, there is no intention of treating the inhabitants otherwise than fairly and generously ...". This proclamation should be specifically directed "towards persuading those still in arms against us that their material interests are bound up with the restoration of tranquillity, and that nothing but the aimless ruin of the country can result from a persistence in hostilities".[13]

On 10 December Chamberlain gave Milner more details on how the proposed proclamation should be circulated. He suggested that influential peace emissaries should be found in South Africa to take the proclamation to the Boers in the veld and that these people should then act as "pacificators, particularly by making known the contents of our proclamations".[14]

Towards the end of October 1900 Milner had been in favour of sending peace emissaries to the fighting burghers, but on 11 December he said in answer to Chamberlain's proposals that he doubted whether these people would be able to exercise the desired influence. He also felt that at that particular point in the conflict the Boers might interpret a proclamation as a sign of weakness.[15] Nevertheless he forwarded Chamberlain's suggestions to Kitchener,[16] and on 15 December Kitchener replied. He expressed his reservations about the peace emissaries who had thus far been sent to the Boers, but was nevertheless in favour of Chamberlain's proposals and admitted that they might perhaps meet with some success.[17] Developments outside South Africa, then, were certainly influenced by Wolmarans and Erasmus, who had succeeded in inculcating the idea of a peace movement on Chamberlain. Their suggestions had been conveyed to Kitchener, who was prepared to act upon them.

As far as developments within the republics were concerned, Meyer de Kock of Belfast in the Transvaal was destined to play a leading role. Prior to the war De Kock had worked as a member of the land commission, a postal agent, an auctioneer, a land assessor and had also solemnised marriages.[18] He was a worthy, dignified person and "was in every way ... a man of substance and authority – a man one would listen to".[19] At the outbreak of war he was in charge of the guards on the railway and bridges in the Belfast district and then he had done commando duty as an ordinary burgher until his decision to lay down his arms on 10 December 1900.[20] According to De Kock, he had surrendered to protect his property and to make sure that his wife and children were not subjected to any hardships in the veld. Furthermore he wanted to raise complaints about the burning of homes with the British authorities.[21]

After his surrender De Kock was taken to the "Rest Camp" in Pretoria, and then on 14 December he was sent to Colonel D. Henderson, director of the British intelligence service in South Africa. De Kock aired his grievances to Henderson and apparently also mentioned the possibility of peace emissaries, to which Henderson responded by saying: "I think you will have to appear before Lord Kitchener tomorrow."[22] The interview with Kitchener took place on 15 December 1900 – the very day that Kitchener told Milner that he was in favour of Chamberlain's proposals to send peace emissaries to the Boers.[23] By this time it was clear that Kitchener was giving the possibility his serious consideration. At the same time De Kock was also thinking along the lines of peace.[24]

According to De Kock, in the course of the interview Kitchener told him that the British government was anxious to prevent any further bloodshed and destruction of property and that after the war the burghers of the Transvaal would be granted their own local parliament subject to the authority of the British government. In the light of this Kitchener then asked De Kock "to be of assistance to me in restoring peace. I wish to employ every means to prevent further bloodshed and destruction. I know it will be taken as a sign of weakness, but this I can bear, but God help the Transvaal if my endeavours for peace have no effect and that I have to turn over a new leaf ... I give you leave to consider with your fellow Burghers and to point out a way to me by which peace may be obtained. But ... beware Transvaal if I have to take any other means."[25]

De Kock then left for Belfast and on 17 December 1900 he addressed a meeting of surrendered burghers who had gathered from all over the Transvaal. At the meeting the following unanimous decision was taken: "A committee will be set up comprising Gentlemen [sic] from the more important towns such as Pretoria, Johannesburg and other places as may be necessary. The men must be of good position, having influence among the Burghers and must draw up a document outlining the true state of affairs in the Transvaal and the Orange River Colony at the present time and the fact that it is hopeless to expect any European or other intervention. This information sheet should then be attached and sent out together with the proclamations."[26]

On 18 December De Kock handed in his report on the proceedings thus far. He said that the meeting had been "most orderly and the speakers cool and calm, and offered their suggestions in all good faith". His report included four suggestions: that surrendered burghers be sent to their various districts and be sheltered there by British garrisons; that selected people be sent to the Boer lines to distribute the documents and proclamations; that the proclamations also be sent to the homes of the fighting burghers, their friends and family members; and lastly, that prominent people from the most important towns should form a committee to compile the information brochure in which the "true" state of affairs would be explained. This information sheet should then be distributed among the Boers in the veld.[27]

De Kock's last suggestion, namely to form a committee of responsible people, was the first to be realised. After Kitchener had addressed a gathering of surrendered burghers on 21 December 1900,[28] the formation of the committee began. A central peace committee was established in Pretoria and on 27 December Kitchener informed Milner of these developments.[29] The central committee comprised General Andries P.J. Cronjé from Potchefstroom,[30] the brother of General Piet Cronjé who had surrendered at Paardeberg; D. Kriel, the magistrate of Carolina; W.J. Steyn, former member of the First *Volksraad* for Standerton; L.C. de Gier of Pretoria, who was to act as secretary; and Karl Rood, a businessman from Pretoria, who acted as chairman until H.P.F.J. van Rensburg, a member of the Second *Volksraad* for Heidelberg (1895–1898) and member of the First *Volksraad* from 1899 to 1900, took over the chairmanship at the beginning of January 1901. During January 1901 the following people were co-opted as members of the central committee: Field-cornet S.J. Roos of the ward Crocodile River, Pretoria; J.F. de Beer of Pretoria, the former inspector of offices who had already been involved in peace initiatives in June and November 1900; W.P. Pistorius, an attorney from Middelburg; O.C. Weeber, who was also an attorney in Middelburg and was W.P. Pistorius's father-in-law; B.C. Bezuidenhout, a prosperous farmer from Heidelberg; Commandant A.J. Dercksen from Boksburg, who had dabbled ineffectively with peace attempts in October and November 1900; and D.G. Steyn, a brother of W.J. Steyn.[31] Revd H.S. Bosman of Pretoria, who had been approached to undertake a peace mission to the Boer lines in November 1900, was also asked to serve on the central committee, but he did not react to the offer.[32] Meyer de Kock was not a member of the central committee, because he had decided of his own accord that he wished to work exclusively in Belfast.[33]

Various local committees were also established. Before the end of January 1901 there were peace committees in six Transvaal towns. These towns, with the people who served on the committees as chairmen, were as follows: Middelburg (O.C. Weeber), Belfast (M. de

Kock), Volksrust (G.J.W. de Jager), Utrecht (M.J. Gregon), Standerton (A.J. Boshoff) and Krugersdorp (F. du Toit).[34] During May 1901 a similar committee was formed in Zeerust with A.F. Bulmer as chairman,[35] while in Heidelberg there was also a movement in favour of peace led by Field-cornet P. Groesbeek, but this did not lead to the establishment of a committee.[36]

Four of the people who played a leading role in the peace committees, namely H.P.F.J. van Rensburg (chairman of the central committee), W.J. Steyn (member of the central committee, who also embarked on a peace mission in January 1901), Meyer de Kock (chairman of the Belfast peace committee, who had done important spadework for the peace movement) and G.J.W. de Jager (chairman of the Volksrust peace committee) had aligned themselves with the so-called "progressive" Joubert group against the "conservative" Kruger group before the war.[37] It cannot simply be inferred, as has been implied previously, that pre-war political differences were responsible for the division in Afrikaner ranks during the war.[38] Among the bitterenders there were also men such as Generals J.H. de la Rey and S.W. Burger who were in the "progressive" camp before the war.[39] In certain republican circles Commandant-general Botha was also considered "progressive".[40] Indeed, P. Pienaar (who was with Steyn and De Wet on commando and was in the Transvaal in September 1900 when President Kruger left for Europe) claimed: "Most burghers who are still fighting are Progressives, and are by implication Paul Kruger's political opponents ... I say to you that most Boers still in the veld are avidly Progressive, those who the world imagines are as strongly politically opposed to Paul Kruger as the English themselves. You might ask why they are still fighting. For their independence!"[41] Pienaar is perhaps guilty of exaggeration when he says that nearly all the Boers in the veld were "progressives", but it is nevertheless clear that the cleavage in Afrikaner ranks cannot be ascribed to the pre-war "progressive" and "conservative" grouping. The division is far more likely to have arisen because the peace committees wanted to see hostilities ended at all costs, whereas at that stage the leaders in the veld were not prepared to accept peace without independence.[42]

Another question is whether the pre-war political orientation of the people who took the lead in the peace committees played a role in their peace initiatives during the war. This might well have been the case, but then only in the sense that they mistakenly saw the war as "Kruger's war".[43]

Kitchener saw the peace committees as "an outside independent organization allowed by me, to do their best to induce the boers in the field to see the hopelessness of their struggle for independence and to show them that a considerable local feeling exists against the continuance of the war which must ruin their country".[44] In an interview on 26 December, Colonel D. Henderson also told D. Kriel, A.P.J. Cronjé, P.F. Zeederberg and W.J. Steyn: "This committee was the beginning of a political party in the states, and it should be run on those lines, as if it were a political party seeking election. They must take every step to bring people to their way of thinking ...".[45]

The relationship between the British army authorities and the central peace committee was, however, of such a nature that the members of the committee could not expect any voice at all in matters of policy. When Kitchener addressed a number of surrendered burghers in Pretoria on 21 December 1900, he touched on the question of post-war government, indicating that "he foreshadowed an enlightened progressive Government, in which the burghers themselves would take a prominent share, and which would ensure to them and their children all the rights of property, as well as their ancient laws and customs." Kitchener's speech was printed in the form of a flyer so that it could be distributed to the Boers in the veld.[46] Members of the central committee were not satisfied with the contents of the pamphlet and on 29 December K. Rood, M. de Kock and P.F. Zeederberg visited Maxwell at his home to discuss the matter. The deputation dealt specifically with the question of post-war government and stressed the following: "The lines as set forth in the pieces ... as to the intentions of Her Majesty's Government are vague, especially as regards the measure of self Govt. to be accorded to the O.R.Colony and the Transvaal." They also wanted greater clarity on the compensation for farms and property which had been purposely damaged, and wanted to know whether the British government would be prepared to provide the farms with livestock after the war. Further, they requested that there be no differentiation made between the burghers of the Free State, Transvaal, colonial rebels and mercenaries. The delegation made it very clear that "[these] steps ... are the only ones that will produce a result".[47]

Maxwell discussed the matters that the members had raised, but Kitchener was not prepared to heed their requests. The military governor had to report back to Rood that "he [Kitchener] does not approve of your committee discussing questions of policy which he considers outside their scope".[48] According to Maxwell the members of the peace committee had to concentrate on the following aspects: they had to enlighten the burghers in the veld about what the British saw as the "true" state of affairs; then the fighting Boers also had to be made aware that there was not the remotest possibility that foreign powers would give them active support. They also had to be told that burghers who surrendered voluntarily would be placed in camps as near as possible to their home towns. "Beyond this," said Maxwell in closing, "the committee is not authorized to touch on the political side, but must clearly understand that the present object is to let the Burghers know the truth and what they are fighting for."[49]

The fact that the British authority was not prepared to give the peace committee any voice at all in matters of policy shows, on the one hand, that even at that stage the British realised that if peace talks were eventually initiated it would be the fighting Boers, and not the group of surrendered burghers, who would play the crucial role. On the other hand, Milner was afraid that the committees might perhaps hold out the prospect of peace terms that were far too liberal, thus giving the fighting burghers the wrong impression. In his view the purpose of the peace committees was "simply to remove misconceptions of our intentions and make known the treatment they [the Boers] will receive [when they surrender voluntarily]".[50]

Mention has already been made of the fact that Britain's erratic policy meant that the surrendered burghers were often treated unjustly.[51] In Chamberlain's telegram of 10 December 1900 he warned Milner that "the essential thing for success ... appears to be that the measures taken should be applied consistently on a systematic plan and not sporadically without fixed principles".[52] The treatment that could possibly be meted out to a person who laid down his arms convinced some burghers not to take this step. Burgher C. Potgieter of the Carolina commando, who had surrendered voluntarily, testified that "there are so many Boers belonging to the Carolina commando who would surrender if they could be assured of fair treatment. The general impression amongst the Boers is that prisoners surrendering are deported and treated with extreme harshness".[53] The purpose of the peace committee was thus primarily to correct this impression and inform the burghers in the veld that people who might be planning to surrender in the future would be more effectively protected and handled better than before. In this way it was hoped to thin out the ranks of the fighting burghers to an even greater extent. The peace committees had to deliver their message verbally and by means of pamphlets to the ordinary burghers and their leaders, because Kitchener was not prepared to have any official communication with the fighting burghers.[54]

Nevertheless, on 20 December 1900 Kitchener gave indications of the direction his policy would take. On that day he issued a government notice in which he mentioned that the surrendered burghers would be placed in protection camps.[55] This notice was in essence the same as Maxwell's notice of 22 September 1900.[56] On 21 December Kitchener raised the question again in a circular to all his commanding officers: "The General Commander-in-Chief is desirous that all possible means shall be taken to stop the present guerrilla warfare. Of the various measures suggested for the accomplishment of this object, one which has been strongly recommended, and has lately been successfully tried on a small scale, is the removal of all men, women and children, and natives from the districts which the enemy's bands persistently occupy. *This course has been pointed out by surrendered burghers, who are anxious to finish the war*, as the most effective method of limiting the endurance of guerillas, as the men and women left on farms, if disloyal, willingly supply. Burghers, if loyal, dare not refuse to do so."[57]

Largely on account of this circular, various historians have accepted that the surrendered burghers, and by implication the members of the burgher peace committees, recommended the idea of concentration camps to Kitchener.[58] Some of the republican leaders also held this opinion.[59] This interpretation cannot simply be accepted without reservation. The concentration camp policy was certainly initiated before 21 December 1900, and indeed by means of protection camps set up for surrendered burghers which were in practice nothing other than concentration camps.[60] The only possibility which remained was that the members of the peace committees might have been instrumental in encouraging Kitchener to expand this policy and implement it on a wider scale. However, recent research seems to indicate that members of the peace committees did not in fact make any written suggestions to the British authorities to place the women and children of loyal burghers in camps.[61] This present study has not revealed any evidence to the contrary.

It might well be that Meyer de Kock made such suggestions verbally to Kitchener. Forty-one years after the war, a burgher, C. Quinlan, who had been in the "Rest Camp" with De Kock, maintained that "Meyer de Kock was the instigator of these camps [concentration camps]. He told General Kitchener that the Boers would surrender if their wives were taken off the farms."[62] Although Quinlan's evidence is valuable because he was with De Kock in the "Rest Camp", and could possibly have been aware of what took place there, it cannot be seen as irrefutable evidence that De Kock was indeed responsible for the proliferation of the concentration camp system. As early as 4 December 1900, even before Kitchener had negotiated with the peace committee, he had thought in terms of concentration camps and had notified Roberts: "The women question is always cropping up and is ... difficult. There is no doubt the women are keeping up the war and are far more bitter than the men ... I really think the only solution that will bring them to their senses is to remove the worst class to Kaapmuiden and form a camp there."[63] The allegation that members of the peace committees made Kitchener aware of the idea of concentration camps thus seems highly questionable.

Although it appears that the surrendered burghers cannot be held responsible for the proliferation of the concentration camp policy as such, they did indeed grant their approval for this line of action. On 26 December Colonel D. Henderson told W.J. Steyn, D. Kriel, A.P.J. Cronjé and P.F. Zeederberg that "they [the British] wanted ... to show ... their good faith by ... moving the women and children into laagers in their respective Districts". Kriel agreed wholeheartedly with Henderson and was of the opinion that "if this had been done from the very first, there would have been a general surrender".[64]

In addition to the central peace committee and local committees which were set up in the Transvaal, similar committees were set up in the Free State. Piet de Wet, a former assistant commander-in-chief of the Free State army and a brother of General Christiaan de Wet, mentioned the possibility of peace committees in the Free State to Kitchener. According to Piet de Wet there was a spontaneous desire for peace among a certain section of the Free State population.[65] By 30 December 1900 the following people were serving on the central committee in Kroonstad: Piet de Wet (chairman); P.M. Botha, C.J. Bornman and C.J. Cloete, all former members of the *Volksraad*; D.H. Botha and F.P. Naudé, former justices of the peace; G.F. Minnaar, reportedly an influential member of the church council at Kroonstad; and Adv. C.L. Botha, subsequently a judge in the Union of South Africa, who acted as secretary.[66] Early in January 1901, G.J. van Tonder, a member of the executive council, held an interview with Kitchener in Pretoria to discuss the formation of a peace committee in Bloemfontein and shortly afterwards a subcommittee was set up in the Free State capital. The members of this committee were: J.G. Fraser (chairman); G.J. van Tonder; J. Palmer, former member of the executive council; J.S. Theron and D.J.H. van Niekerk, former members of the *Volksraad* and H.F.D. Papenfus (secretary), a former civil servant.[67] Thereafter local committees were established before May 1901 in Harrismith, Bethlehem and Winburg.[68]

The peace movement soon began to spread. During January 1901 the prisoners of war who were on parole in Durban formed a committee with the following members: J.L. Bosman (chairman), a businessman from Standerton; J.P. van Zyl, former magistrate of Winburg; J. Olivier of Winburg, a son of the Free State's General J.H. Olivier; C. Visser of Fauresmith; A. Badenhorst of Harrismith and G.C.J. Breedt of Standerton. The members of the committee were aware that their word would quite possibly carry very little weight with the fighting burghers because they had voluntarily laid down their arms. With the cooperation of the British military authorities they therefore wanted to bring men whom they regarded as representative of the Boer prisoners of war, namely General P.A. Cronjé in St Helena and General J.H. Olivier in Ceylon, back to South Africa to convince the Boers in the veld that there was a general feeling against the continuance of war among the people of the Transvaal and Free State. Then they also wanted to liaise with the surrendered burghers in other parts of the country to establish what their views were. The goal was to establish a countrywide united front of all surrendered burghers who were prepared to work towards ending the war. Members of the committee did not want their names to be published, because this might jeopardise their plans. But Kitchener was not in favour of this idea. He felt that "intercommunication between surrendered burghers in different parts of the country [was] not yet possible".[69] Because of Kitchener's objection there was very little cooperation between the various peace committees, but the central committees at Pretoria and Kroonstad on occasion liaised with the subcommittees at Volksrust and Bloemfontein respectively.[70]

By the end of December 1900 the various peace committees were ready to begin their work. A report on Meyer de Kock's meeting at Belfast on 17 December 1900 and Kitchener's address on 21 December at Pretoria were printed; there were 28 000 copies to be circulated. These flyers were sent to 56 commanding officers of British columns as well as to the occupying forces in the cities, towns and districts. Six South African newspapers also published reports in the same vein.[71] A large-scale propaganda campaign was thus launched in which the members of the peace committees were to play an important role.

2 Work of the burgher peace committees and renewed peace initiatives in the Transvaal

As a result of Meyer de Kock's suggestion that a number of carefully selected people should be sent to the Boer lines with the pamphlets, 24 surrendered burghers were chosen by the central committee in Pretoria as peace emissaries who were to leave on 28 December 1900 for different parts of the Transvaal. These people received £1 to cover their personal expenses and rations for two days.[72]

F.G. Hughes, a resident of Kaapsche Hoop, was sent to the Barberton district. He was originally a British resident who had taken on Transvaal citizenship during the war and had decided to surrender on 15 November 1900. According to Hughes, some of the men who were still fighting in the district where he was operating were considering laying down their arms, but they were anxious to have more information about the camps where they would be settled and wanted to know whether the people who were living in the towns would be permitted to stay on in their homes if they were self-supporting. Apart from answering these general enquires Hughes had very little success and he remained in the Barberton district until the end of March 1901, after which the British authorities allowed him to go to Johannesburg for the duration of the war.[73]

Hughes was very fortunate that the Boers in the veld did not capture him. On 13 January 1901 Botha informed his officers about the formation of the peace committees. He warned them to be on the lookout for people who were using all sorts of proclamations and letters to try to persuade the burghers to lay down their arms. The officers had also been given instructions to summarily arrest such people – even were they to approach the Boer lines with a white flag.[74]

Botha was perfectly justified in his instruction to ignore the white flag under these particular circumstances. Article 32 of the Hague Convention does indeed state that the bearer of a white flag "has the right to inviolability" but no provision is made in this article for deserters who depart on a peace mission under a white flag.[75] L. Oppenheim puts the article into clearer perspective. He states: "It is his mission and not the white flag itself, which protects the flagbearer. This mission protects everyone who is charged with it, whatever his rank and whether a civilian or a soldier; *but it does not protect a deserter. A deserter may be detained, courtmartialled, and punished ...*".[76]

A number of peace emissaries were arrested in the veld. W.H. Swaine, who was sent to the district of Carolina, was captured near Oshoek on 14 January.[77] It is not known what punishment he received. Then too, D.C. Joubert and C.E. Fourie, both of whom came from Lydenburg,[78] did not operate for long as peace emissaries. On 17 January 1901 Joubert sent a letter to his cousin, Field-cornet J.M. de Beer of Lydenburg, with a request to be allowed to address the burghers.[79] The request was granted and the following day Joubert held an interview with a number of burghers in the vicinity of

Lydenburg. He presented Kitchener's policy as well as the new governmental system which would possibly be implemented after the war and encouraged the burghers to accept Kitchener's offer to lay down their arms. To Joubert it seemed as if "they [the burghers] were anxious to surrender and recognize their cause as hopeless, but fear punishment and doubt intention of Government".[80] C.E. Fourie sent a letter to Field-cornet P. Taute in which he requested Taute's help to persuade the burghers to lay down their arms.[81] Before Joubert and Fourie could take the matter any further their activities were brought to an abrupt halt. On 21 January Joubert was taken into custody and on 29 January he and Fourie had to appear before a special court martial on charges of high treason. The court found them guilty, but because they were not the leaders (*voormannen*) of a peace committee, they escaped the death penalty and were each sentenced to a fine of £500 or five years imprisonment with hard labour.[82]

On 29 January J.C.P. Grobbelaar and P.B. Coetzee, who were sent as peace emissaries to the Middelburg district, were also tried at Roossenekal. Before they were able to distribute any of the peace committee's pamphlets they were arrested. In their defence Grobbelaar and Coetzee claimed that they had not come with the intention of distributing the documents, but that they merely wanted to use the opportunity to rejoin the commandos. Because of lack of evidence that they expressly tried to persuade the burghers to lay down their arms, the court accepted some aspects of their defence. Nevertheless their right to vote was suspended for a period of ten years and they were ordered to take up arms again. Furthermore the chairman of the court, G.W.J. de Toit, laid down that if in the future they undertook any suspicious activities, the "fullest extent" of the law would be enforced.[83]

J.G. van Helsdingen and J.L.K. Trichardt were sent as peace emissaries to the Rustenburg district. On 2 January Van Helsdingen was captured and tried for high treason at Wolmaransstad. The charge as such could not be proved, but Van Helsdingen was obliged to go back to do commando duty. However, he was on commando for only ten days before he again laid down his weapons and returned to his farm until 3 April 1901. On 4 April he heard a rumour that the Boers were planning to arrest him and he fled to Rustenburg where he

131

reported to Captain J.M. Graham of the British military intelligence service. Graham felt that neither Van Helsdingen nor Trichardt had carried out their duties as peace emissaries properly. According to Graham they could have reported back on their activities far earlier. Van Helsdingen was held for a while as a prisoner of war in Pretoria, but after making convincing representations to the military governor he was released. On 25 April 1902 he joined the National Scouts.[84]

The activities of the peace committees were seriously handicapped by the vigilance of the Boers. Some men did indeed succeed in slipping through the net of watchfulness, but then they came up against the resoluteness of the bitterenders. J.A. Mostert, who was operating in the Krugersdorp district, was warned that if he came near the commandos he would be shot as a traitor. From correspondence with some of the members of the commando, Mostert came to the conclusion "that many of the men are anxious to come in, but they are uncertain as to how they will be treated: the Commandants tell them not to believe the promises of the British".[85]

M.C. Coetzee, a peace emissary in the Johannesburg and Heidelberg area, succeeded in contacting some commando members personally. According to him these people chose to go on fighting because the British had confiscated all their livestock and damaged their property.[86] J.H.G. Adendorff and C.G. Joubert, who were sent to Bethal, succeeded in distributing the peace committee's flyers without the knowledge of the Boer leaders. When the leaders came to hear of this, they forbade the burghers to lay down their weapons in reaction to the appeals in the pamphlets.[87] R. Johnson distributed leaflets in the Piet Retief region and was also active in the Barberton district and Swaziland. He claimed that he had persuaded "a considerable number of burghers" to surrender, but Major F.C.L. Steinaecker, commander of Steinaecker's Horse, considered Johnson "a source of danger in Swaziland, being much hated by the Natives and having no influence with the Boers".[88] The activities of three other peace emissaries appointed by the central peace committee were also investigated. These three people did not take the peace committee's cause seriously at all. They merely went out with the purpose of rejoining the commandos. P.J. Adendorff and I.M. du Plessis, for example, left for Middelburg on 28 December 1900 and went directly from there to their former field-cornet, a burgher called Gous. They handed the pamphlets to him and declared that they were ready to take up their weapons again. According to Adendorff, he and Du Plessis did not agree with the other peace emissaries that the republican war effort was a lost cause. Each of the two men was sentenced to 14 days imprisonment or a fine of £20. They both elected to pay the fine and promptly joined the commando again.[89] D. Coetzee who was sent to the Klerksdorp district was a similar example. He immediately linked up with General P.J. Liebenberg's commando and continued fighting until he was seriously wounded on 27 October 1901. Liebenberg then sent him to the hospital in Klerksdorp and in an accompanying letter to the British commander, requested that Coetzee should be treated well because he was a brave burgher who had sacrificed everything for his country and his people.[90]

In addition to the peace emissaries sent out by the central committee, the local committees also made some attempts to persuade the fighting burghers to change their minds. On 10 January 1901 the peace committee at Middelburg sent a letter to the officers and burghers of their district, making the point that President Kruger had left the country and that, although he had been well received in Europe, there was certainly no likelihood that any European power would intervene on behalf of the Boers. "Why then," the peace committee asked, "continue the struggle when there is only one possible ultimate result?" In conclusion the committee expressed the hope that the officers would make the contents of the letter known to the ordinary burghers "as ... they may ... demand it as a right [so] that they may decide for themselves whether or not to carry on this unfortunate war".[91] Along with this letter, O.C. Weeber, chairman of the committee, also sent a letter to his sons in the commando, advising them to lay down their arms. Botha received these letters but did not divulge their content to the burghers. E.J. Weeber, one of O.C. Weeber's sons who served for a while on the commandant-general's staff, only learned from Botha about the letters and the nature of their content after the war. According to Weeber, Botha did not consider it advisable to give him the information and would have said to him: "Old boy, I did it for your own good. Just think a little about how things were going for us that time. Every day groups of men who had formerly been faithful comrades were leaving us. We could not trust anyone any more. I did not even trust my own brothers. In any case I did not want to add heartache to all that you and your brother were already enduring on the battlefield."[92]

At the end of January 1901 the local committee at Utrecht also tried to use peace emissaries to influence the fighting burghers. According to reports by the British intelligence service, looking at the war situation in retrospect, the burghers in this area showed little enthusiasm to go on fighting, but at the same time they were disinclined to accept the proposals of the peace emissaries.[93] The committee at Krugersdorp held a meeting on 19 January 1901 which was attended by more than 92 surrendered burghers. The following four decisions were accepted in principle: that the burghers in the veld were being kept in the dark by their leaders and that it was necessary to inform them accordingly; that there was no hope of foreign intervention; that the women, children and prisoners of war were suffering unnecessarily because of the continuance of the war; and lastly that the fighting burghers had to be told that the British government was prepared to treat them leniently if they laid down their arms. These decisions were then printed in pamphlet form. The committee also agreed that it was a good idea to publish a letter that J.B. Wolmarans (the man who had approached the Colonial Office as a peace emissary in October 1900) had written to his brother-in-law, J. Els, in which Wolmarans had expressed his firm conviction that no foreign power would come to the aid of the republics. In his view the republican leaders had "loaded a bunch of lies on our necks". He was convinced that "the sooner the burghers and Afrikaners abandon the cause, the better for them".[94] Wolmarans's letter and the decisions of the committee were circulated among the burghers.[95] It could not be established what reaction this provoked among them.

On 24 January 1901 the Volksrust committee members held a meeting. They suggested to the British military authorities that people who had surrendered voluntarily, but who were nevertheless being held as prisoners of war in Natal, should be permitted to return to their various districts. But Kitchener was not prepared to accede to this request at the time.[96] The peace committee also sent a letter to the officers and burghers of the Wakkerstroom district saying that to continue the struggle was futile and could only lead to unnecessary bloodshed. "We, regardless of all self-interest," wrote the committee, "are ready to do everything in our power to bring this sad state of affairs to an end." The committee members hoped that after receiving the letter the officers and fighting burghers would work with them in the interest of immediate peace.[97] But their hopes were unfounded and it appears that the Wakkerstroom burghers were not prepared to cooperate at all with the peace committee. On 28 January H.P.F.J. van Rensburg, chairman of the central committee, informed Maxwell that "I regret to say ... no good results are apparent from the labours of the different local committees ...".[98]

Meyer de Kock acted as peace emissary for the Belfast committee. On 18 January 1901 he wrote a letter on behalf of the Belfast branch to the officers of the Lydenburg commando and two days later, in an earnest discussion with burghers of this commando, he tried to persuade them to lay down their arms. On 22 January De Kock continued his campaign, setting off for the Boer front line with a white flag to deliver the peace committee's pamphlets to General Ben Viljoen. But that same day he was arrested and had to appear before a court martial at Roossenekal on 29 January 1901 on charges of high treason. He was found guilty of the following offences: that he had left his commando unlawfully and had handed over his weapons to the enemy; that he had, in cooperation with the enemy, unlawfully plotted to persuade the loyal burghers to lay down their arms; that he was in possession of the peace committee's pamphlets which were designed to entice the burghers away from the commando; that he had played an important role in the committee; and lastly, that in his personal capacity he had actively tried to persuade the burghers to lay down their arms. De Kock pleaded guilty to three of these charges.

In his defence he claimed that it was not his intention to deceive the people, but that he merely wanted to gain a speedy and honourable peace, which in his opinion would be to the advantage of the whole country. The assistant state attorney, L.J. Jacobsz, admitted in his closing statement that De Kock's actions had possibly been well-meant, but pointed out that he had nevertheless damaged the republican cause and the Boer military operations by trying to persuade some of the fighting burghers to abandon the struggle. The court found De Kock guilty of high treason and the magistrate, Gideon F. Joubert, sentenced him to death. A number of burghers submitted a petition pleading for mitigation of De Kock's sentence, but on 9 February the acting president, S.W. Burger, in consultation with the executive council, upheld the court's decision. On 12 February 1901 De Kock was executed beside an open grave by a firing squad of eight men.[99]

The De Kock incident had many repercussions. In the middle of April 1901 St John Brodrick, the British state secretary for war, asked Kitchener whether the Boers were indeed empowered to execute De Kock. "The only justification I know of," Kitchener replied, "was that De Kock had surrendered, but several surrendered burghers had previously gone back and returned safely."[100] Kitchener's answer is conspicuously vague and misleading. In comparison with the other peace emissaries, De Kock's offences were of a more serious nature. He had actively tried to persuade some of the fighting burghers to surrender and was also one of the leading figures in the peace movement.[101]

Meyer de Kock was the only peace emissary in the Transvaal who had to pay with his life, and under these specific circumstances the Boers were perfectly justified in the action they took. The *Times History* rightly says that the peace emissaries "in taking the risk of attempting to reduce the men on commando ... acted with their eyes open according to their own sense of patriotism ... The fighting burghers holding a different standard of patriotism, were within their rights in applying even extreme penalties."[102] Ironically enough, Gideon F. Joubert, the magistrate who had sentenced De Kock to death, also withdrew from the war at the end of May 1901. "I have surrendered," Joubert wrote to Kitchener, "because I conscientiously consider that any further resistance is hopeless and in my opinion criminal." Kitchener felt that a full judicial investigation should be instigated regarding De Kock's death sentence and was planning to consult Joubert personally on the matter.[103] After consultation with the British legal adviser, however, Kitchener came to the realisation that there were no legal grounds for re-opening the case.[104]

Members of the central committee also acted as peace emissaries. W.J. Steyn, the former member of the First *Volksraad*, departed in the middle of January to Van Tondershoek in order to distribute flyers among the fighting burghers. He was taken into custody, but apparently succeeded in escaping and spent the remainder of the war in Standerton.[105]

The central committee continued its work through the medium of correspondence. On 24 January the members wrote a letter to Botha and his officers. The only objective of the letter, the committee wrote, was to bring about peace as speedily as possible. In motivation of this the members emphasised the suffering of the women and children, the position of the prisoners of war and the destruction of property. If the Boers in the veld refused to stop the war, the committee predicted a dark future for the inhabitants of the country. Botha answered the letter a week later. To Van Rensburg, the chairman, he expressed his amazement to "see that you have absolutely no shame for betraying your land and people". Botha declared unequivocally that "It is impossible for me to negotiate with traitors and I can even say murderers of the *volk*." [106]

The central committee was not at all pleased with this reply from Botha. On 27 February it planned to send the following letter to him: "In the first place we have to point out that we expected a reply not alone from yourself, but also from the Assistant-Generals, Commandants, Field-cornets and other subordinate officers in the field, and we are therefore, not convinced that we should regard your letter as an answer too from your fellow-officers. Secondly, your letter contains no answer to our communications, but teems with accusations ... which have nothing to do with the big question whether the time has not arrived for you as Commander-in-Chief, to solicit the British Government for peace and release the people from further suffering and destruction."[107] In the event, circumstances were such that by the end of February 1901 this letter was not sent to Botha.[108]

In addition to the activities of the delegated peace emissaries, the local committees and the central committee, the elderly former president M.W. Pretorius, who had no official links with any of the peace committees, also acted as a peace emissary. On 17 January 1901 – according to Kitchener entirely on his own initiative – Pretorius departed for the Boer lines.[109] For the duration of his visit the members of the central committee, who were themselves planning a personal interview with Botha, decided to shelve this idea in the hope that Pretorius's mission would be fruitful.[110] Pretorius first held an interview with Generals Ben Viljoen and Schalk Burger, but they were not impressed by his arguments.[111] A day or so later he also talked to Commandant-general Botha about the possibility of peace and on 30 January Pretorius filled Kitchener in on his visit.[112]

By 7 February Pretorius was back in Potchefstroom. Prompted by a telegram from Maxwell to the district commissioner of Potchefstroom, in which he inquired after Pretorius's welfare and referred to his visit, the district commissioner alleged that Pretorius was not to be trusted. According to him, on his way to Kitchener Pretorius had encouraged some of the burghers to continue fighting.[113] It is doubtful whether the district commissioner's suspicions were indeed justified. Botha had given the instruction on Pretorius's departure for home that he should on no account be allowed to talk to members of the commandos.[114] Furthermore Kitchener attached little value to the district commissioner's allegations. He issued orders that Pretorius should be treated "with every kindness and consideration".[115] For his services Pretorius received £50.[116]

On 30 January Kitchener sent a telegram to inform Brodrick and Milner about the results of Pretorius's visit. He explained that "They [Botha and Schalk Burger] would not discuss any questions of peace, stating only that they were fighting for their independence and meant to do so to the bitter end."[117] Later Kitchener provided more information on the visit when he replied to Brodrick's inquiry, saying that "he [Pretorius] told me Botha would not listen to anyone who was a burgher but he thought that if I met Botha matters could be easily arranged".[118] A similar version appeared in *The Bloemfontein Post*. According to this news report, Botha said to Pretorius: "I would not discuss the matter with such men [as Pretorius]. If the British had any proposals to make they must be in writing from Lord Kitchener himself."[119]

Prompted by Pretorius's visit, Mrs Annie Botha, Louis Botha's wife, left to see her husband early in February.[120] According to Kitchener, her message was similar to the one which Pretorius had taken to Botha.[121] It is not clear whether Annie decided of her own accord to deliver this message to her husband, or whether she did so under pressure from Kitchener.[122] In either event, she went to see him and arrived back on 22 February with the following letter from Botha to Kitchener: "With reference to the verbal message received from Your Excellency, I have the honour to inform Your Excellency that no one desires more than I to bring this bloody strife to an end, and also that I would very much like to meet Your Excellency for the purpose of mutual discussion to see if it is not possible to discover terms under which this can be done. With reference to the place of meeting I would suggest Middelburg or a spot in the vicinity thereof."[123] Six days later (28 February 1901) Kitchener, who was himself also anxious for peace,[124] met Botha at Middelburg.

At the Middelburg discussions Botha made it very clear to Kitchener that "you ... will never be able to force me to negotiate for peace with traitors".[125] In the light of this it can be accepted that Botha was not influenced at all by the surrendered burghers who had acted as peace emissaries, nor did they play any role in his decision to enter into the Middelburg discussions. The visit of ex-president Pretorius – who was not a surrendered burgher but identified with the convictions of the peace committee members – had however paved the way for the discussions, in that Botha had informed Pretorius that he (Botha) was not opposed to negotiating directly with Kitchener.[126] Kitchener had then followed up on this with Mrs Botha's visit. Pretorius died a few months after the Middelburg discussions.[127]

The full details of what transpired in the discussions at Middelburg are not important for the purposes of this study. It can, however, be indicated that Botha had his say about certain aspects of the British policy – aspects which had been proffered by the peace committees as reasons why the republics should abandon the struggle. He registered his objections to Kitchener about the treatment that the women and children had received at the hands of the British and also the unnecessary destruction of property by way of the burning of homes.[128] According to Botha's biographer, F.V. Engelenburg, Botha was fully aware that the republics could not expect any active support from foreign powers.[129] Nevertheless Botha was not prepared at that stage to sacrifice the republican independence, which he accurately termed "our just cause".[130]

After a discussion lasting a full five hours, Kitchener and Botha parted to continue the negotiations by correspondence. The official British conditions for peace that would end the republican independence were sent to Botha on 7 March. On 15 March the negotiations were halted when Botha announced that the British conditions were unacceptable to the Boers.[131]

The abortive discussions at Middelburg brought the organised activities of the Transvaal peace committees to a close, but the surrendered burghers persisted in their conviction that the war should be stopped at all costs. They continued along the well-worn path of the peace committees by making a few sporadic persuasive attempts.

W.M. Edwards, who considered himself a personal friend of Botha,[132] was one of the people who tried to persuade the Transvaal Boer commanding officer to abandon the struggle despite the abortive attempts by the peace committees and by Kitchener. Edwards had previously been a highly regarded member of the republican army. As one of Botha's most proficient spies he was chosen to lead a special unit of 50 men. Botha had personally selected the members of this corps. They were provided with good, strong mounts and fieldglasses, and during the first part of the war had done excellent work for the Boers. However, on 6 December 1900 Edwards voluntarily laid down his arms.[133] On 28 March 1901 he wrote a letter to Botha and with Kitchener's approval it was sent to the commandant-general a week later. In the letter Edwards raised much the same arguments as the peace committees – the fate of the women and children and the "unnecessary" bloodshed – in an attempt to persuade Botha to abandon the war. With reference to the discussions at Middelburg he wrote: "If the reports in the papers are correct, Your Honour had an interview with Lord Kitchener, and the peace negotiations were broken off because the British Government declined to pardon or take no steps against the Colonial Africanders, who took part in the war, and that consequently the war had to be carried on. Is this sufficient reason for continuing the bloodshed and misery?"[134]

His information here was inaccurate because the negotiations between Kitchener and Botha had not in fact been suspended merely because the British were not prepared to grant amnesty to the colonial rebels. The most important reason why the Boers were continuing to fight was their determination to retain republican independence.[135] As has been shown, Botha had expressed himself as strongly opposed to this kind of letter and it is doubtful whether he would have condescended to reply to Edwards. Some of the surrendered burghers also went back to the commandos in an attempt to induce their former comrades to lay down their arms. On 24 April a man called Conrad Scholtz from Mapochs Gronden left for the Boer lines with this objective in mind, but before long he was taken into custody and, after receiving corporal punishment, was ordered to resume active commando service.[136]

The last real attempt by a surrendered burgher to change the convictions of the fighting burghers took place in May 1901. On 27 May P. Fouché, who had been an officer in the Transvaal State Artillery, wrote a letter to the members of his former unit. According to Fouché the Boers were fighting for a hopeless cause. He was convinced that the republics would receive excellent treatment at the hands of the British government if they made peace without delay. To expedite the end of the war he encouraged the members of the State Artillery to lay down their arms. "I do not write this letter," wrote Fouché in closing, "because I am compelled to do so or because I am paid for it, but only out of sympathy for you. Think it over and come in. Say I was brave, [but] it did not help, the cause is lost and all to whom you shall speak thus will say: you are a man."[137] As far as can be ascertained, Fouché received no response to his letter.

By the end of August 1901 the church also reacted to the protracted Boer struggle. Revds W.F. Knobel and J.P. Wolhuter, who were in Volksrust, wrote a letter to Revd H.S. Bosman and told him about the high death toll among the women and children in the concentration camps. They informed him that the Boer cause was beyond redemption and that they were writing on behalf of the "men of influence" at Volksrust. It was felt that the church was the only body that could possibly effect a speedy peace and thus avoid "even greater disaster". They saw the matter as being of the utmost importance and wanted to know from Revd Bosman "whether the time has not come for us to act as Peacemakers on behalf of the Church". As the first step in this direction they suggested a general meeting of the N.H. of G. Kerk (Dutch Reformed Church) in the Transvaal to discuss the matter in consultation with the Free State and Cape synods. But

Revd Bosman did not see his way clear to being involved in this undertaking. In his reply he said that although he had given the issue a "great deal of thought", he was not in a position and was also not empowered to take action on such an important matter.[138]

The number of peace initiatives undertaken by surrendered burghers in the Transvaal dropped sharply from March to September 1901. In time the British authorities also refused to grant permission for such attempts. When Commandant S.P. Grobler, who had fled to Bechuanaland, offered his services as a peace emissary in mid-January 1902, Lieutenant-colonel R.M. Poore, the provost marshal, expressed the opinion that, "It is very questionable whether he would be of any assistance to us ... unless he was prepared to fight, as his influence among other burghers will probably be nil." [139]

From the foregoing discussion it is clear that the Transvaal burghers were adamant in their decision not to give up the struggle even when under pressure from their fellow burghers who had surrendered. The prevailing position in the Free State will be discussed below.

3 Work of the burgher peace committees and other peace initiatives in the Free State

Although the central committee at Kroonstad met regularly and the subcommittee in Bloemfontein held weekly meetings from January to November 1901,[140] the peace committees in the Free State, in comparison with those in the Transvaal, did not make as many concerted efforts to send peace emissaries to the republicans in the veld. Those who did in fact leave for the Boer lines rapidly learned at their own cost that the Free State burghers did not share their convictions

This was particularly true in the case of Johannes Jacobus Morgendaal and Andries Bernardus Wessels, two prominent and well-known figures in the Kroonstad region. Prior to the war, Morgendaal had extensive farming interests in the Kroonstad district. He was also a special justice of the peace for the Onder-Valsrivier ward and had also acted for a period as secretary for the N.G. Kerk (Dutch Reformed Church). When the republican forces occupied Griqualand

West in the first month of the war, Morgendaal was appointed magistrate with full jurisdiction over this region. After the Boer evacuation of the area, he returned to Kroonstad where he once again entered the Free State civil service. With the British occupation of Bloemfontein on 13 March 1900 and Kroonstad on 12 May 1900, Morgendaal came to the conclusion that further resistance was absolutely fruitless. He was so certain that the republics would not be able to retain their independence that he took the oath of allegiance to the British crown as a British citizen. On 6 July the British administration appointed him as justice of the peace for Kroonstad.[141]

The 60-year-old Andries Wessels (snr), Morgendaal's father-in-law, was a very prosperous Free State farmer of the farm Paardekraal, halfway between Kroonstad and Heilbron. As a member of the *Volksraad*, before the war he was a strong supporter of the Free State policy to align itself with the Transvaal in the case of armed conflict with Great Britain. Wessels was also on friendly terms with both republican presidents. During the extraordinary sitting of the Free State *Volksraad* on 22 September 1899 he gave his "unqualified vote" for the "full implementation of the Political accord with our brothers … and faithful fulfilment by us of the obligations prescribed in that agreement". However, during the course of the war Wessels changed his mind and on 1 July 1900 he decided to lay down his arms. Just like his son-in-law, Wessels was convinced that no purpose would be served by continuing to fight. During the first week of July 1900 he planned to go to the Boer lines to try to persuade the burghers to stop fighting, but at that stage Roberts was not prepared to give his permission for such an undertaking.[142]

Some six months later Wessels was given the opportunity to effect his proposed plan when he and Morgendaal departed voluntarily on 28 December 1900 for General Christiaan de Wet's laager.[143] Before they could even reach De Wet they were picked up by a Boer patrol and taken into custody 32 kilometres outside Kroonstad, and on 6 January 1901 in the Heilbron district they were brought before a military court comprised of General C.C. Froneman and two other Boer officers. No sentence was passed and the case was referred to a higher court. Morgendaal and Wessels were then placed in a commando of about 70 men under De Wet and General C.C. Froneman.

De Wet gave orders that they had to be heavily guarded and, according to the evidence of Wessels, Froneman warned them explicitly that if they moved away from the wagon in which they were being held without permission, they would be shot.[144] Morgendaal and Wessels spent the night of 8 January with the commando on the farm Nobelsfontein. The account of what befell Morgendaal the next day is based on six eyewitness accounts, two sworn statements, a statement by Dr J.H. Poutsma (a Boer doctor) and the reminiscences of two ex-burghers.[145] A discussion of the incident in a recent doctoral thesis was also examined carefully.[146]

Early in the morning of 9 January 1901 an African man reported that a British force was approaching. Although it was later established that the man had been mistaken, the warning immediately transformed the whole camp into a hive of activity and most burgers hastily harnessed the horses and saddled up. According to an eyewitness by the name of O.T. de Villiers, who was a colonial rebel and member of General de Wet's commando, De Wet was aware that the African's report was untrue and tried to calm the burghers down. H.A. van Heerden, another eyewitness who only recorded his account 48 years after the war, claimed that a few burghers realised that it was a false alarm. Be that as it may, Morgendaal was unperturbed by the confusion and left the wagon to go to wash himself. General Froneman then ordered him to help with harnessing the oxen to the wagon, but Morgendaal ignored his instruction. Eyewitness Izak de Wet (General de Wet's son) claims that Froneman repeated the order to Morgendaal three times, upon which, according to De Villiers, Morgendaal retorted: "I am not a Hottentot." By this Morgendaal presumably implied that he was not prepared to be rudely ordered to obey all Froneman's orders. Froneman had reached the end of his patience with Morgendaal. According to Izak de Wet, Froneman, who was already on his horse, flogged Morgendaal with his horsewhip, but Morgendaal managed to wrest the sjambok out of his hands. Another eyewitness, G.L. Muller, claims that at this stage Froneman threatened Morgendaal: "[You piece of] rubbish, I'll shoot you." With that, General de Wet, who had seen the altercation between the two men shouted to Froneman: "General, shoot him dead on the spot." ("*Generaal, skiet hom op die plek dood.*") De Wet's son swears that these were his father's exact words, and Dr Poutsma's statement corroborates this. However, eyewitness G.L. Muller and Mrs S.E. Morgendaal, in her sworn testimony, claim that De Wet bellowed: "Shoot the bastard." In contrast, De Villiers says that De Wet specifically ordered Froneman: "Shoot him down, he is worth no more than that." The other eyewitnesses, Neudecker and Wessels, make no mention of De Wet issuing an order of this kind, while eyewitness H.A. van Heerden says that De Wet was not even present at that particular moment. The latter evidence is, however, not only contradicted by the previous witnesses, but also by the reminiscences of ex-burghers G.J. Joubert and General M. van Schoor, as well as the sworn statement of J.A. van Biljon, who received his information from Froneman. All the people involved, however, are in agreement that Froneman immediately shot Morgendaal. There is also unanimity (apart from Van Heerden, whose evidence is unacceptable on this point, and that of Wessels, whose version is somewhat vague) that Froneman acted in response to a direct order from De Wet. The bullet struck Morgendaal under the shoulder and he collapsed, seriously wounded. The whole episode took less than five minutes. De Villiers then took care of Morgendaal's welfare, but his request to De Wet that Morgendaal be taken to the hospital at Lindley was refused. Dr Poutsma, who confirms De Villiers's evidence, was however permitted to treat Morgendaal on a neighbouring farm. According to De Villiers, Morgendaal repeatedly said on his sickbed that he only wanted to persuade the burghers to abandon the struggle because this would be in the best interests of the whole country. Ten days after the incident, on 19 January 1901, Morgendaal died of the wound he had received.

On 10 January 1901 Andries Wessels appeared before a court martial of 15 Boer officers with General de Wet as chairman. With one dissenting vote he was found guilty of high treason and sentenced to death. His friends submitted a petition to President Steyn in which they pleaded that his life be spared. In the end, Steyn did not ratify the sentence, apparently because of Wessels's age and because as an individual he was considered harmless. At no stage did Wessels ever learn what punishment Steyn had laid down, and the matter simply remained unresolved. According to Izak de Wet, a number of the youngsters who were on commando subjected Wessels to a somewhat illegal thrashing. On 7 August 1901 Wessels was released by a British force.[147]

Morgendaal's death caused a considerable commotion. Both Major-general W. Knox, the British commander at Kroonstad, and Kitchener initially regarded it as cold-blooded murder.[148] Dr Poutsma was highly critical of the incident and refused to greet General Froneman. He considered Froneman guilty of murder. As a result of the episode Poutsma wanted to resign as doctor, but under pressure from the burghers he agreed to change his decision.[149] Among the ordinary burghers there was also a measure of dissatisfaction over the way in which Morgendaal had met his end. Some of them felt that Froneman had been unjustified in shooting Morgendaal before his case had been properly heard. Had he then been sentenced to death, they argued, he should have been executed by a firing squad.[150] According to Kitchener, at the Middelburg negotiations Commandant-general Botha was unable to justify Morgendaal's death, and Botha put it down to the demoralisation which had set in because of the war.[151] Kitchener later learned from one of the members of the Free State government who had been captured at Reitz that the Free Staters considered Morgendaal's death to be a case of manslaughter because the false report that a British force was approaching had caused such great consternation that Morgendaal's shooting had not been premeditated. Kitchener believed that a judicial inquiry would quite possibly also have indicated that it was manslaughter.[152]

There is no clear-cut criterion according to which the legality of the Boer action against Morgendaal can be measured. The Hague Convention and other international legal standards do not make provision for such incidents. However F. Despagnet, a French jurist who has studied the Anglo-Boer War from a legal point of view, throws some light on the matter. He is of the opinion that the emissaries who were sent to De Wet's commando were agents of the enemy and real traitors. In the light of this he concludes that although Morgendaal's death was cruel, it was indeed in accordance with the criteria of warfare in civilised nations.[153] Seen in this wider perspective, Despagnet's conclusion can thus be endorsed.

As far as can be established Morgendaal was the only peace emissary who was shot dead in the Free State. According to Piet de Wet and the members of the subcommittee in Bloemfontein, two peace emissaries from the Harrismith peace committee, C. Snyman and H. van Wyk, were sentenced to death, but there is no mention of whether the sentence was ever in fact carried out.[154]

Shortly after Morgendaal's fatal mission, M.J. Beukes, a former member of the *Volksraad* for Vrede, tried to arrange a meeting with the burghers from the Vrede and Harrismith districts. About 200 burghers were prepared to listen to Beukes and left for the meeting place. However, when General Philip Botha came to hear of this he promptly sent the burghers back. Two of his officers were allowed to see Beukes to inform him that the burghers did not want to hear what he had to say and that he had no right to address them.[155] Clearly the Boer generals were determined to keep the peace committee propaganda away from the burghers who were still fighting.

J.S. Theron, former *Volksraad* member for the ward of Kaalspruit in the Bloemfontein district, was the final republican peace emissary from the Free State who went to the Boer lines. On 17 January 1901 he went to the Petrusburg region as a delegate from the peace committee in Bloemfontein. He contacted a certain field-cornet called Grobbelaar and through him tried to gain an interview with Commandant van der Berg, the commanding officer in the region. But Grobbelaar was not prepared to act as mediator. He also refused to let Theron return to Bloemfontein and told him that the Boers were not prepared to forfeit their independence. On about 21 January Theron was tried in a military court at Petrusburg. Because he was not in possession of any leaflets for distribution from the peace committee and had also not managed to get as far as to persuade the burghers to lay down their arms, he was freed. However, he had to remain on parole in Petrusburg and on 1 February Theron was released when a British force occupied the town.[156]

Other than this, the activities of the peace committees in the Free State took the form of writing letters to the republicans who were still fighting, and they also organised the distribution of brochures and flyers. African people and British troops were used to place this material where it would come to the attention of the bitterenders.[157]

A leaflet that was widely distributed was one written by P.M. Botha, a former member of the *Volksraad* and a member of the central committee at Kroonstad. From this brochure it appears that Botha was strongly opposed to continuing the war. "I feel that it is my duty to speak," he wrote, "and to speak as strongly as I can, for I burn with indignation when I see the ruin around me. I ask my people to remember that I am one of themselves – a Boer with no better advantage or education than they have had. I have a right to be heard, for I am an old man and I belong to the soil of the country and come of a family which has fought and done as much as any other to make the Orange Free State." His objective with the brochure was to "appeal to my fellow-countrymen to admit their own faults and to recognize that it is best for South Africa, under the present circumstances to become one harmonious whole under the British flag". He also wanted to show his compatriots "what these [Boer] leaders really are, and how they were misled and duped by them".

However, in his attempt to underscore his argument P.M. Botha made a number of unsubstantiated accusations against Steyn and Kruger. He blamed the republican presidents for the outbreak of the war and was of the opinion that if J.G. Fraser had been elected as president of the Free State in 1896, the war would not have taken place at all. He continued in a similar unrestrained fashion: "I feel that I could curse Marthinus Theunis Steyn and the Kruger gang – Steyn, a Free Stater born, used his country as a steppingstone for his ignoble ambition and sacrificed his whole people for the furtherance of his private ends." Botha then closed the plea to his countrymen as follows: "Steyn ... and others still fulminate fire and sword in proclamations but has Steyn or his gang ever been heard of on the battlefield? I truly believe that these braves will also retire at the convenient moment to villas in Sicily. But YOU, where are YOU? YOUR blood has been spent like water, YOUR homes have been destroyed. YOU have been deported to strange countries and your women and children ... reduced to live on the charity of your enemy."[158]

The blatant untruths and poor taste that Botha showed in this brochure did not pass unnoticed. Revd J.A. Steytler of Cape Town made reference to it in a letter to *The South African News*, saying that, "Mr. Botha's recently published pamphlet literally bristles with inaccuracies and glaring misstatements ... For courtesy and good taste we shall search in vain through the ... pages of Mr. Botha's appeal.

All those who have the audacity to differ from him are vilified in turn. Experience, however, happily teaches that when abuse takes the place of argument, the cause it is sought to defend is in tottering condition. And therefore the vituperations of Mr. Botha, though they may rouse disgust, can nevertheless be borne with equanimity."[159]

It stands to reason that Milner was far more impressed by Botha's brochure. He described it as "a remarkable pamphlet" and informed Kitchener: "He [Botha] writes as a Boer to a Boer and preaches peace, denounces the war and goes for the O.R.C. and T.V. in a most effective style. I am sending you 100 copies. It is worth taking some pains to get them spread abroad. A man like Botha ought to be made every use of."[160] Kitchener complied with Milner's request and copies of Botha's leaflet were distributed overseas for propaganda purposes.[161] The district commissioners of Wepener, Smithfield, Boshof, Heilbron and Harrismith each received 100 copies to distribute among the Free State residents.[162]

Where Botha's brochure came into Boer hands, one and all expressed themselves very strongly against the content. A wartime republican paper in the Free State dubbed it "nauseating", "degenerate" and "filthy". The Boer leaders also expressed their dismay that Botha, with his "foolish accusations about our legitimate Rulers and leaders" had tried to "mislead the simple Boers and to instigate suspicion against the honest, well-trusted and wise policy of our leaders". They concluded the protest against Botha's brochure by saying: "We have seen a great deal of hypocrisy and deceit in the world, but never anything quite as bad as this brochure by Botha; no, not ever. It is just too dreadful."[163] Botha's brochure evoked only criticism from his fellow countrymen. He did not live to see the peace that he had championed in such an undiplomatic, controversial manner, because he died of pneumonia on 16 August 1901.[164]

The flyers which had been distributed by the peace committee also evoked a stormy reaction on the republican side. In one of these, dated 21 December 1900 and headed the "Second Meeting of the Burgher Peace Committee", Kitchener outlined his proposal for an enlightened, progressive government with a civilian element, to be implemented after the war.[165] With remarkably prophetic insight this promise was analysed by the Boer leaders in the Free State: "The most important, when one comes to the main issues, is the Management that they (the English) plan to give us. If you look closely you will see that we are to be granted: A Top Management structure comprising Chamberlain, Milner, Paul Botha, Piet de Wet and other traitors, (namely the 'Civilian element' they plan to introduce). This also for just as long as it suits them, because no time has been stipulated ... That is the SELF GOVERNMENT that we get, and it comprises the English and the MOST ROTTEN SCUM of the Afrikaners. This, then, is the ENLIGHTENED PROGRESSIVE Government proposed by Mr. Chamberlain, the one of which Kitchener spoke at the meeting of *Handsoppers* [surrendered burghers] at Pretoria."[166] After the war the former republicans did indeed receive a system of government that was cast in this mould.[167]

The peace committees then tried to contact the republican leaders by means of correspondence. On 11 January 1901 Piet de Wet appealed to his brother to stop the fighting. He referred to the scant possibility of European intervention and begged him to put his emotions aside and to admit what would be in the best interests of the *volk*, to surrender and subject themselves to the British government. According to Piet de Wet, if the war continued for a few more months the whole country would be ruined and reduced to beggary. He was convinced that the Boers did not know the true state of affairs and that the ordinary burghers were being misled by their leaders. He went on to say that the motivation to continue fighting was not "true patriotism", and if the ordinary burghers knew what the "truth" was, "the great majority would already have laid down their arms". In conclusion De Wet "implored" his brother to stand still for a moment and to think in silent prayer about the "true interests of the Afrikaner people". Only then should he decide whether he should perhaps start moving in a different direction to "extinguish the fire of war instead of fanning it".[168] Christiaan de Wet apparently ignored this letter and merely sent a terse message to tell his brother that he would shoot him on sight if he ever saw him.[169]

On 15 January 1901 the peace committee at Bethlehem, with C.J. Cloete, a former member of the *Volksraad* as chairman, also sent Christiaan de Wet a letter. As Piet de Wet had done, they emphasised the destruction of the country and the bloodshed on both sides. "Will you," the committee asked De Wet, "whose name as a warrior will be recorded in every language for posterity, not also ... cause to be written that, at the same time, your feeling of humanity was not extinct, for when there was an opportunity to prevent bloodshed, you were the man who wished to mitigate the tears of wives, widows and orphans, and who wished to save the country from greater misery?"[170] In all likelihood De Wet ignored this too. The peace committees in the Free State did not make any further attempts to contact the officers and burghers in the veld after January 1901. According to J.G. Fraser, Morgendaal's death had put a damper on their activities.[171]

In May 1901 there was censure from within the ranks of the surrendered burghers about the methods used by the peace committees. E.R. Grobler, a former member of the Free State *Volksraad* for Philippolis, who had been chief commandant of the southern section of the Free State forces in the first months of the war, felt that the "farcical manner" in which the peace committees had tried to stop the war had not had the remotest chance of any success.[172] Grobler, who had surrendered at the end of March 1900,[173] suggested to Kitchener that he should secure a quorum of Free State *Volksraad* members who were against the continuance of the war. These people should then try to use constitutional grounds to persuade President Steyn and the Boer generals to abandon the war.[174] Grobler's suggestion was not as far-fetched as it seems as first. Adv. C.L. Botha of the central peace committee at Kroonstad made reference in May 1901 to the fact that nine out of the 59 *Volksraad* members in the Free State had actively promoted peace, while a further 29 members had voluntarily distanced themselves from the republican war effort.[175] On the Boer side concern was expressed over the large number of *Volksraad* members who had become "unfaithful to their *volk*". The ordinary burghers were then also warned to follow their military officers rather than the leaders of the *Volksraad*.[176] Some of the burghers were indeed influenced by the fact that so many of the *Volksraad* members had stood on the sidelines as far as the war was concerned. After the war a bitterender from De Wet's commando who called himself "a misguided burgher" expressed the opinion that it would have been better for everyone if "we had just followed the example of the majority of our *raad* [parliamentary] members".[177] Kitchener sent a copy of Grobler's letter to the provost marshal, Lieutenant-colonel R.M. Poore,[178] but did not take his (Grobler's) suggestion any further. As has been shown, Kitchener was not in favour of allowing the surrendered burghers to maintain contact among themselves.[179]

Revd Charles Murray of Graaff-Reinet and Revd J.F. Botha of Richmond, who had no official links with the peace committees, made a final attempt in September 1901 to persuade Steyn and De Wet to abandon the war.

Murray planned this peace mission on his own initiative. On 26 August he informed the peace committee at Bloemfontein that he had tried in vain to get Dr T. de Water and T.P. Theron of the Afrikaner Bond to join him on his journey to the Boer leaders. He had also approached various ministers of religion in the Cape Colony, but only one, a Revd Botha was agreeable. Murray chose to remain independent of the peace committee, because he was wary of acting as a representative of any particular faction. He argued that in this way he could not be accused of taking sides. His objective was to persuade Steyn and De Wet to withdraw their commandos from the Cape Colony and then to call off the war against Great Britain.[180]

The two ministers held separate interviews on 9 September 1901 with Steyn and De Wet. But they had to return home with absolutely nothing accomplished. Steyn had apparently told them that he was not prepared to pull the commandos out of the Cape Colony unless the full independence of the republics was recognised and general amnesty was granted to all colonial rebels. De Wet expressed the same opinion and added that arrangements were being made to send more commandos to the Cape Colony.[181]

As a result of this abortive attempt Fraser remarked to A.Thynne, a government official in the British administration in Bloemfontein: "Don't you think the intervention of the Commissioner for Lunacy ought to be called in and warrants issued to place Steyn and De Wet into the Asylum till their sanity returns?"[182] Fraser's somewhat irrational outburst illustrates the desperation in the Free State peace committees when they took stock of their activities. When it became patently obvious that they were unable to evoke the desired reaction in the Free State, they began to focus their attention on influential people in the Cape Colony. For Piet de Wet this was the only other alternative.[183]

4 Activities of the burgher peace committees in the Cape Colony

As early as 8 January 1901 the members of the central peace committee at Kroonstad called upon the people in the Cape Colony to help them try to work towards peace. In an open letter they referred to the widespread destruction in the republics and the suffering of the women and children. The blame for all this, according to the central committee, lay with a small stubborn minority who would not accept the inevitable. The Cape Afrikaners were asked to hold a congress at which they were to choose delegates from their ranks, men who would then try to persuade President Steyn and General Christiaan de Wet to initiate peace negotiations with Britain. The central committee was of the opinion that De Wet and Steyn were the only two obstacles on the path to peace.[184] This letter was not well received by certain pro-republican people in the Cape Colony. The writer of a letter to *The South African News* referred to Piet de Wet as a jingo and said he found it unbelievable that the brother of a hero and patriot like Christiaan de Wet could ignore all ties of blood and do such harm to the republican cause.[185]

Because their letter had not produced the desired result, the members of the Bloemfontein peace committee decided to approach the Cape Afrikaners personally. D.J.H. van Niekerk went to Burgersdorp where he addressed a gathering of about 200 people in the town hall on 26 January 1901. In his speech Van Niekerk described the conditions in the Free State and suggested the possibility of setting up a peace committee at Burgersdorp. Those present did not go so far as to actually establish a committee, but according to Van Niekerk the meeting was a success and there were a considerable number of interested people in the audience. C.A. Schweizer, an attorney from Burgersdorp, offered his unreserved support to Van Niekerk and also proposed that the peace committees in the Free State visit various towns in the Cape Colony to inform the residents about conditions in the republics so that they could work together towards peace.[186]

The peace committee in Bloemfontein did not see its way clear to visiting a large number of towns in the Cape, but on the suggestion of Piet de Wet decided to send a deputation to Cape Town. The aim was to gain the support of influential people and ministers of religion who would be prepared to speak out against continuing the war. In this way the committee hoped to erode the sympathy for the Boer cause in the Cape Colony and make the Boer leaders realise that they were fighting a futile war. On 6 February Piet de Wet and Adv. C.L. Botha departed for Cape Town and it was arranged that D.J.H. van Niekerk would join them on 15 February.[187] Revd H.E. du Plessis also arrived during February.[188]

Once in Cape Town, the deputation decided in consultation with Sir Gordon Sprigg, the Cape premier, to approach T.P. Theron, the chairman of the Afrikaner Bond. By negotiating with Theron these men hoped to gain the approval of the Afrikaner Bond for their peace movement.[189] Piet de Wet regarded Theron as a man of "sound opinions".[190] On 1 February, before the arrival of the delegation in Cape Town, the advice of chief justice of the Cape, John Henry de Villiers, was sought on the possibility that some of the members of the Afrikaner Bond might become active in a move to precipitate peace. De Villiers answered that it was a delicate matter, because Britain was not prepared to recognise the independence of the republics and the republics, for their part, were not prepared to sacrifice their independence. "Under such circumstances," he concluded, "individuals like you and me are quite powerless, and we can only trust that Providence will direct matters for the ultimate good of poor distracted South Africa."[191]

Between 15 and 19 February Theron met the deputation at Wellington.[192] In the light of the fact that Theron was considering the possibility of using the Afrikaner Bond's influence in an attempt to end the war, it is not surprising that he was initially prepared to negotiate with the delegation. On the other hand, previous researchers have mentioned the possibility that Theron was unaware of the status of the delegation, because he lived in a district which was under military rule (Britstown) and was not fully conversant with the situation in the Free State and the Transvaal.¹⁹³ Be that as it may, during the interview the delegation asked Theron to give his support to the peace movement in the republics. He would also be expected to send a deputation to the republican leaders to inform them that they should not expect any military aid from the Cape Afrikaners and that it would be advisable to abandon the war.¹⁹⁴ According to Piet de Wet, Theron was "in spirit ... totally in agreement with us", but he wanted to consult the other members of the management of the Afrikaner Bond before giving a final answer.¹⁹⁵

However, on 20 February Theron broke off all further negotiations with the delegation. This struck the members of the committee "like a bombshell".¹⁹⁶ As the reason for his decision Theron said that it was impossible for him to recognise the "legality" of the deputation. Although he claimed to be strongly in favour of peace, in terms of the constitution of the Afrikaner Bond he could not negotiate any further with them on an official level.¹⁹⁷ After the war Theron reiterated this point of view in the Cape parliament. He claimed that he had been prepared to work for peace, but then only if he was approached by the official British authorities. Of his negotiations with the deputation he said: "Unfortunately these requests [for peace] came from outside people, and did not come from those in authority, who had the power to make such requests ... ."¹⁹⁸ According to Davenport, Theron was obliged to act on behalf of the members of the management of the Afrikaner Bond and politically speaking it was impossible for him to follow any alternative policy.¹⁹⁹

Theron's refusal to cooperate with the deputation did not find favour in all Afrikaner circles. In the Cape Colony there was a small minority of Afrikaners who openly expressed their dissatisfaction,²⁰⁰ and in Bloemfontein the peace committee received the news of the failure of the negotiations with disappointment. Nevertheless these people still clung to the hope that there would be other well-meaning and influential people who would be prepared to give their support to the deputation.²⁰¹ The peace committee in Zeerust in the Transvaal also expressed its dismay. According to this committee the Afrikaner Bond had surely not been aware of the urgent necessity for peace, or it would have devoted more attention to the deputation's pleas. One of its resolutions reads: "At the action of such men as Mr. Theron, Chairman of the Bond, and others, we express our greatest indignation ... That they will not help to save their own people, but leave them in a course likely to utterly ruin them, is discreditable in the extreme."[202] This resolution shows a lack of insight into the *locus standi* of the deputation to the Cape and Theron's particular predicament.

The deputation then turned its attention to influential clergymen in the Cape Colony. In this initiative it received active support from Revd H.E. du Plessis of Lindley. At the beginning of February 1901 Du Plessis sent an open letter to the ministers of the N.G. Kerk (Dutch Reformed Church) in which he sketched the situation in the Free State. As far as he was concerned the republics had already lost the war and the commandos were now scuttling around making themselves guilty of uncivilised warfare without accomplishing anything of strategic significance. He felt that the Free State people were being kept in the dark about the republics' chances of a victory and the true state of affairs in their country. He warned his fellow clergymen in the Cape Colony to discourage the holding of congresses and meetings, because they would promote the spirit of rebellion in the people and encourage them to continue the war. In conclusion he claimed that the Cape clergymen were acting against God's Word by supporting a hopeless struggle, because God had already made it clear that it was against His will that the republics should retain their independence.[203]

Milner regarded Du Plessis as an influential Free Stater, but he had his doubts whether Du Plessis would receive much support from the Cape clergy.[204] He was perfectly correct in this assumption. Revd J.A. Steytler of Cape Town reacted by making a systematic analysis of Du Plessis's letter and exposed many of its inaccuracies. In a logical manner most of Du Plessis's unfounded allegations about the struggle in the Free State were refuted. On a theological level too, Du Plessis's interpretation of the will of God as regards the war was seriously questioned. Steytler closed his critical analysis of Du Plessis's letter by saying, "I for one, can afford to treat your insinuations with the contempt it deserves."[205] Some of the Boers in the Free State also studied the Du Plessis letter and came to the conclusion that he was merely repeating the "crazy stories of the Khakis".[206]

This reaction did not deter Du Plessis. He once again appealed to the Cape clergymen and called for a joint sitting of the N.G. Kerke in the Cape Colony, Free State and the Transvaal. The aim here would be to appoint a mediator who would act as a facilitator between Kitchener and the Boer forces.[207] Nothing came of this. Du Plessis also decided to answer his critics. He claimed that Steytler was not in a position to make an accurate judgement on the state of the war. "Coming recently from the seat of war," he wrote, "I happen to know a great deal more than you, who grow enthusiastic from the comfortable security of your study chair. I do not care," he went on, "what motives are ascribed to me for having written that letter. One thing I know: that, in having it published, I was only obeying an internal constraint which I could no longer suppress ... I am sorry that you, through your uncalled for reply, have diverted my attention from the point at issue, namely the cessation of hostilities ... I only wish to see hostilities cease, and solicit the support of my brother-ministers to that end, because the country is being ruined, the people are being demoralized, valuable lives are being lost, and the development of the situation points just in one direction: it is the will of God to bow to the British Empire." Du Plessis then turned to a discussion of divergent theological interpretations, failing to address Steytler's particular points of criticism.[208] In his defence he did try to prove his sincerity, but at the same time he quietly persisted in his factually false convictions about the war situation.

Towards the end of February 1901 Du Plessis conducted an interview, on behalf of the peace committee's delegation, with the well-known Revd Andrew Murray of Wellington, an influential minister of the Cape N.G. Kerk. Du Plessis asked Murray if he would perhaps be prepared to work with the peace committee in the interests of peace. But Murray did not want to be associated with the peace committee at all and Du Plessis had to inform the deputation that Murray was only prepared to work towards a peace that was based on the restoration of republican independence. Although Murray's attitude dismayed the delegates, they approached him again to see if he would perhaps reconsider the matter. To them his opinion on peace was unacceptable as they were in favour of peace at any price. In their view the war had already been lost and the restoration of republican independence was impossible under the circumstances. "We have sound reasons," they said in trying to win Murray over, "to believe that if the leaders of the fighting Boers could be persuaded to lay down their arms immediately and to call upon the mercy of the English, there would be every chance of receiving such help and support from Great Britain that would save our impoverished nation from complete disintegration ... ". But Murray was simply not impressed by these arguments and he informed the deputation that he would willingly chop off his right hand if this could bring peace, but the path along which the peace committees were travelling would not lead to an honourable and desirable peace.[209]

On 8 March the members of the deputation appealed to Revd J.H. Hofmeyr, moderator of the Cape synod. In their letter to him many of the peace committee's arguments were repeated, and they also claimed to be the representatives of a sizeable portion of the Free State population. By the end of March Hofmeyr had still not answered their letter.[210] Later, representations were also made to the moderator of the Free State synod, J.T.T. Marquard. Marquard, who was in Cape Town at the time, had first been held by the British as a prisoner of war, but through the intercession of John X. Merriman, the well-known Cape politician, he had been released on bail. On the grounds of his parole, he said, he could not become involved in politics and was thus not in a position to promote the peace committee's cause.[211]

Revd J.H. van Wyk of Adelaide was the only Cape clergyman who said that he was prepared to cooperate with the peace committee. At the time of the deputation's visit, Van Wyk was in Cape Town. In an interview with Piet de Wet and C.L. Botha he agreed to go to General Christiaan de Wet and Commandant-general Botha to try to persuade them to initiate negotiations with Britain. Kitchener gave his consent for the visit, but Van Wyk then became ill and the trip had to be cancelled. In a letter to Kitchener in June 1901, Van Wyk offered his services again as a peace emissary.[212] The sources do not show whether Kitchener gave his consent for a visit at this time, or indeed whether it took place at all.

The deputation then concentrated its efforts on the prisoners of war in the concentration camps in Cape Town. Among the inmates there were considerable differences of opinion and lack of agreement on whether the war should be continued. A relatively small minority was in favour of the republics immediately calling a halt to the war. One of them was F.J.J. Celliers from the Kroonstad district, who was in the camp at Green Point. On 21 January 1901 he sent the following request to the peace committee in Bloemfontein: "I request you, brothers, to proceed to the Boer camps and tell them there that Steyn is nothing more but a ruffian refugee on British territory and that Kruger has fled to Europe with his stolen millions [sic] ... Make them [the prisoners] understand that a further continuation of the strife is absolutely hopeless ... It is of no use to talk about independence."[213] H.S. Viljoen, a former member of the Free State *Volksraad* for the ward Wittebergen in the district of Bethlehem, also declared himself to be in favour of immediate peace. He and five other prisoners of war informed Milner that "it is sheer folly on the one hand, as well as the greatest sin on the other, to continue this hopeless struggle".[214] But the majority of the prisoners of war retained their loyalty towards the republican cause. People in the camps who became involved in the move for peace at the expense of independence were often treated roughly and on the whole could find only meagre support for their ideas.[215]

When Piet de Wet and Adv. C.L. Botha visited the camp at Green Point, they received "definite opposition" and were booed by some of the inmates. Nevertheless the two men were convinced that some of the prisoners of war were in favour of their visit and claimed that these people had not been given the opportunity to air their opinions.[216] The delegation's visit caused so much upheaval in the Green Point camp that Lieutenant-colonel H.C. Money, the commanding officer of the camp, expressed his concern over the "serious and frequent disturbances". Later he said, "Owing to the visit by the peace Commissioners, a large faction of the Anti-English prisoners banded themselves together and attacked those more peacefully inclined. They organized parties at night to duck these men in the latrine-troughs, and otherwise maltreated them, several in fear of their lives appealed to me for protection".[217]

The delegation discussed the matter in an interview with Milner and proposed that it would be desirable to set up a separate "peace camp" at Simonstown. The purpose of such a camp would be to keep together all the prisoners of war who were in favour of peace, and to separate them from the loyal republican burghers who supported the idea of continuing the war.[218] Milner was impressed by the idea. To Kitchener he wrote: "The more I see of [Piet] de Wet etc., the more sure I am that it is very much to our interests for the future to adopt any sensible suggestions made by them without delay."[219] Milner then told Kitchener that he insisted on "a separation in the camps between the moderate minority, and the majority of rowdy irreconcilables. Whenever the former get together, and try to pass any resolution, they get bullied out of it by the rowdies. The position is an intolerable one, and they will not really speak out until they are by themselves. When they are, I feel confident that they will make their voices heard".[220] He furthermore hoped that the people in the camp would perhaps be able to influence the commandos to abandon the struggle. Even if this was not the case, such a separation, in his view, could only be beneficial and the "pacific section" would thereby be placed in a privileged position.[221]

Kitchener was somewhat hesitant about setting up such a camp because he did not want to forfeit British troops for duties as camp guards,[222] but Milner did not see this as an insurmountable obstacle and decided to go ahead and implement the plan.[223] Inmates for the camp were selected mainly on the grounds of their attitude towards continuing the war and the selection process was carried out by the deputation, assisted by Major A.R. Stuart, a British officer, and Adv. A. Lange-Brink, an attorney from Johannesburg. By 20 March 1901 there were about 800 people in the camp.[224]

These numbers soon increased rapidly. On 8 April Lieutenant-colonel C. Heyman, the commanding officer of all the prisoners of war in Cape Town, reported that there were already 1600 people in the camp. According to him, most of these prisoners of war had either surrendered with General Piet Cronjé on 27 February 1900 at Paardeberg, or had been captured when General M. Prinsloo had surrendered in the Brandwater Basin on 29 July 1900.[225] It was decided that they were to be treated as political prisoners of war and would not be sent out of South Africa.[226] Although the British regarded most of these men as moderates, there were also some of them who were considered "irreconcilable". One of the inmates in the camp differentiated between three distinct classes: "(1) the rabids or irreconcilables; (2) the reasonable moderates anxious for peace; (3) the 'rocky' roosters (beloved by Rhodes), and section No. 2 undoubtedly predominates largely."[227] The fact that there were also so-called irreconcilable prisoners of war in the camp disturbed the British authorities. Adv. C.L. Botha was told to work more selectively, and the irreconcilable element would in time be weeded out and sent to overseas camps.[228] By the end of the war there were 1026 inmates in the Simonstown camp.[229]

At the request of Adv. Botha, General Andries P.J. Cronjé of the central peace committee in Pretoria came to Cape Town to address the prisoners of war in the Simonstown camp. Those inmates who had been taken captive with General Piet Cronjé at Paardeberg were apparently prepared to listen to his brother, Andries.[230] Piet Cronjé himself had been sent to St Helena. In comparison with Piet de Wet's visit to the Green Point camp, Andries Cronjé had a very favourable reception. Major A.R. Stuart reported as follows on Cronjé's visit: "Andries Cronjé's arrival at Bellevue was the signal for a great outburst of rejoicing. The Transvaalers look much happier, and I think he is doing good." Adv. Lange-Brink, who was in the camp at the time of Cronjé's visit, also remarked that "Cronjé received a very hearty reception and is doing good work amongst them [the prisoners]."[231] With Cronjé's encouragement a number of prisoners of war signed a petition in favour of peace. According to Cronjé it was a spontaneous gesture and the people involved planned to send the petition to President Steyn, General Christiaan de Wet and Commandant-general Botha.[232] This petition was indeed delivered,[233] but it is not known how the Boer leaders reacted to it.

While the deputation was on its mission in Cape Town, the members visited the Simonstown camp regularly. Discussions were held with the inmates and some of the prisoners of war decided to form a peace committee in the camp to continue the work of the delegates. The committee comprised W.G. de Klerck of the Transvaal as chairman, P.H. Fauré of Smithfield was the secretary, and there were four additional members. They agreed to devote their endeavours "to increase the numbers of prisoners of war who are peacefully inclined by drafting them from Greenpoint Camp and elsewhere and also to work generally in the interests of peace".[234] On 16 April 1901 the committee sent a letter to General Piet Cronjé on St Helena in the hope that he would be prepared to involve the prisoners of war there, and that by means of petitions they could then persuade the republican leaders in the veld to abandon the war.[235] It is highly doubtful that Piet Cronjé took any heed of this request.[236]

Another outcome of the delegation's work in Cape Town was the establishment of a commission of inquiry to investigate the capture of certain prisoners of war. The deputation justifiably claimed that many surrendered burghers who were honouring the oath of neutrality they had taken had nevertheless been captured unfairly by the British. "Such people," in the view of the deputation, "certainly feel that they have been treated unfairly, and an investigation into these cases ... will go a long way to satisfying their grievances."[237] Milner recognised the necessity of such a commission and was also in favour of sending certain people to the concentration camps to work specifically as peace emissaries. He informed Kitchener that "mistakes were bound to occur, but it is most desirable when they are directly proved, to rectify them, ... some of the men ... would be useful if they returned to their own districts, remaining of course, in refugee camps until the business is over ... I am sure that ... the separation of the sheep from the goats, and the release – under control – of a few particularly white sheep would have a most salutary effect".[238] Kitchener approved this undertaking[239] and the first of Milner's "particularly white sheep" was a former member of the *Volksraad* in the Free State, H.S. Viljoen, and five others who were regarded as influential. They were approved as people who would be able to further the peace committee's cause and were sent to Bloemfontein on 25 February 1901. From there it was planned that they would be sent to concentration camps in Winburg and Kroonstad where they would then influence the women and children in favour of peace, so that the women could in turn put pressure on their men to abandon the struggle.[240]

Over and above the people who were sent as peace emissaries to the concentration camps, on 2 March the commission of inquiry began its work to establish which people had been unjustly captured. The commission comprised Major A.R. Stuart, Adv. Lange-Brink and

Adv. Botha, who represented the central peace committee in the Free State. They had to restrict their inquiry exclusively to surrendered burghers who had been unjustly captured and they had no jurisdiction over those who had been taken prisoner on the battlefield.[241] To begin with, the commission certainly did not have an easy task. Many of the surrendered burghers who applied to return to the Transvaal or Free State did not know under which of Roberts's many proclamations they had surrendered. To avoid this problem an attempt was made to treat each case on its merits.[242] Their work was not always faultless. There were 22 people whose applications were approved to go to concentration camps, but were subsequently returned on the grounds that they had refused to submit themselves to the British authorities.[243] However, the commission's mistakes did not prevent Kitchener from issuing the blanket instruction in May 1901 that all surrendered burghers should be sent to the concentration camps without any further investigation. This instruction made the work of the commission unnecessary and on 10 June 1901 it held its last meeting.[244] By the end of the war there were 3194 surrendered burghers who had been sent out of the prisoner-of-war camps in South Africa to the concentration camps.[245]

As far as the activities of the peace committees in the Cape Colony are concerned, it should be noted that the attempts to gain the support of influential Afrikaners was an abject failure. With the prisoners of war they were able to accomplish somewhat more by being instrumental in the establishment of a separate "peace camp" and also by having success in the release of bona fide surrendered burghers from their prisoner-of-war camps. The influence and significance of the peace movement as a whole will be assessed in the section which follows.

5 Results and significance of the peace movement

From the discussion on the activities of the various peace committees it is clear that they were very active, but that their foremost initiatives often failed to produce any positive results. This does not of course mean that their work bore no fruit at all. To assess these results it is necessary to look at the original objective of the peace committees. On the one hand, this was to persuade the ordinary burghers in the veld to lay down their arms, while on the other, they tried to convince the republican leaders to enter into peace negotiations with Britain.[246] The committees themselves were not empowered to initiate peace discussions on behalf of Britain and the British authorities were also very opposed to their making any move whatsoever in this direction.[247]

Firstly, then, it should be assessed whether the propaganda material used by the peace committees succeeded in persuading the fighting burghers to lay down their arms. There is evidence that, although some burghers continued to fight, they were very sympathetic towards the peace committee's cause.[248] After the war, Commandant-general Botha made mention of burghers who left the commandos from about February to March 1901 to lay down their arms.[249] According to members of the peace committee at Bloemfontein, burghers also deserted from General de Wet's commando.[250] General C.F. Beyers, too, mentioned that in August 1901 burghers in the Waterberg district surrendered in reaction to the efforts of the peace emissaries.[251] J.G. van Dijk of the Waterberg district, who had laid down his arms in the first three months of 1901, admitted that he had taken this step after hearing one of the peace committees' arguments which led him to realise "the folly of fighting against one who is stronger ... ".[252] Milner conceded that the foremost peace initiatives had failed, but still felt that "no doubt the activities of these Committees are making itself [sic] felt in unseen ways".[253] It is remarkable that during January 1901 – when the Boers took strong action against peace emissaries and disloyal burghers – according to the British records only 78 burghers dared to lay down their arms. In February and March 1901, however, 501 and 406 burghers respectively abandoned the struggle.[254] The sudden increase in the number of surrendered burghers possibly indicates that the peace committee propaganda only began to bear fruit after January 1901 and played a part in influencing some burghers to lay down their arms. However, it must also be remembered that Kitchener began to step up his military drives during February and March and also widened the scope and intensity of his concentration camp system.[255] These must also be seen as important contributing factors in the sudden increase of surrendered burghers.

Secondly, it is necessary to investigate the peace committee's attempts to persuade the republican leaders to enter into peace negotiations. These attempts were without any doubt an unqualified failure. What were the reasons behind this lack of success? Two historians put it down to the fact that, *inter alia*, the time was poorly chosen, because the successful Boer incursion in the Cape Colony at the beginning of 1901 had given the republican forces new heart.[256] Milner too was of the following opinion: "I do not think they [the Boers] have any idea of making peace while the Colony question is so prominent."[257] Although the advance into the Cape Colony, during which many rebels joined the Boer ranks, did indeed give the republican leaders new courage,[258] this cannot be seen as an important factor.

The most significant reason for the failure of the peace movement in the Transvaal and Free State lies in the determination of the Boer leaders that republican independence had to be preserved, and their utter refusal to allow the members of the peace movement any say at all over the continuation of the war.[259] The attitude of the Boer leaders was the direct result of the fact that the members of the peace movement had withdrawn voluntarily from the war and had then cooperated with the British. This branded these men as traitors in the eyes of their bitterender compatriots; by their conduct the collaborators thus forfeited any hope of functioning as an effective pressure group. A. Cartwright, the editor of *The South African News*, provides a balanced view of the status of the peace emissaries when he writes: "If the British Commander sent to a Republican camp a so-called 'envoy' who is a burgher of either Republics, the Republican commander would not only be justified under the laws of their states in regarding that messenger as a deserted soldier, but would be bound to so regard him." On addressing the issue of peace through the agency of republican peace emissaries he writes: "If Lord Kitchener were to send to the Republican armies an envoy whose mission was peace, we should rejoice, as we believe all justice loving people would rejoice ... But ... it would be necessary for a peace envoy to be a citizen of a neutral state, ... a condition which is not fulfilled by a surrendered member of either of the Republican armies, whose President or Commandant-general would necessarily treat him as a deserter."²⁶⁰ In the light of this, the initiatives of the peace envoys can certainly be seen as highly unrealistic.

There is no convincing evidence that the members of the peace committees benefited financially from their endeavours. Cartwright insinuated that the deputation to Cape Town was remunerated by the British, and that the members were thus "bought" by the enemy.²⁶¹ This allegation is unsubstantiated. The peace committees apparently financed their own initiatives and received no repayment or salary. The accommodation costs and expenses incurred by the delegation to Cape Town were carried by the peace committee in Bloemfontein. Some of the surrendered burghers in the Free State also made contributions by means of collection lists to cover the expenses of the peace committees.²⁶² As far as can be established, ex-President M.W. Pretorius, who had no official links with the peace committees, was the only peace envoy who received a significant amount of money (£50) for his services.²⁶³ It may well be that the British authorities made promises of better treatment or certain advantages to some peace emissaries. Kitchener, for example, quite conceivably made such a promise to Meyer de Kock without the nature of such an undertaking ever becoming evident.²⁶⁴

Although the members of the peace movement received no remuneration, this does not necessarily mean that their activities were morally justifiable. It is not the historian's task to make moral judgements, but because moral considerations were an integral part of the peace movement it is necessary to go into this briefly. Under normal circumstances the peace movement could perhaps be regarded as loyal resistance. But in time of war the parameters are different. The opinion of an outsider, J.A. Farrar, a nineteenth-century expert on warfare and military practices is pertinent here. Under the heading "The Limits of Military Duty", he writes: "It is surely something like a degradation to the soldier that ... his capacity for blind and unreasoning obedience should be accounted his highest attainable virtue. [This] idea has ... produced a ... conception of honour ... fitter for conscripts than for free men, that a man is held as by a vice to take part in a course of action which he believes to be wrong, and the assertion of his own personal moral responsibility is regarded as a source of infamy."[265] If Farrar's basic point of departure is accepted, it lends a measure of moral justification to the peace movement. This is particularly so if one takes into consideration the fact that the members or former members of the republican forces – in practice a people's army – regarded themselves as "free men" and not as members of a strongly disciplined professional army.[266] However, the jingoistic *Bloemfontein Post* took this argument too far in its leading article when it gave a skewed portrayal of the war situation and tried as follows to put the peace movement in general, and Piet de Wet in particular, into a more favourable light: "Of the brothers De Wet, the one is shooting peace envoys [sic], ambushing convoys or wrecking a train; the other having fought a good but ineffectual fight, is appealing to Afrikaner public opinion to help him to bring about peace in the land. Which is playing the better, the more patriotic part?"[267] It would be superfluous to supply an answer to this question.

Revd J.A. Steytler, despite his strongly republican stance, adopts another very clear view of this issue. By basing his arguments on searching questions he explains the ethical aspects of the question. Because of the convincing impact of his exposition, a long excerpt is quoted here. "I should like to say a word on the Ethics of the New Patriotism," he writes. "I hardly think that we shall find, upon examination, much to be enamoured of in the morals of this latest phase of Patriotism … I should like to put these excellent gentlemen, who represent … the New Patriotism, a few pertinent questions. I appeal, first of all, to your sense of honour, which I am anxious to believe is not wholly dead … Do you experience no qualms of conscience when your thoughts revert to that President who trusted you to support him to the end, but who today is being hunted like a partridge on the mountains, because duty and his oath of office call him to defend his country to the last ditch? Have you felt no sting of remorse as you looked across the fence at your brother who was made prisoner in honourable fight, and who now sits guarded by Maxims and bayonets, while you are basking in the short-lived sunshine of Imperialist popularity? And will not these considerations induce you at least to hold your peace and refrain from issuing appeals which can only embarrass and aggravate your former comrades, and estrange your … friends? … These are some of the questions … which I am anxious to put to the New Patriots. They are questions, I venture to think, which should give them pause in the course they are now pursuing – a course which I feel convinced is fraught with great dishonour to themselves."²⁶⁸

Would it not have been better if the republican leaders had decided to initiate negotiations with Britain and stop the war in reaction to the pressure from the peace committees? This type of question is obviously highly speculative. The fact is that the war continued for another 15 months. V.E. Solomon places great value on the pleas made by the peace committees. In a recent article he claims that "what concerns us ... is the fact that it was eventually [31 May 1902] decided to conclude peace on the very same grounds that the Handsoppers had for so long been advocating."²⁶⁹ This argument cannot be accorded too much weight. Conditions in the republics had deteriorated a great deal by May 1902 and cannot reasonably be compared with circumstances during the first three months of 1901. Hattingh's opinion appears to be more valid in this regard. According to him, the termination of the war at the beginning of 1901 would indeed have saved many lives and the destruction of property, but "the fact that the war ... still continued, and that it did so in the face of overwhelming odds, gave the Boer people a heroic image of almost supernatural endurance ... Despite the fact that the Afrikaner eventually lost the war, it was the way in which this came to pass and the price which had to be paid, which meant that the heirs of this generation of heroes could look back with great pride on their achievement."²⁷⁰ Then too, if the republican leaders had abandoned the war in reaction to the efforts of the peace committees, it might well have accorded the committees an exalted status after the war and a different niche in South African history.

The peace committees represent an important milestone in the history of the surrendered burghers. Whereas these burghers initially tried to remain neutral, it was not long before certain members of the group began, at first sporadically and then in a more organised fashion, to work towards ending the war. The organised peace movement was also a stark manifestation of the growing dissatisfaction of the surrendered burghers about the continuation of the war by their fellow countrymen. This was mirrored in the sharp polarisation

CHAPTER 3: THE BURGHER PEACE COMMITTEES, DECEMBER 1900 – SEPTEMBER 1901

which developed in Afrikaner ranks. Some Afrikaners clung to their belief in the unconditional continuation of the struggle; others were in favour of peace at any price. Certain surrendered burghers could not come to terms with the fact that they were unable to sway the republican leaders, and in collaboration with the British they turned to more militant means of acting against their own people. Thus, at the end of September 1901 the central peace committee at Kroonstad decided to suspend its activities and to form a well-organised burgher corps that would provide military support for the British columns.[271] The National Scouts and the Orange River Colony Volunteers, who were to come strongly to the fore in the last phase of the war, were thus, in this sense, an outcome of the abortive peace movement.[272] In the meantime, a considerable number of disloyal burghers continued to abandon the struggle, and the emphasis will now focus on the role of the surrendered burghers in the last 17 months of the war.

Notes

1 CO 417/307/37785A (FK 410, p. 568), J. Buttery – J. Ardagh, 16 November 1900.
2 See *Staats-almanak voor de Zuid-Afrikaansche Republiek*, 1898, p. 329.
3 *The South African News*, 15 February 1901 (news report).
4 CO 417/307/37785A (FK 410, p. 568), J. Buttery – J. Ardagh, 16 November 1900; Transvaal Archives, Inventory T99, Z.A.R., *Volksraad* lists.
5 *Telegrams and Letters ... Roberts*, v, p. 135, telegram C5821, Roberts – High commissioner, 29 October 1900; MGP 67/1283/00, R. Loveday – Maxwell, 30 December 1900.
6 *Telegrams and Letters ... Roberts*, vi, p. 10, telegram C5984, Roberts – Milner, 3 November 1900; CO 417/307/37785A (FK 410, p. 584), Roberts – British secretary of state for war, 11 November 1900 (copy); Spies, "Civilians", p. 153.
7 CO 417/307/37785A (FK 410, p. 566), Ardagh – Ommaney, 20 November 1900.
8 CO 417/307/37785A (FK 410, pp. 568, 571), Buttery – Ardagh, 16 and 17 November 1900. On the peace initiative of General Hendrik Schoeman to which Erasmus refers here, see Chapter 2, section 5 above.
9 CO 417/307/37789 (FK 410, p. 582), Chamberlain's margin notes, dated 26 November 1900.
10 CO 417/307/37785A (FK 410, pp. 573–6), Chamberlain – Milner, 1 December 1900; CO 417/316/40668 (FK 451, pp. 878–80), Wolmarans and Erasmus – Chamberlain, 12 December 1900.
11 CO 417/316/40668 (FK 451, p. 877), Milner – Chamberlain, 1 December 1900.
12 CO 417/316/40668 (FK 451, p. 877), Chamberlain's undated margin notes. Erasmus (and apparently also Wolmarans) spent the rest of the war in Britain and Europe. (PMO 3/323, report on Members of the Transvaal *Volksraad*, 30 June 1902).

Wolmarans wrote a letter from Paris on 23 January 1901 to *The Cape Times* in which he advised the Boers to give up the struggle. *The Cape Times*, 13 February 1901.

13 CO 417/315/40064 (FK 446, pp. 1014–6), Chamberlain – Milner, 7 December 1900. The version of this telegram in Cd. 547, 5, p. 10 is incomplete.

14 CO 417/315/40064 (FK 446, pp. 1017–9), Chamberlain – Milner, 10 December 1900. The version of this telegram in Cd. 547, 6, pp. 10–1 is incomplete.

15 *Milner Papers*, 45, (FK 1205, p. 1049), Milner – Kitchener, 31 October 1900; CO 417/296/40658 (FK 356, pp. 489–90). Milner – Chamberlain, 11 December 1900. By about June 1900 Milner also had his doubts about peace envoys. Spies, "Civilians", p. 138.

16 WO 32/882/8960 (A382), Milner – Chamberlain, 11 December 1900.

17 HC 26/92, Kitchener – Milner, 15 December 1900.

18 Hattingh, "Meyer de Kock", p. 171.

19 Translated from the Afrikaans. Hattingh, "Meyer de Kock", p. 171. See also Muller, p. 113.

20 PMO 23/1612, annexure C, sworn statement by M. de Kock, 29 January 1901; Hattingh, "Meyer de Kock", p. 170; Muller, p. 112.

21 PMO 23/1612, annexure C, sworn statement by M. de Kock, 29 January 1901.

22 PMO 23/1612, annexure C, sworn statement by M. de Kock, 29 January 1901.

23 HC 26/92, Kitchener – Milner, 15 December 1900.

24 Hattingh, "Meyer de Kock", p. 175.

25 PMO 23/1612, annexure C, sworn statement by M. de Kock, 29 January 1901. De Kock's version of the interview between him and Kitchener is the only one which could be traced.

26 Translated from the Dutch. WO 32/8960 (A382), "Burgher Peace Committee: Minutes of a Meeting held by Mr M. de Kock", 20 December 1900. This is a published Dutch copy which is to be found in the War Office records. The date (20 December) is however incorrect. Handwritten English minutes dated 17 December are in MGP 206/C/62/00. Typed minutes with handwritten alterations (PMO 70/P29) carry the same date (17 December). The latter date is correct because De Kock handed in his report of the meeting on 18 December. PMO 70/P29, De Kock – Poore, 18 December 1900; Spies, "Civilians", p. 278.

27 PMO 70/P29, De Kock – Poore, 18 December 1900.

28 MGP 206/C/62/00, "Second Meeting of Burgher Peace Committee held in Pretoria", 21 December 1900; PMO 70/P29 "Second Meeting ..." (typed and handwritten versions). See also Cd. 547, pp. 50–1 and WO 32/882/8960 (A382) for printed versions.

29 HC 27/93.

30 A.P.J. Cronjé should not be confused with General A.P. Cronjé of the Free State who was captured on 11 July 1901 at Reitz. When A.P.J. Cronjé voluntarily laid down his weapons on 14 June 1900 at Klerksdorp, according to the *Official History*, III, p. 230, he held the rank of commandant. However, the *Times History*, VII, p. 89, gives his rank at this specific time as general. The *Times History* appears to be correct. Although it is not exactly clear when he was promoted to the rank of general, a number of Boer commanding officers referred to him as "general" prior to his laying down his arms. Leyds Archive, 725(e), telegram 10 of 22 May 1900, General du Toit – Kruger; Leyds Archive, 725(e), telegram 32 of 22 May 1900,

General J.C. Smuts – General Oosthuizen; Leyds Archive, 725(e), telegram 43 of 22 May 1900, General Smuts – General A.P.J. Cronjé. A.P.J. Cronjé, who was in the vicinity of Christiana by 22 May 1900, also sent telegrams in which he referred to himself as "general". Leyds Archive, 725(e) telegram 58 of 22 May 1900, General Cronjé – General du Toit.

31 This explanation and identification of the members of the central committee is based on the following sources: MGP 67/1271/01, Van Rensburg – Maxwell, 28 January 1901; MGP 206/C/62/00, Maxwell – Chairman, central committee, undated and Maxwell – Kitchener, 30 December 1900; HC 27/93 Kitchener – Milner, 29 December 1900 and Milner – Kitchener, 3 January 1901; Transvaal Archives, Inventory T99, Z.A.R. *Volksraad* lists; MGP 207/C/70/00, S.J. Roos – Maxwell, 11 January 1901; MGP 206, C/62/00, Maxwell – Van Rensburg, 16 January 1901; PMO 70, P29, "Notes of a meeting held in the Office of Colonel Henderson, D.M.I.", 26 December 1900; PMO 79/P101, "Roll of P.O.W.'s in Pretoria since the British Occupation", 27 March 1901; PMO 30/2072, F.M. Fisher – Poore, 16 September 1901; E.J. Weeber, *Op die Transvaalse Front*, p. 216; Buys, p. 212; Spies, "Civilians", p. 311; Chapter 2, section 5 above.

32 MGP 207/C/87/01, Maxwell – Bosman, 14 February 1901. See Chapter 2, section 5 for Bosman's previous attitude to peace initiatives.

33 PMO 23/1612, annexure C, sworn statement by M. de Kock, 29 January 1901.

34 MGP 206/C/62/00 undated memorandum from Maxwell, but prior to 1 February 1901; PMO 1/9, O.C. Weeber – Poore, 16 January 1901; CO 417/323/9118 (FK 484, pp. 106–9), Milner – Chamberlain, 20 February 1901 and enclosure G.W.J. de Jager – District commissioner Volksrust, 24 January 1901 and M.J. Gregon – District commissioner Utrecht, 23 January 1901; MGP 165/2029/01, Commanding officer Krugersdorp – Maxwell, 18 January 1901.

35 *The Times*, 3 June 1901 (news report); CO 291/28/27112 (FK 900, p. 769), "Minutes of a public meeting held at Zeerust", 27 May 1901.

36 MGP 55/7967/00, Vallentin – Maxwell, undated and Groesbeek – Vallentin, 19 December 1900.

37 See C.T. Gordon, *The Growth of Boer Opposition to Kruger, 1890–1895*, pp. 158, 178–80 and *passim*; Hattingh, "Meyer de Kock", p. 171, note 54; Batts, pp. 131–3; *The Star*, 30 April 1902 (news report).

38 J.A. Coetzee, *Politieke Groeperinge in die Wording van die Afrikanernasie*, pp. 313–16. Coetzee's statement is based only on H.P.F.J. van Rensburg's political stance prior to the war.

39 Gordon, p. 279 and *passim*; Oosthuizen, "De la Rey", pp. 54–5.

40 Barnard, *Botha*, p. 7.

41 Translated from the Dutch. Pienaar, *Met Steyn en De Wet*, pp. 182–3.

42 For the standpoint of the burgher peace committees in this regard, see for example A787, Preller Collection, 28, pp. 26–7, H.P.F.J. van Rensburg and others – Botha, 24 January 1901 and *Verslag der Deputatie die naar de Kaap Kolonie werd afgezonden door de Vredes Comites in de Oranje Rivier Kolonie* (hereafter *Verslag der Deputatie ...*), p. 8, P.D. de Wet and others – Revds A. Murray, 6 March 1901. On the standpoint of the Boer leaders in the veld on 28 February 1901, see Anicus (pseudonym for L. Bierens de Haan), *De Onderhandelinge van Lord Kitchener en Louis Botha, zooals De Commandant-Generaal mij deze gebeurtenis verteld heeft*, p. 7 (hereafter *De Onderhandelinge ...*). For identification of the author of this pamphlet, see Spies, "Civilians", p. 321.

43 MGP 9/993/00, H.P.F.J. van Rensburg – Loveday, 9 July 1900; IOP 8/915, G.J.W. de Jager – Officers and burghers, district Wakkerstroom, 16 January 1901. In both cases it is insinuated that President Kruger was thus responsible for the outbreak of the war.
44 Kitchener Letters, I, (FK 1621, pp. 92–3), Kitchener – Brodrick, 7 March 1901.
45 PMO 70/P29, "Notes of a Meeting ...", 26 December 1900.
46 WO 32/882/8960 (A382), "Second Meeting ...".
47 MGP 206/C/62/00, Maxwell – Kitchener, 30 December 1900.
48 MGP 206/C/62/00, Maxwell – Rood, undated.
49 MGP 206/C/62/00, Maxwell – Chairman, central committee, undated. See also IOP 6/222, "Rules and Regulations for the guidance of local Peace Committees", undated.
50 CO 417/322/3943 (FK 480, p. 645), Milner – Chamberlain, 30 January 1901. See also *Africa (South)*, 636, pp. 42–3.
51 See Chapter 2, section 2 above.
52 CO 417/315/40064 (FK 446, p. 1019), Chamberlain – Milner, 10 December 1900. The version of this telegram in Cd. 547, 6, p. 10 is incomplete.
53 PMO 14/1022, Commanding officer Machadodorp – Poore, 29 March 1901. C. Potgieter's evidence is enclosed.
54 PMO 70/P29, "Notes of a Meeting ...", 26 December 1900.
55 Cd. 547, p. 50.
56 Spies, "Civilians", p. 280. See also Chapter 2, section 4 above.
57 MGP 258, "Circular Memorandum", 29, 21 December 1900. Italics: A.G.
58 M.A. Gronum, *Die Engelse Oorlog*, pp. 40–1; Martin, p. 7; *Times History*, V, pp. 86–7; Kruger, *Good-bye Dolly Gray*, p. 391. Le May, p. 96 goes a step further and alleges, without convincing documentation, that the peace committees suggested to Kitchener that the inmates of the concentration camps "should be subjected to a certain amount of hardship".
59 Muller, p. 112; Viljoen, *Reminiscences*, p. 203. In the Dutch version of Viljoen's book (*Mijne Herinneringen uit den Anglo-Boeren-Oorlog*, p. 208) he is not as categoric that it was the members of the peace committees and particularly Meyer de Kock who recommended the concentration system to Kitchener. Some Free State bittereinders were also under the impression that a member of the Free State peace committee, Piet de Wet, was the "father" of the concentration camp policy. Van Rensburg, "Ekonomiese Herstel", p. 181.
60 Spies, "Civilians", p. 282; Chapter 2, section 4 above.
61 Spies, "Civilians", p. 282; Hattingh, "Meyer de Kock", p. 176.
62 Stallard Papers (unsorted), C. Quinlan – C.F. Stallard, undated but received on 7 October 1943.
63 Roberts Papers (National Army Museum, R33/4) as quoted by Spies, "Civilians", p. 283. See also G. Arthur, *Life of Lord Kitchener*, II, p. 12; P. Magnus, Kitchener, p. 180.
64 PMO 70/P29, "Notes of a Meeting ...".
65 *The Bloemfontein Post*, 6 February and 1 March 1901 (letters from van P.D. de Wet); Spies, "Civilians", p. 312.
66 See HC 27/93, Milner – Kitchener, 30 December 1900; *The Bloemfontein Post*, 8 January 1901 (letter from peace committee at Kroonstad); *The Bloemfontein Post*,

21 May 1901 (letter from C.L. Botha); Van Rensburg, "Ekonomiese Herstel", p. 166.
67 CSO 3/105/01, "Minutes of Bloemfontein sub-committee", 9 and 21 January 1901; *The Bloemfontein Post*, 21 May 1901 (letter from C.L. Botha).
68 *The Bloemfontein Post*, 21 May 1901 (letter from C.L. Botha); GOV 257/20, H.S. Viljoen (chairman, Winburg peace committee) – Fraser, 2 August 1901 (copy).
69 WO 32/882/8960 (A382), Lieutenant-colonel Hull (commander, Durban) – Kitchener, 22 January 1901 and Kitchener – Commanding officer Natal, 5 February 1901.
70 MGP 73/2023/01, Assistant district commissioner Volksrust – Maxwell, 18 February 1901; CSO 3/105/01, "Minutes of Bloemfontein sub-committee", 4 February 1901.
71 WO 32/882/8960 (A382), memorandum by H.Y. Buller, 5 January 1901.
72 PMO 70/P29, De Kock – Poore, 18 December 1900; MGP 205/C/31X/00, list of peace envoys, 28 December 1900.
73 PMO 79/P101, "Roll of P.O.W.'s in Pretoria since the British occupation", 27 March 1901; MGP 206/C/62/00, Assistant provost marshal Kaapsche Hoop – Director of military intelligence, undated; MGP 166/3021/01, Hughes – Military governor, 21 March 1901; IOP 10/1375, Military governor – Military intelligence officer, 28 March 1901.
74 A787, Preller Collection, 14a, telegram 32 of 13 January 1901, Botha – General Spruyt, Commandant Mears, Commandant Erasmus and Field-cornet Pretorius.
75 Cd. 800, p. 25.
76 Oppenheim, II, p. 540. Italics: A.G.
77 MGP 206/C/62/00, General Stephenson – Director of military intelligence, 15 January 1901.
78 MGP 205/C/31X/00, List of peace envoys, 28 December 1900; PMO 79/P101, "Roll of P.O.W.'s ...", 27 March 1901.
79 Cd. 663, pp. 15–6, D.C. Joubert – J.M. de Beer, 17 January 1901 (translated published copies).
80 MGP 65/1011/01, Intelligence officer Lydenburg – Director of military intelligence, 20 January 1901, Joubert's report enclosed.
81 Cd. 663, p. 14.
82 Middelburg Archive, 75, minutes of the Special Military Court, "State vs D.C. Joubert and C.E. Fourie", 29 January 1901. The annexures pertaining to the case are not included in these minutes. For a full account of the trial of Joubert and Fourie, see Cd. 663, pp. 12–6. Compare also *Journal of the Principal Events*, X, p. 6 (translated published copies).
83 Middelburg Archive, 75, minutes of the Special Military Court, "State vs J.C.P. Grobbelaar and P.B. Coetzee", 29 January 1901.
84 PMO 15/1098, J.M. Graham – Director of military intelligence, 5 April 1901 and J.G. van Helsdingen – Military governor, 11 April 1901; WO/unsorted (A462), "Certificates of Engagement National Scouts, no. 5 Wing". The report on the court case in which Van Helsdingen was involved could not be traced.
85 MGP 73/2053/01, Military commissioner of police, Johannesburg – Director of military intelligence, 2 February 1901. Report on Mostert's activities.
86 IOP 6/159, Military commissioner of police, Johannesburg – Director of military intelligence, 7 January 1901. Report on Coetzee's activities.

87   *The Bloemfontein Post*, 7 January 1901 (news report). The names of the peace emissaries are not mentioned in the report. For identification, see MGP 205/C/31X/00, list of peace envoys, 28 December 1900.

88   PMO 17/1219, R. Johnson – Maxwell, 23 April 1901 and General Stephenson – Director of military intelligence, 11 March 1901, including General Stephenson's report on Johnson's activities.

89   PMO 20/1460, sworn statement by P.J. Adendorff and I.M. du Plessis, undated, translated. See also Spies, "Civilians", p. 315.

90   PMO 35/2410, Major H.F. Coleridge – Poore, 5 November 1901 and General P.J. Liebenberg – British commanding officer, Klerksdorp, 28 October 1901 (translated copies).

91   PMO 1/9, O.C. Weeber and six others – "Officers and Burghers of the Middelburg Commando still under arms", 9 January 1901, (translated copy) and O.C. Weeber – Poore, 11 January 1901.

92   Translated from the Afrikaans. Weeber, p. 223.

93   MGP 266, "Summary of Intelligence S.E. Districts", 27 January and 3 February 1901.

94   Translated from the Dutch. MGP 73/2053/01, resolutions of Krugersdorp peace committee, 19 January 1901 and letter by J.B. Wolmarans, 10 October 1900.

95   MGP 73/2053/01, Military commissioner of police Johannesburg – Director of military intelligence, 2 February 1901.

96   SOP/Natal, 5/406, G.J.W. de Jager – Assistant district commissioner Volksrust, 25 January 1901 and W.J. Congreve – Officer in command Natal, 5 February 1901. During May 1901, however, Kitchener gave orders that all surrendered burghers in the prisoner-of-war camps should be allowed to return. See Chapter 3, section 4 above.

97   IOP 8/915, G.J.W. de Jager and 13 others – "Officers and burghers of Wakkerstroom district", 16 January 1901 (translated copy).

98   MGP 67/1271/01.

99   This version of De Kock's peace initiative, his trial and execution is based on the following sources: Middelburg Archive, 75, minutes of the Special Military Court, "State vs Meyer de Kock", 29 January 1901 (no annexures); PMO 23/1612, translated report with annexures of the case against Meyer de Kock, 29 January 1901; Cd. 663, p. 8; Hattingh, "Meyer de Kock", pp. 181–2, 185; Spies, "Civilians", pp. 314–15; A. Kuit, *Kommandoprediker*, pp. 43–4; R.W. Schikkerling, *Hoe ry die Boere ('n Kommando-dagboek)*, pp. 140–1, 14 February 1901; Muller, pp. 112–15; Viljoen, *Reminiscences*, pp. 202–5.

100 WO *Confidential Telegrams* 527 and 528, Brodrick – Kitchener, 15 April 1901 and Kitchener – Brodrick, 16 April 1901.

101 PMO 23/1612, translated report with annexures of the court case against Meyer de Kock, 29 January 1901; Chapter 3, sections 1 and 2 above.

102 *Times History*, V, p. 93. See also Spaight, p. 146; Davitt, p. 476; W.E. Hall, *A treatise on International Law*, p. 656.

103 PMO 21/1532, G.F. Joubert – Kitchener, 22 May 1901 and Kitchener's undated comments in the margin.

104 *Journal of the Principal Events*, X, pp. 44–5, Kitchener – Brodrick, 29 July 1901.

105 MGP 206/C/6200, General Wynne – Henderson, 13 January 1901; *The South African News*, 21 January 1901 (news report); IOP 6/471, District commissioner Standerton – Maxwell, 24 January 1901; PMO 3/233, list of *Volksraad* members, 30 June 1902.

106 Translated from the Dutch. A787, Preller Collection, 28, pp. 26–8, Van Rensburg and other members – Botha, 24 January 1901 and Botha – Van Rensburg and other members, 1 February 1901. For translated versions of this correspondence, see IOP 8/913 and 8/915 as well as MGP 243/2000/01.
107 IOP S/1048, Van Rensburg and other members – Botha (translated copy).
108 This letter was first forwarded to the British military authorities for their approval. On 5 March Maxwell informed Van Rensburg that in the light of the fact that Kitchener had held discussions with Botha at Middelburg on 28 February 1901, the British commander felt it would be inopportune to send the letter. MGP 218/88/01.
109 Kitchener Letters, I, (FK 1621, pp. 34–5), Kitchener – Brodrick, 18 January 1901; Kitchener Letters, I, (FK 1621, pp. 47–8), Kitchener – Brodrick, 25 January 1901; Kitchener Letters, II, (FK 1622, p. 208), Kitchener – Brodrick, 17 May 1901.
110 IOP 7/917, Van Rensburg – Maxwell, 24 January 1901; IOP 8/916, J.F. de Beer – Military intelligence officer, 4 February 1901.
111 *The Bloemfontein Post*, 22 January 1901; Spies, "Civilians", p. 319.
112 WO Confidential Telegrams, 466, Kitchener – Brodrick, 30 January 1901; Spies, "Civilians", p. 319.
113 MGP 243/1945/01 Maxwell – District commissioner Potchefstroom, 7 February 1901; MGP 70/1721/01; District commissioner Potchefstroom – Maxwell, 7 February 1901.
114 A787, Preller Collection, 14 d, Botha – Magistrate Bethal, 26 January 1901.
115 MGP 83/3486/01, Maxwell – Commanding officer and district commissioner Potchefstroom, undated, but subsequent to 7 February 1901 (copy).
116 Milner Papers, 34, (FK 1172, p. 211), Maxwell – Milner, 10 February 1901.
117 WO Confidential Telegrams, 466; HC 27/93.
118 Kitchener Letters, II, (FK 1622, p. 209), Kitchener – Brodrick, 17 May 1901.
119 *The Bloemfontein Post*, 7 February 1901 (news report). See also H.J. May, *Music of the Guns: Based on two Journals of the Boer War*, pp. 159–60 for the same evidence.
120 WO Confidential Telegrams, 475a, Kitchener Brodrick, 8 February 1901; Spies, "Civilians", p. 321.
121 Kitchener Letters, II, (FK 1622, p. 209), Kitchener – Brodrick, 17 May 1901.
122 According to republican sources Kitchener asked her to do so, but British sources claim that she herself requested to go to Botha to propose the possibility of peace negotiations. For a discussion on this, see Spies, "Civilians", pp. 321–2.
123 CO 417/323/6857 (FK 485, pp. 9–10), Kitchener – Milner, 22 February 1901 and enclosure Botha – Kitchener, 13 February 1901. See also *Times History*, V, p. 183.
124 Kitchener Letters, I, (FK 1621, p. 47), Kitchener – Brodrick, 25 January 1901.
125 Translated from the Dutch. *De Onderhandelinge ...*, p. 10.
126 See Spies, "Civilians", pp. 321, 361.
127 On a chilly winter evening in May, Pretorius was interrogated by suspicious British soldiers on the front verandah of his home. He subsequently became ill and died a few days later on 19 May 1901. Spies, "Civilians", pp. 320–1.
128 *De Onderhandelinge ...*, pp. 8–9.
129 F.V. Engelenburg, *Genl. Louis Botha*, p. 51.

130 *De Onderhandelinge* ..., pp. 7, 12, 15. The excerpt is on p. 15. See also A787, Preller Collection, 16, "Memo voor C.G.", undated.
131 *WO Confidential Telegrams*, 498a, Kitchener – Brodrick, 16 March 1901.
132 PMO 22/1580, W.M. Edwards – Botha, 28 March 1901 (translated copy).
133 Breytenbach, *Geskiedenis*, III, pp. 5–6, 210, 438; PMO 22/1580, Edwards – Kitchener, 21 May 1901.
134 PMO 22/1580, Edwards – Botha, 28 March 1901 (copy) and Major (later Lieutenant-colonel) R.M. Poore's margin notes, 4 April 1901.
135 See Spies, "Civilians", p. 322.
136 PMO 18/1326, Captain H.C. Lother (intelligence officer) – Poore, 7 May 1901.
137 PMO 19/1412, P. Fouché – Major Wolmarans and members of the State Artillery, 27 May 1901 (translated copy).
138 Translated from the Dutch. Sinodale Bylae (Synodal Annexures) 1901, S: 1, 7, Revds W.F. Knobel and J.P. Wolhuter – Revd H.S. Bosman, 26 August 1901 and Revd H.S. Bosman – Revd W.F. Knobel and J.P. Wolhuter, 5 September 1901.
139 PMO 45/3051, Poore – Henderson, 11 February 1902.
140 CSO 3/105/01, "Minutes of Bloemfontein sub-committee", 9, 21 January and 8 November 1901.
141 *The South African News*, 27 February 1901 (weekly edition, news report based on information supplied by a Free Stater who was a close friend of both Morgendaal and Wessels); Breytenbach, *Geskiedenis*, I, p. 403; Spies, "Civilians", p. 312 note 240.
142 Translated from the Dutch. *The South African News*, 27 February 1901 (news report); PMO 29/2013, Assistant provost marshal Kroonstad – Poore, 3 September 1901; *Telegrams and Letters ... Roberts*, iii, p. 42, telegram C2497, Roberts – Methuen, 4 July 1900; WO 32/872/5353 (A374), sworn statement by Sophia Ellen Morgendaal née Wessels, 22 January 1901; Spies, "Civilians", pp. 143, 312; *OVS Volksraadsnotule* (OFS parliamentary minutes), p. 30, 22 September 1899. The excerpt is taken from this latter source.
143 WO 32/872/5353 (A374), Major-general W. Knox – Kitchener, 28 January 1901; Cd. 903. p. 80, sworn statement by Andries Bernardus Wessels, 13 August 1901.
144 A119, Renier Collection, 189, eyewitness account by I.J.C. de Wet on the Morgendaal episode, 27 February 1950; Cd. 903, p. 80, sworn statement by Andries Bernardus Wessels, 13 August 1901.
145 Eyewitness accounts by General de Wet's son, Izak, can be found in A119, Renier Collection, 189, 27 February 1950, as well as in I.J.C. de Wet, *Met Generaal de Wet op Kommando*, pp. 74–80. The eye-witness account of the colonial rebel, O.T. de Villiers, is in his book, *Met De Wet en Steyn in Het Veld*, pp. 67–9. (The specific copy which was consulted in the South African Public Library in Cape Town also has margin notes which were signed by O.T. de Villiers himself in 1917, and these throw somewhat more light on the incident.) The other four men who provided eyewitness accounts were Neudecker (PMO 82/35, 2 June 1901); Gerhardus Lourens Muller (WO 32/872/5353 (A374), 24 January 1901), H.A. van Heerden (A119, Renier Collection, 234, 17 April 1950) and Andries Bernardus Wessels (Cd. 903, pp. 80–1, 13 August 1901). A sworn statement by Sophia Ellen Morgendaal née Wessels (22 January 1901), based on what her husband told her on his deathbed, is in WO 32/872/5353 (A374) and the sworn statement of J.A. van Biljon (17 October 1901), which is based on evidence given to him by General C.C. Froneman, can be

CHAPTER 3: THE BURGHER PEACE COMMITTEES, DECEMBER 1900 – SEPTEMBER 1901

found in PMO 81/35. Dr Poutsma's account (undated) is in WO 32/872/5353 (A374) and the memoirs of veterans G.J. Joubert (undated) and General M. van Schoor (31 May 1950) can be consulted in A119, Renier Collection, 224 and 242 respectively. Their memoirs are based upon information provided by others after the incident.

146 Spies, "Civilians", pp. 313–14.
147 Cd. 903, p. 81; Spies, "Civilians", p. 314, De Villiers, p. 69; De Wet, *Met Generaal de Wet op Kommando*, pp. 79–80.
148 WO 32/872/5353 (A374), Knox – Kitchener, 28 January 1901; H.C. 27/93, Kitchener – Milner, 2 February 1901.
149 WO 32/872/5353 (A374), sworn statement by Sophia Ellen Morgendaal née Wessels, 22 January 1901; *The Bloemfontein Post*, 26 February 1901 (news report).
150 WO 32/872/5353 (A374), sworn statement by Gerhardus Lourens Muller, 24 January 1901; *The Bloemfontein Post*, 26 February 1901 (news report); A119, Renier Collection, 234, eyewitness account by H.A. van Heerden, 17 April 1950.
151 Arthur, *Kitchener*, II, p. 21, Extract from Kitchener – Brodrick, 28 February 1901.
152 Spies, "Civilians", p. 314. In February 1902 Kitchener was of the opinion that Morgendaal's death was one of the reasons why Steyn and De Wet continued fighting as "they fear the personal consequences to themselves of the illegal acts they have committed". Kitchener Letters, III, (FK 1623, p. 541), Kitchener – Brodrick, 14 February 1902. Kitchener's opinion in this regard is patently far-fetched.
153 F. Despagnet, *La Guerre Sud-Africaine au point de vue du Droit International*, p. 308.
154 CSO 3/105/01, "Minutes of Bloemfontein sub-committee", 11 March 1901; WO 32/882/8960 (A382), P. de Wet – Kitchener, undated, but received on 18 April 1901.
155 MGP 206/C/62/00, General Wynne – Kitchener, 15 January 1901 and Wynne – Henderson, 18 January 1901 (copies); MGP 71/1874/01, Major T.H.B. Forster – General Wynne, 8 February 1901.
156 *The Bloemfontein Post*, 17 January 1901 (news report); *The South African News*, 18 January and 8 February (news reports); CSO 3/105/01, "Minutes of Bloemfontein sub-committee", 21 January and 4 February 1901.
157 CSO 3/105/01, "Minutes of Bloemfontein sub-committee", 21 and 28 January 1901.
158 P.M. Botha, *From Boer to Boer and Englishman*, pp. 5, 25, 41–2. There is also a Dutch version of this brochure, which could not be traced.
159 *The South African News*, 28 March 1901 (letter from "Mikros"). In the particular newspaper which was consulted in the South African Public Library in Cape Town, a note written in pencil indicates the identity of the author.
160 HC 26/92, Milner – Kitchener, 6 December 1900.
161 PMO 12/885, R. Lynne (from New York) – P.M. Botha, 28 January 1901 and B. Blackwood (censor) – Poore, 11 March 1901.
162 MGB 3, A.J. Trollope – District commissioner Wepener, 12 January 1900; MGB4, K. Apthorp – Pretyman, 29 December 1900; MGB5, A.J. Trollope – District commissioner Boshof, 12 January 1901; MGB7, District commissioner Heilbron – Pretyman, 27 December 1900 and A.J. Trollope – District commissioner Harrismith, 21 December 1900.
163 Translated from the Dutch. *De Brandwacht*, 25 April 1901 (editorial).

164 WO 32/868 (A359), "Kroonstad Staff Diary", 16 August 1901; CSO 3/105/01, "Minutes of Bloemfontein sub-committee", 19 August 1901.
165 See Chapter 3, section 1 above.
166 Translated from the Dutch. *De Brandwacht*, 13 April 1901 (editorial).
167 See Chapter 10, section 1 below.
168 Translated from the Dutch. *The Bloemfontein Post*, 6 February 1901 (Piet de Wet's letter in "Onze Hollandsche Kolom" [Our Dutch column]). Translated versions of the letter can also be found *inter alia* in Cd. 547, pp. 64–5 and *The Cape Times*, 11 February 1901.
169 Kitchener Letters, I, (FK 1621, p. 36), Kitchener – Brodrick, 18 January 1901; Spies, "Civilians", p. 316.
170 Cd. 903, pp. 8–9 (translated published version).
171 J.G. Fraser, *Episodes in my Life*, p. 294.
172 WO 32/882/8960 (A382), E.R. Grobler – Kitchener, 3 May 1901.
173 *Telegrams and Letters ... Roberts*, i, p. 82, telegram C767, Roberts – Gatacre, 31 March 1900.
174 WO 32/882/8960 (A382), E.R. Grobler – Kitchener, 3 May 1901.
175 *The Bloemfontein Post*, 21 May 1901 (letter from Adv. C.L. Botha).
176 Translated from the Dutch. *De Brandwacht*, 25 April 1901 (editorial).
177 Translated from the Dutch. *De Vriend*, 13 May 1903 (letter from "Eene Misleide Burger" [A Certain Misguided Burgher]).
178 PMO 21/1495, 5 July 1901.
179 See Chapter 3, section 1 above.
180 CSO 3/105/01. "Minutes of Bloemfontein sub-committee", 26 August 1901.
181 CSO 52/3061/01, Murray – Goold-Adams, 11 September 1901; Spies, "Civilians", p. 362; J.H. Snyman, "Die Afrikaner in Kaapland, 1899–1902" (Unpublished D.Litt. thesis, Potch, 1973), pp. 308–10.
182 CSO 52/3061/01, Fraser – Thynne, 12 September 1901.
183 CSO 3/105/01, "Minutes of Bloemfontein sub-committee", 4 February 1901.
184 *The Cape Times*, 9 January 1901; *The Bloemfontein Post*, 8 January 1901 (open letters from the central peace committee at Kroonstad).
185 *The South African News*, 19 February 1901 (letter from a "South African").
186 CSO 3/105/01, "Minutes of Bloemfontein sub-committee", 28 January 1901.
187 CSO 3/105/01, "Minutes of Bloemfontein sub-committee", 4 and 11 February 1901.
188 PSY/30/28, General W. Knox – Kitchener's private secretary, 25 January 1901.
189 WO 32/882/8960 (A382), P. de Wet – Kitchener, undated, but received on 18 April 1901.
190 Translated from the Dutch. *Verslag der Deputatie ...*, p. 3, general report, 20 March 1901.
191 HC 147/unsorted, Theron – De Villiers, 1 February 1901 and De Villiers – Theron, 4 February 1901 (copies). See also E.A. Walker, *Lord De Villiers and His Times*, p. 383. John Henry de Villiers was the brother of Melius de Villiers, the Free State chief justice. During November and December 1900, Melius de Villiers, who lived for an extended period of time in Paarl during the war, made no bones about the

fact that he disagreed with the republican decision to continue fighting. (Cd. 547, pp. 15–6; M. de Villiers – Revd C. Maeder, [?] November 1900; *The Cape Times*, 4 December 1900 (letter from Melius de Villiers).

192 *Verslag der Deputatie* ..., p. 5, P. de Wet and others – Milner, 19 February 1901. Snyman, p. 384, alleges that Theron refused flatly to undertake any negotiations at all with the deputation. This is incorrect.

193 T.R.H. Davenport, *The Afrikaner Bond, the History of a South African Political Party, 1880–1911*, p. 232; P. Lewsen (ed), *Selections from the Correspondence of John X. Merriman, 1899–1905*, Van Riebeeck Society, 44, p. 351 n. 41.

194 *Verslag der Deputatie* ..., p. 5, P. de Wet and others – Milner, 19 February 1901.

195 Translated from the Dutch. *Verslag der Deputatie* ..., pp. 6–7, P. de Wet and others – Milner, 25 February 1901.

196 Translated from the Dutch. *Verslag der Deputatie* ..., pp. 6–7, P. de Wet and others – Milner, 25 February 1901.

197 *Verslag der Deputatie* ..., p. 7, Theron – P. de Wet and others, 20 February 1901.

198 *Cape of Good Hope: Debates in the House of Assembly*, p. 370, speech by T.P. Theron, 2 October 1902.

199 Davenport, p. 233.

200 H.W. Fourie, *Een Afrikaners Beroep op Afrikaners om te helpen vrede tot stand te brengen in Zuid-Afrika*, pp. 4, 16; *The Bloemfontein Post*, 18 April 1901 (open letter by K.T. van Zijl of Carnarvon taken from *De Graaff-Reinetter*, 11 April 1901).

201 CSO 3/105/01, "Minutes of Bloemfontein sub-committee", 4 March 1901.

202 CO 291/28/27112 (FK 900, p. 771), copy of minutes of the Zeerust peace committee, 27 May 1901.

203 *The Cape Times*, 12 February 1901,"Open Brief aan de Predikanten der Ned. Geref. Kerk in de Kaapkolonie" (Open letter to the ministers of the Dutch Reformed Church in the Cape Colony). This letter was published in both English and Dutch. See also *The Bloemfontein Post*, 6 February 1901 and Cd. 547, pp. 66–7 for printed copies.

204 CO 417/323/8176 (FK 484, p. 78), Milner – Chamberlain, 13 February 1901.

205 *The South African News*, 16 February 1901 ("A Reply to an Appeal" by "Mikros"). For identification of the writer, see Chapter 3, section 3, n. 159 above.

206 *De Brandwacht*, 25 April 1901 (editorial).

207 *The Cape Times*, 9 July 1901 (open letter from Revd H.E. du Plessis). This appeal was similar to that of Revds Knobel and Wolhuter in the Transvaal in August 1901. Chapter 3, section 2 above.

208 *The Bloemfontein Post*, 5 April 1901 ("An answer to the Reply of Mikros", dated 20 February 1901).

209 Translated from the Dutch. *Verslag der Deputatie* ..., pp. 4, 8–9, P. de Wet and others – Revd A. Murray, 6 March 1901 and Revd Murray – P. de Wet and others, 6 March 1901 as well as general report, 20 March 1901. See also Cd. 903, pp. 44–5.

210 *Verslag der Deputatie* ..., pp. 4, 9–10, P. de Wet and others – Revd J.H. Hofmeyr, 8 March 1901 and general report, 20 March 1901; Cd. 903, pp. 47–8.

211 Cd. 903, pp. 65–6, Bloemfontein peace committee – Revd Marquard, 27 May 1901 and Revd Marquard – Bloemfontein peace committee, 14 June 1901; Marquard, pp. 125–7.

212 CO 417/325/24226 (FK 495, pp. 162–6), G. Sprigg – Kitchener, 9 April 1901 and Kitchener – Sprigg, 11 April 1901, as well as Revd J.H. van Wyk – Kitchener, 5 June 1901 (copies). See also *Africa (South)*, 667, pp. 73–4.
213 *The Bloemfontein Post*, 7 February 1901 (letter by F.J.J. Celliers, dated 21 January).
214 HC 147/unsorted, 27 January 1901.
215 M.C.E. van Schoor (ed), "Dagboek van Hugo H. van Niekerk" in *Christiaan de Wet-annale*, I, 1972, pp. 86–8, 97–8, 101–2, 20 and 21 August 1900, 31 October 1900, 13 November 1900; Oosthuizen, "Krygsgevangenes", pp. 481–2.
216 *Verslag der Deputatie ...*, pp. 5–6, P. de Wet and others – Milner, 15 and 25 February 1901. See also HC 147/unsorted, Milner – Chamberlain, 20 February 1901; Cd. 903, pp. 2, 5–6.
217 SO/POW 15/1247, Lieutenant-colonel H.C. Money – Lieutenant-colonel C. Heyman, 28 July 1901.
218 *Verslag der Deputatie ...*, pp. 4, 6, 8, P. de Wet and others – Milner, 25, 27 February, and general report, 20 March 1901.
219 HC 146/unsorted, 5 March 1901 (copy).
220 HC 146/unsorted, 14 February 1901 (copy).
221 Milner Papers, 19, (FK 1137, p. 668), Milner – W. Hely-Hutchinson, 23 February 1901 (copy).
222 HC 146/unsorted, Milner – Walrond, 6 March 1901 (copy); Spies, "Civilians", p. 318.
223 HC 147/unsorted, Milner – Chamberlain, 6 March 1901 (copy).
224 *Verslag der Deputatie ...*, pp. 4, 8, P. de Wet and others – Milner, 27 February and general report, 20 March 1901; CO 48/552/22427 (FK 804, p. 1136), "Report of the Prisoners of War Enquiry Commission", 11 June 1901.
225 PMO 1/93, Lieutenant-colonel C. Heyman – Poore, 8 April 1901. For the circumstances of General M. Prinsloo's surrender see P.J. Delport, "Die Rol van Generaal Marthinus Prinsloo gedurende die Tweede Vryheidsoorlog" (Unpublished MA dissertation, UOVS, 1972), pp. 150–209.
226 SO/POW 19/1634, Poore – Heyman, 25 April 1901.
227 *The Cape Times*, 1 April 1901 (letter from "A Transvaal Burgher", dated 26 March 1901).
228 CO 48/551/14040 (FK 798, pp. 877–8), Hely-Hutchinson – Milner, 1 April 1901.
229 Cd. 1551, p. 17, "Report on Release and Return of Prisoners of War", 3 January 1903.
230 CO 48/551/13173 (FK 795, pp. 810–11), C.L. Botha – Hely-Hutchinson, 15 March 1901 and Hely-Hutchinson – Milner, 17 March 1900; HC 146/unsorted, Milner – Kitchener, 18 March 1901 and Kitchener's undated margin notes.
231 HC 146/unsorted, A.R. Stuart – O. Walrond, 28 March 1901 and A. Lange-Brink – O. Walrond, 28 March 1901.
232 CO 48/551/14040 (FK 798, p. 878), Hely-Hutchinson – Milner, 1 April 1901 and Cronjé's enclosed report; Cd. 903, p. 11.
233 SO/POW 16/1345, P.H. Fauré – General Piet Cronjé, 16 April 1901 (translated copy). Mention is made here of the petition which was sent to the Boer leaders who were still fighting.
234 CO 48/551/13173 (FK 798, pp. 808–9), C.L. Botha – Hely-Hutchinson, 20 March 1901.

235 SO/POW 16/1345, P.H. Fauré – General Piet Cronjé, 16 April 1901 (translated copy).
236 For information on General Piet Cronjé's disposition during his time as a prisoner of war, see H.P. van Coller, "Generaal P.A. Cronjé; 'n Lewensskets" (Unpublished D.Phil. thesis, UP, 1945), pp. 296–301.
237 Translated from the Dutch. *Verslag der Deputatie* ..., pp. 6–7, P. de Wet and others – Milner, 25 February 1901.
238 WO 32/860/5491 (A362), Milner – Kitchener, 14 February 1901.
239 Milner Papers, 19, (FK 1137, p. 668), Milner – Hely-Hutchinson, 23 February 1901.
240 CSO 4/170/01, Milner – Administrator of the Orange River Colony, 25 Februarie 1901. On their efforts in the concentration camps, see Chapter 4, section 2 below.
241 CO 48/552/22427 (FK 804, pp. 432, 436), "Report of the Prisoners of War Enquiry Commission", 11 June 1901; Milner Papers, 45, (FK 1205, p. 1091), Milner – Kitchener, 9 April 1901; *Verslag der Deputatie* ..., p. 4, general report, 20 March 1901.
242 CO 48/552/22427 (FK 804, p. 432), "Report of the Prisoners of War Enquiry Commission", 11 June 1901.
243 CO 48/552/22427 (FK 804, p. 434), "Report of the Prisoners of War Enquiry Commission", 11 June 1901.
244 CO 48/552/18539 (FK 803, p. 146), Hely-Hutchinson – Chamberlain, 29 May 1901; CO 45/1552/22427 (FK 804, p. 434), "Report of Prisoners of War Enquiry Commission", 11 June 1901.
245 PMO 3/240, "State of Boer Prisoners of War", 14 June 1902; *Official History*, IV, p. 704, Annexure 20; Chapter 2, section 2 above.
246 *The Bloemfontein Post*, 1 March 1901 (Letter from Piet de Wet); Chapter 3, section 1 above.
247 CO 471/322/3943 (FK 480, p. 465), Milner – Chamberlain, 30 January 1901; Chapter 3, section 1 above.
248 Brits, *Diary*, pp. 34–5, 13 January 1901; CO 417/300/7262 (FK 659, p. 568), statement by Commandant D.J.E. Erasmus, 21 January 1901 (copy).
249 Weeber, p. 223.
250 CSO 3/105/01, "Minutes of Bloemfontein sub-committee", 4 February 1901.
251 WO 32/869/7782 (A371), Beyers – General Ben Viljoen, 29 August 1901 (intercepted translated copies of republican documents).
252 MGP 136/15890/01, evidence of J.H. van Dijk, 22 November 1901.
253 Cd. 547, p. 63, Milner – Chamberlain, 13 February 1901.
254 SO/POW 16/1343, "Boer casualties during January, February and March", 1901.
255 Spies, "Civilians", pp. 311, 339–40, 364.
256 Le May, p. 96; Buys, p. 222.
257 Cd. 547, p. 35, Milner – Chamberlain, 29 January 1901.
258 See for example Commandant A.H. Malan's reaction to the invasion of the Cape Colony. Writing to his wife on 22 January from Pietersburg he said: "Oh my treasure ... I rejoiced and jumped and sang although it was after twelve o'clock. I could not sleep so I woke up all my men, had the horses saddled and roused the whole of Pietersburg ... Everyone to whom I told the news also shouted ... When I got back [we] sang all the psalms of praise and then I slept well." MGP 69/1645/01 (translated copy of intercepted republican letters).

259 See Chapter 3, sections 2 and 3 above.
260 *The South African News*, 17 January 1901 (editorial).
261 *The South African News*, 14 February 1901 (editorial).
262 CSO 3/105/01, "Minutes of Bloemfontein sub-committee", 4 and 18 March 1901; *The Bloemfontein Post*, 21 May 1901 (letter from Adv. C.L. Botha).
263 Chapter 3, section 2 above. The peace emissaries who were appointed by the central committee in the Transvaal each received £1, but it was given to them for personal expenses on their journey and not as remuneration. Chapter 3, section 2 above.
264 Hattingh, "Meyer de Kock", p. 176.
265 J.A. Farrar, *Military Manners and Customs: The Laws and Observances of Warfare in Ancient and Modern Times*, p. 276. This work first appeared in 1885 and was reprinted in 1968.
266 See Chapter 1, section 1 above.
267 *The Bloemfontein Post*, 18 February 1901.
268 *The South African News*, 28 March 1901 (letter from "Mikros").
269 Solomon, p. 19.
270 Translated from the Afrikaans. Hattingh, "Meyer de Kock", p. 185.
271 WO 32/882/8960 (A382), "Minutes of Extraordinary meeting of central peace committee", 20 September 1901.
272 *Times History*, V, p. 406; Spies, "Civilians", p. 364; Buys, p. 223; Chapter 6 below.

Chapter 4
The surrendered burghers from January 1901 – May 1902

1 Reasons why burghers continued to lay down their arms

According to British records, in the period from January 1901 to May 1902 about 6025 republican burghers voluntarily laid down their arms.[1] Although this cannot be compared with the large number of burghers who surrendered shortly after the British occupation of Bloemfontein and Pretoria (between 12 000 and 14 000 burghers, in round figures),[2] it nevertheless shows that the ranks of this group continued to increase steadily. In the period under discussion, some of these burghers were also destined to undertake active military service on the British side. In this chapter, however, the focus will fall primarily on those who simply withdrew from the struggle and did not provide any active military assistance to the British army.[3]

It has already been shown why many republican burghers chose to lay down their arms after the occupation of their capital cities.[4] During the last 17 months of the war there were also other factors that had a systematic demoralising impact on some members of the Boer forces.

With Kitchener at the helm, the British army went ahead aggressively, extending the campaign of destruction that Roberts had initiated. As a result, the two republics were virtually reduced to desolation. During the war approximately 30 000 homes were destroyed by the British army in the Transvaal and the Free State. Simultaneously the land was stripped of all sustenance and indeed anything which could be of use to the burghers, the aim being to reduce the resist-

183

ance of the Boer army.[5] The outcome of this policy was twofold. On the one hand it embittered some of the fighting burghers and strengthened their resolve. On 29 January 1901, for example, J. Rattray, a member of Commandant A.H. Malan's commando, wrote from Pietersburg to his father: "The Boers are at last really fighting like demons. And there is no question of giving in. I have seen a few fellows whose homes have been burned and everything else destroyed by the English. These men are like lions. They will fight on until every last shot has been fired."[6] On the other hand, to some burghers the British scorched earth policy was an indication that the continuation of the war would merely lead to further destruction of the country. A Boer's property meant a great deal to him – in time of peace it was the focal point of his livelihood. It is therefore understandable that to witness the results of the enemy's policy of devastation left some Boers heartbroken. Smuts remarked on this in January 1902 when he wrote to W.T. Stead: "A weak man is broken by adversity; the sight of the ruin of his property and family is sufficient in most cases to utterly crush his spirit."[7] On 13 May 1901, two weeks before his voluntary surrender, P.J. du Toit, General P.J. Liebenberg's secretary, made the following entry in his diary after watching the destruction of a number of homesteads at Hartebeesfontein: "I am damn certain it is a bloody mug's game to keep on. The whole country is going to blazes and we are daily being reduced to starvation and ruination. The few of us who remain over will eventually be woodcutters and water carriers of the English."[8] There can be little doubt that the British scorched earth policy (under both Roberts and Kitchener) demoralised some burghers and influenced their decision to lay down their arms.

The concentration camp system was another factor that influenced some burghers to abandon the struggle. The concentration camps had become the refuge for the homeless women and children who were left stranded after the British columns had passed. They also served as protection camps for the surrendered burghers so that the republican forces would be unable to re-commandeer them.[9] Indeed, one of the specific aims of the concentration camps was that they should encourage burghers in the veld to lay down their arms. If the fighting burghers wished to join their families, they could only do so by first laying down their arms and then entering the camps. As Smuts rightly says, "This measure was especially expected to hit the Boers in their most vulnerable part. For it is a well-known fact that the Boers are intensely domestic people, that husbands and wives, parents and children are intensely attached to each other."[10]

The concentration camp system by no means influenced the large majority of the fighting burghers to abandon the struggle, but some did indeed lay down their arms in order to rejoin their families, many of whom were living under dreadful circumstances in the camps. In May and July 1901 both Kitchener and Lieutenant-colonel Henderson of the military intelligence service claimed that the number of surrendered burghers was linked directly to the concentration camp system.[11] Some of the surrendered burghers themselves admitted that the reason for their surrender had been to be with their families and that they could not simply stand aside while their wives and children were suffering so much.[12] In November 1901 Milner declared that "A large number of the surrenders which have taken place during the present year, are undoubtedly due to the assurance which was given, that men voluntarily surrendering would be allowed to join their families in camps."[13]

A prominent feature of Kitchener's military strategy, particularly in the closing months of the war, was the construction of blockhouses and his organisation of massive military drives. The outcome was that the republicans came up against thousands of British troops – usually between blockhouse lines. These tactics meant that the freedom of movement previously enjoyed by the commandos was curtailed and that they often had to cover vast distances in order to escape the British network of troops and blockhouses. The combination of lines of blockhouses and drives was not an unqualified military success, but it did indeed cause a measure of demoralisation and physical exhaustion among the Boer forces.[14] Prompted by the voluntary surrender of 126 burghers in the week of 14 March to 21 March 1902, *The Star* reported: "The surrenderers again advanced to the high figures which have for some time been the rule. It is a feature that has ... become prominent since the policy of drive was adopted and it is clearly a direct result of that policy. The new system deprives the Boer of the choice which he usually has enjoyed of the area in which he will operate, and the instant he is driven from the region to which he belongs and to which he clings with utmost tenacity, his enthusiasm for remaining in the field begins to diminish."[15]

Linked to this, the Boers' preferred method of warfare and the influence of the climate must be analysed. The guerrilla warfare which the Boers conducted in the period from January 1901 until May 1902 made extremely high physical and emotional demands on the individual. Then too, by the end of the war there were burghers who no longer had horses and had to join the commandos on foot.[16] It is thus hardly surprising that some burghers were unable to keep up with the pace of commando life. Among the men who surrendered in August 1901 there were those who gave the reason that "they found it impossible to stand the life any longer".[17] The climate taxed the ability of the Boers to persevere even further. On the rigours of the winter of 1901 the *Times History* wrote: "The winter had set in, with all its attendant hardships and disabilities for guerillas whose home was the veld ... and who were destitute of most of the comforts and resources which fortify the army of a rich and powerful nation. Surely, the Boers could not survive the winter."[18] The republican leaders were aware of the dangers inherent in a harsh winter.[19] In January 1901 Smuts commented on the previous winter: "During the course of last winter the future appeared very dark; large surrenders of burghers were feared ... ."[20] In the winter months of 1901 there was indeed a considerable surge in the number of surrendered burghers. The factors that have already been discussed certainly also contributed to this increase, but it is nevertheless noteworthy that in May there were 1055, in June 894, in July 451 and in August 554 burghers who voluntarily withdrew from the war.[21] This gives a total of 2954 men and indicates that about 49% of the total number of burghers who laid down their arms between January 1901 and May 1902 (6025) did so during the winter months. In other words, about half the burghers who surrendered in the last 17 months of the war took this step in the winter and it is thus reasonable to conclude that they did not see their way clear to suffering the rigours of a harsh winter on the barren, open veld.

In a letter which Smuts wrote in June 1901 on behalf of the Transvaal leaders to President Kruger, he refers to the demoralising effect of the many hardships which the republican forces had to withstand and he then asks: "Is it any wonder that a certain portion of our burghers are demoralised and depressed?" Smuts feared that if matters did not improve "a significant number of these men will give themselves over to the enemy".[22] Revd J.D. Kestell, a well-loved national figure and commando preacher from the Free State, was of the opinion that most of the surrendered burghers had abandoned the struggle because of demoralisation[23] – a demoralisation that can largely be ascribed to the issues that have already been raised. The realisation that the republics were fighting against huge odds, coupled with the uncertainty about what the future might hold for the country as a whole and the individual in particular, also intensified the prevailing spirit of despair. Then there were also some of the fighting burghers who still clung to the vain hope that a European power would come to their assistance.[24] When it became clear that this was not going to happen, some burghers lost all hope and unlike their diehard comrades, they were not prepared to continue fighting if the republics were out on their own.[25]

Sheer self-indulgence may have played a role too. Captain C. Walton of the South African Constabulary describes a surrendered burgher by the name of J. van Wyk as "a man [who] prefers peace to fighting, luxury to discomfort, but ... he is also a Boer heart and soul, and will continue to be one within such limits as he considers compatible with his own safety and comfort".[26]

There were also burghers who were influenced by purely material considerations. Those who surrendered were permitted to take their livestock along to the concentration camps for protection if this was at all feasible, the only stipulation being that such livestock had to be their bona fide property.[27] However, in January 1902 Captain W.S. Bannantyne, the assistant provost marshal at Middelburg, in collaboration with the British commanding officer in this district made it known that surrendered burghers could take in all the livestock they could lay their hands on – irrespective of whether it belonged to them or not. And in February 1902 there were far more burghers who laid down their arms in the Middelburg area than in any other Transvaal district. On 19 March 1902, in reply to Lieutenant-colonel R.M. Poore's query about this, Bannantyne provided the following explanation: "In January 1902 the surrenderers in the District amounted to 95 and the cattle they brought in to 400. In February the surrenderers numbered 229 and the cattle 806. So far in March the surrenderers number 103 and the cattle they have brought in 770. I do not think that more than half these cattle belonged to the men who brought them in, but I am sure that many men who owned no cattle and had no inducement to come in have surrendered entirely owing to the knowledge that they would be allowed to keep any stock which they might sweep up and bring in."[28] It thus appears that material considerations were a very strong motivating factor and it is understandable that pro-Boer sources sometimes, with justification, question the argument that surrendered burghers abandoned the struggle because they felt that further resistance would serve no useful purpose. I.J. van Niekerk, a surrendered burgher from Brandfort, put forward this particular argument in his letter to *The Friend*, and in his caustic reaction to this excuse the editor retorted: "I.J. van Niekerk should instead have written that 'I have laid down my arms because I could see that my little herd of sheep would be seized and they were more dear to me than my independence.'"[29] According to the British director of supplies there were some surrendered burghers who even succeeded in collecting more livestock during the course of the war than they had owned before the hostilities began.[30]

On 7 August 1901 Kitchener issued his well-known proclamation, demanding that all burghers in the veld should surrender before 15 September 1901. Military leaders and members of the republican government who continued fighting after this date were threatened with permanent exile from South Africa and confiscation of their property.[31] This threat, which can be interpreted as an attempt to use intimidation to force those who were still fighting to lay down their arms, made very little impact on the number of surrendered burghers. Kestell was not aware of more than 30 burghers who abandoned the struggle as a direct result of this proclamation.[32]

Following the failure of his banishment proclamation, Kitchener sent out a general circular on 25 December 1901 to the commanding officers of the British columns instructing them that henceforth any burghers who gave themselves up individually should be regarded as prisoners of war and not as surrendered burghers. By way of explanation he wrote: "I prefer those that are discontented to remain out with their commandos and use their influence to bring about a complete, not a partial peace, so that all may go back to their farms." However, if a corporal, field-cornet or commandant with 10, 25 and 50 burghers respectively came forward voluntarily to give themselves up, Kitchener explained that they would not be deported and they would be permitted to keep their property.[33] This was an overt attempt on Kitchener's part to allow his threat of banishment and confiscation to sink in, and simultaneously to swell the ranks of the surrendered burghers. The policy was not enforced consistently[34] and by and large the republican forces took little heed of it,[35] but there were, however, a few exceptions. Field-cornet Nicholas Gouws of Middelburg and a number of his men surrendered in January 1902 following Kitchener's announcement,[36] and it was alleged that Commandant A.B. Dannhauser of Vryheid and 100 of his burghers also surrendered in January 1902.[37]

From the above discussion it is clear that there were a variety of factors which motivated certain republican burghers to withdraw from the war. Cumulatively, these considerations meant that the ranks of surrendered burghers were not only maintained but also increased during the last 17 months of the war. It is impossible to gauge the relative importance of each issue. Demoralisation and defeatism caused by the circumstances and the difficult conditions under which they were fighting, as well as the incentive of material gain can perhaps be singled out as the most important reasons. Then it must also be remembered that the decision to continue fighting rested with each individual burgher. He had to decide whether, despite the overwhelming odds and the many trials and tribulations, he was prepared to fight for a just cause to the very end or whether he should instead take the line of least resistance. Confronted by this dilemma, the burgher who took the decision to give up quite simply lacked the inner strength and courage to continue the struggle.

Because the surrendered burghers did not all lay down their arms for the same reason, it follows that they cannot all be labelled with the same tag. Johanna Brandt, who played an important role in the unofficial Boer "Secret Service" in Pretoria, identified three types of surrendered burghers. Firstly, there were those who saw no earthly chance of success for the republican cause. They were convinced that to continue the struggle was futile and wanted to bring all the suffering to a timely end. Secondly, there were those who were warweary and simply did not care any more which side emerged as the winner. They wanted to distance themselves as far as possible from the hostilities and chose not to be involved in any facet of the war. In a third category were the people who were exclusively concerned about their own material well-being.[38] There were certainly also surrendered burghers who might well have been included in all three categories, but this broad division is a useful one.

In absolute contrast to the surrendered burghers, when 31 May 1902 finally dawned there were those diehards who had fought remorselessly on to the very end – the so-called bitterenders. To present a comprehensive explanation of why these leaders and ordinary burghers continued such an unequal struggle for more than 31 months is a complete study in itself. In passing it can be noted that the exceptional leadership and military expertise of the Boer generals, as well as the self-sacrifice and strong desire for freedom of the ordinary burgher played an important role in the decision to continue fighting.[39] A.Cartwright, editor of *The South African News* also puts this will to persevere down to the "the Boer's faith in the leading of God and the justice of his cause".[40] In similar vein Smuts, in his inimitable style, touched on the very heart of the matter in January 1902 when he wrote to W.T. Stead: "I know the difficulty for the modern man of action and intelligence, accustomed as he is to ideas of natural laws and physical or economical explanations of all phenomena, to understand or appreciate the tremendous force of faith in the affairs of the world, but unless he overcomes this difficulty the present war will, in all essential respects, remain for him an insoluble mystery. A mustard seed of real faith avails more in the affairs of the world than mountains of might or brute force – and only he who thoroughly understands this will be able to appreciate the true inwardness of the present struggle ... This view, which will seem strange and unintelligible to matter-of-fact politicians, is today held by the bulk of the Boers in the field and explains much which must otherwise forever remain inexplicable. To call them names ... explains nothing, and one must explore to a deeper level of their national consciousness in order to find the true cause of their unique persistence ... In short the Boer cause has become a Boer religion, adversity has converted their political creed into a religious faith; and thus hope and faith and strength have been wrung from weakness and despair itself."[41]

As far as this close identification between religion and the continuance of the war is concerned, the stance of the surrendered burghers differed vastly from the view which Smuts, as representative of the fighting burghers, expresses here. As self-appointed spokesmen of the surrendered burghers, Piet de Wet, Adv. C.L. Botha and D.J.H. van Niekerk had this to say: "As Christians and faithful burghers we were obedient to our government when they declared war and called upon us to fight, and indeed we fought manfully. However, when we saw that the struggle had been lost, when our capitals had been occupied and our government disbanded, ... we decided that all further continuance of the war was absolutely futile ... it could only lead to proliferation of the dreadful destruction of our country and the disintegration of our nation – yes, to do so would have been a struggle against the Almighty, the Lord of Hosts Himself, who had ordained the outcome of this war against us ... True to our consciences, true to God's word, we could no longer be part of this futile and suicidal guerrilla war."[42] Revd H.E. du Plessis of Lindley, who identified with the cause of the surrendered burghers, reiterated this point of view. He was of the opinion that God had already made it very clear that the republics had lost the war and that it was the duty of the republicans to accept the inevitable.[43] The surrendered burghers were naturally entitled to their own interpretation on this issue, but it cannot be denied that they did not possess the firm convictions and utter willingness to make sacrifices which were so characteristic of the attitude of the bitterenders.

2 Surrendered burghers in the concentration camps and towns

In the second half of 1900 the British authorities began to take the surrendered burghers to protection camps (which were in reality nothing other than concentration camps) to prevent their being commandeered again. From March 1901 surrendered burghers who had been placed in prisoner-of-war camps in error were transferred to concentration camps on the recommendation of Piet de Wet, Adv. C.L. Botha and D.J.H. van Niekerk. In May 1901 Kitchener laid down a general rule that all surrendered burghers could move out of the prisoner-of-war camps to the concentration camps,[44] so most of the burghers who had surrendered in the period January 1901 to May 1902 also landed up in the camps. As a reason for this Kitchener explained: "I am forced to bring in for protection all surrendered burghers and their families until the country is sufficiently secure from Boers raiding to allow them to go out again and live on their farms."[45] This policy was then applied uniformly in the case of all surrendered burghers.[46]

Initially the British authorities differentiated between the food rations provided for the families of loyal republicans and those supplied to surrendered burghers. On 1 December 1900 Kitchener instructed Maxwell to draw up a differentiated ration schedule and "to make marked differences between those who are refugees from Boer oppression (sic) and those who have to be removed from their farms, owing to their families being out in commando".[47] From the weekly scale of rations which Maxwell drew up for the Transvaal it appears that surrendered burghers received the same amount of flour and salt as the other people in the camp, but they were supplied with an additional two ounces of coffee and four ounces of sugar. They also received meat on occasion, a privilege that was not afforded to the other inmates.[48] In the Free State there was less difference between the two sets of rations.[49] The differentiated ration scales were applied for four months at the most and by March 1901 all white inmates of the concentration camps, with a few insignificant exceptions, received the same rations.[50]

There were some surrendered burghers who were dissatisfied with the amount of food they received in the concentration camps. J.A. Roos at the camp in Irene appealed to the superintendent: "Notwithstanding reiterated protests against the starvation scale ... I cannot trace the slightest amelioration ... According to the highest medical authorities the human system demands at least 5 ounces of proteins per diem for bare nourishment; your Government rations here will scarcely yield two ounces. With what pleasure do one and all who have surrendered to a generous foe, hail the opportunity of … a sacredly binding oath; but what gloomy thoughts must spring up when the pangs of hunger remain unappeased."[51] Other surrendered burghers, quite possibly representative of the majority, did not complain about the rations. J.C. Kruger, who had been transferred from the Green Point prisoner-of-war camp to Kroonstad, claimed that, "From the time we arrived at the refugee camp … the treatment was first class, and if anybody complained it would be a lie. We received enough rations and all the articles we were in want of."[52] P.J. Delport of the same camp confirmed Kruger's opinion.[53] In the Transvaal, surrendered burghers in the Middelburg and Volksrust camps also expressed their satisfaction with their treatment and the rations they received.[54]

That the majority of the surrendered burghers were satisfied with the food rations can be attributed to their willingness to cooperate with the British authorities in the camps and thus earn money to supplement their rations at the camp shops.[55] Because the other inmates of the camps were mainly children, women and elderly men, and the surrendered burghers were physically able to undertake all kinds of odd jobs, it is clear that they would have been used for this purpose. Then too, most of the surrendered burghers were prepared to be subservient to the British authorities, particularly if they were paid to do so. The type of work which the surrendered burghers undertook in the camps included the pitching of tents, the repair of camp equipment and the making of camp furniture, bedsteads and coffins. They were also expected to sweep the camps clean.[56] For their services each surrendered burgher was paid between 1s and 2s 6d per day, W.K. Tucker, the general superintendent of the concentration camps in the Transvaal, considered the payment "very moderate", and added that "it cannot be expected that white men, especially Boers, will work very hard for that sum".[57]

Some surrendered burghers were not particularly anxious to ameliorate the hardship suffered by the women in the concentration camps. Mrs H.G. Bekker of the Klerksdorp camp claimed that a fierce windstorm hit the camp on the night of 15 September 1901 and some of the tents blew over. She was ill and went to seek help from the surrendered burghers in the camp. The person she approached refused to help, and swearing at her said: "Now go and call your Paul Kruger!"

According to Mrs Bekker many of the surrendered burgers adopted the attitude that they had not come to the concentration camps to "take care of other men's women".[58] Dr G.B. Woodroffe, the medical superintendent of the camp at Irene, expressed himself strongly on the unwillingness of many of the surrendered burghers to help the Boer women. In his report of July 1901 he wrote: "The idea of helping the helpless does not exist in the conscience of the stalwart burgher. Over and over again a woman whose husband is fighting or a prisoner of war, has to sit and nurse her children, and ask in vain of a fine, well-built, noble 'patriot' to chop her wood or fetch her rations or her medicine, his reply is, 'I have no time' or something to that effect. There is no such thing as gallantry amongst these creatures, unless paid for, when another name will cover the term gallantry."[59]

Some of the surrendered burghers were also harsh with the children in the camps. Mrs M. Fischer makes mention in her diary of a surrendered burgher in the Standerton camp who hit a ten-year-old boy.[60] In the camp at Howick a surrendered burgher forced the wounded twelve-year-old son of Mrs G.W. Joubert to help pitch tents for a full ten days – under the threat that unless the boy helped him he would see to it that the family's food rations would be reduced.[61]

There were only very few surrendered burghers who took the trouble to help the women. Mrs C. Otto testified that a surrendered burgher in the camp at Mafeking took pity on her and organised that she was settled in a tent when she arrived absolutely exhausted at the camp.[62] Adv. A. Dieperink, a Transvaler who had previously been a member of the First *Volksraad* and had distanced himself from the republican war effort, also gave a helping hand to the inmates in the Middelburg camp. Dieperink, who spent seven months in this camp, went to a great deal of trouble to ease the suffering of the women and personally spent £400 in an attempt to reduce the high death toll among the children.[63]

The unsympathetic attitude shown by most surrendered burghers towards the defenceless women and children contributed a great deal to the very poor relationship between these two particular groups. It is thus no wonder that after a while the women preferred to receive assistance from a "Damned Redneck" (a Briton) rather than from a "*Schelm* [dishonest] Boer".[64]

Another factor in the deterioration of this relationship was the disposition of the women towards the surrendered burghers. The women had very little sympathy for them, and despite all the suffering and hardships of life in the concentration camps they still firmly supported their men who were on the battlefield. Captain A. Hume, who was involved in the supervision of the concentration camp at Bloemfontein, informed Goold-Adams: "I have opportunities of gauging the feelings and sentiments of the people on various subjects ... and I have no hesitation in saying that ... those women whose people are still on commando are continually abusing the men in the camps, calling them cowards and those fighting, heroes. This causes a great deal of unrest."[65] The superintendent of the camp at Volksrust also testified about the attitude of the women towards the surrendered burghers: "The feeling between families of men still on commando and those who have surrendered appears to be very bitter and the men of the latter class have to put up with a great deal of abuse, while in the performance of their duties from the wives of men on commando who call them the slaves of the English and 'handsoppers' ... Wordly altercations are frequent."[66] According to W.K. Tucker the women succeeded in making life very unpleasant for the surrendered burghers in the camps.[67] When some women were on friendly or even cordial terms with the surrendered burghers, this behaviour did not meet with the approval of those who were fiercely loyal to the republican cause.[68]

Some surrendered burghers found it unbearable to be constantly reminded of their apostasy. "The Boers and families desiring to be loyal to H.M. Govt., being in the minority, are most unmercifully persecuted by the anti-British sex," complained T.C. Roberts, a surrendered burgher who had apparently been sent to the camp at Irene.[69]

In the Free State, P.A. Groenewald, a surrendered burgher who was in the Heilbron camp, suggested that the two groups should be housed apart because of the constant ructions between the surrendered burghers and loyal women.[70] As far as the surrendered burghers themselves were concerned, the British authorities did not at any stage go so far as to make a formal separation in the concentration camps, but provision was indeed made for those who actively assisted the British army in a military capacity. In the Vereeniging camp members of the local burgher corps were housed apart, and an additional camp exclusively for National Scouts and their families was constructed at Meintjes Kop.[71]

The attitude of the women towards the surrendered burghers contributed in some measure to the decision by some of these men to leave the concentration camps and rejoin the commandos. According to Lieutenant-colonel R.M. Poore, in the Heilbron camp there were "several wives of men on commando who taunt the men who have surrendered, and do their best to induce them to rejoin the enemy".[72] At Nylstroom a certain Mrs E.L. Nel was prepared to give a surrendered burgher Z.C. de Beer permission to marry her daughter only if he agreed to rejoin the commandos.[73] N.J. Scholtz, the superintendent of the Irene camp, was of the opinion that the "continual sneering ... no doubt tends to make some of the men bitter and so drive them from the camp to rejoin the enemy".[74] By 20 July 1901 there were 73 surrendered burghers who had left the concentration camps to take up commando service again.[75] In February 1902 the number had grown to 324. W.K. Tucker puts this down primarily to the "taunts and gibes" of the women.[76]

There were also other reasons why some surrendered burghers left the camps to rejoin the commandos. Maxwell made mention of the fact that many of those who escaped were unmarried and did not have families to care for in the camps.[77] There were also those who came to the personal decision that perhaps, after all, it was their duty to help the Boers in the veld.[78] P.J. de Wet van Aswegen, a 16-year-old burgher who escaped from the concentration camp at Bloemfontein, admitted after he had been recaptured: "I don't think it is right for a man to be in a Refugee Camp, he should either be a Prisoner of War or else fighting." W.C. Nel, his friend who escaped with him, said that they had never asked to be sent back from the prisoner-of-war camp in Green Point. According to Nel the two men had found their camp life at Bloemfontein extremely unpleasant.[79]

During the last 17 months of the war the republican forces still on occasion confiscated the livestock belonging to surrendered burghers and harvested the wheat on their farms. The provisions procured in this way were then sent to the commandos.[80] The Boers no longer really put much effort into forcing those who had surrendered to rejoin the commandos. According to Emily Hobhouse, after the Middelburg negotiations (28 February 1901) the Boers decided "to wash their hands of the surrendered burghers".[81] The fact that most of them were housed in concentration camps under British protection naturally also made it more difficult to re-enlist these men. However, there were a few cases where raids on concentration camps were undertaken expressly for this purpose. On 27 July 1901 Commandant W.D. Fouché and 70 men attacked the camp at Aliwal North, but of the 689 men in the camp only five of them rejoined the commando. A.C. Trollope, the general superintendent of the concentration camps in the Free State, saw this as an indication "that very little sympathy exists between the Boers still fighting and the refugees".[82] An attack on the Pietersburg camp by C.F. Beyers met with more success. Nine surrendered burghers who had managed to escape had informed Beyers prior to the attack that there were many people in the camp who would welcome the opportunity to rejoin the commandos.[83] At half past two in the morning of 23 January 1902, Beyers stormed the camp with between 30 and 40 of his men. Most of the surrendered burghers were keen to rejoin, although there were a few who had to be pressurised to do so. In total there were 148 surrendered burghers who rejoined the commando, four of whom subsequently went back to the British lines.[84]

In some concentration camps there were surrendered burghers and their like who tried to indoctrinate the women by talking to them openly in favour of peace without independence. In the Free State, H.S. Viljoen (a former member of the *Volksraad*) and five other people who had been sent back from the Green Point prisoner-of-war camp through the mediation of Milner, tried to make the women in the camp at Kroonstad and Winburg change their outlook. They worked on the assumption that if the women could be won over, their men on commando would be influenced to lay down their arms.[85]

But Viljoen and his men had little success and the petitions which they circulated in the concentration camps were signed by very few. The surrendered burghers did not enjoy the confidence of the women and they were often regarded as spies. In the Bloemfontein camp a petition which was circulated on the recommendation of J.G. Fraser produced only 80 signatures, and on 10 June 1901 it was decided to abandon these initiatives.[86]

The longer the war lasted, the closer the cooperation between certain surrendered burghers and the British authorities grew. In May 1901 Maxwell recommended that reliable surrendered burghers should be appointed in a supervisory capacity at the Irene concentration camp. In July 1901 there were 25 men appointed in these posts and by November 1901 the number had risen to 50. To strengthen their hands in carrying out disciplinary duties, these burghers were provided with armbands bearing the letter B.C.P. (Burgher Camp Police).[87] In October 1901 Kitchener instructed that each concentration camp should set up a police department manned by surrendered burghers.

The various superintendents were told to accept only those surrendered burghers who offered their services voluntarily. These people received payment of 1s per day as well as one pound of sugar, four ounces of coffee and 1 pound of meat per week in addition to their normal rations.[88]

The camp police had to assist the superintendent. W.K. Tucker claims that such help was imperative because the superintendents were already sorely stretched.[89] Another reason is presumably that the surrendered burghers could communicate more easily with the inmates in their own language. The camp police were responsible for the maintenance of general discipline and the monitoring of sanitary measures in the camps. For example, they had to see to it that the lower part of the tent flaps were rolled up during the day and that the camps were tidy and clean. The superintendent of the camp at Volksrust reported that, "The Camp police ... have proved of great assistance in preventing filthy practices, which hitherto disgraced and polluted the camp."[90] The camp police at Irene also had to fetch the women and children at the station and help them to carry their possessions to the tents.[91]

In the course of their duties the camp police were sometimes harsh towards the women. Mrs D. Jones, who was in the camp at Klerksdorp, reminisced in 1917 that a member of the camp police walked around with the camp doctor to take those who were ill to the hospital and that he had wrested some of the children from their mothers' arms despite "their begging and pleading that the children be given back to them". After the war Mrs I.A. Grobler de Clerq also made mention of the "brutal" behaviour of the "Boer police" or the "witdoeken" (white scarves) as they were called by the women.[92]

Some members of the camp police also had to stand guard at night to prevent anyone from leaving the camp or any unauthorised person from entering.[93] On 4 January 1902, J. Ferreira, the man in charge of the police at Irene, reported that they had arrested six people who were planning to escape,[94] and in March 1902 the camp police also captured ten escapees outside Irene.[95] The camp police at Nylstroom had less success. Assistant Field-cornet S.A. van Emmenis, who was an officer under General Beyers, managed to escape from the camp in broad daylight right under the noses of the camp police. Van Emmenis had voluntarily laid down his arms and gone into the concentration camp to visit his wife for a while and to collect information about the welfare of the women in the camp. His plan was to escape as soon as he had gathered the necessary information. On 25 October Major E.F. Brereton, the assistant provost marshal, was visiting the camp and his horse was tethered in front of the camp office. Van Emmenis casually untied the animal and galloped off before the members of the camp police realised what was happening. In vain they raised the alarm, but in the meantime Van Emmenis had even taken the time to say a last goodbye to his wife before disappearing.[96]

On 25 April 1901 Kitchener ordered that, where possible, all surrendered burghers were to be permitted to bring their livestock to the concentration camps. He also thought it best that the owners of the animals should be issued with Martini-Henry rifles and a limited amount of ammunition in order to protect their livestock and ensure that the Boers did not steal these animals.[97] However, the superintendents of the concentration camps armed only a few carefully chosen surrendered burghers for this purpose. In the camp at Nylstroom the superintendent armed eight members of the camp police to guard the cattle enclosures near the camp.[98] During 1901 a special Cattle Ranger Corps comprising former republican burghers was established to take care of the herds of livestock.[99]

Then there were some surrendered burghers who served as detectives and intelligence agents in the camps and these people were also paid for their services. They were given substantially more than the camp police and could earn from between 5s to 7s 6d per day. Their task was to prevent possible conspiracies in the concentration camp and to inform the camp authorities about the attitudes and disposition of the women.[100] After the attack on the Pietersburg camp on 23 January 1902, Kitchener laid down that there had to be some of these agents in each camp.[101] The intelligence agents aroused a great deal of bitterness because of the manner in which they approached their duties. Forty-seven years after the war, Mrs R. Smith, who had been an inmate in a Free State concentration camp, referred to these men as the people who "did the dirty work with their witch-hunting and eavesdropping outside the tents".[102] Henderson of military intelligence reported that "the Camp authorities rather object to Intelligence men peeping about the camps, and are inclined to say that the Intelligence men give trouble. I can't provide plaster saints for that kind of work, but the men we are using have prevented half a dozen separate schemes of desertion from the Camps."[103] After the war an English-speaking resident of the Transvaal described the actions of the intelligence agents "as ostensibly the cause why the women and children had to suffer in the concentration camps, as they reported every little outburst of womanly indiscretion to the authorities and for which these unfortunates afterwards had to suffer. They were the spies in the camps and they were despised by the women ...".[104]

The women who were reported to the camp officials were usually punished by being placed in an enclosed area – described by Otto as punishment camps – where they sometimes had to remain for more than a day without food or water.[105] With understandable bitterness an anonymous woman later wrote of the surrendered burghers who acted as intelligence agents: "We must teach our children to hate, hate, hate them!"[106]

From January 1901 to May 1902 there were several of surrendered burghers who left the concentration camps to take up military service for the British. This meant that towards the end of the war the camp superintendents experienced a shortage of labourers, tradesmen and camp police because these people were tempted by the better wages they could earn for active military service.[107]

The British government was hesitant to grant permission to leave the concentration camps to surrendered burghers who wished to return to their farms.[108] The British army had been unable to get the better of the commandos in the veld and the risk was too great that surrendered burghers who were living on their farms would be called up again. In an exceptional case a few surrendered burghers from the Volksrust camp were allowed to attend to their farming activities in the district, but the experiment was not a success. On 22 July 1901 the Boers raided these farms and took all the livestock, and in the clash that followed one of the surrendered burghers, F.W. Kock, was killed and two others were wounded.[109]

Surrendered burghers were more readily permitted to live in the towns and cities, provided that they were self-sufficient or could find work.[110] A census that was conducted in Pretoria at the beginning of 1902 showed that 53% of the total male civilian population in the town were republican burghers, while 33% were British citizens and 14% were other nationalities.[111] There were 162 surrendered burghers who had entered municipal service, of whom 122 were labourers.[112] In Johannesburg, too, there were surrendered burghers who were working for the municipality.[113] Those who were better off tried to get their businesses running again. Up until 31 January 1901 the British authorities in the Transvaal received 605 applications for trading licences, of which 121 came from republican burghers.[114] Some of the surrendered burghers argued that there could be no doubt about the eventual outcome of the war, and the sooner they became reconciled to the new dispensation, the sooner they would be financially back on their feet once more.[115]

On a limited scale, surrendered burghers were also taken on by British state departments. In the Free State the British authorities retained certain republican landdrosts (magistrates) in their positions after the occupation of Bloemfontein. It soon became clear that most of these magistrates were still loyal to the republican cause and they were then dismissed.[116] Only a small number of republican magistrates and clerks were retained by the British. By June 1901 the British authorities had adjudged 66 people who had previously been employed by the Free State civil service as suitable for posts in the British administration.[117] In Pretoria there were surrendered burghers in the military governor's office, the government printing works and the post office,[118] but other than this it does not appear that the British gave them any key posts in the Transvaal administration. As far as can be established, there was only one former republican official (N. van den Berg, the assistant magistrate in Johannesburg) who was appointed in a responsible post.[119]

In Johannesburg the superintendent of the local concentration camp tried to get work for the surrendered burghers on the mines, but the mine owners were not in favour of this idea at all. They felt that the loyal British citizens who had left Johannesburg at the outbreak of the war should be given preference. They also did not fully trust surrendered burghers – "the majority of them are still belligerents who came in here to tide over the winter or for a set purpose under the prevailing easy conditions of organising a scheme of some attack or treachery on Johannesburg and the mines".[120]

Certain non-combatant Boers in the cities were sometimes placed in a difficult position. In September 1901 Kitchener made it obligatory for some of those who had taken the oath of neutrality to travel as passengers on trains between Pietersburg and Pretoria. This measure (which had been introduced some time earlier under Roberts's orders)[121] was implemented in the hope that it would discourage the Boers from attacking the trains or damaging the railway line. There were four people who certainly accompanied trains on this route, namely B.J. Vorster, a former member of the First *Volksraad* and native commissioner of the Soutpansberg district; J.L. Brugman, General de la Rey's son-in-law; M. de Villiers, who according to Maxwell owned a great deal of land, and I. Haarhoff.[122] J.S. Smit, the former railway commissioner who had undertaken a peace mission to Commandant-general Botha in June 1900 and was involved in the burgher peace committee, was also instructed to make these train journeys. However, he saw fit to remind the British authorities of his peace mission and also emphasised the futility of this measure. "I have been looked upon by the burghers still fighting, as a traitor to their cause," he stated, "and I am sure that should they know that I am on a train, the safety of that train would be endangered and by sending me on it, would be direct sending me to my death."[123] Smit's objection had the desired effect, but similar pleas by Vorster, De Villiers and Haarhoff fell on deaf ears.[124] After October 1901 this measure – one that did not, in any event, comply with the norms of international law – was no longer enforced by Kitchener. This does not imply that the measure had proved successful or that Kitchener was bothered about the niceties of international law. Seemingly he no longer put burghers on trains because after October 1901 there was no longer any reason to do so. During the closing months of the war the extension of the blockhouse system made it far more difficult for the Boers to damage railway lines; apparently it was then unnecessary for him to make use of this particular ploy.[125]

By way of summary it can be concluded that generally speaking the surrendered burghers in the concentration camps fared far better than the other inmates. By making themselves available for paid service to the British they could obtain more food and supplement the scanty camp rations. In time, certain surrendered burghers were also appointed to positions of authority. Their role in this regard left much to be desired and only in exceptional cases did they try to be of help to the destitute women and children; they were more often surly and heartless. Their behaviour not only exacerbated the already poor relationship between the two groups, but was also in the future to become the source of great bitterness in Afrikaner ranks. The surrendered burghers who lived in the cities went ahead with their business as far as was possible, but this did not indemnify them from Kitchener's futile retaliatory measures and a few burghers were obliged to accompany trains as hostages. Nevertheless there is little doubt that generally speaking the surrendered burghers in the cities lived under far more comfortable and congenial conditions than those in the concentration camps.

3 The oath of allegiance and the impact of the surrendered burghers on the war

In the period from January 1901 to May 1902 the surrendered burghers were still expected to take the oath of neutrality. This was done in the hope that, having sworn to remain neutral, a burgher would be less inclined to escape from the concentration camps to rejoin the commandos.[126] But at this stage the oath of neutrality was a mere formality, and despite having taken it, surrendered burghers still escaped from the camps.[127]

The British did not adhere to the neutrality principal either. Milner issued a proclamation on 12 February 1901 to the effect that special commissioners would be appointed to give the Transvaal and Free State burghers the opportunity to take the oath of allegiance to the British crown.[128] In terms of the oath of neutrality a surrendered burgher swore not to offer any assistance to either one of the conflicting parties, but by taking the oath of allegiance, such a person accepted British citizenship with all the rights and duties which this implied. He could therefore least of all be regarded as neutral.[129] He had agreed to be partisan.

Article 45 of the Hague Convention stipulated that a hostile power could not place any pressure on the population of an occupied territory to take such an oath.[130] Although this particular clause does not make specific mention of an oath of allegiance, it is nevertheless implied in the context and formulation of the article.[131] As far as could be established, no surrendered burgher was ever forced to take the oath of allegiance. In fact, the British instructions on how the oath was to be taken emphasise that "Burghers taking the Oath of Allegiance must do so voluntarily."[132] Thus, if an individual took the oath of allegiance voluntarily, the British actions cannot be regarded as contravening article 45 of the Hague Convention. Nor were any of the surrendered burghers who had become British citizens in terms of the oath of allegiance expected to fight on the British side unless the place where they were living was attacked by the Boers.[133] It therefore appears that the British acted correctly in the administration of the oath of allegiance, but that the validity of the oath should be questioned, because Britain had annexed the republics as British colonies *before* defeating the Boer forces conclusively and was not, at that stage, in a position to occupy these regions effectively.

A few surrendered burghers who served in the British administration took the oath of allegiance as early as 1900,[134] but most others did so in the last 17 months of the war. The British administration had its hands full to appoint the necessary special commissioners and handle all the applications from surrendered burghers who wanted to take the oath.[135] On 2 May 1901 Major T.H.B. Forster, the commanding officer of the prisoner-of-war camps in Natal, reported that more than 600 of the approximately 1000 surrendered burghers in these camps were keen to take the oath of allegiance, but that he was not empowered to conduct the process. Later in May these people were sent to concentration camps where they were given the opportunity to take the oath.[136]

When the special commissioners visited the concentration camps, the surrendered burghers were able to take the oath of allegiance. The superintendents of the various camps were not allowed to undertake the formalities. In the camp at Mafeking the superintendent unknowingly exceeded his powers in this regard and swore in 400 Transvaal burghers as British citizens. Milner considered this highly irregular and he impressed upon Maxwell how important it was that only special commissioners were empowered to do this. Wary that to re-administer the oath could perhaps lead to "charges of bad faith against the British", Milner was prepared to accept the legality of the oaths sworn by the 400 burghers.[137] According to Goold-Adams, up until 27 May 1902 there were 2999 Free Staters who had taken the oath of allegiance.[138] There are no complete statistics on the numbers in the Transvaal. According to reports which appeared in *The Star*, 1340 Transvaal burghers had taken the oath prior to 8 May 1902,[139] but it is doubtful whether this figure includes all the burghers who accepted British citizenship before the end of the war.

The Bloemfontein Post claimed that the surrendered burghers were placed in a particularly privileged position by taking the oath of allegiance. In a report designed to encourage people to take the oath, the following description was provided of the "favourable" situation enjoyed by surrendered burghers in Klerksdorp who had accepted British citizenship: "To the Dutchmen it is a mystery that they are permitted to enjoy the privilege of British citizenship without any wearisome probation or heavy fee. Their own 'free' and 'glorious' Republic did not deal thusly with aliens ... Yet Great Britain simply invites her late enemies to come and share with her own subjects the advantages of membership of the Empire, and the Dutchman takes a long time to convince himself that there is not some hidden conspiracy aloof to humbug and fool him. He is not used to liberal ...

generosity and he is naturally suspicious. He is even asked if he will take the oath in Dutch or English. Fifty of them leaped into the breach and took the oath regardless of consequences and no doubt many more will follow as soon as they understand that the offer is honest and genuine."[140] This portrayal does not take into account that the republican governments were still in existence and that by taking on British citizenship while the war was still in progress, the surrendered burghers had placed themselves in a position of being neither flesh nor fowl. They were in reality still subject to the republican governments, and British citizenship – based on the invalid annexations – did not free them of this obligation.

The fact that republican burghers were prepared to take the oath of allegiance during the war was interpreted by *The Star* as a promising sign for the future.[141] Lieutenant-colonel R.M. Poore was, however, not convinced that taking the oath necessarily implied loyalty towards the British crown. When he was asked by one of the special commissioners about the motives of those who took the oath, Poore answered: "I am afraid there is little doubt that material advantage is the object in view in most cases, and indeed one could hardly expect it to be otherwise, for the average Burgher, one would think, would not at present feel any sentimental affection or patriotic duty to the King whose armies are still in the process of conquering and laying waste the country he has been born in, and has learned to call his own ... Here in Pretoria there is no doubt that a very large percentage became regenerate, merely to escape the irksomeness of reporting daily, or weekly, to the Police, or in order to obtain some trading license but not many confessed that this was the motive."[142] Then too, the negative effect of the surrendered burghers on the republican war effort must be analysed. (Here the specific focus is on the surrendered burghers as such, and not the burghers who undertook active military service for the British.) Three facets of this issue will be examined.

Firstly, to what extent can the surrendered burghers, by their voluntary withdrawal from the war, be held responsible for losses suffered by the republican troops who were liable for military service? In the period of January 1901 to May 1902 the total republican losses (prisoners of war, deaths, wounded, and surrendered burghers), according to the British records, totalled 29 592 of whom 6025 were surrendered burghers.[143] This amounts to about a 20% loss as a consequence of people who withdrew voluntarily from the war in the last 17 months of the war.

The British military intelligence service calculated that during the entire war the republics lost a total of 55 910 burghers (excluding rebels and foreign troops) of whom 23 151 were surrendered burghers.[144] The accuracy of these British records is debatable. In July 1901 Captain W. Bonham, the assistant provost marshal in Pretoria, remarked: "There is great difficulty in getting accurate returns [of surrendered burghers] and it is hard to see how this can be obviated." He put this down primarily to the fact that the commanding officers of the British columns sometimes calculated the number of surrendered burghers and prisoners of war randomly and also included men who were not liable for republican military service.[145] Then too, it is not clear whether the British military intelligence officials had included the surrendered burghers who later rejoined the commandos. Neither the Boers nor the British have absolutely accurate statistics on these men. It can however be accepted that such people who were still in the veld at the end of the war would be counted as bitterenders, and if they had been captured, as prisoners of war. The possibility of duplication – that they would be included in the calculations as both prisoners of war and surrendered burghers – cannot however be ignored. With so many dubious factors, it is obvious that the British estimate of the number of bona fide surrendered burghers, that is, men who were liable for republican military service and had subsequently laid down their arms, is probably far too high.

As far as can be established, the only other records which cover the entire war are those compiled by Gustav Preller. According to him about 15 000 men laid down their arms during the war.[146] Although Preller does not say so in as many words, it appears from the context of his exposition that by this he means bona fide surrendered burghers who were indeed liable for republican military service. In the light of the fact that the British military intelligence service did not take adequate reckoning of those surrendered burghers who later rejoined the commandos and apparently also included men who were not liable for military service, Preller's total of 15 000 bona fide surrendered burghers is probably more realistic. If this number is accepted as approximately correct, further analysis shows that the Boers lost about 27% of the total number of burghers who were liable for military service (54 667) to surrender.[147]

Secondly, an assessment should be made of the extent to which the surrendered burghers decreased the striking power and military capacity of the republics. It does not necessarily follow that the Boer striking power was reduced strictly in proportion to those who surrendered. The quality and not the number of men which the Boers lost is of crucial importance here. Kitchener, however, placed great importance on the number of surrendered burghers and gave everyone to believe that all the people whom the British labelled "surrendered burghers" were men who were liable for republican military service. In March 1902, in response to Brodrick's query, he claimed: "It is impossible to distinguish between fighting and non-fighting burghers unless they are very old or very young ... All surrenderers reported are men liable to serve under commando law."[148] But Kitchener's answer was misleading. The commanding officers of the British lines often regarded non-fighting men (including elderly men and children as young as nine or ten years) as surrendered burghers, regardless of whether they were liable for military service or not.[149] The loss of these people had next to no effect on the Boer striking power. Among the burghers who were indeed liable for military service, those who saw fit to surrender were generally not among the best and toughest fighters. In January 1902 *The Cape Times* reminded its readers "that those still in the field are not only the most obstinate, but [are] perhaps the best fighters of the Old Republics,"[150] and *The Star* wrote in April 1902 that "only the most irreconcilable of the burghers are now in the field".[151] Kestell illustrated the impact of the surrendered burghers with the following images: "The chaff has gone and the wheat remains. The winds of destruction and the ravaging rainstorms have wrought their havoc on the mountain which is the Afrikaner *volk*; the soft loose earth has been blown away and washed out of the crevices – only the solid rock remains behind."[152] In the same vein D.W. Krüger perhaps exaggerates when he says that for the republican forces the loss of the surrendered burghers was a blessing rather than a curse.[153] No army can afford to lose a large number of men through desertion and still consider this an advantage, but it cannot be denied that the weaker element in the republican forces had been removed and, to a large extent, the military striking power of the pure core which remained made up for the loss.

Thirdly, an attempt can be made to determine the extent to which the issue of surrendered burghers had a demoralising effect on the republican leaders and influenced them to think in terms of peace. On 10 May 1901 Commandant-general Botha, Generals Ben Viljoen, Chris Botha and Jan Smuts met at Immigratie between Ermelo and Wakkerstroom. They decided that with Kitchener's help they would make contact with President Kruger and the republican delegation in Europe to inform them about the conditions in the Transvaal and ask their advice on whether the war should be continued.[154] In a letter to President Steyn the Transvaal leaders outlined five reasons for considering this step.[155] The shortage of ammunition and the fact that the people were entitled to know the truth from their leaders were two of the reasons. The other three reasons were related to the influence of the surrendered burghers. The Transvaal leaders explained that "there are continually groups of burghers who are handing over their arms to the enemy, and this exposes us to the danger that our cause could grind to a dishonourable halt if it eventually comes to the point that the Government and the officers are alone in the veld without burghers". Then too, they were concerned that the authority of the republican governments was steadily declining and there was a danger that the people could lose all respect for their legal government. The Transvaal leaders also predicted a progressive disintegration of the *volk* and the danger that the leaders might eventually lose their personal influence and could even be placed under suspicion by the people. It is clear that these reasons are a reflection on the apostasy of the surrendered burghers, and that this had given rise to a situation where the leaders could no longer count on the unconditional support of all the people. Until he received this letter Steyn's "greatest concern was always that ordinary officers and men, by heeding the enemy ... might be persuaded to lay down their arms".[156]

This letter, however, caused him even greater anxiety because he was afraid that the Transvaal government might possibly leave the

Free State in the lurch. On 15 May he expressed his unequivocal disappointment with the Transvalers and exhorted them earnestly to carry on the struggle at all costs. He referred among other things to the fact that the Free Staters had also experienced the problem of surrendered burghers, but this was not being seen as an insurmountable obstacle.[157] On 3 June 1901 the Transvaal government informed President Kruger about the prevailing conditions and also raised the question of the surrendered burghers.[158] Steyn expected that Kruger would advise the republics to conclude peace under the best possible conditions and was pleasantly surprised when the Transvaal president in fact encouraged the leaders to persevere and to continue fighting.[159] At a meeting on the farm Waterval in the Standerton district on 20 June 1901, representatives of the two republics reiterated their decision not to abandon the struggle without the assurance of full independence.[160]

Although it must be remembered that the pessimistic attitude of the Transvaal leaders in May 1901 was the exception rather than the rule,[161] it would seem nevertheless that at that particular time the surrendered burghers were impacting negatively on the morale of the republican leaders to the point that they even debated the possibility of opting for peace.

Thereafter, the demoralising influence of the surrendered burghers declined somewhat. The authors of the *Times History* are correct in their claim that from about May 1901 "two opposite processes were at work, a sifting process and a moulding process, corresponding to the different effects produced by stress of war on individual characters. Outside the existing nucleus of sturdy fighters there was a large class of burghers whose course was undecided. Whilst this class was constantly lessened by surrenderers, under slight pressure or even without pressure, at the same time a counter current was setting in the other direction. Weak men under the same current become strong, some of the weakest, indeed, became the strongest."[162] In August and September 1901 both President Steyn and Acting President S.W. Burger were able to make statements to the effect that the question of surrender no longer weighed as heavily on their minds as previously, and that they were in a position to manage without these men.[163]

During the discussions at Klerksdorp and Vereeniging in April and May 1902, just before peace was concluded, the issue of surrendered burghers was raised again. Acting President S.W. Burger was of the opinion that, "If there is no change, there are many of the burghers who will be forced to go over to the enemy because they are destitute. Among our people there have always been some who are courageous and others who are weak hearted. These two elements are still with us. One burgher who fights among us today will assuredly lay down his weapons tomorrow. Our cause is getting weaker by the day. Each man that we lose means one more that we cannot replace."[164] On 29 May at Vereeniging, General de la Rey said that he was convinced that if the Boers continued the war, one district after another would be forced to surrender and he feared that "the war will therefore grind to a dishonourable halt".[165] Commandant F.E. Mentz of Heilbron said the following day that if the fighting were to be continued, "then here and there [there will be] commandos that will constantly go over to the enemy".[166] General C.F. Beyers was also concerned about this and he interpreted the opinions of his delegates as follows: "There is one matter that troubles me and that is the demoralisation which appears to have set in. From the addresses that have been presented it seems that a large number of our people will go over to the enemy. When they choose to do so, when this spirit possesses these burghers, then it is absolutely futile to grab them by the throat and say: go and fight."[167]

To place the matter in perspective it should be noted that it was only these delegates who specifically mentioned the question of surrender as such.[168] Many other considerations were also taken into account. According to the Boer leaders it was the cumulative impact of the following factors which made it important to conclude peace: the British scorched earth policy and the exhaustion of various supplies which were vital for the continuance of the war; the concentration camp system; the arming of African people; the possibility that the fighting burghers were in danger of losing all their property as a consequence of Kitchener's proclamation; and the overwhelming odds which they faced in terms of numbers.[169] The authors of the *Times History* are, however, of the opinion that the question of surrender had a considerable impact: "[T]here finally took shape in the minds of the fighting leaders an apprehension that if they did not come to terms while there was still time surrenderers might become wholesale. This apprehension had an appreciable effect on bringing the war to an end."[170] This statement is not entirely valid because it does not take full account of the other important considerations which also influenced the Boer leaders to conclude peace. On grounds of all available evidence it can nevertheless be accepted that the issue of surrender did impact upon the outlook of the Boers to a significant extent, although it is doubtful if this was a crucial reason for concluding peace.

The Boer republics were not the only nation that had been involved in a freedom struggle where surrender played a role. In August 1901 Steyn reminded Kitchener that during the American War of Independence (1775-1783) the Americans had had to deal with a similar problem.[171] Indeed, it was a widespread feature of that particular war. In the citizen force units of the American army, "privates were known to select their commanders and considered themselves socially their equals or superiors. Desertion was common, especially to return to the farms," writes an author on the war. In the period from 1777 to 1778 George Washington's force at Valley Forge (Pennsylvania) declined from 17 000 to 5000 primarily as a result of desertion.[172] The same phenomenon occurred in the American Civil War (1861-1865). After the devastating advance of General W.T. Sherman's Union forces through the states of Georgia and Carolina in 1864 and 1865, there were thousands of men from the Southern forces who withdrew from the war.[173]

If it is considered that the republics had to maintain a drawn out and unequal guerrilla struggle, the incidence of surrender is not a reflection on the preparedness of the Boer forces. Indeed, this makes the determination and endurance of the bitterenders all the more impressive. The Boers were not all born soldiers and it would indeed be unrealistic to expect that a large portion of any country's male citizen population, once mobilised would, to a man, prove equal to the emotional and physical demands of waging a major war. Up to this point attention has been focused mainly on those surrendered burghers who did not provide any active military assistance to the British army. Next, a study will be made of those who went a step further and entered British military service after they had laid down their arms.

Notes

1 *Official History*, IV, p. 705, annexure 20. The *Official History* does not differentiate between surrendered burghers and prisoners of war for April and May 1901. The number of surrendered burghers for May 1901 was 1055 and this number was used for the calculation. MGP 289/8258/01, "Boer Casualties for May 1901". The number of surrendered burghers for April 1901 could not be traced.
2 See Chapter 1, section 3 above.
3 See Chapters 5, 6 and 7 below for a discussion on these burghers.
4 See Chapter 1, section 3 above.
5 For details on this aspect of the British military policy, see for example Spies, "Civilians", pp. 163–86, 269–73; Van Rensburg, "Ekonomiese Herstel", pp. 151–85; Otto, pp. 1–18.
6 Translated from the Dutch. MGP 69/1643/01 (intercepted republican documents).
7 Hancock and Van der Poel, *Selections*, I, p. 469, Smuts – Stead, 4 January 1902. Stead apparently did not receive this letter.
8 Brits, *Diary*, pp. 47–9, 13 May 1901.
9 See Chapter 2, section 4 above.
10 Hancock and Van der Poel, *Selections*, I, p. 469, Smuts – Stead, 4 January 1902. See also Spies, "Civilians", p. 290.
11 Spies, "Civilians", pp. 338–9.
12 See PMO 27/1877, Captain R.W. Morley for J.F. van Zyl – Poore, 1 August 1901; PMO 30/2096, S.G. Nicholson – Superintendent Howick camp, 31 August 1901 (copy) and W.P. Wienand – Poore, 30 August 1901; PMO 54/3736, G.J. Horn – Kitchener, 25 April 1902 (copy); A1270, concentration camp memoirs of Mrs L. du Preez, 1971.
13 HC 54/113, Milner – Chamberlain, 15 November 1901. In February 1901, however, Milner had his doubts whether the concentration camp system would encourage burghers to lay down their arms. Spies, "Civilians", pp. 309–10, 350.
14 For information on the British implementation and the success of this military tactic see *Times History*, V, pp. 396–403, 467–94; *Official History*, IV, pp. 114–326, 485, 492–520; annexure 2, pp. 568–76 and C. Burnett, *The 18th Hussars in South Africa*, pp. 119–242. On Commandant-general Botha's opinion on the blockhouses see J.D. Kestell and D.E. van Velden, *De Vredesonderhandelingen tusschen de Regeeringen der twee Zuid-Afrikaansche Republieken en de Vertegenwoordigers der Britsche Regeering welke uitliepen op den Vrede, op 31 Mei 1902 te Vereeniging gesloten*, p. 21.
15 *The Star*, 22 March 1902 (editorial).
16 According to Commandant-general Botha by May 1902 there were 10 816 men in the Transvaal in the veld, of whom 3296 were on foot. Kestell and Van Velden, *Vredesonderhandelingen*, p. 56.
17 HC 30/96, "Capt. Macgregor, Field Intelligence Report, north western districts", 30 August 1901.
18 *Times History*, V, p. 277.
19 P.C.M. Ackermann, "Aardrykskundige invloede in die stryd tussen Brittanje en die Boererepublieke met besondere verwysing na die Tweede Vryheidsoorlog" (Unpublished D.Phil. thesis, Unisa), 1957, p. 221.
20 Hancock and Van der Poel, *Selections*, I, p. 480, Smuts – Stead, 4 January 1902.

21 *Official History*, IV, p. 705, annexure 20; MGP 289/8258/01 "Boer Casualties for May 1901".
22 Translated from the Dutch. Hancock and Van der Poel, *Selections*, I, pp. 395–6, Smuts – Kruger, 3 June 1901.
23 J.D. Kestell, *Met De Boeren-Commando's*, p. 170.
24 Compare the evidence of magistrate H.J. Bosman of Wakkerstroom on 29 May 1902 at Vereeniging. Kestell and Van Velden, *Vredesonderhandelingen*, p. 164.
25 H.G. de Wet, "The Fighter, The Scout, The Spy", pp. LXXXVII – LXXXIX. Unpublished memoirs of a burgher who laid down his arms and later fought on the British side. The memoirs were compiled in 1914 and were in the possession of Prof F.A. van Jaarsveld.
26 PMO 9/691, "Report of Captain C. Walton", 2 February 1901.
27 PMO 48/3304, Poore – Commanding officer Middelburg, 16 March 1902; Chapter 2, section 4 above.
28 PMO 48/3304, Poore – Bannantyne, 17 March 1902 and Bannantyne – Poore, 19 March 1902.
29 Translated from the Dutch. *The Friend*, 23 January 1903 (Dutch column).
30 PMO 71/P32, Director of military supplies – Poore, 5 December 1901.
31 *Journal of Principal Events*, XI, p. 43. Dutch versions of the proclamation appear in several sources including Van der Merwe, II, pp. 25–6 and Kestell, *Boeren-Commando's*, pp. 166–7. For details of the events leading up to the proclamation and its implementation, see Spies, "Civilians", pp. 365–74.
32 Kestell, *Boeren-Commando's*, p. 169.
33 PMO 1/100, Kitchener – Colonel M.F. Rimington, General L. Rundle, General E. Elliot, General G.M. Bullock, General E. Hamilton, Lord Methuen, General C. Tucker, General C. Knox, General R.A.P. Clements, General B. Hamilton, General H.C.O. Plumer, Colonel J.S. Barker, Colonel D. Mackenzie, Colonel R.G. Kekewich, 25 December 1901 (copy).
34 SO/POW 26/2336, Poore – French, undated but after 25 December 1901 (copy); PM. 35/2378, Commanding officer Pietersburg – Poore, 6 January 1902; Burnett, p. 214, 24 January 1902.
35 Kestell, *Boeren-Commando's*, pp. 195–6.
36 CO 417/360/9821 (FK 660, p. 715), Henderson – Altham, 14 February 1902.
37 PMO 46/3112, Commanding officer Natal – Poore, 21 January 1902.
38 Brandt, p. 157.
39 See Barnard, "Grepe uit die Krygskuns van die Boeregeneraals", p. 2.
40 *The South African News*, 23 January 1901 (editorial).
41 Hancock and Van der Poel, *Selections*, I, pp. 477, 479, Smuts – Stead, 4 January 1902.
42 Translated from the Dutch. *Verslag der Deputatie*, p. 9, P.D. de Wet, D.J.H. van Niekerk and C.L. Botha – Revd J.M. Hofmeyr, 8 March 1901.
43 *The Cape Times*, 12 February 1901. "Ope brief aan de Predikanten der Ned. Geref. Kerk in de Kaapkolonie." (Open letter to the ministers of the Dutch Reformed Church in the Cape Colony).
44 See Chapter 3, section 4 above.
45 PMO 17/1278, Kitchener – Officer commanding Lydenburg, 25 April 1901 (copy).

46 As regards the loyal republican families, Kitchener decided that after December 1901 these people should no longer be sent to the concentration camps. The aim was that the fighting burghers should care for them themselves and by doing so hamper the mobility of the commandos. Spies, "Civilians", pp. 402–9. The policy did not affect the surrendered burghers. HC 61/118, "Circulars General Superintendent of Burgher Camps Department", 20 November 1901.
47 MGP 45/6992/00.
48 Cd. 819, p. 21; Spies, "Civilians", p. 284.
49 Spies, "Civilians", p. 285.
50 Spies, "Civilians", pp. 285, 302–7; Martin, pp. 88–93; Hattingh, *Irenekonsentrasiekamp*, p. 131. Otto's allegation (p. 91) that the differentiated scale was stopped only in the last quarter of 1901 is proved incorrect by these authors.
51 PMO 21/1525, 18 June 1901.
52 *The Bloemfontein Post*, 12 July 1901 (letter from J.C. Kruger).
53 *The Bloemfontein Post*, 3 July 1901 (letter from P.J. Delport).
54 A263, Brigadier-general B.N. Smythe Collection, G.J. Grobler and 5 others from the Middelburg camp – Brigadier-general B.N. Smythe, 13 April 1901; *De Getuige*, March 1903 (letter from N.J. van Zijl who was in the Volksrust camp during the war).
55 See Otto, p. 84; Neethling, p. 213.
56 PMO 22/1552, Superintendent Johannesburg camp – General superintendent, 10 June 1901; Neethling, p. 213; Hattingh, *Irenekonsentrasiekamp*, pp. 178–9.
57 GOV 253/20, W.K. Tucker – Maxwell, 13 November 1901.
58 Translated from the Afrikaans. A951, H.W. Huyser Collection, 1,"Verhaal van die Boereoorlog deur mev. H.G. Bekker" (Story of the Boer War by Mrs H.G. Bekker), 1929. See also M.M. Postma, *Stemme uit die Vrouekampe*, pp. 58–9, evidence of Mrs E.J. van Rensburg, 21 June 1921, where mention is made of the same incident in the Klerksdorp camp.
59 Cd. 819, p. 214.
60 M.A. Fischer, *Kampdagboek*, p. 106, 6 April 1902.
61 Postma, p. 80, evidence of Mrs G.W. Joubert, undated.
62 Neethling, p. 191.
63 PMO 35/2589, A. Dieperink – Kitchener, 16 December 1901 (copy) and W.K. Tucker – Maxwell, 21 February 1902.
64 Cd. 893, p. 8, report from Womens' Committee, 12 December 1901.
65 CSO 29/1466/01, 29 April 1901.
66 Cd. 853, p. 103, report from superintendent at Volksrust, October 1901.
67 GOV 253/20, Tucker – Maxwell, 13 November 1901.
68 Fischer, p. 42, 14 September 1901.
69 PMO 27/1872, T.C. Roberts – Poore, 1 August 1901.
70 CSO 89/538/02, P.A. Groenewald – Goold-Adams, 20 February 1902.
71 Cd. 853, p. 41, report from Dr K. Franks on the camp at Vereeniging, October 1901. On the National Scout camp at Meintjeskop, see Chapter 6, section 1 below.
72 PMO 2/192, Poore – Officer in command Bloemfontein, 4 February 1902 (copy).
73 MGP 179/3750/02, Superintendent Nylstroom camp – Maxwell, 5 March 1902.

THE DYNAMICS OF TREASON: BOER COLLABORATION IN THE SA WAR OF 1899–1902

74 PMO 23/1645, N.J. Scholtz – W.K. Tucker, undated copy. See also Cd. 819, p. 239, report of superintendent at Irene, July 1901.
75 MGP 222, p. 764, Maxwell – Kitchener, 20 July 1901.
76 Milner Papers, 44, (FK 1201, p. 312), W.K. Tucker's report, 22 February 1902 (copy).
77 MGP 222, p. 764, Maxwell – Kitchener, 20 July 1901; PMO 21/1520, Maxwell – Poore, 11 June 1901; Spies, "Civilians", p. 351. See also PMO 35/2419, Assistant provost marshal Kroonstad – Assistant provost marshal Bloemfontein, 18 October 1901 (copy); PMO 85/10, Assistant provost marshal Krugersdorp – Assistant provost marshal Potchefstroom, 20 June 1901 (copy) for the same evidence.
78 A1259, memoirs of the Anglo-Boer war by burgher J. du Plooy, p. 16, undated.
79 PMO 42/2881, statements by P.J. de Wet van Aswegen and W.C. Nel, 26 December 1901.
80 WO 32/878/8722 (A379), Assistant general T. Smuts – Field-cornets, wards 2 and 3, Ermelo, 11 and 29 April 1901 (intercepted republican documents).
81 Hobhouse, *Brunt of the War*, p. 102.
82 CO 224/4/31678 (FK 1037, p. 125). A.C. Trollope's report in August 1901, Cd. 819, pp. 211–12.
83 Naudé, *Vechten en Vluchten*, p. 268. By using an African spy the British intelligence service was aware that the Boers might possibly launch an attack on the camp and would enjoy the support of some of the surrendered burghers. MGP 258, "Summary of Intelligence", 15 December 1901.
84 Naudé, *Vechten en Vluchten*, p. 270; MGP 269, "Summary of Intelligence", 25 January 1902; MGP 258, "Summary of Intelligence", 26 January 1902; PMO 47/3226, statements by surrendered burghers D.J.H. Buchling and L.M. Bronkhorst, 28 January 1902; Spies, "Civilians", p. 401; M.A. Gronum, *Die Bittereinders*, pp. 45–6.
85 See Chapter 3, section 4 above.
86 CSO 3/105/01, "Minutes of Bloemfontein sub-committee", 21 January, 11 March, 9 and 15 April, 10 June 1901; Malan, "Fraser", p. 236.
87 Cd. 819, pp. 51–2; Hattingh, *Irenekonsentrasiekamp*, p. 180.
88 HC 61/118, "Instructions for superintendents", October 1901; Cd. 853, p. 14.
89 GOV 253/20, W.K. Tucker – Maxwell, 13 November 1901.
90 Cd. 853, p. 103, report by superintendent at Volksrust, October 1901.
91 Hattingh, *Irenekonsentrasiekamp*, p. 180.
92 Translated from the Afrikaans. Postma, pp. 34, 89, statements by Mrs D. Jones (1917) and Mrs I.A. Grobler de Clercq, undated. See also Neethling, p. 5.
93 HC 61/118, "Instructions for superintendents", October 1901.
94 MGP 144/366/02, J. Ferreira – Superintendent Irene, 4 January 1902.
95 PMO 49/3336, A.B. Dismore (intelligence agent) – Poore, 11 March 1902.
96 PMO 33/3200, statement by Major E.F. Brereton, 13 January 1901; Naudé, *Vechten en Vluchten*, pp. 267–8.
97 PMO 2/102, Kitchener – All commanding officers, 25 April 1901 (copy); Cd. 819, p. 48, "Memorandum for superintendents", 26 April 1901.
98 PMO 35/2410, Superintendent Nylstroom camp – Poore, 18 October 1901. See also Naudé, *Vechten en Vluchten*, p. 268.
99 See Chapter 5, section 4 below.

100 PMO 2/120, Assistant provost marshal Middelburg – Poore, 18 June 1901.
101 CO 417/360/7125 (FK 659, p. 555), Henderson – Altham, 24 January 1902.
102 Translated from the Afrikaans. A 119, Renier Collection, 129, evidence of Mrs R. Smit, 1949.
103 CO 417/360/7125 (FK 659, pp. 554–5), Henderson – Altham, 24 January 1902.
104 *Pretoria News*, 22 March 1904 (letter from "A Transvaal British").
105 Otto, pp. 80–1.
106 Translated from the Dutch. Neethling, p. 5.
107 MGP 246/3189/01, Maxwell – Officer in command Barberton, 18 September 1901; Spies, "Civilians", p. 354. On the payment received by these people see Chapter 6, section 1 below.
108 MGP 166/1971/01, Maxwell – Superintendent Irene, 15 February 1901.
109 PMO 28/1977, statement by M. Brit, 28 July 1901; WO 32/866/7460 (A366), "Staff Diary Volksrust sub-district", 29 July 1901.
110 PMO 85/11, Superintendent Potchefstroom camp – Poore, 29 June 1901; MGP 130/14463/01, Maxwell – Milner, 12 November 1901.
111 MGP 177/2374/02, "Census of Pretoria", 9 February 1902.
112 PMO 54/3748, "Ex-burghers in Pretoria municipal employ", 3 May 1902. See also MGP 158/5590/02 for an earlier version, 2 April 1902.
113 PMO 50/3419, Commissioner of police Johannesburg – Poore, 9 January 1902.
114 MGP 68/1452/01, list of nationalities of people who applied for trading licences, 31 January 1901.
115 Compare PMO 25/1767, J.J. Bosman – Kitchener, 28 May 1901 (copy).
116 CO 224/3/4259 (FK 1032, pp. 62–3), Milner – Chamberlain, 17 January 1901 and enclosed report by Major-general G.T. Pretyman, 13 March to 31 October 1900.
117 CO 224/3/25199 (FK 1035, pp. 702–25), "Returns showing appointments made or proposed to be made in the Civil Service of the Orange River Colony", 13 June 1901.
118 MGP 145/496/02, Maxwell – Fiddes, 9 January 1902 (copy); PMO 15/1092, P.C. Falconer – Poore, 4 April 1901.
119 Spies, "Civilians", pp. 96–7.
120 CO 417/430/28843 (FK 560, pp. 357–9), circular to Transvaal Chamber of Mines, 18 June 1901 and A. Goldring (secretary) – Chamberlain, 28 June 1901.
121 Chapter 2, section 2 above.
122 MGP 123/127618/01 Vorster – Maxwell, 2 October 1901; Hancock and Van der Poel, *Selections*, I, p. 572, "Memoirs". Spies, "Civilians", p. 380. According to W.J. Leyds, H. Bosch, former assistant state secretary, N. van Nikkelen Kuyper, former orphan master, and two prisoners of war were also placed on the trains. Leyds, *Vierde Verzameling*, part I, vol 2, no 691, pp. 637–8, Leyds – W.J. Brown, 11 March 1902. It was indeed suggested that they should possibly make the journeys, but Captain M. Peters, the commissioner of police, did not regard them as suitable for this purpose. MGP 127/13652/01, Peters – Maxwell, 7 October 1901. There does not appear to be any other evidence that they were indeed put onto the trains.
123 MGP 118/11599, Smit – Peters, 10 September 1901.
124 MGP 117/11367/01, Vorster – Maxwell, 5 September 1901; MGP 139/1661B/01, Haarhoff – Maxwell, 6 December 1901; MGP 123/12763B/01, De Villiers – Kitchener, 1 October 1901.

125 Spies, "Civilians", pp. 381–2.
126 PMO 27/1865, Assistant provost marshal Middelburg – Poore, 1 July 1901.
127 See Chapter 4, section 2 above.
128 MGP 75/2401/01, printed English version of the proclamation.
129 In terms of the British annexations of the Free State (24 May 1900) and the Transvaal (1 September 1900) the non-fighting portion of the population were theoretically British citizens and the fighting burghers were rebels. However, in general the British authorities did not in practice regard them as such. As early as August 1900 Milner was of the opinion that all surrendered burghers, even those who had not been in British service in one capacity or another, should take an oath of allegiance in order to become British citizens. Milner Papers, 45, (FK 1134, p. 225), Milner – Pretyman, 30 August 1900.
130 Cd. 800, p. 26.
131 Compare Spies, "Civilians", p. 49; Chapter 1, section 2 above.
132 MGP 128/13805/01, "Army Orders South Africa", 18 March 1901; See also MGP 150/2311/02, Milner – Maxwell, 14 February 1902; MGP 150/2455/02, Milner – Maxwell, 17 February 1902.
133 PMO 1/83, O. Walrond – Poore, 15 April 1901; MGP 139/16713/01, Milner – Maxwell, 16 December 1901; CSO 88/874/02, memorandum by H.F. Wilson, 17 February 1902; HC 145/unsorted, Milner – Special commissioners, 12 December 1901.
134 IOP 6/358A/01, Maxwell – Hughes (information officer), 22 January 1901. See also Chapter 3, section 3 above for the case of Morgendaal who had already taken the oath of allegiance in July 1900.
135 See MGP 140/17065/01, Commanding officer Pietersburg – Maxwell, 6 December 1901; MGP 138/16409/01, Commanding officer Standerton – Maxwell, 19 December 1901; MGP 176/17896/01, Commanding officer Standerton – Maxwell, 30 December 1901; MGP 143/17913/01, Commanding officer Middelburg – Maxwell, 30 December 1901.
136 SOP/Natal 5/420, Major T.H.B. Forster – Poore, 2 May 1901 and Poore – Forster, 4 May 1901.
137 MGP 128/13805/01, Superintendent Mafeking camp – Commanding officer Mafeking, 11 October 1901 and H. Wyndham (Milner's assistant private secretary) – Maxwell, 11 November 1901.
138 Milner Papers 44 (FK 1202, p. 497), Goold-Adams – Milner, 27 May 1902.
139 *The Star*, 10, 18, 26 and 29 March, 11 and 15 April as well as 8 May 1902 (news reports).
140 *The Bloemfontein Post*, 24 July 1901 (news report).
141 *The Star*, 29 April, 1902 (editorial).
142 PMO 12/894, Poore – Special commissioner, 19 March 1902 (copy).
143 *Official History*, IV, p. 705, annexure 20; MGP 289/8258/01, "Boer Casualties for May 1901"; Chapter 4, section 1 above.
144 WO 32/884/9144 (A383), "Strength of Boer Forces on 31st May 1902"; Cd. 1792, p. 445. According to these records the period until 31 December 1901 yielded 22 098 surrendered burghers in both republics. To this the 1053 burghers who laid down their arms from 31 December 1901 to 31 May 1902 must be added. For the latter figure see *Official History*, IV, p. 705, annexure 20.
145 PMO 2/131, W. Bonham – Major F. French, 27 July 1901 (copy).

CHAPTER 4: THE SURRENDERED BURGHERS FROM JANUARY 1901 – MAY 1902

146 Preller, *Hindon*, p. 49.
147 According to Breytenbach, *Geskiedenis*, I, there were 54 667 republican burghers who were liable for military service. There are no accurate figures on the number of burghers who became liable for active service during the course of the war.
148 WO Confidential Telegrams, no 965 and 967, 1 and 2 March 1902. See also *The Star*, 10 March 1902 (leading article).
149 CO 417/361/12428 (FK 661, p. 161), Henderson – Altham, 9 April 1902; Kestell, *Boeren-Commando's*, p. 175; Kestell and Van Velden, *Vredesonderhandelingen*, p. 22, evidence of General C.R. de Wet, 9 April 1901; Van der Merwe, II, p. 31, Steyn – Kitchener, 15 August 1901.
150 *The Cape Times*, 8 January 1902 (editorial).
151 *The Star*, 24 April 1902 (editorial).
152 Translated from the Dutch. Kestell, *Boeren-Commando's*, p. 170.
153 Translated from the Afrikaans. D.W. Krüger, "Die Tweede Vryheidsoorlog 1899–1902" in A.J.H. van der Walt, J.A. Wiid and A.L. Geyer (eds), *Geskiedenis van Suid-Afrika*, p. 425.
154 Spies, "Civilians", pp. 337–8; Scholtz, "Betrekkinge", pp. 168–9; Van der Merwe, II, pp. 72–3; Kestell, *Boeren-Commando's*, pp. 157–8.
155 Translated from the Dutch. Published Dutch versions of this letter appear in Van der Merwe, II, pp. 72–3 and in Kestell, *Boeren-Commando's*, p. 158. The letter fell into British hands on 11 July 1901 when some of the members of the Free State government were captured at Reitz. Published translated versions appear in Cd. 903, pp. 54–5. The letter, dated 10 May 1901, is signed by the Transvaal state secretary, F.W. Reitz.
156 Translated from the Dutch. Van der Merwe, II, p. 70.
157 Kestell, *Boeren-Commando's*, p. 159; Van der Merwe, II, pp. 73–4.
158 Hancock and Van der Poel, *Selections*, I, pp. 395–6.
159 Van der Merwe, II, p. 76; Hancock and Van der Poel, *Selections*, I, pp. 398–9.
160 Hancock and Van der Poel, *Selections*, I, pp. 401–2; Scholtz, "Betrekkinge", pp. 183–5; Spies, "Civilians", p. 342.
161 Compare Hancock and Van der Poel, *Selections*, I, p. 480, Smuts – Stead, 4 January 1902.
162 *Times History*, V, p. 251. Chapter 4. The surrendered burghers from January 1901 to May 1902.
163 Van der Merwe, II, p. 31, Steyn – Kitchener, 15 August 1901; Cd. 903, p. 92, Burger – Kitchener, 5 September 1901.
164 Kestell and Van Velden, *Vredesonderhandelingen*, p. 25.
165 Translated from the Dutch. Kestell and Van Velden, *Vredesonderhandelingen*, p. 162.
166 De Wet, *Boer en Brit*, p. 401. Mentz's version in Kestell and Van Velden, *Vredesonderhandelingen*, p. 199 differs from that in the annexures to De Wet's work. The meaning is, however, more or less the same and reads as follows: "I am afraid that if we do not accept these terms we will gradually fall apart. I can see no future for us if we continue the struggle, and I fear that the longer we go on, the worse our position will become." (This quotation translated from the Dutch.)
167 Translated from the Dutch. Kestell and Van Velden, *Vredesonderhandelingen*, p. 175.

168 The references by Commandant-general Botha, General L. Meyer and magistrate H.J. Bosman concentrate more specifically on the burghers who undertook active military service for the British. Kestell and Van Velden, *Vredesonderhandelingen*, pp. 31, 86, 94, 185, 188. On the influence of these burghers see Chapter 6, section 2 below.

169 Kestell and Van Velden, *Vredesonderhandelingen*, pp. 209–11.

170 *Times History*, V, p. 408.

171 Van der Merwe, II, p. 31, 15 August 1901.

172 P. Wells, *The American War of Independence*, p. 133. Also see in this regard the remark by the German jurist Oskar Hintrager: "How many similarities there are between this war and the American War of Independence! Simple farmers fighting for their independence against England. The tactics they use, their lack of discipline, the apostasy ... waging of war against farm homesteads, women and children ... – everything is repeated here." (Quotation translated from the Afrikaans.) Oberholster (ed) "Dagboek van Oskar Hintrager", p. 127, 26 August 1900.

173 W.B. Wood and J.E. Edmonds, *The Civil War in the United States with Special Reference to the Campaigns of 1864 and 1865*, p. 314.

Chapter 5
In British military service: local burgher corps, guides and scouts

1 British enrolment of burghers and the question of treason

Even as early as the period from June to October 1900 the British army received sporadic help of a military nature from surrendered burghers. On an informal level some surrenderers supplied information to the British on the movements of the commandos,[1] but on a more formal level they sometimes served as guides. Indeed, by 26 June 1900 the commanding officers of the British columns had already received the order: "A guide should always be obtained and should be an influential farmer of the district."[2]

On their own initiative the commanding officers of certain units also received armed assistance from surrendered burghers. In August 1900 the commanding officer of the Provisional Mounted Police in the Jagersfontein district reported that he had armed a few burghers who had joined his unit.[3] During the Boer siege of Ladybrand (1 to 5 September 1900) eight republican burghers fought on the British side. Major F. White, the commanding officer of the British garrison at Ladybrand, was full of praise for them: "Their knowledge of the by-paths and surroundings was invaluable. They are all good shots and contributed their share to the casualties amongst the enemy. Their real knowledge of the people and country is invaluable and they use it freely in our service."[4]

During October 1900 Lieutenant H.H. Aldridge of the Provisional Mounted Police also armed a few burghers from the Rouxville district for scouting purposes. According to Aldridge they were "very useful" to him in this respect.⁵ In the same month a certain Grobler, a Free State burgher, acted as a guide for the British in the Bethlehem district. He also had between 50 and 60 armed Africans under him and on occasion the force even fired on General Christiaan de Wet's scouts.⁶

By the end of October 1900 Milner felt that the leaders of the British army should definitely try to make greater use of the military assistance offered by surrendered burghers. According to him the British columns should concentrate on "chasing the marauders [sic], and in that enterprise I believe it would be possible gradually to associate some of the inhabitants with us. Of course," he added to Kitchener, "this experiment could only be tried at first in small numbers by arming a handful of farmers attached to a considerable force of Police or other mounted men, so that it would be impossible for them to play false."⁷

Milner was not the only one to hold this opinion. In November 1900 he held various interviews with Paul Botha, the former *Volksraad* member from the Free State. Botha, who later played a prominent role in the peace committee movement, maintained that certain burghers in the Kroonstad district were prepared to fight on the British side because they were convinced of the "necessity of putting down the present state of disorder". Milner labelled Botha "a man of extreme sincerity". "I must say," he added to the military governor in Bloemfontein, "I was much struck by the fact that quite independently of any suggestion of mine, he pressed home with great emphasis the points on which all of us had been thinking hard." In his discussion with Milner Botha felt that it was important "to attach to your patrols and flying columns a few people of the country as Volunteers, whose intimate knowledge of their several neighbourhoods will be of the greatest value, and who, having everything to gain by keeping their districts clear, ... and having burnt their boats by openly joining you, will have the greatest interest in your success." According to Botha some burghers would be prepared to assist the military authorities in the organisation of such an undertaking. He provided the names of the following Free State *Volksraad* members: T.C.L. Bergstedt (Winburg); P. Macdonald (Wepener); R. Macfarlane (Harrismith) and C.J. Cloete (Bethlehem).⁸

According to Captain C. Bisset of the Imperial Light Horse about 500 burghers from the Kroonstad district approached him at the beginning of October 1900 and volunteered to fight on the British side. By doing so, according to Bisset, they wanted to protect their district against "De Wet and his band of raiders".[9] Bisset was quite possibly exaggerating the number of burghers who offered their services. It is highly improbable whether as early as October 1900 there were as many as 500 burghers who were prepared to take up arms on the British side. Furthermore, Bisset does not give the impression of being a trustworthy person. The British authorities suspected him of embezzlement and on 17 October Roberts recalled him from the Kroonstad district where he had been buying up livestock on behalf of the British administration.[10]

Although Bisset's claims were exaggerated, by December 1900 a movement to arm republican burghers and organise them into a corps had certainly been initiated in the Kroonstad district. Major-general Pretyman, the military governor in Bloemfontein, briefly sketched Paul Botha's and Milner's recommendations to the district commissioner of Kroonstad, Captain F.R. de Bertodano. De Bertodano's reaction was a positive one. He was convinced that "the time has come for us to take the action mentioned in your letter. There are numbers of intelligent farmers and others who see what the inevitable end is. Their self-interest points out clearly the benefits proceeding from an early end to the war and future prosperity under English rule. Apart from self-interest there are some I know who are intensely bitter over the cowardly treatment [sic] meted out by De Wet's men to their own kindred." Further, the Kroonstad district commissioner pointed out that older men such as Paul Botha could be very useful because of their influence in the district, while there were also enough younger people who were prepared to take up arms. He already had 30 burghers on the staff of his intelligence service, of whom between 12 and 18 were armed. De Bertodano regarded them as reliable and according to him they had done sterling work for the British. Among their achievements there were two occasions on which they had captured some of De Wet's dispatch riders and they had also prevented a number of Boers from rejoining the commandos. After discussions with some of the residents of the district, including the ex-member of the *Volksraad* for Bethlehem, C.J. Cloete, De Bertodano found that "they all concur in the opinion that the time has certainly arrived when the loyal farmers should and will combine to protect their own". De Bertodano suggested a burgher corps with an initial membership of 60 men. Major-general Pretyman was favourably impressed with De Bertodano's proposal and he approved the undertaking, but at the same time the district commissioner was warned to be careful with the selection of members for the corps.[11]

The district commissioner of Heilbron, Colonel C.M. Wighley, planned a similar scheme to De Bertodano's. On 16 November 1900 he asked for Roberts's approval to arm a number of burghers in the Heilbron district. His reasons for this step were that many Boer patrols were active in the area and were harassing the surrendered burghers who were trying to go ahead with the running of their farms. Wighley further maintained that "a great number of men here are willing to bind themselves together to hound these rebel bands [sic]". If permission was granted to arm burghers he also predicted that "the formation of such a corps would have a very disheartening effect on those still remaining on commando, finding men of their own nationality willing to fight against them".[12] Although Roberts realised the possible advantages of such a corps, he was hesitant to give his permission. He was particularly concerned about the possibility that once these people had been armed by the British, they might go back to the commandos. However, Wighley was convinced that the burghers concerned would not play a double role and informed Roberts that their property could stand as the guarantee of their good faith. If they rejoined the commandos all their property would be confiscated by the British.[13] This argument presumably won Roberts over, and he gave Wighley permission to go ahead with the scheme.[14]

However, Colonel A.E. Dalzell, the commanding officer of the British garrison at Heilbron, had serious reservations about the wisdom of the district commissioner's plans. In December 1900 he pointed out to Kitchener – who had taken over from Roberts on 28 November 1900 – that the surrendered burghers were certainly not to be trusted and to arm them "would ... be indeed tempting Providence". This meant that Wighley had once again to direct a detailed request to Kitchener. He described Dalzell as "a most difficult officer to get on with", and went on to say that "I have had more opportunities of studying the Boers of the district than Col Dalzell ... here has." Wighley said that he had spoken to many surrendered burghers in the district and "the general consensus of opinion has been in favour of such a corps being raised". The district commissioner planned to use the corps as follows: "First to find out through my Kaffir Scouts, where Boers were in the habit of sleeping on farms in the vicinity ..., then suddenly sending a party of scouts there making a dash out at night, surrounding the place and attempting to capture the men sleeping there." With the help of Jan Els of the farm Slootkraal – according to Wighley, his "right-hand man in this movement" – by the end of December 1900 he had already selected 20 surrendered burghers to serve in the corps.[15]

Kitchener had no objections to Wighley going ahead with his plan and recommended that he set to work in consultation with De Bertodano. Because Colonel Dalzell at Heilbron was unwilling to give his support to the scheme, Kitchener suggested that the headquarters should be at Kroonstad rather than Heilbron.[16] During January 1901 a start was made with the formation of a corps for the Kroonstad area when about 70 men were enlisted and placed under the orders of Captain H.M.R. Brett, an intelligence service officer. The corps was generally known as the Kroonstad Burgher Scouts, although they were also referred to as Brett's Scouts. They served in cooperation with the British columns and among other duties they helped to find ammunition that the Boers had hidden. Sometimes the corps also did some reconnoitring on their own and while on a scouting expedition on 21 February 1901, they were involved in a skirmish with 50 Boers near Kroonstad. Two members of the Kroonstad Burgher Scouts were killed, while three Boers allegedly died and five were wounded.[17] In February 1902 De Bertodano said that he had no complaints about the corps,[18] but in contrast, Lieutenant J.F.C. Fuller, who had been involved with the corps in December 1901 in the capacity of an information officer, claimed that they were "a mongrel band of renegade Boers". They made an extremely poor impression on him: "This particular body of men was, I think, the most useless I ever came into touch with. Since it was composed of renegade Boers, they naturally were chary of risking their skins."[19]

On 1 January 1901 Kitchener encouraged various commanding officers in the Free State and the Transvaal to organise surrenderers into burgher corps.[20] In the Bloemfontein district Captain C. Ridley of the South African Constabulary took some of them into service to assist the Constabulary. They were initially called the Burgher Police and later became known as the Farmers' Guard.[21] But although Kitchener was in favour of taking local burghers into service, he was not prepared at that juncture to accept the help of Commandant J.H. Olivier of Rouxville, who was a prisoner of war on Ceylon. Olivier, who had played an important role in the Boer victory at Stormberg (10 December 1899), had offered to return to South Africa to guard the "peace" in his district. Both Kitchener and Milner agreed that accepting the assistance of a Boer officer could be construed as a sign of military weakness.[22]

In addition to the burgher corps that were formed in the Free State, by November 1900 there were also some Transvaal burghers who were prepared to offer armed assistance to the British. The district commissioner at Heidelberg, Captain J.M. Vallentin, had plans to organise these men into their own corps to protect the town, and possibly the district as well. Roberts was initially worried that they might later rejoin the commandos, but on 19 November he gave his permission for the issue of arms to a corps called the Heidelberg Volunteers.[23] On 29 November Roberts visited Heidelberg and asked to inspect the Volunteer corps which had "been formed into a town guard".[24] As the name implies, these people had to protect the town from Boer attacks. It can therefore be presumed that their duties were mainly of a defensive nature and that they had to stand guard on the outskirts of the town to inform the military authorities of the possible presence of Boers in the vicinity. From 1 January to 30 June 1901 the Heidelberg Volunteers suffered very few losses – only one of their members was killed and three were wounded.[25]

Initially the British were uncertain whether the members of the burgher corps should be paid for their services. The military governor at Bloemfontein recommended that they should receive free rations but not be paid.[26] Colonel Wighley of Heilbron was of the opinion that these men were in effect merely protecting their own property by fighting with the British. He wrote to Roberts: "I would offer no pay as the men would be virtually fighting for themselves."[27] Kitchener decided that they could only receive pay or be allowed to take some of the animals once they had proved themselves in the veld.[28] Captain de Bertodano, who had enlisted the Kroonstad Burgher Scouts, had mentioned a figure of 5s 0d per day to them. He disagreed with Kitchener's ruling and felt strongly that all the members of the burgher corps should be paid. "It practically amounts to this," he argued, "that should these men not be paid, they will immediately consider that they were enlisted under false pretences and we have committed a great breach of trust. So far as the ... Kroonstad Scouts is concerned, these men have performed valuable services and would certainly be entitled to pay. If they are paid, then arises a question of an invidious distinction."[29] H.F. Wilson, the secretary of the British administration in the Orange River Colony, agreed with De Bertodano, and the burgher corps in the Free State subsequently received 5s 0d per day, but the policy was not followed uniformly in the Transvaal.[30]

In the last two months of 1900 and in January 1901 the basis was laid for the sustained enrolment of republican burghers into British war service. This is far earlier than is generally accepted in the historiography of the Anglo-Boer War.[31] From the foregoing discussion it appears that the British provided the framework within which burghers could enter service in an active military capacity. Had there not been a real conviction on the part of some burghers to give active support to the British army, the scheme would not have become so viable. It is clear from the evidence of ex-*Volksraad* member Paul Botha and that of the district commissioners of Kroonstad and Heilbron, which has been discussed above, that this conviction was indeed present. The longer the war continued, the more prepared some burghers were to fight on the British side. There are no full statistics to show the rate at which republican burghers went over to the British. According to Kitchener, however, by the middle of January 1902 the total had reached 1660 and by February this had risen to about 2500.[32] On 27 April 1902, according to the British military intelligence, there were 3963 burghers in British service and on 1 June 1902, the day after the Peace of Vereeniging, the total stood at 5464.[33]

In popular parlance, the people who undertook active military service for the British were known as "joiners" or *verraaiers* (traitors).[34]

One Anglo-Boer War historian points out that "the anguished decision of people under enemy occupation is a recurring theme among the tragedies of war. Aside from the rank opportunist or coward, one man sees 'collaboration' as his highest duty towards his own people as sincerely as another believes in dogged opposition at any cost". But he adds: "The fact remains that 'collaboration' enjoys little esteem."[35] Another historian bluntly described the action of the "traitors" as a "deed which was no less than despicable".[36]

On what grounds can the accusation of treason be made? The jurist J.M. Spaight gives the following definition of treason as it applies to the Anglo-Boer War: "Treason means a conspiracy against the established authority in a State. Now the established authority in an occupied territory is the de facto ruler."[37] This explanation of treason hones in on an important issue, namely who really was the de facto power in the Free State and the Transvaal? Britain had certainly annexed the republics (24 May and 1 September 1900), but did not exercise full and effective control over them. The legitimate governments of these regions, the governments with whom Britain had to negotiate at the Peace of Vereeniging, were still in place. For all practical purposes Britain cannot therefore be seen as the de facto ruler. The burghers who helped the British army thus found themselves in an invidious legal position. They were fighting on the side of an apparently established British authority but in reality this authority, as President Steyn put it to Kitchener, only stretched about as far "as Your Excellency's cannon can reach".[38] The war was still in progress and the British authority was only formally recognised once the Peace of Vereeniging had been signed. It is therefore clear that the actions of these collaborators can indeed be regarded as treason. They had taken up arms against their own legitimate government, a government which was in place right up until 31 May 1902.

Constitutionally, therefore, the bitterenders had every right to regard those of their fellow countrymen who were in British war service as war traitors and they were fully entitled to take action against them – regardless of the traitors' motives. Spaight points out that "it is quite immaterial what the motives of the war-traitor are – whether patriotic and noble or base and mercenary".[39] The punishment for treason in terms of republican law was the death penalty or

15 years imprisonment.[40] Clearly the republican authorities had every right to impose these penalties.

It is also appropriate to scrutinise whether the British army acted in accordance with acceptable contemporary wartime practice by enlisting republican burghers into its service. Article 44 of the Hague Convention lays down the following: "Any compulsion of the population of an occupied territory to take part in military operations against its own country is prohibited."[41] The surrendered burghers were not compelled to render active British military service and thus the British action was not a contravention of this article. However, the contemporary French jurist, Despagnet, has some reservations about this issue. According to him the encouragement to commit treason, particularly if it involves the promise of payment, can generally be regarded as blameworthy.[42] Of course this does not mean that such action was at variance with the existing norms of warfare. According to the Netherlands attachés who were with the Boer forces, "When one warring party serves its interests by making use of the voluntary services of subjects of the enemy State, it does not break any rules or practices by so doing."[43] Spaight put the whole issue into a neat nutshell: "The man who volunteers to fight against his native land commits the penal offence of treason against the latter, but the belligerent who accepts his services breaks no war law."[44]

The burghers who actively participated in the military sphere on the British side went a step further than the ordinary surrendered burghers. It was indeed a radical step, and one which ensured that their names became indelibly recorded in South African history as traitors. By entering British service they were also taking an almost irrevocable step, because they would not be able to join the Boer forces again to make up for their disloyalty. The Boers would certainly never trust these traitors again and with good reason; some of them were afraid that if they tried to rejoin the commandos they would be shot.[45]

The so-called joiners served in the British army in a number of capacities. From the records of the British military intelligence service the following groups can be differentiated: the local burgher corps (for example the Kroonstad Burgher Scouts), the guides and scouts, and lastly the Orange River Colony Volunteers (hereafter

ORC Volunteers) and the National Scouts.[46] There were fundamental differences between the local burgher corps as well as the guides and scouts on the one hand, and the National Scouts and ORC Volunteers on the other.

As a rule the local burgher corps and the guides and scouts were recruited randomly by the British. They were not bound by any official service conditions and did not always receive fixed payment. Depending on circumstances they received either money or a percentage of the cattle which they took as booty. Sometimes they were given both money as well as some of the captured livestock.[47] Nor were they certified soldiers. Although they had taken the oath of allegiance and had thereby become British subjects, they were not sworn in as soldiers of the imperial army.[48] Likewise they did not receive a distinctive British uniform.[49] Initially the British leaders chose to accept their services on as informal a basis as possible and they were hesitant to recognise them officially.[50] With the exception of the Farmers' Guard in the Bloemfontein district, the local burgher corps also comprised a comparatively small number of men, and were not widely used in military operations.

In contrast to this, the National Scouts corps was placed on a substantial organisational basis during the last phase of the war (October 1901 – May 1902) and it was a completely separate corps. Members were bound by official service conditions and received fixed remuneration, with the system of payment by means of cattle being largely phased out.[51] In contrast with the local burgher corps, the scouts and the guides, the National Scouts were also sworn in as certified soldiers of the imperial army and they received a characteristic uniform.[52] The National Scout corps, which was organised on a district basis throughout the Transvaal, was also far larger in terms of membership than the local burgher corps[53] and it was involved to a greater extent in military operations. The same applied to the ORC Volunteers that was set up in the northern Free State. The fact that a Boer served as a guide or a scout for the British did not of course mean that he was a National Scout – over and above the National Scout corps there were many burghers who worked for the British as guides and scouts, but were not members of either the National Scout corps or the ORC Volunteers.[54] Lastly, the local burgher corps, guides and scouts did not act in collaboration with the National Scouts or the ORC Volunteers. In the light of these marked differences the various groups will be discussed separately.

2 Local burgher corps in the Free State

In the previous section brief mention was made of the burgher corps that was set up during January 1901 by Colonel C. Ridley of the South African Constabulary in Bloemfontein. On 19 January 1901 the corps comprised 35 men and Ridley was most satisfied with their conduct. "They fought a little action a few days ago under 2 of my officers but without any other to back them up. They did very well," he reported after a skirmish in the Bloemfontein district.[55]

This corps, which was known as the Burgher Police, gave assistance to the Constabulary in the Bloemfontein area in the removal of livestock from farms belonging to the fighting burghers. They also acted as guides for this same British unit and according to one opinion "their knowledge of the country adds greatly to their usefulness".[56] Their numbers increased and on 10 March the corps had 70 members. A Reuter correspondent described them as "keen-eyed, at home on their horses and expert in the handling of their rifles". He continued: "Unpressed men they were too, who have of their own initiative taken up arms not – to use their own words –'to carry on an offensive warfare against their former compatriots, but to protect lives and property from marauders and robbers [sic]'."[57]

Milner welcomed the enlistment of these burghers. "This will widen the breach which it is all in our interest to widen," he remarked to Kitchener on 20 March.[58] About a week later he wrote to the British commander in chief saying, "… so far they [the Burgher Police] have done really well, and are dead keen to shoot anyone who comes cattle-lifting within their lines. Of course, one of their great objects in taking up arms for us at all is to protect their property, and, with British posts all about, I believe they will be reliable and very useful."[59]

The establishment of the Burgher Police tied in well with Milner's idea of demarcating the areas around the republican capitals and

Johannesburg. He called them "protected areas" and they were supposed to be so well guarded that the Boer commandos would be unable to penetrate them. At the end of March 1901 Milner pointed out to Kitchener the great advantages this system would hold for the British. If they could occupy these areas effectively it would be a clear indication that Britain had conquered them irrevocably and could justifiably control and administer them. In these demarcated protected areas Milner hoped to normalise conditions so that local government and farming activities could go ahead unhindered. Once a particular region was effectively occupied, its boundaries could then be systematically extended. Milner also believed that the creation of protected areas "will encourage the tendency of the Boers under our protection to take up arms, to help to keep the other Boers off. They will fight for their cattle on their own ground as for nothing else."[60]

Milner's scheme was implemented only on a limited scale. The military tactics used by the commandos made its effective application virtually impossible, and the South African Constabulary, which was supposed to occupy and protect these areas, was instead used by Kitchener as a "flying column". As a result the Constabulary could devote little attention to the demarcation and protection of these areas.[61]

Nevertheless, in May 1901 a move was made to mark out an area around the perimeter of Bloemfontein and by the middle of July it stretched for about 32 kilometres around the town. Apparently the Boer commandos were unable to penetrate this region for more than a month and this was ascribed to "the good work of the burgher police".[62] According to the authors of the *Times History*, "The protection of Bloemfontein was soon assured by an almost impenetrable screen of posts manned largely by surrendered farmers."[63]

On occasion the Burgher Police came face to face with their compatriots. At the beginning of March members of the corps were involved in a skirmish with a Boer patrol near Brandfort. A newspaper report claimed that the corps itself had not suffered any casualties, but that four Boers were captured, three of whom were wounded.[64] On 19 June they were caught up in a clash lasting several hours with a force of 60 Boers near Vlakfontein (south of Sannaspos). They apparently managed to ward off the Boer attack and in the process wounded three of their former comrades.[65]

The Burgher Police did not always meet with success. On 8 September six members of the corps fell into the hands of the Boers during a reconnoitre in the vicinity of Smaldeel (a railway halt in the Winburg district). The six men (J.J. Eva, J. Adendorf, T.D. Wasserman, H.J. de Bruijn and the brothers N.J. and J.C. Coetzee), escorted by Field-cornet P. R. Erasmus and his force, were taken to General C.C.J. Badenhorst in the Boshof district. In half-hearted defence they claimed that they had wanted to rejoin the commandos, but had been taken prisoner before they had been able to do so. In response, Erasmus pointed out that they had tried to run away when they saw him and his men. Although the six turncoats then gave the feeble excuse that they were only waiting for their pursuers to catch up before making a move to rejoin the commando, General Badenhorst was obviously not prepared to believe this naive fabrication. On 18 September all six men were sentenced to death by a court martial under the chairmanship of Badenhorst. The court's finding was sent to President Steyn for ratification. Steyn and the executive council were extremely accommodating towards two of the traitors, J.J. Eva and J. Adendorf. Although Eva had deserted from the commando and had fought on the British side, it was taken into consideration that he had only been a resident in the Free State a mere eight months before the outbreak of the war. It was argued that he was not really a republican burgher and he was sent back to the Boer lines as an ordinary prisoner of war. Adendorf's age (18 years) and his defence that he had been influenced by his father to fight on the British side were accepted in his case as mitigating factors. He was sentenced for the entire duration of the war to imprisonment with periods of hard labour and was also to receive 25 lashes with a stirrup leather. The sentences on the other four men were ratified and they were executed by firing squad on a date after 11 October 1901.[66]

The danger that members of the Burgher Police could receive the death sentence when they were captured by the Boers did not prevent the number of members from increasing during the last nine months of 1901. According to a report that Milner sent to Chamberlain in December 1901, there were about 500 men in the corps at the time. In the same report Milner described their role in cooperation with the South African Constabulary as "a noticeable and gratifying feature of the operations". "These men," he added, "are not enrolled as ordinary members of the South African Constabulary, but are an auxiliary force, attached to it for the Special duty of protecting a particular area – the country immediately round Bloemfontein ... The area protected by this force is of considerable extent, and within it farming operations have been conducted for months past practically without disturbance."[67] The extent of the "farming operations" to which Milner referred were less expansive than he perhaps cared to admit to Chamberlain. Members of the Burgher Police who owned farms in the protected area were permitted to continue their farming activities on a part-time basis,[68] but other than this it does not appear that agricultural activities were taking place on any significant scale.

In November 1901 the British administration in Bloemfontein considered the feasibility of placing the surrendered burghers and their families in the protected area. H.F. Wilson felt that if the scheme could be successfully implemented it would serve as tangible proof of permanent and effective British occupation. It would also meet the needs of the surrendered burghers. Wilson explained: "Many of those who have surrendered have now taken the oath of allegiance, and would be only too glad to have an opportunity peacefully to settle down to their former occupations. Men of standing and influence are to be counted amongst them. At present they are hanging about the towns and refugee camps with no employment, and are naturally becoming weary and discouraged at the long delay."[69] Milner agreed wholeheartedly with the plan in principle, but he notified Wilson, "I have the greatest difficulty in getting the C-in-C to agree to anything of the kind."[70]

Kitchener himself expressed the hope in May 1901 that they would be able to move the surrendered burghers who were in the concentration camps out to the protected areas,[71] but by November he evidently thought that the time was not yet ripe to do so. Nevertheless, in December 1901 he gave orders that the protected area around Bloemfontein should be extended and that the Burgher Police should henceforth be known as the Farmers' Guard. This name change was to reflect the new role which they would fill in the future – the protection of surrendered burghers who would be farming in the Bloemfontein area,[72] but by May 1902, over and above the members of the Farmers' Guard, there were in fact very few surrendered burghers farming in the protected area.[73]

In order to extend the protected area it was necessary to take on more men as members of the Farmers' Guard. Major E. Lyon of the South African Constabulary, who was responsible for the recruitment of members, hoped to form an additional wing of the corps comprising 500 men, and to this end regular recruitment advertisements appeared in *The Bloemfontein Post*. People had to be prepared to join for three months and would receive 5s 0d per day.[74] There were certain prisoners of war in the camp in Simon's Town who were keen to join the Farmers' Guard in December 1901, but the authorities concerned did not consider it advisable at the time to make use of their services.[75] By the end of the war there were 615 men in the Farmers' Guard.[76] It would appear that the military authorities had experienced some difficulty in recruiting the proposed 500 men for the new section.

By January 1901 Kitchener had given the commanding officers of the British columns the authority to swear in as British citizens those people who joined the burgher corps.[77] Milner was not, however, prepared to regard the standard oath of allegiance administered by military officers as valid in this instance. "Lord Milner feels," his private secretary wrote in November 1901, "that while such authority may be necessary for the purpose of having a more complete hold on former burghers when they are enlisted in Burgher Corps, or for intelligence purposes, the Civil authorities cannot recognise such oaths, and it will be necessary for them to be re-taken before a Special Commissioner appointed by him as High Commissioner in strict accordance with the Instructions and on the proper forms."[78] This meant that in February 1902 members of the Farmers' Guard had to take the oath of allegiance – many of them for the first time – before a special commissioner called Boswell.[79] The sources provide no evidence on the reasons why Milner saw fit to regard this special oath of allegiance, administered by the civil authorities, as the only oath that would be valid. Perhaps he felt that the granting of British citizenship fell more properly under the civil authorities that would later form the basis of the future government of the republics, and it was outside the ambit of the military authorities who would after all be leaving the country when the war was over.

There are very few sources from which an overall picture of the pre-war occupations of the members of the Farmers' Guard can be compiled. From one available list of 80 members it seems that most of them (65) were involved in farming before the war. The others practised a variety of professions, some having been clerks, blacksmiths, bricklayers and butchers, and one was even a photographer. Of the 80 members, 42 came from the Bloemfontein district, while the others came predominately from the districts in the southern and eastern Free State.[80]

By February 1902 the protected area stretched for about 64 kilometres around Bloemfontein. A number of border posts, which were about nine kilometres apart, were set up on the boundary. Between five and ten members of the Farmers' Guard manned each of these and patrolled the area between the different posts.[81] In addition the Farmers' Guard had to patrol the area within the boundaries. Major E.M. Morris considered that the extra patrols were necessary "to protect the people living on their farms with their stock, as well as the Government cattle".[82] After the war H.G. de Wet, who had been a member of the corps for a while, said of the man who went out on these regular patrols: "he soon had the whole sistem [sic] at his finger points, and was always the first to find out if ... any Republican scouts were in the neighbourhood, which he reported to his commander."[83] From March to the beginning of May 1902 the Farmers' Guard captured a total of 20 Boers.[84]

The protected area was not really as safe as the British would have liked it to be and the Farmers' Guard could not always prevent the fighting Boers from finding their way inside. On 22 January 1902 the Boers succeeded in capturing 600 sheep and 60 cattle that were grazing just inside the boundary.[85] Three months later they went even further. On the night of 27 April 1902, 250 Boers under Commandant van der Berg managed to enter the western sector of the protected area. They split up so as to collect livestock from various farms, and they also took clothing and blankets from people who lived there. Members of the Farmers' Guard tried in vain to raise the alarm and a dispatch rider who was sent to Bloemfontein to get help was stopped by the Boers. Meanwhile, a skirmish had broken out between the Farmers' Guard and the Boers and three men from the Farmers' Guard were seriously wounded, with two others suffering light injuries. Afterwards it was reported that the Boers had left one of the wounded men lying naked in the veld. On the Boer side one burgher died, while Field-cornet C.T. van Schalkwyk, who was seriously wounded, was captured. In the early hours of the morning the Boers slipped out of the area again, taking with them 1135 head of livestock, of which 235 belonged to the Farmers' Guard.[86]

This incident, which took place shortly before the Peace of Vereeniging, underlined the resilience and single-mindedness of the Boer forces. It was a rude awakening for the military authorities and they promptly set up a commission of inquiry to investigate the incident. It was found that under the circumstances the Farmers' Guard had acquitted themselves well, but the Boer attack had been cunningly planned and they had also outnumbered the Farmers' Guard in the western sector of the protected area. It was nevertheless clear that the protected area scheme had not really met its objectives and thus the commission thought it wise "to reduce the protected area very much".[87]

The Farmers' Guard was an all-white corps which was active in the Bloemfontein district. During 1901 the Boer forces in the Free State also came up against a local corps which had both white and African members. This corps, which was under the command of Captain O.M. Bergh, a Free State citizen, together with a number of surrendered burghers and Africans from the Winburg area, not only attacked the republican forces, but apparently also burnt farmsteads in the district and molested the defenceless women and children.[88]

In his memoirs General De Wet made mention of between 400 and 500 black people who fought under Bergh.[89] P.A. Nierstrasz puts the number of Africans at about 300 men.[90] It is not known what this corps called itself. Indeed, it is doubtful whether it had any official name at all. In his work on the concentration camps Otto describes the corps in a footnote as the "kafferkommando"[91] – the name by which this corps was widely known in local parlance.[92] By describing Bergh as a National Scout, De Wet gives the impression that this corps had some link with the National Scouts,[93] but this was certainly not so because the National Scouts corps operated in the Transvaal.[94] In any event, Bergh's corps was under the overall leadership of a British officer, Colonel J.S.S. Barker, and was well known among the Boers in the Winburg district.[95]

On 26 May 1901 the surrendered burghers and Africans under Bergh were responsible for the death of Jan Scott, a burgher from the Winburg district. According to the memoirs of two burghers from the same town, P. Beukes and P.J. Muller, as well as William Scott (the grandson of the man who died), Jan Scott was murdered in cold blood during a raid by Bergh's corps.[96] This evidence is also corroborated by Mrs J.J. de Klerk of the farm Candy in the Winburg district, on whose farm Scott is buried. On the gravestone are the words: "Died at the hands of traitors."[97]

De Wet also mentions four other burghers who were "brutally murdered" by Bergh's corps. These four burghers were members of Commandant Sarel Haasbroek's commando.[98] Nierstrasz also alleges that the men were "gruesomely slaughtered".[99] The evidence of burgher G.J.S. van den Heever, who saw three of the corpses, serves to confirm that the men met their end under horrific circumstances. He claims that in September 1901 the "surrendered burghers and blacks" under Bergh surrounded some of the members of Haasbroek's commando at Doornberg, about 48 kilometres north-east of Winburg and 32 kilometres west of Senekal. Van den Heever alleges that the Boers were "too relaxed" and is of the opinion that the encirclement would not have occurred if there had been "proper guards in place during the night". It seems that Bergh's corps was able to catch the Boers unawares and 24 Boers were captured while four were killed. Regarding the death of three of these burghers, Van den Heever relates that a man called Potgieter had been butchered and that his "whole head was broken open and his brains lay on the ground. Ampie Botha had also been bludgeoned to death, with both his arms smashed to a pulp as he turned around. Then he was shot again in his left eye by a bullet from a Martini [Henri rifle] and his head was blown away. You could see that they had held the rifle against him because he was burnt by the gunpowder, and he was also shot again in his stomach. Ampie van Schalkwyk, the 2 Ampies were cousins, ...

had one shot through his head ... and he had also been shot 5 times almost in a ring around his heart ... it looked as if the rifles had been pressed against him." Van den Heever closes the gruesome account by saying: "The 3 young Afrikaners were murdered in this terrible way by fellow-Afrikaners and Kaffirs and the English."[100]

De Wet was determined to take revenge for these murders in early December 1901. He planned an attack on Colonel Barker's columns, because Bergh's corps was under Barker's command. However, in the vicinity of Kafferskop, 30 kilometres north-west of Bethlehem, De Wet came up against three combined British columns and he was forced to abandon his plans.[101] Later in December a number of burghers from Commandant Haasbroek's commando captured 18 of Bergh's Africans and they were shot immediately.[102]

Next, the attention falls on those who were not attached to a particular corps, but were active in the two republics as guides and scouts in the service of the British columns.

3 The guides and scouts

By the end of November 1900 a worried General Smuts wrote from the Krugersdorp district to Reitz, the state secretary: "... it is all too true (how depressing also) that the enemy are being led around by traitors from among our people, which means that they can do so much more than they would otherwise have been able to accomplish."[103] The use of surrendered burghers as guides increased dramatically in 1901 and the last months of the war, and in April 1902 Kitchener was able to report that all the columns of the British army had surrendered burghers available to serve as guides.[104]

Most of these guides were recruited from the concentration camps.[105] They were not normally taken into service for a fixed period and in the words of Major E.H.M. Leggett their numbers varied according to "the exigencies of their Military employment". When their services were not required for a while, they were sent back to the concentration camps.[106] In the Irene camp a large tent was pitched to serve as a "barrack room" for them.[107] The guides were not permanently employed because they were used mainly in the areas they were most familiar with, and the British columns to which they were attached were frequently moved from one area to another. In a new vicinity these guides would be relatively less valuable.[108] By the end of the war the British had 3042 surrendered burghers in service as guides, scouts and interpreters. The large majority of these men were scouts and guides.[109]

The guides each received 5s 0d per day, but if they gleaned particularly useful information on the movements of the Boers they were given between £3 and £7 extra.[110] Nor were the British above bribing the burghers with large sums of money to get information from them. P.H. Bezuidenhout, for example, formerly the assistant magistrate of the Heilbron district, wrote to the director of the military intelligence service in January 1902: "When I was captured on the 20th [of January 1902] near Heilbron I agreed with Mr. Walker, M.I.O.[military intelligence officer] with General Rimington, to give all the information that I knew of the Boer commandoes etc. In return for which I would receive £5 000 from the British Government and get my liberty, and that also my family who is still on the farm where I lived would be fetched in to live with me at Boksburg or elsewhere in the Cape Colony." Bezuidenhout was sent to Pretoria with the promise and understanding that the director of the intelligence service "will settle matters with me". When he arrived in Pretoria, however, he was regarded as a prisoner of war. In view of the fact that he had indeed provided certain information, Major G.F. Milne of the information service and the provost marshal, Lieutenant-colonel R.M. Poore, were prepared to classify him as a surrendered burgher rather than as a prisoner of war. It was decided that he should be sent to Bloemfontein at the expense of the information service and that he should be allowed to remain there on parole.[111] Quite understandably no further mention was made of the £5 000 and in all likelihood it was never paid. If Bezuidenhout, who as assistant magistrate must have been a reasonably intelligent man, had been bribed in this way to give information to the British, how many of the simple folk, the ordinary burghers, were perhaps persuaded to betray their country in a similar fashion? It is also known that on occasion the British threatened some of the prisoners of war with the death sentence to get information about where the Boers had stored ammunition.[112]

On the other hand, republican burghers who were taken prisoner by the British columns were sometimes prepared to act as guides immediately after their arrest. According to Captain M. Miller, a British officer in one of the columns in the eastern Transvaal, this was not an infrequent occurrence. "These Boers are funny fellows," he wrote in February 1902. "We caught one the other day who immediately offered to be a guide and took part the day after in a night march, and brought in one of his pals, as pleased as Punch – and this is a common thing."[113] Nor was Miller exaggerating, because the same allegation was made on the Boer side. J. le Roux, a Transvaal burgher who succeeded in escaping after he had been captured, claimed: "I am very sorry that I must say that the burghers who surrender at once, are ready to guide the enemy, and they do everything in their power for our destruction."[114] The preparedness of some burghers to act as guides immediately after their capture can possibly be ascribed to the fact that the British authorities then classified them as surrendered burghers and did not send them out of South Africa.[115]

How important was the role that these guides played in the British army? From a report compiled by the British field intelligence department in June 1902 it appears that guides who knew the terrain – particularly during the guerrilla warfare phase – were in great demand by the commanders of the columns. Indeed, it is claimed that "Column Commanders have, almost without exception, constantly applied for an increase of their Intelligence Staff ... in capacities of Guides, Interpreters and Agents."[116] Whereas the Boers knew the terrain like the palm of their hand, the British often had very sketchy information, and they had only a limited number of their own specialist guides and scouts. "No successes," according to the authors of the *Times History*, "should obscure the fact that scouting as one of the elementary military duties was neglected." These same writers also claim that it was "in the capacity of scouts and spies that the [surrendered] burghers were most useful", and they refer to the British columns having "so to speak, borrowed eyes when it should have had as many eyes as it had mounted men".[117] The surrendered burghers who served as guides thus filled what was a very significant gap in the British army. They were residents of the country and had an intimate knowledge not only of the war terrain but also of the military

241

tactics of their former comrades. As such they were in a position to supply both information and advice to the commanders of the British columns, information to which they would otherwise not have had access, or perhaps would have acquired with far more effort.[118]

In the light of this it is not surprising that the commanding officers of the British columns often commended the services of the guides. In the Harrismith district the Imperial Light Horse under Brigadier-general J.G. Dartnell captured a number of burghers on 30 November 1901. At the time E. Pentz and P. Marais were serving as guides for the unit and Lieutenant-general L. Rundle, commanding officer of the eighth division at Harrismith, expressed the following opinion on their conduct: "Undoubtedly the success of General Dartnell's troops on the 30th November, when 24 prisoners were captured, was chiefly due to the guiding of these two men."[119] On W. Erasmus of Rouxville, who was a guide for one of the British columns in the Bethulie district, Colonel T.D. Pilcher, the commanding officer, reported: "On November 2nd [1901], Erasmus was with Captain Walters and six men, when fire was opened on them at a range of 50 yards. He [Erasmus] galloped back through a hail of bullets, without being ordered to do so, to where the main body of the patrol was, some 3 miles off, and urging the Officer commanding to hurry, he brought the patrol up just in time to take 21 men prisoner before dark." Colonel Pilcher considered Erasmus a great asset and hoped that he would be able to stay on with his column as a guide – "in which capacity he is excellent".[120] In February 1902 the information officer for Colonel F.S. Garrat's columns in the Heilbron district said of J.G.M. Benadi: "I was extremely short of guides who knew this part of the country ... and found that he [Benadi] was willing to act temporarily as [a] guide in the recent general drive. He accordingly acted as guide for several days and also gave useful information concerning the enemy."[121] In the eastern Transvaal J.C. Cochins, of the farm Driefontein in the Middelburg district, acted as a guide for Colonel E.C. Williams's column and also provided the British with information about Jack Hindon, the renowned Boer train looter. Cochins had been appointed by Captain C.B. Vandeleur, Colonel Williams's information officer, and impressed his new employer with the quality service he rendered: "I approached him on the point of the whereabouts of Hindon and he agreed to do his best to discover his hiding place," wrote Vandeleur. "On the 24th February [1902] I sent him out to obtain information with 2 of my scouts; he returned the same night with 2 prisoners (Hindon's men) and stated [that] he [had] wounded 2 others. These wounded men have since been brought into Middelburg ... I consider this man will be of the greatest service and use to me."[122] Colonel W.P. Campbell who operated in the eastern Transvaal had 38 burgher scouts. In the period from 18 to 31 August 1901 these guides managed, entirely on their own, to capture 14 Boers and Campbell regarded them as "most useful".[123] They were also able to inform the British where the Boers had hidden ammunition and cannons. Indeed, in April 1901 Dr J.C.J. Bierens de Haan of the Netherlands Ambulance expressed the opinion that in most cases the British would not have been able to trace these strategic supplies had it not been for treason.[124] This help from the guides was highly rated and they received an additional bonus in appreciation for work well done.[125] The British officers' satisfaction with the guides does not only reflect the valuable service which they provided, but is at the same time also an indication of the gravely negative impact these services had on the republican cause.

On the other hand, it must be kept in mind that all the guides taken into British service were not equally reliable. On 14 January 1902 J. Pretorius and J. Botha, who were active in the Lindley district as guides under Lieutenant colonel J.H.G. Byng, deserted the columns and vanished without trace. This matter was regarded in a serious light and a commission of inquiry was set up, but it could not be established why the guides had left or where they had gone.[126] In the same vein, the diary kept by P.J. du Toit, who served as a guide with E.H.H. Allenby's columns for about nine months, appears to indicate that he was able to provide very little active or significant assistance to his former enemies.[127]

Nevertheless, in the night attacks which the British launched, particularly those from July 1901 onwards on the Transvaal highveld, the guides did indeed play an important role. The columns led by Lieutenant-colonel G.E. Benson and later General B. Hamilton were well known for these attacks. A. Woolls-Sampson – an *Uitlander* who was a member of the Reform Committee in Johannesburg at the time of the Jameson Raid in 1896 – was Benson's information officer. He used the guides in Benson's column to organise regular and systematic night attacks on the Boer laagers. In cooperation with African spies these guides kept Woolls-Sampson and Benson informed about the places where the Boers might possibly camp for the night. On the basis of this information Benson's columns, led by the guides, were able to launch lightning night attacks, almost invariably surprising the Boers and taking them captive.[128] In September 1901 Benson made appreciative comments about the Boer scouts who had helped his column to take 117 Boer prisoners of war in the course of that particular month.[129] Benson's tactics did alarm the Boers to some extent. On 23 October Commandant-general Botha ordered that the commandos should hit back hard at Benson's "restless column" to wipe it out.[130] On 31 October Benson was killed in the battle of Bakenlaagte, a notable Boer victory. Thereafter General B. Hamilton continued the night drives, with Woolls-Sampson still filling the role of chief planner, and he continued to base his system on information gleaned by Boer guides and scouts. The *Times History* claims that, "A surrendered Boer named [J.] Lange who acted as Sampson's head man, besides controlling a number of skilled guides, had an agent in nearly every Kaffir kraal."[131] J. Lange's services in this spy network were highly commended and in December 1901 he was singled out in Kitchener's report for honourable mention.[132]

In the Free State the British columns also launched night attacks on the Boer commandos with the help of burgher guides they had taken into service. By doing so De Wet claims that the British "discovered a way of inflicting a great deal of harm on us, but they would not have been able to undertake these night attacks had they not been assisted by our very own flesh and blood".[133] At the end of September 1901 Colonel C.J. Briggs of the Imperial Light Horse, which was stationed near Bethlehem at the time, undertook such an attack on Reitz in the hope of capturing De Wet. The Imperial Light Horse covered the distance of about 50 kilometres at a great pace on the night of 26 September, but although a number of burghers were captured, the British were unable to lay their hands on the elusive De Wet.[134] De Wet later described their speedy night ride as a "nice piece" of work, but according to him the columns had been guided by the son of a Free State member of the *Volksraad*, whose name he declined to mention.[135] Lieutenant G.F. Gibson, who was attached to the intelligence service of the Imperial Light Horse and was the author of a work on the history of this regiment during the Anglo-Boer War, disputes this and says: "The column was led by a native named Klaas and Intelligence Agent L.F. Drake, both under the immediate control of the I.L.H. Intelligence Officer. A point is made of this, as General de Wet in his book ... attacks the son of a well-known member of the O.F.S. Volksraad, who he incorrectly states guided the column that night."[136] There does not appear to be any other evidence to establish exactly who guided the Imperial Light Horse on that night of 26 September.

De Wet was, however, perfectly correct in claiming that in July 1901 "treason was taking place" when a Free State burgher, J. Steenekamp, acted as a guide for the British columns – the columns that captured members of President Steyn's bodyguard and other government officials on 11 July at Reitz.[137] Together with Steenekamp there were 10 other "disloyal burghers" who accompanied these British columns.[138] A number of government officials and members of Steyn's military staff were taken captive when a force of about 400 British soldiers under the command of Brigadier-general R.G. Broadwood stormed the town of Reitz in the early hours of the morning. They were Thomas Brain, the government secretary; General A.P. (Andries) Cronjé, a member of the executive council and the military commission; General J.B. Wessels, a member of the military commission; Field-cornet P. Steyn, a member of the military commission and President Steyn's older brother; Rocco de Villiers, secretary of the executive council; Gordon A. Fraser, President Steyn's private secretary; A. McHardy, secretary of the military commission and Commandant O.A. Davel with about 21 men. The British also took possession of £11 500 and President Steyn's correspondence. The president himself only just managed to escape in time.[139]

The capture of so many key people was a cruel blow to the Free Staters, and the fact that treason had played a role made it even more difficult to accept the loss.[140] Had the apostasy of Steenekamp and the others also led to the capture of President Steyn – who together with De Wet to a large extent personified the republican freedom struggle – it might well have had an extremely far-reaching and demoralising impact on the republican cause. After the war Steenekamp was summoned to appear before the Frankfort church council to account for his conduct. He admitted that he had led Broadwood's columns to Reitz, but claimed that the British had forced him to act as a guide. The church council felt that this was highly unlikely and decided that he was merely trying to make an excuse to clear himself. They indicated that Steenekamp had to show true remorse for his unacceptable behaviour and it was only when he eventually admitted that he was sorry that the church council decided to let the matter rest.[141]

If any of these guides fell into Boer hands they were usually given the death sentence. On 26 December 1900 three guides who were attached to the columns under Major-general C.W.H. Douglas were captured near Hartebeesfontein. The three traitors (P.C. de Bruin, J.A.B. de Beer and H.C. Boshoff) were summarily tried and two of them, De Bruin and De Beer, were executed by firing squad early the following morning. Boshoff was set free on account of his age.[142]

In addition to the guides who assisted the British columns to track down the Boer commandos, there were also Boer guides who led the British columns to the farms of the fighting burghers so that the homesteads could be burned down and the women transported to concentration camps. Mrs C.P.M. van Dijk of the Rustenburg district makes mention in her memoirs of "two tame khakis" (impostors pretending to be British soldiers), Willem Roos and Casper Buitendach, who were guides in the columns under Major-general F.W. Kitchener (the brother of the commander-in-chief).[143] Heated verbal exchanges between the guides and the Boer women were not uncommon. Mrs van Dijk remembered the following argument that transpired when she was removed from her farm on 7 February 1901: "Mr L.Grey, a tame khaki came to me from among the throng of troops and asked: 'Where is your husband, what are they still fighting for?' 'He is on commando and he is fighting for his country,' was my answer. To this Grey retorted: 'They are fighting in vain, they have already lost the war. Where is old Paul Kruger now and where is your Bible in which you believe so firmly? We are here to load you up to go to the camps and if you don't cooperate we will toss you onto the wagons. It would be better for your husband to come and surrender because then he would be allowed to stay with you.' And I said 'Look, Uncle Lewies, that is the very last thing my husband would ever do, he will fight to the death.'"[144]

The guides sometimes prevented the women from loading the wagons with all the possessions that they might need in the concentration camps,[145] and certain guides also showed very little respect for the women who were being sent off to the camps. Mrs M.C. Joubert of the Carolina district was taken to a concentration camp and she provides evidence on the treatment that she and her mother received: "The wagons which were provided to transport us were on top of the mountain and we had to climb up there on foot while they hurried us along. The one handsupper [surrendered burgher] rode behind us on a big white horse and he threatened to stab us with the bayonet at the end of his rifle if we wanted to rest or drink some water. My mother was blind and was a very stout woman. She weighed more than 300 pounds and she could hardly walk, but he forced her to obey."[146] This reprehensible and heartless attitude shown by some of the guides towards defenceless women tends to put their act of treason in an even poorer light.

Then there were surrendered burghers who gave active assistance to the British military intelligence service as scouts. Initially, this service of the British left much to be desired and by November 1900 it had only 30 officers and 250 other white members.[147] Even by May 1901 the British still did not have an organised system for collecting information on the Boer movements in a coordinated and effective manner. On the one hand, they relied on African men and on the other they gleaned snippets of information from surrendered burghers. According to the authors of the *Times History* these burgher informants were by and large "the lower class of Boers, bywoners [share-croppers] or landless men, who had no stake in the country and held the ties of the commando very lightly".[148]

However, during the last months of the war the British tried to put their intelligence service on a sounder footing. The staff was increased to 132 officers and 2321 other white staff members and in almost every district they also organised a number of so-called "intelligence posts", each manned by an intelligence agent and a few scouts. This system was only made possible by the blockhouse lines which provided a modicum of security for the small outposts. The intelligence agents and their helpers used the posts as their base and moved out from these as inconspicuously as possible to pick up information on the Boer commandos before passing it on to the British columns. The intelligence agents who controlled the outposts were usually members of the British army. Sometimes surrendered burghers were also given this responsibility, but more often they were expected to act as scouts to do the spying.[149] The headquarters of the military intelligence service in Pretoria reported that, "the information so obtained has been very valuable and accurate. These small posts kept the enemy in a state of disquiet and the enterprise and activity of the Scouts resulted in a large number of captures in every district in which the posts were established."[150] According to the British, the surrendered burghers who did service as scouts played an important role in this information network.

The disloyal burghers could sometimes provide the British with first-hand information. For example, on 18 December 1901 Brigadier-general J.G. Dartnell, commander of the Imperial Light Horse, was alerted that De Wet was planning an attack on one of his convoys at Tierkloofspruit (on the road between Bethlehem and Harrismith). The first whisper of this attack was provided by an African scout on 17 December and early the following morning an anonymous burgher from De Wet's commando, who had come to hand himself over to the enemy, confirmed the rumour and voluntarily offered to provide additional information.[151] The *Official History* maintains that, "This was one of the rare occasions during the campaign on which information as to De Wet was absolutely reliable."[152] De Wet, who was probably unaware of this act of treachery, was determined to overwhelm the British convoy,[153] but because of the information the British had received, they were on the alert and sent out only a compact mounted force, protected by light artillery.[154] The element of surprise which was such a crucial factor in De Wet's tactics had been neutralised by this particular treachery. At 11 o'clock about 200 of his men fired on the British columns from both sides of the road, but the enemy was well prepared and managed to ward off the attack. Not all De Wet's men were equally enthusiastic about taking part in the skirmish and later when writing about the incident at Tierkloofspruit De Wet said wryly: "Everything culminated in disaster."[155]

Some republican burghers represented an even greater threat to their compatriots than did the person who informed the British about De Wet's planned attack at Tierkloofspruit. Although they remained on commando they were in fact British spies. Colonel D. Henderson of the British military intelligence service maintained that, "In the O.R. Colony we have a man with De Wet, but he gets very little chance of reporting. There are three or four others who move from commando to commando …"[156] Towards the end of the war General C.H. Muller of the Boksburg commando also suspected that the British had planted traitors among his ranks.[157]

In addition to the traitors who have been discussed in this section, there were also several local burgher corps in the Transvaal which merit closer attention.

4 Local burgher corps in the Transvaal

There is little evidence of systematic planning in the establishment and organisation of the various local burgher corps that arose in the Transvaal during 1901. By the end of the war a correspondent of the London *Times* reported: "The Burgher corps sprang into existence spontaneously and haphazardly. They were essentially local bodies distinct as regards conditions of service and internal organization, acting independently or attached to a column leader. One point only they had in common – a claim to prize-money."[158] Most of the members of these corps were recruited from among the surrendered burghers in the concentration camps.[159] In October 1901 all superintendents were instructed to bring the existence of burgher corps to the attention of surrendered burghers in the camps.[160]

The Vereeniging burgher corps, established in February 1901, was apparently one of the first in the Transvaal in 1901. Under the leadership of the district commissioner of Vereeniging, Captain W.G. Bentinck, a meeting was held on 9 February in the Vereeniging concentration camp and 23 surrendered burghers decided to throw in their lot with the British. During the period from February to November

1901 this number remained more or less constant.[161] The corps was mainly concerned with rounding up the livestock belonging to fighting burghers whose farms were in the district. The corps members then took care of some of these animals as well as government-owned cattle in the vicinity of the concentration camp. The corps usually worked in collaboration with the British columns, but also sometimes went out to collect cattle on its own. From February to November 1901 corps members rounded up 622 head of cattle and 2588 sheep in the district, and working with the columns they were responsible for collecting 488 cattle and 9975 sheep. Of these, 60% were given to the burgher corps, to be divided among the members by way of payment, while 40% went to the authorities. The corps did not receive any wages and according to Captain Bentinck the members were satisfied with this arrangement.[162] If they chose to do so they were also free to sell some of their livestock to the British administration, and some of them elected to do this.[163]

Members of the Vereeniging burgher corps received separate accommodation near the concentration camp. Dr K. Franks, a medical doctor who visited the concentration camp in September 1901, was not impressed with the camp where they lived. "Being employed as scouts," he reported, "they are not under the same supervision and discipline as those in the other camp; hence their camp is neither so clean nor so orderly as the other."[164] Their camp was perhaps not as tidy, but in other respects the British, who were in close contact with the corps, received no complaints from them. "There has never been the slightest discontent," wrote Captain Bentinck, "[and] a nicer selection of men I have never had to deal with outside the service." He did however have his reservations about their fighting spirit and thought that certain members of the corps "cannot be quite depended on to stand in a tight corner".[165]

In the Pretoria district there was a burgher corps known as Morley's Scouts. The earliest reference that could be traced on the existence of this corps is March 1901.[166] It operated under the leadership of Captain R.W. Morley, a British officer. A member of Morley's Scouts, W.S. Hubbel, used particularly flowery language to describe the capabilities of his commander: "It were better for England's cause if there had been more men like Morley out here, a more hard working, loyal or conscientious specimen of a true Briton and a natural nobleman I have never seen."[167] The members of Morley's Scouts were not all republican burghers. By June 1901 there were 40 members in the corps of whom 20 were of mixed nationalities – among them were Americans, Germans, Russians, Frenchmen and Englishmen. The other 20 were Transvaal burghers.[168]

According to W. Milward, a member of the corps, they were not soldiers "in the ordinary acceptance of the term, as we were never attested or sworn in".[169] Furthermore, the commissioner of police in Pretoria did not regard them as "recognised soldiers of the S.A. Forces".[170] In fact, Morley's Scouts and other similar corps were only informally recognised by the British army command.[171]

An anonymous member of Morley's Scouts said after the war that "the conditions of service were rather unusual. The men had to find their own horses and uniforms, the Government supplying arms and rations. We received no pay but were entitled to 75 per cent of all stock taken from the enemy. None of the members of the corps was attested; and the burghers who belonged to it had not even taken the oath of allegiance to the sovereign they were serving. There were no N.C.O.'s and there was no drill or discipline in the accepted sense of the term".[172] According to the members of the corps, the military authorities also made certain promises to them, namely "that every possible step would be taken to provide them with employment suited to their capacities immediately after the conclusion of hostilities".[173]

The corps's main task was to round up as much livestock as possible in the Pretoria district. This livestock was almost without exception the property of the fighting burghers. Once the livestock was collected it was disposed of by a special member of the corps at a public auction in Pretoria. Morley's Scouts received 75% and the authorities 25% of the money raised and the corps then divided its share equally among the members. By the end of November 1901 each member of the corps was entitled to about £348.[174] The full amount was, however, not paid out to them. In the meantime Kitchener had laid down that they should sometimes operate with the British columns, and because the corps was under the protection of the columns on these occasions, it could not lay claim to a full 75% of the proceeds.[175] This particular regulation caused a great deal of dissatisfaction, especially after the war. Many members of the corps felt that financially they had received a raw deal,[176] but Captain Morley claimed that "they did very well on the whole ... and ... the men were very well treated in generally being given such a large percentage".[177]

According to W. Milward the corps was very active: "Absolutely all the active work of rounding up, driving and guarding the cattle developed upon Morley's Scouts ... In addition to this work Morley's Scouts supplied guides, and local intelligence to the columns, captured several prisoners, inspanned and drove the captured Boer waggons to Eerste Fabrieken."[178] As can be seen from Milward's account of the work done by the corps, Morley's Scouts did not simply round up cattle, but also served in the British columns as guides. In this respect it was the burghers in the corps who acquitted themselves particularly well. "Report most highly of Dutchmen with me. No column should be without them," wrote Captain Morley.[179]

On 18 August 1901 Morley's Scouts, in collaboration with a patrol from the South African Constabulary under a Captain Wood, did some reconnoitring in the vicinity of Bronkhorstspruit. When they came upon a number of Boers a frenzied skirmish broke out. The *Times History* describes the encounter as follows: "With admirable pluck Wood has rushed upon the Boers, who, before they could recover from the shock of the surprise, lost 23 men killed, a large number wounded and 11 taken prisoners. Then, however, they had collected their wits and, pursuing Wood's gallant little force towards the railway, had succeeded in regaining their prisoners, and in taking a few from Wood."[180]

When the burghers in Morley's Scouts were taken prisoner by the Boers they were shown little mercy. Three of them (a man called Drotsky, J.D. Reynders and J.L. van der Walt) were executed by a firing squad in July 1901 after appearing before a court martial.[181] The 17-year-old J. van Heerden, who had also been captured, escaped the death sentence on the grounds of his youth, and was given a six-year prison sentence instead. But after a mere two months with the commandos in the veld he escaped and rejoined Morley's Scouts. Morley claimed that the Boer commanders then issued orders that

Van Heerden "is to be shot on sight without a trial".[182] Apostasy of this kind was of great concern to the Boer leaders. "Alas, when will our burghers discontinue this treachery?" asked General P.R. Viljoen despairingly on 26 July 1901. "Our agents from Pretoria assure us that the war would have been over long since, but the traitors cling with hands and teeth to the enemy."[183]

Morley described his "Dutch scouts" as "very plucky". As far as he was concerned they rendered good service, but he found it remarkable that "they do not like being questioned about casualties on the other side, and will not talk afterwards".[184] However, C. McKay, a British intelligence agent in the Pretoria district, did not trust the burghers who were members of Morley's Scouts. He suspected that they might be playing a double role, and were passing on information to the Boers.[185] Morley categorically denied these allegations and Maxwell likewise attached little credibility to them.[186] Colonel Henderson of the military intelligence service, who followed up McKay's allegations, expressed his feeling thus: "Morley's Scouts are not exactly plaster saints, but I don't believe there is any truth in the report of their treachery. I can get no evidence, only yarns about them ..."[187] In the light of this it is doubtful whether the burghers in Morley's Scouts were as untrustworthy in the service of the British as McKay suggested.[188]

In addition to the Vereeniging burgher corps and Morley's Scouts, there were also four other burgher corps in the Transvaal, namely the Cattle Ranger Corps, Beddy's Scouts, the Lydenburg Volunteer Burgher Corps and the Lebombo Scouts.

Kitchener granted permission for the establishment of a Cattle Ranger Corps on 2 April 1901. It was responsible for the protection of government-owned livestock in Pretoria and was also expected to bring animals from the neighbouring districts into the town. The main objective of the corps was thus to help remove livestock from the farms so that the British columns could devote more attention to the Boers in the veld. At the outset members were to receive 6s 0d per day. However, Kitchener decided in May 1901 that they would not be paid any wages, but would instead be given some of the livestock as payment for their efforts. They were each issued with a rifle, bandolier and ammunition, but had to provide their own saddles and bridles and did not receive a uniform. The director of military supplies issued them with horses that were unsuitable for use by the British columns. By the end of April 1901 the Cattle Ranger Corps comprised about 25 men.[189] Some members of the corps were described as "never-do-well, bar loafers".[190] Two members, A.C. Muller and A.A. van der Merwe of Pretoria, had joined with the idea of being sent out to collect livestock. When they realised that they might also be involved in fighting, they both resigned immediately.[191] Other members were more prepared to fight and in July 1901 the Cattle Rangers killed four burghers near Hammanskraal.[192] Apparently the members of this corps made very good financial pickings from the livestock which they received in return for their services. J. Botha sold the animals he was allotted and he then had more than enough money to live in Pretoria and support his family.[193]

A burgher corps under Captain W.H. Beddy was operative in the Waterberg district by January 1902. Beddy, who had been an information officer in the Kroonstad district, was described as "a farmer of little education who has been employed as Intelligence Agent in several minor Colonial campaigns, and appears to have given satisfaction ...". His involvement in illegal financial transactions led to his being recalled from the Kroonstad district.[194] His financial indiscretions apparently did not prevent him from being placed in control of the burgher corps and Colonel D. Henderson regarded him "as a very good partisan leader".[195] Beddy and his corps were involved in a skirmish on 23 January 1902 with a small group of Boers under Field-cornet C. Snyman near Nylstroom. One of the Boers was killed, three were wounded and three were captured, while one member of Beddy's Scouts, P. Botha, was wounded.[196] The funeral service for the dead Boer was held in the Nylstroom concentration camp on 26 January. An inmate of the camp, J. van Rooyen, conducted the service and he launched a bitter attack upon Beddy's Scouts whom he alleged had "spilt the blood" of their compatriot.[197] Beddy himself was seriously wounded in March 1902[198] and it appears that his corps was not very active after this date.

The Lydenburg Volunteer Burgher Corps that was established in about July 1901 had 44 members by November, and concentrated mainly on removing livestock from the farms which belonged to fighting burghers. By December of that year they had not received any wages, but were entitled to keep 75% of the cattle they collected.[199]

There is very little information on the activities of the Lebombo Scouts. It is, however, known that they were active in the eastern Transvaal and that in February 1902 they captured six Boers. The families of three members of the corps (J.C.P. Nell, D.J van der Heever and F.C. Potgieter) were also permitted to leave their various concentration camps and to join their men.[200] It is reasonable to presume that the activities of the Lebombo Scouts did not differ to any great extent from those of the other burgher corps.

On 14 October 1901 Brodrick asked Kitchener "whether there is any truth in the reports that looting corps have been formed in South Africa, composed of men who find all their own equipment except guns and ammunition but receive no pay, remunerating themselves by selling stock etc. which they capture". On the following day Kitchener sent a brief reply in which he denied the existence of such corps,[201] but in January 1902 he sent a detailed report to Brodrick in which he contradicted his previous statement and discussed the role and activities of these burgher corps. "The plain facts regarding these corps are as follows," he wrote. "The whole of the cattle of surrendered Burghers were confiscated by the Boers still in the field. It is only occasionally that cattle captured by our troops can be identified as the private property of ... surrendered Burghers. In order to surrender, the men in this ... category have been forced to sacrifice their stock, and it seemed only just that they should have an opportunity afforded them of recovering it from the irreconcilables who have seized it. I am particularly anxious to give them this opportunity, inasmuch as those farmers who are willing to accept British rule, and are eagerly waiting for peace, realize that they will have the utmost difficulty in replacing the cattle they possessed before the war ... I therefore authorised the formation of those Forces which the enemy, and pro-Boers who hold them in particular horror, have sometimes held up to opprobrium under the designation of Looting Corps. I need hardly say that this name is entirely misleading." On Kitchener's report, which was also sent to the Colonial Office, H.W. Just, one of the head clerks noted: "Lord Kitchener's defence of his arrangement is adequate, though the system is one which might no doubt be abused if not carefully worked."[202]

Kitchener's defence that the corps were not "looting corps" is, however, not at all convincing. It has already been shown in this section that the corps did not receive any wages, but instead could lay claim to a percentage of the livestock they had rounded up – livestock which did not belong to them. In fact, in 1903 even the members of Morley's Scouts referred to their former corps as an "unpaid guerilla looting body".[203] Then too, R. Granville Nicholson, an acquaintance of the historian Gustav Preller, described Morley's Scouts as "a marauding band and the only remuneration they were to receive was the loot they took captured or stole".[204] The authors of the *Times History* also regarded the various burgher corps (that according to them were made up of the "lower class of Boer") as "privateer corps whose *raison d'être* was loot".[205] Despite Kitchener's protestations, the local burgher corps were indeed nothing other than "looting corps".

By paying the members of these corps mainly in livestock, the British were actually encouraging them to collect as many animals as possible. It is a well-known fact that the British army was trying to take away every possible means of sustenance from the fighting Boers and this was why they removed as much livestock as they could. In other words the burgher corps were filling a specific role in the British scorched earth policy.

From November 1901 onwards some of the local burgher corps disappeared from the scene. Captain Morley was the first to disband his corps. He gave the following reasons for his decision to do so: "I find that the corps (being mostly composed of Dutchmen) is invariably considerably outnumbered. More Burghers have wished to join, but they were not to be trusted to fight and I would not have them. I have found that the Burghers are afraid of joining small Corps, but will willingly join a big one or a column, where they have something to fall back upon when pressed. A Burgher Corps of 500, would rapidly increase to 1000 in my opinion from experience of my own Dutchmen." In the light of this Morley made the following suggestion: "It would be a good move to amalgamate all small Corps into a larger one."[206] Kitchener approved Morley's recommendation[207] and in 1902

Piet de Wet – the brother of Christiaan de Wet and a prominent leader of the collaborators in the Free State.

Farmers' Guard, Bloemfontein.

A gathering of the National Scouts of No 5 Klerksdorp Wing.

A group of National Scouts who have clearly been fitted out for a harsh winter.

Some members of the Farmers' Guard take up a threatening attitude.

The National Scouts leave Klerksdorp to fight against their countrymen.
A.P.J. Cronjé is in front on the white horse.

Some of the members of the Farmers' Guard, photographed at their outpost in front of their shelter; apparently they plan to fight against their compatriots with all possible vigour.

Photograph with handwritten caption: "Town Guard Trompsburg during the Anglo-Boer War comprising Traitors to our country that had to keep the Boer commandos away from Trompsburg."

National Scouts (*Kakieboere*) at Winburg, under the command of Captain O.M. Bergh.
Standing: Hendrik Coen, Albertus Kok, Jan van Jaarsveld, Gert Kok, Jan Coen, Christiaan Pienaar and Pieter Mellon (or Millan).
Seated: J. van Huysteen (father), H. van Huysteen (son), Paul Nel, Captain O.M. Bergh, Theo Ferreira, Thys Kritzinger and F. Viviers.
Front: P. Viviers, P. Meiring and Carl (or Karel) Tempelhof.

Farmers' Guard, Bloemfontein.

A.P.J. Cronjé – a prominent leader of the surrendered burghers in the Transvaal.

most of the local Transvaal corps were amalgamated into one large corps – the National Scouts.[208] In the Free State too, the Kroonstad Burgher Scouts were integrated into the ORC Volunteers in April 1902.[209]

The National Scouts and the ORC Volunteers, both of which took on different characteristics compared to the local burgher corps during the last months of the war, are discussed in the next chapter.

Notes

1 MGB 5, District commissioner Boshof – Pretyman, 12 October 1900. See also Chapter 2, sections 1 and 2 above.
2 MGP 258, "Circular Memorandum, Instructions for Officers engaged in foraging Duties", 26 June 1900.
3 PMP 5/75, Officer in command, Provisional Mounted Police Jagersfontein – Pretyman, 23 August 1900.
4 PMP 5/70 White – Pretyman, 22 September 1900. The burghers were A.J. Fouché, J.A. Fouché, J. Nell, C. Wilson, H.J. Engelbrecht, J. Venter, J. Vermeulen and B. Payne. For details on the siege, see *Times History*, V, p. 6.
5 MGB 4, Lieutenant H.H. Aldrige – District commissioner Smithfield, 9 October 1900.
6 Roberts Papers, WO 105/26 (A392), De Wet – Knox, 6 October 1900. Grobler was captured by De Wet and executed – very likely after a military trial.
7 Milner Papers, 45, (FK 1205, p. 1048), Milner – Kitchener, 31 October 1900.
8 Milner Papers, 46, (FK 1135, pp. 201–7), Milner – Pretyman, 24 November 1900 and enclosure P.M. Botha – Milner, 20 November 1900.
9 *Africa (South)*, 667, p. 10, Bisset – Chamberlain, 3 July 1901; CO 417/334/29279 (FK 536, pp. 335–6).
10 Report on the commission of inquiry into the late administration of the Kroonstad district since the Annexation, p. 23, 16 April 1901; *Telegrams and Letters ... Roberts*, v, p. 109, telegram C5618, Cowan – De Lisle, 17 October 1900.
11 CSO 3/100/01, De Bertodano – Pretyman, 9 December 1900 and Pretyman – De Bertodano, 13 December 1900.
12 Roberts Papers, WO 105/15 T80/2 (Vol. 59/277/74), District commissioner Heilbron – Roberts, 16 November 1900.
13 *Telegrams and Letters ... Roberts*, vi, p. 40, telegram C6370, Roberts – District commissioner Heilbron, 16 November 1900; Roberts Papers, WO 105/15 T80/3 (Vol. 59/277/76) District commissioner Heilbron – Roberts, 19 November 1900.
14 The subsequent correspondence between Wighley and Roberts was apparently mislaid, but on 28 December 1900 Wighley informed Pretyman: "Lord Roberts sanctioned my forming a corps of Boers ..." MGB 7.
15 MGB 7, Dalzell – Kitchener, 18 December 1900 and Wighley – Kitchener, 28 December 1900 (copies).
16 MGB 7, Kitchener – Wighley, 3 January 1901 (copy).

17 WO 32/863/5985 (A364), "Staff Diary Kroonstad", 21 February 1901; WO 32/877/8622 (A378), "Staff Diary, Lines of Communication, northern section", 18 and 24 February 1901; *The Bloemfontein Post*, 8 May 1901 (news report dated 10 March 1901).

18 CSO 3/100/01, De Bertodano – Wilson, 21 February 1901.

19 J.F.C. Fuller, *The Last of the Gentleman's Wars*, pp. 165, 173. For the activities of other burgher corps in the Free State, see Chapter 5, section 2 below.

20 MGP 67/1324/01, Kitchener – Generals Rundle, Wynne and French (copy).

21 Milner Papers, 19, (FK 1134, p. 163), Milner – Chamberlain, 29 January 1901 and enclosure Ridley – Wilson, 19 January 1901. See also Chapter 5, section 2 below.

22 *Africa (South)*, 650, pp. 1, 16, Chamberlain – Milner, 3 January 1901 and Milner – Chamberlain, 9 January 1901; CO 417/322/3336 (FK 479, p. 229); Spies, "Civilians", p. 310.

23 *Telegrams and Letters ... Roberts*, vi, pp. 40, 48, telegrams C6369 and C6459, Roberts – District commissioner Heidelberg, 16 and 19 November 1900.

24 *Telegrams and Letters ... Roberts*, vi, p. 63, telegram C6674, Roberts – Commanding officer Heidelberg, 28 November 1900.

25 *List of Casualties in the Army in South Africa*, p. 104, 1 January 1901 to 30 June 1901.

26 CSO 3/100/01, Pretyman – De Bertodano, 13 December 1900.

27 Roberts Papers, WO 105/15 THO/2 (Vol 59/277/74), District commissioner Heilbron – Roberts, 16 November 1900.

28 MGP 67/1324/01, Kitchener – Generals Rundle, Wynne and French, 1 January 1901 (copy).

29 CSO 3/100/01, De Bertodano – Wilson, 21 February 1901.

30 CSO 3/100/01, memorandum by Wilson, 25 February 1901. See also Chapter 5, section 4 below.

31 Compare for example Gronum, *Die Bittereinders*, p. 6 and Solomon, p. 17, that give July and September 1901 respectively as the dates when this was initiated.

32 WO Confidential Telegrams, 831 and 1095, Kitchener – Brodrick, 15 January 1902 and 17 April 1902.

33 CO 417/361/20859 (FK 663, pp. 579–80), "Return of Ex Burghers serving under British", 27 April 1902; CO 417/362/26810 (FK 665, pp. 14–5), "Return of Ex Burghers serving under British", 1 June 1902.

34 See Van Rensburg, "Die Skandkol wat nie wou toegroei nie" in *Die Huisgenoot*, 8 August 1969.

35 Kruger, *Good-bye Dolly Gray*, pp. 460–1.

36 Translated from the Afrikaans. M.C.E. van Schoor, "Boere-verraaier se Dagboek" in *Die Volksblad*, 15 November 1974 (book review).

37 Spaight, pp. 334–5.

38 Translated from the Dutch. Van der Merwe, 11, p. 30, 15 August 1901.

39 Spaight, p. 334.

40 *Buitengewone Staatscourant der Z.A.R.*, 10 November 1899 (proclamation).

41 Cd. 800, p. 26.

42 Despagnet, p. 144. I.J.C. de Wet, General de Wet's son, considered it a "scandal to enlist the one brother against the other ... " (Translated from the Afrikaans). De Wet, *Met generaal De Wet op Kommando*, p. 45.

43 Translated from the Dutch. Leyds Archive, 781(ii), report by Ram and Thomson, p. 523.
44 Spaight, p. 144.
45 See De Wet, "The Fighter, The Spy, The Scout", pp. 140–4, 155.
46 CO 417/361/20859 (FK 663, pp. 579–80), "Return of Ex Burghers serving under British", 27 April 1902; CO 417/362/26810 (FK 665, pp. 14–15), "Return of Ex Burghers serving under British", 1 June 1902.
47 *Rand Daily Mail*, 25 December 1902 (letter from a former member of Morley's Scouts – a local burgher corps in Pretoria – under the pseudonym "Sumnier"). See also Chapter 5, section 4 below.
48 CSO 87/409/02, Major E.M. Morris (commanding officer Farmers' Guard, a local burgher corps in the Bloemfontein district) – H.F. Wilson, 11 February 1902; CO 291/43 (FK 977, p. 312), "Intermediate Report on Resettlement, National Scouts, ORC Volunteers and Ex-Military Burghers", 15 September 1902 (Hereafter "Intermediate Report"). Major E.M.H. Leggett, who was by that time involved with the burgher corps and the National Scouts, compiled this report.
49 *Rand Daily Mail*, 25 December 1902 (letter from "Sumnier").
50 Compare WO Confidential Telegrams, no. 681 and 685, Brodrick – Kitchener and Kitchener – Brodrick, 14 and 15 October 1901 in which Kitchener denies the existence of burgher corps that receive a portion of the looted cattle as payment. On 9 January 1902, however, he admitted to Brodrick that such corps did indeed exist. CO 417/360/9713 (FK 660, pp. 717–20) (copy); Chapter 5, section 4 below. See also *Times History*, V, pp. 249, 406, 571, that mentions the corps "informally in British pay". Kitchener's reluctance to make the existence of the corps known worldwide was presumably because the pro-Boer circles in Britain suspected that the corps were undisciplined "looting corps". See Chapter 5, section 4 below.
51 "Certificates of Engagement, National Scouts, 5 Wing"; Buys, p. 225; see also Chapter 6, section 1 below.
52 WO/unsorted (A462), "Certificates of Engagement, National Scouts, 5 Wing"; CO 291/43 (FK 977, p. 312), "Intermediate Report", 15 September 1902; see also Chapter 6, section 1 below.
53 HC 165/121, records on numbers of members and officers of National Scouts, 24 June 1902; see also Chapter 6, section 1 below.
54 CO 291/43 (FK 977, p. 312), "Intermediate Report", 15 September 1902. In the light of this, the title of the diary of P.J. du Toit, *Diary of a National Scout* (edited by J.P. Brits) is misleading. In spite of the fact that Du Toit acted as a guide for the British columns, there is no evidence at all in the diary that he had specifically joined the National Scout corps as such.
55 Milner Papers, 45, (FK 1134, p. 163) Milner – Chamberlain, 29 January 1901 and enclosure Ridley – Wilson, 19 January 1901.
56 *The Bloemfontein Post*, 28 February 1901 (news report).
57 *The Bloemfontein Post*, 8 May 1901 (news report dated 10 March 1901). The claim by the authors of the *Times History*, V, pp. 248–9, that "several hundred Burgher Police" assisted the South African Constabulary prior to May 1901 appears to be inaccurate in the light of the March 1901 membership of 70 men.
58 Milner Papers, 19, (FK 1135, p. 311); Headlam, ii, p. 237.
59 Milner Papers, 45, (FK 1205, p. 1086), 29 March 1901.

THE DYNAMICS OF TREASON: BOER COLLABORATION IN THE SA WAR OF 1899–1902

60 Milner Papers, 19, (FK 1135, pp. 311–12), Milner – Kitchener, 20 March 1901. See also Headlam, ii, pp. 237–8; Milner Papers, 45, (FK 1205, pp. 1085–7), Milner – Kitchener, 29 March 1901; *Times History*, V, pp. 260–2.
61 Spies, "Civilians", pp. 347–8; Buys, pp. 238–40.
62 *The Bloemfontein Post*, 16 July 1901 (news report). The *Times History*, V, p. 261 claims that the area stretched for 40 kilometres (25 miles) around the town of Bloemfontein.
63 *Times History*, V, p. 261.
64 *The Bloemfontein Post*, 8 May 1901 (news report dated 10 March 1901).
65 *The Bloemfontein Post*, 20 June 1901 (news report).
66 A69, N.C. Havenga Accession, General C.C.J. Badenhorst – General J.B.M. Hertzog, 15 September 1901; A239, Major A.L. la C. Bartrop Accession, statement by J.J. Eva, 1 November 1901; Van der Merwe, II, pp. 43–4; Badenhorst, pp. 104–5.
67 HC 2/45, 14 December 1901 (copy); Cd. 903, p. 199; *The Star*, 7 March 1902 (printed versions).
68 *The Bloemfontein Post*, 31 Mei 1901 (news report).
69 GOV 480/129, L.C. Dalton (secretary, "Land Settlement Board") – Wilson, 19 November and Wilson – Milner, 27 November 1901; *Africa (South)*, 669, pp. 185–6.
70 *Africa (South)*, 669, pp. 186–7, 4 December 1901.
71 Spies, "Civilians", p. 347.
72 WO 108/16/997 (A407), evidence of Major E.M. Morris, officer in command of the Farmers' Guard, 5 May 1902; *The Cape Times*, 4 December 1901 (news report).
73 WO 108/16/997 (A407), evidence of Major E.M. Morris, 5 May 1902.
74 *The Bloemfontein Post*, 9, 16, 18, 23, 26, 27, 28 and 31 December 1901 (advertisements).
75 SO/POW 28/2552, Commanding officer Simon's Town camp – Heyman, 12 December 1901.
76 CO 417/362/26810 (FK 665, p. 14), "Return of Ex Burghers serving under British", 1 June 1902.
77 MGP 67/1324/01, Kitchener – Generals Rundle, Wynne and French (copy).
78 HC 145/unsorted, Walrond – G.V. Fiddes, 28 November 1901.
79 CSO 87/409/02, Wilson – Milner, 12 February 1902.
80 CSO 94/792/02, 18 March 1902.
81 WO 108/14/417 (A406), Colonel Pilkington – Wilson, 10 February 1902; WO 108/16/997 (A407), evidence of Major E.M. Morris, 5 May 1902.
82 WO 108/16/997 (A407), evidence of Major E.M. Morris, 5 May 1902.
83 De Wet, "The Fighter, The Scout, The Spy", p. 133. De Wet compiled his memoirs in the third person.
84 WO 108/16/997 (A407), evidence of Lieutenant P. Hale of the South African Constabulary, 5 May 1902.
85 WO 108/14/417 (A406), Colonel Pilkington – Wilson, 10 February, 1902.
86 WO 32/872/8882 (A374), Sergeant P. Gettings – Commanding officer South African Constabulary, 30 April 1902; WO 108/16/968 (A407), evidence of Lieutenant P. Hale of the South African Constabulary and Sergeants C. Kruger and C. Oertel of the Farmers' Guard, 5 May 1902.

87 WO 108/16/997 (A407), findings of the court of inquiry, 8 May 1902.
88 Personal interview with Mrs J.J. de Klerk of the farm Candy, Winburg district, 10 July 1976 (Mrs de Klerk has personal information, passed down in her family, on the corps.); *The Cape Times*, 30 March 1917 (letter from J.H. Brand Wessels); An editorial addition to the article by L. Scholtz, "Hoofregter Melius de Villiers se Mededeling oor 'Swart Troepe' in die Oorlog", in *Historia*, 21(2), September 1976, p. 137.
89 De Wet, *Boer en Brit*, p. 237.
90 Leyds Archive, 774(b), 16, Nierstrasz, p. 1343.
91 Otto, p. 46 note 19.
92 Personal interview with Mrs J.J. de Klerk of the farm Candy, Winburg district, 10 July 1976.
93 De Wet, *Boer en Brit*, p. 237. It appears that in his memoirs De Wet uses the term "National Scout" throughout as a collective name to indicate all the burghers who fought on the British side. Compare De Wet, *Boer en Brit*, pp. 161, 168, 195, 207 note 1, 229, 233.
94 For the National Scout corps, see Chapter 6, sections 1 and 2 below. There were indeed 29 Free State burghers who joined the National Scouts but they fought in the Transvaal and not in the Free State. Cd. 1551, p. 61, report on the resettlement of burghers who fought on the British side, March 1903.
95 Pienaar, "De Wet", pp. 220; De Wet, *Boer en Brit*, p. 237; Personal interview with Mrs J.J. de Klerk of the farm Candy, Winburg district, 10 July 1976.
96 A119, Renier Collection, 85, memoirs of P. Beukes, 1949; A119, Renier Collection, 130, memoirs of P.J. Muller, 1949; A119, Renier Collection, memoirs of William Scott, 1950.
97 Translated from the Dutch. Personal interview with Mrs J.J. de Klerk of the farm Candy, Winburg district, 10 July 1976.
98 De Wet, *Boer en Brit*, p. 237.
99 Leyds Archive, 774(b), 16, Nierstrasz, p. 1343.
100 Translated from the Afrikaans. A119, Renier Collection, 1099, memoirs of G.J.S. van den Heever, pp. 60–2, 1944.
101 De Wet, *Boer en Brit*, pp. 237–8; Pienaar, "De Wet", pp. 220–1.
102 A119, Renier Collection, 1099, memoirs of G.J.S. van den Heever, p. 62, 1944.
103 Translated from the Dutch. Hancock and Van der Poel, *Selections*, 1, p. 345, 29 November 1900.
104 WO Confidential Telegrams, no. 1095, Kitchener – Brodrick, 17 April 1902.
105 MGP 93/5356/01, Intelligence officer in Major-general S. Beaton's columns – Maxwell, 16 May 1901; MGP 251/4260/01, Maxwell – Commanding officer Palapye, 11 November 1901; MGP 244/2601/01, Maxwell – Superintendent Irene, 17 May 1901; MGP 117/11386/01, Maxwell – Commanding officers Johannesburg and Bloemfontein, 5 and 6 September, 1901.
106 CO 291/43 (FK 977, p. 312), "Intermediate Report", 15 September 1902. An apparent exception to the rule was the case of P.J. du Toit who was in Colonel E.H.H. Allenby's columns for an unbroken period of nine months. Brits, *Diary*, pp. 51–93, 31 May 1901 to 2 March 1902.
107 Cd. 902, p. 72, report on Irene camp, October 1901.

108 PMO 55/3717, Assistant provost marshal Middelburg – Poore, 20 April 1902; PMO 42/2845, Captain A.W.J. Baird – Director of military intelligence service, 22 December 1901 (copy).
109 CO 417/362/26510 (FK 665, pp. 14–5), "Return of Ex Burghers serving under British", 1 June 1902.
110 SNA 165, pp. 128, 228, "Rates of Pay to Scouts" and "Rewards and Special Payments to White men", undated.
111 PMO 55/3690, P.H. Bezuidenhout – Director of military intelligence service, 31 January 1902, Major G.F. Milne – Poore, undated and Poore – Commanding officer Bloemfontein, 24 April 1902.
112 Compare Buurman, *Oorlogswolke oor die Republieke: Die Herinneringe van 'n Boere-offisier* (Commandant M.J. Bornman), pp. 80–8.
113 M. Miller (ed), *A Captain of the Gordons*, 1900–1909, p. 127, 28 February 1902. See also PMO 42/2845, Major-general W.S. Fetherstonaugh – Poore, 21 January 1902; PMO 56/3845, information service Frankfort – Poore, 17 May 1902 for similar evidence.
114 WO 32/869/7782 (A371), J. le Roux – Botha, 27 August 1901 (translated intercepted republican documents).
115 PMO 42/2827, Major G.F. Milne – Poore, 21 December 1901 and Poore – Milne, 22 December 1901; PMO 48/3243, Poore – Commanding officer Kroonstad, 7 March 1902 (copy).
116 WO 32/884/9164 (A383), "Report on Field Intelligence", 13 June 1902.
117 *Times History*, V, pp. 249, 269.
118 The British made use of African people on a large scale in this respect. Spies, "Civilians", pp. 434–6. The role of African guides and scouts as such falls outside the scope of this study. It can however be noted that the Boers experienced many problems as a result of armed Africans who provided information on the movements of the Boers to the British. Preller, *Hindon*, pp. 230–3. The well-known General Ben Viljoen was in fact captured in January 1902 as a consequence of information that the British received from an African named Wildebeest. For providing this information Wildebeest was rewarded with a payment of £5. SNA 165, p. 234 "Rewards and Special Payments to Native Scouts", March 1902; Viljoen, *Reminiscences*, p. 273.
119 PMO 41/2755, Rundle – Poore, 5 December 1901.
120 PMO 41/2790, Pilcher – General C. Knox, 9 December 1901 (copy).
121 PMO 40/3128, Information officer in Colonel F.S. Garrat's column – Director of military intelligence service, 10 February 1902.
122 PMO 48/3247, Vandeleur – Director of military intelligence service, undated, but apparently early in March 1902.
123 WO 32/869/7868 (A372), "Staff Diary, Colonel W.P. Campbell's Column", August and September 1901.
124 Leyds, *Vierde Verzameling*, vol II, annexure Z, memorandum from Dr Bierens de Haan, pp. 104–5, 24 April 1902.
125 PMO 29/2026, Captain A. Burrows – Assistant provost marshal Machadodorp, 7 August 1901, Assistant provost marshal Machadodorp – Assistant provost marshal Middelburg, 11 August 1901 and Assistant provost marshal Middelburg – Assistant provost marshal Machadodorp, 12 August 1901; PMO 45/2057, Lieuten-

ant H.S. Craig – Assistant provost marshal Potchefstroom, 18 May 1902 and Captain I. Richardson – Assistant provost marshal Potchefstroom, 20 May 1902.

126 PMO 45/3013, proceedings of a court of inquiry at Lindley, 16 January 1902 (copy).
127 Brits, *Diary*, pp. 51–93, 31 May 1901 to 2 March 1902.
128 *Times History*, II, p. 108; V, pp. 329–30, 451–2.
129 WO 32/869/7868 (A372), "Col. Benson's Column, Staff Diary", September 1901.
130 Botha – General C. Botha, as quoted in the *Official History*, IV, p. 305.
131 *Times History*, V, pp. 451–2.
132 Cd. 824, p. 21, 8 December 1901.
133 De Wet, *Boer en Brit*, p. 229.
134 G.F. Gibson, *The Story of the Imperial Light Horse in the South African War, 1899–1902*, pp. 303–4.
135 De Wet, *Boer en Brit*, p. 230.
136 Gibson, p. 303.
137 Translated from the Dutch. De Wet, *Boer en Brit*, pp. 212–13.
138 M.C.E. van Schoor (ed), "'Dagboek' van Rocco de Villiers" in *Christiaan de Wet-Annale*, 3, 1975, p. 30.
139 Van der Merwe, II, pp. 20–4, *Times History*, V, pp. 300–1; *Official History*, IV, pp. 247–8; Van Schoor (ed), "'Dagboek' van Rocco de Villiers" in *Christiaan de Wet-Annale*, 3, 1975, p. 29.
140 De Wet, *Boer en Brit*, p. 212.
141 N.G. Church council minutes, Frankfort, 8 and 30 January, 3 April and 13 May 1905. See also Van Schoor (ed), "'Dagboek' van Rocco de Villiers" in *Christiaan de Wet-Annale*, 3, 1975, p. 30 n 59.
142 Brits, *Diary*, p. 32, 26 and 27 December 1900. See also De Wet, *Boer en Brit*, p. 234, in which he mentions a certain De Lange who was sentenced to death for high treason at the beginning of November 1901 by a court martial on the farm Blijdskap in the Free State.
143 A951, A.W. Huyser Collection, account of the Anglo-Boer War by Mrs C.P.M. van Dijk, 25 April 1929. See also W.C. Groenewald, "Bedreiging in die Nag" (Threat in the night) in *Die Huisgenoot*, 6 May 1938.
144 Translated from the Afrikaans. A951, A.W. Huyser Collection, account of the Anglo-Boer War by Mrs C.P.M. van Dijk, 25 April 1929.
145 Fischer, p. 9, 30 May 1901; Postma, p. 47, evidence of Mrs M.J.J. de Waal, undated.
146 Translated from the Afrikaans. Undated statement by Mrs M.C. Joubert as quoted by F.J. Grobler, "Die Carolina-kommando in die Tweede Vryheidsoorlog, 1899–1902" (unpublished MA dissertation, Potch), 1960, p. 140.
147 WO 32/884/9164 (A383), "Report on Field Intelligence", 13 June 1902.
148 *Times History*, V, p. 249.
149 WO 32/884/9164 (A383), "Report on Field Intelligence", 13 June 1901; CO 291/43 (FK 977, p. 313), "Intermediate Report", 15 September 1902; Fuller, p. 159.
150 WO 32/884/9164 (A383), "Report on Field Intelligence", 13 June 1902.
151 *Times History*, V, p. 429; *Official History*, IV, p. 386; Gibson, p. 313.
152 *Official History*, IV, p. 391.

153 De Wet, *Boer en Brit*, p. 238; *Times History*, V, p. 431.
154 Gibson, p. 313; *Times History*, V, p. 431.
155 Translated from the Dutch. De Wet, *Boer en Brit*, p. 239.
156 Milner Papers, 45, (FK 1206, p. 1297), Henderson – Altham, 21 June 1901 (copy). See also Kitchener Letters, II, (FK 1622, pp. 262–3), Kitchener – Brodrick, 28 June 1901.
157 Muller, p. 174.
158 *The Times*, 21 May 1902 (news report).
159 PMO 22/1584, Captain R.W. Morley – Poore, 14 June 1901; MGP 109/92688/01, Captain J.M. Vallentin – Maxwell, undated.
160 Cd. 853, p. 14, circular to all superintendents, October 1901.
161 MGP 132/14824/01, Captain W.G. Bentinck – Kitchener's private secretary, 9 November 1901. Report on Vereeniging burgher corps.
162 MGP 132/14824/01, Captain W.G. Bentinck – Kitchener's private secretary, 9 November 1901.
163 MGP 132/14824/01, Major W.S. Birdwood – Maxwell, 12 November 1901.
164 Cd. 853, p. 41, report by Dr K. Franks, October 1901.
165 MGP 132/14824/01, Captain W.G. Bentinck – Kitchener's private secretary, 9 November 1901.
166 MGP 83/3465/01, Captain R.W. Morley – Commissioner of police, 30 March 1901.
167 MGP 156/4791/02, W.S. Hubbel – Maxwell, 20 March 1902.
168 MGP 102/7404/01, "Present State of Morley's Scouts", 23 June 1901; MGP 149/1913/02, W. Milward – Maxwell, 16 January 1902.
169 MGP 149/1913/02, W. Milward – Maxwell, 16 January 1902.
170 MGP 143/17982/01, Commissioner of police – Maxwell, 11 October 1901.
171 *Times History*, V, p. 406; Chapter 5, section 1 above.
172 *Rand Daily Mail*, 25 December 1902 (letter from a former member of Morley's Scouts under the pseudonym "Sumnier").
173 *The Friend*, 6 March 1903 (letter signed by 183 "Ex-Irregulars", including some members of Morley's Scouts).
174 *Rand Daily Mail*, 25 December 1902 (letter from "Sumnier"); HC 64/121, C.J.S. Hartley (a member of Morley's Scouts) – Chamberlain, 13 September 1903.
175 HC 64/121, Morley – Military secretary, 30 November 1903.
176 *Rand Daily Mail*, 25 December 1902 (letter from "Sumnier"); *The Friend*, 6 March 1903, (letter from 183 "Ex-Irregulars"); HC 64/121, C.J.S. Hartley – Chamberlain, 13 September 1903.
177 HC 64/121, Morley – Military secretary, 30 November 1903.
178 MGP 149/1913/02, W. Milward – Maxwell, 16 January 1902.
179 MGP 107/8867/01, Morley – Maxwell, 16 July 1901.
180 *Times History*, V, pp. 330–1. See also HC 30/96 "Field Intelligence Report, Capt. Macgregor", 18 August 1901.
181 WO 32/869/7782 (A371), news of the war by N.J. de Wet of Middelburg, 6 July 1901 (intercepted translated republican documents); Spies, "Civilians", p. 364.
182 PMO 30/2055, Morley – Poore, 7 September 1901.

183 CO 417/360/10274 (FK 660, p. 791), General P.R. Viljoen – Commandant H. Alberts and burghers, 26 Julie 1901 (intercepted translated republican documents).
184 MGP 102/7404/01, Morley – Maxwell, 23 June 1901.
185 MGP 117/11334B/01, C. McKay – Maxwell, 5 September 1901; PMO 31/2138, C. McKay – Intelligence officer Kaalfontein, 20 September 1901.
186 PMO 30/2055, Morley – Poore, 7 September 1901; MGP 229/85/01, Maxwell – Military secretary, 27 November 1901. See also MGP 107/8658B/01, Morley – Maxwell, 14 July 1901.
187 PMO 43/2901, Henderson – Poore, 6 November 1901.
188 There is probably also little truth in the allegation by Buys, p. 282, that the "joiners" in Morley's Scouts were "very unreliable" in their service to the British.
189 PMO 1/92, signed copy by Kitchener of the conditions of service for the Cattle Ranger Corps, 2 April 1901; *The Times*, 22 April 1901 (news report); PMO 23/1621, Major R. Ford – Poore, 2 May 1901.
190 HC 52/111, "Civil Intelligence", 7 May 1901.
191 PMO 23/1620, Director of military supplies – Poore, 21 June 1901.
192 PMO 27/1869, Poore – Director of military supplies, 31 Julie 1901.
193 MGP 83/3378/01, Staff officer "Refugees" – Maxwell, undated.
194 Report on the Commission of Enquiry into the late Administration of the Kroonstad District since the Annexation, 16 April 1901.
195 CO 417/361/15424 (FK 663, p. 138), Henderson – Altham, 30 March 1902.
196 *The Star*, 24 January 1902 (news report); *The Bloemfontein Post*, 24 January 1902 (news report); MGP 149/2056/02, Major E. Brereton – Maxwell, 4 February 1902.
197 PMO 44/2999, Major E. Brereton – Poore, undated; Poore – Commanding officer Pretoria district, 1 February 1902.
198 CO 417/361/15424 (FK 663, p. 138), Henderson – Altham, 30 March 1902.
199 MGP 131/14613/01, Resident magistrate Middelburg – Maxwell, 4 November 1901; MGP 139/16775/01, District commissioner Lydenburg – Maxwell, 12 December 1901 and Maxwell – District commissioner Lydenburg, 13 December 1901; MGP 137/16314/01, Maxwell – Director of military supplies, 14 December 1901; MGP 50/2105/02, District commissioner Lydenburg – Maxwell, 6 February 1902; PMO 47/3158, District commissioner Lydenburg – Poore, 17 February 1902.
200 PMO 50/3420, Henderson – Poore, 22 February 1902; MGP 180/5899/02, Commanding officer Lebombo Scouts – Maxwell, 7 April 1902.
201 WO Confidential Telegrams, 681 and 685.
202 CO 417/360/9713 (FK 660, pp. 717–20), 9 January 1902 (copy) and H.W. Just's margin notes, 16 March 1902. See also *Africa (South)*, 680, pp. 310–11.
203 *The Friend*, 6 March 1903 (letter from 183 "Ex-Irregulars").
204 A787, Preller Collection, 116, p. 3, R. Granville Nicholson – Preller, 5 December 1903.
205 *Times History*, V, p. 406.
206 MGP 135/15698/01, Morley – Maxwell, 21 November 1901.
207 MGP 135/15698/01, Major W.S. Birdwood – Maxwell, 24 November 1901.
208 *The Times*, 21 May 1902 (news report); MGP 177/1993/02, Commanding officer Lydenburg Volunteer Corps – Maxwell, 4 February 1902 and Maxwell – Com-

manding officer Lydenburg Volunteer Corps, 5 February 1902; *Reprint of Circulars issued by Director of Supplies*, p. 83, in which mention is made of the disbanding of the Cattle Ranger Corps on 24 January 1902; PMO 60/4183, amalgamation of the Vereeniging burgher corps with the National Scouts, 23 November 1901.

209 CSO 208/347/03, Captain P.H. Blakemore – Assistant colonial secretary, 23 January 1903.

Chapter 6
In British military service (continued): the National Scouts and Orange River Colony Volunteers

1 Establishment, recruitment and organisation of the National Scouts and Orange River Colony Volunteers

According to the authors of the *Times History*, the National Scout corps was only formed during the last phase of the war (October 1901 to May 1902).¹ But despite the fact that the National Scouts only came to the fore at this time, a corps of the same name was evidently established far earlier. Johanna Brandt mentions that the British held a public meeting near Church Square "a few months after the surrender of Pretoria" in order to "recruit National Scouts from among the burghers who were in Pretoria",² but the date of this meeting is unknown. Certainly, by 15 February 1901 there was already a National Scout corps comprising 60 men. They were stationed in a camp to the south-west of Proclamation Hill under the command of Captain W.P. Anderson of the Transvaal Constabulary. From here, among other duties, they undertook scouting expeditions and supplied information on the Boer commandos to the British authorities.³ But this was not their only task, nor the most important one. By the end of February 1901 Poore said in his report on the corps: "In view of the uselessness of the present struggle the Corps called National Scouts was formed firstly for the purpose of denuding the enemy now in the field of cattle, horses, wagons, etc. ..."⁴ Poore's remarks suggest that initially the National Scouts had a great deal in common with the local burgher corps which were discussed in the previous chapter. However, during the last phase of the war the National Scout corps was destined to undergo widespread expansion

267

and it began to operate throughout the Transvaal. Later on their primary function was no longer to round up livestock; instead they began to fulfil a more active fighting and reconnoitring function within the framework of the British army.[5]

Early in October 1901 the British authorities in the Transvaal began to place the military assistance provided by the surrendered burghers on a better organisational footing. On 2 October it was decided to extend the scope of the National Scouts, which was at that stage the largest burgher corps in the Transvaal, and to absorb it officially into the British army.[6] Each member of the corps had to take the oath of allegiance. In contrast with members of the local burgher corps they were also formally sworn in as members of the imperial army.[7] In order to curb undisciplined plundering, something which had been prevalent in the local burgher corps, it was laid down that "no looting of farms or dwelling houses will be allowed".[8] As far as was possible, members of the existing local burgher corps were absorbed into the National Scouts. Major Leggett, who was responsible for the amalgamation, had an unenviable task on his hands. To Poore he said despairingly: "The winding up of these old loot corps is no joke I can assure you. I am trying to clean up other people's messes."[9]

On 9 October Kitchener received a letter dated 21 September 1901 from the central peace committee in Kroonstad. From the letter it appears that the peace committee had finally accepted that its efforts to change the outlook of the republican leaders who were still actively involved in the war had been fruitless. In the light of this the committee decided to take a more drastic stance. In its view, "The time has arrived that each one who is concerned with the true welfare of the O.R. Colony must contribute his share in order to bring about an end to this destructive strife, and [the committee] resolves to propose to Lord Kitchener to dissolve the Peace Committee and in future to allow no communication whatever with the fighting party. And also to propose to Lord Kitchener a scheme for the raising of a properly organised Guide Corps."[10] Because the British had decided on 2 October that they would expand the National Scout corps, there can be no direct connection between the letter which reached Kitchener on 9 October and the British decision of seven days earlier. It appears that the British acted entirely on their own initiative.[11]

The expansion of the National Scout corps nevertheless coincided with the growing feeling among some surrendered burghers that the burghers in the veld were fighting a futile, losing battle and that the time had come to take a stronger line towards their "stubborn" compatriots. In January 1902 C.L. Theunissen, a burgher from Krugersdorp and seemingly an acquaintance of President Kruger, wrote a letter to the president saying "that the dissatisfaction on account of the burghers still in the field is so great, that many of our people have joined the English and fight against their own kindred ... The result can only be civil war. The most horrible event which has ever befallen South Africa, and which will result in the destruction of the Africander race."[12] At a meeting of about 200 surrendered burghers held in Potchefstroom on 6 January 1902, General Andries P.J. Cronjé, a former member of the central peace committee in Pretoria, declared that he was convinced that petitions for peace would carry no weight at all with the republican leaders, and especially General De la Rey. He was in favour of sending a letter to De la Rey "telling him that if he did not come in and surrender, stronger measures would be taken ... to induce him to do so". The meeting followed up on Cronjé's suggestion and a letter was sent to the general.[13] A week previously, Field-cornet N. Meyer of the Rustenburg district had also communicated with De la Rey and his men. Meyer felt that the women were being made to suffer unnecessarily because of the continuation of the war and that the Boers had achieved very little success with their current tactics. "Brother Afrikaners," he wrote, "you are simply fleeing here, there and everywhere around the country. When the British troops are still miles away you are already off again ... and you leave your poor women and children to the mercy of the troops. That is less than one would expect from a kaffir ... Burghers, there is still a way out; make use of it and give yourselves up. Your women are dying of sorrow. And the British Government will *never, never* give up the country ... if you chose not to react to this friendly warning ... then I, together with thousands of other burghers – the burghers who still have some respect for their families – will be forced to take up arms against you for the sake of our women and children, and in so doing we shall cleanse our land of all the robbers and murderers in the veld."[14] By all accounts General de la Rey's answer to both the Potchefstroom meeting and Meyer's letter were brusque and brief.[15] In the eastern Transvaal a former member of the Volksrust peace committee, J.W. Steenkamp, promised active military assistance to the British authorities to help end the war. "I beg to take the liberty again to offer my services," he wrote to Maxwell in February 1902. "I am able to raise, here in Volksrust alone, over 60 capable men who would be willing to do service under me, and who are all reliable men."[16] This shows clearly that a widespread tendency towards offering more concerted help to the British was emerging among the ranks of surrendered burghers.

What was the motive behind the British decision to make use on a greater scale of the military help offered by the surrendered burghers? For Kitchener the National Scouts were more than just a military tool to force the war to an end. Even as early as June 1901 he had proposed the implementation of a policy of divide and rule. "There are already two parties amongst them [the Boers] ready to fly at each other's throats," he wrote to Brodrick. By emphasising the division which was already evident in Afrikaner ranks, Kitchener hoped that "the Boers could be induced to hate each other more than they hated the British", and in this way "the British objective would be obtained". If a more or less permanent state of civil war among the Boers could be nurtured, Kitchener thought that the British would be able to rule them far easier. However, in June 1901 Kitchener was "by no means convinced that a sufficient degree of hatred could be permanently and artificially sustained".[17] About seven months later Kitchener's opinion on the proposed division in Boer ranks had changed somewhat. At the beginning of 1902, when the recruiting campaign for National Scouts was in full swing, he informed Brodrick that the National Scouts "can never be trusted by or join the irreconcilable element again, and we shall therefore have a party amongst the Boers themselves depending entirely on British continuity of rule out here".[18] This statement by Kitchener has direct bearing on the British political agenda for the National Scouts, and he reiterated it to Brodrick in March 1902: "the result on the future of the country of having a considerable party who have fought with us must be very great".[19] In January 1902 *The Star* hoped that after the war the National Scouts would form "a most valuable political nucleus", while the director of the British military intelligence service was sure that "the 'khaki burgher' will prove a third political party in the State".[20] On the Boer side the expansion of the National Scout corps was seen as a "diabolical weapon" which Kitchener had hatched in order to "sow hatred and enmity, division and bitterness among the Boer people".[21]

Milner, who was the representative of the British civil authority in the Transvaal and Orange River Colony, did not at this juncture express his thoughts on the possible political value the National Scouts might hold after the war. In 1905 he did, however, impress upon his successor, Lord Selborne: "Here let me say one word, and it is once for all, about my view on the Scout question. Personally I never favoured – on the contrary I had always the greatest misgivings about – the action of the military in engaging a number of Boers to fight their own countrymen."[22] Milner's excuse is not entirely acceptable. By the end of 1900 he was strongly in favour of the enlistment of republican burghers in British military service and although in the last phase of the war he was not involved as such with the National Scouts, he gave his approval to the movement.[23] Furthermore he did not hesitate to use the National Scouts as a political argument when it suited him to do so. While at a reception organised in his honour in Johannesburg in January 1902, he spoke disparagingly about the pro-Boer movement in Britain and went on to say: "The moment the Boer surrenders, the pro-Boers take no further interest in him whatsoever ... And what of those of our enemies who ... are actually fighting for us to-day in order to bring peace to the country?"[24]

From October 1901 onwards, with the help of former Boer officers, the military authorities began to recruit members for the National Scouts on a larger scale. In the eastern Transvaal Commandant J.G. Celliers did some recruiting in the vicinity of Middelburg and by the beginning of November 1901 his section already numbered 100 men.[25] Later, Celliers was also involved in the same capacity in the Soutpansberg district.[26] Meanwhile, in the south-western districts of the Transvaal, General Andries Cronjé took it upon himself to establish a National Scouts section in the region.[27] Field-cornet N. Meyer did some recruitment for the National Scouts in the Rustenburg district and by November 1901 he had enlisted a considerable number of men. *The Times* expressed the hope that these Rustenburg burghers who had joined the National Scouts would prove to be "an important addition to the field force".[28] They were not to be disappointed – by the end of the war there were 147 burghers from the district who were members of the National Scouts.[29]

In December 1901 regular recruitment meetings were held in the various Transvaal concentration camps. Captain T.S. Allison, a British officer, was active in this campaign, but there were also some members of the corps who addressed the surrendered Boers in the camps in the hope of being able to persuade their fellow burghers to join up.[30] Recruitment agents were also busy in the "Rest Camp" at Pretoria and burgher J.P. la Grange Lombard met up with one of the agents there. He preferred not to mention the agent by name, but described him as having an "imposing personality", a "melodious voice" and being "very well spoken". According to La Grange Lombard the agent visited the camp on a regular basis to enlist burghers who were prisoners of war and were due to be sent to overseas camps. He would explain to them that by joining the National Scouts they would be able to avoid imprisonment and in some cases the men decided to take his advice.[31]

Kitchener himself also had a hand in the recruitment of National Scouts. In December 1901 he visited several concentration camps with this in mind.[32] Subsequent to an address Kitchener delivered in the Belfast camp, Leggett reported: "After Chief's speech to Burghers in Belfast Camp today, the men ... decided themselves to raise a corps of 100 men ..."[33] According to Kitchener's aide-de-camp, F. Maxwell, between 200 and 300 men from four different camps in the eastern Transvaal joined the National Scouts after Kitchener's speeches.[34] On 6 January 1902 Kitchener also addressed a gathering of about 200 surrendered burghers in Potchefstroom. He told them that Steyn and De Wet were only able to keep the burghers in the field by feeding them lies. "Military operations were now more in the nature of police work," he told his audience, "and it was becoming increasingly difficult to find any Boers." He hoped that the surrendered burghers present would realise "that their own interests demanded that they should take some active part in bringing matters to an end. If they would only come in and find the Boers ... the troops would deal further with them". Kitchener also stressed "that Louis Botha disliked more than anything else to have men of his own race fighting against him because in most cases the hiding places of the Boers were known to them". In conclusion he expressed the hope that members of the audience would join the National Scouts, "which was a corps formed on lines to which they were accustomed. They would be under their own officers who would be elected by themselves and they would be allowed to fight in their own way." Sixteen people joined up after Kitchener's address and two days later another 30 men from Krugersdorp followed suit.[35] Later in January the number of National Scouts in the southwestern districts showed a significant increase.[36]

In some concentration camps the conditions of service for the National Scouts were pasted up so that they could be brought to the attention of the inmates.[37] The conditions were presented in a very favourable light in order to attract as many surrendered burghers as possible. It was for example suggested that to join forces with the enemy would be a noble deed because it would restore peace in their troubled land.[38] In addition to this appeal to the "patriotism" of the National Scouts there was also the more explicit financial overture. Until January 1902 the members of the corps received 50% of the captured livestock and 2s 6d per day. In order to satisfy the demands made by the members of local corps that were absorbed into the National Scouts, a percentage of the livestock had to be included. However, according to a war correspondent from the *Times* of London, objections were soon raised against this practice, "not only at headquarters, but by the scouts themselves, and it was soon abandoned".[39] After the war a former National Scout, J.H. Joubert, maintained that the Scouts preferred receiving a regular payment to getting a percentage of the livestock, "because we then had cash on hand at the end of the month".[40] Each member of the National Scouts had to join up for a period of 6 months and from January 1902 they received 5s 0d per day plus rations. A corporal in the National Scouts earned a wage of 7s 0d, while a field-cornet and a commandant in the corps received 10s 0d and 15s 0d respectively.[41] The wages were certainly reasonable in such times of hardship and poverty.

273

Other offers made to recruits were couched in rather vague terms. Members of the National Scouts who rendered particularly valuable services to the British were promised "gifts", but the actual nature of these gifts was not disclosed.[42] They were also informed that they would be given privileged positions after the war. "Unofficially," according to the authors of the *Times History*, "it was put before every burgher that at the end of the war he would obtain certain preferential advantages in the settlement of the land. To the officers the hopes held out were necessarily more shadowy; but all were led to believe that they would hold in one way or another a privileged position."[43] An officer of the National Scouts in Klerksdorp, G. Linton, was even promised that he would be given a farm after the war. Linton did not doubt the veracity of the offer in the least and in January 1903 he made enquiries about the promise that had been made to him. Leggett was cornered and categorically denied Linton's claim: "I am able to state definitely that at no time was a promise of a farm or of any special bonus made by myself nor by any authorised officer, nor so far as I knew by any unauthorised officer to Mr Linton or to any other of the National Scouts officers."[44] Despite Leggett's categoric denial there is evidence that even Kitchener made unrealistic promises to the National Scouts. Ironically enough, it was Leggett himself who provided this evidence. In July 1904 he admitted candidly to Milner: " ... it is further a fact known to His Excellency that promises were undoubtedly made by the Commander-in-Chief, during the War, to the Scouts, which promises have not been and indeed could not be carried out."[45] This evidence makes it clear that the British did indeed make extravagant promises to the Scouts – in Linton's case even a farm – in order to secure their services. In this respect the National Scouts were certainly recruited for military duty under false pretences.

Some burghers in the concentration camps were unmoved by the recruiting campaign that was launched for the National Scouts. In the Johannesburg concentration camp an inmate by the name of J.F. Brand said: "We must not make fools of ourselves and join the National Scouts and fight against our own people ... The old Colony is rising and the British had no more troops fighting for them and that was why they wanted the Boers to fight for them."[46] H.F. Nel in the

Pietersburg camp spread a rumour that all young men who did not join the National Scouts would be sent away as prisoners of war.[47] The British authorities brooked very little opposition in this regard and people who tried to deter surrendered burghers from joining the National Scouts were either fined or sent away as prisoners of war.[48]

It was not only surrendered burghers from the concentration camps and prisoners of war from the "Rest Camps" who joined the National Scouts. Sometimes republican burghers who were captured in the veld immediately offered to join the National Scouts.[49] In the concentration camp at Simon's Town there were also volunteers who were keen to join up. When J.C. Henning and 39 burghers heard in November 1901 that "a corps of Volunteers has been raised by our own Countrymen in the two late Republics", they themselves approached Kitchener to request that they be allowed to fight on the British side. "We are convinced," they claimed, "that they [the Boers in the field] by their prolonged resistance against the inevitable, are only ruining the country, and inflicting untold misery and suffering upon thousands of helpless women and children and seeing that they will not accept the generous terms which have from time to time been offered them by His Majesty's Government, we wish to assist as far as lies in our power in compelling them to come to a peaceful settlement."[50] This request was granted and on 23 February 1902 there were 49 burghers who left the camp to join the National Scouts.[51]

There were also requests that came from men in overseas concentration camps to render military service to the British. In September 1901, for example, there were 200 prisoners of war in Ceylon who were keen to fight under the British flag in India.[52] This news was welcomed by the jingoistic *Bloemfontein Post* and the paper even held out the prospect of an "Afrikander Horse, providing a guard of honour for the Sovereign at some great State function",[53] but according to Chamberlain this idea fell through because of "legal and other difficulties". Nevertheless, 163 prisoners of war in Ceylon were still prepared to come back to South Africa to fight against their former comrades.[54] On Bermuda and St Helena too, there were 158 and 298 prisoners of war respectively who were willing to take up arms against their countrymen in the last seven months of the war. An analysis of the 298 requests from those on St Helena shows that the large majority (274) had been taken prisoner at Paardeberg (27 February 1900) or shortly afterwards.[55] This appears to indicate that during their long, tedious and lonely exile these people gradually lost touch with the national aspirations of their fellow countrymen. Some of the prisoners of war on Bermuda who were prepared to fight on the British side argued that the bitterenders in the republics were in any case fighting a losing battle, saying: "We feel justified and consider it our duty to participate in any movement that might tend to bring an early termination to the war."[56] But Lieutenant-general H.L. Geary, the commanding officer and governor of Bermuda, had his doubts about these prisoners of war and claimed: "They did not belong to the more respectable classes".[57]

Sir J. West Ridgeway, the British governor of Ceylon, was nevertheless of the opinion that it would be to the advantage of the British authorities in South Africa to give serious consideration to the applications of these prisoners of war. "The political advantages would be enormous," he wrote to Chamberlain. "If we could only divide the Boers and create a strong loyal party, it would I am sure grow rapidly."[58] Milner and Kitchener were in favour of these prisoners of war joining the corps provided that they were reliable and met with the approval of the other members of the National Scouts. However, according to Kitchener it was Chamberlain who had to take the final decision.[59] But Chamberlain was reluctant to give his approval. Presumably he did not want to antagonise the Indian government: "They consider that the raising of regiments from the prisoners of war might not be understood by the Native troops and the Indian population," he informed the governor of Ceylon.[60] The matter was thus settled and none of the overseas prisoners of war ever served on the side of the British. However, the names of those who had been prepared to do so were placed on a list so that at the end of the war they could return to South Africa before those who had remained loyal to the republican cause.[61]

Although certain researchers claim that the recruiting campaign for National Scouts met with little success,[62] the British authorities were satisfied with the results. According to Milner the National Scouts movement had reached "considerable proportions" by January 1902 and at the same time the director of the British military information service reported: "The Burghers are now rolling up well for the National Scouts."[63] In April 1902 Kitchener was also well pleased with the recruiting campaign.[64] British records show that at the beginning of January 1902 the corps had 950 members, and by April 1902 this had grown to 1125. By the end of the war the number of National Scouts stood at 1359 men.[65] Only volunteers and bona fide Transvaal burghers were accepted as members of the corps. Existing members who had already been sworn in were also consulted on the reliability of all new recruits, and only those who met with their approval were permitted to join up.[66] Well-nigh all the members of the National Scouts had fought previously on the Boer side.[67] To now fight on the opposite side was a strange experience and possibly they felt somewhat conscience-stricken. "I have watched these burghers," wrote a correspondent of the London *Times*, "I have seen them join a column, every expression, every attitude displaying shyness and mistrust; … a little later on they will, perhaps, take you into their confidence." The same correspondent also claimed that the British officers and troops readily accepted the presence of "Brother Boer" in their ranks.[68]

As with the British troops, the National Scouts were provided with full military kit. Captain M.C. Jamieson, who was appointed as adjutant for the corps, testified after the war that the National Scouts were issued with a horse, saddle, bridle, rifle and ammunition as well as "a distinctive regular uniform consisting of Khaki, the tunic of which had brass buttons which buttoned up to the neck where it was fastened with a clasp hoop; the letters N.S. also in brass appearing on a badge; the tunics were without epaulettes and had pleated top pockets only over the chest, there were no side pockets. The rest of the uniform consisted of riding breeches, felt hat, etc."[69] The provision of a complete set of military equipment to the members of the National Scouts was in marked contrast to those who served in the local burgher corps who, with the exception of rifles and ammunition, had to provide all their own kit.[70] The National Scouts were also placed under British military jurisdiction and were subject to the same disciplinary code as the British troops.[71] Similarly, after the war they received South African War medals for their services in the imperial army.[72]

Major E.M.H. Leggett, who had previously been attached to the Imperial Military Railways, was appointed as staff officer in charge of the organisation of the National Scouts. Captain T.S. Allison of the South African Mounted Irregular Forces was assistant staff officer and Captain M.C. Jamieson of the same regiment, as mentioned above, was the adjutant of the corps. The British commander of the National Scouts as far as military operations were concerned was Major A. Hoskins of the North Stafford Regiment. The headquarters of the National Scouts was in Pretoria, but depots were also opened in other parts of the Transvaal to enlist new members and kit them out for service. In the eastern Transvaal depots were opened at Belfast, Middelburg, Lydenburg and Kaapsche Hoop. In the southwestern districts there was one at Klerksdorp and a depot was also opened at Pietersburg to serve the northern districts.[73]

By the end of the war the National Scouts comprised nine sections, each under its own officers. Most of these branches were in the eastern Transvaal. At Belfast there were two sections comprising 141 and 175 men who were under Commandants P.A. van Vuuren and N.J. Breytenbach respectively, with seven field-cornets and 15 corporals. The largest concentration of National Scouts was stationed at Vlaklaagte, which was about 32 kilometres northwest of Standerton. Two sections of the corps, comprising 110 and 194 men, were under the orders of Commandants P.J.J. van Vuuren and J.W. Steenkamp respectively, and had 17 field-cornets and 16 corporals under them. At Middelburg there was a section of 110 men under Commandant G.L. Vosloo with three field-cornets and four corporals. There were also National Scouts based at Kaapsche Hoop and Lydenburg. At Kaapsche Hoop, Field-cornet H.J. Joubert and one corporal were in charge of 31 men, and at Lydenburg there were 41 men under the orders of Commandant J.J. Erasmus and one corporal. In the north at Pietersburg, Commandant J.G. Celliers and Field-cornet A.Z.A. Briel were assisted by three corporals and had a corps of 113 men, while at Klerksdorp in the southwestern Transvaal, General Andries Cronjé and Commandant A.B. Pickard with seven field-cornets and ten corporals, were in command of 266 men.[74] The British authorities thought it advisable to station the members of the National Scouts as close as possible to their own districts. This was done because the men knew their own local vicinity very well and were thus of greater value to the British columns in a specific area. Another reason was that the National Scouts were not always prepared to operate outside their home districts.[75]

Although the commanders were in control of their various sections, they were still subordinate to Major Leggett and the other British officers on his staff. A British lieutenant was assigned to each section of about 50 National Scouts, and in the sections that had more than 150 men there was a lieutenant and a captain. The British officers with the National Scouts were paid on a slightly higher scale than the corps' own officers.[76]

Then the British authorities also paid particular attention to the families of the National Scouts. On 30 October 1901 a general circular was sent out to all superintendents instructing them that wherever possible the families of Boer people who were actively involved in British military service should be allowed to live in houses in the various towns.[77] In Vereeniging two families of burghers who were still in the veld had to vacate the house they were renting in November 1901, so that there was accommodation for the families of National Scouts.[78] By April 1902 in Krugersdorp, Klerksdorp and Potchefstroom there were 172, 460 and 1300 people respectively (including men, women and children) who had been given permission to live in these towns rather than in concentration camps. The large majority of these people were family members of the National Scouts.[79]

In Pretoria, Pietersburg, Standerton and Belfast many of the families of National Scouts were also housed in the towns.[80] This naturally meant that they were receiving preferential treatment because the loyal republican residents had to live in tents in the concentration camps. This distinction can be seen as yet another British ploy to enlist members for the corps. In this way the inmates of the concentration camps could also be shown that if they made an open declaration of their loyalty to the British authorities it would be to their material advantage.

Because of practical considerations the British authorities could not accommodate all the families of National Scouts in houses; some of them still had to live in the concentration camps. Feelings were understandably very tense between the families of National Scouts and those of the loyal burghers. So much so that the general superintendent of the concentration camps thought it wise to send out a circular in which he requested that the families of National Scouts should be separated from the other inmates when they were given their rations, "as complaints have reached Head Quarters that in some cases the members of National Scouts' families are being subjected to unpleasantness at the hands of other Refugees".[81]

To protect these families and to meet the needs of the National Scouts as far as possible, the British decided in December 1901 to set up separate camps for the National Scouts' families.[82] At Meintjeskop in Pretoria one such camp was formally opened on 11 January 1902; it was well sited and water was led to the camp from the town.[83] The British authorities made special arrangements to transfer the families of National Scouts who had previously been housed in other concentration camps, to Meintjeskop.[84] By February 1902 there were 326 people in the Meintjeskop camp; by March of the same year this number had risen to 427 and in April 1902 the total was 458. In this period only one person died in the camp.[85] In March 1902 National Scouts from Vlaklaagte were permitted to visit their family members in the camp, and while they were there, the British officers who were attached to the National Scouts in Pretoria organised a dance for the visiting members and their families.[86] Separate camps for National Scouts and their families were also established at Belfast and Pietersburg.[87]

As far as could be established, the families of National Scouts were not on a better scale of rations than the other inmates of the concentration camps. In other respects, however, they were favoured in that they were not subjected to the same disciplinary measures and enjoyed greater freedom of movement.[88] They also received excellent medical treatment.[89] Likewise, there was a concerted effort to make the Meintjeskop camp as comfortable as possible for the inmates. The superintendent of this camp, Major A.M. Lloyd, requested special recreational facilities for the young boys and also put up a large tent to serve as a place where the inmates could gather. Church services, for example, were also held in this tent, but because there was not a single minister from Pretoria who was prepared to visit the camp, the inmates themselves conducted the services. At the end of April 1902 Commandant J.G. Celliers visited Meintjeskop and expressed his satisfaction with conditions at the camp.[90]

The ORC Volunteers – the Free State equivalent of the National Scouts – fell under the same service conditions as the National Scouts.[91] This corps came into being largely owing to the efforts of Piet de Wet and Commandant S.G. Vilonel of Senekal. In September 1901 Piet de Wet, the chairman of the central peace committee at Kroonstad, felt that there was a need for such a corps "because ... there is always a want for sufficient guides who are acquainted with the position of the country where they must act as guides. We could even name instances, if necessary, where on account of the want of sufficient (or satisfactory) guides the results wished for have not been obtained ... By having a standard corps the Officers are better able to get to know and to trust these persons, where such is now almost impossible on account of the continual change of guides".[92] The matter was delayed for some months and only at the beginning of 1902 did it receive attention again.

On 11 January 1902 Commandant Vilonel wrote a letter to President Steyn, giving him a choice that was in any event already a fait accompli: "If you wish to proceed with the needless continuance of a devastating war, which can only have as a basis the total decline and destruction (extinction) of your own people, and the making of woodcutters and watercarriers of all ex-burghers of both Republics, you will be the cause of me with other ex-officers and burghers taking up arms against you in civil war, to thus accelerate the end."[93] Steyn's reaction to this letter is undocumented.

Vilonel's initial objective was to form one large corps which could take action against General Christiaan de Wet.[94] In January and February 1902 he started recruiting in the Bloemfontein concentration camp, but could not raise enough men to meet his purposes,[95] and the idea of forming one large corps to attack De Wet was dropped. In March 1902 Piet de Wet held various discussions with Captain P.H.J. Blakemore of the British intelligence service at Heilbron and it was decided rather to form two sections of the ORC Volunteers.[96] According to the British records, by 27 April 1902 the corps comprised 385 men and by the end of the war the number was 448.[97] One section of 220 men was stationed at Winburg under Vilonel's command, while Piet de Wet had 248 men under him at Heilbron. Captain Blakemore was in general control of the ORC Volunteers and recruiting depots were opened at both Winburg and Heilbron.[98]

With the organised enlistment of the National Scouts and ORC Volunteers the breach in Afrikaner ranks widened dramatically and was used to full advantage by the British. Seen in broad perspective, the National Scouts and ORC Volunteers – two corps which were formally incorporated into the Imperial army – were the pinnacle (or the nadir) of the campaign initiated by Roberts with his early proclamations of February and March 1900. While some surrendered burghers had thought in 1900 that the war was already over and had launched a series of unrealistic peace initiatives, they now took a much more radical step by electing to fight against their own compatriots on an organised, formally recognised basis.

2 Participation and its impact

At no stage did the different sections of the National Scouts act together as a combined unit against the Boers. Nor did the individual sections fight as separate task forces against the Boers. Instead they were assigned to various British columns as guide and reconnaissance corps, which meant that sometimes, independent of the British columns, they undertook spying campaigns.[99] Although the National Scouts were used primarily as guides and scouts, they were also caught up in a number of clashes and pitched battles against their countrymen. The latter aspect of their participation in the war is examined first; thereafter their work as guides and scouts is discussed.

On 1 April 1902, a group of 40 National Scouts was involved in the battle of Boschmanskop in the eastern Transvaal. Boschmanskop is about 29 kilometres south-east of the town of Springs. On the night of 31 March, under command of Colonel R.T. Lawley, Lieutenant-colonel H.D. Fanshawe and 312 members of the Queen's Bays launched an attack on the commandos under General J.J. Alberts and General Piet Viljoen. The National Scouts acted as guides and succeeded in sneaking the British force past the Boer sentries. The unexpected British attack initially caused havoc among the burghers, but they soon recovered and a few hundred mounted Boers drove the British back in a storming counter-attack. The British lost about 77 men and approximately 33 Boers were killed,[100] while one National Scout was wounded.[101] The battle of Boschmanskop was really the only significant battle in the eastern Transvaal in which the National Scouts played a role.

In the western Transvaal the Scouts under General Andries Cronjé were involved in several pitched battles. One of these was the battle of Ysterspruit on 25 February 1902. Thanks to careful planning and some intrepid mounted attacks in the early hours of the morning of 25 February, the commandos of Generals de la Rey, J.G. Celliers and J.C.G. Kemp succeeded in capturing a convoy under Lieutenant-colonel W.C. Anderson at Ysterspruit about 14 kilometres from Klerksdorp. In the fierce encounter the British lost about 187 men, while the Boer losses were approximately 51. During the battle, De la Rey's men managed to seize a large quantity of ammunition, something that the Boers sorely needed at the time.[102] When the news of the British reverse became known in Klerksdorp, reinforcements comprising 80 National Scouts under General Andries Cronjé and 250 British troops under Major C. Roy set off at about half past six for the scene of the battle. At the suggestion of Cronjé the men galloped past the Boer front at a distance of about 600 metres, unleashing a hail of bullets on the burghers. Undaunted, the Boers returned the fire and it soon became clear that the British reinforcements would not be able to drive the Boers back. General Cronjé was forced to retreat to Klerksdorp with the news that the Boers had scored a resounding victory. The National Scouts did not suffer any casualties during the attack.[103] The victory at Ysterspruit was an important one for the Boers and they were able to replenish their supplies significantly, but the fact that General Cronjé and the National Scouts had been in action against them was greeted by dismay in many circles. When President Kruger, who was in the Netherlands at the time, read in the press that Cronjé had also been involved in the battle, he sat for a moment with closed eyes as if deep in thought, and then moaned: "Cronjé, Cronjé, Cronjé, can it be true that you are fighting against us?"[104]

General de la Rey followed up his success at Ysterspruit with the renowned victory over Lord Methuen on 7 March 1902 at Tweesbosch. Lord Methuen was wounded in this battle and captured by the Boers. Expansively, De la Rey released Methuen so that he could go to Klerksdorp to receive medical treatment. On the military defeat which the British had suffered the *Official History* says: "It was long since so complete a catastrophe had befallen the British arms. Other disasters there had been of a similar kind during the campaign, but none involving the capture of an officer of high rank, moreover, not even much honour had been saved at Tweebosch, for the personal gallantry of Lord Methuen and the few who emulated him could not cloak the pusillanimity of those whose flight had sacrificed their comrades."[105] An unknown number of National Scouts were also involved at Tweebosch and apparently performed poorly when it became evident that the British were being outclassed.[106] According to P.S. Lombard, a heliographer who took part in the encounter, the "gang of joiners" had fled in a north-westerly direction over the Bechuanaland border. The Boers gave chase and a couple of National Scouts were shot dead before they could cross into safety.[107]

On 11 April 1902 the National Scouts were also involved in a battle which took place at Rooiwal, which is about 100 kilometres to the west of Klerksdorp. The fighting was the outcome of an extended British drive against the western Transvaal commandos which was initiated on 8 April by the columns under Colonel R.G. Kekewich, Major-general F.W. Kitchener and Colonel H. Rawlinson. At the time, General J.C.G. Kemp was acting as commander of the western Transvaal commandos in the place of General de la Rey, who had left to participate in peace negotiations at Klerksdorp. After consultation with his fellow officers, Kemp decided to attack the right flank of the enemy, which was under Colonel Kekewich's command. On 11 April 1902 at half past seven in the morning the Boers commenced their assault. The British commanders were initially caught unawares, but recovered quickly and positioned their troops to respond to the Boer attack. About 800 Boers rode knee to knee and fired remorselessly from the saddle while they stormed the British lines. This mounted attack by the Boers is widely regarded as one of the most remarkable assaults of the war.[108]

Commandant F.J. Potgieter of Wolmaransstad was the Boer commander, and according to the memoirs of P. le Roux, a burgher who took part in the encounter, about 200 National Scouts under General Andries Cronjé hid in a corn field in order to attack the Boer flank.[109] It was to the advantage of the National Scouts that Commandant Potgieter was also under great pressure from the British columns. From their hiding place, which gave them good cover, the Scouts fired with great ferocity on their countrymen and this attack, accompanied as it was by that of the other British troops, forced the Boers back.[110] Potgieter died in the encounter, reputedly shot by one of the National Scouts.[111] Eventually, because of the enemy's numerical advantage, the Boers were obliged to retreat and they were then pursued by some of the men under Kekewich and Rawlinson. Andries Cronjé and a group of National Scouts also joined the pursuit. The Scouts managed to seize some of the Boer cannons (in reality they were British cannons that had fallen into Boer hands at Tweebosch) and Andries Cronjé himself captured three Boers. In recognition of his actions in this encounter he was given an honourable mention in a report that Kitchener later compiled on the battle.[112]

According to the *Official History* 51 Boers died in this battle, while 77 were captured, 41 of whom were wounded – a total of 128 men lost.[113] As far as can be established the National Scouts did not suffer any casualties. After the encounter Andries Cronjé and several of the National Scouts walked around the battlefield offering water to the wounded Boers, some of whom flatly refused to accept any such comfort from the hands of the National Scouts.[114]

Rooiwal was the last of the battles in the western Transvaal in which the National Scouts were involved.

In the northern parts of the Transvaal the Scouts played no role in any major battles, but together with the British forces they did become involved in a number of skirmishes against the commandos under General Beyers.

According to Colonel D. Henderson, the director of the British military information service, Beyers was unusually inactive at the beginning of January 1902, which Henderson put down to the "reformed burghers who are sitting opposite him, and as he knows that these men, who have deserted him, are better men than those he has been able to keep with him, he is a little careful".[115] Henderson was clearly exaggerating. On 23 January 1902 Beyers had little difficulty in attacking the concentration camp at Pietersburg and even risked an attack on the town itself.[116] By the middle of February 1902 the members of his commando made it very apparent that they were far better fighting material than the National Scouts. Beyers anticipated that a group of National Scouts would be waiting for him at the foot of the Houtbos Mountains about 62 kilometres north-east of Pietersburg and he ordered about 100 burghers to reconnoitre the area and then to surround the National Scouts who were indeed found hiding there. It is not known how many Scouts were there that day, but when they saw the Boers coming they retreated hurriedly without offering any resistance at all.[117]

On 20 March 1902 Beyers occupied Fort Edward, one of the northern-most British outposts. The fort was sturdily built and manned by 50 British troops, and under the circumstances Beyers thought it wise not to attack directly but rather to cut off its water supply and besiege it. Lieutenant-colonel H.C. Denny was promptly sent from Pietersburg to relieve the fort, and was accompanied by 550 men including 150 former republicans. The British troops attacked Beyers and his force of about 400 Boers on 23 March. The Boers beat off the attack without much difficulty and Denny was forced to retreat.[118] The National Scouts did not fight with great commitment in this encounter. According to Denny the "converted Burghers [were] loyal and brave, but fighting as with a rope around their necks, in respect of their conversion".[119] Subsequent to Denny's abortive attempt, Lieutenant-colonel J.W. Colenbrander and a stronger force were despatched to relieve Fort Edward. On 28 March 1902 he succeeded and the Boers were obliged to fall back to the east towards Malepspoort.[120]

At the beginning of April 1902 Colenbrander planned to pin Beyers down with an encircling movement in the vicinity of Malepspoort, about 37 kilometres south-east of Pietersburg. On 5 April 1902 he sent the National Scouts under Commandant J.G. Celliers and some men of Steinaecker's Horse under Captain McQueen to reconnoitre the area. They were also instructed to make sure that the south-eastern and south-western escape routes from Malepspoort were blocked off. On 7 April 1902 Colenbrander and his main force of about 2000 men left Pietersburg to launch a direct attack on Beyers. Colenbrander hoped that Beyers would flee before being attacked and that the National Scouts and Steinaecker's Horse would then be on hand to intercept his men. On 8 April 1902 Colenbrander launched the attack and with some brief interruptions the fighting went on until 10 April 1902. Initially Beyers was able to resist Colenbrander's onslaught, but later, being greatly outnumbered by the British, he and his men left the *poort* (a narrow defile in the hills) and moved off in a south-westerly direction. The National Scouts and Steinaecker's Horse, who had been charged with guarding the exit, were unable to stop Beyers and most of his men got through,[121] but in the skirmish which ensued the National Scouts killed three Boers and took 20 captive. According to British records the total Boer losses for the entire operation were eight dead, seven wounded and 97 prisoners of war. On the British side one man was killed and eight were wounded, while two members of the National Scouts also suffered injuries.[122]

Six days after the encounter at Malepspoort, Beyers captured "a few joiners" who were subsequently court-martialled and executed by firing squad.[123] At the beginning of May 1902 the National Scouts under Celliers were again engaged with Colenbrander in an effort to pin down some of Beyers's men in the vicinity of Malepspoort. According to the *Official History*, Colenbrander's force, which comprised a total of 900 men, followed 150 Boers and succeeded in capturing 104 of them.[124]

From the participation of the National Scouts in skirmishes in the Transvaal it appears that their presence in the British army was by no means a crucial factor which tipped the scale in favour of the British. The authors of the *Times History* are correct in saying that the National Scouts "never turned the issue of a fight in the open field".[125] The British troops of course far outnumbered the National Scouts and therefore played a much larger and more significant role in battle, but apart from this the National Scouts were indifferent fighting stock. According to Kitchener they were "as a rule ... not very keen on severe fighting". In skirmishes they were only prepared to fight "when they are convinced of being much stronger and have the best positions; then they show dash and are very good at following up scattered and flying Boers".[126] A good example of this was the battle at Rooiwal. When the National Scouts, as has been shown, were under good cover and were backed up by British soldiers, they fought bravely and then followed up their advantage by pursuing the Boers. On the other hand, it was certainly evident at both Tweebosch and Fort Edward that the National Scouts were very reticent to fight; and they were apparently very wary of being involved on equal terms with their former countrymen in an open confrontation.

Whereas the National Scouts were of relatively little value to the British on the battlefield, the same cannot be said of their services as guides and scouts. In this capacity they made a far greater contribution to the British war effort. The National Scouts were familiar with the terrain and could provide the British with valuable information on the movements and habits of the Boers. These services were particularly useful to the British because there were very few outstanding scouts and guides in the British ranks.[127] Le May referred to the fact that the National Scouts' "value to the British was out of proportion to their ... numbers; they knew the country, they knew the habits of the commandos, and they were particularly valuable as guides and scouts".[128] Kitchener too, is on record as saying: "The National Scouts have done very good work."[129]

From February 1902 the various sections of the National Scouts in the eastern Transvaal were assigned to the columns under Lieutenant-colonel E.B. Urmston, Colonel C.W. Park and Colonel E.H.H. Allenby.[130] By means of night attacks and military drives these columns tried to capture the senior Transvaal government officials who had moved out of Pretoria, and the commandos under Commandant-general Louis Botha.[131] The National Scouts were actively involved in these military manoeuvres and right up until the end of May 1902 the British leaders frequently referred (often as regularly as every week) to their role alongside the British columns. On occasion they also did reconnoitring on their own, independent of the columns.[132]

Colonel Henderson of the military intelligence service was more than satisfied with the information that he received by way of the National Scouts. He was particularly pleased with the Middelburg district where "our Intelligence is really good".[133] On the grounds of this information and guided by the National Scouts, the British columns were able to trace the positions of the Boer laagers more easily.

In an effort to trap the Transvaal government, three columns under Colonel Park, escorted by 300 National Scouts, undertook an attack on Bothasberg (about 60 kilometres north-east of Middelburg) on 20 February 1902. Following a rapid night march the British launched the attack early in the morning of 20 February. The republican government had, however, already left its stronghold and so in this respect the British attack failed. Nevertheless the British succeeded in capturing 153 Boers including three field-cornets called G. Joubert, H. de Jager and A.J. Viljoen.[134] The authors of the *Times History* claim that: "It was mainly due to the assistance of a strong wing of National Scouts that these captures were effected."[135]

In the western Transvaal the Boer commandos were constantly uneasy because they realised that with the National Scouts to help them as scouts, the British columns were a very real threat. This was certainly the case after a surprise attack in the early hours of the morning of 5 February 1902, when a British force headed by Major H.P. Leader, accompanied by an unknown number of National Scouts, captured between 100 and 132 burghers under Commandant Sarel Alberts at Gruisfontein (about 24 kilometres east of Lichtenburg).[136] This unexpected night assault made the Boers more jumpy than ever. According to General Kemp, they then decided to take the precaution of halting at one place during the day and then moving quietly on to another position after nightfall, "so as to muddle up the maps used by the men who have betrayed our nation".[137] As far as General de la Rey was concerned the knowledge that the British commanders were making use of the services of the National Scouts was another negative factor which he had to take into account when he was planning his military strategy.[138]

In the northern Transvaal the British made very effective use of the services of Commandant J.G. Celliers, who was stationed at Pietersburg. On 23 February 1902 he received a personal instruction from Kitchener to be on the lookout for General Beyers's dispatch riders who were expected to be departing soon to deliver reports to the Transvaal government. While out reconnoitring on 9 March, Celliers and a few of his National Scouts succeeded in capturing five of the dispatch riders and the reports they were carrying. The British regarded the content of the reports as very significant and Celliers earned high praise for his endeavours: "His work has been very smart and he has covered great distances in effecting this."[139]

The British records on the independent scouting campaigns (those without the assistance of the columns) conducted by the National Scouts in all parts of the Transvaal claim that they were responsible for killing 19 men in action and capturing approximately 255 Boer prisoners of war.[140] These statistics do not really reflect the true value of the National Scouts to the British, because they were more often than not in joint action with the columns and it is impossible to establish with any degree of accuracy how many Boers perished or were captured as a consequence of the information and help provided by the National Scouts. It is, however, reasonable to assume that the Boers would have suffered fewer losses during the last five months of the war – in total the British records claim that 431 Boers died and 5193 were taken prisoner in this period[141] – had it not been for the active assistance of the National Scouts. A war correspondent of the London *Times* who was with the National Scouts in the veld was fully convinced of their valuable contribution to the British columns, and wrote: "Of the usefulness of these National Scouts there can be no doubt. In operations in their own districts their local knowledge renders them invaluable. It is a knowledge such as can never be acquired by any one who has not lived all his life on the veld – the instinct that takes them unerringly across a trackless expanse of grass on a dark night, that knows the undulations of the ground, imperceptible from a distance, by which a body of men can pass unobserved hard by an enemy's camp. At night one often has occasion to admire the silence and despatch with which a body of these scouts will fall out from a column on the march, round up a farm a mile or two off the line of route, and rejoin, it may be with a dozen or more prisoners, the force a few miles further on."[142]

Kitchener also regarded the National Scouts as excellent horsemen and was particularly impressed by the speed with which they mounted their horses. In March 1902 he sent out a general circular on the particular routine used by the National Scouts and how it differed from that in the British drill book. Soon afterwards all commanding officers received the instruction that "The General Commander-in-Chief has noticed that the method of mounting and dismounting their horses adopted by the National Scouts, is very quick and wishes all mounted troops to practise in it."[143] There were other areas in which the British were able to learn much from the National Scouts. "Their resourcefulness is unfathomable," wrote the war correspondent of the London *Times*, "ranging as it does from the shoeing of a horse to a cure for incipient dysentery culled off the veld …"[144] Furthermore the National Scouts were generally true to their new masters. Prior to the general extension of the corps in February 1901, Poore found it necessary to dismiss a few National Scouts because he felt that they were not entirely trustworthy.[145] These were, however, isolated cases and according to Kitchener there was not a single National Scout in the last phase of the war who let the British down.[146]

The intrinsic value of the National Scouts to the British was, of course, at the same time, to the distinct disadvantage of the Boers. Johanna Brandt emphasised that the National Scouts were an added threat to the Boers. "Before long the National Scouts were a strong and well-organised force, knowledgeable about all the Boer military tactics and familiar with the countryside – a dangerous and treacherous addition to the difficulties that the trustworthy burghers had to contend with."[147] Kestell also remarked on the "valuable assistance" that the "Afrikaner collaborators gave to the English by acting as scouts". According to him, had it not been for these burghers the British would have experienced far greater difficulty in driving the republican leaders into a corner. "These Afrikaners," he wrote, "made it possible for the English to cover great distances by night and, being aware of the habits of their fellow Afrikaners, they put the enemy in a position to capture the Boers and steal their cattle. Had it not been for them the enemy would not have been able to do this – or at least it would have been infinitely more difficult for them to do so."[148]

In contrast to the National Scouts the ORC Volunteers were not involved in any major battles. Their participation in the war was confined to reconnaissance campaigns and to accompanying British columns.

The northern section of the ORC Volunteers under Piet de Wet was stationed at Heilbron.[149] It appears that Piet de Wet was primarily concerned with the recruitment of members and the organisation of the corps and was himself not actively involved in the veld. As far as can be established he acted as a guide for the British on only one occasion.[150] Most of the members of his section were integrated into the British columns as guides and scouts. From 5 to 13 April a group of ORC Volunteers did some reconnaissance work to the north-east of Heilbron, but in this period they were able to capture only one Boer.[151]

The southern section of the ORC Volunteers under Vilonel was more active, and on 22 March 1902, according to a British report, they captured seven Boers near Winburg.[152] The director of British military intelligence claimed that on the whole the Free State was very quiet in April and that Vilonel was responsible for the only disturbance "when he took his tame Boers out from Winburg and had a stiffish skirmish with a party of wild ones. In this fight ... none but Dutchmen were engaged".[153] In this encounter on 18 April near the present Marquard, Vilonel captured one Boer, while in comparison two Volunteers perished and the Boers took five turncoats captive.[154] G.J.S. van den Heever of Senekal, who took part in this clash, remembered years later in 1944 that Vilonel himself was very nearly captured by the Boers. He alleges that had Vilonel not been "mounted on a veritable racehorse ... he would certainly have been caught". Van den Heever claims that the five ORC Volunteers who were captured by the Boers were an 18-year-old boy called Steyn from Winburg, two brothers by the name of Ellison from Thaba Nchu, as well as two men called Meiring and Tromp who came from Trompsburg. They were all sentenced to death by a court martial under the chairmanship of General Froneman. Steyn was later reprieved on account of his age and Tromp managed to escape. The sentences of the other three ORC Volunteers were carried out at Kafferskraal, a farm between Senekal and Ficksburg. "It was such a sad scene to see them begging for mercy," said Van den Heever.[155] From the available evidence it appears that the ORC Volunteers, in comparison with the National Scouts, did not play as significant a role in the war. A possible explanation for this is that the ORC Volunteers was the smaller of the two units – it numbered only 448 compared with the 1359 National Scouts – and added to this the ORC Volunteers only became functional in March 1902, right at the end of the war.[156]

In March 1902 the Free State leaders were nevertheless worried at the notion that in addition to fighting the enemy they would encounter their own men too. They saw in this the danger that the ordinary burghers might possibly become thoroughly demoralised. "Hold fast, brothers, do not despair!" they warned, "To take up arms against your own people is to commit suicide and even worse, it is tantamount to killing your own family with the very same blow you use to take your own life."[157]

In the Transvaal the actions of certain National Scouts against their loyal republican counterparts exceeded all the norms of civilised warfare. As if treason was not bad enough, some National Scouts sank even lower by being guilty of certain atrocities such as those committed at an incident in the eastern Transvaal. In the closing stages of the war Commandant-general Botha's scouting corps was involved in a skirmish with a British force, accompanied by a few National Scouts, at Panstasie near Middelburg. Because of the British numerical advantage the Boers had to give way. A young 20-year-old burgher, also called Botha, was wounded in the leg by the British as the Boers retreated. He fell from his horse and was unable to move. Willem Mels, a National Scout from Middelburg, came upon the wounded man and according to Captain C.J. Trichardt, an officer in Louis Botha's scouting corps, Mels took his stirrup and "beat the poor helpless young Botha until he died of his head wounds". Trichardt gleaned this information from Botha's *agterryer* (mounted manservant), a young black man who had succeeded in escaping. After the war Botha's father reburied his son's body with the bullet wound in his leg and the stirrup marks on his head. "This is the way these murderers behaved," said Trichardt.[158]

Boer prisoners of war also came into contact with the National Scouts. On 19 February 1902 two burghers named S.A. Coetzee and W.P. Coetzee were captured by the National Scouts in the Lydenburg district. The Scouts did not harm them but stole their money, an amount of £26, and their watches,[159] which was in contravention of article 4 of the Hague Convention.[160] The treason of which the National Scouts were guilty and the unacceptable behaviour of some members of the corps towards their countrymen naturally gave rise to a great deal of bitterness in Boer ranks. R.W. Schikkerling, a mem-

ber of Commandant W.J. Viljoen's commando, expressed himself with regard to the collaborators as follows: "These despicable traitors were once our brothers-in-arms; they ate from the same bowl; sang and prayed with us, shared our triumph and our setbacks; and now in exchange for gold they have turned against us. Because of their falsehood they are hated with such venom that the blackest revenge is sworn against them. They can expect no mercy at all from us ... Time is about as likely to wash the black pollution from their souls as it is to erase the blue from the skies above."[161] These feelings of contempt and abhorrence are also mirrored in the contents of an anonymous letter received by G.L. Vosloo, leader of the Scouts in Middelburg:
Traitor, brute, curse of the Earth,
Degraded wretch of nature,
May God's wrath which has spared you until now
Exterminate you with the fire and brimstone of hell.[162]

When members of the National Scouts fell into Boer hands they could certainly not expect any mercy from their countrymen. When the name "National Scout" first became known in May 1901 among the Boers on the highveld, General Ben Viljoen captured a Scout and after a court martial the man was executed by a firing squad.[163] Then too, during the discussions between the two republican governments on 20 June 1901 on the farm Waterval near Standerton, a National Scout who had been captured by Commandant-general Botha was tried and executed. "What use has humanity for a man having been favoured by destiny with the opportunity of giving his all for an ideal ... and throws that down and takes service against it because a long purse hires him," said Commandant Ben Bouwer, when asked about this incident.[164] In March 1902 two National Scouts, Piet Bouwer en Dolf Emmenis were captured near Heidelberg and were sentenced to death by a Boer court martial. Emmenis was shot five times, but still showed signs of life. Apparently the Boers then cut open his jugular so that he bled to death.[165] Another National Scout, J.D.S. Swanepoel of Klerksdorp, was captured by the Boers in March 1902 near Hartebeesfontein and he too was subsequently tried and executed.[166]

The National Scouts must have realised full well that if they were captured by the Boers they would not be regarded as prisoners of war, but would almost certainly be given the death sentence. As has already been mentioned, this was apparently also one of the reasons why they were hesitant to fight with absolute commitment in battles against their former comrades. However, when the Boers drove them into a corner and there was no chance of escape some National Scouts fought with great determination.

In March 1902, for example, a group of Boers trapped four National Scouts in an abandoned homestead in the Lydenburg district. R.W. Schikkerling gave a dramatic account of the fighting which ensued: "They [the National Scouts] realised the deadly earnestness of the fight only too well and made no move at all to surrender. The Boers directed most of their fire at the doors and windows and using the cover of a garden wall they crept closer. The poor wretches inside answered every volley with furious fire. It seems they could not fight with the same precision and dedication as men who were fully committed to a cause, but instead they were imbued with a hopeless determination and calm courage which takes over when one realises that there is no chance of rescue and no way out. Even when the men who had encircled the house were directly outside, there was no sign of surrender. Among those who were trapped in the house were a father with two of his sons and they continued to fire even after the thatch roof was set alight and the whole homestead was filled with billowing smoke. When the roof finally fell in, the poor scum, suffocating and scorched, dived out of the windows, only to be riddled mercilessly with bullets. Their bodies were simply left lying there …"[167]

All kinds of far-fetched rumours about the treatment which the National Scouts suffered at the hands of the Boers were spread in Pretoria in March 1902. Among other things it was said that the Boers captured 12 Scouts and castrated them. According to Leggett this was simply gossip, "believed by the Dutch (especially the *vrouw's* [women])".[168] In spite of the fact that the Boers bore a bitter grudge towards the National Scouts, they did not, as far as can be established, ever assault and maim these traitors who had forsaken the peoples' cause, nor were they shot without a court martial if they were captured. The Boers were of course fully entitled to execute the National Scouts after a proper hearing.[169]

What impact did the National Scouts have on the Boers' military morale? On the one hand Colonel Henderson claimed in January 1902 that the National Scout "movement is having a depressing effect on the Boers still on commando".[170] Henderson cannot be accused of undue exaggeration. According to E.J. Weeber, who was a member of Commandant-general Botha's staff for some time, this "blackest treachery" by their "erstwhile comrades" made this final phase of the war "indeed the very darkest period in the history of the war ... Utter dejection, born of hopelessness and aggravated by treachery ... was a dark shadow which dimmed and embittered the nation's soul."[171] Weeber's description makes it very clear that the question of treachery within the ranks had a demoralising effect on some Boers. On the other hand, there is also evidence that the British enrolment of the National Scouts made certain Boers so embittered that it motivated them to continue fighting at all costs. In October 1902 some of the prisoners of war in the "Rest Camp" at Pretoria told Dr James Kay, an English-speaking medical practitioner from Pretoria: "They [the British] can see the war is no nearer the end now than it was two years ago, and Kitchener acknowledges he can't beat us. If he can, why is he getting Boers to help him? We know about the traitor Celliers; he was with Beyers for a long time, then he surrendered and has been trying to raise some men for cattle raiding. It is all he is fit for."[172] The jurist J.M. Spaight is of the same opinion: "The employment of such auxiliaries [National Scouts] may have been a mistake of policy, as [it may have the effect of] embittering the commando Boers and prolonging their resistance."[173] Thus, on the one hand, the National Scouts had a demoralising effect on some Boers; on the other, the British use of National Scouts embittered and strengthened certain Boers in their resolve to continue the struggle. The *Times History* is absolutely correct when it says; "Their [the National Scouts'] moral effect upon the fighting men is not easy to gauge. In the case of a stubborn nation such an example operates in two ways. For every man it attracts, it embitters and hardens ... others."[174]

The influence of the National Scouts can also be examined by asking whether the republican leaders regarded it as significant in their decision to conclude peace. If so, how crucial, in their view, was this particular consideration? Here it is important to remember that it was not only the National Scouts and ORC Volunteers who were fighting against their own countrymen. As previously mentioned, there were no fewer than 5464 republican burghers in British war service.[175] The Boers were thus confronted by an appreciable number of disloyal burghers who were actively supporting the British war effort.

The negative influence of these burghers can, to some extent, be gauged by examining what the republican leaders had to say at the peace negotiations. In addition, it is also relevant to look carefully at the post-war opinions expressed by republican officers, other contemporary people and of course the burghers who went on fighting to the bitter end, the so-called bitterenders.

In Vereeniging on 16 May 1902 a worried Commandant-general Botha, the commander of the Transvaal forces, said that "there are also some of our own people who have taken up arms against us". He even expressed the improbable eventuality that "if this continues, there will soon be more Afrikaners fighting against us than for us". Botha repeated this again on 30 May 1902, just before the final conclusion of peace. "One great difficulty", which in his view militated against continuing the war, was "the apostasy of so many of our burghers" and the "great damage" this had done to the republican cause.[176] The acting state president of the Transvaal, General Schalk Burger, also referred to the negative effect of the disloyal burghers. In a plea to the other delegates that they accept the notion of peace he said: "Each man we lose in this way makes the enemy stronger ... the enemy is learning about us; they are learning from our own people, those who are fighting with them against us, how they should go about fighting against us ... If you refuse to see these things then it is impossible for me and others to open your eyes."[177] General Lucas Meyer, a representative of the Transvaal government, fully supported Burger in this regard: "We have taught the English how to wage war. Our people are with them and are showing them how to move about at night and where the footpaths are."[178] For General Hertzog, the Free State leader, the fact that "some thousands of our own people ...have taken up arms against us" was one of the reasons why the Boers should perhaps consider concluding peace.[179] A delegate from the Wakkerstroom commando, acting magistrate H.J.

Bosman, bemoaned the fact that the position of the Boers had been weakened by these defectors. On 17 May he pointed out to the meeting that "many burghers have been disloyal to our cause and have thus strengthened the enemy. Had it not been for the help rendered by our own people, we would not now be in such a parlous position. If we continue we will simply get weaker and weaker ..."[180] These pronouncements, all of which refer specifically to the negative impact of the disloyal burghers, gain even more significance when a study is made of the post-war opinions of republican officers, other contemporary people and the bitterenders.

Captain Henri Slegtkamp, the capable Boer officer who inflicted a great deal of damage on the British communication network by blowing up trains, attached considerable importance to the negative impact of the National Scouts. He was of the opinion that the war could have continued: "But the treachery!"[181] For General Christiaan de Wet, who felt very strongly indeed about the whole question of collaborators, it was "easier to fight against the mighty army of England than against such lousy scum among my own people".[182]

There were other contemporary figures who also expressed their opinion on the influence of the disloyal burghers. Shortly after peace was declared, John X. Merriman had contact with certain bitterenders. As a result of his discussions with these particular Boers, this sharp-witted Cape politician wrote to one of his London correspondents: "I fancy – for it is a subject which I do not care to discuss with those I have met – that they [the Boers] attribute the surrender to the arming of the Natives and in the second place to the 'National Scouts' who betrayed their hiding places and acted as guides to the [British] columns."[183] For Hansie van Warmelo (Johanna Brandt), who together with her mother was involved in the Boers' unofficial Secret Service, it was neither the deaths in the concentration camps nor the armed Africans that had forced the Boers to surrender, but was in fact the "National Scouts – the Judas Boers". According to her they were not committed fighters, but "they have broken our strength because they have besmirched our ideal, dampened our spirit, robbed us of our inspiration – our conviction, our hope".[184]

After the war there were bitterenders who expressed the view that the National Scouts were the reason why the Boers had been obliged to abandon the struggle. In 1903 an anonymous burgher in Carolina said: "Those people were the cause of our defeat,"[185] and according to R.W. Schikkerling, "Had it not been for that dishonourable scum [National Scouts] … the enemy would never have penetrated our positions."[186] In the opinion of the heliographer P.S. Lombard, "Furthermore, had there not been so much treachery on the Boer side, the burghers could have held out for longer and would have stood a good chance of winning the war."[187] Burgher F.D. Conradie thought that the National Scouts were "jointly responsible for our losing the war",[188] and I.J.C. de Wet, General de Wet's son, held a similar view.[189]

In the light of all this, it is hardly surprising that an anonymous English-speaking Transvaal resident was moved to write in February 1904 that, "Rightly or wrongly there is a feeling existing in South Africa at the present moment and it is universally believed by the Africander side, that the game the National Scouts played in the War has cost the Boers their independence, a fact which might be forgiven, but will never be forgotten."[190] Clearly, the National Scouts and other burghers in British military service made a deep impact on the Boers' emotions and they blamed their defeat to a large extent on the treachery of these people. However, undue emphasis should not be placed on the value of all this evidence. After the war the Boers harboured such bitterness towards the collaborators that they were inclined to lose perspective and heap all the blame for the republican surrender on their shoulders. On a journey through the Free State and the Transvaal in 1902 and 1903, E.F. Knight, a special correspondent from the British newspaper *The Morning Post*, came into contact with many bitterenders. He made the point that "it is the theory of the Dutch, satisfying to their self-esteem, … that we [the British] could never have beaten the Boers without Boer aid."[191] Knight put this down to the bitter grudge the Boers held towards the National Scouts and the fact that some bitterenders grossly overestimated the number of collaborators.[192]

Nevertheless, on the basis of all the quoted evidence and with due allowance for the necessary reservations, it can be concluded that the National Scouts and the other burghers in British military service in May 1902 were indeed a consideration in the decision to conclude peace. Because of their great value to the British as guides and scouts and the effect, in some measure, which they had exercised on the demoralisation of the Boers, the treachery of these disloyal Boers did indeed contribute to the downfall of the republics.

To what extent was the influence of these collaborators an important reason for concluding peace? According to the authors of the *Times History* the fact that the Boers were also confronted by their fellow republicans in the military sphere was perhaps "the weightiest reason of all" behind Botha's decision to conclude peace.[193] L.S. Amery, the editor of the *Times History*, wrote in a work which he compiled 37 years after the war: "Two factors more than any others, accounted for the imminent breakdown of their [the Boers'] resistance." One was the concentration camp policy and the other was "the ever-growing strength and efficiency of the National Scouts commandos of 'tame' Boers, who ... were prepared to help the British put an end to the war, and, for their particular purpose, were extremely efficient troops".[194] This statement does not give due attention to the other factors which also influenced the Boer decision – factors such as the overwhelming British numerical advantage, the arming of Africans, and the shortage of provisions in some districts. It cannot thus be accepted that the National Scouts, second only to the concentration camp policy, as Amery puts it, was the most important reason why the Boers decided to sign the peace agreement.

The republican leaders themselves identified six reasons which were behind the decision to conclude peace. In a document drawn up by General Smuts and General Hertzog, and subsequently approved by 54 of the 60 republican delegates at Vereeniging on 31 May 1902, the following six important reasons, in the order on the original document (although not necessarily in order of importance), were provided for the Boer decision: firstly, the British scorched earth policy and the wanton destruction of all the resources which were necessary to sustain the continuance of the war; secondly, the concentration camp policy that had led to the deaths of thousands of women and children; thirdly, the arming of black people who were guilty of committing "atrocities" and "murders"; fourthly, the distribution of the British proclamations which threatened the fighting burghers with the confiscation of all their property; fifthly, the fact that the circumstances of the war were such that it had become impossible for the Boers to hold British prisoners of war, which meant that the Boers were only able to inflict "comparatively little damage" on the British forces. As opposed to this the republican prisoners of war were sent overseas which meant that only a very "limited number" of men remained in the Boer fighting force; sixthly, the "remaining fighting burghers" constituted only a "tiny minority of our people" and they were obliged to fight under circumstances which "in fact amounted to starvation and privation" against an overwhelming British numerical advantage.[195] This document, in which no mention at all was made of the collaborators, was drawn up specifically with posterity in mind and must therefore be treated with some degree of circumspection. The implication is that the reasons given by the Boers were not necessarily the most important reason for their surrender.[196] It is also highly doubtful whether in a document such as this the Boers would have been inclined to admit to posterity that there had been internal dissent on the question of continuing the struggle, or indeed that the traitors within their own ranks had played an important role in their defeat.[197]

As far as the outspoken General de Wet was concerned, the question of treachery was the most crucial reason for the Boer decision to abandon the struggle. Just before his burghers had to hand over their rifles on 14 June 1902 near Brandfort, he addressed them for the last time and singled out the "Handsuppers" and "National Scouts" as the people responsible for the final "lunge to the jugular". "It was their doing," he said, "that dealt us the death blow which drove us to this fatal decision."[198] De Wet made a similar statement in his memoirs.[199] Commandant-general Botha was not quite as dogmatic on this particular issue, but he did mention the collaborators in a speech delivered at Vereeniging on 30 May, when he declared unequivocally: "I say to you: we were so broken and weakened that had we gone on any longer we would not have been able to function as one party."[200]

It would be unwise to conclude on the basis of this evidence that the influence of the burghers who fought on the British side was the most important reason, or even that it was one of the significant reasons, why the republican leaders abandoned the struggle in May

1902. There were indeed so many issues at stake for the Boers that it is impossible to arrange them in order of importance with any measure of certainty. Would it indeed be too far-fetched on the grounds of these statements by De Wet and Botha, the two commanders of the republican forces, to presume that the question of treason perhaps influenced the republican leaders to a greater extent than they were prepared to admit in the document drawn up for posterity?

Notes

1 *Times History*, V, p. 406.
2 Translated from the Dutch. Brandt, p. 158.
3 WO 32/863/5985 (A364), "Staff Diary Pretoria", 15, 16 and 21 February 1901.
4 PMO 46/3107, report by Poore, 27 February 1901.
5 See Chapter 6, section 2 below for the contribution of the National Scouts during the war.
6 PMO 76/P66, "National Scouts Memorandum", signed by Leggett and approved by Kitchener, 2 October 1901; *The Times*, 23 November 1901 and 21 May 1902 (news reports); MGP 160/6605/02, Leggett – Acting military governor, 15 June 1902.
7 PMO 76/P66, "National Scouts Memorandum", signed by Leggett and approved by Kitchener, 2 October 1901; CO 291/43 (FK 977, p. 312), "Intermediate Report", 15 September 1902; WO/unsorted (A462), "National Scouts Certificates of Engagement, no 5 Wing"; Chapter 5, section 1 above.
8 PMO 76/P66, "National Scouts Standing Orders", 2 October 1901.
9 PMO 45/3014, Leggett – Poore, 7 February 1902.
10 WO 32/882/8960 (A382), "Minutes of Extraordinary Meeting of the Central Peace Committee held at Kroonstad", 20 September 1901 (translated copy with covering letter sent on 21 September 1901 and received by Kitchener on 9 October 1901).
11 In the *Times History*, V, p. 406 the impression is created that Kitchener acted in response to the letter from the peace committee. The authors of this work do not, however, mention that Kitchener only received this particular letter after he had already granted his approval for the formation of the National Scout corps. Their version of this particular aspect is therefore not quite accurate.
12 WO 32/874/8206 (A375), C.J. Theunissen – Kruger, 23 January 1902 (translated copy).
13 GOV 108/25, W.S. Duxbury (resident magistrate Potchefstroom) – Walrond, 8 January 1902. Report on the meeting, 6 January 1902. See also CS 64/870 and Milner Papers, 44 (FK 1201, p. 262) for the same report.
14 Translated from the Dutch. A copy of this letter dated 29 December 1901 appears in Oosthuizen, "De la Rey", pp. 533–33a. The letter is the private property of Oosthuizen, the author. For a published English version, see *Klerksdorp Mining Record*, 6 February 1903.
15 *The Times*, 8 February 1902 (news report).
16 MGP 152/2854/02, 15 February 1902.
17 Kitchener Letters, II, (FK 1622, p. 253), 21 June 1901. See also Magnus, p. 186.

18 Kitchener Letters, IV, (FK 1623, p. 511), 17 January 1902.
19 Kitchener Letters, IV, (FK 1624, p. 579), 16 March 1902.
20 *The Star*, 9 January 1902 (news report); CO 417/360/5871 (FK 659, p. 495), Henderson – Altham, 17 January 1902.
21 Translated from the Afrikaans. Conradie, p. 200.
22 Milner Papers, 105, (FK 1194, p. 327), 27 September 1905.
23 CO 417/348/2274 (FK 602, p. 536), Milner – Chamberlain, 17 January 1902. See also Chapter 5, section 1 above for Milner's initial attitude on the British arming of surrendered burghers.
24 *The Star*, 9 January 1902 (news report). For Milner's post-war attitude towards the National Scouts, see Chapters 8, 9 and 10 below.
25 MGP 131/14613/01, Resident magistrate Middelburg – Maxwell, 4 November 1901.
26 See Chapter 6, section 2 below and also Chapter 7, section 2 below, for more information on J.G. Celliers.
27 MGP 174/14587/01, Leggett – Maxwell, 4 November 1901; *The Bloemfontein Post*, 23 November 1901 (news report); *The Cape Times*, 23 November 1901 (news report).
28 *The Times*, 9 December 1901 (news report).
29 Lt. Gov. 141/115, list of names of National Scouts in the Rustenburg district, 12 March 1903.
30 *The Times*, 16 December 1901 (news report); *The Bloemfontein Post*, 18 December 1901 (news report); *The Cape Times*, 31 December 1901 (news report); MGP 252/4652/01, Maxwell – Superintendent Belfast concentration camp, 18 December 1901; PMO 48/3233, Allison – Poore, 25 February 1902.
31 Translated from the Afrikaans. J.P. la Grange Lombard, *Bang Plekke*, p. 116.
32 *The Cape Times*, 31 December 1901 (news report); Spies, "Civilians", p. 437.
33 MGP 143/17989/01, Leggett – Maxwell, 17 December 1901.
34 C.A. Maxwell (ed), *Frank Maxwell, Brigadier-general V.C., C.S.I., D.S.O., A Memoir and some Letters*, pp. 91–2; Spies, "Civilians", p. 437.
35 GOV 108/25, W.S. Duxbury – Walrond, 8 January 1902. Report on the meeting at Potchefstroom and Kitchener's speech, 6 January 1902.
36 HC 145/unsorted, Duxbury – Milner, 18 January 1902.
37 *The Star*, 22 February 1902 (news report).
38 Brandt, pp. 158–9.
39 *The Times*, 21 May 1902 (news report).
40 Translated from the Afrikaans. Magistrate Louis Trichardt, Civil Case, 181/1930, J. Steyn vs. G. Lyon, evidence of J.H. Joubert, p. 54, September 1930.
41 *The Times*, 21 May 1902 (news report); SNA 165, p. 130 "Rates of Pay National Scouts", undated.
42 *The Times*, 21 May 1902 (news report); *Times History*, V, p. 407.
43 *Times History*, V, p. 407.
44 GOV 361/46, Linton – Kitchener, 12 January 1903 and Leggett – W.E. Davidson, 10 March 1903.
45 GOV 668/17, Leggett – Milner, 1 July 1904.
46 *The Star*, 21 February 1902 (news report).

47 MGP 137/16237/01, W.K. Tucker – Maxwell, 2 December 1901.
48 MGP 149/2046/02, Maxwell – Assistant provost marshal Klerksdorp, 5 February 1902 (copy); Cd. 1423, p. 144, punishments imposed on burghers.
49 PMO 47/3204, Colonel C.W. Park – Poore, 25 February 1902.
50 PMO 40/2731, J.C. Henning and 39 others – Kitchener, 27 November 1901 (copy).
51 PMO 63/4402, "Roll of Prisoners of War who left Bellevue Camp, Simonstown", 23 February 1902; PMO 3/240, "State of Boer Prisoners of War", 14 June 1902.
52 *Africa (South)*, 650, p. 221, Sir J. West Ridgeway (of Ceylon) – Chamberlain, 9 September 1901.
53 *The Bloemfontein Post*, 31 October 1901 (news report).
54 Cd. 903, p. 126, Chamberlain – Milner, 5 December 1901.
55 PMO 54/3688, Lieutenant-general H.L. Geary (at Bermuda) – Milner, 25 February 1902 (copy); SO/POW 42/3921, Lieutenant-colonel C. Heyman – Poore, 8 May 1902 (copy); PMO 74/51 "Roll of names of men in Bermuda who are willing to take part in the field", undated; SO/POW 31/2887, Lieutenant-colonel T.J.P. Evans (at St Helena) – Lieutenant-colonel C. Heyman, 29 November 1901; PMO 54/3751, list of names of prisoners of war (with dates of surrender) on St Helena who wished to join the National Scouts, 22 February 1902; SO/POW 44/4155, Poore – C. Heyman, 6 June 1902. See also Oosthuizen, "Krygsgevangenes", p. 510 in which mention is made of prisoners of war on St Helena who wished to fight on British side. Oosthuizen does not, however, give further details.
56 *The Bloemfontein Post*, 27 February 1902 (printed version of a letter signed by A. Venter and seven others).
57 HC 90/1449, H.L. Geary – Chamberlain, 12 February 1902 (copy).
58 *Africa (South)*, 650, p. 221, Sir J. West Ridgeway – Chamberlain, 9 September 1901.
59 CO 417/348/2274 (FK 602, p. 536), Milner – Chamberlain, 17 January 1902; WO Confidential Telegrams, no. 920, Kitchener – Brodrick, 14 February 1902.
60 *Africa (South)*, 681, p. 24, Chamberlain – Sir J. West Ridgeway, 3 March 1902.
61 CO 417/356/26207 (FK 640, p. 213), Chamberlain – Viceroy India, 30 June 1902 (copy).
62 Buys, p. 227; Solomon, p. l7.
63 CO 417/348/2274 (FK 602, p. 536), Milner – Chamberlain, 17 January 1901; CO 417/360/5871 (FK 659, p. 495), Henderson – Altham, 17 January 1902.
64 WO 108/16/941 (A407), Kitchener – Leggett, 15 April 1902.
65 *The Star*, 9 January 1902 (news report); CO 417/361/20859 (FK 663, pp. 578–80), "Return of Ex Burghers serving under British", 27 April 1902; CO 417/362/26810 (FK 665, p. 14), "Return of Ex Burghers serving under British", 1 June 1902. In the light of this statement it appears that the number given in the *Times History*, V, p. 408, namely that there were 1480 National Scouts by the end of the war, is somewhat high.
66 *The Times*, 21 May 1902 (news report); CO 417/348/2274 (FK 602, p. 536), Milner – Chamberlain, 17 January 1902; PMO 51/3463, Lieutenant L. Symnes (National Scouts) – Poore, 14 March 1902.
67 CO 417/348/2274 (FK 602, p. 536), Milner – Chamberlain, 17 January 1902; Spies, "Civilians", p. 437.
68 *The Times*, 21 May 1902 (news report).
69 Landdrost (magistrate) Louis Trichardt, Civil Case, 181/1930, J. Steyn vs. G. Lyon, summarised evidence of Captain M.C. Jamieson, p. 98, September 1930.

70 See Chapter 5, sections 1 and 4 above.
71 PMO 76/P66, "National Scouts Standing Orders", 2 October 1901.
72 CS 461/3427, R.H. Brade on behalf of "Army Council" – Colonial secretary, 9 May 1904 and Colonial secretary – Lieutenant-governor, 8 June 1904.
73 CO 291/43 (FK 977, pp. 312–13), "Intermediate Report", 15 September 1902.
74 HC 165/121, numbers of National Scouts and officers, 24 June 1902. With the exception of General A.P.J. Cronjé, Commandant J.G. Celliers and Field-cornet A.Z.A. Briel, the National Scouts' officers did not necessarily hold the same rank in the republican forces.
75 GOV 108/25, W.S. Duxbury – Walrond, 8 January 1902. Report on the meeting at Potchefstroom and Kitchener's speech, 6 January 1902; *The Times*, 21 May 1902 (news report).
76 *Times History*, V, p. 407; *The Times*, 21 May 1902 (news report).
77 Cd. 902, p. 47.
78 MGP 135/15749/01, Maxwell – Commanding officer Vereeniging, 20 November 1901 and Commanding officer Vereeniging – Maxwell, 23 November 1901. Also Maxwell – Commanding officer Vereeniging, 23 November 1901.
79 CO 417/351/23939 (FK 619, pp. 415–20), reports on the concentration camps at Krugersdorp, Klerksdorp and Potchefstroom, April 1902.
80 MGP 174/15570/01 Commissioner of police Pretoria – Maxwell, undated; KK Supplementary Items, 2, report on Pietersburg camp, April 1902; MGP 177/1783/02, Commanding officer National Scouts Standerton – Maxwell, 14 January 1902; CO 417/351/23939 (FK 619, p. 417), report on Belfast concentration camp, April 1902.
81 KK Supplementary Items, 2, general circular, 30 April 1902. See also N. Devitt, *The Concentration Camps in South Africa*, p. 24; Martin, pp. 106–7, annexure B.
82 MGP 251/4496/01, Maxwell – Commanding officer Standerton, 2 December 1901 (copy).
83 Cd. 936, p. 12, Maxwell – Milner, 28 January 1902; KK Supplementary Items, 2, report on Meintjeskop camp, March 1902.
84 MGP 176/17911/01, Major A. Hoskins – Maxwell, 29 December 1901; MGP 144/406/02, Superintendent Irene concentration camp – Maxwell, 6 January 1902; MGP 180/3847/02, Major A. Hoskins – Maxwell, 6 March 1902.
85 KK Supplementary Items, 2, report on Meintjeskop camp, March 1902; Otto, p. 172, annexures.
86 *The Star*, 15 March 1902 (news report).
87 MGP 254/5202/02, Maxwell – Superintendent Belfast concentration camp, 10 February 1902; MGP 178/2442/02, Superintendent Belfast concentration camp – Maxwell, 11 February 1902; Magistrate Louis Trichardt, Civil Case, 181/1930, J. Steyn vs. G. Lyon, evidence of H.B. Dunn and W. Golding, pp. 48, 66, September 1930; KK Supplementary Items, 2, report on Pietersburg camp, April 1902. The number of people in the National Scout camp at Belfast could not be established. The Pietersburg camp was small – by April 1902 there were only 17 residents. Most of the families of the National Scouts lived in houses in the town of Pietersburg.
88 CO 417/351/23939 (FK 620, p. 420), report on the Volksrust camp, April 1902; *The Times*, 21 May 1902 (news report); KK Supplementary Items, 2, report on Meintjeskop camp, May 1902.
89 CS 71/1933, Dr R. Fox Symons – W.E. Davidson, 3 March 1902.

THE DYNAMICS OF TREASON: BOER COLLABORATION IN THE SA WAR OF 1899–1902

90 MGP 178/2279/02, Major A.M. Lloyd – Maxwell, 8 February 1902; KK Supplementary Items, 2, reports on Meintjeskop camp, March and May 1902.
91 CO 291/43 (FK 977, pp. 312–13), "Intermediate Report", 15 September 1902; *The Star*, 9 April 1902 (news report); *The Times*, 10 April 1902 (news report).
92 WO 32/882/8960 (A382), "Minutes of Extraordinary Meeting of the Central Peace Committee held at Kroonstad", 20 September 1901.
93 CO 417/360/10274 (FK 660, p. 790), translated copy of Vilonel's letter. See also *The Bloemfontein Post*, 27 February 1902 for a printed version of the particular letter.
94 *The Times*, 21 May 1902 (news report).
95 SO/POW 33/3056, permit issued to S.G. Vilonel, 20 January 1902; PMO 47/3172, Vilonel – Kitchener, 18 February 1902.
96 WO 108/16/879 (A407), Leggett – Lieutenant-general Ian Hamilton (chief of staff), 30 March 1902.
97 CO 417/361/20859 (FK 663, pp. 579–80), "Return of Ex Burghers serving under British", 27 April 1902; CO 417/362/26810 (FK 665, p. 14); "Return of Ex Burghers serving under British", 1 June 1902. The *Times History*, V, p. 408, gives the number of Volunteers as 480, but in comparison with the aforementioned statistics this appears to be somewhat high.
98 CO 291/43 (FK 977, p. 313), "Intermediate Report", 15 September 1902.
99 WO 32/883/9121 (A378), Lieutenant-general Ian Hamilton – Kekewich, 16 April 1902; G. Preller, "Die National Scouts", in *Die Burger*, 1 July 1926; Brits, *Diary*, p. 92, 20 February 1902.
100 WO 32/878/8721 (A378), General J.J. Alberts – Assistant commandant C. Britz, 3 April 1902 (translated, intercepted republican documents); Leyds Archive, 775 (17)(a), Nierstrasz, p. 1465; Standertonner [pseudonym], "Die Laaste slag op die Hoëveld, Boesmanskop, 1 April 1902", in *Die Huisgenoot*, 29 October 1937; *Times History*, V, pp. 559–61; *Official History*, IV, pp. 518–19.
101 De Wet, "The Fighter, The Scout, The Spy", p. 214.
102 WO 32/877/8622 (A378), "Staff Diary Potchefstroom sub-district", 25 February 1902; *Times History*, V, pp. 497–99; *Official History*, IV, pp. 410–15; Oosthuizen, "De la Rey", pp. 548–50; Gronum, *Die Bittereinders*, pp. 86–97; J.C.G. Kemp, *Vir Vryheid en Vir Reg*, pp. 446–8; Naudé, *Vechten en Vluchten*, pp. 323–7.
103 WO 108/15/658 (A406), Captain E. Greenway – Leggett, 3 March 1902, report on role of National Scouts in the encounter; *Times History*, V, p. 500; H.M. Guest, *With Lord Methuen and the First Division*, p. 108.
104 Translated from the Dutch. A.G. Oberholster (ed), *Dagboek van H.C. Bredell, 1900–1904*, p. 61, 6 March 1902.
105 *Official History*, IV, p. 420. See also *Times History*, V, pp. 502–8; Gronum, *Die Bittereinders*, pp. 98–106; Kemp, *Vir Vryheid en Vir Reg*, pp. 448–53; A313, De la Rey Collection, 2, De la Rey – De Wet, 13 March 1902.
106 Guest, *With Lord Methuen*, p. 114.
107 Lombard, p. 152.
108 *Official History*, IV, pp. 498–503; *Times History*, V, pp. 527–537; Gronum, *Die Bittereinders*, pp. 119–126; Kemp, *Vir Vryheid en Vir Reg*, pp. 461–468; Naudé, *Vechten en Vluchten*, pp. 352–354.
109 A422, G.L. Brits Collection, undated memoirs of P. le Roux on the battle of Rooiwal, 11 April 1902. Gronum, *Die Bittereinders*, p. 123 claims, without giving a source, that

500 National Scouts under Piet Cronjé were involved in the battle of Rooiwal. He obviously confuses Andries Cronjé with his brother, Piet, who was sent to St Helena as a prisoner of war after Paardeberg (27 January 1900). The number of National Scouts that he mentions also appears to be incorrect. Only the Klerksdorp section of the National Scouts, which numbered 266 men in total, took part in the battle. See Chapter 6, section 1 above for numbers in the Klerksdorp section. For this reason, burgher P. le Roux's figure of 200 men appears to be more realistic.

110 A422, G.L. Brits Collection, undated memoirs of P. le Roux on the battle of Rooiwal, 11 April 1902; undated memoirs of Field-cornet G.J. van Wyk of Wolmaransstad on the battle of Rooiwal, 11 April 1902, as repeated verbatim in Oosthuizen, "De la Rey", p. 606; A787, Preller Collection, 81, p. 177, "Geskiedenis van Onder-Hartsrivier kommando"; *The Bloemfontein Post*, 19 April 1902 (news report).

111 A787, Preller Collection, 81, "Geskiedenis van Onder-Hartsrivier kommando", p. 177.

112 Cd. 986, p. 14, Kitchener's report of 1 June 1902 in which a description of Andries Cronjé's contribution to the success of the encounter is provided.

113 *Official History*, IV, p. 503. The *Times History*, V, p. 537, puts the total Boer losses at 110 men.

114 Undated memoirs of Field-cornet G.J. van Wyk of Wolmaransstad on the battle of Rooiwal, 11 April 1902 as repeated verbatim in Oosthuizen, "De la Rey", p. 606.

115 CO 417/360/4848 (FK 659, p. 470), Henderson – Altham, 10 January 1902.

116 *Official History*, IV, p. 446. See also Chapter 4, section 3 above on the attack on the Pietersburg concentration camp.

117 Naudé, *Vechten en Vluchten*, p. 360.

118 *Official History*, IV, pp. 446–7; Naudé, *Vechten en Vluchten*, pp. 360–1. Naudé is incorrect in mentioning Colonel Kenny.

119 WO 32/879/8757 (A379), "Staff Diary Pietersburg District and Lines of Communication", 23 March 1902.

120 *Official History*, IV, p. 447; Naudé, *Vechten en Vluchten*, p. 361; G.D. Scholtz, *Christiaan Frederik Beyers, 1869–1914*, p. 84.

121 WO 32/881/8918 (A381), "Staff Diary Pietersburg District and Lines of Communication", 5, 7, 8 and 9 April 1902; Cd. 986, p. 4, Kitchener's report, 1 June 1902; *Official History*, IV, pp. 447–9; Naudé, *Vechten en Vluchten*, pp. 362–3.

122 WO 32/881/8918 (A381), "Staff Diary Pietersburg District and Lines of Communication", 9 and 12 April 1902.

123 Naudé, *Vechten en Vluchten*, p. 363; Leyds Archive, 774 (16)(b), Nierstrasz, p. 1392.

124 *Official History*, IV, p. 451.

125 *Times History*, V, p. 408.

126 Kitchener Letters, II, (FK 1623, p. 513), Kitchener – Brodrick, 17 January 1902.

127 Cd. 1791, p. 110, case 13941, evidence of Lieutenant-general J.D.P. French, 12 February 1903. See also Chapter 5, section 3 above.

128 Le May, p. 126.

129 Kitchener Letters, II, (FK 1623, p. 512), Kitchener – Brodrick, 17 January 1902.

130 WO 32/877/8622 (A378), "Staff Diary, Head Quarters, Eastern Line and District", 1 February 1902.

131 *Official History*, IV, pp. 512–21; *Times History*, V, pp. 464–6, 557–63.

132 WO 32/877/8622 (A378), "Staff Diary, Head Quarters, Eastern Line and District",

2, 3, 5, 14, 17, 18, 19, 21, 23 and 24 February 1902; WO 32/877/8622 (A379), "Staff Diary, Head Quarters, Lines of Communication East", 1 and 12 March, 1902; WO 32/879/8757 (A379), "Staff Diary Barberton District", 19 March 1902; WO 32/881/8918 (A381), "Staff Diary, Head Quarters, Lines of Communication East", 1, 4, 14, 15, 18 and 21 April 1902; WO 32/883/9121 (A383), "Staff Diary, Head Quarters, Lines of Communication East", 5, 9, 10, 11, 12, 21 and 22 May 1902.

133 CO 417/361/10924 (FK 661, p. 125), Henderson – Altham, 21 February 1902.

134 WO 32/877/8622 (A378), "Staff Diary Col. Park's Column", 20 February 1902; WO 32/877/8622 (A378), "Staff Diary Lieutenant-colonel Urmston's Column", 20 February 1902; Cd. 970, p. 4, Kitchener's report, 8 March 1902; *The Star*, 24 February 1902 (news report); *Times History*, V, p. 465, *Official History*, IV, p. 516.

135 *Times History*, V, p. 465.

136 Kemp, *Vir Vryheid en Vir Reg*, pp. 444–5; *Official History*, IV, pp. 408–9; *Times History*, V, pp. 496–7. According to Kemp there were 100 prisoners of war, but according to the British works cited here 131 and 132 men were captured respectively.

137 Translated from the Afrikaans. Kemp, *Vir Vryheid en Vir Reg*, p. 445.

138 A313, De la Rey Collection, 2, De la Rey – De Wet, 13 March 1902.

139 WO 32/877/8622 (A378), "Staff Diary, Lines of Communication North", 23 February 1902; WO 32/879/8757 (A379), "Staff Diary Pietersburg District", 9 and 10 March 1902.

140 The British kept regular records (although they were not necessarily entirely accurate and complete) of the number of Boers captured and killed by the National Scouts when they were in action on their own (rather than as part of the British columns). The following sources were used in the compilation of the statistics used in the discussion: WO 32/877/8622 (A378), "Staff Diary, Lines of Communication North", 6 February 1902; WO 32/879/8757 (A379), "Staff Diary Pietersburg District", 9 March 1902; WO 108/16 (A407), Leggett – Kitchener, 12 March 1902; MGP 154/3705/02, "P.O.W. Lists", 4 March 1902; MGP 151/2719/02, "P.O.W. Lists", 21 February 1902; MGP 149/1777/02, "P.O.W. Lists", 28 January 1902; *The Star*, 9 January, 15 and 27 February (news reports); CO 417/361/16650 (FK 664, p. 318); Henderson – Altham, 6 April 1902; WO 32/883/9121 (A383), "Staff Diary Colonel Park's Column", 12 May 1902; WO 32/881/8918 (A81), "Staff Diary, Head Quarters, Lines of Communication East", 4 and 21 April 1902.

141 *Official History*, IV, p. 705, annexure 20.

142 *The Times*, 21 May 1902 (news report).

143 WO 108/16/771 (A407), general circular issued by Kitchener, 16 March 1902.

144 *The Times*, 21 May 1902 (news report).

145 PMO 70/18, report by Poore, 25 February 1901; PMO 46/3107, report by Poore, 27 February 1901.

146 Kitchener Letters, IV, (FK 1624, pp. 578–9), Kitchener – Brodrick, 16 March 1902.

147 Translated from the Dutch. Brandt, p. 159.

148 Translated from the Dutch. Kestell, *Boeren-commando's*, p. 181.

149 See Chapter 3, section 1 above.

150 De Wet, *Boer en Brit*, p. 238.

151 WO 32/881/8918 (A381), "Staff Diary Heilbron District", 5 and 15 April 1902.

152 *The Bloemfontein Post*, 24 March 1902 (news report).

153 CO 417/361/18627 (FK 664, p. 349), Henderson – Altham, 20 April 1902.

154 WO 32/881/8918 (A381), "Staff Diary Orange River Colony, Winburg District", 18 April 1902; A119, Renier Collection, 1099, Memoirs of G.J.S. van den Heever, p. 63, 1944.
155 Translated from the Afrikaans. A119, Renier Collection, 1099, memoirs of G.J.S. van den Heever, pp. 63–4, 1944.
156 CO 417/362/26810 (FK 665, p. 14), "Return of Ex Burghers serving under British", 1 June 1902; Chapter 6, section 1 above.
157 Translated from the Dutch. *De Staatscourant der Oranje-Vrijstaat*, 8 March 1902.
158 Translated from the Afrikaans. A422, G.L. Brits Accession, sworn statement by C.J. Trichardt, 1960.
159 PMO 58/4014, evidence of prisoners of war, S.A. Coetzee and W.P. Coetzee, 22 February 1902.
160 Cd. 800, p. 23. Article 4 laid down, with reference to prisoners of war, that their "personal belongings, except arms, horses, and military papers, remain their property".
161 Translated from the Afrikaans. Schikkerling, p. 378.
162 Translated from the Dutch. A422, G.L. Brits Accession, sworn statement by C.J. Trichardt, 1960. See also C.C. Eloff (ed), *Oorlogsdagboekie van H.S. Oosterhagen, Januarie – Junie 1902*, p. 86, annexure F.
163 Preller, "Die National Scouts" in *Die Burger*, 1 July 1926.
164 P.J. le Riche, "Memoirs of Ben Bouwer", quoted in Scholtz, "Betrekkinge", pp. 184–5. (These memoirs are in the possession of Dr C.L. Scheepers Strydom of Bellville, Cape Town.)
165 PMO 58/4070, Lieutenant J. Nixon (National Scouts) – Poore, 29 March 1902; PMO 56/3883, statement by Sergeant R. Fowlds of the National Scouts, based on information from Field-cornet A. Greyling, who was present at the execution and was subsequently a prisoner of war, 11 May 1902.
166 WO 108/16/878 (A378), Commanding officer National Scouts Klerksdorp – Leggett, 30 March 1902.
167 Translated from the Afrikaans. Schikkerling, pp. 378–379.
168 WO 108/16/203 (A407), Lieutenant H. Shipley – Leggett, 14 March 1902 and Leggett's undated margin notes. See also Spies, "Civilians", p. 437.
169 Spaight, pp. 145–6; Chapter 5, section 1 above.
170 CO 417/360/5817 (FK 659, p. 495), Henderson – Altham, 17 January 1902.
171 Translated from the Afrikaans. Weeber, p. 266.
172 *Africa (South)*, 669, p. 54, Kay – Chamberlain, 18 October 1901.
173 Spaight, p. 145.
174 *Times History*, V, p. 408.
175 CO 417/362/26810 (FK 665, p. 14), "Return of Ex Burghers serving under British", 1 June 1902; Chapter 5, section 1 above.
176 Translated from the Dutch. Kestell and Van Velden *Vredesonderhandelingen*, (peace negotiations), pp. 86, 188.
177 Translated from the Dutch. Kestell and Van Velden, *Vredesonderhandelingen*, p. 201.
178 Translated from the Dutch. Kestell and Van Velden, *Vredesonderhandelingen*, p. 185.
179 Translated from the Dutch. Kestell and Van Velden, *Vredesonderhandelingen*, p. 181.

180 Translated from the Dutch. Kestell and Van Velden, *Vredesonderhandelingen*, p. 94.
181 Translated from the Afrikaans. D. Mostert, *Slegtkamp van Spioenkop: Oorlogsherinneringe van Kapt. Henri Slegtkamp*, p. 268.
182 De Wet, *Boer en Brit*, p. 94.
183 Lewsen, *Selections, 1899–1905*, p. 350, Merriman – Bryce, 21 July 1902. Merriman does not provide the names of the Boers with whom he was in contact.
184 Translated from the Dutch. Brandt, pp. 394–5.
185 Translated from the Dutch. *Land en Volk*, 27 February 1903 (letter from "Barbarus").
186 Translated from the Afrikaans. Schikkerling, p. 378.
187 Translated from the Afrikaans. Lombard, p. 160.
188 Translated from the Afrikaans. Conradie, p. 201.
189 De Wet, *Met genl. de Wet*, p. 45.
190 *Pretoria News*, 22 March 1904 (Letter from "Transvaal British").
191 E.F. Knight, *South Africa after the War: A Narrative of Recent Travel*, p. 99.
192 Certain bittereinders, according to Knight, p. 99, estimated the number of collaborators to be as high as 15 000 men.
193 *Times History*, V, p. 589.
194 L.S. Amery, Days of Fresh Air, being Reminiscences of Outdoor Life, p. 164.
195 Quoted phrases translated from the Dutch. Kestell and Van Velden, *Vredesonderhandelingen*, pp. 208–11.
196 See Le May, p. 152; Spies, "Civilians", p. 443.
197 In certain Boer circles there was sometimes the feeling that it would be wiser not to acknowledge the deeds and the influence of the Boer traitors to future generations. In his study of the published autobiographical sources on the Anglo-Boer War, J.F. Stemmet came to the conclusion that: "Because of their Christian convictions and in order to protect the families and descendants of surrendered burghers and collaborators, most of the authors of works on the war decided to commit these deeds of disloyalty to oblivion." (Translated from the Afrikaans), J.F. Stemmet, "Gepubliseerde Outobiografiese Bronne oor die Tweede Vryheidsoorlog" (Unpublished MA dissertation, Potch), 1973, p. 430. For example, Captain Henri Slegtkamp told Dirk Mostert, who compiled his war memoirs in 1935: "Tell them [posterity] the naked truth but do not record in the book any of the names of those men who wavered. We must not open up old wounds again."(Translated from the Afrikaans), Mostert, pp. 2–3. At the end of 1902 General Botha, after consultation with General de Wet and General de la Rey, decided to destroy a list of names of the National Scouts which the Boers had acquired during the war. He thought this wise "because as far as the descendants of the 'National Scouts' are concerned it is better that the names should remain unknown". (Translated from the Afrikaans), G.D. Scholtz, *In Doodsgevaar: Die Oorlogservarings van Kapt. J.J. Naudé*, p. 232.
198 Translated from the Dutch. Badenhorst, p. 161.
199 De Wet, *Boer en Brit*, p. 195.
200 Kestell and Van Velden, *Vredesonderhandelingen*, p. 188.

Chapter 7
The rationale of treason and the implications of the final peace negotiations at Vereeniging

1 Motives of the rank and file

In December 1901 the pro-British *Cape Times* welcomed the extension of the National Scout corps, but did see fit to remark that "the idea of ... men serving against their own kith and kin is one that under most circumstances would be repugnant to all ethics that pertain to the bearing of members of a race to each other".[1] In this section an attempt will be made to offer an explanation for this unethical phenomenon by looking at the possible reasons why the rank and file, the ordinary members of the Scouts, fought on the British side. Although the emphasis will fall primarily on the National Scouts, the other burghers who fought for the British will also receive some attention.

Gustav Preller was of the opinion that "the reasons why these people [the National Scouts] came to the point where they took up arms against their own flesh and blood are perhaps just as varied as the causes of poverty".[2] This is certainly true. It is virtually impossible to consider every individual's reasons; they will all differ to a varying extent. In such circumstances the historian can merely try to identify and discuss certain basic common factors.

Donald Denoon, who has written on the post-war period in the Transvaal, attempts briefly to explain the phenomenon of National Scouts in purely economic terms. According to him, before the war most of the National Scouts had not owned land but were poor landless men in the employ of a landed proprietor (so-called *bywoners*), while the bitterenders were the landowners. He therefore attributes the division in Afrikaner ranks to "economic differentiation".[3] Because of a lack of substantiation, Denoon's generalisation that the National Scouts were landless *bywoners* cannot be accepted unreservedly.[4] The hypothesis does however bear closer examination.

The jurist J.M. Spaight has the following to say on the economic position of the National Scouts: "Some of the National Scouts were very wealthy men. I have it on unimpeachable authority that one who was captured with five others by Chris Botha, offered £80 000 if his life was spared. The six were shot."[5] In contrast to Spaight's comment (which clearly applies only to some of the National Scouts) the authors of the *Times History* are categoric that most of the National Scouts were *bywoners* before the war.[6] An analysis of the possession of property by individual National Scouts adds more weight to the hypothesis that most of them were in fact in a poor economic position prior to the war. From the enrolment certificates of the National Scouts at the Klerksdorp section, in which recruits were required to state whether they owned property, it appears that of the 213 men in the age group 20 to 60 years there were 154, that is 72%, who did not own any property at all.[7] The Klerksdorp section of the National Scouts – the only section for which there are enrolment certificates available – cannot, however, be seen as representative of all the National Scouts in the Transvaal. Nevertheless it would appear that in the eastern Transvaal there were also many *bywoners* in the corps. The resident magistrate of the Ermelo–Carolina district, J.C. Wedgewood, who was in close contact with the people living there, made the statement shortly after the war that "with few exceptions, the 'Joiners' are of the poor 'bywoner' class".[8] A contemporary author from the Netherlands who wrote on economic conditions in the Transvaal divides the Boer population before the war into two classes, namely the progressive "modern" farmers and what he termed the *takhare*. A *takhaar* is a derogatory word meaning a hillbilly, an impoverished individual of dubious character, and in this group the author included the *bywoners* on farms and the poverty-stricken whites who lived in squalid conditions in the cities and towns. According to him it was particularly the *takhare* who were the "troublesome element in the war, the ship-wrecked people, those who were self-confessed failures with no property to defend ... those who even served the enemy in the expectation of booty".[9] John X. Merriman, the Cape politician, also wrote after the war, "The takhaar when he surrendered became a 'National Scout' in many cases."[10] According to General Smuts the National Scouts in the Rustenburg section were an uneducated and backward group of burghers, "who are found in the back parts of the Rustenburg district".[11] After conducting interviews in the Free State to discuss repatriation with many ORC Volunteers and other burghers in British military service, Lieutenant-governor H. Goold-Adams said in August 1902 that he had come to the conclusion: "I gather that the majority of these men are persons without property."[12] On the basis of all this evidence it can be accepted that before the war most of the National Scouts and ORC Volunteers were either *bywoners* or impoverished whites living in the cities and towns.

As a result of conditions prior to the war, such as the excessive subdivision of farms, a shortage of good agricultural land, the rinderpest epidemic and a changing economic system, the number of *bywoners* and indigent whites in the Transvaal prior to 1899 had escalated rapidly.[13] In the Free State there was a more even distribution of wealth, but in this republic there were also poor whites and *bywoners*.[14] The *bywoner* was usually entirely dependent for his livelihood on the landowner – on whose property he worked primarily as a farm labourer – and he himself showed little initiative and sense of responsibility.[15] Many impoverished farmers also sought refuge in the cities in the last decade of the nineteenth century. They usually found it difficult to adjust and were eventually so poverty-stricken that they became a social burden. Material decline was accompanied by psychological degeneration. The poor whites in the cities and towns and the *bywoners* on the farms thus formed the lowest white class in pre-war republican society.[16] Many people in this social class were often associated with traits such as "laziness", "immorality" and "thieving".[17] It is therefore hardly surprising that a bitterender, E.J. Weeber, expressed himself on the National Scouts in similar terms when he said: "The so-called 'National Scouts' were by and large the people on the lowest rung of development, ignorant, uneducated and totally unprincipled – many had criminal tendencies and were absolutely dishonourable."[18] Preller alleges that he knew "dozens" of

313

National Scouts before and during the war and that many of them were "people without any culture, really mindless, perhaps also stupid in some cases".[19]

It is a useful exercise to reflect on the disposition of some *bywoners* and poor burghers towards commando service. Even as early as 1883 a reader who called himself "Jan without land and soldier without pay" complained in *De Volksstem* that a large part of the population owned no land, but that it was expected of them to do commando service and to defend the property of landowners while their own families were in dire need.[20] A year later a burgher from Utrecht referred to the landless poor "who are the soldiers of the nation [and] exposed to life-threatening danger and yet they must serve without pay", and he went on to complain that when they returned from commando they were even summonsed because they were unable to pay their tax within the required time.[21] In 1891 C.F. Bezuidenhout and 39 other *bywoners* from Vrede informed the *Volksraad* that they were having financial difficulty in equipping their sons with full kit for commando service.[22] When war broke out in 1894 against the African leader Malaboch, the impoverished burghers in the Waterberg district felt very angry that they had been called up for commando duty. They claimed that they were so poor that they would have to go into debt to acquire the necessary commando equipment and that they would then have to fight without being paid while their families did not even have bread to eat.[23] Shortly before the Anglo-Boer War began, G. Ferreira and 14 other needy burghers from Parys approached President Steyn for financial assistance. Because of their dire economic straits they said that they doubted whether they would be in a position to meet their obligations in the war they presumed was imminent.[24] During the war H.F. Wilson, secretary of the Orange River Colony, alleged that many *bywoners* had been forced by their "immediate landlords" to join the commandos.[25]

It thus appears that even before the Anglo-Boer War, some *bywoners* felt aggrieved about the fact that they had to render commando service without pay in order to protect (as they saw it), other peoples' property, while they themselves possessed no land at all. They also had to incur expense in acquiring the necessary commando equipment. Then too, while the *bywoner* was absent on commando his family was sometimes bereft of the meagre provisions he had previously provided for them. As a "disadvantaged" group who had occupied a very lowly economic and social position in pre-war republican society, it is understandable that they were relatively easy prey to the vague British promises that if they enlisted in the National Scouts they would be ensured of a privileged position in post-war society. In addition, they were being paid to fight for the British – and this while they were feeling aggrieved that they received no remuneration for commando service on the republican side. It is also to be doubted whether as a uneducated and backward group of people they were equipped to see through the hollow British promises or to realise exactly what was at stake in the war.

In contrast to this, the "the cultured young burghers" were in General Christiaan de Wet's words, "the flower of our army".[26] Weeber also claimed that the "educated Afrikaner was in general a more ardent patriot than his less privileged fellow Afrikaner".[27] It thus follows that these men presumably had a better understanding of the full implications of the war and the ideals they were fighting for.[28]

The wartime metamorphosis from a republican burgher to a traitor in a British uniform did not take place overnight. It was usually a long process stretching over a number of months. From the enrolment certificates of the Klerksdorp National Scout section it appears that the large majority (79%) of these men laid down their arms during 1900.[29] By withdrawing themselves voluntarily from the struggle they distanced themselves publicly from the republican war effort. As surrendered burghers their continued detachment from the republican cause meant that in time they lost all contact and sympathy with their fighting compatriots. From this point on it was merely a simple step to renounce the republican cause completely.

The circumstances in which some of the surrendered burghers found themselves during the war also contributed to their taking this step. Here the prevailing conditions in the concentration camps (where most of the surrendered burghers were housed and where the majority of the National Scouts and members of other burgher corps were recruited) were particularly significant.

It is well known that the British administration of the concentration camps left much to be desired and that there was an extremely high death toll in most camps, particularly in the winter months of 1901 among the women and children. A National Scout commented on this after the war when he wrote: "You should not imagine for one moment that the Refugee camp was paradise ..., that is borne out by the many graves and other things that they [the bitterenders] did not see with their own eyes ... The aim of the N.S. [National Scouts] was in essence to make the people stop fighting; to effect a peace that would be in the interests not only of those who had surrendered, but also for those [who] had stood firm to the end. Because while everyone was suffering, the poor women and children were suffering infinitely more than anyone else."[30] H.M. Guest, editor of the *Klerksdorp Mining Record*, expressed similar sentiments after the war: "They [the National Scouts] sat in concentration camps month after month, witnesses to the abnormal mortality which occurred among the women and children ... They saw the poor creatures pining for the wide veld, and droop and die; they knew of the destruction of ... houses and fields and the future was so black and hopeless that their action in first demonstrating with ... friends outside and afterwards taking up arms against them, was perfectly intelligible and reasonable."[31]

These explanations, both of which were written after the war in apologetic terms so as to justify what the National Scouts had done, cannot be accepted unreservedly as a convincing reason why certain National Scouts sided with the British. By and large the surrendered burghers in the concentration camps displayed little evidence of any sympathy for the women and children.[32] Furthermore it is highly doubtful whether their concern for these women and children was such that they would be prepared to take up arms against their countrymen for this specific reason.

A more acceptable reason is that members of the National Scouts were paid well by the British and were thus able to take better care of their families; that added to this, their families also received preferential treatment in the concentration camps. By joining the British army the National Scouts could also earn more than they would get for labouring work in the concentration camps.[33] H.A. Cornelisse, a war correspondent from the Netherlands who spent six months in the concentration camps at Irene and Pietersburg, also reported on this aspect: "These corps [National Scouts and others] are comprised of the inmates of the concentration camps who are living there with women and children. These men must earn something extra to be in a position to buy additional food for their women and children ..."[34] According to Cornelisse it was a general trend that men joined the National Scouts in order to take better care of their families. And then there were certain National Scouts who were absolutely destitute. For example G.S. Cruse of Pretoria applied in December 1901 to join the Scouts so that he could receive an income to support his ten children. During the war he had lost everything.[35]

Boveri, in his extensive study of the phenomenon of treason in the 20th century found that as a result of the destruction and misery caused by wars, "each one must search out his own way and make a new life for himself, drawing only from his own resources ... Once he has lost his home, the last prop is removed and he must face the world alone and unprotected ... As a rule it is accompanied by the loss of courage which springs from total insecurity. In the midst of inner disunity ... the courage to seek a new way ... is the blossom that can unfold in our landscape [of treason]."[36] To a certain degree Boveri's conclusion is also true of the National Scouts who joined the corps while living in the concentration camps. Once they had lost all their meagre possessions they took the radical step of fighting on the British side because of despair and inner turmoil. After the war Guest described these emotions as follows: "They [the National Scouts] were sitting idly in the doors of their tents in concentration camps, 'cribbed, cabin'd and confined', chafing in their limited grounds, despair settling in their hearts as they saw ... the country being gradually but surely devastated, stock destroyed, dwellings falling into ruins and a black future rising like a blank wall before them."[37] For the surrendered burghers in the concentration camps the war was to all intents and purposes over, but they were still forced against their wishes to remain in the camps. After the war N.J. Lotz of Luckhoff, who joined the ORC Volunteers, was stricken with remorse for his actions and testified that the concentration camp life had just become too much for him to bear. He was anxious that the war should end so that he could be relieved of the tedium and frustrations of camp life. Because of this he had given in to "the temptations" and had decided to fight on the British side because of sheer "despair and misery".[38]

In the concentration camps there was very little taking place that was edifying or uplifting. No provision worth mentioning was made for recreation and the monotony of camp life was depressing and tiresome for the inmates.[39] Both Kitchener and the director of the British military information service mentioned that many young men who were bored with sitting in the camps joined the National Scouts.[40] These people apparently found the camp life so monotonous that with very little thought for the consequences of their actions they grasped avidly at any opportunity to exchange it for a more adventurous existence and one that earned them some money. It is significant that 28% of the members of General Andries Cronjé's National Scout section were under the age of 20 years.[41] Because of their youth these people were apparently also impressionable and were easily influenced to join the National Scouts when they heard the British promises.

Some National Scouts were bitterly dissatisfied with the way the burghers in the veld treated them after they had laid down their arms. To get their own back they then decided to fight against them on the enemy side. Although under the circumstances the Boer attitude towards the surrendered burghers was not unduly harsh, the Scouts did not see it as such.[42] G.H. Muller, a National Scout from Frankfort, said after the war that he had felt very aggrieved about the corporal punishment (25 lashes with a stirrup leather) he had received. He was determined to avenge this treatment, which he regarded as highly degrading, as well as similar punishments which had been meted out to other surrendered burghers.[43] In an open letter compiled in March 1906 a group of National Scouts put forward a number of reasons why they had fought on the British side. Among other things they alleged that the treatment they had been subjected to as surrendered burghers had driven them to take this step "because the continuance of the war by an informal fighting force no longer gave us personally nor our possessions any protection, particularly as regards our women and children".[44] Another National Scout said after the war: "When someone surrendered to a superior force he was hounded by the others; his possessions were confiscated, his farm destroyed and so on. And this desperate war had gone on for so long that eventually the surrendered burghers did not know what to do because they had been stripped of everything and had very little money; the little they had was used up and what were these men supposed to do then?"[45] Kitchener's views on the motives of the members of the different burgher corps are somewhat ambiguous: "Their chief desire is to recover sufficient breeding cattle before it is too late to enable them to restock their farms and make a living in the immediate future."[46] This motive had its origin in the desire for revenge and in selfish, personal gain – both of which reflect very negatively on the burghers who fought on the British side.

From the available documentary evidence it is also noticeable that many National Scouts were either directly or distantly linked by family ties. Major Leggett gave a typical example of this kind of relationship which stretched from a father-son link to the in-laws: "J.G. Bremmer is a National Scout, J.G. Bremmers's brother, D. Bremmer, is a National Scout, J.G. Bremmer's eldest son, Jacobus, is a National Scout, J.G. Bremmer's second son, Martinus, is a National Scout, J.G. Bremmer's son, Jacobus, married the daughter of Dinkelman, corporal in the National Scouts. Dinkelman married a sister of Trollope, corporal in the National Scouts. These are connected by family with the Van Rooyens, who are connected with the National Scouts."[47] In their correspondence various other British officers and the National Scouts themselves made mention of similar family ties between the members of the Scouts.[48] This would seem to indicate that family considerations and influences might also have played a role in the decision of some people to fight on the British side.[49]

As mentioned already, during the closing phase of the war there was a growing feeling among some of the surrendered burghers that, in the interest of the *volk*, the war had to be ended at all costs. In order to achieve this goal, they argued, they had offered to assist the British army in a military capacity.[50]

This motive is examined more closely below so as to establish whether or not it was a crucial consideration among the ordinary members of the National Scouts. The evidence here can conveniently be divided into humanitarian and political arguments.

P.J. du Toit, who acted as a guide for the British, justified his actions on humanitarian grounds: "Because I am convinced in my mind that nothing in the world can save us, then why should I wait to do my share towards bringing this horrible and miserable state of affairs to a speedy termination, for the sake of the country at large, for the sake of humanity, and lastly for the sake of the women and children in refugee camps and the prisoners of war ... ? This I consider the duty of every true patriot."[51] *The Cape Times* maintained: "The Boers who are forming the National Scouts refused to be classed as traitors or as unpatriotic, but justify themselves on the ground of the interests of the greater number, for the sake of common humanity and in the name of ordinary common sense."[52] After the war M.A. Botha of Kroonstad said that for humanitarian reasons it was the duty of the National Scouts to step into the breach and on behalf of the entire nation "to influence the misconception of those foolish countrymen to bring this fatal war to an end and to assist in bringing about peace as quickly as possible".[53]

As far as the political argument is concerned, the existing evidence points to the unfounded grievance which the ordinary members of the National Scouts harboured against the republican leaders in general, and more particularly against President Steyn and President Kruger. This becomes evident in this somewhat disjointed statement by a National Scout by the name of P.L. Swart: "Steyn, with his gospel, is always there to ruin the country more and more, he is very smart at turning round the meaning of the Bible in order to get undeserved glory ... Why did ... brave General de Wet invade Foreign Territory? No doubt Kruger had misled ... all. Kruger vowed to Sir Alfred Milner at Bloemfontein that no one has a right to steal another man's land, and that it is God's Word. Why did he not stick to his Christianity, instead of mocking God and Man and instead of sneaking into other People's houses like a murderer? He wanted to make out that Natal was our country, he wanted to reconquer it by force ... We in Africa have to bear the brunt of all his mean lies, while he quietly slips off to Europe to ask for assistance ... It is all very well for the Field-cornets to tell us all sorts of stories; it is all very fine for a Deputation to go to Europe. They say from Delagoa Bay that we will have our country back within a fortnight. On the strength of these lies they kill an ox and have a great feast. They then pray to God that there may no longer be any Guerilla war to disturb our Peace. We will therefore fight ... for our king and Fatherland."⁵⁴ This political argument was refined and formulated more clearly in 1906 in an open letter from 11 National Scouts in which they stated that they had fought on the British side "because we then no longer had a lawful government in terms of the Constitution of the Z.A. Republic. We were instead, in obedience to God's will, under Great Britain which had lawfully conquered and taken over our country, occupied our capital cities, taken over the entire administration and had set up an orderly and stable government in the land. We were thus duty bound to honour this government in obedience to God's Word, just as the 'bitterenders' were later also obliged to do."⁵⁵

When these humanitarian and political arguments are analysed, it is clear that the National Scouts were using them in an attempt to justify and exonerate their actions. In the first place, it is dubious whether purely humanitarian considerations are acceptable as a bona fide reason for an unethical deed of blatant treason. Their political arguments, too, are not always based on the true state of affairs. It is a generally accepted fact, for example, that the republics did not advance into Natal and the Cape Colony as aggressors with the objective of conquest, but that they did so for defensive reasons. Furthermore, reference has already been made to the obvious flaws in the argument that Britain had established a legal and efficient administration during the war.⁵⁶

Nevertheless it is possible that some National Scouts were sincere in their belief that these issues may have motivated them to take up arms against their countrymen. Even 28 years after the war J.H. Joubert still insisted: "I joined the National Scouts in an attempt to bring the war to an end. I did so for the love of my country. I was a true patriot."⁵⁷ But Joubert's evidence is far from conclusive. In the final analysis it is therefore questionable whether humanitarian and political considerations can be regarded as the most important reason why the National Scouts fought on the British side. A statement made by a disillusioned Milner after he had left South Africa in 1905 is perhaps closest to the truth: "I know that a great many of them [National Scouts] were men of a low type, and actuated by base motives, thought I do not, for a moment, admit that this is universally true. I believe that ... there were some men who were honestly convinced that the war had become criminal from the moment it had become hopeless and that their duty to their own countrymen was to do all they could to bring it to an end."[58]

By way of summary it can be said that most National Scouts were already *bywoners* or other poor whites prior to the war, and that precisely for this reason they could be relatively easily persuaded and manipulated to enter the British ranks and receive payment for their services. This can thus be regarded as the single most important motivating factor. Circumstances during the war, such as the treatment that the surrendered burghers received at the hands of the fighting burghers and the conditions in the concentration camps also played a role. Family considerations appear to be a secondary issue. In conclusion there was apparently also a prevailing conviction among a minority of the rank and file of the National Scouts that it would be serving the best interests of the country to fight on the British side and, by so doing, bring the war to an end. Whatever reason is advanced, it can only serve as a possible explanation for their actions; in no way can it be seen as an excuse for their act of treason. As an anonymous Australian officer so rightly remarked after the war, "All history has commended the man who fights for his country to the last, and has condemned the man who turns against his own country."[59]

2 Motives of the leaders: the Orange River Colony Volunteers and the National Scouts

Whereas the focus in the previous section fell mainly upon the rank and file members of the National Scouts and ORC Volunteers, the Free State and Transvaal leaders of these corps – Piet de Wet, S.G. Vilonel, A.P.J. Cronjé and J.G.Celliers – are discussed in this section. Within the scope of this study it is impossible to give full biographical descriptions of these leaders. Instead the emphasis falls on their careers up until the end of the war and more particularly on the circumstances which led to their laying down their arms against the

British and the reasons why they subsequently decided to fight against their own countrymen.

Of these particular leaders, the most widely known is Piet de Wet. His prominence is largely due to his blood relationship to the famous Christiaan de Wet. In comparison with Christiaan de Wet, whose renowned career has been discussed widely over the years, the career of Piet de Wet, the disgraced, disloyal brother is in stark contrast. In March 1902 Major Legget remarked dryly: "Piet de Wet is also his brother's brother."[60]

Pieter Daniël de Wet was born on 18 August 1861 (seven years after his famous brother) on the farm Nuwejaarsfontein in the Dewetsdorp district. As a member of a large family – his parents Jacobus Ignatius de Wet and Aletta Susanna Margaretha de Wet (born Strydom) had 14 children – Piet de Wet, like most of the children of that time, spent his youth on the farm. Although he received little formal education he was intelligent and well spoken. Until his eighteenth year he helped his father on the farm, but in 1879 he went with his brother Christiaan to the Transvaal where they began farming in the Heidelberg district. Apparently the two brothers were very attached to each other at the time. On 8 December 1880 they were together at the great gathering of the *volk* at Paardekraal where the Transvalers decided to resist the British annexation of 1877, and together the brothers fought in the First Anglo-Boer War (1880–1881). They also participated in the storming and conquest of Amajuba on 27 February 1881, where Commandant-general P.J. Joubert gained a celebrated victory over General Colley. In 1882 Piet de Wet was again involved in a war when he was under arms for seven months against Njabela, an African leader.

In 1883 he returned to the Free State and in the same year he married Susanna Margaretha de Wet (her maiden name was also De Wet) of Lindley. They settled on the farm Vinkfontein in the Lindley district and five sons and six daughters were born of their marriage. Piet de Wet was a progressive farmer who enjoyed the confidence of his fellow burghers. At the end of 1893, at the age of 32 years, he was elected as a member of the *Volksraad* as the representative for the ward of Middel-Liebenbergsvlei in the district of Bethlehem, defeating his opponent, H.S. Viljoen, by 145 votes to 47.[61]

As a member of the *Volksraad* Piet de Wet showed a lively interest in the issues of the day and he was able to make his point and express his opinions well.[62] At this juncture, as was also the case with the majority of the Free Staters, he was intolerant of any British interference in Transvaal affairs. Following the Jameson Raid in January 1896, he described the Chartered Company as a "nest of bandits" and accused Cecil John Rhodes of being "the person who is responsible for all that has happened". Piet de Wet wanted to assist the Transvaal militarily and he felt strongly that the Free State burghers "who enjoyed their own freedom should be prepared to move into the South African Republic and help her when her independence is at stake".[63]

For unknown reasons he resigned as a member of the *Volksraad* in 1897 and moved temporarily to Pretoria in 1898 where President Kruger was a personal friend of his. Just before the war he went back to Lindley where he was chosen as the field-cornet of the local commando.[64]

According to Van Rensburg, Piet de Wet was inclined to be headstrong and self-willed.[65] Hintrager, who had contact with De Wet in June 1900, described him as "somewhat difficult" and "emotionless".[66] Nevertheless he was a popular member of the *Volksraad* and a deeply religious man who was concerned about the welfare of his burghers when on commando.[67]

Before the Anglo-Boer War began Piet de Wet had no doubts about the wisdom of the Free State policy of supporting the Transvaal in the event of war. On the contrary, according to his nephew, Barend de Wet, he was in favour of this policy and about two weeks before the war he openly said as much in the home of his brother, Christiaan.[68] Piet de Wet also wrote a letter to President Steyn on 25 September 1899 in which he said categorically and ardently that if the war broke out "then I am going on commando".[69] He also wrote to his brother in January 1901 to say: "You know that similar to you and the others, I am critical of the political [pressure] the British Government is putting on the Transvaal."[70]

When the war broke out he was the 38-year-old field-cornet in charge of 200 Lindley burghers who left with the Bethlehem commando for the Natal front. In Natal he was involved in the battle of Nicholson's Nek on 30 October 1899 – an encounter in which about

850 British troops were forced to surrender and during which Piet de Wet led his men with distinction. From 2 November 1899 he took part in the siege of Ladysmith, but by the end of the month he was transferred to the southern front. Prior to his departure with 500 burghers he requested that the Free State government make provision for sufficient fodder for his animals and food for his men who were en route to Norvalspont.[71]

Under his leadership on 16 December 1899 the Boers succeeded in taking the important British position at Vaalkop near the town of Arundel. On account of his previous military experience and the leadership potential that he had shown thus far, at the end of December 1899 President Steyn offered him the chief commandant position, with the rank of general, of the Free State commandos to the south of the Orange River. Of the younger Free Staters Piet de Wet was one of the first to attain the rank of general. He replaced General E.R. Grobler, who at the time was unable to continue his command because of ill health. Piet de Wet opposed the passive military tactics of his predecessor and those of the Transvaal's General H.J. Schoeman and in time, together with General de la Rey, he began to implement a more aggressive approach. The Boers' stubborn resistance under De Wet and De la Rey was one the reasons why the British gradually had to move their offensive further west towards the Modder River.[72]

As the senior commandant on the Cape front, Piet de Wet insisted that the Free State and Transvaal burghers respected the private property of the local residents. When certain Transvaal burghers took a number of horses and cattle from the wife of a man called Roberts, De Wet objected to this and described it as being in contravention of Free State policy. De la Rey, who had not sanctioned the action, promised to set the matter right.[73] It appears that Piet de Wet attached considerable importance to waging war in an orderly manner.

On President Kruger's insistence, President Steyn gave Piet de Wet orders on 16 February 1900 to go to the western front as a reinforcement for General Piet Cronjé. De Wet with his staff and about 1000 men went via Bloemfontein to Modder River, but on the way he heard the news that Piet Cronjé with about 4000 men had surrendered at Paardeberg on 27 February. Soon afterwards Piet de Wet and his brother, Christiaan, took part in the encounters at Abrahamskraal

(10 March), Sannaspos (31 March) and Dewetsdorp (20 April) – all of them battles in which, under the circumstances, he acquitted himself well.[74] In May 1900 he was back in his home district of Lindley and from here he launched sporadic attacks on the British columns that were making their way towards Pretoria.[75] At the end of April 1900 Piet de Wet was of the opinion that the Free State forces should summon all their resources and make a concerted effort to halt the British advance. In contrast, Christiaan de Wet felt that a strong force should depart for Norvalspont to attack the enemy from the rear.[76] This difference of opinion between Piet de Wet and his brother was a mere whisper of what was to follow. It also shows that Piet de Wet was geared to more conventional methods of warfare than his brother. Under these circumstances, to meet the British advance head on and thereby to accept that the areas occupied by the British were irredeemably lost was the conventional pattern of defence which held no element of surprise. Christiaan de Wet's plan to infiltrate the regions which had already been conquered by the British, and to attack the British forces from the rear involves a more unconventional element of surprise. During the later phases of the guerrilla war this became an integral part of Christiaan de Wet's military strategy. His brother, on the other hand, regarded this unregulated, mobile warfare as pointless.[77] Near the town of Lindley on 31 May 1900, using military tactics which were largely conventional and working in cooperation with General Marthinus Prinsloo, Piet de Wet succeeded in capturing the 13th Battalion Imperial Yeomanry, comprising 468 men under Colonel B.E. Spragge. The prisoners of war, who included many members of the British aristocracy, were some of the last prisoners which the Boers could send to Pretoria. This victory by the Boers under Piet de Wet, a victory in which the British had 80 other casualties in addition to the prisoners of war, was a sobering setback after the success they had achieved thus far in the Free State. For the Boers it was a sweet victory coming as it did so soon after Roberts's annexation of the Free State on 28 May 1900; it was one of the encouraging signs that the war could perhaps be continued.[78] On Piet de Wet's military acumen, mainly during the phase of conventional warfare, there is very little disagreement. Van Rensburg makes mention of his "calm undauntedness" and Oberholster underlines this,

while Van Schoor refers to him as the "accomplished brother" of Christiaan de Wet.[79] The Irish pro-Boer author, Michael Davitt, who by and large could not abide surrendered burghers, made the following comment about Piet de Wet: "He had been an admirable fighter from the beginning of the war, and had shown himself a most capable officer when in command of men. In the campaign around Colesberg, December and January (1899–1900), he exhibited some of the very best qualities of Boer generalship."[80] H.G. de Wet, a burgher who had been on commando with Piet de Wet and who also later fought on the British side, was of the opinion that "Piet de Wet was without a question the best tactician in the Boer army, a man that fought with his brains."[81] In the *Times History* Piet de Wet is also accorded high praise: "In fact, almost up to his surrender ..., Piet de Wet enjoyed a higher reputation as a leader than his brother."[82] H.G. de Wet and the authors of the *Times History* are perhaps guilty of exaggeration in their assessments of Piet de Wet, but his British opponents certainly had great respect for his military capabilities. In May 1900 Roberts wrote of him: "Piet de Wet ... had given us a considerable amount of trouble from the day we entered the Orange Free State."[83] Lieutenant-general Ian Hamilton, who was involved in a skirmish with De Wet as the British marched to Pretoria, mentioned his "military capacity" as a Boer leader.[84]

Despite his creditable military career it appears that Piet de Wet began to have doubts about continuing the war by the middle of May 1900. Even before his victory over the Yeomanry on 31 May 1900 he had entertained the idea of a voluntary surrender, and had tried to put this into effect. On 18 May he was involved in an exchange of correspondence with Lieutenant-general Ian Hamilton in which he suggested that he might voluntarily lay down his arms. Because De Wet had thus far played an important role in the war, Roberts, in terms of his Proclamation III of 15 March 1900, was not prepared to accept De Wet's offer.[85] Piet de Wet's victory of 31 May did not imbue him personally with a new sense of urgency and courage to continue the struggle. Instead, at this time he showed increasing signs of war-weariness. In the first week of June 1900 he negotiated again with the British and agreed to allow Lord Methuen a cease-fire of six days. Following this incident, Methuen informed Roberts:

"I know for certain Commandant [P.] De Wet and his Commando are heartily sick of fighting, and long to give in their arms." Once again, Roberts was reluctant to give his permission for this step.[86] In the event, President Steyn intervened and gave orders that the ceasefire should be ended immediately.[87] The Boer siege of Lindley which commenced immediately thereafter was characterised by lethargy and lack of planning, and Piet de Wet was partly to blame for this negative attitude. He was with the commandos only during the day and at night he slept at his home.[88] On 22 June, after he had spoken to General Hertzog and Piet de Wet, Hintrager wrote in his diary: "On his face [Piet de Wet's] one can read sadness and despair."[89]

On 19 July 1900 Piet de Wet fought for the last time on the Boer side when, together with Captain Danie Theron, he was involved in a rearguard skirmish at Karroospruit (11 kilometres north of Lindley) against Brigadier-general R.G. Broadwood's force. By this time Piet de Wet was clearly struggling with the notion of surrender and in any event, because the British numerical superiority was too great for the Boers, they were forced to retreat.[90] For Piet de Wet this fight was most probably the final evidence that it would be pointless to continue the war.

The next day (20 July 1900) at Blesbokfontein, north-west of Lindley, Piet de Wet asked Christiaan whether he was still prepared to carry on fighting. Christiaan de Wet reacted instantly; he was furious with his brother and shouted: "Are you mad?"[91] Piet de Wet went back to his commando and called a meeting of the members of his staff, where the question of voluntary surrender was discussed. On 24 July he and six of his staff members, including his staff officer, Thomas Craven, left for Lindley to negotiate with the British.[92] On the way he told some of the burghers that "Our cause is now hopeless," and when one of them asked what their next step should be, De Wet answered: "I am not going to give anyone advice, each man must do what he thinks best, but I am going home."[93] Without any further ado Piet de Wet and the six members of his staff voluntarily surrendered at Kroonstad on 26 July 1900.[94]

As has been shown, from May 1900 Piet de Wet had been showing clear signs that he was losing heart. His depression can certainly be partly ascribed to the general feeling of desperation that had descended on the Free Staters after the battle of Paardeberg and the occupation of Bloemfontein.[95] He himself said in January 1901 that when he saw that the British numerical advantage was so great and that it "was a hopeless task" to regain what they had already lost, he had not laid down his weapons "irresponsibly" but had stated his case in a letter to President Steyn and suggested that he negotiate peace with the British "rather than ruin the country and making the people suffer such poverty".[96] It is not known what President Steyn's reaction was to this letter, but it can be presumed that he found Piet de Wet's suggestion totally unacceptable. Thereafter De Wet became "more convinced than ever that it was better for our people to lay down their arms and accept God's will, and in so doing, to sustain ourselves for the future".[97] As mentioned above, Piet de Wet was not in favour of informal, mobile warfare – the type of warfare that the Boers began to use increasingly in the second half of 1900. Then too, years after the war, Piet de Wet told a reporter from *Die Volksblad* that the "main reason" why he had withdrawn from the war was that "I agreed with President Kruger that [it would be best] to stop the war, to give up the two republics under protest, and not to sign any oath of allegiance to the king of England."[98] There is no evidence that Piet de Wet was anything other than convinced that the republics could gain nothing by continuing to fight; however, this was not the only reason why he laid down his arms.

After his agreement with Lord Methuen on a ceasefire in the beginning of June 1900, Piet de Wet had incurred the resentment of his brother. On 6 June Christiaan de Wet convened a meeting of the war council in order to discuss his brother's actions. Prior to the meeting Christiaan de Wet was "angry" and snapped: "Everything here is so false that I don't even trust my own jacket on my back."[99] At the meeting apparently no disciplinary steps were taken against Piet de Wet,[100] but according to what is seemingly the only available source on the proceedings of the meeting, there was a very heated exchange of words between Piet and Christiaan. At the meeting Piet de Wet also spoke out about the futile expectation that there might be active foreign intervention in South Africa. In his memoirs H.G. de Wet gives the following account (which is perhaps not entirely accurate) of the exchange of words between the two brothers, as well as Piet de Wet's opinion on the possibility of foreign intervention: "General Piet de Wet ... told them that he considers it time to stop this fight; that the talk of the intervention of other Powers was manufactured to mislead the Burghers to keep them in the veld, and that the European Powers could not come to the assistance of the Republics if they wished, and that he refused to be a party to this deliberate falsehood. It will only end in the complete ruination of the country and innocent women and children will be the sufferers. General [Christiaan] de Wet, great fighter as he was, was well known to be very hotheaded and could not tolerate views that did not tally with his sentiments. He lost his temper and insulted his brother Piet. General Piet de Wet ... then ... said: 'I wash my hands, I will not order another man into a fight to be killed in a hopeless cause. I will not be a part to the complete ruin of my country.'" [101] After this confrontation with his fiery brother, the rivalry between Piet and Christiaan increased. C.P. van der Merwe, a burgher who took part in the siege of Lindley, remembered that Christiaan de Wet, as is understandable, "completely ignored" his brother. "If the burghers ask him [Piet de Wet] what the instructions are, he answers that I should go and find out the orders from the other burghers."[102]

The poor relationship between Piet and Christiaan de Wet at this time was exacerbated late in June 1900 with the election of a commanding officer of the Free State forces. Four men were in the running for the position, namely Generals Piet and Christiaan de Wet, General Marthinus Prinsloo and Commandant J.H. Olivier.[103] The fact that none of these four people were formally appointed as commanding officer and thus did not have the final word led to a great deal of confusion and unpleasantness. In addition to Piet de Wet's difference of opinion with his brother, he also quarrelled with General Marthinus Prinsloo.[104] To resolve the crisis, President Steyn appointed Christiaan de Wet as chief commandant, but Commandant Olivier objected to this and demanded that the chief commandant be elected rather than appointed by the president.[105] Piet de Wet was also dissatisfied with the procedure that had been followed and was of the opinion that the officers themselves should choose the new chief commander. According to Henning Olivier, Commandant Olivier's son, Piet de Wet said to President Steyn: "You are the cause of this bickering. I am going home. I am finished with all of you. Why don't you have an election?"[106] Christiaan de Wet was not prepared to accept the position until he was certain that he enjoyed the confidence of all his officers. Using a secret ballot he organised an election to clear the air. The result showed conclusively that President Steyn had appointed the right man. Christiaan de Wet received 26 votes while Commandant Olivier and General Marthinus Prinsloo polled three and two votes respectively; Piet de Wet received only one vote.[107] After the election Piet de Wet was a disappointed man. To burgher G.J. Joubert who had contact with him at that time, it "appeared that he had been looking forward to becoming the chief commandant and was far from satisfied [with the result]".[108]

It would seem that Piet de Wet's clash with his brother, his view on the possibility of foreign intervention, his dissatisfaction with the appointment of Christiaan de Wet as chief commandant and his poor showing in the election which followed were also factors in his decision to lay down his arms.

Then there is also some evidence that points to the fact that Piet de Wet's wife, Susanna, played a role in his decision. On 20 June 1900 Hintrager and General Hertzog arrived at De Wet's farm and when they learned that he was not at home they spoke to his wife for a while. According to Hintrager, she was "very worried because the English had recently been setting so many farmhouses alight and had taken all the property, specially livestock". Hintrager claimed that she was "talking incessantly about 'burning down homes' and she wanted to know whether it was true what people in the laagers were saying about all the burghers being treated as rebels if they continued fighting". On the evening of 23 June Hertzog and Hintrager were in Piet de Wet's house again when Mrs de Wet repeated her complaints about "homes being set alight", the confiscation of property, "sheep being seized" and the "rebel proclamation". Piet de Wet then fetched some copies of Roberts's proclamations and showed them around to the others. Later, when Hintrager heard about Piet de Wet's surrender he expressed the opinion that Mrs de Wet had had a great deal to do with it. On 1 August 1900 he wrote in his diary: " 'Cherchez la femme!' Try to fathom the mind of a woman: for her, the home and hearth are more important than our independence and our fatherland. Now this decision *is the result of all the complaints that I often heard in her home.*"[109]

Piet de Wet's voluntary surrender and his later involvement in British military service signalled the final break between him and his brother. When Christiaan de Wet heard the news of his brother's surrender, he was so emotional he could hardly speak and his remark to General C.C.J. Badenhorst was barely audible: "If only he had rather been shot dead."[110] Assistant Lieutenant J.F.C. Fuller, who was stationed in Kroonstad for a while after the war, remembered the following meeting between the two brothers shortly after peace was signed, when they chanced to come upon one another in the Grand Hotel in Kroonstad: "Piet was having a drink when Christia[a]n came in. On seeing each other they fell to and had an awful row, which would have undoubtedly led to a free fight had they not been separated. Christia[a]n then turned away and said that he would not remain under the same roof with so black a traitor."[111] In 1915 when Christiaan de Wet had to sit in gaol awaiting trial as a leader of the rebellion, Piet de Wet wanted to go and talk to him "to mend the trouble between him and his brother", as he put it. But his brother sent back the message: "I have nothing to say to him!"[112] There were also other members of Piet de Wet's family who rejected him after his surrender. On 8 January 1901 his nephew, Barend de Wet, wrote to him as follows: "A time will still come when the whole of South Africa will be very much too small for you …, your day will come and the righteous punishment earned by you, you cannot and will not be able to escape. To me your nephew …, to your whole family, yes, I say to the whole Africander nation, you do not exist any more."[113] After his surrender Piet de Wet spent a short while in Kroonstad. Here he told the British commanding officer that if Christiaan de Wet was made aware that General Marthinus Prinsloo had surrendered on 29 July 1900 in the Brandwater Basin, "he [C. de Wet] would do so also, but that he would not believe it unless one of Prinsloo's men was sent to him".[114] This advice that Piet de Wet gave to the British has been interpreted in a earlier work as an indirect and "subtle attempt" on Piet de Wet's part "to put an end to [C.] de Wet's eagerness to go on fighting".[115] The British apparently attached a great deal of value to Piet de Wet's advice because Adjutant Albert

Grobler was sent with this message from Prinsloo to Christiaan de Wet. The commander of the Free State forces was, however, unmoved; the information made no difference to his passionate conviction and his determination to continue the war.[116]

Piet de Wet's voluntary surrender made him an unpopular figure among the loyal republicans. Yet immediately after his surrender he showed himself to be genuinely concerned about the fate of the civilian population. Not only did he mention this in the letters he subsequently wrote on behalf of the burgher peace committee,[117] but he also approached the British to complain about the way in which they were treating the women and children. While he was in Kroonstad he went to see Lieutenant-general Kelly-Kenny and raised objections against the British "methods of carrying on the war with reference to Boer women". Kelly-Kenny sent De Wet's complaints by letter to Roberts, who sidestepped the issue and replied: "I have never heard a rumour of the women having been treated disrespectfully."[118] By February 1902 Piet de Wet appears to have changed his stance on this matter. At a public meeting in Kroonstad he even helped the British army defend itself against valid allegations that they were treating the women inhumanely.[119]

During the first week of August 1900 De Wet apparently moved of his own volition from Kroonstad to Durban, where he remained for four months on parole.[120] On 11 December he asked Kitchener for leave so that he could return to the Free State and set up a burgher peace committee there.[121] On the way he paid a visit to Christiaan de Wet's wife, Cornelia, who lived in Johannesburg at the time. Piet de Wet tried to persuade her to influence her husband to abandon the struggle, but she described the visit as a "source of unpleasantness" and asked the military commissioner of police to inform her brother-in-law "not to make any further visits to me in the future".[122] From January to March 1901 Piet de Wet played an active role in the Free State peace movement.[123] When these peace committees achieved only limited success he became progressively more closely aligned to the British and more estranged from the Boer cause. On 6 May 1901 P.J. du Toit, General P.J. Liebenberg's secretary, wrote in his diary that, according to reports from the Free State, Piet de Wet had acted as a guide for the British columns, but Du Toit added that he was not certain whether this was true or not.[124] However, by June 1901 Piet de Wet was definitely serving the British as a guide for Major-general E. Elliot's columns.[125] Towards the end of September 1901, as chairman of the central peace committee in Kroonstad, De Wet suggested to Kitchener that it would be a good idea to form a well-organised corps of guides in the Free State.[126] This suggestion did not receive immediate attention in the Free State and it was only in March 1902 that the ORC Volunteers, partly as a result of Piet de Wet's efforts, was formally established. He himself was given the command of the northern section of the ORC Volunteers based at Heilbron.[127]

Next, the thorny issue of why Piet de Wet decided to take the additional step must be addressed. What motivated him to provide active military help to the British? During the last phase of the war Piet de Wet identified himself almost entirely with the idea of British authority in South Africa. In a speech delivered at a public meeting in Kroonstad on 25 February 1902 he said: "I love my people with the same love wherewith I loved them before the war, and ever strived to procure their best interests, and ... we can thank God, that, having lost our independence, it has been taken from us by a Government that treats us as well as can be wished ... [W]e will go on hoping to have peace soon and that the day will soon dawn when we all in Africa, as Afrikanders that have one interest, will live together as brothers and will faithfully support our Government, which Government is at the present day ... the greatest in the world."[128]

By this time Piet de Wet had lost all sympathy with the republican war effort. For him the decision to continue the war was based entirely upon emotion and sentiment. Even in August 1900 he had spoken out against "that sentiment," which in his words was "the curse of my Race". According to the available evidence he was also determined to act forcefully if the republican leaders would not change their minds. To H.G. de Wet he said: "I ... will give them [the republican leaders] six months to get their foreign intervention going or to produce the Party ... that has guaranteed [sic] our independence, and if they don't do so in six months, I will take *any* action that I may feel that is necessary to stop the war."[129]

As indicated above, after his four months in Durban Piet de Wet established the burgher peace committee in the Free State. The futile efforts of this organisation to convince the republican leaders to abandon the war presumably made him decide to resort to more drastic measures. He was apparently also angered by the death of Morgendaal. According to H.C. de Wet, "When the tragic death of Mr Morgendaal was communicated to General Piet de Wet, he decided to give the British active military assistance to bring the war to an end."[130] By September 1901 he was convinced that anyone who had the interests of the Free State at heart should make a concerted effort to put an end to the devastating war.[131]

This evidence throws some light on the motives behind his conduct. It seems that after his surrender Piet de Wet was determined to help end the war at any cost. As shown above he was a stubborn and headstrong person who persisted in his chosen path regardless of the consequences. As time went by he identified fully with the British war effort and regarded the republican cause as pure sentiment. In all probability he did not see it as an unethical step to fight on the British side. As early as January 1901 he mentioned to his brother that the Free State government "against which I could have been committing treason" no longer existed.[132] This was patently untrue,[133] but nevertheless it seems that De Wet was utterly convinced that his misplaced view of the war was accurate, and this was one of the reasons why he took up arms against his countrymen. In January 1903 he reiterated his standpoint to Chamberlain: "He wished Mr Chamberlain to understand the feeling of those who took the part of the English ... Their idea was that they had no Government and that the guerilla war was devastating the country." For this reason, he maintained, he felt called upon to fight with the British.[134] As far as can be established there is no evidence to the contrary, but there are indeed sources which indicate that this was not the only reason why Piet de Wet fought on the British side.

In the blueprint of the proposed Free State burgher corps that Piet de Wet put before Kitchener on behalf of the central Free State peace committee in September 1901, it was recommended that with, the approval of the military authorities, the members of the corps should receive part of the captured livestock as a reward for their efforts. The livestock could remain in the possession of the military government, but should be registered in the name of the corps so that after the war the members could either claim the livestock or elect to be paid a cash amount, according to their circumstances. The motivation for this recommendation was that after the war there would not be enough livestock available for farming to be resumed.[135] Such an arrangement would have suited Piet de Wet very well. Indeed, even before the war he had speculated with livestock. In September 1899 he had written to President Steyn and offered to buy slaughter oxen, horses and other livestock in his district and then to sell the animals at a profit to the government for use during the war.[136] In reaction to De Wet's stipulation that the proposed corps should be given a portion of the captured livestock, in his enclosed letter to Kitchener Major-general Knox wrote: "The members, I have no doubt, are beginning to feel the pinch of loss of business and aim at making a livelihood."[137] This creates the impression that in Piet de Wet's case there were also material considerations at stake.

Then it can also be accepted that during the war Piet de Wet was remunerated for the military service which he rendered to the British. The burgher commandants in the ORC Volunteers received 15s 0d per day.[138] However, there is no proof that Piet de Wet received any money for military service rendered to the British after the war. The money that he did in fact receive in the post-war period was not connected with his wartime service.[139]

Nor could any documentary evidence be found to corroborate the following statement in an article on Piet de Wet: "Unlike his famous brother, Christiaan, this De W. [Piet de Wet] was always prosperous."[140] At the time of his death in 1929 Piet de Wet lived in Lindley. The movable assets in his estate comprised only the contents of his house and a motor car, and he left behind no movable assets or cash. The total estimated assets of the estate (including the contents of the house and the car) totalled £1 047 15s 0d, of which £484 00s 9d was debt. A balance of £563 15s 3d thus remained for distribution.[141] By comparison, the assets in Christiaan de Wet's estate on his death in 1922 totalled £10 340 9s 10d. After subtracting a debt of £7 204 7s 4d, Christiaan's estate stood at £3 135 12s 6d,[142] which was far greater than the value of Piet de Wet's estate. Judging from these figures it is clear that at the time of his death Christiaan de Wet was in a far better financial position than his brother was when he died. It might, of course, be true that at an earlier stage Piet had been more prosperous than Christiaan, or that the figures given in the two estates are not entirely reliable; either way, it is impossible to be dogmatic on this issue.

Together with Piet de Wet, S.G. Vilonel was the other important leader of the ORC Volunteers. Stephanus Gerhardus Vilonel was born on 1 November 1865 at Edenburg in the Free State. His parents were Francois Philipus Vilonel and Hendrina Johanna Adriana née Griessel. Little is known about his youth, but as a young man, after his school education, he must have studied further to qualify as an attorney – a profession which he practised until his death in 1918. At the beginning of the 1890s he settled in Senekal where he soon built up a flourishing legal practice. That he was prosperous is confirmed by the fact that during the period 1896–1899 there were only three people in the district of Senekal who paid more municipal tax than he did. Vilonel also had farming interests and owned the farm De Rust as well as a third share in another farm in the Senekal district. In addition to his professional activities he showed a lively interest in civic affairs in Senekal and at 27 years of age he was elected as town clerk of the local municipality, a post which he held from 1892 to 1899.[143] He was also a keen sportsman and was particularly good at target shooting, walking off with the laurels as the best shot at the Free State championships in 1894.[144] In September 1896 he married Sarah du Toit Luttig and two sons and a daughter were born of the marriage.[145] Michael Davitt described Vilonel as "a man ... of good address and education"[146] and the local correspondent of *The Friend* at Senekal regarded him "as one who has the rare ability of winning golden opinions from all".[147] In his pre-war career then, Vilonel distinguished himself as a prosperous and versatile person who at a comparatively early age had already distinguished himself as an attorney, town clerk and an award-winning marksman.

There is no evidence that Vilonel had any reservations about the Free State policy of providing military support for the Transvaal during the war. When the conflict began the Senekal burghers had so much confidence in him that he was chosen as commandant of the local commando. During the first phase of the war he took part in several of the battles in Natal and in February 1900 he was transferred to the western front. Because of General Piet Cronjé's surrender on 27 February 1900 at Paardeberg the Boers had to fall back and Vilonel was involved in this retreat. On 10 March 1900 at Abrahamskraal he was one of the Boer commanders who tried unsuccessfully but with great determination to halt the British advance to Bloemfontein. On this occasion Vilonel acquitted himself well under difficult circumstances.[148]

On Vilonel's military expertise Adjutant J.N. Brink, who had close contact with him, had the following to say: "He was respected by the burghers as a brave man. He showed outstanding ability as one of the commanders at the battle of Abrahamskraal where the men fought bravely under him. He was in every way capable and was a man of mature experience."[149] Brink's statement is corroborated by Oosthuizen who remarks on the "brave" action by Vilonel and his burghers at Abrahamskraal when they succeeded in resisting an attack under heavy fire from Brigadier-general R.G. Broadwood.[150] Oberholster also describes Vilonel as a "capable leader".[151]

However, when the British occupied Bloemfontein (13 March 1900), Vilonel began to lose heart for the republican cause. This can be detected in a letter he wrote in March 1901 in which he claimed that in mid-March he had made a suggestion at a war council meeting that the republics should consider stopping the war. His suggestion was unanimously rejected.[152]

Shortly before the battle of Sannaspos (31 March 1900) Vilonel was involved in a serious dispute with General Christiaan de Wet. At the time De Wet was making a determined effort to rid himself of the cumbersome laager of wagons that often accompanied the commandos and seriously impeded the mobility of the burghers. Vilonel disagreed with this measure and said that he did not want to "impose any discomfort" on his burghers. He blatantly disregarded a written order from De Wet that he should dispense with about 30 of the wagons that were with his commando. He also requested that a war council meeting be convened to revoke De Wet's decision on this. General de Wet, who was busy with the preparations for the battle of Sannaspos, refused point blank to waste any time on Vilonel's impractical suggestion. Vilonel then objected to placing his burghers in the firing positions which De Wet had assigned to them;

he claimed that he first wanted to reconnoitre the positions, despite the fact that this had already been done, before he sent his men out. Furthermore, Vilonel then asked De Wet to delay the proposed attack so that he could first spy out the situation at Sannaspos through his binoculars. De Wet's patience with Vilonel snapped. He gave him the choice of handing in his resignation as commandant or being relieved of his post by De Wet. Vilonel chose the former and promptly wrote his letter of resignation in front of the general. "What a weight it was off my neck," wrote De Wet in his memoirs, "when I was freed of such a perverse commandant."[153]

Vilonel continued to serve as an ordinary burgher in the Free State forces.[154] Although he had been demoted in rank, according to Adjutant Brink he still gave the Boer forces the benefit of his good advice prior to the battle of Biddulphsberg on 29 May 1900.[155] However, by now Vilonel was seriously entertaining the idea of withdrawing voluntarily from the war. When General A.J. de Villiers, the republican commander at the battle of Biddulphsberg, was seriously wounded, Vilonel took him to the hospital in Senekal where the British offered to nurse De Villiers, but shortly after being admitted to hospital the Boer general died.[156] General de Wet presumed that Vilonel had taken this opportunity of talking to the British about the possibility of surrender,[157] and this was indeed the case. On 6 June 1900 Roberts informed the British commanding officer at Senekal that if Vilonel surrendered voluntarily he should be permitted to remain in the town on parole.[158]

Despite Vilonel's demotion, he was still highly regarded in the Free State army and after his visit to Senekal he returned to the commandos for a while. With General de Villiers's death a new general had to be chosen and the officers who had to make the appointment decided after careful consideration that on account of his military capabilities Vilonel would be the right person. Quite possibly they were unaware that Vilonel had already been in touch with the British authorities. When he was offered the position Vilonel openly admitted to them that he was unworthy of the nomination because he had already decided to withdraw from the war. The officers let him have his way and during the second week of June 1900 Vilonel formally laid down his arms at the British garrison at Senekal.[159]

Michael Davitt gives the following as a reason why Vilonel made this decision: "A too ardent ambition to rise rapidly in military rank caused him [Vilonel] to become insubordinate and he was, in consequence relegated ... This ... was the anti-climax to his dreams of distinction, and he became discontented. From this frame of mind to actual treachery was a transition resulting from wounded vanity, and he deserted to the British."[160] It can be accepted that Vilonel was probably upset about being demoted to the rank of an ordinary burgher, but this was not necessarily the reason for his surrender. If Vilonel had really been as hurt about his demotion in the Free State army as Davitt suggests he was, he could after all have accepted the rank of general that was offered to him before his formal surrender; this would have put him into a prominent leadership role again. The fact that Vilonel openly turned this offer down seems to indicate that his lowly status as an ordinary burgher was not a serious consideration in his decision to lay down his arms.

According to Adjutant Brink, Vilonel withdrew from the struggle because he was convinced that " the war would not last much longer; that the Boer deputation to Europe would come to naught; [and] that Lord Roberts's proclamations, by which the opportunity was provided for the protection of private property if burghers were prepared to surrender, would contribute substantially to lower the already deteriorating and depressed morale of those burghers who were still fighting".[161] In March 1901 Vilonel himself stated that he had laid down his arms because he was of the opinion that "our independence was hopelessly lost, ... and that it was absolute folly to continue the struggle, as it would only lead to total destruction of private property and ultimate destitution ..."[162] It therefore seems plausible that this must have been an important reason why he surrendered.

However, his view on the state of the war was not his only reason for taking this step. At the beginning of June 1900 Vilonel learned that if he did not surrender in the foreseeable future the British were planning to destroy his office and its contents, including all his title deeds, documents and papers. Prevention of this possible damage – which according to him would also have placed many of the burghers in the district in a desperate position after the war – was an

CHAPTER 7: TREASON AND THE FINAL PEACE NEGOTIATIONS AT VEREENIGING

additional reason why Vilonel decided that he should rather withdraw from the struggle.¹⁶³

Shortly after his surrender Vilonel wrote to Field-cornet Hans van Rooyen of the Ladybrand commando in an effort to persuade him and his men to lay down their arms. Previously, while Vilonel was still on commando, Van Rooyen had shown some interest and had asked Vilonel questions about Roberts's proclamations. Vilonel's letter to Van Rooyen was intercepted by a Captain Pretorius who handed it over to the Boer general, General J. Crowther. Crowther regarded the matter in a serious light and decided to go all out to catch Vilonel red-handed. Field-cornet van Rooyen was asked to prove his innocence in the incident by signing a letter which gave the impression that he and his men were prepared to surrender but which stated that he wished to meet Vilonel and a British officer at an appointed time and place in order to discuss the matter further. The letter was delivered to Vilonel in Senekal by an African man. Without suspecting anything, Vilonel set off for the appointed place, which was not far outside the town. Captain Pretorius and a number of men were waiting for him and when he arrived they promptly arrested him. Astounded and indignant, Vilonel protested in vain at the manner in which he had been captured.¹⁶⁴

In mid-June 1900 Vilonel was accused of treason and tried before a special court martial at Reitz under the chairmanship of General Hertzog. He was found guilty and sentenced to five years imprisonment with hard labour. Hertzog regarded this as a relatively light sentence and said that Vilonel was lucky to come out of it with his life.¹⁶⁵

However, Vilonel regarded his sentence as unjust and lodged an appeal. The appeal court hearing, which Vilonel handled himself, took place from 10 to 14 July 1900 at Fouriesburg. Vilonel claimed that he had merely acted in accordance with his convictions and with what he saw as the best interest of the people. His somewhat meagre defence did not impress the appeal court and quite understandably the sentence of the court martial at Reitz was unanimously upheld.¹⁶⁶ When General Hertzog repeated the judgement he also determined Vilonel's place in the historiography on the war: "… as long as the history of the Free State is read, thus long the name of S.C. [read S.G.]

Vilonel will remain there as an eternal blot of shame."¹⁶⁷ Hertzog's judgement has merit within a certain context, but in the light of Vilonel's pre-war reputation and his early wartime career it is clear why an eyewitness at the hearing said: "One cannot but feel deep sympathy that there was such a tragic end to such a promising career. Today an honoured patriot, tomorrow a disgraced traitor, despised by all but a few of his countrymen."¹⁶⁸

Since by this time the Boers no longer had prisons where Vilonel could be effectively detained, during July 1900 they were obliged to move him from one place to another with the mobile commandos. In this way, towards the end of July he landed up with General Marthinus Prinsloo's force.¹⁶⁹

On 29 July 1900, with about 4300 men, Prinsloo surrendered unconditionally to the British in the Brandwater Basin. Many of the Boers had serious doubts whether Prinsloo really had no other option than to surrender.¹⁷⁰ Prinsloo's biographer comes to the following conclusion on the circumstances surrounding the incident: "Considered objectively, the position of the Boer commandos in the Brandwater Basin was indeed difficult, but conditions were by no means so bad that there was any justification for Prinsloo's attitude."¹⁷¹ It falls outside the parameters of this study to go into greater detail with regard to Prinsloo's surrender, but Vilonel's role in the incident does merit closer examination.

On 29 July Prinsloo used Vilonel as a go-between to conduct final negotiations on his behalf with Lieutenant-general Hunter.¹⁷² Vilonel had acted as an interpreter and according to Van Everdingen was also the "most prominent spokesperson" present on an earlier occasion when Prinsloo had held a personal interview with Hunter about his (Prinsloo's) possible surrender.¹⁷³ Prinsloo had apparently made use of Vilonel's services in the hope that, owing to his previous contact with the British, Vilonel might be able to organise favourable conditions for him, but in the event Vilonel was unable to do so.¹⁷⁴ There is no conclusive evidence that Vilonel directly influenced Prinsloo to surrender,¹⁷⁵ but it can be accepted that he would certainly not have tried to convince Prinsloo to resist the British aggressively. And his surrender would of course have been to Vilonel's advantage if the British were prepared to release him (Vilonel) from his imprisonment. The fact that Prinsloo involved Vilonel, a person who was regarded by the Boers as a traitor, in the negotiations, gave rise to niggling suspicions that Prinsloo's actions had perhaps been deliberate treason.[176]

After the surrender in the Brandwater Basin, Vilonel was not – in contrast with Prinsloo and the rest of his men – regarded as a British prisoner of war. The British freed him and Vilonel thought it wise to take himself off to Basutoland (Lesotho) for a while[177] – more than likely because he was still a convicted prisoner as far as the Boer court martial was concerned and he did not want to take the risk of falling into Boer hands again.

By March 1901 Vilonel was back in the Free State. It is interesting that at this stage he did not serve on any of the Free State peace committees. A possible explanation for this is that at the time when the committees were set up in December 1900 and January 1901 he was still in Basutoland. He must also have realised that his status as a convicted prisoner would most probably have been held against him if he had approached any of the Boers about making peace. In March 1901 he said that personally he was against the idea of writing an open letter "because many persons are so ready to construe it in a different manner to what it was intended".[178] As far as can be ascertained, for the next nine months Vilonel took no active part in the war at all.

As mentioned above, in January 1902 Vilonel sent a letter to President Steyn in which he said that if those who were still fighting were not prepared to stop the war he would organise a corps to fight against them. He then began to do some recruitment work for the ORC Volunteers and in March 1902 he was in command of the southern section of this corps that was based at Winburg.[179]

Vilonel himself said that he regarded it as his duty to fight on the British side to try to terminate the war. He claimed that a radical step such as this was necessary in order to bring the Boers to their senses and make them see that to continue the war was futile. According to him the Boers had absolutely no chance at all of being the victors at the end of the war. "I have carefully followed the general course of the war," he wrote on 11 January to President Steyn, "and I have up to the present moment, not seen anything whatsoever to justify the continuance of the war ..."¹⁸⁰ This particular outlook probably contributed to Vilonel's decision to support the British cause.

However, it would also appear that after his surrender in July 1900, Vilonel became increasingly bitter towards his former countrymen. He felt aggrieved about the Boer trap he had walked into when he had wanted to negotiate with Field-cornet van Rooyen about surrendering arms; as far as he was concerned the tactics that had been used on that occasion amounted to "treason".[181] The fact that he lodged an appeal in a higher court against the prison sentence that he had received is proof that he was also dissatisfied with the sentence that had been passed. Vilonel was clearly a man who had a very high self-esteem[182] and it was more than likely a humiliating experience for him to be handled as a convicted prisoner by his countrymen. As time went by he began to project his personal dissatisfaction onto the republican leaders and their cause. By March 1901 he was antagonistic towards anybody who was taking up the cudgel for republican independence. He criticised the pro-Boers in the Cape Colony in bitter terms about the moral support they gave to the republican efforts to maintain their independence. As far as he was concerned it was "the greatest crime that could be perpetrated under the present circumstances". He also made the unfounded allegation that the Boer determination to continue fighting was absolute "robbery".[183]

After January 1902, once he had decided to fight on the British side, he went even further and rejected, as a pure figment of the imagination, the firmly held and genuine religious beliefs which the Boers displayed during the war. "The large majority of the people of the Orange Free State and the South African Republic," he wrote to Steyn, "never had any true and sincere belief or trust in the protection and support of the Almighty and Just God, and have now even less; but it was always, and is still now, even an imaginary impression, and exists only from a wish rather than any immediate or actual belief..."[184] For a man who was so alienated and embittered towards his people's war effort that he could stoop to a public criticism of their Christian beliefs it would in all likelihood not have been too difficult to renounce those same people by taking up arms on the British side. In the light of this, after the war Adjutant Brink was probably not far from the truth when he identified Vilonel's "revenge" as the reason for the radical action that he took.[185]

In the Transvaal, General Andries P.J. Cronjé, the brother of General Piet Cronjé, was the best-known leader of the National Scouts. Andries Petrus Johannes Cronjé was born on 18 June 1849 at Colesberg. When he was barely three years old his parents, Andries Petrus Cronjé and Johanna Christina née Geldenhuys left the Cape Colony and settled in the Potchefstroom district. Andries Cronjé spent his youth on the farm Goedgevonden and at 18 he started up on his own farm, Palmietfontein, which was also in the Potchefstroom area. Shortly afterwards he married Catharina Wilhelmina Basson and the couple had one daughter. Cronjé's first wife died in 1870 and he later married Johanna Elizabeth Dorothea Steyn who bore him four sons and four daughters. When Johanna died in 1904 Cronjé married, for a third time, Isabella Johanna Lombard (née Botha), but this last marriage was childless.[186]

In 1885 Cronjé was chosen as field-cornet of the Klerksdorp commando. In this capacity he took part in the following campaigns against African leaders: Massouw (1885–1886), Modjadji (1890–1891), Malaboch (1894), Magoeba (1895), Magato (1898) and Mphefu (1898). In 1896 he also helped to nip the Jameson Raid in the bud.[187] In addition to his military activities Cronjé took a lively interest in church affairs and for the ten years before the outbreak of the Anglo-Boer War he served an unbroken term as an elder on the local church council.[188]

According to H. Bramley, the assistant sheriff at Klerksdorp, Cronjé was an extremely popular and respected figure in the district. Bramley kept a diary of local events before and during the Anglo-Boer War and on 31 September 1899 he made the following comment on Cronjé: "Andries Cronjé is in charge of our commando and a fairer specimen of humanity would be hard to get. He is rather below the medium height and of slender build and looks sickly, but is nevertheless active and as brave as you make them. He is a little over 50 I should say, and speaks very slowly and in a low tone, and is one of the most popular men in the district, being loved and respected by all for his generosity, good tact and friendliness to all ... Should he fall the sorrow will be greatly felt."[189]

No evidence could be found to support the idea that Cronjé was reluctant to join the war. At the beginning of October 1899, probably on the basis of his earlier military experience against the African communities, he was promoted from field-cornet to commandant.[190] It is not clear exactly when he was promoted to general, but it was certainly before his surrender in June 1900.[191]

At the outbreak of the Anglo-Boer War on 11 October 1899 Cronjé headed the Potchefstroom commando. In November he was stationed on the south-western border of the Free State and on 28 November, together with General De la Rey, he was involved in a confrontation against Lord Methuen at Modder River; a few weeks later, on 11 December 1899, he also fought at Magersfontein.

In February 1900 Cronjé took part in the military activities in the vicinity of Paardeberg and on 11 February, on the orders of his brother General Piet Cronjé, Andries Cronjé and General Christiaan de Wet tried to halt the British march to Kimberley under Major-general J.D.P. French. Despite their efforts, French succeeded in breaking through and he relieved Kimberley on 15 February. Meanwhile the circumstances of General Piet Cronjé and his encircled main army at Paardeberg continued to deteriorate. Andries Cronjé and Generals Philip Botha and C. de Wet tried in vain on 23 February 1900 to free Piet Cronjé from the outside, and eventually, on 27 February 1900, he was forced to surrender with about 4000 men. The battle of Paardeberg was a tragic episode for Andries Cronjé in more ways than one. Over and above his brother's defeat, Cronjé lost one of his sons in the battle; a bomb landed directly on the young A.P. Cronjé, and he died immediately, horribly disfigured.

Following this, Andries Cronjé took part in the battle of Abrahamskraal (10 March 1900) and after Roberts's occupation of Bloemfontein on 13 March he left for the Transvaal western front where, with about 1200 men, he was given the task of safeguarding the drifts over the Vaal River at Christiana. Cronjé kept on the move and in April he even went as far afield as Boshof, where he harried Methuen's force.

The republican forces were unable to prevent the British advance towards the Transvaal. On 16 May 1900 Lieutenant-general A. Hunter took Christiana without any opposition and shortly afterwards

Cronjé left for Klerksdorp. By this stage Cronjé was seriously ill and on 14 June 1900 he and 150 of his men voluntarily surrendered their arms to a section of the Kimberley Mounted Corps under the orders of Captain H. Lambert at Klerksdorp.[192]

Even in the early stages of the war Andries Cronjé had experienced problems with his health. According to Piet Cronjé, he had overworked himself and in January 1900 had had to undergo medical treatment for a while. The smoke and gas from the British lyddite bombs apparently also affected him adversely.[193] These bombs gave off a gas that under some circumstances could be poisonous.[194] Cronjé's poor state of health at the time of his surrender undoubtedly played an important role in his decision to lay down his arms. Field-cornet (later Commandant) J.A. van Zyl of Griqualand West, who did not himself surrender but was with Cronjé when he laid down his arms, said that Cronjé was "dead-sick and utterly exhausted … He just could not take any more … Nevertheless he exhorted his commanders to do their duty to the best of their ability for as long as possible. But alas, when Andries Cronjé was no longer there to take the lead, all the Boers in his commandos just went home … "[195] Cronjé was so ill at the time of his surrender that President Steyn was under the incorrect impression that he had actually died that same day.[196]

After his surrender Cronjé recuperated in Klerksdorp. On 25 July 1900 when the Boers took the town, which had in the meantime been occupied by the British, they presumably left Cronjé in peace on account of his health. In November 1900 the Boers had to evacuate Klerksdorp again. By this time Cronjé's state of health had improved considerably and he began to cooperate more closely with the British. According to J.H. Voss, the magistrate who had been appointed by the British at Klerksdorp, Cronjé had come to the realisation that the Boers were fighting against all odds with little hope of any favourable outcome of the war. Cronjé also promised Voss that he would "use what influence he had at his command" to persuade his countrymen that it was futile to continue the war.[197]

By the end of December 1900 Cronjé was serving on the central peace committee in Pretoria, and in March 1901, on behalf of that committee, he addressed the prisoners of war at the Simon's Town camp.[198] On his return to the Transvaal he lived in the Klerksdorp concentration camp, where he rendered "very valuable unpaid assistance in the management of the garden". The superintendent of this camp was full of praise for Cronjé's attitude towards the British and even went so far as to describe him as "the best Dutchman in South Africa".[199]

When a section of the National Scouts was set up in the western Transvaal, a recruitment meeting was held on 6 January 1902 at Potchefstroom and on this occasion Cronjé gave the following reasons why, in his opinion, such a section was necessary: "We know perfectly well that we have no chance against the British forces, so in consideration of the prisoners of war, the families who are in Burgher Camps, for our own sakes we must do our best to stop the war without bloodshed if possible, but stop it, and that right early ..." According to the resident magistrate at Potchefstroom Cronjé then continued: "He [Cronjé] did not wish them [the surrendered burghers] to join with any thoughts of vengeance in their hearts towards those still in the field. The great object was that each one should do his utmost and use every means in his power to secure peace and prosperity for the country and the people, and stop the ruin and devastation which must result from continued resistance to law and order."[200] The sources do not provide any other clues as to why Cronjé decided to fight on the British side. However, M. McFie, the post-war British magistrate at Potchefstroom, regarded Cronjé as an honourable man with a "high personal character".[201] Of course it can perhaps be argued that as a British magistrate McFie was not entirely unbiased, but if his evidence is accepted it gives greater credibility to the sincerity of Cronjé's own statement that he had fought on the British side to terminate the war for the well-being of his people.

Commandant J.G. Celliers of the Soutpansberg district is the last of the important leaders of the National Scouts who will be discussed in this section. Compared to the other leaders, Jan Gabriël Celliers is a relatively unknown figure. According to C.J. Scheepers Strydom, Celliers (who should not be confused with General J. Celliers of the Free State or General J.G. Celliers of Lichtenburg) was born on 12 July 1862 at Fraserburg in the Cape Colony.[202] It is not known when he moved to the Transvaal or what his profession was. At the outbreak of the Anglo-Boer War Celliers was appointed as commandant and was stationed on the Transvaal northern border to prevent a possible British attack from Rhodesia.[203] He was then transferred to the Cape front where he participated in military operations in the Colesberg vicinity together with Generals de la Rey and Piet de Wet. In skirmishes with the British he was lightly wounded several times.[204] On 20 February 1900 he was ordered to move with his men to Bloemfontein and on 10 March he took part in the battle of Abrahamskraal.[205] Thereafter Celliers returned to the Transvaal and in the second half of 1900 he joined the commandos under General Beyers. In April 1901 he gave himself up voluntarily to the British at Potgietersrus,[206] and from October 1901 onwards he undertook recruitment work for the National Scouts.[207]

By all accounts Celliers was a brave but reckless fighter. Preller describes him as a man without "a single fearful hair on his head" and "as brave as a lion".[208] After the war J. Krige, who was under Celliers's command on the Cape front, provided similar evidence on his former leader: "General Celliers did not know the meaning of the word calmness and was ever restless and impetuous ... He was always burning to be in the saddle and charging (our more expressive word was 'storming') the enemy."[209] J. van Dal, who was for a time also with Celliers on commando, was of the opinion that "as a fighting man he has few equals", but he added that on occasion Celliers also acted irresponsibly.[210] During the battle of Abrahamskraal, it was alleged that simply to impress his men Celliers left his position and, under heavy enemy fire, lit up his pipe and calmly surveyed the surrounding countryside.[211]

His unbridled recklessness led to a confrontation between him and General Beyers in April 1901. When Celliers was on the Cape front he had been promoted to acting general, but Beyers refused to ratify his appointment to this rank. "Uncle Jan, you are much too reckless and you will just let my burghers shoot everyone," said Beyers. However, Celliers was extremely annoyed with Beyers and felt very aggrieved; he left the commando and apparently said that he felt like "shooting Beyers".[212]

In a Dutch newspaper Celliers was described as "someone with unbounded courage, but completely without any sense of morals".[213] An episode from Celliers's pre-war career corroborates this statement to a large extent. On 19 October 1891 he had to appear before the circuit court at Pietersburg on a charge of culpable homicide. Celliers had been involved in an exchange of words with Mathijs Martinus Bezuidenhout, the owner of the farm Doornfontein. He had lost his temper and stabbed Bezuidenhout several times with a knife in the chest and back and shortly after the incident Bezuidenhout had died. Celliers maintained that he was innocent, but the court found him guilty and sentenced him to two years imprisonment with hard labour.[214]

In the light of Celliers's personal irresponsibility and his criminal background it is not surprising that without any pangs of conscience, particularly after his clash with Beyers, he was able to take the unethical step of taking up arms against his own countrymen. However, Celliers is alleged to have said to H.S. Lombard, a surrendered burgher from Pretoria "that he is averse to the continuation of the war by the Boer leaders and considers it his duty to take up arms for the British in order to assist in bringing the war to as speedy a termination as possible".[215] Whether Celliers, a convicted criminal, really regarded it as his duty to help the British is highly debatable. According to R. Orsmond, the post-war magistrate at Pietersburg, Celliers was a "regular scoundrel" who was only prepared to support the British "as long as there is a prospect of getting anything [out of the British]".[216]

Because of his dubious background the British could not trust Celliers either. They received a report to the effect that he was playing a double role and might well be secretly helping the Boers. According to the provost marshal in Pretoria, who investigated the case, there was no truth in this allegation, so it can be accepted that it was exaggerated.[217]

From the discussion in this section it appears that, with the exception of Celliers, the leaders of the ORC Volunteers and the National Scouts were educated and respected people in pre-war republican society. This is in marked contrast to most of the rank and file members of these corps. If another comparison is drawn, it would seem that the leaders, far more so than the majority of the ordinary members, were convinced that it was in the interest of the republican people to try to help end the war by taking drastic steps, and even by taking up arms on the British side. However, as has been shown, this was not always their only consideration. It is also noteworthy that the leaders had to exercise their command over the very lowest class of Boer and that these leaders were apparently unable to attract very many others of their own social standing to the ranks of the collaborators. Initially it had been Piet de Wet's intention to recruit "well-to-do cattle farmers",[218] but here the leaders were clearly unsuccessful and they were obliged to accept any type of recruit they could find.

3 The Peace of Vereeniging

When peace was signed on 31 May 1902 the war came to an end for the surrendered burghers, National Scouts and other burghers in British military service. As far as the Boers were concerned, the prisoners of war and by implication also the surrendered burghers were *hors de combat*, outside the arena, or as President Steyn put it, "dead" as far as taking any civil role was concerned.[219] As a result they had no say at all in the decisions taken at Vereeniging. It could perhaps be argued that the National Scouts were already British citizens and that the British representatives were acting on their behalf.[220] Be that as it may, the fact that not one of the National Scouts was present at Vereeniging did not bode well for their future.

Because the British negotiated only with the representatives of the bitterenders, the burghers who had continued to fight until the end, the implication was that the republican delegates were recognised not only as the spokesmen of the Boer forces, but also as the leaders of the entire Boer nation. As the authors of the *Times History* so rightly remark, "The fighting men ... [came] in clothed with that moral and political superiority with which we had hoped to invest those who had thrown in their lot with the conquerors." In truth, the British had no other practical alternative. Significantly, the writers of the work mentioned above ask: "Could we ever rob the Boer leaders of their prestige? ... Could we ever set the fighting Boer below the National Scout? Assuredly not." And they then go on to point out how the situation influenced the position of the National Scouts: "Their position was strangely paradoxical. Kitchener, who was primarily responsible for the raising of the Scouts ... did not hold with any approach consistent with the policy which could invest them [the National Scouts] at a future date with influence and esteem. Bent on ending the war by every legitimate means within his reach he snatched in perfectly good faith at the military expediency offered him, with too little concern for the military consequences ... Coming into existence amid all these ambiguities, the Scouts, therefore, held a position which ... was precarious."[221] Writing about this issue in 1939, L.S. Amery was perfectly correct in saying: "As it was they [the National Scouts] were out of the picture and in a false position the moment the fighting leaders retained their leadership for the future by an agreed peace."[222] By negotiating with the Boer leaders about peace, the British by implication also recognised that despite the annexation proclamations the republican governments were still legally in existence. In this way the British thus indirectly, and quite possibly unconsciously, gave notice that the National Scouts who had fought with the enemy against their own lawful authorities were nothing less than traitors. The utterly subordinate position of the National Scouts at Vereeniging also seriously limited their possible potential as a post-war political pressure group.[223]

In April 1902, J.G. Fraser had predicted in a discussion with Milner that the burghers who were in British military service would be placed in a very disadvantageous position by a negotiated peace which involved only the bitterenders. Fraser pointed out that people such as Piet de Wet and S.G. Vilonel "are men of importance" and that they should have had some input in the peace negotiations. Milner could offer Fraser little in the way of assurances. He gave Fraser to understand that "it is the vice of all negotiations with the men who have stuck it out that it to some extent gives away the men who have already come in". According to Milner, Fraser was however "most insistent, that we should bear this in mind and minimise it as much as possible".[224]

During the peace negotiations, however, the British made no attempt to discuss the position of the National Scouts or to gain any specific benefits for them. Presumably they realised that any talk of this kind would merely antagonise the bitterenders and might even possibly prejudice the negotiations.

The British silence in this regard did not only impact negatively on the position of the National Scouts; it also caused considerable confusion after the war. This was particularly so in the case of article 10 of the peace treaty which deals with post-war repatriation and compensation. The word "*volk*", meaning "the people" in the relevant article[225] was later to prove too vaguely defined and led to queries about whether the National Scouts and other defectors were also part of "the *volk*" who were entitled to compensation.[226] Nor did the republican leaders even try to gain clarity on this specific issue.

The invidious position in which the disloyal burghers found themselves after the war was not entirely unexpected. Revd J.A. Steytler of Cape Town, with prophetic insight, had warned the members of the burgher peace committee in March 1901 not to put too much trust in the British: "If you suppose that, in the event of the resistance of the Republics being finally overcome, you will retain their [British] goodwill ... I make bold to prophesy that you will soon be undeceived. Even they have sufficient knowledge of human nature not to trust implicitly men who are able to forswear their allegiance as easily as they change their coats. So long as you can serve their interests they will flatter you and make all possible use of you, but so soon as they have attained their purposes they will fling you aside with no more compunction than you cast away a worn-out shoe."[227]

Despite the fact that the National Scouts were marginalised during the peace negotiations, had the war been resumed, Kitchener would not have hesitated for a moment to make as much use as possible of their services. On 11 May 1902 he had seriously considered the possibility of establishing protected areas in large parts of the eastern Transvaal with the help of the National Scouts if the Boers did not accept the peace proposals.[228] He also gave orders to Colonel C.W. Park on 21 May 1902 to initiate "vigorous operations ... with a view of capturing the [Boer] government by means of National Scouts" should the peace negotiations fail.[229]

With the conclusion of peace the military service of the National Scouts in the Imperial army came to an end. After the war they still maintained their ties with the British military officers for a short while, but in time they fell increasingly under the dispensation of the British civil authority. As far as the civil authorities were concerned the Scouts were appreciably less useful than they had been for the military, who had made good use of their services during the war. Although the civil authorities could not simply distance themselves completely from the National Scouts after peace was declared, the Scouts soon realised that the civil authorities were far less concerned about them than the military authorities had been in the heat of the struggle. In the chapters which follow the post-war role and position of the dissident burghers will be examined.

Notes

1. *The Cape Times*, 4 December 1901 (news report).
2. Translated from the Afrikaans. Preller, "Die National Scouts" in *Die Burger*, 1 July 1926.
3. D. Denoon, *A Grand Illusion: The failure of imperial policy in the Transvaal Colony during the period of reconstruction, 1900–1905*, pp. 17–8. See also D. Denoon, "Participation in the Boer War: People's War, People's Non-War or Non-People's War?" in B.A. Ogot, *War and Society in Africa*, pp. 117–18; D. Denoon, *Southern Africa since 1800*, p. 131.
4. Denoon based this statement in part on the erroneous perception that Piet de Wet was the "landless brother" of Christiaan de Wet. Denoon, "Participation in the Boer War", p. 117. In reality Piet de Wet was a landowner. A.P.J. van Rensburg, "Pieter Daniël de Wet" in *DSAB*, II. Denoon's only other source is CO 291/43, "Intermediate report on resettlement of National Scouts", 15 September 1902. According to Denoon in this document the British officers who were in charge of the National Scouts expressed the view that "the recruits comprised a few middle-aged and propertied men, while the bulk comprised landless *bijwoners* attracted by the prospect of loot, land, stock and firearms". Denoon, *Grand Illusion*, p. 17. In this particular document in the Transvaal Archives, housed in the National Archives, Pretoria, no evidence could be found that the British officers in command of the National Scouts made this statement. Denoon's hypothesis does have merit, but there is no knowing where he obtained his information. It may perhaps be, although this seems unlikely, that the photostat copies of the particular document (FK 977, pp. 311–20) in the Transvaal Archives differ from the original that Denoon consulted in die Public Record Office, London.
5. Spaight, p. 146 note 1.
6. *Times History*, VI, p. 54.
7. WO/unsorted (A462), "Certificates of Engagement, National Scouts, no. 5 Wing". The age group 20 to 60 years was chosen because on account of their age they were more likely to have had the opportunity to acquire land than the younger group under the age of 20.
8. *Transvaal Administration Reports for 1902: Judicial*, magistrate's report, District Ermelo–Carolina, p. 15.
9. Translated from the Dutch. J. Visscher, *De Ondergang van een Wereld: Historisch-economische Studie over de Oorsaken van den Anglo-Boer Oorlog (1899–1902)*, pp. 39–40. This work was published in 1903.

10 Lewsen, *Selections 1899–1905*, p. 352, Merriman – J. Bryce, 21 July 1902.
11 Compare Hancock en Van der Poel, *Selections*, I, pp. 614–15, "Memoirs".
12 CSO 139/3001/02, "Memorandum to Central Repatriation Board", Bloemfontein, 7 August 1902.
13 A.N. Pelzer, "Die 'arm blanke' in die Suid-Afrikaanse Republiek tussen die jare 1882–1899 in *Historiese Studies*, III and IV, 1941 and 1942, pp. 1–29; 55–67; P. Naudé, "Die Verskynsel van Gebrek aan Grondbesit by die Burger van die Zuid-Afrikaansche Republiek" in *Historia*, 1(1), 1956, pp. 49–52; J.P. Kotzé, "Die Runderpes in Transvaal en die onmiddellike gevolge daarvan, 1896–1899" (unpublished MA dissertation, RAU, 1974), pp. 203–39.
14 Van Rensburg, "Ekonomiese Herstel", p. 141. See also G.J. Lamprecht, "Die Ekonomiese ontwikkeling van die Vrystaat van 1870–1899" (Unpublished D.Phil. thesis, US), 1954, pp. 48–50.
15 *Report of the Transvaal Indigency Commission, 1906–1908*, pp. 72–4; R.W. Wilcocks, "Die Arm blanke" in *Carnegie Kommissie – Die Arm Blanke Vraagstuk in Suid-Afrika*, II, p. 64; P.J. de Vos, "Die Bywoner: 'n Sosiologiese Studie oor die Bywonerskap in sekere Hoë- en Middelvelddistrikte van Transvaal en Vrystaat" (Unpublished MA dissertation, UP), 1937, pp. 102–5.
16 Pelzer, *Historiese Studies*, II, 1942, pp. 182–5; Visscher, pp. 39–40.
17 Translated from the Dutch. Visscher, p. 39.
18 Translated from the Afrikaans. Weeber, p. 159.
19 Translated from the Afrikaans. Preller, "Die National Scouts" in *Die Burger*, 1 July 1926.
20 *De Volksstem*, 16 May 1883 as quoted by J.L. Hattingh, "Die Trekke uit die Suid-Afrikaanse Republiek en die Oranje-Vrystaat 1875–1895" (Unpublished D.Phil. thesis, UP), 1975, p. 475.
21 Translated from the Dutch. *De Volksstem*, 12 February 1884 (letter from a burgher at Utrecht) as quoted by Hattingh, "Trekke", p. 548.
22 Hattingh, "Trekke", p. 568.
23 Hattingh, "Trekke", p. 574.
24 Steyn Collection, 156/1/–156/1/1a, p. 79. G. Ferreira and 14 others – Steyn, 26 September 1899.
25 Milner Papers, 19, (FK 1135, p. 254), Wilson – Milner, 3 July 1900.
26 Translated from the Dutch. *Official report ... Brandfort, 1 and 2 December 1904*, p. 84. Address by General de Wet.
27 Translated from the Afrikaans. Weeber, p. 159.
28 The *bywoners* were naturally not found exclusively in the ranks of the National Scouts. It can be accepted that there were also *bywoners* among the loyal burghers. Kitchener and H.E. McCallum, the governor of Natal, gave evidence that this was in fact the case. Spies, "Civilians", p. 372; *Africa (South)*, 650, p. 160, McCallum – Kitchener, 17 July 1901.
29 WO/unsorted (A462), "Certificates of Engagement, National Scouts, no. 5 Wing".
30 Translated from the Dutch. *De Volksstem*, 28 November 1903 (letter from a National Scout under the pseudonym of Da Gama).
31 *Klerksdorp Mining Record*, 4 September 1903 (leading article).
32 See Chapter 4, section 2 above.

33 See Chapter 4, section 2 above and Chapter 6, section 1 above respectively for the remuneration in the concentration camps and the payment received by the National Scouts.
34 Translated from the Dutch. Leyds Archive, 866, p. 10, typed copies of press reports. This report appeared on 21 December 1901 in the *Algemeene Handelsblad*.
35 MGP 142/17735/01, G.S. Cruse – Maxwell, 30 December 1901.
36 M. Boveri, *Treason in the Twentieth Century*, pp. 46–7.
37 *Klerksdorp Mining Record*, 6 February 1903 (leading article).
38 Translated from the Dutch. *De Vriend*, 23 December 1904 (letter from N. J. Lotz).
39 See Hattingh, "Irenekonsentrasiekamp", p. 127.
40 Roberts Papers 33/60 ("National Army Museum"), Kitchener – Roberts, 22 November 1901 as quoted by Spies, "Civilians", p. 437; CO 417/360/7125 (FK 659, p. 555), Henderson – Altham, 24 January 1902.
41 WO/unsorted (A462), "Certificates of Engagement, National Scouts, no. 5 Wing".
42 See Chapter 2, section 1 above for the manner in which the Boers treated the surrendered burghers.
43 N.G. Church council minutes, Frankfort, 8 January 1905, evidence of G.H. Muller.
44 Translated from the Dutch. *Stemmen des Tijds*, March 1906 (open letter signed by C.S. Grobler and 10 other National Scouts).
45 Translated from the Dutch. *De Volksstem*, 28 November 1903 (letter from a National Scout under the pseudonym Da Gama).
46 CO 417/360/9713 (FK 660, p. 719), Kitchener – Brodrick, 9 January 1902 (copy).
47 MGP 154/3973/02, Leggett – Maxwell, 28 February 1902.
48 Compare PMO 21/1530, "Enquiry re Burghers wishing to join Morley's Scouts", 13 June 1901; PMO 29/1990, J.C. de Klerk – Captain A. Reid, 29 July 1901; PMO 37/2535, S.J. de Lange – Poore, 13 September 1901; PMO 54/3718, S.J. Kamfer – Captain T. Allison, 17 April 1902; PMO 55/3832, Major A. Hoskins – Leggett, 5 May 1902; PMO 55/3821, Captain T. Allison – Leggett, 5 May 1902; PMO 56/3884, Lieutenant H. Shipley – Leggett, 15 May 1902; PMO 56/3876, Lieutenant A. Gibson – Leggett, 22 May 1902.
49 There were of course also incidents where family members fought against one another. (La Grange Lombard, pp. 104–5). The classic case here is between Piet and Christiaan de Wet.
50 Chapter 6, section 1 above.
51 Brits, *Diary*, pp. 54–5, 14 June 1901.
52 *The Cape Times*, 4 December 1901 (news report).
53 Translated from the Dutch. *De Getuige*, June 1903 (letter from M.A. Botha).
54 *The Times*, 4 June 1902 (translated statement by P.L. Swart, 2 May 1902).
55 Translated from the Dutch. *Stemmen des Tijds*, March 1906 (open letter signed by C.S. Grobler and 10 other National Scouts). Although the circumstances are by no means comparable, it is nevertheless interesting to note that members of the resistance movement against the Hitler regime in Germany and during the Second World War (1939–1945) used more or less the same arguments to explain their actions. Their point of departure was that the Nazi government "represented naked force with no constitutional basis. Therefore, since the very state was criminal, there can be no question of treason to it" (Boveri, p. 307).

56 Chapter 1, section 2 above and Chapter 5, section 1 above.
57 Translated from the Afrikaans. Magistrate Louis Trichardt, Civil Case, 181/1930, J.J. Steyn vs G. Lyon, evidence of J.H. Joubert, p. 54, September 1930.
58 Milner Papers, 105, (FK 1194, p. 327), Milner – Selborne, 27 September 1905.
59 *Pretoria News*, 20 January 1903 (letter from "An Australian Officer").
60 WO 108/16/879 (A407), Leggett – Lieutenant-general Ian Hamilton, 30 March 1902.
61 This version of Piet de Wet's pre-war career is based on the following sources: Estate 21437, P.D. de Wet, 1929, Master of the Supreme Court, Bloemfontein; *The Friend*, 4 March 1929 (obituary); *Die Volksblad*, 1 and 2 March 1929 (obituaries); Van Rensburg, "Pieter Daniël de Wet" in *DSAB*, II; Oberholster, "Dagboek van Oskar Hintrager", p. 40 note 129; Pienaar, "De Wet", pp. 1–5; *OFS Volksraad minutes*, 1894, p. 4, result of election, 24 November 1893.
62 Compare *OFS Volksraad minutes*, 1894, pp. 36, 99, 101, 119–20, 141, 175 and 187 for his part in debates on 9, 11, 15, 17, 18, 22 and 23 May on the question of African labour, locusts, the construction of bridges and the emigrations which left the Free State at that time. See also *OFS Volksraad minutes*, 1895, pp. 45, 73, 91, 159 and 199 for his contributions in the *Volksraad* on 3, 5, 6, 16 and 19 April on the postal service, the railways, the police force, district councils and customs.
63 Translated from the Dutch. *OFS Volksraad minutes, Extraordinary Session*, pp. 48, 58, 10 and 11 January 1896.
64 *Die Volksblad*, 1 March 1929 (obituary); Van Rensburg, "Pieter Daniël de Wet" in *DSAB*, II.
65 Van Rensburg, "Pieter Daniël de Wet" in *DSAB*, II.
66 Translated from the Afrikaans. Oberholster, "Dagboek van Oskar Hintrager", p. 43, 21 June 1900. The word *"temperamentlose"* (translated here as "emotionless") in Hintrager's diary is a direct translation from the original German manuscript by Oberholster. In the published German version of Hintrager's diary *(Steijn, de Wet und die Oranje-Freistaater, Tagebuchblätter aus dem südafrikanische Kriege)* on p. 12 Hintrager uses the word "temperamentloze" to describe Piet de Wet. It is not quite clear what he means by this word. Presumably it means that Piet de Wet did not have a fiery temperament. Compare PC Schoonees and others, *Verklarende Handwoordeboek van die Afrikaanse Taal*, p. 880 for the word "temperament".
67 Van Rensburg, "Pieter Daniël de Wet" in *DSAB*, II; Kestell, *Boeren-Commando's*, p. 163; A119, Renier Collection, 77, evidence of G.J. Joubert on Piet de Wet, 1939.
68 PMO 7/497, Barend de Wet – P.D. de Wet, 8 January 1901. This letter was sent to Piet de Wet, c/o the military governor, Pretoria.
69 Translated from the Dutch. Steyn Collection, 156/1/1–156/1/1a, pp. 57–9.
70 *The Bloemfontein Post*, 6 February, 1901 (letter from P. de Wet – C. de Wet in the Dutch columns, dated 11 January 1901).
71 *Die Volksblad*, 1 March 1929 (obituary); Van Rensburg, "Pieter Daniël de Wet" in *DSAB*, II; *Times History*, II, pp. 245, 385; A371, S.P. Engelbrecht Collection, 18, p. 121, P.D. de Wet – Steyn, 27 November 1899.
72 *Die Volksblad*, 1 March 1929 (obituary); Van Rensburg, "Pieter Daniël de Wet" in *DSAB*, II; *Times History*, III, pp. 126, 128, 134–5, 461.
73 Leyds Archive, 760, p. 154, P. de Wet – De la Rey, 24 January 1900; Leyds Archive, 762, p. 64, De la Rey – P. de Wet, 26 January 1900.

74 Leyds Archive, 716 (b), telegram 19 of 13 February 1900, Kruger – Steyn; Leyds Archive, 717 (a), telegram 27 of 16 February 1900, Steyn – Kruger; *Die Volksblad*, 1 March 1929 (obituary); Van Rensburg, "Pieter Daniël de Wet" in *DSAB* II; *Times History*, III, pp. 470, 574; IV, pp. 30–9, 46–47, 67, 129, 246.

75 Roberts Papers, WO 105/16 (Vol 5/90/42), Lieutenant-general Ian Hamilton – Roberts, 27 May 1900; *Official History*, II, pp. 209–11; III, pp. 64, 93, 126.

76 De Wet, *Boer en Brit*, p. 72.

77 For an overview of Christiaan de Wet's military tactics see Pienaar, "De Wet", pp. 281–3, 290 and for his brother's reaction to this see *The Bloemfontein Post*, 6 February 1901 (letter dated 11 January 1901 from P. de Wet – C. de Wet in the Dutch columns).

78 For De Wet's victory at Lindley see *Times History*, IV, pp. 252–9; *Official History*, III, p. 115–20; De Wet, *Boer en Brit*, p. 83; B.N. Reckitt, *The Lindley Affair*, pp. 6, 31–49; Delport, pp. 134–6; Van Rensburg, "Pieter Daniël de Wet" in *DSAB*, II; Roberts Papers, WO 105/40 (A395), "Court of Enquiry (25 September 1900) re Surrender of Col. Spragge at Lindley".

79 Van Rensburg, "Pieter Daniël de Wet" in *DSAB*, II; Oberholster, "Dagboek van Oskar Hintrager", p. 40 note 129; Van Schoor, *De Wet en sy Verkenners*, p. 20.

80 Davitt, p. 488.

81 De Wet, "The Fighter, The Scout, The Spy", p. LV.

82 *Times History*, II, p. 245.

83 Roberts Papers, WO 105/40 (A399), undated report by Roberts on his march to Pretoria. From the content of the report it appears, however, that Roberts must have written the remark about Piet de Wet in May 1900.

84 Roberts Papers, WO 105/16 (vol 32/70/149), Hamilton – Roberts, 18 May 1900.

85 Roberts Papers, WO 105/16 (vol 32/70/148 and 149), Hamilton – Roberts, 18 May 1900; *Telegrams and Letters ... Roberts*, ii, telegrams C1675 and C1714, pp. 47 and 52, Roberts – Hamilton, 18 and 19 May 1900; *The Times*, 21 May 1900 (news report). See Chapter 1, section 3 above for the terms of the particular proclamation.

86 Roberts Papers, WO 105/108 (vol 6/99/100), Methuen – Roberts, 4 June 1900; *Telegrams and Letters ... Roberts*, ii, p. 80, telegram C1901, Roberts – Methuen, 4 June 1900; *Official History*, III, p. 227.

87 Van der Merwe, II, pp. 16–7.

88 Delport, p. 138; Pienaar, "De Wet", pp. 120–1; Pretorius, pp. 90–1; Oberholster, "Dagboek van Oskar Hintrager", p. 40, 20 June 1900.

89 Oberholster, "Dagboek van Oskar Hintrager", p. 44.

90 Compare Pretorius, pp. 77–8, 90–1; Lombard, p. 63.

91 Translated from the Dutch. De Wet, *Boer en Brit*, p. 115. See also Van Rensburg, "Pieter Daniël de Wet" in *DSAB*, II; Pienaar, "De Wet", p. 142; Pretorius, p. 89. With the exception of the latter, the other sources mentioned give the farm's name as "Rivierplaas", but the documentation provided by Pretorius, pp. 88–9 shows that it was in fact Blesbokfontein.

92 A60, D.J. Malan Collection, 23, "Oorlogdagboek van D.J. Malan", 23 and 24 July 1900.

93 Translated from the Afrikaans. A119, Renier Collection, 77, evidence of G.J. Joubert on Piet de Wet, 1939.

94 *Telegrams and Letters ... Roberts*, iii, p. 99, telegram C3024, Roberts – Kelly-Kenny, 27 July 1900.
95 Van Rensburg, "Pieter Daniël de Wet" in *DSAB*, II.
96 Translated from the Dutch. *The Bloemfontein Post*, 6 February 1901 (letter dated 11 January 1901 from P. de Wet – C. de Wet in the Dutch columns). Piet de Wet's letter to Steyn could not be traced, but De Wet, "The Fighter, The Scout, The Spy", p. 103 mentions that such a letter was indeed sent.
97 Translated from the Dutch. *The Bloemfontein Post*, 6 February 1901 (letter dated 11 January 1901 from P. de Wet – C. de Wet in the Dutch columns).
98 *Die Volksblad*, 1 March 1929 (obituary). For President Kruger's attitude in May 1900 which corroborates Piet de Wet's statement, see Van der Merwe, II, pp. 59–60; Chapter 2, section 5 above.
99 Translated from the Afrikaans. Van Schoor, *De Wet en sy Verkenners*, p. 20. See also C.M. van den Heever, *Generaal J.B.M. Hertzog*, p. 108.
100 Compare Van den Heever, p. 108.
101 De Wet, "The Fighter, The Scout, The Spy", pp. 103–4.
102 Translated from the Dutch. A1250, C.P. van der Merwe Accession, memoirs of the Anglo-Boer War, undated.
103 De Wet, *Boer en Brit*, p. 104.
104 Oberholster, "Dagboek van Oskar Hintrager", pp. 41, 44, 45; 20, 23 and 24 June 1900; Delport, pp. 139–40.
105 De Wet, *Boer en Brit*, p. 104.
106 Translated from the Afrikaans. A1237, memoirs of Henning Olivier, 1940.
107 De Wet, *Boer en Brit*, p. 104.
108 A119, Renier Collection, 77, evidence of G.J. Joubert on Piet de Wet, 1939.
109 Translated from the Afrikaans. Oberholster, "Dagboek van Oskar Hintrager", pp. 40–1, 44, 98; 20, 23 June and 1 August 1900. Hintrager added the part in italics to his diary at the beginning of 1902. On the proclamations to which Piet de Wet's wife was referring, see Chapter 2, section 2 above.
110 Translated from the Dutch. Badenhorst, p. 45.
111 Fuller, p. 283. See also E. Holt, *The Boer War*, p. 286. It is somewhat strange that Christiaan de Wet was in the Grand Hotel where his brother was enjoying a drink. Pienaar, "De Wet", p. 9 note 26 mentions in passing that Christiaan de Wet was a teetotaller.
112 Translated from the Afrikaans. Van Schoor, *De Wet en sy Verkenners*, p. 21.
113 PMO 7/497 (translated copy).
114 *Telegrams and Letters ... Roberts*, iii, p. 113, telegram C3154, H.V. Cowan – Hunter, 30 July 1900, with reference to a telegram from the commanding officer, Kroonstad.
115 Pretorius, p. 191.
116 Pretorius, p. 191.
117 See *Verslag der Deputatie*, pp. 9–10, P.D. de Wet and others – Revd. J.H. Hofmeyr, 8 March 1901; Chapter 3, sections 3 and 4 above.
118 *Telegrams and Letters ... Roberts*, iv, p. 28, Roberts – Kelly-Kenny, 14 August 1900. In this source Roberts refers to a letter that Kelly-Kenny sent to him on 6 August and in which Piet de Wet's complaint is mentioned.

119 *The Bloemfontein Post*, 3 March 1902 (translated printed version of speech presented by P. de Wet at Kroonstad, 25 February 1902).
120 *Telegrams and Letters ... Roberts*, iii, p. 120, telegram C3223, Roberts – Buller, 2 August 1900; *The Bloemfontein Post*, 6 February 1901 (letter dated 11 January 1901 of P. de Wet – C. de Wet in the Dutch Columns); De Wet, "The Fighter, The Scout, The Spy", p. 119.
121 See Chapter 3, section 1 above.
122 Translated from the Dutch. Leyds Archive, 861, p. 61, Mrs C. de Wet – Military commissioner of police, Johannesburg, 31 December 1900. See also Van Schoor, *De Wet en sy Verkenners*, p. 16; Davitt, p. 167.
123 See Chapter 3, sections 3 and 4 above.
124 Brits, *Diary*, p. 47, 6 May 1901.
125 De Wet, *Boer en Brit*, p. 207, note 1.
126 WO 32/882/8960 (A382), "Minutes of Extraordinary meeting of the Central Peace Committee held at Kroonstad", 20 September 1901. See also Chapter 3, section 5 above and Chapter 6, section 1 above.
127 See Chapter 6, section 1 above.
128 *The Bloemfontein Post*, 3 March 1902 (translated printed version of speech delivered by P. de Wet at Kroonstad, 25 February 1902).
129 De Wet, "The Fighter, The Scout, The Spy", p. 119. Italics: A.G.
130 De Wet, "The Fighter, The Scout, The Spy", p. 133. See Chapter 3, section 3 above for the way in which Morgendaal died.
131 WO 32/882/8960 (A382), "Minutes of Extraordinary Meeting of the Central Peace Committee held at Kroonstad", 20 September 1901; Chapter 6, section 1 above.
132 Translated from the Dutch. *The Bloemfontein Post*, 6 February 1901 (letter dated 11 January 1901 from P. de Wet – C. de Wet in the Dutch columns).
133 See Chapter 1, section 2 and Chapter 5, section 1 above.
134 Milner Papers, 46, (FK 1207, p. 71), "Summary of the proceedings of a deputation which met Mr. Chamberlain at Sunnyside", 14 January 1903 (copy).
135 WO 32/882/8960 (A382), "Minutes of Extraordinary Meeting of the Central Peace Committee held at Kroonstad", 20 September 1901.
136 Steyn Collection, 156/1/1–156/1/1a, pp. 57–9.
137 WO 32/882/8960 (A382), Knox – Kitchener's private secretary, 21 September 1901.
138 See Chapter 6, section 1 above.
139 In September 1903 he received £113 for his services as repatriation officer. GRD 92, "Salaries, Board members", 4 September 1903. He used some of this money to buy wagons and mules from the repatriation board. Lindley magistracy, 1.9, P. de Wet – F. Eglin, 9 November 1903.
140 Translated from the Afrikaans. Van Rensburg, "Pieter Daniël de Wet" in *DSAB*, II.
141 Estate 21437, P.D. de Wet, 1929, Master of the Supreme Court, Bloemfontein.
142 Estate 15186, C.R. de Wet, 1922, Master of the Supreme Court, Bloemfontein.
143 This discussion of S.G. Vilonel's pre-war career is based on the following sources: Estate 2081, S.G. Vilonel, 1918, Master of the Supreme Court, Bloemfontein; Senekal Municipality register of rates and taxes, 1896–1899; Senekal Municipality, Outgoing Correspondence, 1892–1899.

144 *The Friend*, 6 April 1894 (local news). See also Leyds Archive, 866, p. 17, press reports. Undated typed copy of a report that appeared in the *Nieuwe Rotterdamsche Courant*.
145 *The Friend*, 14 September 1896 (local news). See also A.M. Grundlingh, "Die Stigting van Senekal en Ontwikkeling in die dorp en wyk Onderwittebergen tot 1899" (Unpublished BA Hons essay, UOFS), 1971, p. 38.
146 Davitt, pp. 562–3.
147 *The Friend*, 14 September 1896 (local news).
148 Oberholster, "Dagboek van Oskar Hintrager", p. 69, note 172; *Times History*, III, p. 480, 547, 577; VI, p. 30, 514; Leyds Archive, 866, p. 17 (press reports, undated typed copy of a report that appeared in the *Nieuwe Rotterdamsche Courant*); A1259, memoirs of L.J. du Plooy of the Anglo-Boer War, undated; *De Volksstem*, 16 March 1900 (news report).
149 Translated from the Afrikaans. J.N. Brink, *Oorlog en Ballingskap*, p. 69. Brink does not mention Vilonel's name, but refers to him as "Mr X". From the context it is however clear that he means Vilonel.
150 Oosthuizen, "De la Rey", p. 239.
151 Oberholster, "Dagboek van Oskar Hintrager", p. 69 note 172.
152 *The Bloemfontein Post*, 19 March 1901 (letter from S.G. Vilonel).
153 De Wet, *Boer en Brit*, pp. 56–7. See also Pienaar, "De Wet", pp. 68–70; Brink, p. 93.
154 De Wet, *Boer en Brit*, p. 75.
155 Brink, p. 69.
156 De Wet, *Boer en Brit*, p. 75; Van Everdingen, *Tweede Tijdvak*, I, p. 239.
157 De Wet, *Boer en Brit*, p. 75.
158 *Telegrams and Letters ... Roberts*, ii, p. 84, telegram C1926.
159 Brink, p. 69; A119, Renier Collection, 1056, "Die Ervarings van vk. I.A. Meyer van die Ladybrandse kommando in die Engelse oorlog, 1899–1902", p. 15, 1929; *The Bloemfontein Post*, 19 March 1901 (letter from Vilonel).
160 Davitt, p. 563.
161 Translated from the Afrikaans. Brink, p. 69.
162 *The Bloemfontein Post*, 19 March 1901 (letter from S.G. Vilonel).
163 Brink, pp. 69–70. See also Solomon, p. 15.
164 Brink, pp. 70–5; De Wet, *Boer en Brit*, pp. 75–6; A119, Renier Collection, 1056, "Die Ervarings van vk. I.A. Meyer van die Ladybrandse kommando in die Engelse oorlog", p. 15, 1929; Solomon, p. 15.
165 Pienaar, *Met Steyn en De Wet*, p. 148.
166 Brink, p. 177; Davitt, p. 563; Van Everdingen, *Tweede Tijdvak*, II, p. 4; Pienaar, *Met Steyn en De Wet*, p. 148.
167 Translated from the Dutch. News report in *De Bazuin*, 17 July 1900 as reproduced in Badenhorst, p. 40. See also Oberholster, "Dagboek van Oskar Hintrager", pp. 69–70 for the same reproduction. The minutes of the court case could not be traced.
168 Translated from the Dutch. Pienaar, *Met Steyn en De Wet*, p. 148.
169 Van Everdingen, *Tweede Tijdvak*, II, p. 52; Brink, p. 77.
170 De Wet, *Boer en Brit*, pp. 109–13; Van Everdingen, *Tweede Tijdvak*, II, pp. 52–3; Brink, pp. 92–3.

171 Translated from the Afrikaans. Delport, p. 166.
172 Roberts Papers, WO 105/24 (A390), Hunter – Roberts, 4 August 1900.
173 Van Everdingen, *Tweede Tijdvak*, II, p. 53.
174 Roberts Papers, WO 105/24 (A390), Hunter – Roberts, 4 August 1900; Delport, p. 204.
175 Adjutant J.N. Brink, who was captured in the Brandwater basin, suspected this but did not state this explicitly. Brink, p. 77.
176 Delport, p. 205.
177 Boldingh, p. 42; Van Everdingen, *Tweede Tijdvak*, II, p. 53. See also Chapter 2, section 3 n. 144 above.
178 *The Bloemfontein Post*, 19 March 1901 (letter from Vilonel, written from the Winburg district).
179 See Chapter 6, section 1 above.
180 *The Bloemfontein Post*, 27 February 1902 (letter from Vilonel – Steyn). See also CO 417/360/10274 (FK 660, pp. 789–90).
181 De Wet, *Boer en Brit*, p. 76.
182 Brink, p. 93.
183 *The Bloemfontein Post*, 19 March 1901 (letter from S.G. Vilonel).
184 *The Bloemfontein Post*, 27 February 1901 (letter from Vilonel – Steyn, dated 11 January 1902).
185 Brink, p. 77.
186 Estate 50957, A.P.J. Cronjé, 1923, Transvaal Archives, Pretoria; Van Coller, pp. 1–8.
187 A787, Preller Collection, 81, p. 158, "Geskiedenis van Klerksdorpse kommando", *Die Volksstem*, 24 February 1923 (obituary); *The Star*, 24 February 1923 (obituary).
188 *Almanak voor de Nederduitsch Hervormde of Gereformeerde Kerk in Zuid*-Afrika, 1898–1899.
189 A782, H. Bramley, "Anglo-Boer War Diary", pp. 8–9.
190 KG 332 (3), p. 206, Commissioner of mines, Klerksdorp – Commandant-general, 2 October 1899, in which mention is made of Cronjé's appointment.
191 See Chapter 3, section 1, note 30 above.
192 For this information on Cronjé's exploits during the war see *Times History*, II, pp. 343–4, 362; III, pp. 382, 477, 574; IV, pp. 28, 95, 210, 215, 255, 513; *Official History*, III, pp. 108–9, 230; Badenhorst, p. 16; H.M. Guest, *Vicissitudes of a Transvaal dorp*, annexure A, "Local Boer losses" (no page numbers); J.P. Brits, "Andries Petrus Johannes Cronjé", unpublished manuscript for *DSAB*, III; *Telegrams and Letters ... Roberts*, ii, p. 103, telegram C2063, Roberts – Baden-Powell, 14 June 1900.
193 Roberts Papers, WO 105/27 (A393), translated intercepted version of a conversation between General Piet Cronjé en President Kruger, 6 January 1900.
194 See Bakkes, p. 67 note 18.
195 Translated from the Dutch. *Nieuwe Rotterdamsche Courant*, 10 November 1900 (news report).
196 Leyds Archive, 727 (c), telegram 41 of 17 June 1900, Steyn – Kruger.
197 WO 32/867/4737 (A367), report by J.H. Voss on the Boer occupation of Klerksdorp, 17 October 1900. See also Guest, *Vicissitudes*, pp. 28–31.

198 See Chapter 3, sections 1 and 4 above.
199 Cd. 893, p. 137, report on Klerksdorp concentration camp, October 1901.
200 GOV 108/25, W.S. Duxbury (resident magistrate Potchefstroom) – Walrond, 8 January 1902. Report on the meeting and Cronjé's speech, 6 January 1902.
201 CS 1079/29, confidential report from resident magistrate Potchefstroom, 9 March 1904.
202 C.J. Scheepers Strydom, *Ruitervuur*, p. 149. On p. 200 Scheepers Strydom confuses Jan Gabriël Celliers with the Lichtenburg general, but in the context where Jan Gabriël Celliers's date of birth is discussed it is clear that he had the correct person in mind.
203 PMO 22/1585, sworn statement by J. van Dal, 1 October 1901.
204 *Times History*, III, pp. 461–3, 466; PMO 22/1585, sworn statement by J. van Dal, 1 October 1901.
205 *Times History*, III, p. 470; De Wet, "The Fighter, The Scout, The Spy", p. LXII.
206 PMO 22/1518, sworn statement by J. van Dal, 1 October 1901.
207 See Chapter 6, section 1 above.
208 Translated from the Afrikaans. Preller, "Die National Scouts" in *Die Burger*, 1 July 1926.
209 J. Krige, *American Sympathy in the Boer War: A plain tale of Commando Life in the Boer War of 1899–1900 and subsequent Adventures in the United States of America*, p. 4.
210 PMO 22/1585, sworn statement by J. van Dal, 1 October 1901.
211 De Wet, "The Fighter, The Scout, The Spy", p. LXII.
212 Translated from the Afrikaans. Preller, "Die National Scouts", in *Die Burger*, 1 July 1926. See also W133, Wypkema Collection, 2, news report in an unidentified Netherlands newspaper, taken from the *Temps*, 11 February 1902.
213 Translated from the Dutch. W133, Wypkema Collection, 2, news report in an unidentified Netherlands newspaper taken from the *Temps*, 11 February 1902.
214 ZTPD 3/48, case 1143, "The State versus Jan Gabriel Celliers", 19 October 1901. See also PMO 22/1585, C.R. Gardner – Commanding officer Middelburg, 17 June 1901 and M.R. Greenless, police staff officer – Maxwell, 25 October 1901.
215 PMO 22/1585, sworn statement by H.S. Lombard, 1 October 1901.
216 EC 35/456/03, confidential report from resident magistrate Pietersburg, 17 July 1903.
217 MGP 208/4154/01, M.R. Greenless – Maxwell, 25 October 1901; PMO 22/1585, M.R. Greenless – Maxwell, 25 October 1901 (copy) and Poore – Maxwell, 27 October 1901 (copy). See also Spies, "Civilians", p. 436.
218 WO32/882/8960 (A382), "Minutes of Extraordinary Meeting of the Central Peace Committee held at Kroonstad", 20 September 1901.
219 Kestell and Van Velden, *Vredesonderhandelingen*, p. 40. See also Spies, "Civilians", p. 440.
220 Spies, "Civilians", p. 440.
221 *Times History*, V, pp. 571, 572, 409–10.
222 Amery, *Days of Fresh Air*, p. 165.
223 For another discussion of this aspect see Chapters 8, 9 and 10 below.
224 Milner Papers, 41, (FK 1191, pp. 113–14), Milner – Chamberlain, 23 April 1902 (copy).

225 Kestell and Van Velden, *Vredesonderhandelingen*, p. 136.
226 See Chapter 8, section 3 below.
227 *The South African News*, 28 March 1901 (letter from "Mikros", pseudonym of Revd J.A. Steytler).
228 Kitchener Letters, IV, (FK 1624, p. 650), Kitchener – Brodrick, 17 May 1902.
229 WO 32/883/9121 (A383), "Staff Diary, Head Quarters, Lines of Communication East", 21 May 1902.

Chapter 8
British assistance in South Africa after the war

1 Repatriation

After a struggle lasting 32 months there was peace once more in the two former republics. Many bitterenders accepted the peace and the loss of independence that of necessity came with it with very heavy hearts. The British of course saw it quite differently. The news that peace had been concluded on 31 May 1902 was greeted with great excitement among the British troops and pro-British residents of Pretoria. At long last the British were victorious and at last the Transvaal and the Free State were formal British colonies.

To celebrate the British victory a "grand celebration of the Peace" was held at the beginning of June 1902 on Church Square in Pretoria. "It was the usual sort of thing," a British journalist wrote 21 years after the event, "cheering, hymns, a short address from the Archbishop of Cape Town, General Salute, a clerical procession to the words of Kipling's tawdry 'Recessional' and so on. However, when someone shouted: 'Cheers for Kitchener' – the whole square went wild. Helmets, hats, and caps of every cut flew into the air, or were waved on the muzzles of rifles. The troops and people cheered as though they could never stop, and the shouting went on long after Kitchener himself had disappeared into the Government Buildings behind him."[1] The National Scouts were not left out of these festivities and 500 of them were present on Church Square as an integral part of the Imperial army, sharing in the euphoria.[2]

Kitchener made a point of paying a personal visit to Meintjeskop shortly after the conclusion of peace and the 500 National Scouts formed a guard of honour and cheered him enthusiastically. In a short address Kitchener thanked them for their contribution during the war and "told them that he had not forgotten their services, and promised them that they would be looked after in future".[3]

Despite this promise from Kitchener, who was the senior representative of British military authority in the country, that the National Scouts would be looked after, even at this early stage there were signs that the civil administration would not be as kindly disposed to the Scouts as their military predecessors had been. A. Richmond, one of Milner's imported officials who worked in the office of the colonial secretary, regarded the celebrations on Church Square as "a thrilling event in the Imperial history", but he was unhappy that the National Scouts had also been involved. "[T]here was one discordant note," he wrote. "A commando of Boers who had surrendered and enrolled in a corps which was known as the 'National Scouts' took part in the ceremony of triumph. Some of us felt that that should not have happened."[4] Because of the attitude of some British people as he travelled through the Transvaal, the journalist E.F. Knight remarked that "[there is] a tendency to despise these scouts who fought for us and to deny them all sympathy".[5]

Shortly after peace was declared, there were a number of burghers who had fought on the British side during the war who were apprehensive that their expectations would not be met. P.D. Schutte and 30 members of the ORC Volunteers contacted Major Leggett in July 1902. "We joined ... under the distinct promise," they wrote, "that at the end of the war we would have the first chance and privilege to commence farming, and that we would be assisted and supported by the authorities. But to our surprise and disappointment we have noticed that nothing has been done for us, and the promises made to us under which we joined have not been carried out." In the light of this they asked Leggett to place them in a position to begin their farming activities as soon as possible. Leggett referred the request to H. Goold-Adams, the Lieutenant-governor of the Orange River Colony. According to Leggett this kind of request was "indicative of general ex-military burgher opinion".[6] Many other ORC Volunteers and members of the Farmers' Guard either wrote to Goold-Adams during the second half of 1902 or approached the civil authorities for help on the basis of the promises made to them during the war.[7] Goold-Adams wrote in a memorandum that he had also held discussions with various "individuals and deputations from different parts of the Colony representing parties of ex-burghers who have served His Majesty during the late war in one way or another, either as Volunteers, Farmers' Guard or Column Guides. They one and all urge that the services which they have rendered to the Military entitles them to some special consideration in the shape of help to enable them to earn their livelihood, and they one and all ask for special government help."[8]

Transvaal burghers who were in British military service also demanded that the promises that had been made to them should be honoured. In the Volksrust district 50 National Scouts gave a local firm of attorneys, Rademeyer and De Beer, instructions to bring their position to the attention of the civil administration. "The National Scouts were promised by the Military Commanders," read the document from the attorneys, "that each man would receive a gratuity of 9 oxen, a wagon, and two cows, as soon as Peace was concluded, in order to enable them to restart their various occupations, and that they have not been furnished with these or any other considerations despite repeated applications. As they have rendered valuable service ... and are all poor men, they would be pleased to hear whether the Government intends fulfilling its promise."[9] From Krugersdorp the local magistrate reported in August 1902 that "many if not all of them [the National Scouts] were under the impression that a separate organisation would be provided for their repatriation."[10] In Pretoria H.W.J. van der Brugge, who had been attached to the British information service for a considerable period, was extremely disappointed that the civil administration would not offer him a position. He then approached the assistant provost marshal and told him of another "very disagreeable circumstance". He explained: "I have to stand the sympathising smiles of my ex-Countrymen who with an 'of course' or 'I've told you so long ago', or 'British Government all round', rejoice in my unfortunate position." Van der Brugge hoped that with the help of the assistant provost marshal he would be given a position in the civil administration "to enable me to show other people that I have not been 'chucked out' as they think".[11]

In January 1903 Captain P.H.J. Blakemore, the British commanding officer of the ORC Volunteers, summed up the feelings of the burghers who had fought on the British side as follows: "The feeling existed when peace was declared that the British Government would drop them and leave them to the mercy of the Boers ..., by whom naturally, they were very much hated."[12]

Shortly after peace had been declared these burghers thus found themselves in an unenviable position. They had given the British active support during the war on the understanding that after the war they would be in a privileged position. And now it seemed that the civil authorities had forsaken them. With justification the *Times History* wrote: "To the military they were auxiliaries whose services were no longer needed; to the civil administration they were just ordinary Boers requiring repatriation."[13]

Milner, the architect of the British post-war policy, clearly felt that the administration was obliged to devote special attention to the burghers who had stood by the military authorities. "Without openly stating it," he informed Goold-Adams, "I think that every reasonable advantage should be given, in the settlement of the country, to those who have shown themselves conciliatory or have fought for us."[14] But it would be incorrect on the basis of this statement by Milner – or in the light of his overt anglicisation policy towards the Afrikaner[15] – to claim that by means of special assistance with repatriation he was also hoping to harness the National Scouts (who had already shown their pro-British tendencies) to help widen the existing division in Afrikaner ranks and thus advance the British cause in the post-war period.

Despite the fact that Milner had encouraged the initial enlistment of burghers into British military service and had also approved the National Scout movement in the last phase of the war,[16] he in fact showed little concern for these burghers once the war was over. For him it was simply a matter of keeping the promises, as far as this was practical, that the military authorities had made to the National Scouts during the war. In an interview with Eugène Marais, the editor and owner of *Land en Volk* (a Dutch newspaper that was subsidised by the British), Milner said early in 1903 that he saw it as his "duty to protect the people who had helped us". Leon Rousseau, Marais's biographer, even goes so far as to say that it was clear to Marais "that the Governor has the greatest contempt for the Boer traitors. Often when he talks of them he does so sneeringly."[17] There is other evidence that Milner felt under a moral obligation to the National Scouts. In 1905 he told his successor, Lord Selborne, how he felt about the collaborators. He explained that his commitment to them had arisen from the vague promises the military authorities had made to the National Scouts, giving them the impression that they would be privileged after the war.

The onus was thus on him to carry out this policy as best he could. "[W]hen the war was over I succeeded to the consequences of this policy," he wrote to Selborne, "and ... whether we were right or not in inducing these men to take our side, we could not but be wrong in allowing them to suffer for what we had induced them to do. I still get hot when I think of the attitude which a good many of our people, after the war was over, took towards the men whom, while the war was still going on, the military had not scrupled to make so much use of."[18]

W.E. Davidson, the Transvaal colonial secretary, expressed a similar opinion on the National Scouts in somewhat stronger terms than Milner. To Gustav Preller he said: "You know we despise these people as much as you do, but we are bound to protect them."[19] In the light of this it is understandable that G.B. Beak, who was busy with repatriation in the Orange River Colony at the time, could write: "The constitution of burgher corps to fight on the British side may have been undertaken originally from political motives, but the line adopted by the ... Administration in connection with the repatriation of the volunteers goes far to disprove that it desired in any way to perpetuate the political and social breach produced by the war."[20] There is naturally the possibility that the civil administration might have been hoping for political dividends after meeting the promises made by the military as far as was possible. However, there is no evidence at all that points to this. Nor, in practice, did special resettlement assistance provided for the National Scouts and their ilk bring any political advantages for the British. It can thus be accepted that political considerations were not a significant factor in the resettlement of the dissident burghers.

The question can justifiably be posed: why did the civil administration have so few political designs as far as the repatriation of the burghers who had fought on the British side was concerned?

In the first place it must be remembered that it was the military authorities and not the civil administration who had regarded the National Scouts as a political factor.[21] It does not necessarily follow that after the war, and under different circumstances that the civil administration was bound to adopt a similar stance.

Secondly, it must be kept in mind that an enormous task awaited the administration to repatriate a dislocated Boer society in its entirety.[22] Repatriation was obviously an absolute necessity in order to normalise a society that was in tatters; it was not a system that was directed primarily towards gaining political advantage.

Thirdly, even at the Peace of Vereeniging the National Scouts had already lost the political initiative.[23] Quite correctly the *Times History* states: "As it was the political influence to which the ex-military burghers might reasonably have aspired, if the guerilla war had been carried out to the bitter end, had been given away by peace negotiations which practically ignored them. The only thing remaining was to provide a material recompense sufficient to prevent any sense of injustice or betrayal ..."[24]

Fourthly, the number of burghers that fought on the British side (5464 men) was small in comparison to the combined total of bitterenders and former prisoners of war (about 43 000 men).[25] In addition, the National Scouts and their like were rejected to such an extent by the majority of the Boer people that their influence was largely restricted to their own circle and the chances were thus small that they would attract many more followers. Fifthly, Milner was aware that most of the National Scouts belonged to the lower class of Boer society and he did not see them as a potential political pressure group.[26] Primarily, then, to avoid losing face over the promises the British had made, Milner thought it would be wise to pay close attention to the repatriation of the National Scouts and their like. Goold-Adams agreed. As a result of the aforementioned interviews that he had conducted with a number of the collaborators, he wrote to the Central Repatriation Board in Bloemfontein: "I recognize that something more than what is done for the ordinary impecunious person should if possible, be done for these people, and I do not think that they should be able to say that loyalty to the British does not pay."[27]

By August 1902 two special repatriation boards had been set up in Pretoria and Bloemfontein, exclusively for burghers who had rendered service to the British. Major Leggett headed the Transvaal board and Captain Blakemore was in charge of the one in the Orange River Colony. Other British officers who had been involved in the military organisation of the National Scouts and ORC Volunteers during the war also remained in the country to give the necessary repatriation assistance to the collaborators and Piet de Wet, Andries Cronjé and S.G. Vilonel were also involved in the process. These boards functioned independently and were not under the civil administration, but there was some mutual consultation. The main aim of the two boards was to ensure that special relocation assistance was provided for the National Scouts and ORC Volunteers through the local repatriation boards. They also had to organise suitable work for those who were unemployed.[28]

Leggett maintained in February 1904 that "no greater measure of repatriation aid could be afforded to the burghers who had joined the British Forces, than to the rest of the people",[29] but his statement was inaccurate. Each burgher who had fought on the British side received goods to the value of £50 from the two special boards. These goods, depending on the circumstances of the particular individual, included seed, implements, animals or wagons. A sum of £38 000 cash was also made available for distribution among all British military burghers.[30] In contrast to this, the bitterenders and the prisoners of war who had returned received no such assistance and they experienced many repatriation problems.[31] The National Scouts and their ilk were supposed to pay back £25 of the original £50 after two years. However, they were under the impression that it was a free gift for the services they had provided to the British during the war. By 1906 not a single one of these men had repaid his portion, and the British authority decided to cancel their debt.[32] In contrast to this, the crown colony government expected the bitterenders and ex-prisoners of war to produce the first payment of their repatriation debt by April 1907.[33]

Through the two special boards that had been set up for them the National Scouts and ORC Volunteers were favoured above the bitterenders in other ways too. These boards saw to it that as far as possible the collaborators received preferential treatment from the local repatriation boards as well. In the Soutpansberg district, for example, the National Scouts who owned property were settled on their farms before the bitterenders.[34] In the Pretoria district the National Scouts also received preferential treatment; in September 1902 there were only 46 wagons available for transporting displaced families to their farms and not only were the National Scouts and their families transported first, but they were also allowed the use of more wagons than the other burghers.[35] Similarly, in the Krugersdorp district the National Scouts were given preference with transportation.[36] The National Scouts could also acquire additional supplies of seed, livestock, ploughs, wagons and rations from their local boards.[37] Indeed, it came down to the fact that, over and above the repatriation assistance they received from the two special boards, the burghers who had fought on the British side also received preferential treatment from the local repatriation boards, where the majority of the staff were pro-British people.

On the basis of a promise made by Kitchener, the National Scouts were also under the impression that they would each be provided with a firearm after the war, and that this rifle would then remain their personal property. Leggett claimed that he had received "a large number of letters" from National Scouts in which they requested that this particular promise be honoured. According to Leggett the promise was as follows: "That to every man of our Corps to whom a permit to carry arms might be issued by the proper authority, should be given free of charge from Army Stores one Martini rifle and one hundred rounds of ammunition." Leggett considered it important that the British should keep their word on this. "I feel sure that you will agree with me," he wrote to the colonial secretary, "that men who have already taken the Oath of Allegiance and have proved their fidelity by the extreme step of taking the field on the British side, would feel deeply any decision now depriving them of what they consider the highest possible privilege."[38] Leggett made a similar plea to the civil administration in the Orange River Colony.[39] As the head of the civil administration Milner was also involved in the question of the possession of firearms. Despite misgivings he agreed that the promise made by the military would have to be honoured. He notified Goold-Adams: "Lord K[itchener], I fear, undoubtedly promised the National Scouts that they should retain their arms. This is going too far, but inasmuch as, greatly to my dismay, the Military were quite liberal in their distribution of arms to the men who surrendered at the end, it is only fair that our friends should be allowed to retain arms ... I think ... it is a question of prestige [among the National Scouts]."[40] It is clear that Milner, as the governor of the two colonies, had his reservations about this. Initially the Transvaal colonial secretary, W.E. Davidson, had laid down certain conditions on the issue of firearms to National Scouts. He had ruled that only those who owned "landed property" and really had the need for a weapon should receive one. Leggett subsequently insisted that any National Scout who had been approved by him had to be issued with a rifle. The colonial secretary let Leggett have his way and the conditions were duly scrapped.[41] In practice the National Scouts had been able to acquire rifles relatively easily even before Davidson's conditions.[42]

It would appear that at the beginning of 1903 the National Scouts were satisfied that the British had met their obligations as far as assistance with repatriation was concerned. E.F. Knight, who visited a number of different repatriation camps in January 1902, found that the officials there had been as accommodating as possible towards the National Scouts. A former National Scout from Rustenburg had reportedly said to him: "This has shut the mouths of those who once jeered at us ... We can now laugh at those who used to ask mockingly what we had gained by serving the British."[43] Captain Blakemore commented in January 1903 that the repatriation assistance that the two special boards had rendered to those who had formerly been part of the British military "has not only shown these particular Burghers that the British Government stood by them, but it has also given the lie to those Boers who said that the British Government would drop them as soon as their services from a Military point of view were no longer required".[44] Beak was of the same opinion: "Doubtless it was a source of satisfaction to them [the Volunteers] to be treated differently from the ordinary ex-burgher."[45] In January

1903 S.G. Vilonel also expressed his gratitude to Chamberlain for the repatriation assistance that had been provided for the ORC Volunteers.[46]

Seen in broader terms it is doubtful whether the civil administration followed a wise policy by giving the defectors better treatment than the bitterenders. As has been shown, they did so because they felt morally obliged to honour the promises made by the British military as far as this was practical. Had they not done so, the burghers who had fought on their side could have laid serious and justifiable charges of breach of faith against them. It would have served to prove yet again to the entire Boer population that by and large they could not rely on British promises. However, the administration erred in that they gave undue preference to the National Scouts and their like. By doing so, the majority of the Boer population (the bitterenders and the returned prisoners of war) grew even more antagonistic towards their disloyal compatriots in particular, and the British authority in general.[47] The editor of *The Friend* was fully justified in his opinion that the repatriation policy did not show sufficient concern for the feelings of the bitterenders: "We acknowledge that the British Government, having made a mistake in the first instance in ever allowing the Boer to fight against the Boer, must make the best of a bad job and see it through, but there is no reason whatever why a man who fought against his own country should be better treated than the man who stuck to his guns to the last ... We honestly believe that the British Government are doing what they consider their best for the Boers, but we ask any right-thinking man if he can place his hand on his heart and truly answer in the affirmative as to whether it is fair, honest or justifiable that the National Scout should receive better treatment than the faithful burgher."[48]

In addition to the resettlement of land-owning National Scouts on their farms, the special repatriation board in Pretoria also undertook to find jobs for poverty-stricken and unemployed National Scouts. By the middle of September 1902 there were 25 National Scouts who had been appointed as gaolers to guard black prisoners in Pretoria. After representations by Leggett the Department of Postal Service offered to take on six National Scouts, and at the same time the railways agreed to employ 70 members of the corps. The railways also accepted a further 30 young National Scouts as apprentices in the railway workshop. In addition to technical instruction, it was envisaged that they would be taught English, History and Geography. The Department of Native Affairs and the Public Works Department also offered to take on National Scouts as foremen and game rangers respectively, and the transport section of the army also agreed to provide temporary employment for 40 National Scouts for a period of six months.[49]

At the end of December 1902 Leggett reported on how the National Scouts were coping in their new positions. It appeared that not everyone was suited to the type of work he had been hired to do. Three gaolers had simply walked off the job and one had been discharged because of misconduct. Furthermore, the 30 young National Scouts who had been taken on as apprentices by the railways had not acquitted themselves satisfactorily. "I regret to say," Leggett reported, "that the Railway has definitely intimated that it could not see its way open to take cognizance of these lads out of Workshop hours. The result was that the boys, freed from all restraint and finding themselves in possession of money received as wages, lost the sense of discipline, and in several cases absconded." Because of this, the proposed plan to teach the young National Scouts subjects like English and History also had to be abandoned. In the post offices at Johannesburg and Pretoria in December there were still vacant positions for postmen, but "owing to the lack of educationally qualified men" Leggett could not fill these jobs with National Scouts. The Department of Native Affairs did appoint a few National Scouts as foremen, but the Public Works Department had no vacant positions available for National Scouts as game rangers.[50]

The National Scouts and their ilk were also employed as members of the colonial police force, the South African Constabulary. This force, having functioned as a military unit during the war, was relieved of its military duties shortly after the conclusion of peace. Even while the war was still on, Captain W.H. Beddy of Beddy's Scouts had given the burghers in his corps the impression that once hostilities had ceased they would be able to get posts in the Constabulary with relative ease.[51] In July 1902 Milner gave his permission that burghers who had fought on the British side could become members of the Constabulary.[52] Initially they were expected to join for a period of three years, but very few of these burghers were prepared to commit themselves for such a long period, so the service requirements were changed so that they were also able to join for a three-month term. The result was that a greater number of National Scouts were interested in the police force and 150 from the Transvaal were accepted into the Constabulary.[53] In the Orange River Colony some of the surrendered burghers also took refuge in the Constabulary.[54] Provision was also made for the bitterenders in the police force and before the end of September 1902 about 150 bitterenders from both colonies had joined up.[55] The commanding officer of the Constabulary hoped that the National Scouts and bitterenders would be a "link with the people". Both the National Scouts and the bitterenders were used individually as "interpreters, guides and plain-clothes agents". Because of the bitterness between the two groups, they were not placed together in the same sections of the police force.[56]

According to Leggett, because of their "knowledge of the topography and different dialects" the National Scouts were particularly useful to the Constabulary, but many of them were not, however, very keen on the "too marked insistence upon details of drill and dress". Leggett felt that it was understandable that strict discipline "[would] annoy men accustomed to the open life of the veld".[57] Some National Scouts even left the police force because the junior officers of the Constabulary, in their view, placed far too much emphasis on disciplined military drill.[58]

The reality was that the officers of the Constabulary experienced more than just disciplinary problems with the National Scouts. In Pretoria a Scout named A.L. Botha was fired in February 1903 "because he is quite unsuitable for a constable, is a bad rider and has had very little education".[59] Colonel Pilkington of the local police force in Bloemfontein was prepared to employ only a limited number of ORC Volunteers because he could not see his way clear "to enroll illiterate men in the S.A.C.". To overcome the problem S.G. Vilonel requested that special evening classes be arranged for these uneducated ORC Volunteers, but the authorities were not prepared to do this.[60]

The bitterenders were vehemently opposed to the idea that their countrymen, who had fought against them in the war, were now appointed in the police force and were supposed to protect them. "Many of the S.A.C. posts have a Boer in the Corps," said the resident magistrate in Pretoria, "and in one instance this Boer happens to have been a National Scout and the farmers refuse to allow him into their houses."[61] In August 1905 Captain Wood of the local police force in Heidelberg gave evidence before a commission of inquiry into the Constabulary: "I do not think you would get a good class of Boer to join the Constabulary. The farmers do not like the Boer policemen. They would sooner deal with the English policemen, if both parties could understand one another."[62] Colonel Pilkington, who was not very keen on appointing ORC Volunteers in the Constabulary, predicted as early as July 1902 that there would be problems in this regard. To Goold-Adams he said: "There may be a strong feeling against the Volunteers among those who held out, and it seems a pity to array this feeling against the constabulary."[63] Certain National Scouts also misused the little authority they were afforded as members of the Constabulary. "They took advantage of their position," said Captain Wood, "and imposed upon the farmers by putting their horses up at the farms, and by making themselves objectionable in other ways. They were not of a good class." Wood dismissed 18 National Scouts who were not equipped to be policemen and three others were fired because of "immorality" and "assault".[64] It is not known how many other policemen, including bitterenders, were also dismissed.

Twenty members of the National Scouts chose not to be employed in the Transvaal as policemen and instead joined the British South African Police in Rhodesia and the Cape Police in Bechuanaland.[65] Other National Scouts went even further afield. About 27 National Scouts and surrendered burghers from the Transvaal and, according to reports, 40 members of the Farmers' Guard in the Free State had joined the British army by the end of 1902 to serve in Somaliland to help suppress an uprising under Muhammed Abdallah Hasan (or "the mad Mullah" as the British called him).[66] From 1900 the British had experienced continual sporadic problems with "the mad Mullah" and his followers, and he was only finally subdued in 1920.[67] Leggett was of the opinion that the National Scouts – "who were the first Boers to wear the King's uniform" – would be a "valuable backbone to the Boer Contingent" in Somaliland.[68]

National Scouts were consequently not appointed on a large scale in responsible positions in the British administration. As far as can be established, the only exception was Andries Cronjé, who was appointed as a justice of the peace in Potchefstroom.[69] S.G. Vilonel complained specifically about this to Chamberlain in January 1903 when he said "that offices like that of 'J.P.' [Justice of the Peace] and other appointments of public trust ... had not been entrusted to them. This looked as if the Government held them of little esteem, and caused a soreness of feeling on their part."[70] The bitterenders were nevertheless concerned that the British might decide to place the National Scouts in important positions of authority. A bitterender from Carolina, for example, was under the false impression that the British were possibly planning to appoint a National Scout as justice of the peace in the town. "If that should happen," he wrote, "then our Government must think very little indeed of our loyal burghers. Why not appoint a raw Englishman instead? We would first have to lose our self-respect, ... before we would be willing to be under such disloyal men. We have had more than we can stomach of them. They are too low to tread on this beautiful land, and then that they should be in authority over us! No, never!"[71] Major-general Walter Kitchener (the brother of the British commander-in-chief during the war) had reiterated this point shortly after peace was signed. In his report on the manner in which the bitterenders had laid down their arms he wrote: "At every meeting the burghers begged me to submit their earnest request that they may not be put under the magistracy of one of their countrymen who has fought against them. In my opinion, they honestly intend to become good subjects, but they foresee bitterness on both sides if their political differences during the war are emphasised by making one side rulers over the other." According to Walter Kitchener the bitterenders preferred to have "high class Englishman" in the civil service.[72]

This antagonism that the bitterenders felt towards the burghers who had defected is also evident in their vehement protest against the appointment of National Scouts and surrendered burghers on local repatriation boards. Each local repatriation board comprised a magistrate as chairman, three official and three unofficial members. In the Transvaal the names of these members were published in the

Government Gazette on 8 July and 1 August.[73] Ramsay Macdonald – the outspoken pro-Boer who later became British prime minister – commented on the composition of these boards after a journey that he undertook through the Transvaal in October 1902. He claimed that the bitterenders and former prisoners of war were disproportionately represented on the repatriation boards compared with the National Scouts and surrendered burghers.[74] Macdonald's allegation is corroborated by the available lists in the colonial secretary's office. Using these lists, the status of the board members can be ascertained. Despite the fact that the lists are incomplete, it appears that in July 1902 there were 102 members who had been appointed to the boards in the Transvaal. Of these, 33 had been British subjects before the war (Constabulary officers and magistrates), while the National Scouts and surrendered burghers had 36 representatives and the bitterenders and ex-prisoners of war had 33 members.[75] In view of the fact that the bitterenders and former prisoners of war made up by far the greater percentage of the Boer population, it is clear that they were indeed very poorly represented on the boards. In the Orange River Colony, Beak claimed that the repatriation boards had a majority of bitterender representatives,[76] but a historian who has researched the post-war economic position of the bitterenders in this colony has analysed the name lists and has proved conclusively that this was not the case.[77]

Reacting to requests submitted by National Scouts, Leggett claimed that representation by surrendered burghers and National Scouts was necessary on the boards to give them a justifiable say in the process of repatriation assistance and compensation.[78] Milner claimed that he did not want to favour the one group over the other, but these appointments were being made to protect the National Scouts "who being in a minority are in danger of being bullied locally".[79] The National Scouts were indeed in the minority and the administration could not really be faulted for giving this group, who had their own identity and expectations, some representation on the boards. But they did err in giving them greater representation than was justified by their numbers. If they had been serious about being fair to both parties, the reasonable solution would have been to increase the size of the boards to make proportional representation possible.

During the visit of the Boer generals to Europe and Britain, Louis Botha complained to Chamberlain in September 1902 about the unfair representation on the Transvaal repatriation boards. According to Botha the loyal burghers were very dissatisfied about these appointments. Furthermore, he told Chamberlain that he realised that the British administration had an obligation to the National Scouts, but did not see why this meant that they should be placed on a better footing than the bitterenders and ex-prisoners of war. Chamberlain responded by saying that they could not leave the National Scouts high and dry, but he tried to use a fallacious argument to avoid being drawn into a discussion on the real issue of unequal representation.[80] Earlier Botha had also failed in his attempt to broach the subject with Milner,[81] and Schalk Burger had made a similar, and equally fruitless, attempt to procure more representation on the repatriation boards for the bitterenders.[82] In the Orange River Colony there was also dissatisfaction about these boards. Anonymous bitterenders from the Wepener district complained to E.F. Knight that the surrendered burghers on the boards "belonged to a class which they could no longer trust". The bitterenders also accused the surrendered burghers of favouritism. "My informants," wrote Knight, "also accused the Dutch ['handsupper'] Commissioners of favouring their own friends and snubbing other poor applicants for assistance."[83]

General J.C.G. Kemp had another complaint against the surrendered burghers and National Scouts on the repatriation boards. He singled out article 10 of the peace agreement, which laid down the broad parameters of repatriation, claiming that this article, by implication, made provision for bitterenders and former prisoners of war only. He thus saw it as his duty "to most strenuously protest against the ... action, that people who have willingly become subjects of a foreign Govt. in time of war, enlisted in that Govt.'s ranks as soldiers ... when their own Govt. was at war with this Foreign Govt., should have a right to be considered by a Commission formed out of the conditions of the Treaties of Peace between representatives of their former Govt. and their newly adopted Govt."[84] Kemp's protests fell on deaf ears and he promptly resigned his membership of the Krugersdorp repatriation board.[85] The administration also received complaints about this same matter from bitterenders in Braamfontein.⁸⁶ Even a British magistrate registered an objection against G.L. Vosloo, the National Scouts representative on the Middelburg board; according to him, Vosloo did not do his work properly.⁸⁷ However, all these complaints failed to have any impact on the composition of the repatriation boards.

Thus far, attention has been paid only to the repatriation of burghers who had fought on the British side. In contrast to these people, the surrendered burghers who had not participated actively in the British war effort received no special repatriation assistance at all. It can however be accepted that they would not have experienced many difficulties with repatriation in light of the fact that provision was made for them on the local boards.

By way of summary it can be concluded that, although the burghers who joined the British military initially feared that the civil administration would ignore their interests, the administration did indeed honour the promises made by the military authorities. Those who owned farms or land received special repatriation assistance to commence farming, while the unemployed who had no land were given a new start in civil society – an opportunity that because of their poor background they did not in every instance put to good use. Six months after the conclusion of peace, most of the National Scouts and their ilk had found a means of livelihood, but there were still a number of indigent people who needed assistance. The discussion will now turn to the assistance that was provided for these people.

2 Land settlement

Towards the end of October 1902 a correspondent of the London *Times* reported as follows on the activities of the special repatriation board in Pretoria: "When all the National Scouts who have farms to go to, either as owners, part owners or bywoners, shall have been repatriated, and as many as possible of the rest have been found employment in one way or another, it is reckoned that, a few of the hopelessly indolent being eliminated, there will still be some 400 indigent ex-burghers left on the hands of the organization."⁸⁸ Leggett accepted the placement of these National Scouts as his responsibility. His sympathetic interest in the National Scouts had its origin in his former military links with them and, according to Milner, after the war Leggett felt personally responsible for these people.[89] The governor regarded Leggett as an accomplished person, but felt that he had "inadequate experience in controlling the expenditure of money".[90]

Towards the end of 1902 Leggett initiated an ambitious scheme to assist those National Scouts for whom he had not yet been able to find a refuge where they could get back on their feet. "They had no money," said Leggett, "no means of obtaining security, and ... by reason of political estrangement are unable to find land on which to squat by leave of the landowners." Whereas Leggett had been able to organise employment in lowly capacities for the other impoverished National Scouts, these needy people were according to him unsuited for such posts, or they had chosen instead to try their hand at some type of farm labour. Four months after the conclusion of peace they were still in the concentration camps. Leggett divided this group of National Scouts into two categories: "(a) the deserving class, anxious to work on the land and whose misfortune it is our duty to repair both to the advantage of themselves and of the country as a whole, (b) the doubtful class, apparently lazy, and satisfied to remain in the Burgher Camp as long as they are fed by the Government."[91] On this latter category the following report appeared in an English newspaper in the Transvaal: "Life in the concentration camp is one prolonged loaf – an ideal state of existence to a 'bywoner'. To them the concentration camp is a palace of plenty."[92]

In order to offer this group of National Scouts a livelihood, Leggett set up five land settlement farms. These settlements were known as the Standerton Farmers' Association, Middelburg and Belfast Farmers' Association (situated between these two particular towns), North Pretoria Farmers' Association (about 56 km north-west of Pretoria), Vaal River Farmers' Association (situated between Heidelberg and Standerton) and the Potchefstroom and Klerksdorp Farmers' Association (between these two towns). The settlement that was established between Potchefstroom and Klerksdorp was the one with the largest area (145 square km). The smallest settlement farm (about 12 square km) was the one north of Pretoria. The settlement schemes were financed in part by the colonial government and partly by private undertakings. In the case of the settlement north of Pretoria a few wealthy National Scouts accepted a number of their less fortunate comrades as *bywoners* on their farms.[93] In the Orange River Colony similar settlements were established, but these were on a much smaller scale. The colonial government acquired nine different farms in total and made them available to about 65 impoverished ORC Volunteers. Piet de Wet was also prepared to employ a number of *bywoner* ORC Volunteers on his own farm.[94]

In a report to Chamberlain, Milner mentioned that some bitter-enders were unwilling to employ their pre-war quota of *bywoners*, particularly if these *bywoners* had fought on the British side during the war. "And even where they were taken back," he continued, "the ex-Military Bywoners found themselves unpleasantly situated and exposed to social ostracism." The settlement farms that Milner had sanctioned, in his view, had two advantages. On the one hand they would be a refuge for the poverty-stricken National Scouts who were being rejected by their fellow countrymen, and on the other it would be a worthy assistance project to give these unfortunate people some economic stability.[95]

Each settler received a farm of about half a square kilometre of arable land. Farming implements were supplied by the colonial government and private undertakings, and the new farmer undertook to pay back the price of these with interest. The settlers also had to hand over 50% of their yield to the government or to the private company concerned. Leggett, who was closely associated with the organisation of the settlement farms, described the scheme as "a combination of capital, brain, and muscle, in a truly co-operative and profit-sharing union".[96] In 1904 he provided a general overview of these settlements, or as he put it, "a bird's-eye view of any one of the groups of Settlement farms". His description, which perhaps painted a picture that was too idyllic, was as follows: "Fifty or sixty settlers' houses – huts in many cases, but nevertheless homes – dotted over the veld, three or four hundred yards from one another, ... or perhaps in small clusters around the farm dams. Below them the holdings or irrigated land in the valleys; above dry lands ploughed for the summer mealie crops; and behind these, against the wide expanse of unenclosed veld, is the common grazing ground ... It cannot be doubted," wrote Leggett in conclusion, "that these centres will grow in importance year by year and ... record the larger hopes for the future."[97]

Government schools were also opened on the settlements, but the school attendance and scholastic progress of the pupils left much to be desired. The resident magistrate at Standerton put this down primarily to "the low social and intellectual standard of the majority of the parents."[98] The low social level that these people occupied was also reflected in their mutual interaction. According to Leggett, stealing a fellow settler's implements was common practice. He also referred to another aspect of their social behaviour: "Another feature – also generally associated with the lowest stratum of the population in all countries – has been the comparative laxity in married life, wives leaving their husbands to live with other settlers, and vice versa."[99]

The National Scouts on these settlement farms received a visit in January 1903 from no less a figure than Chamberlain. As part of his tour through South Africa, the Colonial Secretary visited the settlements at Standerton and Potchefstroom-Klerksdorp. The welcome that Chamberlain received on these settlements was quite possibly the warmest that he experienced in the Transvaal. On his visit to the Standerton settlement farm on 4 January he was reportedly introduced to "an Ex-National Scout named Roets, with whom Mr Chamberlain shook hands cordially. Mr Roets then offered Mr Chamberlain an address on behalf of the National Scouts of the Colony on the farm Vlakfontein, expressing the gratitude of these burghers for what the new Government had done for them."[100] In Pretoria, where Chamberlain called four days later, he was confronted by the Boer generals – including Louis Botha, Schalk Burger, Christiaan de Wet, De la Rey and Smuts. They expressed their dissatisfaction with the British administration to Chamberlain in no uncertain terms.[101] In contrast to the Boer leaders' unequivocal criticism of the administration, on 23 January Chamberlain was greeted by a number of apparently satisfied and almost jingoistic National Scouts on the Potchefstroom-Klerksdorp settlement. At the entrance to the settlement they had hung a large banner that read "Welcome in our midst" and "Long live

Chamberlain". Union Jacks were flapping in the breeze and the tents that housed the National Scouts were draped with British flags.[102] When Chamberlain and his entourage, which included his wife, approached the settlement in their coach, they made a somewhat unconventional entrance. "Quantities of Boers met us on the borders of the farm and we drove under a triumphal arch of welcome, escorted by a cavalcade," wrote Mrs Chamberlain to her mother. "We drove on, and then fancy our astonishment, when we found them removing the horses and we made the final stage of the drive drawn by Boers, old and young, all smiling and waving and enthusiastic. Who could have foreseen that such a thing could ever happen to Joe and me?"[103] Andries Cronjé then thanked the colonial government for the assistance that had been provided for the National Scouts. In his reply to this Chamberlain said: "We do not wish and we do not intend to forget those who have been our friends, those who have at any time served us, who have helped to bring about the restoration of peace."[104]

Chamberlain's visits to the settlements, the reaction of the National Scouts there and his promise to them, create the distinct impression that the secretary of state attached great importance to the political loyalty of the National Scouts. But the truth was that the Scouts on the settlement farms had very little political value to the British.

The British did not regard the settlements as exclusive entities of political loyalty, nor did they see the National Scouts on the settlement farms as political allies against the bitterenders. This is verified by the fact that from January 1903 the administration also allowed needy bitterenders to settle there. "Applications poured in from Bywoners of every shade of political sympathy," said Milner, "and Major Leggett and his fellow workers wisely decided to make no distinctions, but to extend the system of these burgher settlements ... to embrace Bywoners of the 'wild' Boer class as well as 'ex-military burghers' and men who had surrendered and remained neutral."[105] According to Leggett the total number of National Scouts placed on all the settlement farms was about 400 men.[106] He did not provide a comparative total as such for the bitterenders, but he did confirm that by August 1903 they were in the majority on the farms and had been for some time.[107] If the British administration had entertained any political motives in the placement of the National Scouts on the settlements, it is to be doubted whether they would also have included the bitterenders in the scheme; by doing so they would have effectively scotched the idea of turning the settlements into loyal political entities. The administration might, of course, have argued that the National Scouts would exert a positive political influence on the bitterenders, but this does not appear to have been the case. Although the settlements were initially used to house National Scouts, the fact that the bitterenders were also involved later seems to indicate that the most important objective in creating these settlements was to give economic help to all impoverished Boers, irrespective of their political outlook.

This view of the negligible political role played by those National Scouts who were on the settlement farms is also apparent in the following example. Captain R.W. Morley, commander of Morley's Scouts during the war, approached Leggett at the beginning of 1903 to see what he felt about the idea of merging all the National Scouts on the settlements into a "Farmers' Association" with the "main object [being] to oppose any ... insurrectionary movement from any Party, ... such as the Bond". (Here he was presumably referring to the Afrikaner Bond in the Cape Colony, a movement that, according to him, could possibly spread it tentacles into the Transvaal – something that did not, in the event, take place.)[108] Morley was convinced that "we should secure a great number of names, which would have an influence in politics". But Leggett simply ignored this suggestion.[109]

Other evidence gives more weight to this particular opinion. Captain T.S. Allison, who was a staff officer of the National Scouts during the war, and was appointed as manager of the Standerton settlement after peace was declared, had poured so much of his own capital into the settlement when it was set up that in 1904 he was on the verge of bankruptcy. He then went to the colonial government to seek financial assistance. Patrick Duncan, the treasurer, would not agree to help and informed him "that as the Assocation and Captain Allison have made their bed, so they must lie on it". Allison was furious. He threatened that if he did not get financial aid he would inform the National Scouts that it was thanks to him (he alleged) that they had been settled there and that the colonial government had given no assistance at all. Allison also claimed "that if asked what were the promises made to the Scouts, in the name of the Imperial Government, during the War, I will reply to such questions very differently to the sense of all that has been said officially since the Peace". Leggett told Milner about Allison's threats and also informed him that Allison wielded so much influence over the National Scouts that he might well be able to colour their attitude towards the British in a negative way. "I do not regard the Scouts as reliable or as individually important," Leggett continued, "but I do feel that an overt influencing of these people into the opposite Camp would have serious consequences, and they would perhaps be more bitter than any other section." In his reply Milner was unequivocal that the National Scouts did not, as far as he was concerned, have any political clout at all: "In my opinion the bywoner class, whether on or off the Settlements, and whether 'National Scouts' or 'handsoppers' or 'bitterenders' will ultimately fall into line with the general Boer Nationalist movement. I absolutely put aside all political consideration in this case." Milner was more concerned about the "promises made to the 'scouts', which influence me, I own, more than any conjectural estimate of the political value of the 'Scouts', which I believe to be *nil*". Milner did, however, recommend that Allison should be given financial assistance; but only because the government had also invested a substantial amount of money in the settlement and Milner saw it as "a piece of Repatriation work" that held some promise.[110]

Milner was to be disappointed in his hopes that the settlements would show economic viability as repatriation projects. By the latter half of 1904 it had become clear that the settlers were unable to make a living on their designated land. In August 1904 Leggett reported that the majority of the settlers did not even produce enough food for their own consumption. He put this down to the drought and the laxity of the settlers.[111] Leggett himself was not without blame either; in September 1905 Milner pointed out that his financial administration of the settlement farms left a great deal to be desired.[112]

Then too, the private undertakings that had a stake in the settlements also left the settlers in the lurch. This was particularly so in the case of the Potchefstroom-Klerksdorp settlement in which the African Agricultural and Finance Corporation Limited had a large holding. Even in the initial stages of the scheme, L. Hess, the editor of *The Transvaal Critic*, had expressed serious doubts about the integrity of the director of this syndicate, W. Carliss. Hess regarded him as a person with the "most questionable antecedents". He pointed out: "Mr Carliss seems chiefly to have profited by the exceptional gullibility and pliancy of a Government infatuated with belief in its own business capacity ... He turns out the most colossal and complicated schemes with all the fluency and ease with which Abbé Siéyes turned out constitutions for the First French Revolutions, and to little more profit to himself or any one. These settlement schemes of his are foredoomed to failure simply because he has mistaken his people. The Afrikaner is even more unlike a Russian serf than is a Britisher, and it would be only where Russian serfdom was possible, that these schemes would be possible also."[113]

Hess's worst fears were realised. In July 1903, on behalf of the Potchefstroom-Klerksdorp settlers, L. Wahl expressed his concern about the lack of progress on the settlement. He complained: "The Syndicate is very behind hand with all their promises and that up to date only three houses are nearing completion; the settlement cannot obtain implements and have to purchase themselves." According to Wahl, "the whole settlement [was] very disheartened."[114] Many of the settlers left their land during 1904 and in April 1905 the African Agricultural and Finance Corporation Limited was declared bankrupt.[115] A similar fate befell other Transvaal settlements. By May 1907 there were only 20 National Scouts still on the settlement farms. The others had all gone elsewhere to seek a livelihood as transport riders or labourers.[116] In the Orange River Colony things were not a great deal better. At the beginning of 1907 the secretary of the Land Board reported that, although the "late Burgher Scouts" had been given good agricultural land, "the management was ... unsatisfactory from the start and ... the Association was forced ... into liquidation." On the eventual fate of these settlers he commented that "they have all obtained employment elsewhere as bywoners, to which class they originally belonged."[117]

The poor management and financial breakdown of these settlements made some of the National Scouts resentful. For example, A.B.

Pickard, a former National Scout officer who had lost a substantial amount of money in the Potchefstroom-Klerksdorp settlement, wrote to Leggett: "I regret very much that for the services I have rendered the Government since the start of the National Scouts, I should be thanked in this manner ... I feel very sore under the treatment I have received." Andries Cronjé also lost money in the undertaking.[118] It is clear that the British political detachment from the National Scouts on the settlements, the economic failure of the scheme and the dissatisfaction of people like Pickard all played a role in the breakdown of any solidarity the collaborators might have had as an independent group. It also meant, of course, that in the political arena they were more easily integrated into Afrikaner ranks.[119] This integration did not, however, take place overnight. Bitter feelings were still very prevalent between the two groups and the compensation issue, which is discussed in the next section, was to aggravate this antagonism even more.

3 Compensation

In terms of article 10 of the peace agreement, Britain undertook to make £3 000 000 available for the repatriation of the republican *volk*. In the same article provision was made for the payment of British military receipts and republican promissory notes. Loans would also be granted at an interest of 3% (repayable after two years) to all residents of the two former republics – excluding foreigners and rebels.[120] Although this article did not appear at first glance to hold any ambiguities, both the British and the Boers attached different interpretations to it. For example, the Boers saw it as compensation for war losses, while the British were more inclined to interpret it in the sense of repatriation assistance.[121]

For the purposes of this study the most important controversy revolves around the interpretation of the word "*volk*" in article 10. The surrendered burghers and burghers who had entered British military service were not involved in the peace negotiations and they thus had no voice in the formulation of the peace terms.[122] On the basis of this the Boer leaders presumed that the surrendered burghers and National Scouts would not have a share in the £3 000 000. On 29 July, just prior to the departure of the Boer deputation from Cape Town to Britain and Europe, Botha wrote to Milner about this issue. Botha did not regard the surrendered burghers and National Scouts as part of the *volk*, on behalf of whom the peace agreement had been signed. In his view the word *"volk"* in article 10 referred only to the bitterenders and those Boers who had been prisoners of war,[123] and by implication it can be accepted that Botha also included the widows whose husbands had been killed in the war. Milner, however, placed a far wider interpretation on this particular article. With reference to Botha's letter he wrote to Chamberlain: "I give to this statement the most unqualified denial ... It is plainly quite contrary to the language of clause 10 which, while it might easily be stretched to cover other inhabitants of the two Republics besides burghers, cannot possibly be twisted so as to exclude any class of burghers. The words are 'the people'. To contend that the expression 'the people' means half the people is preposterous." In closing, Milner also warned Chamberlain: "If Botha makes any statement in England of this kind I hope he will be informed that I flatly deny his assertions."[124]

Botha did indeed raise this issue in an interview with Chamberlain on 11 November 1902. Chamberlain maintained that the political attitude of the National Scouts and surrendered burghers was immaterial and that they were part and parcel of the "people". Botha replied that the National Scouts, by entering British service as soldiers, had already aligned themselves with the British. According to Botha, Chamberlain's interpretation would mean that the British troops would theoretically also qualify for a share of the £3 000 000. Chamberlain retorted that the British soldiers were certainly not part of the "people" and that it was essential that the National Scouts, like the other members of the republican *volk*, also be given financial assistance. The argument did not end there. Botha went on to insist that he did not want to be prejudicial to the National Scouts, but that they already enjoyed many privileges over the bitterenders. To this Chamberlain simply replied that this was merely the way the war had turned out – as far as the National Scouts were concerned it had been a risk to elect to fight on the British side, and in view of the fact that the British were the victors, the National Scouts were fortunate enough to reap the benefits of this victory.[125]

It is clear that Botha and Chamberlain each had their own interpretation of article 10. Because the word "*volk*" was not qualified in the article, it is difficult to reach a conclusive answer on the controversy. On the one hand Botha was indeed correct in saying that the National Scouts had made their own agreement with the British and had not been involved as part of the *volk* when the agreement was compiled.[126] On the other hand, it must be remembered that right up until just before the Peace of Vereeniging the bitterenders treated the National Scouts as a part of the *volk* who owed allegiance to the republics. They were, for example, not regarded as British prisoners of war when they were captured, but as members of the *volk* who had committed treason.[127] However, at the peace talks the Boer leaders certainly did not regard the National Scouts as part of the *volk*, on whose behalf they had negotiated. In the light of this, their specific interpretation of article 10 of the peace terms does carry more weight. As far as the British interpretation of the article is concerned, it appears that they realised too late that there were loopholes in the wording that was used. They were cornered and were obliged to place as wide an interpretation as possible on the word "*volk*" so that the National Scouts would not be left out in the cold.

Some of the burghers who had fought on the British side were afraid that because of the wording of article 10 they would not be given a share of the £3 000 000. In the Orange River Colony Captain H.M.R. Brett claimed on behalf of 26 burghers in his corps that they had just as much right to compensation as did the bitterenders.[128]

Some surrendered burghers did not only claim a share of the £3 000 000, but were even under the impression that they were entitled to more compensation than the bitterenders. In the Orange River Colony, E.F. Knight reported that certain surrendered burghers claimed "that as they were guaranteed protection by Lord Roberts's proclamation, and acted faithfully in accordance with it, they are entitled to some special compensation for their losses. They ... consider – and they feel very strongly on the matter – that they should be put on a different footing from those who now throw it in their faces that after all the 'handsuppers' are not better off than those who went out on commando. It is claimed that these men should receive compensation before any distribution is made among the Boers." Knight considered it important to try to meet these people halfway: "There is no doubt that our neglect to act with justice in this case would rankle deeply in the minds of these people, and would be quoted all over the country, and for years to come, by our enemies, as yet another instance of Great Britain's breach of faith. It is a very old tradition in South Africa that Great Britain's pledges cannot be trusted."[129] In the Transvaal H.C. Marais, a surrendered burgher from Pretoria, alleged that there was a similar attitude among the surrendered burghers in the district. According to him they were angry because both the British and the Boers had driven off their livestock during the war and it now looked as if they were not going to receive any compensation. In an injured tone he wrote: "Ask any man in Pretoria who laid down arms under Lord Roberts's proclamation ... and who owned horses or stock what treatment he experienced. You will be surprised to hear the accumulated fund of bitterness that is still existing and how valuable horses and mules were seized three times in succession."[130]

During Chamberlain's visit to South Africa a deputation of surrendered burghers and burghers who had fought for the British made a point of discussing this matter with the Colonial Secretary and Milner on 14 January 1903. Andries Cronjé, W.J. Steyn (who had been a member of the central peace committee in Pretoria during the war) and J.H. Voss (a surrendered burgher who had been appointed by the British as magistrate in Klerksdorp in 1900) represented the Transvaal surrendered burghers and National Scouts. For the Orange River Colony Piet de Wet and S.G. Vilonel acted as spokesmen. The well-known Revd S.J. du Toit, who had a great deal of sympathy for the surrendered burghers and National Scouts, also took part in the interview. Andries Cronjé was the first to speak. According to him the surrendered burghers and National Scouts were particularly dissatisfied because the promises of compensation that had been made to them had not yet been met and now it appeared that the peace terms at Vereeniging excluded them from compensation. "At the present time," he continued, "those who had stood out to the last against the British Government were laughing at the men whom he represented, and saying that it would have been better for them if they also had fought to the last and shared in the terms which the Boer Generals had secured at Vereeniging." W.J. Steyn supported Cronjé on this point. The next speaker, Piet de Wet, did not address the matter of article 10 of the peace terms as such. On behalf of his group he appealed "that they should be treated in the matter of compensation not like the Boers who had surrendered last, as they did not want to come under Article 10 of the Terms of Surrender. They had nothing to do with the Terms of Surrender. They stood upon their rights and previous promises of the British Government. With them it was a question of principle rather than of money. What they claimed from the British Government was a claim of right and justice, and not of gratuity and of grace. They had a moral claim which the other party had not; yet the other party came to them and said: 'We had to make terms for you.'" S.G. Vilonel also made the following point as far as compensation was concerned: "They relied upon the proclamations which were issued by the highest Military Authority." Revd S.J. du Toit spoke on behalf of the "loyal Dutch" in the Cape Colony and expressed the hope that Chamberlain would also grant them an interview.

Chamberlain assured the delegation that they would indeed be included in the compensation process and that the promises that had been made by the military would, as far as possible, be honoured. He then went on to say that "those who came in early and stood by the British, would be better off than those who fought to the end. The British were grateful to them for their services in the cause of Peace, and it was desirable that it should be recognised that it was not a bad thing to stand on the side of the British Government, and that it did not forget its friends." Milner also conceded that they had a moral right to compensation – "based on the promises of the British Military Authorities" – and that it was desirable to honour these promises.[131] About three weeks after the interview Chamberlain repeated his promise of compensation at Bloemfontein.[132] Chamberlain's assurances apparently satisfied the collaborators and according to E.F. Knight, "the 'hands-uppers' regarded him as their saviour".[133]

Chamberlain kept his promise. The surrendered burghers not only had a share of the £3 000 000, but a special fund of £4 500 000 (the

Protected Burgher Fund, that was initially known as the Military Compensation Fund) was also established for them. The funds were administered by the Central Judicial Commission that controlled all the compensation funds. "It was urged on behalf of these classes," reads a report compiled by the commission, "that they had rendered services which merited recognition beyond the relief mentioned in Article X to which relief all ex-Burghers were, in the terms of Article X, equally entitled." As justification for the surrendered burghers being entitled to a share of two funds (£3 million and £4,5 million) it was maintained that: "Many of those allowed to rank as Protected ex-Burghers had suffered losses before they became entitled to rank as Protected ex-Burghers. Thus their losses were: (1) As ex-Burghers, (2) As Protected ex-Burghers. The first were allowed against the ex-Burgher Fund. The second were allowed against the protected ex-Burgher Fund."[134] The surrendered burghers thus enjoyed a double advantage from the compensation process.

As far as can be established there is no evidence that the Protected Burgher Fund was set up for political motives. According to Goold-Adams it owed its origin primarily to the efforts of Chamberlain and "the money was given on his recommendation by the Imperial Government as an act of grace to redeem certain undefined pledges made in the Proclamations".[135] In essence these "undefined pledges" came down to the fact that in his proclamations Roberts had promised the surrendered burghers protection of their property – a promise that had not been kept during the war.[136] It seems likely that the Protected Burgher Fund was established purely to honour the promises that had been made to the surrendered burghers.

Burghers who had been active during the war in British military service were given an even better deal. In addition to the fact that they were entitled to a share of both the funds mentioned above, they could also submit their claims to a special fund of £2 000 000 (that was established for British subjects, neutral foreigners and black people).[137]

This dispensation certainly favoured the surrendered burghers and British military burghers above the bitterenders who could only share in the £3 000 000. L. Hess of *The Transvaal Critic* commented on this issue: "The case of the National Scouts is an interesting one, chiefly because it seems extraordinary that it should have escaped notice that if the services of these men were accepted on special promises, special compensation would necessarily have to be given to them. It now appears that compensation to them will add another enormous amount to the general bill of costs."[138] The British authority was indeed under a moral obligation to honour its obligations to the surrendered burghers and British military burghers on the basis of the promises made by the military authority, but it cannot be considered reasonable that these people were compensated so far out of proportion in comparison to the bitterenders. As the editor of *The Friend* so rightly remarked: "We can quite see that Mr Piet de Wet and his section are entitled to compensation if they surrendered under Lord Roberts' proclamation, the terms of which, ... were in many cases not carried out, and he has every right to ask that the contract should be fulfilled." But he adds, "where are the rights of those men who had surrendered last, and are now just as much entitled to the privileges of a British citizen as Mr Piet de Wet? Why should they be treated on a different footing?" In a carefully worded protest he then goes on to say: "We certainly do not want to see the Christiaan de Wet man get more compensation than the other individual. They should both be treated on the same basis, both on the lines that they are now all British subjects and come into the Empire on an equal footing, no matter what they did ... during the war. The British Government have made many mistakes in South Africa, of which the raising of the National Scouts was not the least, and it appears they are going to add another grave one."[139] The government's compensation policy was ill-advised in the sense that it made the bitterenders even more antagonistic towards the new government. In order to prevent a loss of faith in the British promises the administration went too far overboard and in so doing they alienated the bitterenders even more. Furthermore it contributed nothing towards making the bitterenders more forgiving towards their disloyal countrymen. "This was statesmanship at its weakest", in the words of a historian who commented on the compensation paid to the bitterenders.[140]

With the payment of compensation claims the Central Judicial Commission found it very difficult to determine exactly who was a surrendered burgher and who was not. This problem existed because some burghers had laid down their arms only to rejoin the commandos a short while later.¹⁴¹ There were also people who in truth took no part in the war at all, giving themselves over to the British troops at the very first opportunity. Ironically enough, these people, unless they surrendered specifically in reaction to a British proclamation, were denied access to the Protected Burgher Fund. The Central Judicial Commission reasoned that because these people had never joined the commandos, their withdrawal from the war did not weaken the republican army. Goold-Adams was aware that "many instances of ... hardship will ensue from the strict observance of this principle, but I fear that there is no intention on the part of the Central Judicial Commission from departing from it".¹⁴² By March 1903 it was laid down that the burghers who had fought in the war and could prove that they had surrendered voluntarily because of a British proclamation and had not subsequently rejoined the commandos, would for the purposes of compensation, be regarded as surrendered burghers.¹⁴³

Compensation officials experienced problems with the execution of this provision. In November 1903 it was reported from the Bethlehem district that there was great confusion over which people were entitled to claim from the various funds.¹⁴⁴ "Confusion was consistently compounded," writes Denoon. "For one thing, it proved impossible to distinguish clearly between the various sums involved. Some applicants could claim under ... theoretically distinct headings, since their status had changed from *bittereinder* to *hensopper* (or vice versa) during the war. The bureaucratic solution for confusion was to issue more instructions, advice and notices to the officers in charge of distribution."¹⁴⁵

This confusion caused delays in the payment of the compensation claims to the surrendered burghers, but their claims were still paid out before those of the bitterenders. The first surrendered burghers received their money on 13 May 1903 at Pietersburg.¹⁴⁶ In comparison to this, the bitterenders in the Orange River Colony had to wait for more than two years before their first claims were paid in October 1905.¹⁴⁷

In the entire Transvaal a total of £736 979 was paid out as compensation to surrendered burghers. In the Orange River Colony the amount was £1 157 976. Because the surrendered burghers could claim from two different funds they naturally received more compensation than the bitterenders. Generally speaking the surrendered burghers received about 10s 0d in the pound for their estimated claims. In contrast, the bitterenders were eventually allowed about 2s 0d in the pound. Furthermore, the bitterenders' repatriation debt was also subtracted from their compensation claims.[148]

The burghers who joined the British military fared even better financially than the surrendered burghers and the bitterenders. On 23 January 1904 the magistrate in Pietersburg reported as follows on the payment of compensation claims to the various groups: "1. The National Scout has been treated well as regards compensation – even it might be said liberally. 2. The ex-burgher who surrendered and kept neutral has also been paid out well for his losses. 3. The man who stayed in the field to the end has at present received nothing except aid from the Repatriation."[149] British military burghers who experienced problems with compensation could also count on their former British officers coming to their rescue. One such case was P.J. Botha of Bloemfontein who had served as a British intelligence agent during the war. He was hesitant to appear before the local board "as one of the members of this Board is Ex-Commdt. Andries Bester, and naturally he is averse to state the part he had played in the Campaign". However, Colonel D. Henderson, the head of the British military intelligence service during the war, glossed over Botha's role so that he did not have to appear before the board and he duly received £400 of his claim of £572.[150] In the light of the generous manner in which these people were treated it is not surprising that Johanna Brandt could allege that a few National Scouts who were poor people before the war received so much from the British that after the war they were known as *"zak patriotten"* (pocket patriots).[151] It is doubtful, however, whether this was generally the case.

Despite the fact that the surrendered burghers were given comparatively better treatment, there was still widespread dissatisfaction in their ranks about the compensation issue; like the bitterenders, many of them were angry. After the payments had been made to the surrendered burghers in the Rustenburg district on 30 and 31 May 1904, the magistrate reported: "There was considerable dissatisfaction expressed amongst the protected burghers at the amount received ..."[152] In other parts of the Transvaal there were similar grievances about the payment of compensation claims,[153] In the Orange River Colony too, many surrendered burghers also felt that they had been sold down the river.[154]

The dissatisfaction of the surrendered burghers over compensation can be ascribed to a number of different factors. In the first place, the compensation officials were sometimes not careful enough when they investigated the claims submitted by the surrendered burghers. A number of cases came to light where a person who was a surrendered burgher was incorrectly classified as a bitterender and the claim was paid out accordingly.[155] Linked to this, the way some of the compensation officials behaved towards the surrendered burghers left much to be desired. This was particularly so in the case of Major I.M. McInnery who, as vice-chairman of the Central Judicial Commission, personally controlled some of the payments to the surrendered burghers.[156] Milner described McInnery as "a great big bullying Australian, who would make even an agreeable duty unacceptable by his method of discharging it, but perfectly fearless in the discharge of his duty".[157] McInnery sometimes showed some of his rough character traits in his dealings with the surrendered burghers. In Vrede a claimant who apparently had good reason to be unhappy with the compensation he had received was simply chased out of McInnery's office.[158]

A second reason for dissatisfaction was expressed by those surrendered burghers who acted on Roberts's proclamations of 15 March and 31 May 1900. These proclamations promised surrendered burghers that their property would be protected.[159] In the Ermelo district two surrendered burghers, A. Boshoff and N. Lombard, expected that their claims would be paid out in full because they had laid down their arms in reaction to Roberts's proclamations. They were soon disillusioned. Boshoff received only £1800 for his claim of £9000 and Lombard £450 for his claim of £1800. Boshoff refused to accept similar payments, while Lombard reckoned that "half an egg is better than an empty shell". Other surrendered burghers in the district followed Boshoff's example and refused to accept the payments. A reporter from *De Volksstem* remarked correctly that the surrendered burghers were busy reaping the bitter fruits of the "Comedy of Proclamations".[160] In the Orange River Colony Goold-Adams mentioned in a report on the surrendered burghers' dissatisfaction that "it is the generally accepted idea amongst those who surrendered under Proclamations ... that a guarantee of absolute protection for all property was given, and that it was not in any way qualified by the proviso that the Government would protect them 'as far as compatible with the successful operations of the war' ... This being the case, it can be easily imagined that there is a feeling amongst many of the claimants that they are justified in asking for everything they have lost, and they consequently feel aggrieved because they have not been treated in this manner." According to Goold-Adams this dissatisfaction was not always justified because the surrendered burghers did not take full account of the precondition that their property would only be protected in as far as military operations allowed.[161] It must however be mentioned that only Roberts's proclamations of 31 May and 6 June 1900 to the residents of the Transvaal included this precondition. In the proclamations of 15 March 1900 to the Free Staters, no such precondition is mentioned.[162] On this basis the surrendered burghers in the Orange River Colony thus had a valid argument. Because Roberts's proclamation to the residents of the Transvaal did indeed include the relevant precondition, they had less cause for complaint. But it must be kept in mind that after the occupation of Johannesburg and Pretoria, the surrendered burghers, on the basis of the British promises, were under the distinct impression that the war was over and that their property was absolutely safe.[163] Be that as it may, most surrendered burghers expected, in the light of Roberts's proclamations, that they would be well compensated for the damage that they had suffered during the war. When they realised that their high hopes were to be dashed, they claimed that the British had not kept their promises.

A third reason for the dissatisfaction of the surrendered burghers also lies in Roberts's proclamations. On 14 August 1900 Roberts withdrew the proclamations under which republican burghers could lay down their weapons and swear an oath of neutrality. (The most important reason for this step was that some of the surrendered burghers had rejoined the commandos.) However, in practice many burghers still continued to lay down their arms – something that Roberts naturally encouraged. On 22 September 1900 Roberts then also altered his proclamation of 14 August, laying down uniform measures for the treatment of all surrendered burghers regardless of the date on which they laid down their arms.[164] A few compensation officials took the view that Roberts had withdrawn his proclamations on the oath of neutrality on 14 August so that people who surrendered after this date could not claim to have withdrawn in reaction to Roberts's proclamations. The fact that Roberts had changed his policy on 22 September 1900 was not taken into consideration by these compensation officials. On the surrendered burghers' reaction to this Goold-Adams commented: "I do not think that many of the claimants interpret it in such a manner. I know that claims have been made by persons who surrendered after that date [14th August] which have been thrown out, greatly to their annoyance."[165] The surrendered burghers who were treated in this manner clearly had very good reason to complain.

Fourthly, some surrendered burghers who had taken the oath of allegiance during the war, and had thereby become British citizens, felt that they should also be entitled to compensation as British citizens. However, the Central Judicial Commission laid down that unless persons had played an active role in combat on the British side, they could not claim from the £2 000 000 fund that had been set aside for British citizens. "There are again cases of grievance due to a misunderstanding of the circumstances under which the special fund of two millions was given," explained Goold-Adams.[166] As far as the dissatisfaction of these people was concerned Milner felt obliged to say: "Compensation has, on the whole, been rather a curse than a blessing. You give a man a pound, and he hates you for it, because he asked for four and expected two, and all his neighbours, who have not got anything hate you equally."[167]

The fifth and final reason for the dissatisfaction was that, as has been mentioned, people who had not been on commando were excluded from a share in the Protected Burgher Fund. Goold-Adams sketched their position as follows: "It is a fact that, during the occupation of this country by our troops, many persons were found residing in their homes who, as burghers were liable to be called out, and were in possession of arms. These surrendered, believing that in doing so they were conforming to the conditions laid down in the

Proclamations, yet, owing to the fact that they had never taken an active part against us, these persons have been debarred from getting compensation from the Protected Burgher funds. They consequently consider that they have been unjustly dealt with."[168]

The dissatisfaction in the ranks of surrendered burghers reached such a pitch, and according to Goold-Adams some of these men had valid complaints, that he thought it wise to re-examine the claims submitted by these people.[169] Milner was very opposed to this idea: "[T]o reopen these questions would be little short of a disaster," he wrote in March 1905.[170] The new governor, Lord Selborne, also spoke out against such a step in August 1905.[171] About a year later a commission headed by Sir John West Ridgeway investigated circumstances in the two colonies prior to the granting of self-government, and consulted Piet de Wet for his opinion on this. In October 1906 De Wet said that he felt the matter should be dropped: "I don't think it is advisable to reopen this 'grievance' again, because by so doing the dissatisfaction which has almost died away, will appear with renewed strength."[172] The outcome was that no further steps were taken to satisfy the aggrieved surrendered burghers.

The whole issue of compensation paid to the surrendered burghers had an important influence on the mutual relationship between the bitterenders and the surrendered burghers. It worked like a double-edged sword. Initially the two groups were estranged because the surrendered burghers were favoured to a considerable extent in the payment of compensation.[173] However, it appears that although they received more than the bitterenders, they too were dissatisfied. The grievances of the surrendered burghers on the manner in which their claims were handled gave rise to a common grievance with the bitterenders. This tended to bring the two groups somewhat closer together, and at the Brandfort congress in December 1904 this in fact proved to be an important unifying factor.[174] Before this could occur, however, the surrendered burghers, particularly those who had fought on the British side, had to survive a period of social ostracism.

The tensions between the surrendered burghers and the British military burghers on the one hand, and the bitterenders on the other, and how these eventually came to a head in the religious sphere are discussed in the next chapter.

Notes

1 H.W. Nevinson, *Changes and Chances*, pp. 322–3.
2 Magistrate Louis Trichardt, Civil Case 181/1930, J.J. Steyn vs G. Lyon, evidence of J.H. Joubert, September 1930, pp. 10, 57; KK Supplementary items, 3, report on Meintjeskop camp, June 1902.
3 *The Star*, 12 June 1902 (news report); see also *The Bloemfontein Post*, 12 June 1902 (news report).
4 A. Richmond, *Twenty-Six Years, 1879–1905*, p. 192.
5 Knight, p. 209.
6 CSO 127/2443/02, P.D. Schutte and 30 others – Leggett, July 1902 (the exact date is not given in the letter) and Leggett – Goold-Adams, 12 July 1902.
7 CSO 135/2815/02, J.H. Vivier and 38 others – Goold-Adams, 24 July 1902; CSO 138/2961/02, P.H. Botha and 19 others – Goold-Adams, 2 August 1902; CSO 157/3905/02, J.F. Bester and 12 others – Goold-Adams, 18 September 1902.
8 CSO 139/3001/02, "Memorandum to the Central Repatriation Board", Bloemfontein, 7 August 1902.
9 CS 282/3762, Rademeyer and De Beer – Colonial Secretary, 7 April 1903. The names of the 50 National Scouts are attached to this same letter.
10 CS 1078/71, Resident magistrate Krugersdorp – Davidson, 12 August 1902.
11 PMO 16/1167, H.W.J. van der Brugge – Captain W. Bonham, 22 September 1902.
12 GOV 624/391, Blakemore – Leggett, 4 January 1903.
13 *Times History*, VI, p. 53.
14 Milner Papers, 19, (FK 1135, pp. 354–5), 10 August 1902. Headlam, II, p. 376, in his version of this letter, left out this sentence.
15 On Milner's policy of anglicisation see Van Rensburg, "Ekonomiese Herstel", pp. 186–7, 204–6; C.P. Jamneck, "Die Milner-regime in Transvaal 1902–1905" (Unpublished MA dissertation, Unisa), 1947, pp. 1–7, 63–72, 74–101; M.A. Basson, "Die Britse invloed in die Transvaalse onderwys, 1836–1907" in *Archives Yearbook for South African History*, 19 (II), 1956, pp. 136–8.
16 See Chapter 5, section 1 and Chapter 6, section 1 above.
17 Translated from the Afrikaans. L. Rousseau, *Die Groot Verlange: Die Verhaal van Eugène N. Marais*, p. 169. *Land en Volk* received a subsidy of £2000 per year from the British administration. See CT 290/3, Secretary of the Treasury – Lieutenant-governor, 15 January 1904.
18 Milner Papers, 105, (FK 1194, pp. 327–8), 27 September 1905.
19 Preller, "Die National Scouts" in *Die Burger*, 1 July 1926.
20 Beak, p. 67.
21 See Chapter 6, section 1 above.
22 See Van Rensburg, "Ekonomiese Herstel", p. 272.
23 See Chapter 7, section 3 above.
24 *Times History*, VI, p. 53.
25 For the number of burghers who fought on the British side see Chapter 5, section 1 above, and for the number of republican prisoners of war and bitterenders, see *Official History*, IV, pp. 704–5, annexures. Botha put the total number of bitterenders and prisoners of war at 55 000 men. Cd. 1284, p. 20, interview with Chamberlain, 5 September 1902.

26 GOV 668/17, Milner – Leggett, 2 July 1904; Milner Papers, 105, (FK 1194, p. 328), Milner – Selborne, 27 September 1905.
27 CSO 139/3001/02 "Memorandum to the Central Repatriation Board", Bloemfontein, 7 August 1902.
28 CO 291/43 (FK 977, pp. 311–12) "Intermediate Report", 15 September 1902; *The Times*, 21 October 1902 (news report); GOV 827/17, Leggett – Director "Government Relief O.R.C.", 8 February 1904 (copy); Beak, p. 66.
29 GOV 827/17, Leggett – Director "Government Relief O.R.C.", 8 February 1904 (copy).
30 GOV 495/129, "Report on Volunteer Repatriation O.R.C.", 26 February 1904 (copy); Cd. 1551, pp. 60–64; Beak, p. 66; Van Rensburg, "Ekonomiese Herstel", p. 240.
31 For discussion on the problems that faced the bitterenders and former prisoners of war, see Van Rensburg, "Ekonomiese Herstel", pp. 280–7; J.C.G. Kemp, *Die Pad van die Veroweraar*, pp. 82–8.
32 *Africa (South)*, 853, p. 28, report of the West Ridgeway Commission, 30 July 1906.
33 Van Rensburg, "Ekonomiese Herstel", pp. 289.
34 *The Star*, 17 September 1902 (news report).
35 *Land en Volk*, 26 September 1902 (news report).
36 GOV 255/20, S.J. Thompson – Buchan, 25 September 1902.
37 CO 291/43 (FK 977, p. 313), "Intermediate Report", 15 September 1902; GOV 495/129, "Report on Volunteer Repatriation O.R.C.", 26 February 1903.
38 CS 99/6063, Leggett – Davidson, 7 July 1902.
39 CSO 138/2963/02, Leggett – Goold-Adams, 4 August 1902.
40 Milner Papers, 19, (FK 1135, pp. 356–7), 10 August 1902.
41 CS 246/1667, Davidson – Leggett, 11 September 1902 and Leggett – Davidson, 17 September 1902 and undated margin notes by Davidson.
42 CS 134/10538, Resident magistrate Pietersburg – Davidson, 3 September 1902; CS 135/10703, Resident magistrate Pietersburg – Davidson, 5 September 1902. In the light of this, Denoon is incorrect in saying, without acceptable evidence, that "National Scouts were ignored ... completely in the economic sphere ... Neither transport nor arms were given." Denoon, *Grand Illusion*, p. 81.
43 Knight, pp. 244–5.
44 GOV 624/391, Blakemore – Leggett, 4 January 1903.
45 Beak, p. 67.
46 GOV 625/372, "Summary of the proceedings of a deputation which met Mr. Chamberlain at Sunnyside", 14 January 1903.
47 Jamneck, p. 77.
48 *The Friend*, 24 January 1903 (editorial).
49 CO 291/43 (FK 977, p. 314), "Intermediate Report", 15 September 1902.
50 GOV 624/391, "Second Intermediate Report on Resettlement of National Scouts, ORC Volunteers and Ex-Military Burghers", 31 December 1902 (hereafter "Second Intermediate Report").
51 MGP 173/1586/01, Beddy – Maxwell, 18 November 1901. On Beddy's corps see Chapter 5, section 4 above.
52 CO 291/40/29793 (FK 962, p. 261), Milner – Chamberlain, 21 July 1902.

53 CO 291/43 (FK 977, pp. 314–15), "Intermediate Report", 15 September 1902.
54 Van Rensburg, "Ekonomiese Herstel", p. 193.
55 CO 291/43 (FK 977, p. 315), "Intermediate Report", 15 September 1902; *The Star*, 4 August 1902 (news report); *The Bloemfontein Post*, 5 August 1902 (news report).
56 Cd. 1551, p. 196, report by Major-general R.S.S. Baden-Powell, December 1902. See also CSO 115/1839/02, Baden-Powell – Colonel Pilkington, 19 July and 15 September 1902.
57 GOV 624/391, "Second Intermediate Report", 31 December 1902.
58 HC 2/45, Leggett – Colonel W. Lambton, 15 December 1902.
59 SAC Papers, 11, "Records of Conduct and Service".
60 CSO 114/1776/02, Pilkington – Goold-Adams, 11 July 1902 and Vilonel – Blakemore, 15 July 1902 and Pilkington – Goold-Adams, 17 July 1902.
61 EC 67/142/03, confidential report of resident magistrate Pretoria, 10 February 1903.
62 *Report of the South African Constabulary Commission 1905, with Minutes of Proceedings, Minutes of Evidence and Annexures*, p. 305, Item 2773, 28 August 1905.
63 CSO 114/1776/02, 11 July 1902.
64 *Report of the South African Constabulary Commission 1905, with Minutes of Proceedings, Minutes of Evidence and Annexures*, p. 305, Items 2770–2772, 28 August 1905.
65 CO 291/43 (FK 977, p. 315), "Intermediate Report", 15 September 1902.
66 GOV 629/401, "Somaliland Campaign", 1902–1903; *The Bloemfontein Post*, 4 November 1902 and 13 January 1903 (news reports).
67 I.M. Lewis, The Modern History of Somaliland, pp. 63–85; Encyclopedia Brittanica, 20, p. 967.
68 HC 2/45, Leggett – Colonel J.S. Nicholson, 19 December 1902.
69 *Government Gazette, Transvaal Colony*, 5 September 1902. Appointments in the Legislative Council that cannot be regarded as administrative appointments as such are discussed in Chapter 10, section 1.
70 GOV 615/372, "Summary of the proceedings of a deputation which met Mr. Chamberlain at Sunnyside", 14 January 1903.
71 Translated from the Dutch. *Land en Volk*, 24 April 1903 (letter from a burgher in Carolina).
72 Cd. 988, p. 30, report by Major-general W. Kitchener, 14 June 1902.
73 Government Gazette, Transvaal Colony, 18 July and 1 August 1902.
74 J. Ramsay Macdonald, *Wat ek in Suid-Afrika Gesien Het*, pp. 132–7 (Translated by J.A. Coetzee).
75 CS 1091/5870, "Commission under Article 10 of the terms of Surrender", 17 July 1902.
76 Beak, pp. 48–9.
77 Van Rensburg, "Ekonomiese Herstel", p. 267.
78 CS 113/8084, Leggett – Davidson, 23 July 1902.
79 Milner Papers, 19, (FK 1135, p. 355), Milner – Goold-Adams, 10 August 1902; Headlam, II, p. 376.
80 Cd. 1284, pp. 20–1, interview with Chamberlain, 5 September 1902. Chamberlain's statement came down to the following: "[W]e must be true to those who

supported us. But although that is a principle which we must lay down, it is not the fact that the National Scouts, or those who surrendered in the early portion of the war, have been represented in any much larger proportion than others. They have been placed with others – the burghers who surrendered later – upon commissions, but taking the average the proportion is not much larger than the rightful proportion according to mere numbers [sic]."

81 Milner Papers, 44, (FK 1203, p. 590), 29 July 1902. For copies of Botha's letter see GOV 585/281; Cd. 1284, p. 5; EC 27/178/51; Lt. Gov. 76/84/1.
82 GOV 255/20, Burger – Milner, 6 August 1902.
83 Knight, p. 97. See also CS 146/12093, Resident magistrate Standerton – Colonial Secretary, 17 September 1902.
84 CS 131/10200, Kemp – Milner, 6 August 1902. For article 10 of the peace agreement see Kestell and Van Velden, *Vredesonderhandelingen* (Peace negotiations), p. 136.
85 *Land en Volk*, 10 October 1902 (news report).
86 Lt. Gov. 76/84/17, Pienaar and Durandt (of Braamfontein) – Lawley, 26 January 1903.
87 CS 1079/42, confidential report by resident magistrate Middelburg, 10 August 1903.
88 *The Times*, 21 October 1902 (news report).
89 Milner Papers, 34, (FK 1171, p. 75), Milner – Loveday, 9 July 1902.
90 Milner Papers, 105, (FK 1194, p. 323), Milner – Selborne, 27 September 1905.
91 CT 290/522, Leggett – Duncan, 11 October 1902.
92 *The Transvaal Leader*, 11 October 1902 (news report).
93 GOV 624/391, "Second Intermediate Report", 31 December 1902; Transvaal Administration Reports for 1902: General Report on Burgher Land Settlements (Transvaal), pp. 12–4; General Administration Report, Burgher Land Settlement (Transvaal), for 1903–04, pp. 6–7.
94 GOV 624/391, Blakemore – Leggett, 4 January 1903; Cd. 1551, p. 67.
95 Cd. 1551, pp. 7–8, 14 March 1903. These settlements were not in accord with Milner's large-scale immigration policy for British settlers. On this policy see M. Streak, *Lord Milner's Immigration Policy for the Transvaal, 1897–1905*, (Published series RAU B1), pp. 21–68; Van Rensburg, "Ekonomiese Herstel", pp. 206–29.
96 *Transvaal Administration Reports for 1902: General Report on Burgher Land Settlements (Transvaal)*, p. 14. See also Lt. Gov. 37/39/7, "Holdings for Squatter Settlers", 14 May 1903; CO 291/45/2350 (FK 991, pp. 722–3), circular with contractual conditions to all inmates of the concentration camps, 17 November 1902.
97 General Administration Report, Burgher Land Settlements (Transvaal), for 1903–04, pp. 14–5.
98 CS 1079/41, confidential report from resident magistrate Standerton, 14 June 1903.
99 General Administration Report, Burgher Land Settlements, (Transvaal) for 1903–04, p. 13.
100 *Pretoria News*, 5 January 1903 (news report).
101 J. Amery, *The Life of Joseph Chamberlain*, IV, 1901–1903, pp. 304–10; *Times History*, VI, p. 80.
102 *Pretoria News*, 24 January 1903; *Klerksdorp Mining Record*, 27 January 1903 (news reports).

103 Quoted by Amery, *Chamberlain*, p. 344.
104 *The Star*, 23 January 1903 (news report). See also *Pretoria News*, 24 January 1903 (news report).
105 Cd. 1551, p. 8, Milner – Chamberlain, 14 March 1903.
106 GOV 668/17, Leggett – Robinson, 1 July 1904. See also *The Times*, 21 October 1902 (news report).
107 GOV 1254/94, Leggett – Glyn, 21 August 1903.
108 See also Davenport, pp. 256–7.
109 CT 289/255, Morley – Leggett, 8 January 1903 and Leggett – Duncan, 10 January 1903.
110 GOV 668/17, Leggett – Milner, 1 July 1904 and Milner – Leggett, 2 July 1904. See also Denoon, *Grand Illusion*, pp. 81–2.
111 Lt. Gov. 135/112/113, Leggett – R. Solomon, 17 August 1904. See also Lt. Gov. 40/42/6, Leggett – Glyn, 27 October 1904.
112 Milner Papers, 105, (FK 1194, pp. 323–4), Milner – Selborne, 27 September 1905.
113 *The Transvaal Critic*, 27 February 1903 (editorial). See also *The Transvaal Critic*, 20 February 1903 (editorial).
114 Lt. Gov. 141/115/5, L. Wahl – Lawley, 31 July 1903.
115 Lt. Gov. 135/112/113, Leggett – R. Solomon, 17 August 1904; Lt. Gov. 142/115/134, H.B. Bourne – Lawley, 15 April 1905.
116 *Transvaal Indigency Commission, Minutes of Evidence*, p. 286, Item 6823, evidence of Captain W.S. Scott on the Potchefstroom-Klerksdorp settlement, 30 April 1907; p. 296, Item 7044, evidence of A.H. St. C. Baker on the Vaal River settlement, 7 May 1907; p. 301, Item 7278, evidence of J.F. de Bruti on the Vaal River settlement, 7 May 1907.
117 GOV 1262/unregistered correspondence, report by T. Dickson, 7 January 1907.
118 Lt. Gov. 142/115/34, A.B. Pickard – Leggett, 3 May 1904 and A.P.J. Cronjé – Leggett, 9 May 1904.
119 On this aspect see Chapter 10, sections 1 and 2 below.
120 Compare Kestell and Van Velden, *Vredesonderhandelingen*, p. 136.
121 On this aspect see Kriel, pp. 161–6; Beak, pp. 39–45, 238–40; Van Rensburg. "Ekonomiese Herstel", pp. 230–6.
122 See Chapter 7, section 3 above.
123 Milner Papers, 44, (FK 1203, p. 500).
124 CO 291/41/33248 (FK 66, p. 97) 11 August 1902; HC 91/38 (copy). General Christiaan de Wet claimed at the Brandfort congress in December 1904 that both Milner and Kitchener had said at the peace negotiations that the £3 000 000 was meant only for the bittereinders and former prisoners of war. (*Officieele Verslag ... 1 en 2 Desember 1904*, p. 34). In the official minutes of the peace negotiations (Kestell and Van Velden, *Vredesonderhandelingen*), as well as in the minutes that appear as an annexure in De Wet, *Boer en Brit*, pp. 299–409, no evidence could be found to substantiate this. It is possible that Milner and Kitchener might have made such statements but that they were not recorded.
125 CO 291/52/49359 (FK 1020, pp. 210–11), "Private and Confidential interview of Chamberlain with Botha and De la Rey", 11 November 1902; Lt. Gov. 134/115/29; HC 111/160 (copies); Van Rensburg, "Ekonomiese Herstel", pp. 236–7.

126 Although the prisoners of war, like the National Scouts, were not involved in the compilation of the peace terms, it can be accepted that the Boer leaders acted as spokesmen on their behalf. See Kestell and Van Velden, *Vredesonderhandelingen*, p. 40; Milner Papers, 44, (FK 1203, p. 500), Botha – Milner, 29 July 1902.
127 See Chapter 6, section 2 above.
128 CSO 208/347/03, H.M.R. Brett – Goold-Adams, 12 January 1903.
129 Knight, pp. 123–4. See also *The Bloemfontein Post*, 16 December 1902 (report on an interview with F.A.S. Schimpers, a surrendered burgher from Winburg).
130 *Transvaal Advertiser*, 8 January 1903 (letter from H.C. Marais).
131 GOV 615/372, "Summary of the proceedings of a deputation which met Mr. Chamberlain at Sunnyside", 14 January 1903.
132 *The Friend*, 6 February 1903 (report on Chamberlain's speech in Bloemfontein).
133 Knight, p. 177.
134 Cd. 3028, pp. 57, 81, report of Central Judicial Commission, 6 March 1906. See also CSO 243/2075/03, instructions of Central Judicial Commission, February 1903.
135 HC 120/165, Goold-Adams – Milner, 31 January 1905.
136 See Chapter 1, section 2 above and Chapter 2, section 2 above.
137 Cd. 3028, pp. 87–8, report of Central Judicial Commission, 6 March 1906; Van Rensburg, "Ekonomiese Herstel", p. 241.
138 *The Transvaal Critic*, 22 May 1903 (editorial).
139 *The Friend*, 24 January 1903 (editorial).
140 Translated from the Afrikaans. Van Rensburg, "Ekonomiese Herstel", p. 257.
141 Cd. 3028, pp. 79–80, report of Central Judicial Commission, 6 March 1906. See also Chapter 2, section 1 above on the surrendered burghers who rejoined the commandos.
142 CSO 303/5100/03, Resident magistrate Heilbron – Goold-Adams, 11 July 1903 and Goold-Adams – Resident magistrate Heilbron, 4 August 1903. See also CSO 298/4802/03, Resident magistrate Bethlehem – Goold-Adams, 30 June 1903; Van Rensburg, "Ekonomiese Herstel", p. 241.
143 Beak, p. 289, annexure H(II), "Instructions issued on 14th March 1903"; Cd. 3028, p. 90, report of Central Judicial Commission, 6 March 1906.
144 CSO 368/8308/03, A. Skene – Goold-Adams, 28 November 1903.
145 Denoon, *Grand Illusion*, p. 64.
146 Cd. 3028, p. 81, report of Central Judicial Commission, 6 March 1906.
147 Van Rensburg, "Ekonomiese Herstel", p. 252.
148 Cd. 3028, p. 81, report of Central Judicial Commission, 6 March 1906; Beak, pp. 241, 251; Van Rensburg, "Ekonomiese Herstel", pp. 250, 253; Van Rensburg, "Die Skandkol wat nie wou toegroei nie" in *Die Huisgenoot*, 8 August 1969.
149 CS 1082/5, confidential report from resident magistrate Pietersburg, 23 January 1904.
150 GOV 361/46, Lt. A. Bartrop – Henderson, 4 February 1903 and Henderson – Milner, 28 February and 15 March 1903.
151 Brandt, p. 159.
152 CS 1082/65, confidential report from resident magistrate Rustenburg, 12 June 1904.

153 CS 472/4235, Resident magistrate Belfast – Colonial Secretary, 27 July 1904; *De Volksstem*, 12 August 1903 and 5 October 1904 (news reports from Ermelo).
154 *The Friend*, 12 July 1904 (news report from Dewetsdorp); *De Vriend*, 31 October 1904 and 10 November 1904 (news reports from Winburg); HC 120/165, Goold-Adams – Milner, 31 January 1905.
155 HC 120/165, Goold-Adams – Milner, 31 January 1905.
156 Cd. 3028, p. 81, report of Central Judicial Commission, 6 March 1906.
157 Milner Papers, 105, (FK 1194, p. 273), Milner – Selborne, 14 April 1903.
158 Van Rensburg, "Ekonomiese Herstel", p. 247.
159 See Cd. 426, pp. 3, 7–9 and Chapter 1, section 2 above for these proclamations issued by Roberts.
160 Translated from the Afrikaans. *De Volksstem*, 12 August 1903 (news report).
161 HC 120/165, Goold-Adams – Milner, 31 January 1905.
162 Compare Cd. 426, pp. 3, 7–9.
163 See Chapter 1, section 2 above.
164 See Cd. 426, pp. 14–5, 18 and Chapter 2, section 2 above for these proclamations issued by Roberts.
165 HC 120/165, Goold-Adams – Milner, 31 January 1905.
166 HC 120/165, Goold-Adams – Milner, 31 January 1905.
167 Milner Papers, 105, (FK 1194, p. 207), Milner – Lyttelton, 13 March 1905.
168 HC 120/165, Goold-Adams – Milner, 31 January 1905.
169 HC 120/165, Goold-Adams – Milner, 31 January 1905.
170 Milner Papers, 105, (FK 1194, pp. 206–7), Milner – Lyttelton, 13 March 1905.
171 HC 120/165, Selborne – Lyttelton, 21 August 1905.
172 Sir John West Ridgeway Collection, P.D. de Wet – Ridgeway, 2 October 1906. This letter from Piet de Wet was traced in September 1975 by means of correspondence with Lord V. Tollemache, Helmingham Hall, Stowsmarket, Suffolk, England. Lord Tollemache is in possession of Ridgeway's documents. A reference to the particular letter appears in J.P. Pearson (ed), *A Guide to Manuscripts and Documents in the British Isles relating to Africa*, p. 279.
173 N.C. Weideman, "Die politieke naweë van die Anglo-Boereoorlog in Transvaal tot 1907" (Unpublished D.Phil thesis, UP), 1955, pp. 112–13.
174 Van Rensburg, "Ekonomiese Herstel", p. 263; Chapter 10, section 2 below.

Chapter 9
Afrikaner disunity after the war and the attitude of the British authority

1 Interpersonal relations within Afrikaner ranks

The disunity that had arisen within Afrikaner society during the war continued in the post-war period. It was exacerbated by the fact that the surrendered burghers and those who had entered British military service received a substantially better deal as far as compensation was concerned than did the bitterenders and the former prisoners of war. Many bitterenders also held the disloyal burghers partly responsible for the republican demise[1] – which was not conducive to a spirit of forgiveness.

Although there had also been defectors among the prisoners of war,[2] the large majority of the former prisoners aligned themselves with the bitterenders on their return from captivity and treated the National Scouts with contempt. Indeed, even in May 1902 the commanding officer of the prisoner-of-war camp at St Helena mentioned that the National Scouts "will for a long time be a source of extreme hatred ... to the Boer Prisoner on his return".[3] Tension and antagonism between the bitterenders and the defectors in the two former republics were thus initially dominant features of post-war Afrikaner society.

Two weeks after the conclusion of peace, General de Wet told a reporter of *The Bloemfontein Post* that harmony among the people was certainly desirable, but that the disloyal burghers presented a serious obstacle to the realisation of this goal.[4] In an address to the inmates of the Kroonstad concentration camp at about the same time, De Wet referred to the collaborators as murders of their own *volk*.

According to him they belonged in a pigsty and he would not condescend so much as to greet any surrendered burgher.[5] General Hertzog felt the same. On his return to Bloemfontein after the conclusion of peace he "heartily despised" the traitors and refused to greet them.[6]

In a blistering editorial in *Land en Volk*, Eugène Marais expressed the general attitude towards the National Scouts in no uncertain terms. "The hate is there," he wrote, "as deep as the ocean and as wide as God's earth: and do not for one instant ask that we smother it. We hate these people from the very depth of our hearts because they have besmirched our honourable name throughout the world. It is impossible to forgive and even less to forget."[7] Gustav Preller also endorsed the presence of antipathy towards the National Scouts. In reaction to the Marais article he wrote: "We all felt like this. On occasion we came upon people in the street, old acquaintances we knew before the war, but we would not even look in their direction, let alone greet them. The hate was certainly there."[8] In the Orange River Colony the editor of *The Friend* quoted an extract from the Marais article and pointed out that although Marais had accurately reflected the general feeling, the article only served to intensify the existing bitterness towards the National Scouts. With an eye to the future, he warned that it was going to be necessary to live alongside those who had defected. No matter how unpleasant this would be, he wrote, "The Afrikaners who fought to the end must regard the surrendered burghers and National Scouts as fellow Afrikaners and accept them again in their ranks."[9]

In the Transvaal there was also a moderate voice. Despite his condemnation of the National Scouts, J.P.L. Lombard, a bitterender who was apparently from Pretoria, pleaded that the bitterenders be more conciliatory. "Now that we have peace we should show these people forgiveness, then ... we can pick ourselves up again and try to move forward," wrote Lombard to *De Volksstem*.[10] His plea was not well received. Commandant Ben Bouwer, a Boer commander who had been active in the Cape Colony, replied that he could perhaps reconcile himself to the burghers who had surrendered, but that the "Afrikaner *volk*" should completely ostracise those men who had gone so far as to actually fight on the British side. According to him, the *volk* could in any event never again rely on these people who had so "shamefully" abandoned the bitterenders during the war.[11] A similar opinion was expressed by a bitterender from Marico.[12]

Despite their conduct during the war there were some collaborators who felt that they should be fully accepted back into Afrikaner ranks. Barely two weeks after peace had been signed, Piet de Wet and Revd H.E. du Plessis, who had been actively involved in the peace committee movement, wrote an open letter to the press in which they called for reconciliation between the two groups. "To prevent a schism," they wrote, "and [to] strive with united effort for the upbuilding of the desolate country, we must sink all petty differences in the sea of oblivion and let the dead bury their dead." The moment of peace for which all had longed had finally arrived, and in their view it was the appropriate time to forget all such differences. They closed their letter with a biblical quotation: "Blessed are the peacemakers, for they shall be called the children of God."[13]

Under the prevailing circumstances this plea for harmony was somewhat unrealistic. The wartime role of De Wet and Du Plessis was of such a nature that they could hardly have expected the bitterenders simply to forgive them without any further qualms. The war was only just over; its wounds were still far too raw. "Who can take exception when a brave and noble *volk* despises a traitor in the same way that an honest person hates the devil, sin and all that is filthy and horrible?" asked Eugène Marais in the same editorial.[14] Any reconciliation between the two groups would certainly not be effected as easily as Piet de Wet hoped it would. About six months after his open letter he informed Chamberlain that the collaborators "thought ... to bring about a reconciliation, but the other side had not met them in the same way. They were branded, distrusted and hated".[15]

On a social level, the bad blood between the different groups became evident in various ways. Shortly after the peace, when certain bitterenders and National Scouts met one another in Pretoria, insults were flung from both sides and abusive language apparently became the order of the day.[16] Even in October 1903 the issue of the National Scouts was such that "social life in Pretoria is split into all kinds of cliques".[17] In the rural areas the feelings against the National Scouts were every bit as bad. In the districts of Standerton and Pretoria bitterenders refused to send their children to school with those of the National Scouts.[18] In the Klerksdorp district a school inspector, J.A. Corbett, was obliged to close one of the schools because of the "violent opposition between National Scouts and bitterenders".[19] In the districts of Lindley, Bethlehem, Hoopstad, Heilbron and Vrede bitterenders initially wore small white buttons to distinguish themselves from the burghers who had defected.[20] The traitors were left in no doubt at all that they were social outcasts. At a picnic held in the Ladybrand district to celebrate the birthdays of Presidents Kruger and Steyn, steps were taken to ensure that only bitterenders attended the function.[21] There were even some disloyal burghers in the Ladybrand district who were still tasting the bitter fruits of their actions in 1906. A.J. Fouché, a former member of the Farmers' Guard who joined the South African Constabulary after the war, had to resign from the police force in July 1904 for health reasons. He then searched for a permanent job as a labourer for two whole years without success; by his own admission none of his countrymen were prepared to employ a Boer who had fought on the British side during the war.[22]

The property of surrendered burghers was also damaged on occasion. In mid-June 1902 an officer of the South African Constabulary claimed that some of the bitterenders in the Ficksburg district had set light to the pastures on farms belonging to surrendered burghers who had hidden away in Basutoland (Lesotho) during the war.[23] The magistrate in the Vrede district also reported that the bitter feeling between the two groups "is showing itself in the removal of horses and cattle from one farm to another and also in the destruction or removal of iron roofing and woodwork, etc."[24] In July 1903 the magistrate in Lydenburg at the time reported two cases where livestock belonging to surrendered burghers was mishandled: "A horse of one Broeksma, an early surrendered burgher, had its ears cut off and its tail hogged ... and ... his father-in-law, Botha, had two of his horses similarly treated."[25]

The two groups often became involved in scuffles. In November 1903 in the district of Christiana a National Scout, Swanepoel, became embroiled in an exchange of words with three bitterenders and according to the local British magistrate (who was clearly not au fait with the local language!), "called them 'thunder and lightning', which it seems is a very dreadful thing to do". A fist fight ensued and Swanepoel knocked out two of the bitterenders. The magistrate later compelled him to apologise for his behaviour.[26] In the Ermelo district the two groups tackled each other on a larger scale. In June 1903 *De Volksstem* reported that "fisticuffs between guerillas, handsuppers and joiners occur frequently in the neighbourhood".[27] J. van Rensburg, a bitterender from the same district, landed up in court after a fight with a National Scout called Ballot. Van Rensburg appeared on charges of assault, was found guilty and given a fine of £20. "These parties can never live together," commented an Ermelo bitterender on the incident, "and we cannot blame Mr van Rensburg for laying his hands a little too heavily on that rubbish; it is a pity that we do not have more freedom, then we would indeed put those women [the Scouts] in their place a little bit."[28] In the Pietersburg district in June 1902 there were also fist-fights between National Scouts and bitterenders.[29] The tension between the two groups was so intense that the Krugersdorp magistrate reported shortly after the conclusion of peace: "I believe the Scouts were in real fear of returning to their farms unarmed."[30] Some National Scouts apparently thought that after the war the bitterenders were intent on taking revenge by shooting them.

In the Volksrust district in February 1903 there was a big uproar about an alleged murder of four Van Oudtshoorn brothers. All four of them had been National Scouts. According to an account of the murder in *Land and Volk*: "One was found eighteen miles from his farm ... with his throat cut, and the other three on their farm."[31] On this occasion the press was certainly guilty of sensation mongering. The four Van Oudtshoorn brothers had indeed been National Scouts – but they had not been murdered. The local magistrate reported: "The Van Oudtshoorn murders as reported ... are entirely imaginary, but the announcement in print has caused some excitement among early surrenderers and National Scouts who have been asking for revolvers etc."[32] Without providing any credible evidence, V.E. Solomons claims in an article that within two months of the peace negotiations 22 National Scouts had been shot,[33] but this could not be satisfactorily confirmed, and in the light of these other unsubstantiated reports it is doubtful whether there is any truth in the allegation. The bitterenders were in any case not so filled with hatred towards the National Scouts that they would have gone so far as to murder them.

Some National Scouts nevertheless found their social position so unbearable that they preferred to leave the Transvaal and find refuge elsewhere. On behalf of 100 members of the corps, G.S. Cruse, a National Scout from Pretoria, lodged a written request to the Rhodesian administration that they be permitted to settle there. As the motivation for their proposed move Cruse claimed that land was unavailable in the Transvaal, "and what is more, our social position will not admit of our staying here".[34] The Rhodesian authorities were prepared to receive the National Scouts, but the proposed emigration apparently fell through because the National Scouts lacked the necessary funds and there was an outbreak of a cattle disease in Rhodesia.[35] In January 1904 a certain A. Erasmus of the Lydenburg district and an unknown number of people considered moving to Uganda. The local magistrate interviewed them and outlined the following as two of the reasons provided by the prospective emigrants: "1. They have lost the position of influence which they used to have in the District. 2. As they are all National Scouts or 'handsuppers', their relations with their neighbours are not so pleasant as they used to be."[36] No evidence could be found to confirm whether Erasmus and company did indeed go to Uganda or not.

In the Ermelo district there were also certain "National Scouts and Surrendered Boers, who have lost 'caste' through their action in the late war", who in October 1906, according to an inspector of the local constabulary, had planned to relocate to British East Africa. But it appears that this proposed move by Ermelo residents did not take place.[37] However, a historian who has done research on the question of the East African emigrants has established, by conducting personal interviews with several war veterans, that there were indeed certain individual National Scouts who moved to British East Africa. He does not, however, mention from which districts these Scouts originated, nor does he give their approximate date of departure.[38]

Six years after the war, C.J. Cloete, a former member of the *Volksraad* (parliament) in the Free State and chairman of the Bethlehem peace committee during the war, considered going to settle in British

East Africa. By 1908 he was still so unpopular among the Boers that he felt it would be wise to move away. Cloete and another representative decided to undertake a fact-finding journey to East Africa in 1908 on behalf of 20 residents of the Bethlehem district. Initially they were not impressed by the conditions there; Cloete and his travelling companion returned to the Free State, and interest in the initiative waned. However, three years later, in 1911, Cloete and 10 other families did indeed settle permanently in British East Africa.[39] Tension between them and the bitterenders thus motivated a number of collaborators even to consider moving to other British colonies, but only a few ever came to the point of actually moving. The large majority remained in the Transvaal and the Orange River Colony. Their conduct during the war was to a large extent the reason behind their discomfiture and the disunity in Afrikaner ranks.[40] As has been shown, this dissension found expression in an informal way on the social level, but the tension between the groups was not confined to the secular sphere; it also surfaced in other circles. There was considerable division in the religious sphere for example, and this dissent became apparent in a more formal manner in the Transvaal.

Attention will now be given to the friction in religious circles in the Orange River Colony and the Transvaal, and an attempt will be made to establish just how significant this formal division in Afrikaner ranks became.

2 Friction in religious circles and the formation of a new church

In the Orange River Colony, Revd H.E. du Plessis, who had been the minister at Lindley since 1894,[41] emerged as a serious stumbling block for the bitterenders in his congregation. They simply could not reconcile themselves to his conduct during the war. Revd du Plessis's close ties with the peace committee movement are well documented.[42] After the limited success of the peace delegation to the Cape, Du Plessis provided regular religious support to inmates in the concentration camp at Kroonstad.[43] On 25 January 1902, on the grounds of his "treason", the Free State government no longer allowed him to conduct marriage ceremonies. He was still permitted to practise as a minister, but "in future no marriage solemnised by him"[44] would be legally recognised.

Furthermore, after the war Du Plessis was no longer welcome as a minister among his congregation. The bitterenders refused to attend his services. "How can a burgher who continued to fight until the very end listen to a sermon with the people [presumably ORC Volunteers] that had tried to shoot him?" asked the editor of *De Vriend*.[45] There was so much dissatisfaction in the congregation that Du Plessis was asked to resign. Under circumstances such as these he could hardly expect to reap any religious benefit from his endeavours, and on 13 December 1902 he felt obliged to relinquish his ties with the Lindley community.[46] After his resignation Du Plessis went to the Standerton land settlement area in the Transvaal.[47]

The breach in the Lindley congregation centred around Du Plessis as an individual rather than the antipathy between the bitterenders and the surrendered burghers. This becomes evident in a letter from four local bitterenders to Goold-Adams, in which they expressed themselves in favour of "mutual reconciliation" and asked the lieutenant-governor's permission to hold a large gathering on 16 December 1902 (the Afrikaner's Day of the Covenant), "in order to remove all differences".[48] In May 1903 the minister from Reitz, Revd D.J. Viljoen, who had also spent a short time at the helm of the Lindley congregation, was able to attest that "conciliation and forgiveness took place at Lindley between the two parties that had previously been antagonistic towards each other".[49]

The tense relationship between the two groups also led to disunity in the Vrede congregation. The conduct of three church council members during the war was the reason behind the refusal of members of the congregation to attend church, and they demanded that the people concerned should step down. These men refused to do so and the end result was that the other church council members resigned in March 1903. This made it necessary to hold a full church council meeting to elect a new governing body, and it was significant that only bitterenders were subsequently chosen as members.[50] Similarly, in Bethlehem feelings also ran high. The disposition between certain members of the congregation was so strained that the local minister was obliged to postpone the first Holy Communion service until January 1903.[51]

From 1903 until 1906 there was continual friction in the Frankfort congregation owing to the war record of four men (J. Steenkamp, G. Muller, R. van Rensburg and J. Benade) who had fought on the British side. The church council initially tried in vain to get them to admit to their breach of moral conduct. R. van Rensburg in particular felt very aggrieved about this. In April 1904 he went so far as to say that the bitterenders were responsible for the deaths of the women and children in the concentration camps. He was also very outspoken in his criticism of Revd J.D. Kestell of Ficksburg and said that Kestell "deserved to be turned to stone before he crossed the threshold of the Church".[52] Van Rensburg and a few of his kind were censured by the church and as a result they could not partake of the sacraments.[53] However, in 1905 this church council decision was overruled by both the presbyterial executive and the synod.[54] There was nevertheless so much antagonism that Van Rensburg and some of the other protestors joined the *Kruiskerk* under the Revd S.J. du Toit in 1906.[55]

In most of the other congregations in the Orange River Colony there was a more forgiving spirit and the wartime differences did not lead to any serious conflicts in religious circles. Even as early as 14 August 1902 Revd J.C. Hefer of Parys was able to write: "With regard to the good progress of Peace in my Congregation, I may state that through God's blessing and gracious workings of the Spirit of Peace, all bitterness is being removed. Some of the Kerkeraden of the late burghers refused coming to church and taking their places alongside their fellow Kerkeraden, who had, after surrender, assisted the British Army – last Sunday, however, the most determined, who repeatedly refused, an ex-commandant, at the repeated injunction of God's word, came and resumed his place, joining also in the evening prayer."[56] In the available minutes of the respective church councils of Bloemfontein, Harrismith, Hoopstad, Kroonstad and Vredefort there is also very little indication of serious tension between members of the congregation in as far as the different stances they adopted during the war are concerned.[57]

A factor that contributed to the gradual waning of antagonism was the influence of the synod of the N.G. Kerk (Dutch Reformed

Church) in the Orange River Colony. The problem of these strained relations was discussed at a sitting held on 5 May 1903. The majority of the representatives were of the opinion that the "sharp lines of demarcation" that were drawn during the war had to be removed. The general attitude of the synod was accordingly laid down as follows: "The Church will do everything in her power to facilitate peace and reconciliation, and Evangelism will triumph through the medium of forgiveness and grace."[58] In August 1903, with the coming church council elections in mind, the official church magazine warned: "We are presently in danger of allowing our votes to be influenced by the politics of the past. May God protect us from this! The Christian outlook should override a standpoint based on nationhood or politics."[59]

In the Orange River Colony, after 1903, with the exception of the Frankfort congregation, the pressure between the two groups in church circles had been reduced to the absolute minimum. The acceptance of the burghers who had defected into church ranks also implied that they would be accepted more readily into society again.[60]

In the Transvaal, however, matters did not run as smoothly. "Nothing on earth would ever induce me to make peace or to countenance the making of peace with the National Scouts," wrote Eugène Marais to Milner in June 1903.[61] In November 1902 a bitterender from Balmoral expressed the hope that all bitterenders would remain steadfast in their determination "not to have anything to do with the traitors".[62]

This attitude towards the National Scouts, then, manifested itself strongly in religious circles in the Transvaal. In the N.H. of G. Kerk in Pietersburg, Lichtenburg, Ventersburg and Ermelo the National Scouts were placed under censure by the church. Unless they agreed to confess their guilt openly they were not permitted to partake of the sacraments.[63] National Scouts from the congregations at Belfast and Piet Retief found that the ministers were not prepared to baptise their children without a confession of guilt from the parents.[64] In the congregations of Schweizer-Reneke, Carolina and Utrecht the presence of the National Scouts or surrendered burghers as members of church councils caused a great deal of unpleasantness.[65] From Heidelberg the magistrate reported in January 1903: "The feeling in the District against the National Scouts still remains intense, and the Magistrate is afraid we shall have no assistance from the Reverend Mr Louw in healing it."[66] The magistrate's judgement on Revd A.J. Louw was not entirely accurate. Louw claimed that he did indeed try to reconcile the two groups but that the "root of bitterness" had grown extremely deep.[67] This clearly shows that problematic relations between the two groups affected many of the Transvaal congregations.

Four months after the conclusion of peace, the N.H. of G. Kerk of the Transvaal gave an indication of its official stance towards the National Scouts. On 2 October 1902 the synod executive in Pretoria expressed the hope that church council members in the congregations would be chosen with the "utmost circumspection with an eye to satisfaction".[68] It is doubtful whether the executive thought that the election of National Scouts and surrendered burghers to the church councils would have been the cause of any satisfaction at all in the congregations. On 10 October the church stated its position with greater clarity in a pastoral letter that was sent out to all the congregations. The division among churchgoers was lamented, but on the other hand it was found necessary that "we give the members of the congregations the reason behind this bitterness; namely that those who have been guilty of infidelity and treason must with all earnestness be urged to atone and to repent. They have sinned against God and their people, and unless they are truly sorry and have come to repent of their wrongful ways, … they cannot conceivably partake of the sacraments with a clear conscience."[69] In effect this recommendation by the church meant that unless the National Scouts were prepared to admit their guilt openly they were to be subjected to strict church discipline. Certain National Scouts interpreted this pastoral letter as clear evidence that the highest office bearers of the church were in favour of their being deprived of church privileges.[70] A few National Scouts reportedly felt so aggrieved that they left to join English churches.[71]

There is justification in asking why it was that the church, as a religious institution, found itself at the centre of an issue about the secular relationship between the bitterenders and the National Scouts, and why in the process it had recommended pastoral discipline as punishment for the collaborators. After all, the church had no doctrinal or theological dispute with the National Scouts; the issue was purely one of their conduct during the war.

In this regard it is important to bear in mind that after the war the church was the only Afrikaner institution that remained intact. The Afrikaners' state institutions had been terminated by the Peace of Vereeniging, and in the immediate post-war period the church was in fact the only surviving mouthpiece available to the majority of the *volk*.[72] After the war the church and the *volk* were so closely connected that the two were virtually synonymous. This is clear from the official church magazine of the N.H. of G. Kerk: "As the Church of the *volk* we have a grave responsibility towards our people. It is no surprise, then, that one of our leaders has said of our General Meeting that it is now the *Volksraad* [parliament] of our *Volk*."[73] It is thus understandable why the church felt itself called upon to pass judgement on the National Scout question. The church could really not do otherwise; it was confronted by the problem and had to take a stance. It was also the only body that was in a position to enforce discipline.

The close connection between church and *volk* naturally also had thorny theological implications. "Such an absolute identification of people and church ... raises serious doubts as to where the church's first loyalty belongs. Who is the real Master of the Church? Which voice is heard loudest – God's or the people's?" writes a theologian on the question of nationalism and the Afrikaner churches.[74] It is not the purpose of this study to examine the theological implications in any detail. Nevertheless it is necessary to briefly outline the postwar attitude of the church and to explain why it recommended that pastoral discipline be applied in the case of National Scouts. The church was very careful not to give any political slant to its action against them. Its primary point of departure was that the National Scouts had not as such committed a political offence, but were guilty on ethical and moral grounds by having taken up arms against their own compatriots.[75] In October 1903 H. Luckhoff, a bitterender from Pretoria, justifiably emphasised the unethical aspect of the National Scouts' conduct: "The National Scouts have done a mean thing. It was not through a conscientious belief [that] by doing so they would put a stop to the sufferings of their kin; it was because they were paid for the disgraceful and dastardly act."[76] As has already been shown, political and humanitarian considerations were not the predominant reasons why the majority of ordinary members of the National Scouts decided to fight on the British side. Even the pro-British *Cape Times* identified this manifestation of treason in Boer ranks as unethical.[77] It is therefore understandable why the church did not regard the conduct of the National Scouts as political in nature – as indeed did various English newspapers[78] – but saw it instead as a moral offence. In terms of the church ordinance at the time, the church was in fact permitted to express its stance on moral misdemeanours. In the section on pastoral discipline the following church statute applied: "The Church Management keeps it in mind that its surveillance is not only concerned with misdemeanours that are punishable by the civil authorities, but also over all manner of misconduct. Everything that is in contravention of the Holy Communion formula ... everything that disturbs the good and correct order of things ... as well as continued immorality ..."[79] Measured by contemporary norms then, and seen in the light of the motivation of the majority of the National Scouts, it would appear that the church did not exceed its spiritual brief to any great extent.

Whether the Transvaal church should not rather have approached the whole question of the relationship between bitterenders and National Scouts in the same spirit as the synod of the church in the Orange River Colony is an open question. It should nevertheless be remembered that in the Transvaal the church was confronted by a far greater problem than was the case in the Orange River Colony. In the Transvaal there was much more dissent in local congregations and there were also certain National Scouts who obstinately refused to be subjected to pastoral discipline.

At the first post-war sitting of the synod of the Dutch Reformed Church in May 1903 the question of the National Scouts gave rise to lengthy debate. There was no agreement among the delegates on what action to take against them. Some of the members were in favour of placing the Scouts under very strict church discipline. Eventually the various representatives agreed to accept the recommendations of a legal commission of the church as the official decision of the synod. In terms of this decision the church adjudged the conduct of people who had been "unfaithful" to their government and their *volk* to be a "serious sin", one that could not be allowed to pass "unreprimanded". Since peace had been concluded and it was the responsibility of the church to maintain good order as well as to promote "welfare and peace" within the church, the commission felt that it was necessary that the people concerned be "admonished most severely to repent and reform their ways before they could again partake of any of the privileges enjoyed by members of our Church with a clear conscience".[80]

This decision had important implications. In the first place it was only applicable to those who had given active assistance to the British. The synod decision did not include the surrendered burghers. In fact, Revd H.S. Bosman, the moderator, announced that the synod had nothing against those who had withdrawn from the war, and that among them, in his view, there were people who were just as honourable as the bitterenders.[81] In the official church magazine Bosman also emphasised that the synod's decision was not applicable to the surrendered burghers.[82] This meant that the surrendered burghers were not involved in the subsequent dispute between the church and some of the National Scouts and that they were more readily accepted back into Afrikaner ranks as well as church membership per se.[83] In the second place the decision was worded in more moderate terms than it had been in the pastoral letter of October 1902. Whereas the circular letter stated that the National Scouts had to admit their guilt before they could take Holy Communion, the synod decision of May 1903 put more emphasis on a warning and did not, as such, summarily withhold the sacraments from these people. According to ecclesiastical law a warning in the spirit of this particular decision cannot be regarded as an extreme form of pastoral discipline.[84] Despite this, some of the National Scouts were under the impression that the synod's decision gave official approval to a particularly strict form of church discipline.[85]

In the third place the synod's decision provided no clarity as to what action congregations should take against the National Scouts if they paid no heed to the warning. Revd C.E. Anderson of Vryheid and Revd J.P. Wolhuter of Piet Retief had drawn attention to this particular shortcoming at the meeting of the synod and had warned the delegates that it might well lead to "additional confusion and dissatisfaction" in the congregations.[86]

In the event, this was indeed the case. In the execution of the synod's decision congregations applied the prescribed discipline on National Scouts in a number of different ways. In February 1904 Revd Bosman expressed his concern that some ministers and church council members were not showing a sufficiently forgiving attitude towards the National Scouts. He was of the opinion that if all ministers acted in accordance with the spirit of the synod's decision – and "it was just as much a mission and a duty as it was an instruction" – there would have been far less bitterness in the congregations. "These members must be visited in their own homes," he wrote in the official church magazine, "and above all no church council member should ever raise his hand against his fellow burgher. It is because of incorrect handling that most of the trouble has arisen."[87] To a reporter from the *Pretoria News* Bosman admitted in October 1903 that some ministers had not acted in the spirit of the synod's decision, but added that the church as such could not be held responsible for the conduct of individuals. The moderator went on to say: "Personally I am no extremist. We have extremists amongst us who would be glad to see the Scouts go, but I am not one of them, nor are they in the majority in our Church."[88] As far as can be established, the ministers and church council members in Pietersburg, Standerton, Volksrust, Carolina and Ermelo applied more stringent disciplinary measures on the National Scouts than were required in terms of the synod decision.[89]

With the exception of Pietersburg, these towns were all situated in the eastern Transvaal. The majority of the National Scouts who rebelled against the church's stance after May 1903 were originally from the eastern Transvaal and this was also the region where most of the National Scouts subsequently settled.[90] The resistance by the National Scouts to the church decision was to a large extent focused on a few leading personalities, namely S.P. Grobler from the Bethal district and N.J. Breytenbach, a wealthy farmer from the Ermelo district. Both men had been commanding officers of the National Scouts during the war.[91]

Under their leadership a series of meetings were held in the Ermelo district and adjoining areas from August 1903 to December 1903 to protest against the stance taken by the church. At a meeting on 26 August in the Standerton district, the National Scouts voiced their objection to the action of the N.H. of G. Kerk. They alleged that it was punishing them for political reasons and that the decision taken by the synod was subject to a number of divergent interpretations. They claimed that when they tried to make this point they were summarily "told to 'get out', 'get out', 'get out'".[92] As has been shown, the church did not judge the conduct of the National Scouts specifically on political grounds, but rather as a moral and ethical offence that called for disciplinary measures by the church. The National Scouts were nevertheless correct that the church decision was liable to be interpreted in a number of different ways.

The leaders of the protest took further steps in September 1903. At a meeting at Bethal on 8 September, they demanded a public apology in the press from the N.H. of G. Kerk. They also asked the moderator of the church to retract the synod's decision.[93] The moderator did not have the authority to meet their demands, but replied that he was prepared to talk to the dissatisfied people in order to clear up the "colossal misunderstanding".[94] On 29 September this meeting was held in Pretoria. Revd Bosman tried in vain to find some common ground so that the two parties could settle the matter amicably, but Grobler adopted such an aggrieved and recalcitrant attitude that the discussions simply ground to a halt. In Bosman's view it was clear that Grobler wanted to pose as a martyr for his beliefs and that he was bent on leaving the mother church.[95]

On 8 October Grobler held another meeting, this time at Vlaklaagte. Despite the fact that it was attended only by 76 National Scouts, Grobler was determined to form a new church. N.J. Breytenbach was more compliant, thus Bosman, who attended the meeting on invitation, persuaded Breytenbach to delay the establishment of the new church so that a church commission could clear up all the confusion by providing a full report on the decision of the synod.[96]

However, in Grobler's view the commission delayed its report for far too long. On 8 December he issued an ultimatum to the commission in which he stated that certain National Scouts were planning to leave the church unless they received a satisfactory answer within two days. Grobler again demanded the retraction of the church decision and also insisted on an entirely new election of church council members.[97] In terms of ecclesiastical law it was outside the authority of any church committee to meet such demands.[98]

On 22 December 1903 Grobler arranged another meeting at Bethal and here he persuaded the National Scouts who were present that the answer was to separate from the mother church. The new church, he said, would be known officially as the *Nederduitsch Gereformeerde Kerk van Transvaalkolonie*. This name was, however, seldom used and the breakaway church became better known as the *Scoutkerk*, which has been translated in this work as the Scout Church. The well-known Revd H.E. du Plessis of Lindley and Revd C.J. Brink of Roossenekal, who had both shown considerable sympathy for the National Scouts, would be the ministers of the new church.[99] During the war Brink had been the minister in the Simon's Town concentration camp where the majority of prisoners of war had already reconciled themselves to British paramountcy. He had also been active in the concentration camp at Aliwal North. By his own admission, after the war he had chosen to break his ties with his congregation.[100]

The formation of a separate Scout Church can be regarded as an indication that the division in Afrikaner society had become a formal reality. By publishing a whole series of polemic editorials and other articles, Vere Stent, the editor of the *Pretoria News*, aroused a great deal of publicity about the religious wrangle and the breach in Afrikanerdom. Using this one-sided publicity he created the impression that a schism in the church would bring the Transvaal people to their knees.[101] A church historian is also of the opinion that the formal establishment of the Scout Church meant that "the Transvaal people had been torn apart".[102] Thus it is pertinent to examine whether the formation of the Scout Church did indeed drive a wedge into Afrikaner society.

It would seem that the Scout Church centred almost entirely around Grobler and Breytenbach. They did not succeed in attracting a great deal of interest in the new church among the ordinary members of the National Scouts. According to Leggett the majority of National Scouts did not even become embroiled in the church wrangle. Even if the church had placed them under censure, it did not concern them to any great extent because they were in any case not keen churchgoers.[103] Then too, some National Scouts who were interested in church affairs consented to confess their wrongdoing in the presence of their respective ministers. In February 1904 Bosman announced that many National Scouts had been accepted back into the "bosom" of the local congregations.[104] By the end of 1903 some congregations had also decided to allow all their members, irrespective of their role during the war, to join in the celebration of the Holy Communion and to enjoy the sacraments.[105]

In order to gain support for the new church Grobler and Breytenbach held meetings in January 1904 in the eastern Transvaal. But the response was very poor. Only 47 people attended a meeting held on 5 January in the Standerton district. Of these, ten voted against breaking away from the mother church.[106] At a meeting on 9 January in the Middelburg district there were 22 people present.[107] It is thus not surprising that in April 1904 the magistrates of Ermelo and Standerton mentioned that the Scout Church did not have much of a following.[108] In July 1904 Grobler claimed that congregations had been established in Ermelo, Carolina, Middelburg, Bethal, Standerton and Heidelberg. According to him there were 650 families who were members of the Scout Church.[109] Grobler's statistics do not really indicate a significant breach in Afrikaner ranks. In addition, there is a strong possibility that Grobler may very well have exaggerated the number of members. In March 1904 *Land en Volk* reported that only 28 people (not families) were members of the Scout Church in Ermelo.[110] A month later, according to the local magistrate the Scout Church at Ermelo had 32 members.[111] In contrast, Grobler claimed that there were 100 families (not persons) in the Ermelo congregation three months later,[112] but it is doubtful whether the number of members could have increased so dramatically. Writing in 1923 Bosman recalled that the Scout Church congregations had been extremely small. According to him one of the congregations had comprised of only one family: a man, his wife and six children.[113]

During June 1904 the leaders of the Scout Church also tried to establish a number of congregations in the western and northern regions of the Transvaal,[114] but they met with little success. In 1906 the Scout Church comprised seven small congregations at Bethal, Standerton, Heidelberg, Zeerust, Ventersdorp, Breyten (in the Ermelo district) and Skeerpoort in the district of Pretoria. The Zeerust congregation numbered only 35 people in May 1905, but the total number of members in all these congregations is unknown. In any event, the Scout Church showed hardly any viability. Only at Breyten was a small church building erected. In Zeerust construction began on a church, but by May 1905 the local magistrate cast doubt on whether, owing to a lack of funds, it would ever be completed.[115]

By way of conclusion it can be said that the tense interpersonal relationships that existed on a social level after the war also became evident in church circles. This led to the formation of a new church – an indication that the post-war division in Afrikaner society had been formally realised in a separate organisational entity. It would, however, be unrealistic to regard the Scout Church as a very significant breach in Afrikanerdom. The new church was the brainchild of a few aggrieved individuals and did not ever find much appeal in the rank and file of the National Scouts.

Next it is necessary to examine the attitude of the British colonial authority to this religious schism in Afrikaner ranks and to establish how the Scout Church eventually disappeared.

3 The attitude of the British authority and the demise of the Scout Church

In previous works historians have accepted, without any convincing evidence, that the British colonial authority encouraged the religious friction in Afrikaner ranks so that the British cause could benefit politically. This opinion appears to have been based on the premise that because the National Scouts had been used by the British during the war to undermine the republics militarily, they would also be exploited by the British in the post-war period to counteract the bitterenders in both the religious and political spheres. G.D. Scholtz, for example, writes: "Events that played themselves out during the war placed the British in a position to launch an attack on the Dutch Reformed Church after the conclusion of peace. In this instance the National Scouts, the men who had taken up arms against their own countrymen during the war, were used as a battering ram against the walls of the church."¹¹⁶ To what extent can this interpretation be accepted as accurate?

In December 1902 Sir Arthur Lawley, the lieutenant-governor of the Transvaal, gave the first clear indication of his personal standpoint on the matter. He held an interview with Bosman about certain National Scouts who had been excluded from the sacraments by their local congregations. Lawley thought it necessary that Revd Bosman should use his influence to promote a more forgiving attitude in the church community. In the Orange River Colony Goold-Adams held a similar discussion with the moderator, Revd J.J.T. Marquard. Both Bosman and Marquard undertook to use their influence to end the friction in religious circles.¹¹⁷ From this evidence it is already clear that right from the start neither head of the civil administration in the two colonies was in favour of encouraging the division in Afrikaner society.

As the overall head of the civil administration in both colonies, Milner, significantly enough, seldom bothered to pay any attention to the friction within the Afrikaner church. Nevertheless, in 1902 he made a few remarks about the matter. On 10 August he mentioned to Goold-Adams that he had no wish to support the National Scouts in a religious wrangle. However, if the ministers persisted in their overt campaign to force the National Scouts to confess their guilt, the government would be obliged to protect the National Scouts.¹¹⁸ On 11 August in a letter to Chamberlain, Milner described the action by the ministers towards the National Scouts as laughable. He was of the opinion that they had political motives for their action. "It may seem foolish of the Afrikander wirepullers to attack a number of their own race," he wrote, "but they evidently think that they can bring sufficient pressure to bear on those who have taken our side to make them recant, and thus consolidate a Nationalist Party throughout South Africa with which to carry on the old fight for supremacy in the political field." In this letter Milner did not, however, make any mention that the colonial administration had plans to use the National Scouts to enter the political arena.¹¹⁹ In October 1903, when the breakaway by Grobler and his group was in full swing, Milner made it clear that he did not want to compromise the colonial authority. In reply to a request from Grobler for assistance from the government to acquire some of the property that belonged to the mother church, Milner simply noted: "The Govt. has no power to interfere."[120]

Then the attitude of Chamberlain, the secretary of state for the colonies, can also be noted. In February 1903 Bosman made mention of the unfortunate friction in church circles in a letter to Chamberlain and expressed the hope that the colonial authorities would not exacerbate the disunity. Chamberlain gave Bosman the assurance "that there is no desire on the part of the Government to meddle in Church matters ..." He nevertheless warned Bosman "if on the other hand the exclusion of these men [National Scouts] from Church Commissions were to continue, the natural result would be a division in the Church which would be much to be regretted".[121] The reality was that Bosman and Chamberlain both agreed that the friction within church ranks was unfortunate. The only difference was that they disagreed about how it should be contained. Bosman felt that the best solution was to apply a lighter form of discipline on the National Scouts so that morally they would be acceptable once more not only to other members of the congregation, but also, by implication, among themselves.[122] For Chamberlain the best way around the problem was that the National Scouts should simply be accepted back into church ranks without any further ado. According to him the ministers were discriminating against the National Scouts on the basis of a political offence, and if this was so then the authorities would be obliged to take sides. While on his visit to South Africa, Chamberlain said at Lichtenburg: "We do not want to take sides, but we must put forth all the strength we possess to prevent the persecution of those who helped us."[123] Chamberlain was not in fact correct in his assumption that the National Scouts were being punished for a political offence,[124] but the main issue here is that, like Bosman, he condemned the wrangle in the church. With Chamberlain as its spokesperson, the British authority was only prepared to take sides with the National Scouts if the ministers persisted in their actions and continued to place the Scouts under strict church discipline.

Major Leggett, who was closely associated with the Scouts, was also dismayed about the tensions in the church. After a visit to Standerton in October 1903 he wrote to the lieutenant-governor's private secretary as follows: "A man told me in his house that his children and other children of the Scouts were now being baptised by the Rev. Theunissen, but only if the godfather (sponsor) is a 'bitterender' or a prisoner of war. All this is very sad." For Leggett it was "a pleasure to return to the Western Transvaal. At the last Nachtmaal at Rustenburg, old John Steenekamp, the district commandant who surrendered with De la Rey, stood at the Church door and welcomed every man, National Scout or Handsupper."[125]

Of all the British officials Sir Arthur Lawley was most closely involved with the breach in Afrikaner church ranks. In May 1903 the lieutenant-governor was confronted by the N.H. of G. Kerk about the activities of Revd H.E. du Plessis on the Standerton settlement farm. After leaving his congregation in December 1902, Du Plessis accepted an offer from Leggett in February 1903 to go to the Standerton settlement. There were a considerable number of National Scouts living there who, in reaction to the first pastoral letter of October 1902, thought that the doors of the church had been permanently closed to them.[126] In March 1903 Du Plessis requested formal church approval from the moderator to serve as assistant minister on the Standerton settlement farm.[127] At the synod of May 1903 it was decided that unless Du Plessis received his calling in accordance with the prescribed procedure by a church council, in terms of ecclesiastical law his request could not be granted. On 16 May a delegation of the synod also laid a complaint with Lawley that Du Plessis was apparently providing religious direction at Standerton without the official sanction of the church.[128]

To this Lawley replied that "the Government has never contemplated the assumption of powers to *appoint* Ministers of Religion with the ecclesiastical functions appertaining to Ministers of any particular denomination".[129] In mitigation Du Plessis also claimed that his work on the settlement farm was not really of the same nature as the usual church activities; it was for this very reason that he had approached the moderator.[130] Furthermore, in his reply Lawley admitted that he had extended the invitation to Du Plessis to work on the settlement estate. He realised that such a step had been out of the ordinary, but as motivation Lawley explained: "Towards the end of last year [October 1902] there was a general adoption by the Ministers of your Church of the attitude that a political difference was to be construed as a moral offence and that the so-called offenders in this respect should be ostracised by their neighbours and denied the sacraments of the Church."[131] Lawley also referred to the pastoral letter of October 1902. In accordance with this, he said, the National Scouts had been censured in even stronger terms than in the synod decision of May 1903.[132] Because certain National Scouts had complained to him about this letter, Leggett had approached Du Plessis, who was at the time without a congregation, to work on the Standerton settlement.[133] "Since then," Lawley wrote in conclusion, "I am happy to know that wiser counsels have prevailed and that the attitude of the Church is towards the promotion of peace throughout the country."[134] Lawley's letter can be interpreted as an indication that he sympathised with the National Scouts, but it cannot be used as evidence that he was trying to kindle the division in church ranks in order to glean political advantage from the situation.

A mere four months later the issue reared its head once more and Lawley was confronted by a similar problem. On 22 September 1903 Grobler asked the government whether it would be prepared to provide assistance if the National Scouts decided to form a new church in the eastern Transvaal.[135] It is important to note that Grobler only made his request on 22 September. Before this date he had already organised two meetings, one on 26 August and another on 8 September, in the Standerton and Bethal districts respectively. At both these meetings the National Scouts present had raised objections about the synod's decision of May 1903.[136] The British had not had any input to these meetings at all. Thus it cannot be alleged that the National Scouts only objected to the church decision after encouragement by the British colonial authority. Lawley's reaction to Grobler's letter gives additional insight into the British attitude: "I find some difficulty in acceding to these requests, not because I do not sympathise with the sense of injury felt by members ..., but because the dispute in question is a purely Church matter, and I do not consider that, at this juncture, the intervention of the Government would be likely to restore that harmony within the Church, which in my opinion, is most desirable."[137] It is clear that at the time Lawley was not in favour of becoming embroiled in the church dispute.

In an interview with Grobler and his dissatisfied Scouts on 30 September, the day after their abortive discussions with Bosman, Lawley adopted the same attitude. During the interview he made the point that he had already warned Bosman previously that if the ministers persisted in their campaign to place the National Scouts under the censure of the church, it might well put the unity of the church at grave risk. Lawley made it very clear to Grobler and his group that "the last thing that I wish to see is discord and friction among the various sections of the community". He also emphasised that "it is impossible for the Government to take sides with one party at the present juncture and I can give no definite pledge at present. It is the last thing the Government could do to appear to be intriguing with one party against the other ... I am not in a position, nor should I feel justified, to give any definite pledge just now. That is not because I fail to sympathise with you, gentlemen, but it is because I do not wish as head of the Government to interfere in any way between a congregation and its minister." In addition Lawley clearly advised them that they had to make the decision about the proposed breakaway for themselves: "I want you to understand that in so far as the secession from the Church goes, that is a matter in which you must make up your own minds. You are men of intelligence and independent spirit and you are capable of forming an opinion. Until you have made up your minds one way or the other, I cannot interfere and you must not expect me to interfere."[138]

Lawley's attitude at the interview is proof that he was not trying to encourage friction within the church. He did indeed sympathise with the position in which the National Scouts found themselves, but they could not expect the government to interfere on their behalf in a church dispute. If Grobler interpreted Lawley's sympathy as an indication that the government would support their unconditional breakaway, this could only have been Grobler's personal interpretation of the facts; Lawley himself did not encourage the secession. It is also significant that Lawley took no further part in the dispute in Afrikaner religious circles until Grobler and his supporters themselves decided on 22 December 1903 to break away from the mother church.[139]

It was only on 28 January 1904, when the secession had already taken place, that Lawley again conducted an interview with Grobler and his group. On this occasion Grobler requested the government to provide the new church with financial support. Lawley pointed out to Grobler that he had told them previously that the government did not want to choose sides in a dispute that was purely a church matter and "for that reason it was impossible for the Government to give any guarantee or any pledge while a dispute in the Church or on Church matters was going forward". In this interview Lawley once again emphasised: "I deprecate the mixing up of politics and church matters and I would rather not do so to-day." On this basis he then went on to pass judgement on the issue as follows. He argued that the colonial government had made money available for the mother church as a whole for the restoration of its buildings; in the light of the fact that the breakaway group was no longer part of the mother church it was unable to enjoy the privileges of the church in these buildings. Lawley thus agreed to give limited financial support to the Scout Church, but in the course of the interview he did not commit himself to any specific amount that the new church could reckon on receiving.[140]

Lawley's argument as to why the Scouts were entitled to financial support is perhaps not entirely watertight. The authorities gave money to the N.H. of G. Kerk for the repair of their churches that had been damaged during the war – the Scout Church had no such church buildings that could have been destroyed during the war. The crux of the matter is, however, that Lawley based his argument for financial help to the National Scouts on the reasons given above – and not on political grounds. It would appear then that it was only after the breakaway of the Scout Church that Lawley considered that it was justified to show his sympathy with the National Scouts in a tangible manner in the form of promised financial support.[141]

In a broad perspective, the attitude of the British colonial authority can be summarised as follows. In the initial stages of the dispute it warned the ministers of the N.H. of G. Kerk, the biggest Afrikaner church, not to place the National Scouts under church discipline because this would lead to increased disunity and in this eventuality the government might well be forced to choose sides. The colonial authority took this stance because it was of the mistaken opinion that the National Scouts were being punished unnecessarily for a political offence. When it subsequently became clear that the enforcement of church discipline did indeed instigate obstinate and exaggerated opposition from Grobler and his kind, the authorities were very careful in the course of the subsequent dispute and the breakaway of the National Scouts not to encourage them to take such a step. Denoon is thus justified in his comment that, "On one hand the administration was discouraging the National Scouts from breaking Afrikaner ranks, and on the other warning the bittereinder ministers against the consequences of provoking the National Scouts. If the administration was less than zealous, at least its intentions were honourable."[142] It was only after Grobler and his National Scouts had left the church that the British authority chose sides by promising them financial support. Lawley also made it very clear to Grobler that he was not supporting them for political reasons, but only because he sympathised with their position; in his judgement they had a claim, as a separate church, to financial assistance. The allegation that the British authority purposely attempted to take political advantage of the church dispute in Afrikaner ranks and that they actively encouraged the breach in the church thus appears to be somewhat far-fetched. It is possible that the British authority, and more specifically Chamberlain, might secretly have hoped in January 1903 that the breach in Afrikaner society would be serious enough for the British to glean political advantage from the situation,[143] but in practice, however, the colonial authorities did not follow such a policy. Furthermore, Chamberlain, as Colonial Secretary, in contrast with Lawley, the lieutenant-governor, had exercised no influence at all in the church dispute in the Transvaal during the second half of 1903. Indeed, in September 1903 Chamberlain had resigned his ministerial position.[144]

The reality was that the post-war British authority in South Africa had no real political interest in the National Scouts. In October 1903 Eugène Marais remarked correctly that although the military authority had made use of the National Scouts during the war, these people would gradually come to the realisation that the British had "no greater love" for them than they did for any other civilised nation in the world. If the National Scouts were to rely unreservedly on

British support, said Marais, they would most certainly be disappointed.[145] Grobler and his group of breakaway National Scouts did indeed soon experience problems with the British authorities. By June 1904 they had still seen no sign of the promised financial support from the government.[146] In a confidential letter to the lieutenant-governor's private secretary, Leggett provided the reasons for the delay. After an interview with the head committee of the Scout Church in March 1904, Leggett came to the conclusion that the committee had gone to work in a disorganised and fumbling manner. "They do not seem able to frame their proposals in a business-like way," wrote Leggett, "and, although they promised to put their position and requests in written form, they did not bring with them … any documents for presentation to the Government."

Furthermore, there was a difference of opinion among the members of the committee of the new church because the government was not prepared to pay them personal salaries. As a result, Leggett decided to keep the committee in the dark about the amount of money the government was planning to give to them.[147] In April 1904 Leggett also found it necessary to point out to Breytenbach that the government was only prepared to carry a portion of the Scout Church's building costs. Administrative and travelling expenses and the ministers' salaries would have to be covered by the new church itself. "In this you will see," said Leggett, "the Government would be following the precedent established by itself in granting aid to the older Dutch churches towards the restoration of their buildings after the War."[148] It would appear that the authorities were consistent in the principle that Lawley had laid down for financial assistance. Lawley's private secretary likewise emphasised in a letter to Grobler that the government could only cover part of the building costs and "that in all other matters the Government will, in all respects, recognise the newly established Church so far as, and no further, than the Church of any other recognised denomination".[149] The authorities were thus very careful not to give the leaders of the Scout Church the impression that the government would carry all their expenses.

It was only towards the end of July 1904 that Leggett informed Breytenbach that the government had made £2 500 available to help the Scout Church with building costs. Breytenbach was disappointed with this amount and expressed the hope that the government would come to the aid of the Scout Church again at a later stage. To this Leggett replied: "You refer to possible requests for further help, and will therefore, I know, forgive me for drawing the attention of yourself and your Committee to the very clear pronouncement ... to the effect that the donation now approved is final so far as concerns any obligations the Government may have kindly assumed."[150] By September 1904 the Scout Church had still not received the £2 500 from the government. "There is undoubtedly a feeling that the Government is rather playing with these people," Leggett said of the National Scouts' reaction to the delay.[151] In October 1904 the money was at last paid out to the new church.[152]

Thereafter, members of the Scout Church tried in vain to request further financial assistance from the government. In August 1905 Revd Brink played openly on Lawley's finer feelings: "God's sake, for the sake of Justice and Truth and Mercy and for the love of God, help the poor and ... oppressed people by financial aid to build their churches."[153] But Lawley had indicated as early as July 1905 that the Scout Church could not count on any additional financial help.[154]

When, in January 1905, Grobler yet again asked for monetary assistance, Leggett was convinced that "Mr Grobler and his friends are attempting to blackmail the Government".[155] Leggett then enquired from Breytenbach whether Grobler's handling of the accounts of the Scout Church was in order. Breytenbach's reply to this question was very significant: "I know absolutely nothing of Mr Grobler; he has refused to give me a reply to six successive letters. It seems to me that this was with him a money making affair; we are trying to find out what he did with most of the money, (Govt. Grant), but he will have to account for it, and I think it is this he wants to avoid."[156]

Grobler's administration of the church funds was certainly suspect. The authorities suspected that he had appropriated a substantial portion of the money for his own use. Consequently, in September 1906, the state laid a charge against him for fraud. During the court hearing it became clear that Grobler had indeed spent the money ill advisedly, but the state could not prove the charge of fraud.[157]

This court hearing delivered the death blow to the Scout Church, an institution which had in any event never really shown any actual viability. Revd du Plessis, who said he was not prepared to work with Grobler, also resigned in February 1905.[158] Du Plessis approached the N.H. of G. Kerk again and was accepted back into the church ranks, and in August 1905 he was officially reinstated as a minister.[159] At the church synod in June 1906, Revd Bosman also decided to commit the "painful Scouts issue" to the realms of the past. In his opening statement he said: "The least said about that, the better for all parties. Let the dark pages in the history of our people ... rest in oblivion, even if they can never be entirely obliterated."[160] Some of the members of the Scout Church who had not in the meantime found their way back to the N.H. of G. Kerk joined Revd S.J. du Toit's *Kruiskerk* by 1906.[161] Thus the existence of the Scout Church as a separate religious body came to an end.

The Scout Church, which was at best an artificial creation, thus represented the only formal breach in Afrikanerdom. The apathy of the colonial authority and the fact that this breach was of marginal significance meant that the disunity in Afrikaner ranks did not have far-reaching political implications. The disunity that was a pervasive reality in the immediate post-war period had largely dissipated by 1906. The factors that helped to heal these war wounds will become evident later on.

Notes

1 See Chapter 6, section 2 above.
2 See Oosthuizen, "Krygsgevangenes", pp. 228–9, 489–521; Chapter 6, section 1 above.
3 CO 417/361/21492 (FK 663, p. 601), report on prisoners of war on St Helena, 1 May 1902.
4 *The Bloemfontein Post*, 14 June 1902 (report on an interview with Christiaan de Wet).
5 CSO 120/2072/02, letter from Dr G. van der Wall of the Kroonstad concentration camp with a report on Christiaan de Wet's speech, 12 June 1902. Van der Walt sent the letter to *The Bloemfontein Post*. The newspaper did not publish it, but sent the letter to the colonial secretary.
6 Van den Heever, p. 178.
7 Translated from the Dutch. *Land en Volk*, 17 October 1902.
8 Translated from the Dutch. Quoted by Rousseau, p. 170.
9 Translated from the Dutch. *The Friend*, 5 November 1902 (editorial in Dutch column).

10 Translated from the Dutch. *De Volksstem*, 16 May 1903 (letter from J.P.L. Lombard).
11 Translated from the Dutch. *De Volksstem*, 20 May 1903 (letter from Commandant Ben Bouwer).
12 *Land en Volk*, 17 April 1903 (letter from a bitterender at Marico).
13 *The Bloemfontein Post*, 18 June 1902 (open letter dated 10 June 1902 from P. de Wet and H.F. du Plessis).
14 Translated from the Dutch. *Land en Volk*, 17 October 1902.
15 GOV 615/372, "Summary of the proceedings of a deputation which met Mr Chamberlain at Sunnyside", 14 January 1901.
16 KK Supplementary items, 3, report on Meintjeskop camp, June 1902; CO 417/344/38516 (FK 583, p. 683), Leggett – F. Perry, 15 August 1902.
17 *Pretoria News*, 15 October 1903 (letter from "A Sympathiser with the Scouts").
18 CS 1079/39, confidential report by the resident magistrate, Standerton, 16 May 1903; EC 30/67/03, confidential report by the resident magistrate, Pretoria, 10 February 1903.
19 Transvaal Educational Department Reports, p. 8, January – December 1903.
20 CSO 199/6118/02, report by the resident magistrate, Vrede, July – December 1902; Knight, pp. 199–200; Van Rensburg, "Die Skandkol wat nie wou toegroei nie", in *Die Huisgenoot*, 8 August 1969; Van Rensburg, "Ekonomiese Herstel", p. 301.
21 *Pretoria News*, 13 October 1903 (news report).
22 CSO 593/1269/06, A.J. Fouché – Lieutenant J.F. Maguire (SAC), 15 February 1906 and certified statement by A.J. Fouché, 2 June 1906.
23 CSO 117/1901/02, Lieutenant C. Oakes – Wilson, 16 June 1902.
24 CSO 139/3007/02, Resident magistrate Vrede – Goold-Adams, 2 August 1902.
25 CS 1079/44, confidential report by the resident magistrate, Lydenburg, 10 July 1903.
26 CS 1081/20, confidential report by the resident magistrate, Christiana, 21 November 1903. The magistrate refers here to the Dutch term "Donder en bliksem!", a highly insulting and aggressive Dutch phrase that has no English equivalent, but which can perhaps be best translated as "Go to blazes!"
27 Translated from the Dutch. *De Volksstem*, 24 June 1903. See also *Acta Synodi, N.H. of G. Kerk, 1903*, p. 81, evidence of the minister, Ermelo.
28 Translated from the Dutch. *Land en Volk*, 27 February 1903 (letter from a bitterender from Ermelo). See also CS 1079/26, confidential report by the resident magistrate, Ermelo, 7 March 1903.
29 KK Supplementary items, 3, report on Pietersburg concentration camp, June 1902.
30 CS 1078/71, Resident magistrate Krugersdorp – Davidson, 12 August 1902. For similar evidence see *Land en Volk*, 24 February 1905 (letter from "National Scout").
31 Translated from the Dutch. *Land en Volk*, 13 February 1903 (news report). See also *Rand Daily Mail*, 5 February 1903.
32 EC 30/67/03, confidential report from the resident magistrate Volksrust, 7 February 1903.
33 Solomon, p. 19.

34 CO 417/344/38516 (FK 583, pp. 680–1), G.S. Cruse on behalf of 100 National Scouts – Administrator Rhodesia, July 1902 (copy). The exact date of the letter is not given. See also Knight, p. 200: "throughout the [Transvaal] colony the National Scouts were regarded by the Dutch population with a hatred so intense that it was doubtful if they would be able to remain in the country."

35 CO 417/345/44395 (FK 585, pp. 68–70), Administrator Rhodesia – Milner, 23 September 1902 and Leggett – F. Perry, 24 September 1902.

36 Lt. Gov. 77/84/24, Resident magistrate Lydenburg – Lawley 18 January 1904.

37 CS 842/13973, C.E. Cornwall (inspector SAC Ermelo) – Secretary SAC Johannesburg, 3 October 1906. L.J.S. Changuion, "Die Verhuising van Boere na Oos-Afrika, 1902–1914" (Unpublished MA dissertation, UP), 1975, p. 23, claims on the evidence of the given source that the National Scouts concerned did indeed move to British East Africa. However, the inspector of the Constabulary only made mention of an "Alleged Immigration", and that it was the "intention" of a few National Scouts to emigrate to British East Africa. Without additional evidence it cannot thus be accepted that these National Scouts did indeed go to British East Africa.

38 Changuion, p. 23.

39 HC 130/456, Resident magistrate Bethlehem – Courtenay, 7 October 1908; Changuion, pp. 23–4, 144–6. For Cloete's role in the Bethlehem peace committee, see Chapter 3, section 3 above. Naturally there were also bitterenders who left South Africa after the war, and one group, for example, went to Argentina. P.W. Grobbelaar (ed), *Die Afrikaner en sy Kultuur, IV, Afrikaners in die Vreemde* (compiled by C.J. Scheepers Strydom), pp. 206, 212.

40 Stanley Trapido maintains that it is incorrect to see the division in Afrikaner ranks in terms of Boers who collaborated and bitterenders. According to him the disunity should rather be regarded as follows: "Milner's land policy (devised, without success, to create a class of English commercial farmers) provided the opportunity for large Afrikaner land and cattle holders to acquire liquid capital, and this, together with the benefits which the same group derived from compensation granted for loss of property, made commercial agriculture viable. Because it was only those with large landed interests who were able to take advantage of Milner's schemes, intra-Afrikaner tensions were soon revived. This conflict is usually depicted as having arisen from differing stands taken by Afrikaners during the war, as being the perpetuation of conflict between *hensoppers* and *national scouts*, on the one hand, and *bittereinders* on the other, and Botha's policy of reconciliation is accordingly depicted in purely party political and nationalist terms ... That Afrikaner society was riven with conflict is apparent. Whether these conflicts were solely the result of positions adopted during the war, is however open to question, and it would appear that a more satisfactory structural explanation is available." (S. Trapido, "The South African Republic: Class Formation and the State, 1850–1900", *University of London Institute of Commonwealth Studies*, 16, Collected seminar papers on the Societies of Southern Africa in the 19th and 20th Centuries, 3, June 1972, p. 61.) This theory is patently flawed. It is not backed by sound evidence. It is also well known that the large majority of Afrikaners were in a poor financial position after the war. Even if certain Afrikaners were in possession of substantial capital, it is not clear why this should necessarily have led to tension and division.

41 P.J. Steyl (ed), *N.G. Kerk Lindley*, 1876–1951, p. 40.

42 See Chapter 3, section 4 above.
43 GOV 250/20, Du Plessis – Walrond, 22 February 1901; *The Bloemfontein Post*, 6 January 1903 (editorial); *The Times*, 7 January 1903 (news report).
44 Translated from the Dutch. *OVS Staatscourant*, (Government gazette) 21 February 1902 (notice dated 25 January 1902). See also Steyn Collection, 156/1/3, p. 3.
45 Translated from the Dutch. *De Vriend*, 28 January 1903 (editorial).
46 HC 108/156, memorandum by Leggett on church matters, 26 June 1903; *De Vriend*, 28 January 1903 (editorial); *The Bloemfontein Post*, 6 and 28 January 1903 (editorial articles); J.A.S. Oberholster, *Die Gereformeerde Kerke onder die Kruis in Suid-Afrika*, p. 278, note 21; Van Rensburg, "Die Skandkol wat nie wou toegroei nie" in *Die Huisgenoot*, 8 August 1969; Van Rensburg, "Ekonomiese Herstel", pp. 301–2.
47 HC 108/156, memorandum by Leggett on church matters, 26 June 1903. On the disagreement that arose in the Transvaal over Du Plessis's activities on the settlement farm, see Chapter 9, section 3.
48 Lindley Magistracy, 1.7, S.A. Celliers and three others – Goold-Adams, 8 December 1902. The Day of the Covenant, or Day of the Vow, was an Afrikaner national day of remembrance of the battle of Blood River (Ncome River) in which the Voortrekker leader Andries Pretorius and his men triumphed over a Zulu force on 16 December 1838. Prior to the battle the Voortrekkers appealed to God for his help and guidance and took a solemn vow to commemorate the day each year.
49 Translated from the Dutch. *De Fakkel*, 14 May 1903, p. 60.
50 *De Volksstem*, 1 July 1903 (letter from a bitterender at Vrede); *De Fakkel*, 30 April 1903, p. 60.
51 M.C.E. van Schoor and A.P.J. van Rensburg, *Die Geskiedenis van Bethlehem, 1864–1964*, p. 55; *De Kerkbode*, 29 January 1903, p. 53.
52 Translated from the Dutch. N.G. Kerk council minutes, Frankfort, 23 July 1904. On the division in the Frankfort congregation, see also the following church council minutes: 31 August, 5 October and 2 November 1903; 11 and 20 January, 4 July and 26 November 1904; 8 and 30 January, 3 April, 13 May 1905; 24 February, 26 May and 2 July 1906.
53 *N.G. Kerk* council minutes, Frankfort, 8 January and 3 April 1906.
54 *N.G. Kerk* council minutes, Frankfort, 13 May 1905; *Stemmen des Tijds*, October 1906, p. 2.
55 *N.G. Kerk* council minutes, Frankfort, 16 April 1906; *Stemmen des Tijds*, October 1906, p. 2; Oberholster, *Kerke onder die Kruis*, pp. 262–3. The *Kruiskerk* (literally: Church of the Cross) was a comparatively short-lived, Afrikaner church movement.
56 CSO 141/3149/02, Revd J.C. Hefer – Goold-Adams, undated.
57 See the *N.G. Kerk* council minutes for the mentioned towns in the period 1902–1904.
58 Translated from the Dutch. *De Fakkel*, 14 May 1903, pp. 59–60. See also *De Kerkbode*, 21 May 1903, p. 245 for an abbreviated version of the discussions during the synod meeting.
59 Translated from the Dutch. *De Fakkel*, 6 August 1903, p. 203.
60 See Chapter 10, section 2.
61 Milner Papers, 34, (FK 1172, p. 284), 26 June 1903.

62 Translated from the Dutch. *Land en Volk*, 14 November 1902 (letter from a bitterender at Balmoral).
63 Religious reports. A–Z, RR III, 4, "Staat van Godsdienst der Gemeente Zoutpansberg", 1902; N.H. of G. Kerk council minutes, Lichtenburg, 29 December 1902; N.H. of G. Kerk council minutes, Ventersburg, 10 January 1903; HC 108/156, memorandum by Leggett on church matters, 26 June 1903; CS 1079/37, confidential report by resident magistrate Ermelo, 18 April 1903.
64 HC 108/1S6, memorandum by Leggett on church matters, 26 June 1903; GOV 1254/94, Revd J.P. Wolhuter, Piet Retief – A.S. du Plessis, 3 March 1903 (translated copy).
65 N.H. of G. Kerk council minutes, Schweizer-Reneke, 1 November 1902; N.H. of G. Kerk council minutes, Carolina, 10 November 1902; N.H. of G. Kerk council minutes, Utrecht, 29 December 1902.
66 EC 30/39/03, confidential report by resident magistrate Heidelberg, 24 January 1903.
67 Religious reports, A–Z, RR, III, 4, "Staat van Godsdienst der Gemeente Heidelberg", 1903.
68 Translated from the Dutch. Synod Commission, minutes, 92–18, S–II, (1), 2 October 1902. G.D. Scholtz, *Die Geskiedenis van die Nederduitse Hervormde of Gereformeerde Kerk van Suid-Afrika, 1885–1910*, p. 125 claims incorrectly that the meeting took place on 21 October 1902.
69 Translated from the Dutch. *Land en Volk*, 10 October 1902, "Herderlike Brief gericht aan die gemeenten der Nerderduitsch Hervormde of Gereformeerde Kerk" (Pastoral letter addressed to the congregations of the N.H. of G. Kerk). This letter was initially worded in stronger terms. See Synod Annexures, 1902, S–I, 7, for the original letter in Dutch.
70 CS 1079/18, confidential report by resident magistrate Potchefstroom, 13 February 1903; *Land en Volk*, 14 November 1902 (letter from an anonymous National Scout who was registering his objection to the wording of the pastoral letter). Scholtz, *Nederduitse Hervormde of Gereformeerde Kerk*, pp. 125–7; Oberholster, *Kerke onder die Kruis*, pp. 275–6 and C.P.H. Olivier, "Die Geskiedenis van die Scoutkerk in Transvaal" (Unpublished proponent paper, UP), 1969, pp. 12–20 make no mention of the pastoral letter of October 1902 and the reaction to this by some National Scouts. As a result they accept incorrectly that the National Scouts reacted only in 1903, and that they only did so after alleged encouragement by the British authority. Because of this error the authors also accept, without further investigation, that from the initial stages the church acted in a conciliatory manner towards the National Scouts.
71 *Pretoria News*, 3 March 1903 (news report).
72 J.J. Oberholster and M.C.E. van Schoor, *Die Nederduitse Gereformeerde Kerk in die Oranje-Vrystaat*, p. 113; G.D. Worst, "Die Naoorlogse Periode" in D.J. Keet (ed), *Wonderdade van God: Jubileum Gedenkboek, 1842–1942*, p. 142.
73 Translated from the Dutch. *De Vereeniging*, 10 February 1904, p. 6.
74 P.G.J. Meiring, "Nationalism in the Dutch Reformed Churches", in T. Sundermeier (ed), *Church and Nationalism in South Africa*, p. 63.
75 *Acta Synodi, N.H. of G. Kerk*, 1903. p. 82.
76 *Pretoria News*, 16 October 1903 (letter from H. Luckhoff).
77 *The Cape Times*, 4 December 1901 (news report); See Chapter 7, section 1.

78 Compare, *Pretoria News*, 2 September 1903 and 11 March 1904 (editorial articles); *The Transvaal Leader*, 8 October 1902 (news report); *Rand Daily Mail*, 14 October 1903 (editorial); *Klerksdorp Mining Record*, 4 September 1903 and 3 November 1903 (editorial articles); *The Star*, 1 October 1903 (news report).

79 Translated from the Dutch. *Wetten en Bepalingen voor het Bestuur van de Nederduitsch Hervormde of Gereformeerde Kerk in Zuid-Afrika, 1903*, pp. 49–50, article 88.

80 Translated from the Dutch. *Acta Synodi, N.H. of G. Kerk*, 1903, pp. 80–90. The specific decision appears on p. 87. In *De Volksstem* of 20 May 1903 there was also a version of the discussions at the synod.

81 *De Volksstem*, 10 February 1904 (letter from Revd H.S. Bosman). Bosman's more moderate attitude is in keeping with his outlook during the war. In November 1900 he even considered undertaking a peace mission to the commandos. However, he did not execute this plan. See Chapter 2, section 5 above.

82 *De Vereeniging*, 21 October 1903, p. 2; 24 February 1904, p. 6.

83 See Chapter 10, section 2 below.

84 There are various degrees of church discipline: (a) a brotherly warning by the minister, (b) censure in the presence of the full church council, (c) censure by denying the person access to the sacraments for a prescribed period, (d) censure by denying the person access to the sacraments for an unspecified period, and (e) complete severance of all contact with the person by means of ex-communication. See J.H. van Loggerenberg, "Kerklike Opsig en Tug in die Nederduitsche Gereformeerde Gemeente Bloemfontein, 1848–1948" (Unpublished MTh dissertation, US), 1972, pp. 44–8; *Wetten en Bepalingen voor het Bestuur van de Nederduitsch Hervormde of Gereformeerde Kerk in Zuid-Afrika*, 1903, p. 55, article 213.

85 HC 108/156, memorandum by Leggett on church matters, 26 June 1903; *Pretoria News*, 2 September 1903 (news report).

86 *Acta Synodi, N.H. of G. Kerk*, 1903, pp. 89–90.

87 Translated from the Dutch. De Vereeniging, 24 February 1904, p. 6. See also H.S. Bosman, *Een Terugblik op Kerkelijke en godsdienstige toestanden in de Transvaal*, p. 74.

88 *Pretoria News*, 15 October 1903 (report on an interview with Revd Bosman).

89 See N.H. of G. Kerk council minutes, Pietersburg, 4 April 1904; EC 39/49/01, confidential report by resident magistrate Ermelo, 24 January 1904; *Pretoria News*, 15 October 1903 (report of an interview with Revd Bosman); *De Getuige*, October 1903, pp. 300–2; *Stemmen des Tijds*, March 1906, p. 7.

90 See Chapter 6, section 1 above for the geographic distribution of the National Scouts.

91 Preller, "Die National Scouts" in *Die Burger*, 1 July 1926; *Stemmen des Tijds*, October 1906, p. 3; *Pretoria News*, 2 September 1903 (news report); Chapter 6, section 1 above.

92 *Pretoria News*, 2 September 1903 (news report).

93 *Pretoria News*, 12 September 1903 (news report); Olivier, p. 30.

94 *De Volksstem*, 10 October 1903 (report by Revd Bosman).

95 *De Volksstem*, 10 October 1903 (report by Revd Bosman); *De Vereeniging*, 24 February 1904, pp. 6–7; Oberholster, *Kerke onder die Kruis*, p. 276; Scholtz, *Nederduitse Hervormde of Gereformeerde Kerk*, p. 129; Olivier, pp. 31–3.

CHAPTER 9: AFRIKANER DISUNITY AFTER THE WAR AND THE BRITISH AUTHORITY

96 *De Volksstem*, 17 October 1903 (report on the meeting); *Land en Volk*, 16 October 1903 (report on the meeting); *Pretoria News*, 17 October 1903 (report on the meeting); *De Vereeniging*, 24 February 1904, p. 7; Oberholster, *Kerke onder die Kruis*, p. 277; Scholtz *Nederduitse Hervormde of Gereformeerde Kerk*, p. 130; Olivier, p. 36.

97 *De Vereeniging*, 24 February 1904, p. 7; Oberholster, *Kerke onder die Kruis*, pp. 277–9; Scholtz, *Nederduitse Hervormde of Gereformeerde Kerk*, p. 131; Olivier, p. 39.

98 *De Vereeniging*, 24 February 1904, pp. 7–8; Oberholster. *Kerke onder die Kruis*, p. 279.

99 Oberholster, *Kerke onder die Kruis*, pp. 279–80; Scholtz, *Nederduitse Hervormde of Gereformeerde Kerk*, p. 132; Olivier, p. 40. Revd Brink was not in favour of the name "Scout Church". To Revd G.J. Rudolph of Rustenburg, who had used the term in a letter to him, Brink replied: "You speak of a 'Scout-kerk' … If our people would indulge in calling names, just mark what names they can resort to: 'Guerillas Church', 'Church of the gepantzerde broeken' [armoured trousers]; 'Kerk der Vluchtende helden' [fleeing heroes], etc." See Synod Annexures, 1904–1909, S–1, II, letter from Revd C.J. Brink, 18 April 1904.

100 Synod Annexures, 1904–1909, S–1, Revd Brink – Revd Bosman, 8 June 1906.

101 See the following editions of the *Pretoria News*: 2, 5 and 12 September; 3, 6, 12, 13, 14, 15, 16, 17 and 30 October; 3 and 30 November; 11, 15, 18, 19 and 29 December 1903; 20, 28 and 29 January; 15 February; 16, 17 and 19 March; 7 June 1904.

102 Translated from the Afrikaans. Olivier, p. 11.

103 HC 108/156, memorandum by Leggett on church matters, 26 June 1903.

104 *De Volksstem*, 10 February 1904 (letter from Revd Bosman).

105 N.H. of G. Kerk council minutes, Lydenburg, 5 December 1903; *De Vereeniging*, 2 December 1903, p. 3.

106 *De Vereeniging*, 24 January 1904, p. 7.

107 *Pretoria News*, 28 January 1904 (news report).

108 CS 1082/20, confidential report by the resident magistrate, Ermelo, 5 April 1904; CS 1082/39, Confidential report by the resident magistrate, Standerton, 19 April 1904.

109 GOV 1254/94, Grobler – Leggett, 20 July 1904.

110 *Land en Volk*, 4 March 1904 (editorial).

111 CS 1082/20, confidential report by the resident magistrate, Ermelo, 5 April 1904.

112 GOV 1254/94, Grobler – Leggett, 20 July 1904.

113 Bosman, p. 75. See also *Transvaal Census Commissioner Report*, 1904, p. XXIV, where it is mentioned that the Scout Church had "very few members".

114 *Pretoria News*, 7 June 1904 (news report).

115 GOV 1254/94, Resident magistrate Zeerust – Colonial secretary, 20 May 1905; *Stemmen des Tijds*, March 1906, p. 7; October 1906, pp. 2, 4.

116 Translated from the Afrikaans. Scholtz, *Nederduitse Hervormde of Gereformeerde Kerk*, p. 124. Similar opinions are expressed by Oberholster, *Kerke onder die Kruis*, pp. 283, 285; Olivier, pp. 15, 35, 42–4 and Solomon, p. 20. It must be pointed out that these authors relied mainly on incomplete information gleaned from the official church magazine *(De Vereeniging)* which did not accurately reflect the attitude of the British authority. They did not consult the archival records of the colonial secretary, high commissioner and governor. The documents in these

collections provide far more insight into the attitude of the British authority towards the breach in the church.

117   HC 108/156, memorandum by Leggett on church matters, 26 June 1903.
118   Milner Papers, 19, (FK 1135, p, 356).
119   HC 91/138 (copy).
120   CS 1081/55, Colonial secretary – Milner, including Grobler's request, 28 October 1903 and Milner's margin notes, 29 October 1903.
121   GOV 1253/114, Bosman – Chamberlain, 22 February 1903 and Chamberlain – Bosman, 10 March 1903.
122   *Pretoria News*, 15 October 1903 (report of an interview with Revd Bosman).
123   Compare Amery, *Chamberlain*, IV, pp. 347–8.
124   See Chapter 9, section 2 above on this issue.
125   GOV 1254/94, Leggett – Glyn, 5 November 1903.
126   Synod Annexures 1903, S–1, 7, Revd H.E. du Plessis – Moderator, 16 March 1903; Lt. Gov. 141/115/4, Leggett – Lawley, 27 March 1903; HC 108/156, memorandum by Leggett on church matters, 26 June 1903.
127   Synod Annexures 1903, S–1, 7, 16 March 1903.
128   *Acta Synodi, N.H. of G. Kerk*, 1903, pp. 85, 86, 88.
129   Lt. Gov. 144/120/6, Lawley – Moderator, 19 May 1903 (copy).
130   Synod Annexures 1903, S–1, 7, Revd H.E. du Plessis – Moderator, 16 March 1903.
131   Lt. Gov. 144/120/6, Lawley – Moderator, 19 May 1903 (copy).
132   See Chapter 9, section 2 above.
133   HC 108/156, memorandum by Leggett on church matters, 26 June 1903.
134   Lt. Gov. 144/120/6, Lawley – Moderator, 19 May 1903 (copy).
135   CS 1081/55, Grobler – Lawley, undated.
136   Olivier, pp. 28–31; Chapter 9, section 2 above.
137   CS 1081/55, margin notes by Lawley on Grobler's letter, 28 September 1903.
138   GOV 1254/94, report on the interview, 30 September 1903.
139   Olivier, p. 35 claims on the basis of a report in *De Vereeniging*, 24 February 1904, p. 8, that the presence of a British officer, Captain Walden, at a meeting at Vlaklaagte on 8 October 1903 should be regarded as a clear indication that the British authority gave active support to the breakaway. Walden, who lived on the Standerton settlement farm for National Scouts was, however, simply attending the meeting as an observer and did not take an active part in the discussions. See GOV 1254/94, Walden – Leggett, 9 October 1903.
140   GOV 1254/94, report on the interview, 28 January 1904.
141   It should be noted that during January and February 1904, Bosman and Lawley were involved in a fruitless debate about the secession of the Scout Church in their exchange of letters. Both Bosman and Lawley agreed that the breakaway was unfortunate; but because they approached the matter from two different corners, they could not find common ground. Bosman argued that the church should impose a lighter form of discipline on the National Scouts, while Lawley's opinion was that this discipline would simply lead to even more disunity. See *De Vereeniging* 24 February 1904, pp. 8–10 for this correspondence.

142 Denoon, *Grand Illusion*, p. 80.
143 In a letter to the British king Chamberlain mentions that the ministers "are very sore ... with the National Scouts who assisted us. This may not be a bad thing for us in the end". Quoted by Amery, *Chamberlain*, IV, pp. 337–8.
144 Le May, p. 162.
145 Translated from the Dutch. *Land en Volk*, 16 October 1903 (editorial).
146 *Pretoria News*, 7 June 1904 (news report).
147 GOV 1254/94, Leggett – Glyn, 30 March 1904.
148 GOV 1254/94, Leggett – Breytenbach, 23 April 1904 (copy).
149 GOV 1254/94, Glyn – Grobler, 13 April 1904 (copy).
150 GOV 1254/94, Leggett – Breytenbach, 22 July 1904 and Breytenbach – Leggett, 29 July 1904 and also Leggett – Breytenbach, 3 August 1904 (copies).
151 GOV 1254/94, Leggett – Glyn, 23 September 1904.
152 *De Volksstem*, 8 September 1906 (evidence of N.J. Breytenbach during a court case in which the Scout Church was involved).
153 GOV 1254/94, Brink – Lawley, 28 August 1905.
154 Lt. Gov. 144/120/6, Lawley – Grobler, 21 July 1905.
155 GOV 1254/94, Leggett – Colonial secretary, 4 January 1905.
156 GOV 1254/94, Breytenbach – Leggett, 25 February 1905.
157 ZTPD 3/144, Case 109, "Rex versus S.P. Grobler", September 1906. See also *De Volksstem*, 8, 12 and 15 September 1906 for reports on the court case.
158 GOV 1254/94, Du Plessis – Leggett, 20 February 1905.
159 *Acta Synodi, N.H. of G. Kerk*, 1906, p. 167.
160 Translated from the Dutch. *Acta Synodi, N.H. of G. Kerk*, 1906, p. 103.
161 Oberholster, *Kerke onder die Kruis*, pp. 273, 287; Olivier, pp. 58–62; D.A. Scholtz, "Ds. S.J. du Toit as Kerkman en Kultuurleier" (Unpublished D.Th. thesis, US), 1975, pp. 343–4.

Chapter 10
Reconciliation in Afrikaner ranks

1 Afrikaner politics as a unifying factor

By their very nature, the terms of the Peace of Vereeniging were such that the Afrikaners were deprived of a political voice; they had no access at all to the management of state affairs. The legislative councils that were set up immediately after the war in both colonies were comprised entirely of British officials. Milner was, however, prepared to enlarge these councils with nominated members, thus giving the local English-speaking residents a measure of representation. The composition of the legislative councils was destined to forge a political link between the Boer generals and the leading collaborators.

In August 1902, after consultations with Goold-Adams, Milner decided on the following nominated members for inclusion in the legislative assembly of the Orange River Colony: J.G. Fraser, R. Macfarlane, J.M. Wessels and J.F.J. van Rensburg. During the war, Wessels and Van Rensburg had both been bitterenders, but according to Milner they were moderate enough to serve on the council.[1] Macfarlane had distanced himself from the republican war effort,[2] as had Fraser, who had served on the burgher peace committee during the war. A legislative council that excluded Afrikaner leaders like General Christiaan de Wet could naturally hardly be regarded as representative of the Boer population in the Orange River Colony, but Milner could not see his way clear to include De Wet. "What seems to me to stand against Christiaan de Wet," he wrote to Goold-Adams, "is that … we could hardly put him on without putting on Piet de Wet, and to have both de Wets in, and tearing one another's hair out, might be both ludicrous and inconvenient."[3] Milner also conveyed this sentiment to Chamberlain and added another of his reservations: "As legislators, moreover, they would probably both be useless."[4] As a result, neither of the two brothers was asked to serve on the legislative council.

In the Transvaal Milner did indeed approach the recognised Afrikaner leaders – General Botha, General Smuts and General de la Rey – to serve in the enlarged council. In August 1902 Milner regarded De la Rey as "a man of spotless reputation" and in his view Botha, too, was "above the average of his countrymen".[5] It is not known what he felt about Smuts at this juncture.[6] Initially Milner could only find one National Scout or surrendered burgher who in his opinion was suitable to serve on the council, namely General Andries Cronjé.[7] But Chamberlain was far from satisfied with this proposed composition of the council. "Cronjé appears to be the sole representative of loyal Boers, 'Hands-uppers' and National Scouts," he complained to Milner. "If this is so, I think they have been insufficiently considered and I am strongly of opinion that they should have another representative ..." Milner's response to this was that "it is difficult to get another representative of the 'hands-upper' class, who has any general reputation ... When you have passed two or three very conspicuous names you come to something like a hundred, who are all much on the same level."[8] It is important to note here that Milner did not want to load the Transvaal's legislative assembly indiscriminately with surrendered burghers and National Scouts because this might afford them a significant political status. On the contrary, he approached the Boer generals, thus indirectly giving notice that they were still recognised as the true leaders of the *volk*.

In February 1903 Botha, Smuts and De la Rey reacted to Milner's invitation. All three turned the offer down and indicated that they felt that the time was not yet ripe for a nominated legislative council. The Boer leaders were also not prepared to take joint responsibility for the actions of the colonial government.[9] The reality of the situation was that they realised that their influence would be very limited on a council in which the government would have overwhelming control.[10] Only after the Boer generals refused to serve did Milner cast about for other representatives. On the recommendation of Andries Cronjé, he then nominated H.P.F.J. van Rensburg, the former chairman of the central burgher peace committee in the Transvaal. Two other people who had deserted the republican cause, namely J. Brink (a former magistrate of Rustenburg) and Z.J. de Villiers (who had been mayor of Johannesburg before the war), were also given a seat in the council. Only one bitterender, P. Roux, a former field-cornet from Marico, was prepared to serve on the council.[11]

Although in comparison to the bitterenders the "unfaithful" burghers had been afforded extensive representation in the legislative council, this by no means placed them in a powerful political position. Quite the opposite was true. By refusing to serve on Milner's legislative council, the Boer generals sent out a clear message to their followers that they were not prepared to associate with the British colonial government on a political level. In this way, in the eyes of the bitterenders, they were able to retain the respect and status that they had earned during the war. This also meant that they were free to express their criticism of the government and begin to forge their own political path.[12] On the other hand, despite the fact that they were represented in the council, the dissident burghers did not have any real bargaining power. In terms of the political dispensation they exercised very little influence and it was the exception rather than the rule for them to take part in the debates.[13] "Our Legislative Council has so far excited very little public attention," wrote Smuts in May 1903 to Merriman. "The Councillors as well as the public know that they are mere puppets in a play [in] which Destiny is the one real actor."[14]

Destiny, to use Smuts's metaphor, was however not the only actor in the post-war political developments. In terms of Afrikaner politics, Botha and Smuts were also important players. The war had brought their leadership qualities to the fore, and after the war it goes without saying that they became the political leaders. As the recognised and accepted leaders of the defeated Afrikaner nation, in the post-war period Botha and Smuts played a very significant role in the formulation of the Afrikaners' political objectives. With this in mind attention will now focus primarily on the policy that Botha followed towards the collaborators.

In May 1903 Botha gave a clear indication of his viewpoint with regard to the National Scouts. At the synod of the N.H. of G. Kerk he addressed the delegates on the issue of the National Scouts and asked them to adopt a conciliatory attitude towards the defectors. "Our nation is a big nation still today," he said, "but it is our duty to keep together and try to bring all our people into the same groove. So as God's ministers I must ask you one and all to try your utmost to bring the lost ones, 'handsoppers', etc., back to the nation to which they belong." According to Botha it would serve no purpose to close the doors of the church to the National Scouts: "No, we must take a broader view of the matter and think of what might happen in the future. We, the Afrikaners, are a great people and let us try to keep all of our people together and try to make ourselves a still greater nation."[15] To a reporter from the *Pretoria News*, Botha emphasised his post-war stance on the National Scouts: "I deprecate and always have deprecated any attack upon the National Scouts ... They are all our people and we must be united."[16]

Botha's stance was far more moderate than that of certain ministers who wanted to place the National Scouts under strict church discipline.[17] As L. Hess of *The Transvaal Critic* so rightly reported, while Botha and De la Rey "are working heart and soul for reconciliation ..., we find the clergy ... keeping the embers of dissension glowing".[18] It is therefore not surprising that Botha wrote to Leyds saying, "... our people are standing immovably firm ... on all important issues ... except on the National Scouts."[19] Why, one might ask, did Botha adopt this conciliatory stance towards the defectors? Part of the explanation is that he called for a spirit of forgiveness simply to reduce the friction in Afrikaner ranks.[20] The political situation in the Transvaal was, however, an even more telling factor – Botha was afraid that the Afrikaners in the Transvaal would be outnumbered by the English speakers. His fears were not entirely unfounded. On the basis of the 1904 census, Garson estimates that the Afrikaners comprised about half of the white population in the Transvaal. In order to combat the political implications of this, Botha was trying to promote Afrikaner unity. In practice this meant that the surrendered burghers and National Scouts had to be absorbed again into Afrikaner society. A conciliatory stance towards the unfaithful Afrikaners was the only realistic alternative to ensure a successful future for Afrikaner politics.[21] Botha's policy of forgiveness towards the National Scouts can be regarded as his "first instalment of conciliation".[22] In a broader perspective he also tried to reconcile the Afrikaners with their English-speaking compatriots and the British empire. This latter aspect, however, falls outside the scope of the present study.[23]

By mid-1903 the Boer generals began the political mobilisation of their followers. In June, Botha informed Milner that matters such as the importation of Chinese labourers were making the Boer people uneasy, and he began to organise a series of public meetings at which this and other issues which concerned the "burgher population" would be discussed.[24] On 2 July 1903 a meeting was held in Heidelberg. It was well attended and gave a clear indication of Botha's popularity as a political leader. "The ex-burghers have responded to Mr Botha's call in a very willing manner," read a report on the meeting. "They have obeyed their leader unhesitatingly and without question, and are evidently imbued with a devoted faith in the wisdom of their late Commander-in-Chief."[25] Although Botha had planned further meetings for 1903, these did not in fact take place. Apparently he did not want to give the impression to the colonial government that by holding these meetings the Boer people were planning to launch an organised protest against the Milner administration.[26]

The next step in the development of post-war Afrikaner politics was the formation of eight *Boerevereenigingen* (Boer associations) in the Transvaal. These societies were set up at the end of 1903 ostensibly to discuss farming issues, but in reality they functioned as quasi-political organisations.[27] Certain of these *Boerevereenigings* also gave attention to the National Scout question. The association in the Soutpansberg area initially refused membership to National Scouts, but Commandant Wynand Viljoen, an influential figure among the local bitterenders, was not in agreement with these sentiments: "Referring to the National Scouts, Mr Viljoen said they were responsible to God alone for their action in the late war. If they wished to join this association, its present members would not say them nay."[28] In the Pretoria district the *Boerevereniging* was, in the words of the local magistrate, "instrumental in getting farmers representing different shades of political faith to join together".[29] Towards the end of March

1904, during the first general meeting of all the Transvaal associations, held at Krugersdorp, Botha proposed the formation of a separate organisation specifically for political purposes.[30] On 23 May 1904 a Boer congress was held in Pretoria and here urgent attention was given to the establishment of such an organisation. The 160 delegates from all parts of the Transvaal chose a committee of seven members to draw up a constitution for a permanent organisation and to lay down the rules for local branches. These seven members were Louis Botha (chairman), Schalk Burger, J.H. de la Rey, C.F. Beyers, J.C. Smuts, E. Esselen and A.D.W. Wolmarans. Under their direction, the necessary arrangements were made over the next six months to form a political party. In Pretoria on 28 January 1905 Botha announced the establishment of *Het Volk* – the first post-war political party for the Afrikaners in the Transvaal. The head committee of *Het Volk* comprised the same seven people who had been chosen in May 1904 to do the initial spadework in setting up a political organisation.[31]

According to Le May the "reunion of Afrikanerdom" was one of *Het Volk*'s specific aims.[32] This was indeed the case. As the organisation of the new party progressed, Botha devoted himself tirelessly to the task of bridging the gap between the bitterenders and the National Scouts. He wrote to Steyn to say that the head committee "planned to bring the *volk* gradually to the sentiment of unity and the realisation of the necessity of standing together faithfully as one".[33] In a letter to Leyds, he mentioned that in the midst of hectic arrangements for the organisation of *Het Volk*, he had still managed to make time to combat the disunity among the people.[34] In his public speeches too, Botha often urged the necessity of reconciliation between the two groups. In his closing address at the congress of May 1904 in Pretoria he made the following appeal to the delegates: "Let us do everything in our power to heal this breach; then we shall regain our stature. Let us remove the words 'handsupper' and 'scout' from our language. The honour of the *volk* is too important and too sensitive to be impaired by such things."[35] In February 1905 at meetings of *Het Volk* at Heidelberg, Bethal and Middelburg, Botha had the same message for those present.[36] And at the re-internment of General Philip Botha in the Vrede district, Botha told the gathering of about 600 burghers and their families that "they must not forget the weaker brethren who had fallen away during the war through various causes, and who must now be taken back amongst us to strengthen our nation and help us to achieve our great aim".[37]

The other members of the head committee supported Botha in his policy of reconciliation. At Klerksdorp De la Rey said in 1905 that it was one of *Het Volk's* aims "to bring together in harmony again their people who, in many cases, were living in open hatred to their kith and kin". Smuts made similar statements at Klerksdorp and Potchefstroom.[38] At a meeting of *Het Volk* at Lichtenburg Smuts said: "Wipe the slate clean and do not let us hear any more of 'handsuppers', 'wild boers' and 'tame boers'."[39] A.D.W. Wolmarans too, at a meeting in the Pretoria district, warned those present: "You must all make peace with the Joiners and National Scouts and be like one man again, and then you will get your country back."[40] Even Beyers, who was by no means always in agreement with Botha's post-war policy,[41] asked his audience at Nylstroom "not to treat the National Scouts in an un-Christianlike manner, but leave them to the Lord to deal with".[42]

The organisers of *Het Volk* also showed that their conciliatory policy towards the National Scouts was not just something spoken about at meetings. The party went further and approached the disloyal burghers to serve on the management of local branches.[43] N.J. Breytenbach, for example, one of the leading figures in the Scout Church, was asked in February 1905 to make himself available as a committee member for the *Het Volk* branch at Ermelo, but Breytenbach turned the offer down.[44] At a meeting at Warmbaths the same offer was made to Jan du Plessis de Beer (a former *Volksraad* member and surrendered burgher who had fled to Bechuanaland and Rhodesia during the war). He indicated that he would be prepared to serve on the local *Het Volk* committee.[45] W.J. Steyn, an ex-member of the *Volksraad* who had been involved in the central peace committee in Pretoria during the war, also accepted an offer to join the committee of the Standerton branch.[46]

By and large the surrendered burghers joined the ranks of *Het Volk*, but there were also exceptions. Commandant A.J. Dercksen, who had made a few futile attempts to promote peace during the war, maintained that although *Het Volk* claimed to have accepted the surrendered burghers they were nevertheless regarded as "suspected people". He had plans to form his own political party whereby "the surrendered burghers ... would be placed in a position to show the world that we are still reputable Afrikaners who wish to promote the rise and welfare of our country with our whole heart and soul".[47] Dercksen's proposed political organisation came to naught and thus posed no threat to Botha's policy of conciliation.

Botha's policy soon showed the desired results. In May 1906 he was able to write to Leyds that the "differences among our ... people" had been all but obliterated.[48] Le May writes that Botha had attained the remarkable political feat "of knitting together the torn fabric of Afrikanerdom, immediately after the war, so that by 1906 the Boer party in the Transvaal – Het Volk – had acquired a monolithic solidarity".[49] Le May perhaps exaggerates the solidarity of *Het Volk* – Beyers and Wolmarans did not always agree with the other members of the head committee – but there is no doubt that through *Het Volk* Botha had made significant progress towards bridging the discord between the bitterenders and the collaborators.

To this must be added that time tends to heal, and after the war, as the years passed so the bitter emotional sentiments against the National Scouts began to ease. Some bitterenders also showed their forgiveness towards the disloyal burghers in a particularly generous manner. One remarkable example of this spirit of forgiveness was that shown by Commandant J.A. Joubert. During the war his arm had been amputated as the result of wounds inflicted by a National Scout. After the war he visited the man concerned and told him that he wanted to reconcile himself with his previous opponents. According to Botha's biographer, Joubert's generous gesture made a deep impression on the public and served as an example to others to adopt a tolerant attitude towards the National Scouts.[50] In the Barberton district a bitterender, Commandant H. Davel, was prepared to invite bitterenders as well as surrendered burghers and Scouts to his daughter's wedding. "This is the first time they have met in this way, and it is solely due to Davel's attitude towards the handsoppers and Scouts," said the local magistrate.[51] From the Ermelo district too, where there had been considerable friction between the two groups, the magistrate reported that a bitterender, Field-cornet W. de Villiers, "has seen the malcontents and pointed out to them the folly of their action and got the personal guarantees of most of them to let the [Scout] matter drop".[52] In light of this, the authors of the *Times History* are perhaps not far from the truth when they describe the waning friction in Afrikaner ranks as "a remarkable testimony ... to the lack of vindictiveness which is one of the most favourable traits of the Boer character".[53]

Botha's conciliation policy and the spirit of forgiveness shown by certain bitterenders were purposeful and undisguised attempts to contain the friction in Afrikaner ranks and promote the reintegration of the disloyal burghers. It would, however, be incorrect to ascribe this reintegration entirely to these overt attempts. Other less obvious factors also contributed to this process of reconciliation.

2 Other factors that contributed to reconciliation

In this section the emphasis will be on the way in which a number of more marginal factors promoted the process of reconciliation in Afrikaner ranks. Among these are the attitude of disinterest shown by the British colonial authority towards the collaborators; the realisation of their guilt that became evident among some members of the dissident group, and the grievances the surrendered burghers held against the colonial authorities as far as the compensation process was concerned.

The apathetic and disinterested post-war British attitude towards the National Scouts as far as repatriation, land settlement, compensation and the church issue are concerned, and the reasons behind this attitude have already been discussed. Briefly, it comes down to the fact that even at the time of the Peace of Vereeniging the National Scouts had lost any political initiative they might previously have had: the British negotiated only with the bitterenders. Afrikaner political power was still in the hands of the bitterenders and their leaders; after the war the British administration did not make any concerted effort to drive a wedge into Afrikaner society by using the National Scouts.[54] As Le May so rightly says about the political situation: "After the war, the 'handsuppers' and the National Scouts had been neglected by the Government."[55]

As early as September 1902 an anonymous surrendered burgher from Bloemfontein expressed the opinion that the administration did not really regard the collaborators as a political factor. "To many of us," he wrote, "it seems that the British in the attempt to reconcile [C.] De Wet and others like him, ... are neglecting and alienating their real supporters amongst the Dutch."[56] According to Leggett, in the Transvaal a few of the National Scouts had come to the realisation that in the eyes of the administration they were political lightweights and that the British were still obliged to recognise the Boer generals as the true leaders of the *volk*. "The whole policy," remarked Leggett, "inclines the moderate Boer to the side of the ... 'indispensable' leaders."[57] The reality was that the disloyal burghers had no other choice. "Brother, with whom is the Khaki Boer [collaborator] now able to take refuge?" asked a disillusioned member of the ORC Volunteers.[58] The magistrate at Lydenburg reported in January 1904 that "the National Scouts are ... inclined to do anything to regain the esteem of their own people."[59] A month later he claimed "that a large number of National Scouts have recently gone over to the Boers. The former gives as a reason for their action that they have been badly treated by the Government."[60] Captain W.H. Beddy, who was the leader of Beddy's Scouts during the war, also made mention of the fact that the ex-burghers in his corps were disgruntled with the government's attitude towards them and that as a result they were being driven "into the arms of the political agitators".[61] It can thus be accepted that the civil administration's indifference towards the collaborators was a factor that promoted their reintegration into Afrikaner society.

Denoon is of the opinion that the colonial administration's attitude towards the National Scouts and surrendered burghers meant that the British damaged their own political cause and that this thus worked to the advantage of the Afrikaner politicians. He expresses this as follows: "incipient distinctions within Afrikanerdom might well have proved useful to imperial manipulators. Consistent support for the *hensopper* churches, financial favours to landless *bijwoners*, political assistance for the *hensopper* spokesmen, might well have confounded Afrikanerdom for a while, thereby delaying their entry into the politics of the urban areas." Denoon is however careful not to propound this suggestion in dogmatic terms. Instead he qualifies his statement by saying: "Until Afrikaner social history is better developed, this argument cannot proceed beyond speculation."[62] Denoon's argument is apparently based on the supposition that the post-war division in Afrikaner society had crystallised to the point that the surrendered burghers and the National Scouts had formed a consolidated, unified group, one that with sustained British support might have been a handy tool to slow down the development of Afrikaner politics. In practice, however, the National Scouts – and the surrendered burghers even less so – did not have that level of solidarity; as far as the British were concerned there was little political advantage to be drawn from them. The division in Afrikaner ranks was experienced for the most part as the accumulated effect of unpleasant incidents and emotional bitterness on the social level and the only formal breach (the Scout Church) was relatively insignificant.[63]

In addition, the solidarity of the dissident burghers as a separate group was also broken down by the realisation of some members that they had chosen the wrong path during the war. This was followed in several cases by public confessions and pleas to be accepted back into Afrikaner society, and this recognition of guilt also became a factor that contributed to reconciliation. One such example was provided by J.Z. Grobler of Pretoria. In the official church magazine he begged his countrymen for forgiveness. "I was a National Scout," he wrote, "and I have made myself guilty before God and my people. I now feel too unworthy ... to be in the midst of my brothers, because I have behaved shamefully towards them ... I worry day and night about these matters ... Oh, dear brothers, please forgive me for what I have done against you. Oh my brothers, I was blinded by sin and dishonesty when I went ahead and became a National Scout ... It is my heartfelt wish to gain forgiveness from God and my people." In the same imploring tone Grobler concludes his letter: "Oh, Oh, my brothers, please forgive me for what I have done."[64] The confession by Hans Grady, a National Scout from the Heidelberg district, was just as grief-stricken: "I feel so unworthy and guilty that I can find no rest in my soul ... I shall thus lie down in the dust and beseech the entire Afrikaner *volk* for forgiveness ... God will forgive me. Will you forgive me too, you men, women and children for whom I have caused so much trouble and sorrow, will you please do so, that I may find rest for my soul! This is the imploring prayer of your grieving and mortified fellow-Afrikaner."[65] J. Cronjé, a National Scout from Potchefstroom, asked for forgiveness in a similar manner. In April 1905 he became a member of *Het Volk* and aligned himself completely with the party. "I promise to be faithful to my fellow burghers from now on and until the grave," Cronjé assured his compatriots.[66] In the Orange River Colony N.J. Lotz from Luckhoff, a former member of the ORC Volunteers, asked his "fellow Afrikaners" for forgiveness and promised that he would "in the future, with God's help, work for the rebuilding of our beloved Afrikaner *volk*".[67] H.S. Botha, a surrendered burgher from the Pretoria district, also felt called upon to make a public confession. The fact that he had left his fellow burghers in the lurch at a very early stage worried him so much that "I have broken down under the burden of sorrow that I am carrying."[68]

These confessions were not isolated incidents. Other collaborators who did not go so far as to ask forgiveness in a public declaration usually confessed in their homes to their local minister, or sent a personal letter to the church council.[69] This about-face by some of the burghers in the group naturally made its reintegration into Afrikaner society far easier and Afrikaner politicians like Botha welcomed this. Significantly, to an anonymous National Scout who sorrowfully asked for forgiveness Botha is said to have replied: "I accept your regrets … The time is coming when I shall require your services."[70]

In May 1904 a very prominent National Scout leader showed remorse for his conduct during the war. General Andries Cronjé, who had played a high profile role in the National Scouts, came to the realisation that his judgement about the state of the war, an assessment that had been instrumental in his decision to take up arms against his countrymen, had been inaccurate. In light of this he wrote a letter to the Klerksdorp church council in which he asked for "the forgiveness of my countrymen in the hope that I shall also receive forgiveness from a Higher Hand".[71] Shortly before his confession, Cronjé's wife had passed away. On the basis of his "conversations with men from the Western Transvaal", Leggett was of the opinion that the "capitulation of Andries Cronjé to the D.R. Church party was induced by his wife, while on her death bed. During her illness she was frequently visited by Rev. Strassheim, who is said to have told her unmistakeably that the family troubles ... were the visitation of God for Andries' conduct during the war ..." According to Leggett it was on the insistence of his wife that Andries Cronjé had agreed to register an apology.[72] It is unknown just how accurate Leggett's information was, but the main point here is that Andries Cronjé – a leading light among the collaborators and someone who had also served as a representative of the National Scouts on the legislative council – had changed his stance. *De Volksstem* "rejoiced" enthusiastically about Cronjé's decision and claimed that many National Scouts had already followed their leader's "good example".[73] Because Cronjé, from his position as a representative of the collaborators, had now distanced himself from them, this group crumbled even more – and this became yet another factor that influenced the process of reconciliation in Afrikanerdom.

The dissatisfaction of the surrendered burghers over the payment of their compensation claims also promoted reconciliation in Afrikaner ranks. "Probably no question arising out of the war has swayed so many minds and caused more heartburning than that of compensation," remarked the editor of the *Rand Daily Mail*.[74] Although in general terms the surrendered burghers were more favourably treated than the bitterenders in the compensation process, the payment of their claims was carried out with so many attendant discrepancies that, just like the bitterenders, they were very dissatisfied with the deal they had received.[75] In the Ermelo district the surrendered burghers held a protest meeting to discuss the manner in which their claims had been paid. They felt that as far as compensation was concerned, they had done no better than the bitterenders.[76] From the Rustenburg district in March 1904 the magistrate compiled a very significantly phrased report on the compensation grievances of the surrendered burghers and the outcome of their dissatisfaction. "The so-called 'Protected Burgher' is most bitter," he wrote. "He is asking what advantage he has derived from keeping his oath and rendering us assistance at great personal loss of prestige among his fellows ... Signs are not wanting of a drawing together of the two parties on this platform."[77]

In the Orange River Colony, where the reconciliation process developed somewhat differently from that in the Transvaal, not only was compensation a common grievance for both the surrendered burghers and the bitterenders; it also played a role in the rise of postwar Afrikaner mobilisation. Unlike Botha in the Transvaal, the Boer generals in the Orange River Colony made no determined effort to reintegrate the disloyal burghers into Afrikaner ranks. At the beginning of 1903 General Christiaan de Wet had not yet given any real indication of a tolerant attitude towards this group. Indeed, in the course of an interview with Chamberlain in Bloemfontein on 6 February 1903, De Wet made it clear that he had no time for the unfaithful burghers.[78] The bitterenders and former prisoners of war also outnumbered the English speakers in the Orange River Colony so there was no danger, as there was in the Transvaal, that the Afrikaners might be at a disadvantage in the political arena because of a numerical minority.[79] In the Orange River Colony it was thus less crucial that the Boer generals should adopt a conciliatory attitude towards the dissident burghers in the interest of Afrikaner unity. In comparison to the Transvaal there was also relative calm in church circles; disloyal burghers were more readily accepted in church circles and by implication into Afrikaner society.[80] Naturally this made reconciliation a less urgent process.

By the end of 1904 Afrikaner resistance to the British colonial administration began to take shape in the Orange River Colony. Under the direction of J. Vlotman a meeting was held on 17 September 1904 at Brandfort, where 19 dissatisfied people aired their grievances against the colonial authority. Those who attended formed a committee of seven members and on 28 September a manifesto was published in *De Vriend*. In this manifesto the committee focused mainly on the ambient dissatisfaction about compensation; they encouraged "people from all groups" to hold local meetings and to choose delegates for a general congress that they planned to hold at Brandfort.[81]

In his study on the rise of party politics in die Orange River Colony, A.H. Marais regards this manifesto as the "beginning of a tidal wave of nationalism, a wave that would not permit itself to be curbed, one that gathered rushing momentum and soon flooded the whole Orange River Colony". However, he pays little attention to the status of the people responsible for compiling the manifesto, or indeed the reasons why they decided to draw up a manifesto in the first place.[82] J. Vlotman, the chairman of the Brandfort committee, was a surrendered burgher who had laid down his arms and withdrawn from the war on 19 May 1900 in the Winburg district. Despite the fact that he had remained true to the oath of neutrality, he was taken prisoner by the British and sent to the Green Point prisoner-of-war camp. He had raised an objection to his internment as a prisoner of war and the military authorities subsequently allowed him to live in Stellenbosch on parole.[83] With the conclusion of peace, Vlotman returned to Brandfort and on 14 September 1904 he learned that the compensation officials had rated his claim for damages below those of the bitterenders.[84] Vlotman was furious. Three days after receiving this disturbing news he held the meeting from which the Brandfort manifesto was born. Three other members of the committee (N.J. Vermaak, G.H. Erwee and G.J. van Graan) were also surrendered burghers, while J.P. Marais had not taken part in the war at all. Only one bitterender, J.J. van Rensburg, served on the Brandfort committee. The remaining member, W.H. Maas, had been in British military service during the war. In an interview that the Brandfort committee held on 3 October 1904 with Goold-Adams, it became very clear that the members were dissatisfied primarily because of the manner in which compensation claims had been processed.[85] In retrospect there is little doubt at all that the first Brandfort meeting and manifesto can be seen as the beginning of the political revival in the Orange River Colony. From the Brandfort meeting matters progressed to the Brandfort congress (December 1904), the Bloemfontein congress (July 1905) and eventually to the formation of the Orangia Unie (May 1906) – developments that can indeed be described as a tidal wave of nationalism. It must, however, be emphasised that the Brandfort committee did not foresee these developments or have them in mind; they were merely concerned about their compensation claims.

The fact that the first open signs of resistance came from the surrendered burghers shows the significance of their dissatisfaction with the compensation process and the extent to which this had already alienated them from the British colonial authority. Alienation from the British authority meant that they had to seek another political home. The most obvious alternative was to reconcile with the bitterenders.

After the Brandfort committee had published its manifesto, its resistance campaign began to gain support in a larger arena. *De Vriend*, the pro-Boer newspaper in the Orange River Colony, gave considerable publicity to the movement and was careful not to denigrate the people who had inspired the initiative as surrendered burghers. The editor of the newspaper, J. Visscher, tried a wider tack with this publicity, attempting to reach all classes of society. Commenting on the manifesto he wrote: "With the inauguration of the Brandfort movement we are beginning a new phase in our history. It is taking shape as a national movement. We trust that it will remain so. This [movement] must reflect the views of the entire Volk."[86]

During October and November 1904 meetings were held in nearly all districts in the Orange River Colony. Initially the surrendered burghers used these meetings to air their compensation grievances, but it would appear that the bitterenders gradually became involved and matters such as the language medium at schools, the bitterenders' dissatisfaction with the South African Constabulary and the question of representative government also received attention.[87] The Frankfort magistrate was perhaps not entirely incorrect in reporting that the resistance movement "was ... being arranged by certain Protected Burghers to further their own interests and ... the Constabulary, Language and School questions were evidently held out by the Brandfort movement to attract the 'Wild Boer'".[88]

On 1 and 2 December 1904, 102 delegates from all parts of the Orange River Colony assembled at Brandfort. In a report on the congress Goold-Adams mentioned that half of the representatives were surrendered burghers and the others were bitterenders[89] – a significant indication that the two groups were prepared to meet each other on common ground. General Christiaan de Wet accepted a special invitation to attend the congress and General Hertzog was also present.[90] The presence of both these recognised and accepted Afrikaner leaders afforded the gathering greater prestige, but at the same time their attendance led to a change in the leadership of the movement. Vlotman, who had been its initiator, was named as honorary chairman and General Hertzog was chosen as chairman of the congress.[91] In real terms, Vlotman's position as honorary chairman was merely a consolation prize for his trouble, while Hertzog, as chairman of the congress, had moved into the driving seat as the true political leader. From that point onwards it was Hertzog who was at the forefront of the political revival of the Afrikaners in the Orange River Colony. Goold-Adams had expected that this would happen. "The result of the Congress," he reported, "has been to confirm my anticipation that, as soon as the actual business of the meeting commenced, the management of the proceedings would be taken out of the hands of the original movers of the Compensation question, and would pass into those of the more important politicians."[92]

At the congress Hertzog gave the surrendered burghers plenty of time to discuss the compensation issue and to show how the British authority had failed to meet their expectations. Many of the surrendered burghers gave vent to their disillusionment in no uncertain terms; the predominant theme was that Roberts's promises had not been met and that the British authorities had handled their compensation claims in an unsatisfactory manner.[93] In an annexure to the official minutes of the congress there are 325 statements by bona fide surrendered burghers who alleged that they had received a raw deal because of the arbitrary decisions of compensation officials.[94]

Characteristic of the speeches at the congress was the manner in which the compensation grievances had engendered a spirit of rapprochement between surrendered burghers and bitterenders. One example was provided by an English-speaking delegate from Vrede, a man called Willis, who had apparently already aligned himself with the bitterenders. He emphasised that the British government, by means of its promises, had alienated the weaker burghers from their faithful countrymen, "and when the promises were not honoured they had to go back ashamedly to look for support from the people they had deserted in the first place".[95] H. Pepler from the Bloemfontein district declared frankly that Roberts's proclamations "has brought this Congress together".[96] De Beer, a bitterender from Lindley, also made it clear that he saw the congress as "the foundation" upon which all the groups of the population could build in the future.[97] In an impressive address General Christiaan de Wet spoke of the new spirit of forgiveness that had been engendered by the compensation question. "As far as the protected burghers are concerned," he said, "even though I hate these people to the extent that I cannot bear to look at them, I still say that they are entitled to their twenty shillings in the pound. Thus, in place of hatred, I will now tell you that my feeling is this: we are now all brothers."[98] At the end of the congress J. Visscher of *De Vriend*, who had acted as secretary, mentioned with justification that the congress had strengthened the "bonds of brotherhood between the Burghers" and had removed the divisions.[99]

By 1906, in both the Orange River Colony and the Transvaal, there was very little friction between the groups. The West Ridgeway Commission was able to declare in July that the surrendered burghers and collaborators in both colonies no longer existed as a separate group: "These men are now being rapidly reconciled and are being quietly absorbed into the general population. None of them would wish us to disturb this peaceful operation by any intervention on his behalf."[100] The process of reconciliation was complete; the unpleasant incidents and open dissent in Afrikaner ranks were largely a thing of the past. The disloyal burghers that had deserted from Afrikaner ranks during the melting pot of the war had been brought back into the fold and were accepted as part of the *volk*. Afrikanerdom could once again show a united front.

The integration of the unfaithful burghers back into the ranks of the *volk* meant that after the granting of representative government to the Transvaal in December 1906, there was no talk of a separate group, or of their putting forward any candidates in the general election that followed in February 1907. By this time they had been absorbed into *Het Volk*, the party that won the election. Indeed, even by February 1906 Botha claimed that he was confident that *Het Volk* could count on the support of the disloyal burghers in an election.[101]

In the Orange River Colony, which was granted representative government in June 1907, the leaders of the ORC Volunteers, Piet de Wet and S.G. Vilonel, were involved in the election of November 1907. De Wet and Vilonel stood as independent candidates in Lindley and Senekal respectively. Their opponents were both representatives of Orangia Unie – Hertzog's *volk* party in the Orange River Colony. But De Wet and Vilonel received very little support in the election. In

Lindley De Wet polled only 236 of the 757 votes cast, and Vilonel fared even worse in Senekal, receiving only 262 from a total of 1024 votes.[102] As early as October 1905 Vilonel had realised that he did not really enjoy any significant political influence. "Even in Senekal where at present I enjoy the entire support of the great majority of the people in business affairs," he admitted to Goold-Adams, "I feel convinced, that if circumstances made it possible for me to devote any part of my time to politics, I would stand no chance in an election."[103] On the one hand the participation of De Wet and Vilonel as independent candidates in the 1907 election possibly indicates that they could not identify fully with post-war Afrikaner politics in the Orange River Colony. On the other hand, their weak showing in the election is a clear indication that in comparison with the Orangia Unie candidates, they had insignificant support. Their participation in the election was however not much more than a futile indication of the limited local and personal support that they enjoyed in Lindley and Senekal. Like *Het Volk* in the Transvaal, the Orangia Unie won the general election, and the Afrikaners had thus regained political control in both these former colonies.

Notes

1. CO 224/8/38562 (FK 1053, pp. 108–117), Milner – Chamberlain, 25 August 1902. See also Van Rensburg, "Ekonomiese Herstel", p. 189; Malan, "Fraser", pp. 246–8. Initially W. Burns-Thompson from Harrismith was named in place of Macfarlane, but Burns-Thompson turned the offer down. When Macfarlane died in 1904, Burns-Thompson took his place.
2. Milner Papers, 46 (FK 1135, pp. 201–7), Milner – Pretyman, 24 November 1900 and enclosed P.M. Botha – Milner, 20 November 1900; Chapter 5, section 1.
3. HC 113/161, 10 August 1902 (copy).
4. CO 224/8/38562 (FK 1053, p. 115), 25 August 1902.
5. HC 27/156, Milner – Chamberlain, 28 August 1902 (copy).
6. By the beginning of 1903, however, apparently as a result of reports from his secret service, Milner had the following opinion of Smuts: "Smuts is one of the most dangerous men in South Africa and is working against us as hard as he can." He also altered his opinion on Botha and apparently believed that "Botha would probably try to deceive both sides." See also Denoon, *Grand Illusion*, p. 83. On Milner's secret service, which was not always very reliable, see Le May, p. 159; N.G. Garson, "'Het Volk': The Botha-Smuts Party in the Transvaal, 1904–1911" in *The Historical Journal*, 9(1) 1966, p. 107 note 22; Denoon, *Grand Illusion*, p. 83.
7. HC 27/156, Milner – Chamberlain, 28 August 1902 (copy).

8   HC 114/162, 27 September and 3 October 1902 (copies).
9   GOV 588/284, Botha, De la Rey and Smuts – Milner, 6 February 1903.
10 Le May, p. 159.
11 HC 105/155, Milner – Chamberlain, 11 April 1903 (copy); Hancock and Van der Poel, *Selections*, I, p. 599, "Memoirs".
12 Garson, pp. 103, 106; G.B. Pyrah, *Imperial Policy and South Africa, 1902–1910*, p. 144; Le May, p. 159.
13 See *Legislative Council Debates*, 1903, 1904, 1905. Andries Cronjé, for example, only took part in debates on 21 July 1903 and 25 July 1905 about blacks and land settlement.
14 Hancock and Van der Poel, *Selections*, II, p. 95, 29 May 1903.
15 HC 108/156, Milner – Chamberlain, 25 May 1903, and enclosed translated copy of Botha's speech, 14 May 1903. Surprisingly, Botha's speech was not noted in the official synod minutes of the N.H. of G. Kerk (*Acta Synodi*). On the reliability of this report Milner mentioned: "These notes emanate from a perfectly trustworthy source ..." Milner also claimed that the Dutch newspapers made no mention of Botha's speech and "probably no reference will ever be made [to it] in public".
16 *Pretoria News*, 14 December 1903 (report on an interview with Botha).
17 On the various attitudes held by the ministers on the National Scout question, see Chapter 9, section 2 above.
18 *The Transvaal Critic*, 29 May 1903 (editorial).
19 Translated from the Dutch. Leyds Archive, 262 (1), 14 March 1904.
20 See Davenport, p. 324; N. Bromberger, "General Botha and the Conciliation Policy" (Unpublished BA Honours essay, UK), 1957, p. 11.
21 Garson, pp. 104, 111. See also Engelenburg, p. 123; B. Spoelstra, "Die Bewindsaanvaarding van die Botha regering oor Transvaal as selfregerende Britse kolonie in 1907" in *Archives Yearbook for South African History*, 16(II), 1953, p. 315.
22 Garson, p. 130.
23 On this issue see Bromberger, pp. 12 70.
24 GOV 587/281, Botha – Milner, 4 June 1903.
25 *Klerksdorp Mining Record*, 3 July 1903 (report on the meeting). See also *De Volksstem*, 4 July 1903 (report on the meeting).
26 Knop (pseudonym for Gustav Preller), *Agt jaar s'n politiek: skoon geskiedenis van die Suidafr. Nasionale Partij, 1902–1910*, p. 14. Garson, pp. 106–107 presumed on the basis of secret British reports on the meeting that Botha did not hold any further meetings in 1903 because the Heidelberg meeting had not really been a success. Judging by the newspaper reports on the meeting (*Klerksdorp Mining Record*, 3 July 1903 and *De Volksstem*, 4 July 1903) it is, however, doubtful whether the Heidelberg meeting was a failure and that it was this that prevented Botha from organising any further meetings during 1903.
27 Davenport, p. 256; Garson, p. 107.
28 *The Transvaal Leader*, 23 January 1904 (report on a meeting at Pietersburg). See also HC 108/156, Captain G. David – Commanding officer (SAC) Soutpansberg, 25 January 1904.
29 GOV 1252/Unsorted, confidential report by the resident magistrate Pretoria, 15 March 1905.

30 Garson, pp. 106–7.
31 *De Volksstem*, 25 May 1904 and 1 February 1905 (reports on meetings); Garson, p. 107; Weideman, pp. 332–3.
32 Le May, p. 173.
33 Translated from the Dutch. Steyn Collection, 156/1/3, p. 443, 19 September 1904.
34 Leyds Archive, 262 (1), 8 October 1905.
35 Quoted by Engelenburg, p. 125.
36 *De Volksstem*, 4 February 1905 and 4 March 1905; *The Star*, 17 February 1905 (reports on meetings).
37 HC 108/156, "Report on the Re-internment of Philip Botha", 22 February 1904.
38 *The Star*, 23 and 24 February 1905 (reports on meetings). See also *De Volksstem*, 25 February 1905 (reports on meetings).
39 GOV 1252/Unsorted, confidential report by the resident magistrate Lichtenburg, 1 March 1905.
40 HC 108/156, translated report of A.D.W. Wolmarans's speech, 13 May 1905.
41 See Scholtz, *Beyers*, pp. 159, 163–4.
42 *Pretoria News*, 26 October 1903 (report on the meeting).
43 Le May, pp. 173–4.
44 GOV 1254/94, Breytenbach – Leggett, 25 February 1904.
45 *The Star*, 21 February 1905 (report on the meeting). On Jan du Plessis de Beer's role during the war see Chapter 2, section 3 above.
46 *Land en Volk*, 10 February 1905 (news report).
47 Translated from the Dutch. *Land en Volk*, 28 April 1905 (letter from A.J. Dercksen). On Dercksen's peace missions during the war see Chapter 2, section 5 above.
48 Translated from the Dutch. Leyds Archive, 262 (ii), 9 May 1906.
49 Le May, p. 215. See also Steinmeyer, *Spykers met Koppe*, p. 30.
50 Engelenburg, pp. 122–3.
51 EC 36/562/03, confidential report of resident magistrate Barberton, 19 September 1903.
52 EC 31/144/03, confidential report of resident magistrate Ermelo, 7 March 1903.
53 *Times History*, VI, p, 53.
54 See Chapter 8, sections 1, 2 and 3. Also Chapter 9, section 3.
55 Le May, p. 173.
56 *The Bloemfontein Post*, 18 September 1902 (letter from a surrendered burgher).
57 GOV 1253/Unsorted, Leggett – Glyn, 14 March 1903.
58 Translated from the Dutch. *De Getuige*, September 1903, p. 258.
59 GOV 1251/50, confidential report by resident magistrate Lydenburg, 25 January 1904.
60 CS 1082/17, confidential report by resident magistrate Lydenburg, 24 February 1904.
61 Lieutenant-governor 75/83/33, Beddy – Colonel S.B. Steels (SAC), 12 January 1905.

62 Denoon, *Grand Illusion*, p. 241.
63 See Chapter 9, sections 1 and 2 above.
64 Translated from the Dutch. *De Vereeniging*, 26 January 1905, p. 9. Grobler's letter also appeared on 10 February 1905 in *Land en Volk*.
65 Translated from the Dutch. *De Vereeniging*, 3 November 1904, p. 4.
66 Translated from the Dutch. *De Volksstem*, 29 April 1905 (letter from J. Cronjé).
67 Translated from the Dutch. *De Vriend*, 23 December 1904 (letter from N.J. Lotz).
68 Translated from the Dutch. *De Vereeniging*, 9 September 1903, p. 6.
69 Religious reports, 1899–1903, A–Z, RR III, 4, "Staat van Godsdienst der Gemeente Klerksdorp", 1903; *N.H. of G. Kerk* council minutes, Belfast, 25 April 1903; *De Volksstem*, 10 February 1904 (letter from Revd H.S. Bosman).
70 Quoted by Devitt, p. 24.
71 Translated from the Dutch. *De Volksstem*, 25 May 1904 (news report).
72 GOV 1254/94, Leggett – Walrond, 3 June 1904.
73 *De Volksstem*, 25 May 1904 (news report).
74 *Rand Daily Mail*, 22 December 1902 (editorial).
75 See Chapter 8, section 3 above on the compensation issue and the reasons why the surrendered burghers were dissatisfied.
76 *De Volksstem*, 5 October 1904 (news report).
77 CS 1082/21, confidential report from the resident magistrate Rustenburg, 6 March 1904.
78 *The Friend*, 7 February 1903 (news report); Badenhorst, pp. 166, 177.
79 See A.H. Marais, "Die Afrikaner verkry Politieke beheer (1902–1910)" in O. Geyser and A.H. Marais (eds), *Die Nasionale Party, Agtergrond, Stigting en Konsolidasie*, p. 65.
80 See Chapter 9, section 2 above.
81 *Officieel Verslag* [official report] ... *Brandfort*, pp. 2–4; *De Vriend*, 28 September 1904 (manifesto), Van Rensburg, "Ekonomiese Herstel", p. 257.
82 Translated from the Afrikaans. A.H. Marais, "Die Ontstaan en ontwikkeling van partypolitiek in die Oranjerivierkolonie, 1902–1912" (Unpublished MA dissertation, UOVS), 1967, p. 23. In Marais, "Die Afrikaner verkry Politieke Beheer", the manifesto as such and its compliers are not mentioned at all.
83 SO/POW 19/1584, J. Vlotman – Staff officer, Green Point concentration camp, 2 May 1901 and memorandum by staff officer, 9 September 1901; Vlotman Collection, Items on Brandfort congress, December 1904.
84 *Officieel Verslag* [official report] ... *Brandfort*, p. 4.
85 In the course of the interview with Goold-Adams the leaders also mentioned their status during the war. On this interview see *Officieel Verslag* [official report] ... *Brandfort*, pp. 8–16. Compare also Van Rensburg, "Ekonomiese Herstel", p. 257.
86 Translated from the Dutch. *De Vriend*, 28 September 1904 (editorial).
87 See *De Vriend*, 4, 10, 14, 15, 20, 22, 24, 25, 26 and 29 October; 3, 8, 10, 12, 17 and 26 November for reports on the discussions at the meeting.
88 HC 120/165, report by the resident magistrate Frankfort, 30 December 1904.

89 CSO 580/1165/05, Goold-Adams – Milner, 31 January 1905 (copy).
90 Van den Heever, p. 200.
91 *Officieel Verslag* [official report] ... *Brandfort*, p. 29.
92 CSO 580/1165/05, Goold-Adams – Milner, 31 January 1905 (copy). See also Van Rensburg, "Ekonomiese Herstel", pp. 257–8.
93 Compare *Officieel Verslag* (official report) ... *Brandfort*, pp. 30–50.
94 *Officieel Verslag* ... *Brandfort*, pp. II–LXXXIV.
95 Translated from the Dutch. *Officieel Verslag* ... *Brandfort*, p. 32.
96 Translated from the Dutch. *Officieel Verslag* ... *Brandfort*, p. 47.
97 Translated from the Dutch. *Officieel Verslag* ... *Brandfort*, p. 47.
98 Translated from the Dutch. *Officieel Verslag* ... *Brandfort*, p. 34.
99 *De Vriend*, 9 December 1904 (editorial).
100 *Africa (South)*, 853, p. 28, 30 July 1906.
101 Leyds Archive, 262 (ii), Botha – Leyds, 16 February 1906.
102 See Malan, "Fraser", annexure F, pp. 365–6, for a list with all the election results for 1907.
103 HC 119/164, 19 October 1905.

A final word

Seen against the background of political developments in Africa in the twentieth century, the Anglo-Boer War was the first anti-colonial or nationalist war of the century that took place on the continent. Despite the fact that there were divergent opinions on what constituted the national interest during this war, these differences did not really present an insurmountable obstacle to the political mobilisation of the Afrikaner in the post-war period. About three years after the war, Milner admitted to Selborne that the "Afrikander party" was an "all-pervading political force" in South Africa. There were indeed, according to him, sometimes petty differences "dividing the political Afrikaners", but significantly he added that "in their aim, and, broadly speaking, in their method also, they are absolutely alike".[1] In the final analysis, the polarisation that took place in Afrikaner ranks during the war was not a significant issue in the subsequent political development of the Afrikaner.

During the Anglo-Boer War certain terms were however born, and these were destined to be reflected in several different ways in South African politics for a number of years afterwards. In September 1910, H. Burton (the minister of Native Affairs in the first Union cabinet) spoke out in criticism of English speakers who were in favour of cooperation with the Afrikaans speakers. According to him those English speakers who were prepared to cooperate were guilty in a most reprehensible manner "of not representing English sentiment, as well as being *renegades, National Scouts and traitors to their blood*".[2] During the rebellion of 1914 and the general election which followed soon afterwards in October 1915, the term "National Scout"

469

was used with another connotation. In August 1915, the prime minister, General Louis Botha, reacted to criticism from certain Afrikaner circles that by providing military support to the British empire during the First World War he had become an "Englishman" and a "Khaki", by saying that: "One can easily dismiss their criticism and denigrate these people precisely because in the Anglo-Boer War so many of them were on the other side and fought against their own people as 'National Scouts'."[3] Just before the 1915 general election General Smuts wrote to Merriman in similar vein: "Of course the Nationalists are now resuscitating all the episodes from our greater past and appropriating credit to themselves although most of them did precious little to build up that tradition. They were the handsuppers and national scouts in those times, and I fear the only thing which is 'national' about many of them is their connection with the national scouts."[4] It is highly unlikely that there was very much truth in these claims by Botha and Smuts – in the heat of the political debate it is probable that they only used these terms to belittle their opponents.

Even 74 years after the Anglo-Boer War the name "National Scout" cropped up in political circles. In May 1976, T.B. Floyd, a guest writer for the newspaper, *Die Afrikaner*, wrote of the contemporary Afrikaner "political struggle": "The weakling who surrenders and turns 'National Scout' on us is unfortunately still in our midst."[5] For quite a long time after the Anglo-Boer War the term "National Scout" was still seen as an abusive term. So much so that in Louis Trichardt in September 1930 it led to a libel case. The case arose from an exchange of words between G. Lyon, a local resident, with J.J. Steyn, the chairman of the National Party branch. Lyon referred to Steyn in public as a "damned National Scout" whereupon Steyn instituted civil proceedings. In order to establish whether Steyn had in fact been a National Scout or not, a number of people who had been in contact with the National Scouts during the Anglo-Boer War gave evidence in the court. The court finding was that although Steyn had surrendered and had helped the British during the war in the Belfast concentration camp, he had not been a National Scout. In handing down his judgement the magistrate, J.A. Verschuur, declared that the term "'National Scout' is of a highly defamatory nature in this country" and that Lyon's utterance "was calculated to bring the Plaintiff [Steyn] into contempt and ridicule and to lower his reputation, more especially in the eyes of the political party he is actively associated with". In the light of this the court decided that Lyon had to pay an amount of £100 damages to Steyn.[6] This particular term in fact lived on for many years after the Anglo-Boer War, but these days those who were unfaithful to the republican cause are now a forgotten generation.

There can be little doubt that the people who lived through the Anglo-Boer War and the post-war period until 1907 experienced some very turbulent years in South African history. This period saw a devastating war in which the ingenious military skills and remarkable endurance of the Boer generals and their burghers quite justifiably earned them high praise from many quarters. Just as remarkable was the resilience shown by the defeated *volk* in their recovery after the war. As far as the dissident burghers who are discussed in this study were concerned, it was a period of despair, divided loyalty, unrealistic peace missions, dishonourable service to the enemy, broken promises, disillusionment and finally, realisation of guilt. They had no share in this heroic period of Afrikaner history.

Notes
1 Milner Papers, 105, (FK 1194, p. 251), 14 April 1905.
2 *The Star*, 9 September 1910 (news report). Italics: A.G.
3 Translated from the Dutch. *De Burger*, 28 August 1915 (report on an address by Botha at Vrede).
4 Quoted by W.K. Hancock, *Smuts, I, The Sanguine Years 1870–1919*, p. 404.
5 Translated from the Afrikaans. *Die Afrikaner*, 14 May 1976 (article by T.B. Floyd).
6 Landdros (magistrate) Louis Trichardt, Civil Case 181/1930, J.J. Steyn vs. G. Lyon, September 1930, pp. 1–108. The extract appears on p. 108. The evidence that was brought before the court in this case has been used previously in this study. See Chapters 4, 5, 6, 7 and 8.

Annexure 1
List of Ex-Burghers of the late O.V.S. who have served the British Army

List of Orange River Colony Volunteers with addresses

Alberts ASJ	Heilbron	Botha PJJ	Edenburg
Alberts JJJ	Heilbron	Botha PP	Rouxville
Alberts NF	Heilbron	Botha TL	Heilbron
Badenhorst LH	Heilbron	Botha W	Heilbron
Bam FJ	Kroonstad	Botha WJ	Heilbron
Barker J	Heilbron	Botma JC	Heilbron
Barkley JJ	Heilbron	Bouwer DJ	Heilbron
Barnard HC	Bethlehem	Bouwer WJ	Heilbron
Becker MJ	Heilbron	Breedt GC	Heilbron
Benade JP	Heilbron	Breedt JJ	Heilbron
Bertram OC	Winburg	Brits MG	Heilbron
Bester AP	Winburg	Brits OMM	Heilbron
Beukes AJ	Heilbron	Bruyns HW	Senekal
Beukes CJ	Heilbron	Bruyns R	Harrismith
Bezuidenhout JA	Heilbron	Calitz HW	Heilbron
Birmingham WD	Winburg	Calitz JCJ	Heilbron
Birmingham WD	Winburg	Castelyn JH	Heilbron
Blignaut ER	Ladybrand	Celliers AJW	Heilbron
Booyens JD	Heilbron	Celliers CP	Bethlehem
Booyens JJ	Heilbron	Celliers JAH	Heilbron
Booyens JO	Heilbron	Celliers JAH	Heilbron
Booysen JJ	Heilbron	Celliers JD	Heilbron
Bornman C	Heilbron	Celliers JW	Ladybrand
Botha CJ	Heilbron	Celliers SJ	Winburg
Botha CJJ	Rouxville	Chandler CJ	Thaba Nchu
Botha FPJ	Heilbron	Christoffel JA	Thaba Nchu
Botha GJ	Heilbron	Classen CJ	Heilbron
Botha H	Heilbron	Classen NJ	Heilbron
Botha JG	Heilbron	Cockram PPJ	Heilbron
Botha JJ	Heilbron	Coetzee IS	Winburg
Botha LR	Heilbron	Coetzee JJ	Winburg
Botha MA	Heilbron	Coetzee LC	Winburg
Botha OJ	Honingspruit	Coetzee WJ	Heilbron
Botha PC	Heilbron	Coleman HB	Heilbron
Botha PR	Heilbron	Collins JW	Heilbron

Craytor J	Winburg	Engels J	Heilbron
Cronjé JJ	Heilbron	England WG	Heilbron
Cronjé JJ	Philippolis	Erasmus AJ	Heilbron
Cronjé PB	Rouxville	Erasmus LWJ	Heilbron
Cronjé WJL	Heilbron	Erasmus MS	Hoopstad
Crous GJ	Heilbron	Ferreira MH	Bethlehem
Dannhauser JA	Heilbron	Ferreira SM	Winburg
De Beer JM	Heilbron	Flint EA	Heilbron
De Bruyn PC	Heilbron	Flint JH	Heilbron
De Bruyn PC	Heilbron	Fouché HJ	Heilbron
De Bruyn TH	Senekal	Fouché MJ	Heilbron
De Clerk S	Winburg	Fourie AJ	Winburg
De Jager SJF	Senekal	Fourie CG	Heilbron
De Jonge JC	Senekal	Fourie JC	Heilbron
De Lange GM	Brandfort	Fourie JJ	Heilbron
De Langer SJ	Lydenberg	Fourie JMA	Ventersburg
De Vos DCP	Winburg	Fourie LJ	Heilbron
De Vos DCP	Winburg	Fourie P	Bethlehem
De Vries JT	Winburg	Fourie TL	Heilbron
De Waal JG	Heilbron	Frann J	Senekal
De Wet BJJ	Heilbron	Franzuer J	Winburg
Delport C	Rietfontein	Fredt HC	Rouxville
Dorfling JC	Heilbron	Froneman CA	Winburg
Draper HK	Winburg	Froneman CAF	Winburg
Dundas JN	Roodepoort	Geere CF	Heilbron
Du Plessis CJ	Heilbron	Geldenhuis BP	Heilbron
Du Plessis GBS	Heilbron	Geldenhuis PA	Heilbron
Du Plessis HJD	Winburg	Gertenbach JJ	Winburg
Du Plessis JH	Winburg	Gouws FBS	Winburg
Du Plessis PJ	Heilbron	Gouws FT	Ladybrand
Du Plessis PJM	Heilbron	Gouws PA	Heilbron
Du Preez CVS	Rouxville	Greeff CJ	Heilbron
Du Toit JH	Heilbron	Greeff WJ	Colesberg
Ebertsohn JH	Heilbron	Grison LHM	Winburg
Ebertsohn JM	Heilbron	Grobbelaar PJ	Heilbron
Ebertson AG	Heilbron	Grobler AC	Heilbron
Eksteen EP	Winburg	Grobler C	Heilbron
Eksteen JA	Winburg	Grobler MJ	Heilbron
Els CW	Heilbron	Grové MC	Heilbron
Els CW	Heilbron	Guse HN	Heilbron
Els JC	Heilbron	Harding JS	Bethlehem
Els MJ	Heilbron	Harding RS	Bethlehem
Els PG	Winburg	Hattingh DJ	Heilbron

Hattingh GJ	Heilbron	Jordaan T	Winburg
Hattingh JH	Heilbron	Jordaan WA	Heilbron
Hattingh PDG	Heilbron	Joubert FJ	Winburg
Hattingh WJW	Heilbron	Joubert G	Heilbron
Hemabas JG	Winburg	Joubert JD	Hoopstad
Hendrick JS	Senekal	Karimaker PA	Winburg
Hendricks JJ	Heilbron	Keeve AP	Heilbron
Henning JC	Brandfort	Keeve PJ	Honingspruit
Henning SK	Winburg	Keyser JPK	Winburg
Henning WJP	Smithfield	Klaasen WJ	Heilbron
Hennop P	Heilbron	Kleinhans JH	Heilbron
Herbst CF	Heilbron	Kleinhans WJ	Honingspruit
Herbst CF	Heilbron	Klopper CC	Heilbron
Herbst WJ	Heilbron	Klopper GPJ	Heilbron
Herholdt JR	Heilbron	Klopper MJL	Heilbron
Herholdt JR	Heilbron	Klopper R	Heilbron
Herman JU	Heilbron	Kock CWA	Heilbron
Hiron CJ	Rouxville	Kock JW	Heilbron
Homan BJS	Winburg	Koekemoer HJ	Bethulie
Homann DT	Heilbron	Koekemoer LF	Winburg
Horak AM	Heilbron	Koetzee D	Bethulie
Ilsley WE	Winburg	Koetzee FSJ	Edenburg
Ingram JL	Heilbron	Koetzee GD	Thaba Nchu
Jackson RC	Philippolis	Koetzee JA	Winburg
Jacobs GC	Heilbron	Kokemaar AC	Bethlehem
Jacobus AS	Winburg	Korff L	Heilbron
Janse van Vuuren JSM	Honingspruit	Kotzee SP	Wepener
Jelliman CH	Senekal	Kraus PJH	Winburg
Jelliman K	Heilbron	Kromer PC	Ventersburg
Jelliman V	Heilbron	Kruger CP	Heilbron
Jellitman WK	Heilbron	Kruger DJP	Heilbron
Johnston J	Heilbron	Kruger JP	Heilbron
Jones AG	Heilbron	Labuschagne MA	Heilbron
Jooste FJ	Heilbron	Labuschagne PJ	Heilbron
Jordaan AJ	Heilbron	Lamprecht GJ	Heilbron
Jordaan BJ	Heilbron	Le Riche JS	Winburg
Jordaan DJB	Heilbron	Le Roux JJS	Senekal
Jordaan FJ	Winburg	Le Roux PJ	Heilbron
Jordaan GWWB	Heilbron	Le Roux WJ	Bethlehem
Jordaan HA	Winburg	Lehmkuhl BGH	Heilbron
Jordaan JJ	Heilbron	Leonard GP	Winburg
Jordaan JJ	Heilbron	Lesson MP	Ficksburg
Jordaan PW	Heilbron	Lindeque GF	Heilbron

Lindeque GJ	Heilbron	Minny HJ	Heilbron
Lindeque JJ	Heilbron	Mitchell C	Ficksburg
Lindeque WJMP	Heilbron	Mordee WJ	Winburg
Lindique D	Heilbron	Mostert AB	Heilbron
Loch WF	Winburg	Muller C	Heilbron
Loggenberg JAW	Heilbron	Muller JF	Heilbron
Loggenberg JH	Heilbron	Myburg JW	Heilbron
Loggenberg JW	Heilbron	Myburg PA	Heilbron
Lombard BJB	Lindley	Nel JD	Heilbron
Lombard CP	Hoopstad	Nel JH	Heilbron
Lotter CW	Heilbron	Nel TMPJ	Kroonstad
Lourens MJ	Heilbron	Nell JT	Smaldeel
Lourens MJ	Heilbron	Nell MD	Winburg
Lourens MJ	Heilbron	Nieuwenhuisen JP	Lindley
Lourens WC	Heilbron	Nortier JS	Heilbron
Louw WP	Winburg	Nothnagel OJ	Heilbron
Lowe JP	Bethlehem	Nothnagel PJ	Heilbron
Lubbe DJ	Heilbron	Odendaal GH	Winburg
Lubbe S	Senekal	Odendaal JP	Honingspruit
Lues PJ	Heilbron	Oliver HJO	Bloemfontein
Maas DA	Bloemfontein	Oosthuizen JA	Heilbron
Maas WH	Bloemfontein	Oosthuizen JM	Heilbron
Malan HJ	Heilbron	Opperman J	Prior Siding
Marais AP	Heilbron	Otto WM	Heilbron
Marais DP	Winburg	Palk R	Potchefstroom
Marais H	Harrismith	Paulson JP	Winburg
Marais JJ	Heilbron	Perry CA	Winburg
Marais LJ	Heilbron	Peterse JP	Heilbron
Marais WJ	Heilbron	Piek JJ	Heilbron
Maree J	Winburg	Pienaar AHJ	Heilbron
Maritz SF	Heilbron	Pienaar HJ	Heilbron
Marshall BG	Heilbron	Pienaar HJ	Heilbron
McKenzie PF	Heilbron	Pienaar PJ	Winburg
McKenzie W	Heilbron	Pieterse DJ	Heilbron
Meintjes AW	Heilbron	Pieterse J	Heilbron
Meyer HP	Heilbron	Pietersen FJ	Ficksburg
Meyer JJ	Winburg	Pieterze AG	Winburg
Meyer JW	Heilbron	Pietsee JM	Winburg
Meyer LJ	Winburg	Potgieter JH	Heilbron
Meyers JP	Heilbron	Potgieter PL	Heilbron
Minnaar AP	Heilbron	Presson JJE	Bethuli
Minnaar HS	Heilbron	Pretorius BPFGR	Heilbron
Minnaar JP	Heilbron	Pretorius JJ	Jagersfontein

Pretorius JP	Brandfort	Smith JS	Winburg
Pretorius NS	Winburg	Smith R	Heilbron
Pretorius PJ	Kroonstad	Smith TFW	Bethlehem
Pretorius PJ Jr.	Kroonstad	Smith TTW	Winburg
Pretorius WJ	Heilbron	Snyman FJ	Heilbron
Prinsloo LE	Winburg	Snyman JT	Heilbron
Prinsloo PR	Heilbron	Steenberg JJ	Heilbron
Prinsloo WJ	Heilbron	Steenkamp JH	Heilbron
Rademeyer CJ	Winburg	Steyn CW	Heilbron
Rademeyer WJ	Bethlehem	Steyn E	Winburg
Rautenbach P	Winburg	Steyn EN	Winburg
Rautenbach RJ	Heilbron	Steyn HT	Heilbron
Remro GWH	Winburg	Steyn JJ	Heilbron
Reynolds R	Ladybrand	Steyn JN	Winburg
Roets JG	Heilbron	Steyn WJ	Heilbron
Roets JGM	Heilbron	Straiz EC	Hoopstad
Roodt CJ	Heilbron	Swanepoel AJJ	Smithfield
Roodt CJP	Heilbron	Swanepoel FH	Thaba Nchu
Roodt JC	Heilbron	Swanepoel HJ	Rouxville
Roodt JC	Heilbron	Swanepoel HJ	Rouxville
Roos CR	Heilbron	Swanepoel JUC	Bethlehem
Roos JI	Heilbron	Swanepoel J	Winburg
Roux JP	Heilbron	Swart AW	Heilbron
Ruthenberg C	Winburg	Swart DJ	Bloemfontein
Ruthenberg WFA	Krugersdorp	Swart J	Winburg
Schimpers M	Winburg	Swartz J	Heilbron
Schumann JJ	Bloemfontein	Swartz J	Winburg
Schumans JJ	Bloemfontein	Swartz JH	Heilbron
Schutte BJP	Heilbron	Swartz K	Heilbron
Schutte CJ	Heilbron	Taljaard MJ	Heilbron
Schutte JJF	Heilbron	Thom JC	Thaba Nchu
Schutte PP	Heilbron	Tolmay SA	Bloemfontein
Senekal BW	Winburg	Trichardt H	Winburg
Senekal PMS	Senekal	Tromp JC	Bethulie
Serfontein DJ	Heilbron	Trompe JJ	Rouxville
Serfontein HP	Heilbron	Truter JO	Heilbron
Smidt JF	Heilbron	Van de Berg WJ	Heilbron
Smit J	Heilbron	Van de Venter PR	Heilbron
Smit JD	Heilbron	Van der Linden JA	Trompsburg
Smit SA	Heilbron	Van der Merwe AA	Heilbron
Smith CE	Roodepoort	Van der Merwe DC	Senekal
Smith FJ	Senekal	Van der Merwe DJ	Senekal
Smith HP	Heilbron	Van der Merwe JS	Winburg

Van der Merwe JT	Senekal		Venter JH	Winburg
Van der Merwe LJ	Senekal		Venter JJ	Winburg
Van der Riet AE	Heilbron		Venter JM	Winburg
Van der Venter WA	Winburg		Venter PA	Heilbron
Van der Walt HP	Winburg		Venter PA	Heilbron
Van der Walt SJ	Winburg		Venter PA	Ventersburg
Van der Westhuizen AA	Heilbron		Venter SJ	Winburg
Van der Westhuizen CJ	Heilbron		Venter SN	Winburg
Van der Westhuizen WMP	Honingspruit		Venter WA	Winburg
Van Jaarsveld JV	Winburg		Vergothen AM	Winburg
Van Niekerk AE	Heilbron		Viljoen AC	Winburg
Van Niekerk JJJ	Winburg		Viljoen AJ	Heilbron
Van Nieuwenhuis HP	Heilbron		Viljoen JV	Winburg
Van Rensburg CV	Heilbron		Villette JL	Fauresmith
Van Rensburg GF	Winburg		Vorster JW	Heilbron
Van Rensburg PJ	Heilbron		Vosloo GJ	Heilbron
Van Schalkwyk OJ	Smithfield		Vosloo GJ	Heilbron
Van Staden JF	Heilbron		Voster SE	Heilbron
Van Wyk AC	Heilbron		Wagner JC	Heilbron
Van Wyk DW	Winburg		Wagner JJ	Heilbron
Van Wyk JH	Winburg		Wagner JP	Heilbron
Van Wyk MC	Winburg		Wagner JW	Heilbron
Van Wyk SJ	Heilbron		Wagner WH	Heilbron
Van Zyl PP	Heilbron		Walker AED	Winburg
Van Zyl TL	Heilbron		Wessels JHW	Heilbron
Velm WA	Heilbron		Wheeler TW	Winburg
Venter AJ	Winburg		Wigram W	Winburg
Venter GJ	Rouxville		Williams WL	Heilbron
Venter J	Senekal		Woest JA	Winburg
Venter JA	Heilbron		Wolmarans JG	Heilbron
Venter JD	Oitensburg		Wordeje PJ	Heilbron
Venter JH	Senekal		Wyk TG	Rouxville

List of Ex-Burghers of the late O.V.S. who served in the National Scouts

Bates LF	Kroonstad	Strydom WJ	Harrismith
Bester BH	Vrede	Strydom PWA	Harrismith
Dippenaar CRO	Bloemhof	Taljaard HF	Vrede
De Jager CJ	Vrede	Van Nieuwenhuisen	Heilbron
De Lange AJ	Villiersdorp	Van der Spuy MS	Vrede
Jacobs LM	Jacobsdal	Venter JA	Vrede
Klassen JJC	Winburg	Van Rensburg JMJ	Vrede
Lourens PC	Vrede	Venter JP	Vrede
Lourens JA	Vrede	Willsen HAS	Vrede
Loack HCL	Vrede		

Annexure 2
Return of Ex-Burghers employed in the Field Intelligence Department,
O.R. Colony District, C0394/02 en 2796

Name & address	Duties	Appointed	Discharged	Character	Family & remarks
Alberts JJ Groodegeluk	Guide	21.06.01	19.07.01		
Alexander W Zoetfontein	Scout	01.02.01	30.06.02	Good	Mother & 2 sisters
Anderson WD Heilbron	Guide	13.09.00	23.10.00	Good & loyal	Family in Kroonstad
Anderson ZB Harrismith	Guide	20.04.00		Good & loyal	Family in Harrismith
Andrews DC Bethlehem	Guide	03.10.00		Good & loyal	Family in Harrismith
Andrews OC Bethlehem	Guide	01.07.00	10.06.02		
Angus AM Utrecht	Guide	01.06.00	01.12.00	Fair	Wife & 1 child, no use
Archbell FT Bethlehem	Guide	04.01.02		Good & loyal	Single
Archbell JW Bethlehem	Guide	10.09.00	23.10.00	Good & loyal	Family in Bethlehem
Armstrong C Brandfort	Agent	23.03.02	30.06.02		
Armstrong SV Brandfort	Scout	14.05.01	30.06.02		
Bam JC Kroonstad	Scout	01.10.01	30.06.02		Best Scout in Corps
Bam SR Kroonstad	Guide	11.09.01			
Barkhuizen Honingdraai	Guide	27.06.01	13.07.01		
Barnard SJ Kroonstad	Guide	23.10.01			Wife
Basson L Brandfort	Agent	01.09.01	30.06.02		
Baxter R Bethlehem	Interpreter	23.09.00		Good & loyal	Single
Beddy EH Fauresmith	Agent	16.10.01	19.01.02	Reliable	Single
Bell AR Bethlehem	Guide	22.06.01	30.06.02	Good & loyal	Family in Bethlehem
Benskes HC Parys	Guide	15.06.01	30.06.01		

Name & address	Duties	Appointed	Discharged	Character	Family & remarks
Bester WA Harrismith	Agent	01.01.02	30.06.02	Very good	Wife, strongly recommended
Beukes BM Harrismith	Scout	10.09.01	31.05.02	Very good	4 Children, useful for Civil Service
Bezuidenhout HPB Bothaville	Agent	01.07.01	24.06.02	Fair (drinks)	Wife & 6 children, good man when sober
Bezuidenhout RB Bothaville	Guide	21.02.02	31.05.02	Very good	Wife & 4 children, useful for Civil Service
Bezuidenhout RJ Kroonstad	Scout	25.06.01	30.01.02	Very reliable	Wife & 7 children
Biddy IS Fauresmith	Agent	20.10.00	18.07.02	Reliable & energetic	Wife & 7 children
Bland JFA Harrismith	Clerk	09.08.00	10.09.00	Good & loyal	Family in Harrismith, did very useful work
Bloem S Fauresmith	Guide	12.06.01	31.12.01	Fair	Wife & 2 children
Booyens AJ Parys	Guide	16.07.01	27.07.01		
Booyens JD Parys	Scout	06.01.02			
Booyens JO Parys	Scout	06.01.02			
Border T Kroonstad	Agent			Very good	Single
Botha CF Kroonstad	Guide	10.02.02		Good	Single
Botha CF Jr Kroonstad	Guide	01.06.01	10.07.01		Wife & 2 children
Botha CJ Heilbron	Guide	29.08.01	18.10.01		
Botha CR Kroonstad	Guide	31.08.01	10.06.02	Good	
Botha F Philippolis	Farrier	21.10.01	15.05.02	Good	Wife & 3 children
Botha H Kroonstad	Guide			Good	Wife & children
Botha JP Wepener	LM	21.10.01	30.04.02	Good	Wife & 2 children
Botha JS Kroonstad	Agent			Very reliable	Single
Botha MP Kroonstad	Guide	11.01.02	01.02.02		
Botha PC Hoopstad	Guide	20.06.01	16.07.01	Good	
Botha SJ Kroonstad	Guide	16.09.01	10.06.02		Wife & 2 children
Botma C Kroonstad	Guide	22.07.01	13.08.01		

ANNEXURES

Name & address	Duties	Appointed	Discharged	Character	Family & remarks
Botma C Kroonstad	Guide	10.04.01	01.09.01	Untrust-worthy	Wife & 5 children
Bouwer PF Heilbron	Scout	06.01.02			
Boyce JJ Harrismith	Clerk	05.12.01	24.03.02	Good & loyal, abilities nil	Single
Brink GJ Winburg	Scout	01.01.02		Good	
Brink PG					
Brown A Jacobsdal	Scout	29.10.00	03.07.02	Reliable	Single
Bryan C Philippolis	Guide	01.05.02	30.06.02	Good	Wife & 7 children
Buck CG Reitz	Guide	10.04.02		Good & loyal	Family in Bethlehem
Campbell A Ficksburg	Scout	09.09.01	30.06.02	Good & loyal	Family in Ficksburg
Celliers FJJ Kroonstad	Scout	15.01.02	30.06.02		Served with Brett
Celliers JG Parys	Guide	12.01.02			
Claasen HL Koffiefontein	Guide & Scout	04.03.02	11.06.02	Trustworthy	
Claasen JH Heilbron	Scout	04.03.02	30.06.02		
Claasen NP Heilbron	Scout	04.03.02	30.06.02		
Claasen WJ Koffiefontein	Guide & Scout	16.08.01	11.06.02	Trustworthy	
Classens WW Bloemfontein	Guide	12.12.00		No good	
Cloete L Edenburg	Guide			Very good	Wife & 2 children
Cochrane EJ Bloemfontein	Clerk & interpreter	13.01.02	15.07.02	Very good & young	Single
Coetze F Fauresmith	Guide	08.05.02	30.06.02	Excellent	Mother & sisters
Coetzee CJ					
Coetzee SP Winburg	Scout	04.03.02	01.04.02	Very good	Married, was not on pay
Coetzee WA Senekal	Guide & Scout	04.03.02	25.05.02	Very good	
Coetzer J Heilbron	Guide	17.07.01	23.09.01		
Coetzer JG Groenfontein	Scout	04.03.02	30.06.02	Reliable	
Coetzer JP Kroonstad	Guide	01.06.01	30.09.01		

THE DYNAMICS OF TREASON: BOER COLLABORATION IN THE SA WAR OF 1899–1902

Name & address	Duties	Appointed	Discharged	Character	Family & remarks
Collins A Vrede	Guide	28.06.01	30.06.02	Good & loyal	Family in Harrismith
Collins JD Heilbron	Guide	01.12.01	31.12.01		
Cowell W Reitz	Guide	28.06.01	30.06.02	Good & loyal	Family in Harrismith
Crocum L Kroonstad	Scout	01.06.01	30.06.02	Good	Wife & 5 children
Cronjé CP Kroonstad	Guide	01.02.02	24.06.02	Very good	Single, served with Brett
Cronjé F Philippolis	Guide	12.12.00	15.07.01	Short period	
Cronjé GP Kroonstad	Scout	01.02.02	30.06.02		
Cronjé JJ Kroonstad	Scout	14.03.02			Wife & 4 children
Cronjé JM Kroonstad	Scout	01.02.02	30.06.02		
Crous J Kroonstad	Scout			Good	Wife
Crous S Kroonstad	Guide			Good	Wife & child
Dannhauser GN Heilbron	Guide	01.02.02	14.02.02		
Dannhauser JA Heilbron	Scout				
Davenish AS Hoopstad	Agent & Scout	18.03.02		Trustworthy	Wanting in energy
Davenish JH Hoopstad	Guide	31.03.01	30.06.02	Reliable	Wife & 6 children
Davis A Harrismith	Guide	29.09.01	18.10.01	Fair & loyal	Family in Harrismith
De Beer CN Heilbron	Interpreter	21.12.01	30.06.02		
De Beer JJL Heilbron	Scout	25.09.01			
De Jager JH Vrede	Scout	28.05.02	30.06.02		
De Jager JP Harrismith	Guide	27.03.02	08.04.02	Good	Single
De Kock VC Winburg	Guide	17.08.01	30.09.01		
De Kok FC Vredefort	Guide	15.09.01	31.09.01		
De Lange Vrede	Guide	07.10.01			Captured 12.10.01, tried & shot
De Lange H Winburg	Scout	05.12.01	30.06.02		

482

Name & address	Duties	Appointed	Discharged	Character	Family & remarks
De Wet HG Kroonstad	Guide	30.09.01	01.03.02		Single
Delport H Kroonstad	Guide			Good	Wife & 3 children
Delport JA Kroonstad	Guide	01.09.01	01.06.02	Reliable	Mother, wife & child
Delport RJJ Kroonstad	Guide	01.09.01	01.06.02	Reliable	
Depenard AW [Dippenaar?]	Scout	10.10.01	07.02.02		[Illegible]
Dixon GS Frankfort	Agent	28.01.02	30.06.02		
Dixon J Frankfort	Agent	05.11.01	30.06.02		
Drake LF Vrede	Guide	27.08.01	26.03.02	Good & loyal	Single
Drake SF Vrede	Guide	27.08.01	26.03.02	Good & loyal	Single
Dreyer PM Harrismith	Guide	01.12.00	03.12.00	Good & loyal	Family in Harrismith
Dunningham H Vrede	Interpreter	03.10.00	12.02.01	Good & loyal	Family in Harrismith
Du Plessis J Winburg	Scout	05.12.01	30.06.02		
Du Plessis JJ Kroonstad	Scout	19.03.02	30.06.02		
Du Plessis JN Kroonstad	Scout	01.02.02	30.06.02		
Du Plessis PJ Kroonstad	Guide	15.06.01	30.06.01		
Du Plessis R Kroonstad	Scout	01.02.02	30.06.02		
Du Toit JH Heilbron	Scout	21.12.01	30.06.02		
Dyason GB Harrismith	Guide	04.01.02	23.03.02	Good & loyal	Family in Harrismith
Ebersohn PJ Bethlehem	Scout	10.04.02	30.06.02		
Ebersohn PJ Winburg	Guide	27.03.02	24.06.02	Good	Single
Eckstein C Winburg	Agent	01.01.02	24.06.02	Very good	Wife & 3 children, very good man
Eckstein CJ Winburg	Agent	11.07.01	30.06.02		
Eckstein H Winburg	Scout	01.01.02	08.01.02		
Eckstein JA Winburg	Scout	01.01.02	30.06.02	Very reliable	

THE DYNAMICS OF TREASON: BOER COLLABORATION IN THE SA WAR OF 1899–1902

Name & address	Duties	Appointed	Discharged	Character	Family & remarks
Edwards GH Ficksburg	Guide	01.03.02	10.04.02		Fernaus' column
Els I Ficksburg	Guide	09.02.02	16.03.02		Pitchers' column
Els JC Heilbron	Scout	2.02.02	01.05.02		
Els MJ Kroonstad	Scout	02.02.02			
Engelbrecht G Heilbron	Guide	14.06.01	17.06.01		
Engelbrecht HBL Kroonstad	Guide	03.08.01	30.06.02		
Erasmus JF Kroonstad	Scout	02.02.02			
Erasmus R Heilbron	Agent	01.12.01	30.06.02		
Ferreira J Kroonstad	Guide	19.09.01	16.10.01		
Ferreira PH Vrede	Scout	28.05.02	18.06.02		
Forbes WG Bethlehem	Guide	08.09.00	12.02.02	Good & loyal	Single
Forbes WH Bethlehem	Guide	11.12.00	28.02.01	Good & loyal	Single
Fouché PHE Heilbron	Guide				
Fourie J Fauresmith	SS	14.05.02	11.06.02	Reliable	Wife & 6 children
Fourie JJ Vrede	Guide	15.12.01	31.05.02	Very good	Single
Fourie P Bethlehem	Guide	24.10.01			
Fourie P Kroonstad	Scout	12.12.01	01.06.01		
Fourie PH Winburg	Guide	21.06.01	16.07.01	Good	
Fourie PR Kroonstad	Guide	21.06.01	01.06.02	Reliable	Wife & 6 children
Fowler JC Philippolis	Guide	21.10.01	30.06.02		
Frank J Brandfort	Scout	01.02.01	01.05.01		
Froneman CA Winburg	Scout	03.02.02	28.02.02		
Froneman NJ Winburg	Scout	01.03.02	30.06.02		
Froneman R Winburg	Scout	03.02.02	17.03.02		

ANNEXURES

Name & address	Duties	Appointed	Discharged	Character	Family & remarks
Galpin EW Ficksburg	Agent	01.04.01	09.06.02	Good	Reliable
Geere CF Kroonstad	Guide	11.09.01	26.02.02		
Gibbins AC Harrismith	Chief Guide	13.05.00		Good & loyal	Family in Harrismith
Gilfillan GGG Roodepoort	Scout	01.02.02	30.06.02		
Glyn L Brandfort	Guide	01.08.00	30.09.00		
Gouws GJ Kroonstad	Guide	16.11.01		Good	
Gouws J Bultfontein	Guide	01.10.01	02.05.02	Good	
Gray D Fauresmith	SS	16.02.02	30.03.02	Trustworthy	Wife & 3 children, not smart enough
Grobler PJ Kroonstad	Guide	21.06.01	16.07.01		
Groenewald BJJ Winburg	Scout	01.01.02	30.06.02	Reliable	
Grové MC Kroonstad	Guide	11.09.01	30.06.02	Good	Wife & 6 children
Guy M Heilbron	Agent	21.08.01	30.06.02		
Haefele PL Kroonstad	Guide	11.09.01	24.04.02	Good	Wife & 1 child
Harvey Springfontein	Guide	01.12.01		Good	Single
Hattingh Heilbron	Scout	01.02.02			
Hefer Kroonstad	Guide	01.09.01	20.04.02	Good	Wife
Henegan Bloemfontein	Guide	26.10.01	30.06.02	Very good	Single, invaluable scout
Henning Smithfield	Scout	25.11.01		Very good	
Henning Edenburg	Scout	10.02.02		Very good	Wife
Herbst Edenburg	Guide	4 months		Very good	Wife & 2 children
Herhold Parys	Scout	01.02.02			
Higgs Thaba Nchu	Interpreter	04.05.01	09.06.02	Good	
Hiscock G Leribe	Guide	08.06.00	29.01.01	Fair	Family in Basutoland
Holtzhauzen JP Transvaal					

Name & address	Duties	Appointed	Discharged	Character	Family & remarks
Holtzhuizen Bethlehem	Guide	24.02.02	10.06.02		
Holtzhuizen Reitz	Guide	20.02.02	31.05.02	Very good	Wife, excellent guide
Hoven Zastron	Guide	15.05.01	30.06.02	Very good	Single
Howard Hoopstad	Agent	01.05.01	30.06.02		
Howard C Leribe	Guide	02.05.01	04.12.01	Fair	Family in Ficksburg
Hoyneau Bethlehem	Guide	20.03.02	15.05.02		
Irwin C Harrismith	Guide	01.10.00	25.10.00	Good & loyal	Family in Harrismith
Jacobs J Smithfield	Guide	21.10.01	31.05.02	Very good	Wife & 2 children
Jacobs S Winburg	Guide	17.05.01	28.09.01		
Jonge Heilbron	Scout	24.10.01	15.05.02	Very good	
Jooste Boshof	Guide	21.02.02	30.06.02	Trustworthy	Wife & 2 children
Jordaan Winburg	Scout	04.03.02	01.04.02	Very good	
Jordaan Kroonstad	Guide	21.06.01	16.07.01		
Joubert JC Vet Rivier	Agent	01.02.02	30.06.02	Very good	
Kennard H Bethlehem	Guide	03.10.00	23.10.00	Good & loyal	Family in Harrismith
Kilian PJ Heilbron	Guide	11.10.01	30.06.02		
Kilian S Heilbron	Scout	11.10.01	30.06.02		
Klassen J	Guide	9 months		Good	
Klopper GPJ Heilbron	Scout	14.03.02			
Klopper HR Heilbron	Guide	23.10.01			
Klopper MJ Heilbron	Scout	06.01.02			
Koekemoer AC Vrischgewaacht	Guide	12.01.02			
Koekemoer HJ Vrischgewaacht	Guide	12.01.02			
Koekemoer WJ Vrischgewaacht	Scout	01.02.02	30.06.02		

ANNEXURES

Name & address	Duties	Appointed	Discharged	Character	Family & remarks
Koekemoer WJ Kroonstad	Guide	15.01.02	24.06.02		Single
Koen P Vrede	Guide	27.03.02	08.04.02	Good	Family in Natal
Kotze JA Winburg	Guide	01.01.02	26.02.02		
Kriek CJ Bethlehem	Scout	14.03.02	30.06.02		
Krogman H Harrismith	Guide	20.04.01	30.06.01	Good & loyal	Family in Harrismith
Krogman H Bagshot	Guide	04.07.01	02.08.01	Good & loyal	Single
Kruger DJP Heilbron	Scout	14.03.02			
Kruger JC Bethulie	Interpreter & censor	01.06.01	20.04.02	Very good	Reliable
Kruger WG	Guide	02.07.01	19.07.01		
Langridge L Harrismith	Guide	03.09.00		Good & loyal	Single
Langridge S Harrismith	Guide	13.09.00		Good & loyal	Family in Harrismith
Law G Harrismith	Agent	01.03.02		Good & loyal	Family in Harrismith
Lawrence MJ Lowries Rust	Bretts	15.01.02	15.03.02		1 Child
Layard B Lindley	Guide	15.01.02	24.06.02	Good	Single
Le Roux JR Kroonstad	Guide	11.01.02			
Le Warne A Heilbron	Scout	06.01.02			
Lehmkuhl BGH Kroonstad	Guide	21.06.01	18.07.01		
Lennon J Harrismith	Guide	01.02.02	30.03.02	Good & loyal	Single
Liddell JG Harrismith	Guide	20.11.01	31.10.02	Good & loyal	Family in Harrismith
Lindeque PJM Heilbron	Guide	16.07.01	25.07.01	Good	
Lingenhayer O Butha Buthe	Guide	12.12.00	12.01.01	Indifferent	Family in Basutoland
Logan JC Ladybrand	Scout	22.12.01	10.05.02	Very good	Married
Louw HW Boshof	Guide	26.05.01	26.09.01		
Lowrens MJ Heilbron	Scout	12.10.01			

Name & address	Duties	Appointed	Discharged	Character	Family & remarks
Lowrens MJ Kroonstad	Guide	13.01.02	15.03.02		
Lowrens WC Heilbron	Scout	14.03.02			
Lubbe PJ Kroonstad	Scout	20.12.01			
Luden W Hibernia	Barkers	01.01.02	28.02.02	Good	
Luthen F Bloemfontein	Interpreter	05.09.01	30.06.02		
Lynch SE Ladybrand	Scout	01.09.01	30.06.02		
Macfarlane T Bethlehem	Guide	25.06.01	14.07.01		
Magnus GE Boshof	Agent	01.02.02	18.06.02	Reliable and trustworthy	Wife & 6 children, policeman
Maher J Bethlehem	Guide	29.09.01	26.03.02	Good & loyal	Family in Harrismith
Mann J Harrismith	Guide	25.12.00	07.01.00	Good & loyal	Family in Harrismith
Marais SJ Bethlehem	Guide		18.07.01		
Mathee HPW Kroonstad	Guide	11.01.02	19.01.02		
McMaster C Bloemfontein	Assistent to censor	01.02.01	30.04.02		Single
McMaster JW Kroonstad	Agent	03.10.01	24.06.02	Fair (drinks)	Wife & 1 child, excellent guide
McMaster P Bloemfontein	Agent	06.02.01	25.02.02	Reliable	Single
Meintjies PJ Kroonstad	Guide	03.08.01			
Meyer DJ Heilbron	Scout	06.01.02			
Meyer H Harrismith	Guide	03.07.01	15.10.01	Good & loyal	Family in Natal
Meyer HW Harrismith	Agent	7 months		Good	
Middelton HM Bethlehem	Clerk	10.03.02	18.03.02	Good & loyal	Family in Harrismith
Miskin AK Reitz	Guide	11.04.02	19.05.02		
Miskin H Reitz	Guide	04.04.02		Good & loyal	Single
Mitchby H Ficksburg	Interpreter & clerk	10.09.00		Good & loyal	Family in Ficksburg
Moore MFJ Fauresmith	Farrier	08.03.02	31.05.02	Fair	Wife & 4 children

ANNEXURES

Name & address	Duties	Appointed	Discharged	Character	Family & remarks
Mooy PE Boshof	Agent	22.06.01	30.06.02	Trustworthy	Wife
Mousby C Bethlehem	Guide	01.12.00	31.06.01	Good & loyal	Family in Basutoland
Mousley S Bethlehem	Guide	01.06.01	06.06.01	Good & loyal	Family in Basutoland
Muller GS Bethlehem	Guide	04.12.01		Reliable	Wife & 5 children
Muller JF Kroonstad	Guide	11.09.01			
Mulligan GF Ficksburg	Guide	12.06.00		Good & loyal	Family in Ficksburg
Myburg JH Heilbron	Interpreter	14.04.01	30.06.02		
Myburg PM Parys	Scout	14.03.02			
Nel J Ladybrand	Guide	07.03.02	09.06.02		
Nel SM Ladybrand	Scout	22.10.01	10.05.02	Very good	
Nel W Ladybrand	Guide	07.03.02	09.06.02		
Nieuman Ventersburg	Scout	01.01.02	28.02.02	Good	
Nortier SJ Lindley	Guide	05.03.02	13.03.02		Single
Norval G Philippolis	Trainer	21.10.01	19.05.02	Good	Wife
Oberholzer JA Winburg	Guide	31.08.01	30.06.02		
Oberholzer MA Heilbron	Scout	14.03.02			
Odendaal AG Vrede	Scout	28.05.02	30.06.02		
Odendaal Alfred Ladybrand		03.05.02	End of War	Good	
Odendaal PJ Vrede	Scout	28.05.02	30.06.02		
Odendaal SC Vrede	Guide	15.01.02			
Olivier HA Heilbron	Agent	05.11.01	30.06.02		
Olivier P Heilbron	Scout		07.04.02		
Oosthuizen JM Bethlehem	Guide	05.03.02	13.03.02		
Orlandi A Edenburg	Guide	4 months		Very good	

THE DYNAMICS OF TREASON: BOER COLLABORATION IN THE SA WAR OF 1899–1902

Name & address	Duties	Appointed	Discharged	Character	Family & remarks
Orlandi S Edenburg	Guide	5 months		Good	
Osmond H Winburg	Scout		30.06.02		
Passmore AE Bethlehem	Guide	01.04.02	30.06.02		
Passmore AE Bethlehem	Guide	23.12.01	10.04.02	Good & loyal	Single
Peacock S Ficksburg	Guide	11.09.00	02.07.01	Fair & loyal	Family in Ficksburg
Peacock W Ficksburg	Guide	09.06.00	01.03.01	Good & loyal	Family in Ficksburg
Peens GJ Kroonstad	Guide	11.03.02			
Pellissier JP	Scout	18 months		Very good	
Pelser John Smithfield	Scout	25.11.01	12.03.02	Very good	
Penny WS Jagersfontein	Guide	01.05.01	30.06.02	Thoroughly loyal	
Piak J Heilbron	Guide	14.04.01	16.06.02		
Pienaar PJ Winburg	Scout	01.01.02	08.01.02		
Pieterse DJ Heilbron	Scout	11.02.02			
Pietersen JM Winburg	Scout	01.01.02	28.02.02		
Pietersen NJ Winburg	Scout	01.01.02	28.02.02	Good	
Potgieter A Bethlehem	Guide	01.01.02	26.03.02	Good	Single
Potgieter JH Bloemfontein	Scout	01.02.02	10.04.02		
Preston JJ Bethlehem	Scout	19.03.02		Good	Single
Pretorius PJ Kroonstad	Guide	11.09.01	14.09.01		
Pretorius WJ Bethlehem	Guide	11.09.01	12.10.01		
Prinsloo JA Vlakfontein	Guide	30.03.01		Thoroughly loyal	
Prinsloo L Vlakfontein	Guide	16.05.01	30.06.02	Thoroughly loyal	
Prinsloo WJ Kroonstad	Guide	01.08.01	08.08.01		
Prinsloo WJ Kroonstad	Guide	15.10.01	13.01.02		

Name & address	Duties	Appointed	Discharged	Character	Family & remarks
Prinsloo WJ Kroonstad	Guide	15.12.01	26.01.02		Single
Pritford WA Harrismith	Guide	10.11.00	30.11.01	Very indifferent	Family in Harrismith
Raaff N Bloemfontein	Guide	14.06.01	01.03.02	Good	Single, well educated, young
Rabie CH Kroonstad	Guide	20.06.01	13.03.02	Good	Wife, 6 children
Rabie CJ Kroonstad	Guide	29.09.01			Single
Rabie G Bethlehem	Scout	03.03.02	30.06.02	Good	
Rabie JB Bethlehem	Scout	03.03.02	30.06.02	Good	
Rademan CJH Harrismith	Guide	Short time		Very good	Wife, 4 children
Rademeyer CJ Winburg	Scout	01.01.02	28.02.02	Good	
Ras PJ Hoopstad	SS	09.02.02	08.03.02	Bad	Deported
Rayner W Harrismith	Guide	01.10.01	05.10.01	Fair	Family in Harrismith
Richter E Vrede	Guide	04.07.01		Good & loyal	Single
Roberts C Eensgevonden	Scout	27.08.01	30.06.02	Good	
Roberts JW Boshof	Agent	24.05.01	11.07.02	Trustworthy	
Roetz CJP Heilbron	Guide	25.06.01	14.07.01		
Rogers H Harrismith	Guide	13.04.01	20.04.01	Good	Family in Harrismith
Roodt JHJ Heilbron	Scout	14.03.02			
Roodt JJ Heilbron	Scout	06.01.02			
Roos CJ Kroonstad	Guide	04.06.01	16.06.01		
Roos CR Bethlehem	Guide	05.03.02	13.03.02	Reliable	Wife, 4 children
Roos FP Bethlehem	Guide	28.06.01			Single
Roos JJ Kroonstad	Guide	05.12.01			
Roos JQM Driewater	Guide	05.03.02	13.03.02		
Roos WC Bethlehem	Guide	20.03.01	12.07.01	Reliable	Wife & children

Name & address	Duties	Appointed	Discharged	Character	Family & remarks
Rosenstein H Senekal	Guide	04.12.00	28.01.01	Good & loyal	Single
Rossouw JJ Fauresmith	SS	24.03.02	21.06.02	Unreliable	Discharged for making false reports whilst in SS
Rossouw P Winburg	Scout	18.02.01	01.04.02	Very good	
Rotey CJ Bethlehem	Guide	20.01.02	13.03.02		
Roux P Winburg	Scout	04.02.01	01.04.02	Very good	
Saaiman JHP Boshof	Guide	22.11.01	30.06.02	Reliable	Wife, 5 children
Saaiman PK Kroonstad	Scout	13.07.01			
Schickerling F Fauresmith	SS	16.02.02	30.03.02	Reliable	Wife, 6 children
Schickerling W Fauresmith	Guide	21.10.01	30.06.02	Good	
Schimper M Winburg	Scout		07.04.02	Very good	
Schingeer J Winburg	Scout		17.02.02	Very good	
Schoeman MJ Kroonstad	Scout	15.01.02	06.04.02		
Schoeman MJ Lindley	Guide	15.01.02	31.03.02		
Schoonfeldt S Fauresmith	Scout	11.05.02	30.06.02	Good	
Schutte CP Heilbron	Scout	01.07.01	31.08.01		
Schutte JJF Heilbron	Scout	14.03.02			
Schutte P Kroonstad	Guide & Agent	27.07.01	30.06.02		Wife, 4 children
Searle H Lindley	Scout	01.02.02	30.06.02		
Searle H Lindley	Scout	15.01.02	06.04.02		
Searle H Lindley	Guide	15.03.02	26.06.02	Good	
Searle N Lindley	Guide	15.01.02	10.04.02	Very good	
Senekal G Parys	Guide	01.02.02	26.06.02	Very good	
Senekal GTJ Heilbron	Scout	11.02.02	30.06.02		

ANNEXURES

Name & address	Duties	Appointed	Discharged	Character	Family & remarks
Senekal HJ Winburg	Scout	01.01.02	09.03.02		
Senekal JM Winburg	Scout	01.01.02	09.03.02		
Senekal NJ Winburg	Scout	01.01.02	09.03.02		
Singleton Bloemfontein	Guide				
Skine A Bethlehem	Clerk	21.04.02		Good & loyal	Single
Small AJP Edenburg	Guide	23.03.02		Very good	Wife, 1 child
Smit AJ Transvaal					
Smit GJA Transvaal					
Smit HJ Kroonstad	Guide	19.03.02	30.06.02		
Smit HJ Bethlehem	Guide	13.03.02	26.06.02	Good	
Smit TG Winburg	Scout	01.01.02	30.06.02		
Smith HRP Kroonstad	Guide				
Smith W Bothaville	Scout	15.01.02	15.03.02		
Smith W Bothaville	Guide	10.01.01	15.03.02		
Snyman C Edenburg	Guide	17.08.01	01.02.02	Very good	Widower
Snyman DB					
Solomon I Harrismith	Guide	02.06.01	28.02.02	Good & loyal	Single
Spangle AC Kroonstad	Scout	14.06.01			
Spies Bloemfontein	Interpreter	18.03.01	15.07.02	Very reliable	
Spilsburg W Harrismith	Guide	25.04.01	26.04.01	Good & loyal	Family in Harrismith
Steenberg JJ Parys	Scout	14.03.02			
Steenkamp C Heilbron	Guide	30.06.01	16.07.01		
Steenkamp JM Parys	Guide	20.06.01	18.07.01		
Steenkamp WD Parys	Guide	21.06.01	18.07.01		

Name & address	Duties	Appointed	Discharged	Character	Family & remarks
Steenkamp WD Parys	Guide	15.08.01	11.09.01		
Stephen John Bothaville	Scout	01.02.01	30.06.02	Reliable (drinks)	
Stephens JS Bothaville	Guide	07.03.02	26.06.02	Fair (drinks)	
Steyn H Lace Diamond Mine	Guide	15.12.01	24.06.02	Excellent	Very plucky
Steyn HT Kroonstad	Guide	02.02.02	30.06.02		
Steyn HT Lace Diamond Mine	Guide	01.02.02	24.06.02	Good	
Steyn JHG Kroonstad	Scout	02.02.02			
Steyn JJ Kroonstad	Guide	21.12.01	30.06.02		
Steyn JJ Lace Diamond Mine	Guide	15.12.01	24.06.02	Fair	
Steyn WC Winburg	Guide	23.10.01	13.03.02		
Steyn WC Ventersberg Road	Guide	15.12.01	10.01.02	Good	
Steytler H Lindley	Agent & Scout	01.12.01	18.06.02		
Swanepoel CJ Parys	Guide	16.07.01			
Swanepoel CJ Kroonstad	Guide	16.06.01	27.07.01		
Swanepoel H Bethlehem	Agent	15.12.01	01.07.02		Wife, 4 children
Swanepoel P Smithfield	Guide	21.10.01	30.04.02	Good	
Swart JC Vredefort	Scout	14.03.02			
Sykes J Bethulie	Scout	05.02.01	30.06.02	Good	
Taljard CJ Bloemhof	Guide	01.02.02	30.06.02	Good	Single
Taljard PJF Bethlehem	Guide	27.04.02	08.06.02		
Theron AW Bethlehem	Guide	17.04.02	30.06.02		
Thompson FA Heilbron	Scout	01.09.01		Good	Single
Thompson WH Bethlehem	Guide	20.04.01	05.10.02	Good & loyal	Single
Thorold F Bethlehem	Guide	01.06.01	06.06.01	Good & loyal	Family in Basutoland

Name & address	Duties	Appointed	Discharged	Character	Family & remarks
Thurston JT Harrismith	Guide	27.06.01		Good & loyal	Single
Turvey A Ladybrand	Guide	19.05.00	26.06.00	Good & loyal	Single
Uys AJ Vrede	Guide	01.04.02	15.04.02	Very good	Married, well off
Uys FJ Ventersburg	Scout	01.02.02	30.06.02	Very good	Single
Van Aswegen SJ Boshof	Guide	12.05.02	30.06.02	Very good	Wife
Van Bloemstein S Hoopstad	Agent	20.02.02	30.06.02	Reliable & useful	Wife & 2 children
Van Coller PJJ Kroonstad	Guide	11.01.02			
Van de Berg V Ladybrand	Scout	01.02.02	10.05.02	Very good	
Van de Riet WH Harrismith	Interpreter	20.04.01	02.07.01	Good & loyal	Single
Van der Merwe AJ Fauresmith	Guide	21.05.02	24.06.02	Good	
Van der Merwe JA Edenburg	Guide	01.11.01	01.05.02	Very good	Wife & 6 children
Van der Merwe PJ Bethlehem	Guide	15.12.01	30.06.02		
Van der Merwe SW Boshof	Guide	07.06.02	30.06.02	Very good & reliable	Wife & 4 children
Van Eden JJ Leeuwkop	Scout	04.03.02			Widower
Van Eden JT Kroonstad	Guide	25.02.02			
Van Maerkerham G	Guide	01.03.02	24.05.02		
Van Niekerk HR Boshof	Guide	15.06.01	20.06.02	Very good	Wife & 5 children
Van Niekerk SW Fauresmith	Guide	21.05.01	30.06.01	Good	
Van Rensburg Heilbron	Guide	25.07.01	05.08.01		
Van Rensburg J Bethlehem	Guide	15.01.01	03.12.01	Good & loyal	Family in Harrismith
Van Rensburg P Philippolis	Guide	06.12.01	30.06.02		
Van Rensburg WR Bethlehem	Guide	29.05.01	30.06.02		
Van Schalkwyk TJ Edenburg	Guide	26.03.01		Very good	Wife, 2 children
Van Staden M Kroonstad	Guide	16.07.01		Good	Wife, 5 children

Name & address	Duties	Appointed	Discharged	Character	Family & remarks
Van Tonder Heilbron	Guide	25.07.01	05.08.01		
Van Wyk A Winburg	Scout				
Van Wyk LJ Heilbron	Guide	17.07.01	19.09.01		
Van Wyk MA Vrede	Scout	28.05.02	16.06.02		
Van Wyk WS Kroonstad	Guide	31.07.01	22.01.02		Wife, 4 children
Van Zyl A	Guide	06.12.01	15.12.01		
Van Zyl J Kroonstad	Guide	27.10.01			
Van Zyl JA Heilbron	Guide	14.03.02			
Van Zyl TG Kroonstad	Guide	21.06.01			
Venter DJ Kroonstad	Guide				
Venter PA Bethlehem	Guide	20.06.01	18.10.01		
Venter WA Winburg	Scout	01.01.02	19.01.02		
Verster AJ Rouxville	Scout		10.05.02	Very good	
Verster J Zastron	Scout	09.10.01	02.04.02	Very reliable	
Victor W Fauresmith	Farrier	08.03.02	14.05.02	Fair	Wife & child
Viljoen HS Bethlehem	Guide	01.09.01	30.06.02		
Visser IJ Trompsburg	Guide	09.02.02			Wife
Vliem WA Heilbron	Guide	27.01.02			
Vosloo GF Kroonstad	Guide	23.10.01		Good	Wife, 4 children
Vyver FH Fauresmith	Guide & Scout	08.01.02	12.06.02	No use	
Wagner JJ Kroonstad	Guide	25.09.01			
Walton AM Bethlehem	Agent	01.02.02	30.06.02	Very good	
Ward CT Winburg	Scout	03.02.02	28.02.02		
Welgemoed C Winburg	Guide	04.01.02	25.03.02	Good	Family in Harrismith

Name & address	Duties	Appointed	Discharged	Character	Family & remarks
Welgemoed CB Bethlehem	Guide	11.04.02	30.06.02		
Wessels JHW Kroonstad	Guide	21.06.01	15.07.01		
Wessels JM Vrede	Agent	09.02.02	31.05.02	Very good	Brother
Wessels RH Vrede	Scout	28.05.02	30.06.02	Trustworthy	
Wessels WCP Vrede	Agent	21.02.02	06.06.02	Very good	Wife, 1 child
Wiggett AH Zastron	Scout	21.04.02	30.06.02		Wife, 1 child
Wildeman FJ Hoopstad	Guide	21.12.01	28.01.02		
Williams D Kroonstad	Guide		13.12.01		
Wilson EH Bethlehem	Guide	09.02.02	19.05.02		
Winter JF Ficksburg	Guide	01.03.02	10.04.02		
Wolmarans J	Guide	20.06.01	16.07.01		
Yelling WE Springfontein	Lieut IO	26.08.01	15.07.02		Single
Young W Harrismith	Guide	01.03.01	07.08.01	Indifferent	Widower, 2 children

Annexure 3
Names of National Scouts
No. 5 Klerksdorp Wing, W032 (A462)

Alexander A	Klerksdorp	De Roos FJ	Potchefstroom
Allen CB	Potchefstroom	De Villiers FC	Klerksdorp
Allen GF	Potchefstroom	De Villiers JC	Potchefstroom
Allen RH	Potchefstroom	Delport JGP	Potchefstroom
Arlow JF	Rustenburg	Delport PA	Rustenburg
Arlow N	Rustenburg	Denken HR	Potchefstroom
Badenhorst HS	Rustenburg	Dermott CR	Rustenburg
Barbarie F	Vryburg	Dermott HL	Rustenburg
Barnard HC	Potchefstroom	Devenish G	Klerksdorp
Barnard OJ	Potchefstroom	Du Plessis ADJ	Rustenburg
Bekker BP	Ventersdorp	Du Plessis AJC	Heidelberg
Bekker CC	Ventersdorp	Du Plessis J	Rustenburg
Bekker J	Ventersdorp	Du Plessis JF	Pretoria
Bekker PJ	Ventersdorp	Du Plessis WJ	Pretoria
Besoples J	Pretoria	Du Toit AS	Rustenburg
Beukes C	Klerksdorp	Du Toit C	Klerksdorp
Bezuidenhout HW	Luca River	Du Toit FH	Rustenburg
Bisschoff SH	Rustenburg	Du Toit GJ	Rustenburg
Booysens N	Pretoria	Du Toit JD	Johannesburg
Boshoff DC	Ventersdorp	Du Toit RF	Rustenburg
Botes J	Potchefstroom	Du Toit RP	Rustenburg
Botha RJ	Pretoria	Duckett F	Pretoria
Breed PG	Pretoria	Durien J	Potchefstroom
Breedt JE	Rustenburg	Durning CP	Klerksdorp
Britz NJJ	Johannesburg	Durning FD	Klerksdorp
Byles H	Pretoria	Edwards OD	Barberton
Carlinsky J	Potchefstroom	Engelbrecht EHJ	Meintjieskop
Celliers JB	Rustenburg	Engelbrecht EJ	Rustenburg
Clark HW	Rustenburg	Erasmus DO	Potchefstroom
Cloete AJ	—	Erasmus JJ	Rustenburg
Collins HO	Pretoria	Erasmus PJ	Rustenburg
Cronje APJ	Klerksdorp	Esterhuizen W	Klerksdorp
Cronje FJ	Klerksdorp	Fourie AJJ	Potchefstroom
Cronje PA	Klerksdorp	Fourie HJ	Klerksdorp
De Beer JC	Pretoria	Fourie HS	Klerksdorp
De Bruyn FS	Potchefstroom	Fredrickson A	Johannesburg
De Klerk NPW	—	Furstenburg F	Kroonstad

498

Geyser PJ	Rustenburg	Labuschagne FF	Klerksdorp
Gloves J	Krugersdorp	Labuschagne NJS	Krugersdorp
Grobler JJ	Rustenburg	Le Roux JC	Burkraal
Grobler JJP	Krugersdorp	Le Roux WRSF	Rustenburg
Haarhoff MJ	Rustenburg	Lee GH	Potchefstroom
Haarhoff PJ	Pretoria	Lennon PA	Potchefstroom
Haarhoff PJA	Krugersdorp	Lizmore D	Rustenburg
Haarhoff PJA	Rustenburg	Lottering CJ	Krugersdorp
Hallath J	Wolmaransstad	Lourens FS	Krugersdorp
Hallath S	Wolmaransstad	Maarsten JN	Meintjeskop
Hammond AJ	Klerksdorp	Mackenzie JH	Bloemfontein
Harmse BD	Rustenburg	Malan FP	Pretoria
Harmse DJ	Rustenburg	Marais H	Pretoria
Hattingh JH	Pretoria	Marais LFJ	Klerksdorp
Havenga BP	Rustenburg	Marx HC	Pretoria
Henry PH	Krugersdorp	Mathews W	Potchefstroom
Herbst G	Pretoria	Matthews JB	Potchefstroom
Homan BJ	Rustenburg	McGrath J	Potchefstroom
Horn JW	Klerksdorp	Meyer FS	Rustenburg
Hugo JP	Krugersdorp	Meyer JH	Potchefstroom
Jacobs JPA	Potchefstroom	Meyer JJ	Bloemhof
Jacobs MJ	Pretoria	Meyer JJ	Rustenburg
Jacobs PD	Rustenburg	Meyer JJ	Rustenburg
Jacobs PP	Klerksdorp	Meyer NJ	Pretoria
Jacobs SC	Potchefstroom	Meyer NP	Rustenburg
Jacobs SJ	Klerksdorp	Meyer PJ	Rustenburg
Janse van Rensburg AW	Meintjeskop	Montgomery JH	Pretoria
Janse van Rensburg CJ	Potchefstroom	Morris JH	Klerksdorp
Janse van Rensburg JH	Pretoria	Morris PJ	Reineke
Janse van Vuuren GPF	Rustenburg	Muller AJ	Potchefstroom
Jonker CJ	Rustenburg	Muller JH	Rustenburg
Jonker CJJ	Rustenburg	Murray C	Potchefstroom
Jonker D	Rustenburg	Naudé PS	Lichtenburg
Jonker JJ	Rustenburg	Neethling JJ	Wolmaransstad
Jonker JP	Rustenburg	Norkee JP	Kurgersdorp
Jooste WJ	Klerksdorp	Oberholzer WJ	Klerksdorp
Joubert HF	Potchefstroom	Olivier GW	Potchefstroom
Kaltwasser PG	Potchefstroom	Otto AF	Krugersdorp
Korb JJ	—	Otto JJ	Rustenburg
Krause MJ	Rustenburg	Pickard AB	Potchefstroom
Kroukamp JJ	Pretoria	Pienaar H	—
Kruger JC	Potchefstroom	Pieterse BA	Potchefstroom
Labuschagne CC	Krugersdorp	Pieterse DJ	—

Pieterse FS	Wolmaransstad	Strydom GS	Klerksdorp
Pietzer PP	Pretoria	Strydom MJ	—
Pitzer GP	Irene (Pretoria)	Strydom PS	—
Pitzer SD	Pretoria	Swanepoel DJ	Johannesburg
Potgieter IP	Klerksdorp	Swanepoel JC	Klerksdorp
Potgieter JJ	Johannesburg	Swanepoel W	Klerksdorp
Pretorius CJ	Johannesburg	Swart GP	Potchefstroom
Pretorius PP	Wolmaransstad	Swart HB	Klerksdorp
Pretorius SJ	Wolmaransstad	Swart JN	Rustenburg
Raath RJ	Potchefstroom	Swart MJ	Rustenburg
Rademan CFC	Rustenburg	Swart SN	Rustenburg
Robbertz HL	Meintjeskop	Swartzel S	Potchefstroom
Robbutz FW	Meintjeskop	Taljaard JN	Rustenburg
Robbutz HC	Meintjeskop	Taylor W	Krugersdorp
Roberts JHI	Rustenburg	Trichardt LG	Pretoria
Robertse DJ	Luca River	Valkenberg G	Rustenburg
Roos PJ	Rustenburg	Van Aswegen HA	Krugersdorp
Roscher AFC	Potchefstroom	Van Baalen SPJ	Potchefstroom
Ross GA	—	Van Biljoen WJ	Potchefstroom
Rossouw C	Wolmaransstad	Van Buissen AM	Wolmaransstad
Rossouw JJ	Klerksdorp	Van Buissen J	Wolmaransstad
Rossouw PJ	Klerksdorp	Van den Beck GP	Krugersdorp
Rouse JP	Keurike	Van den Berg JH	Potchefstroom
Schemel HA	Potchefstroom	Van den Heever CM	Wolmaransstad
Schoeman JP	Pretoria	Van den Heever TJ	Wolmaransstad
Schoeman WJ	Pretoria	Van der Linde AC	Potchefstroom
Schoonbee HS	Rustenburg	Van der Linde WG	Potchefstroom
Schusibee WA	Rustenburg	Van der Merwe GJ	Wolmaransstad
Smit FA	Pretoria	Van der Schyf TJ	Klerksdorp
Smit PJ	Potchefstroom	Van der Walt JN	Rustenburg
Smith CS	Rustenburg	Van der Walt JS	Rustenburg
Smith F	Johannesburg	Van der Westhuizen CF	Rustenburg
Smith OS	Krugersdorp	Van der Westhuizen GS	—
Snyman HGJ	Pretoria	Van der Westhuizen PR	Rustenburg
Spangenberg MH	OR Colony	Van Dyk J	Potchefstroom
Steenberg ZJ	Potchefstroom	Van Eden FJ	Potchefstroom
Steenkamp JH	Ermelo	Van Eden HJ	Potchefstroom
Stewart J	Durban	Van Eeden P	Klerksdorp
Steyn J	Potchefstroom	Van Graan JJ	Potchefstroom
Stopforth J	Klerksdorp	Van Helsdingen JG	Rustenburg
Stopforth SJ	Potchefstroom	Van Rensburg AWJ	Pretoria
Streicher O	Wolmaransstad	Van Rooyen G	Krugersdorp
Streicher SF	Wolmaransstad	Van Staden GJ	—

Van Staden HJ	Bloemhof	Wagner PF	—
Van Tonder F	Krugersdorp	Waite HD	Potchefstroom
Van Vuuren GA	Pretoria	Weber HF	Ventersdorp
Van Vuuren HB	Potchefstroom	Westhuizen JM	Rustenburg
Van Zyl AJ	Rustenburg	Wheeler RH	Krugersdorp
Vermeulen JW	Klerksdorp	Wilkins WJ	Standsfontein
Viljoen AJ	Klerksdorp	Wilthagen WF	Reineke
Viljoen JH	Pretoria	Wolmarans AB	—
Visagie Z	Potchefstroom	Young H	Ventersdorp
Visser C	Wolmaransstad	Zawitsky HF	Luipaardsvlei
Visser GP	Bloemhof	Zawitsky JJ	Johannesburg
Volsleedt HF	Klerksdorp	Zawitsky WP	Klerksdorp
Vos PS	Rustenburg	Zawitsky Z	Johannesburg
		Zawitsky Z	Luipaardsvlei

Sources

A ARCHIVAL SOURCES

I. **Transvaal Archives, National Archival Depository, Pretoria**
Accessions
A239, Major A.L. la C. Bartrop.
A82, H. Bramley.
A422, G.L. Brits.
A412, General S.W. Burger.
A313, General J.H. de la Rey.
A1259, L.J. du Plooy.
A1270, Mrs L. du Plooy.
A371, S.P. Engelbrecht.
A140, F.V. Engelenburg.
W5, W.J. Geerling.
A951, H.W. Huyser.
A1237, H. Olivier.
A787, G.S. Preller.
W125, General H.J. Schoeman.
A263, Brigadier-general B.N. Smythe.
A1147–1148, Temporary archival source research, Europe.
A1250, C.P. van der Merwe.
T99, Volksraadslyste Z.A.R. (Lists, S.A.R. parliament).
A133, A. Wypkema.

Estates
Andries Petrus Johannes Cronjé, Estate no. 50957, 1923.

Joseph Chamberlain Papers (1900–1903)
(Microfilms of original documents, University of Birmingham).
Original series number: J/C Box 13–16. Microfilm series number: D/C 24–26.

Colonial Office Records (1900–1903)
(Photocopies of original documents, Public Record Office, Kew, London).
Original series number: CO 48, 224, 291, 417.
Photocopy series number: FK vols 299–1063.

Archives of Colonial Secretary, Transvaal (1901–1906)
CS vols 3–421, 805, 842, 1076–1092.

Archives of the Colonial Treasurer, Transvaal (1901–1906)
CT vols 1–83, 284–293, 296.

Archives of the Executive Council, Transvaal (1903–1905)
EC vols 30–42.

Foreign Office Records (1900)
(Microfilms of original documents. Public Record Office, Kew).
Original series number: FO 364–368, 508–509.
Microfilm series number: A282, A284.

Secretary of the Governor (1901–1906)
216, 249–257, 327–595, 612–668, 826–830, 880, 906–928,

Archives of ̶ ̶missioner for South Africa (1900–1908)
HC vols 2–16̶.

Hooggeregshofstukke (Supreme Court items) (1893, 1906)
ZTPD vols 3/48, 3/144.

Archives of the Intelligence Officer to the Military Governor, Pretoria (1901–1902)
IOP vols 1–39.

Kitchener Letters (1900–1902)
(Photocopies of original documents. Public Record Office, Kew).
Original series number: Kitchener Letters, PRO 30/57.
Photocopy series number: FK vols 1621–1624.

Argief van die Kommandant-Generaal, Zuid-Afrikaansche Republiek (Archives of the Commandant-general of the South African Republic) (1899–1901)
KG vols 332–334, 353.

Konsentrasiekampstukke (Concentration camp items) (1900–1902)
KK vols 2–4.

Landdrosstukke (Magisterial items) (1900–1901, 1930)
Bloemhof, vol 182, (1900).
Ermelo, vols 2, 3, (1900).
Klerksdorp, vols 9, 116, 145, 146, (1900).
Louis Trichardt, vol 181, (1930).
Middelburg, vol 75, (1901).
Soutpansberg, vols 122, 123, (1900–1901).

Archives of the Legal Assistant to the Military Governor, Johannesburg (1900–1902)
LAJ vols 1–13.

Dr W.J. Leyds Archive (1899–1906)
Leyds Archive vols 94, 103, 109–191, 197–198, 259, 261–262, 579, 709–710, 716–739, 744, 749, 754, 760–764, 766–776, 779–781, 860–869.

Archives of the Lieutenant-governor of the Transvaal Colony (1902–1906)
Lt. Gov. vols 1–165.

Archives of the Military Governor, Pretoria (1900–1902)
MGP vols 2–290.

Milner Papers (1900–1905)
(Photocopies of original documents in the Bodleian Library, Oxford University).
Original series number: Milner Papers 15–105.
Photocopy series number: FK vols 1128–1220.

Archives of the Secretary for Native Affairs (1902)
SNA vol 165.

Archives of the Political Secretary (1900–1901)
PSY vols 28, 38–42, 55–70.

Archives of the Provost Marshal's Office, Army Headquarters, South Africa (1900–1902)
PMO vols 1–85.

Lord Roberts Papers (1900)
(Microfilm of original documents in Public Record Office, Kew).
Original series number: WO Roberts Papers 105.
Microfilm series number: A389–399.
Manuscript accession in Transvaal Archives: vols 6, 25–32, 35–46, 48, 50–65.

South African Constabulary Papers (1903)
SAC vol 11.

Argief van die Staatsekretaris van die Zuid-Afrikaansche Republiek (Archives of the State Secretary of the South African Republic) (1900)
SS vols 8433–8448.

Archives of the Staff Officer Prisoners of War, Cape Town (1900–1902)
SO/POW vols 1–88.

Archives of the Staff Officer Prisoners of War, Natal (1901)
SOP/Natal vols 5–20.

War Office Records (1900–1902)
(Microfilms of original documents in Public Record Office, Kew).
Original series number: WO 32/108.
Microfilm series number: A356–387, 400–417, 462.

II Free State Archives, Bloemfontein

Accessions
A59, A. Fischer.
A69, N.C. Havenga.
A60, Senator D. J. Malan.
A155, Oorlogsmuseum (War museum).
A119, Renier.
A156, M.T. Steyn.
A336, J. Vlotman.

Archives of the Colonial Secretary, Orange River Colony (1900–1906)
CSO vols 3–151, 199, 203–368, 427, 593, 612.

Archives of the Government Relief Department, Orange River Colony (1902–1903)
GRD vols 1–4, 9, 56–59, 75, 92, 103, 104, 141–144.

Magistracy Lindley (1902–1904)
Vols 1–4.

Archives of the Military Governor, Bloemfontein (1900–1903)
MGB vols 1–26.

Archives of the Provisional Mounted Police (1900)
PMP vols 5, 22–24.

Archives of the Municipality of Senekal
Register of taxes and minutes of council meetings, 1893–1907.

III Archives of the Nederduitse Hervormde of Gereformeerde Kerk, Pretoria
Godsdiensverslae (Reports on religious matters) (1899–1905)
Vols A–Z, RR–III, 4–5.

Church council minutes, N.H. of G. Kerk
Belfast, 1902–1906.
Carolina, 1902–1905.
Germiston, 1903–1904.
Krugersdorp, 1903–1904.
Lichtenburg, 1902–1906.
Middelburg, 1902–1906.
Potchefstroom, 1902–1906.
Pretoria, 1902–1906.
Roossenekal, 1902–1904.
Schweizer-Reneke, 1902–1906.
Soutpansberg, 1902–1906.
Utrecht, 1902–1906.
Ventersdorp, 1902–1905.
Wakkerstroom, 1902–1904.
Zeerust, 1902–1904.

Parish minutes, N.H. of G. Kerk
Lydenburg, 1903–1906.
Rustenburg, 1903–1906.
Utrecht, 1903–1905.

Synodal annexures (1906–1909)
Vols S–I, (6–11).

Minutes of Synodal Commissions (1902–1906)
Vols S–II, (92–18).

IV Archives of the Nederduits Gereformeerde Kerk, Bloemfontein
Church council minutes, N.G. Kerk
Bloemfontein, 1902–1904.
Harrismith, 1902–1904.
Hoopstad, 1902–1904.
Kroonstad, 1902–1904.
Vredefort, 1902–1904.

V Local Nederduits Gereformeerde Kerk Archives, Frankfort
N.G. Kerk council minutes, 1903–1906.

B ESTATES, PERSONAL INTERVIEWS, CORRESPONDENCE AND PRIVATE COLLECTIONS

Estates: Master of the Supreme Court, Bloemfontein
Christiaan Roedolf de Wet, Estate no. 15186, 1922.
Pieter Daniël de Wet, Estate no. 21437, 1929.
Stephanus Gerhardus Vilonel, Estate no. 2081, 1918.

Personal Interviews
Mrs J.J. de Klerk, Winburg district, 10 July 1976.

Correspondence
Lord Tollemache, Helmingham Hall, Stowmarket, Suffolk, England, in respect of J. West Ridgeway papers, September 1975.

Private Collections
H.G. de Wet, "The Fighter, The Scout, The Spy" (Unpublished memoirs, 1914). Formerly in the possession of the late F.A. van Jaarsveld, History Department, University of Pretoria.
Colonel C.F. Stallard Papers. In possession of A.J. Fick, formerly of the History Department, University of South Africa, Pretoria (one letter consulted).

C OFFICIAL PUBLICATIONS

I. Britain
Parliamentary Papers published by Command of the Government.
Cd. 35.   *Correspondence with the Presidents of the South African Republic and of the Orange Free State Respecting the War.* 1900.
Cd. 261. *Further Correspondence relating to Affairs in South Africa.* 1900.
Cd. 426. *Army Proclamations issued by Field-marshal Lord Roberts in South Africa.* 1900.
Cd. 457. *South Africa. Despatches,* I, 1900.
Cd. 524. *Return of Buildings burnt in each month from June 1900 to January 1901, including Farm Buildings, Mills, Cottages and Hovels.* 1901.
Cd. 528. *Papers relating to Negotiations between Commandant Louis Botha and Lord Kitchener.* 1901.
Cd. 546. *Letter from Commandant Louis Botha to Lord Kitchener dated 13th February, 1901.* 1901.
Cd. 547. *Further Correspondence Relating to Affairs in South Africa.* 1901.
Cd. 582. *Correspondence between the Commander-in-Chief in South Africa and the Boer Commanders so far as it affects the Destruction of Property.* 1901.
Cd. 605. *Despatch by General Lord Kitchener, dated 8th May, 1901 relative to Military Operations in South Africa.* 1901.
Cd. 608. *Return of numbers of persons in the Concentration Camps in South Africa, June 1901.* 1901.
Cd. 663. *Further papers relating to negotiations between Commandant Louis Botha and Lord Kitchener.* 1901.
Cd. 694. *Further returns of numbers of persons in the Camps of Refugee in South Africa, July, 1901.* 1901.
Cd. 695. *Despatch by General Lord Kitchener, dated 8th July, 1901 relative to Military Operations in South Africa.* 1901.
Cd. 732. *Correspondence relating to the Prolongation of Hostilities in South Africa.* 1901.
Cd. 800. *International Convention with respect to the Laws and Customs of War by Land. Signed at The Hague, July 29, 1899.* 1901.
Cd. 819. *Reports, &c., on the working of the Refugee Camps in the Transvaal, Orange River Colony, Cape Colony and Natal, November 1901.* 1901.

Cd. 820.   Despatches by General Lord Kitchener, dated 8th August, 8th September and 8th October, 1901, relative to Military Operations in South Africa. 1901.
Cd. 823.   Despatch by General Lord Kitchener, dated 8th November 1901, relative to Military Operations in South Africa. 1902.
Cd. 824.   Despatch by General Lord Kitchener, dated 8th December, 1901, relative to Military Operations in South Africa. 1902.
Cd. 853.   Further Papers relating to the working of the Refugee Camps in the Transvaal, Orange River Colony, Cape Colony and Natal, December 1901. 1901.
Cd. 890.   Despatch by General Lord Kitchener, dated 8th January, 1902, relative to Military Operations in South Africa. 1902.
Cd. 893.   Report on the Concentration Camps in South Africa, by the Committee of Ladies appointed by the Secretary of State for War, containing Reports on the Camps in Natal, the Orange River Colony and the Transvaal. 1902.
Cd. 902.   Further Papers relating to the working of the Refugee Camps in South Africa. 1902.
Cd. 903.   Further Correspondence relating to Affairs in South Africa. 1902.
Cd. 934.   Further Papers relating to the working of the Refugee Camps in South Africa. 1902.
Cd. 936.   Further Papers relating to the working of the Refugee Camps in South Africa. 1902.
Cd. 942.   Statistics of the Refugee Camps in South Africa. (May 1902–AMG). 1902.
Cd. 970.   Despatch by General Lord Kitchener, dated 8th March, 1902, relative to Military Operations in South Africa. 1902.
Cd. 988.   Despatch by General Lord Kitchener, dated 23rd June, 1902, relative to Military Operations in South Africa. 1902.
Cd. 1096. Correspondence respecting Terms of Surrender of the Boer Forces in the Field. 1902.
Cd. 1163. Further Correspondence relating to Affairs in South Africa, July, 1902. 1902.
Cd. 1284. Papers relating to an Interview between the Secretary of the State for Colonies and Generals Botha, De Wet and De la Rey on September 5th, 1902. 1902.
Cd. 1463. Further Correspondence relating to Affairs in South Africa, February, 1903. 1903.
Cd. 1551. Papers relating to the Progress of Administration in the Transvaal and the Orange River Colony, April 1903. 1903.
Cd. 1789. Report of His Majesty's Commissioners appointed to inquire into the Military Preparations and other Matters connected with the War in South Africa. 1903.
Cd. 1790. Minutes of evidence taken before the Royal Commission on the War in South Africa, I. 1903.
Cd. 1791. Minutes of Evidence taken before the Royal Commission on the War in South Africa, II. 1903.
Cd. 1792. Appendices to the Minutes of Evidence taken before the Royal Commission on the War in South Africa. 1903.
Cd. 2104. Correspondence relating to Affairs in the Transvaal and Orange River Colony, July, 1904. 1904.
Cd. 2482. Further Correspondence relating to Affairs in the Transvaal and Orange River Colony, May 1905. 1905.
Cd. 2563. Further Correspondence relating to Affairs in the Transvaal and Orange River Colony, July 1905. 1905.
Cd. 3028. Further Correspondence relating to Affairs in South Africa, July, 1906. 1906.
Cd. 3582. Further Correspondence relating to Affairs in the Transvaal and Orange River Colony. 1907.

Confidential Print
Africa (South):
636   Telegrams, 1901.
650   Secret Correspondence, 1901.
653   Memorandum prepared in the Colonial Office on certain Points connected with the Conduct of Hostilities in South Africa.
662   War in South Africa; Correspondence, August and September 1900.
663   War in South Africa; Correspondence, October to December 1900.

664   War in South Africa; Correspondence, January and February 1901.
665   War in South Africa; Correspondence, March and April 1901.
666   War in South Africa; Correspondence, May and June 1901.
667   War in South Africa; Correspondence, July and August 1901.
668   War in South Africa; Correspondence, September and October 1901.
669   War in South Africa; Correspondence, November and December 1901.
680   War in South Africa; Correspondence, January to March 1902.
687   Refugee camps in South Africa; Correspondence, March and February 1902.
694   Affairs in Bechuanaland Protectorate and Rhodesia; Further Correspondence, July to December 1901.
697   Refugee camps; Further correspondence, February 1902 to August 1903.
699   Affairs in South Africa; Further correspondence, July to September 1902.
705   Affairs in South Africa; Further correspondence, October to December 1902.
726   Affairs in South Africa; Further correspondence, April to June 1903.
728   Affairs in South Africa; Further correspondence, July to September 1903.
732   Affairs in South Africa; Further correspondence, October to December 1903.
853   Memorandum on the Transvaal and Orange River Colony, 1906.

War Office Publications
Journal of the Principal Events connected with South Africa. Vols VI–XVI.
Reprint of Circulars issued by Director of Supplies, 1902.
South Africa. Despatches. Vols II–III.
South African War, 1899–1902. Confidential Telegrams, October 1899–October 1902.
Telegrams and Letters sent by Field-marshal Lord Roberts, April 1900–December 1900. Vols I–VI.

II. Zuid-Afrikaansche Republiek (South African Republic)
Staats-Almanak voor de Zuid-Afrikaansche Republiek, 1898.
Wet nr. 20 van 1898, Voor den Krijgsdienst (in the Zuid-Afrikaansche Republiek).
Eerste Volksraadsnotules, 1899 (Minutes of the First Volksraad).
Buitengewone Staatscourant der Zuid-Afrikaansche Republiek, 1899–1900 (Government Gazette).

III. Republiek van die Oranje-Vrijstaat (Republic of the Orange Free State)
Volksraadsnotules, (Parliamentary minutes), 1893–1899.
Wet nr. 10 van 1899, De Krijgs- en Commandowet.
De Brandwacht, 1901.
De Staatscourant der O.V.S., 1901–1902 (Government Gazette).

IV. Cape Colony
Cape of Good Hope: Debates in the House of Assembly, 1902.

V. Transvaal Colony
List of Burghers who have surrendered their arms in the Transvaal and Orange Free State, 1900.
List of Casualties in the Army in South Africa, 1901.
List of Casualties in the Army in South Africa, 1902.
Transvaal Administration Reports for 1902: General Report on Burgher Land Settlements (Transvaal).
Transvaal Administration Reports for 1902: Burgher Camps Department.
Transvaal Educational Departments Reports, 1902–1903.
Government Gazettes, 1902–1904.
Transvaal Administration Reports: Judicial, 1902–1904.
General Administration Report, Burgher Land Settlements (Transvaal), for 1903–1904.
Transvaal Legislative Council Debates, 1903–1906.
Transvaal Census Commissioner Report, 1904.

Report of the South African Constabulary Commission 1905, with Minutes of Proceedings, Minutes of Evidence and Annexures, 1905.
Repatriation Department of the Transvaal: Reports and Financial Statements, 1906.
Transvaal Indigency Commission Report (with Minutes of Evidence), 1906–1908.

VI. Orange River Colony
Report on the Commission of Enquiry into the late Administration of the Kroonstad District since the Annexation, 1901.
Government Gazette, 1902–1904.
Minutes of the Proceedings of the Legislative Council, 1903–1904.
Rapport van de Kommissie door de Regering van de Oranje Rivier Kolonie aangesteld om onderzoek te doen naar den toestand van Arme Blanken in de O.R.K., 1908.

VII. Other
Almanak voor de Nederduitsch Hervormde of Gereformeerde Kerk in Zuid-Afrika, 1889–1899.
Verslag der Deputasie die naar de Kaap kolonie werd afgezonden door de Vredes Comites in de Oranje Rivier Kolonie, 1901.
Wetten en Bepalingen voor het bestuur van de Nederduitsche Hervormde of Gereformeerde Kerk in Zuid-Afrika, 1903.
Acta Synodi, N.H. of G. Kerk, 1903.
Officieel Verslag van de Verrichtingen van het Nasionaal kongres gehouden te Brandfort op 1 en 2 Desember 1904.
Acta Synodi, N.H. of G. Kerk, 1906.

D NEWSPAPERS AND CONTEMPORARY PERIODICALS

Die Afrikaner, 1976.
The Bloemfontein Post, 1900–1905.
De Burger, 1915.
The Cape Argus, 1900–1903.
The Cape Times, 1900–1903.
De Fakkel, 1903–1906.
The Friend, 1894, 1896, 1902–1905, 1929.
De Getuige, 1903–1904.
De Kerkbode, 1900–1904.
Klerksdorp Mining Record, 1903–1905.
Land en Volk, 1899, 1902–1905.
De Natal Afrikaner, 1900.
The Natal Mercury, 1900.
The Natal Witness, 1900.
Nieuwe Rortterdamsche Courant, 1900.
Pretoria News, 1903–1905.
Rand Daily Mail, 1902–1904.
The South African News, 1900–1903.
The Standard and Diggers' News, 1899–1900.
The Star, 1902–1905, 1923.
Stemmen des Tijds, 1903–1907.
The Times, 1900–1904.
Transvaal Advertiser, 1902–1904.
The Transvaal Critic, 1903–1905.
The Transvaal Leader, 1902–1904.
De Vereeniging, 1903–1906.
Die Volksblad, 1929.

De Volksstem, 1899–1900, 1903–1906.
Die Volksstem, 1923.
De Vriend, 1903–1905.
De Zoutpansberg Wachter, 1900.
De Zuid-Afrikaan, 1900.

E SOURCE PUBLICATIONS

Brits, J.P. (ed.), *Diary of a National Scout P.J. du Toit, 1900–1902*. Pretoria: Human Sciences Research Council, 1974.
Curtis, L., *With Milner in South Africa*. Oxford: Basil Blackwell, 1951.
Eloff, C.C. (ed.), *Oorlogsdagboekie van H.S. Oosterhagen, Januarie – Junie 1902*. Pretoria: Human Sciences Research Council, 1976.
Ferreira, O.J.O. (ed.), *Geschiedenis werken en streven van S.P.E. Trichard luitenant kolonel der vroegere Staats-Artillerie Z.A.R. door hemzelve beschreven*. Pretoria: Human Sciences Research Council, 1975.
Fischer, M.A., *Kampdagboek, Mei 1901 – Augustus 1902*. Cape Town: Tafelberg, 1964.
Hancock, W.K. & Van der Poel, J. (eds), *Selections from the Smuts Papers*, I, *June 1886 – May 1902*; II, *June 1902 – May 1910*. Cambridge: Cambridge University Press, 1966.
Headlam, C. (ed.), *The Milner Papers*, II, *South Africa, 1899–1905*. London: Cassell, 1933.
Kestell, J.D. & Van Velden, D.E., *De Vredesonderhandelingen tusschen de Regeeringen der twee Zuid-Afrikaansche Republieken en de Vertegenwoordigers der Britsche Regeering, welke uitliepen op den Vrede, op 31 Mei 1902 te Vereeniging gesloten*. Pretoria: J.H. de Bussy, 1909.
Lewsen, P. (ed.), *Selections from the Correspondence of John X. Merriman, 1899–1905*. Van Riebeeck Society, 47, Cape Town: Van Riebeeck Society, 1966.
Leyds, W.J., *Eenige Correspondentie uit 1899 (Zoogenaamde "Eerste Versameling")*. Second edition, Amsterdam: J.H. de Bussy, 1938.
——, *Tweede Verzameling (Correspondentie 1899–1900). Deel I*, 2 vols. *Deel II, Bijlagen, Index*. 's-Gravenhage: N.V. Geuze, 1930.
——, *Derde Verzameling (Correspondentie 1900). Deel I. Deel II, Bijlagen, Index*. 's-Gravenhage: N.V. Geuze, 1931.
——, *Vierde Verzameling (Correspondentie 1900–1902). Deel I*, 2 vols. *Deel II, Bijlagen Index*. 's-Gravenhage: N.V. Geuze, 1934.
Marquard, L. (ed.), *Letters from a Boer Parsonage. Letters of Margaret Marquard during the Boer War*. Cape Town: Purnell, 1967.
May, H.J., *Music of the Guns: Based on two journals of the Boer War*. London: Hutchinson, 1970.
Oberholster, A.G. (ed.), *Dagboek van H.C. Bredell, 1900–1904*. Pretoria: Human Sciences Research Council, 1972.
Oberholster, J.J. (ed.), "Dagboek van Oskar Hintrager. Saam met Christiaan de Wet, Mei tot September 1900" in *Christiaan de Wet-Annale*, 2. Pretoria & Bloemfontein: S.A. Akademie vir Wetenskap & Kuns & Oorlogsmuseum, Oct. 1973.
Van Schoor, M.C.E. (ed.), "Dagboek van Hugo H. van Niekerk" in *Christiaan De Wet-Annale*, 1. Cape Town, Pretoria & Bloemfontein: S.A. Akademie vir Wetenskap & Kuns & Oorlogsmuseum, Oct. 1972.
——, (ed.), "'Dagboek' van Rocco de Villiers en Bylaes" in *Christiaan de Wet-Annale*, 3. Pretoria & Bloemfontein: S.A. Akademie vir Wetenskap & Kuns & Oorlogsmuseum, Oct. 1975.
Williams-Foxcroft, E. & Van Schoor, M.C.E. (eds), "Die dépêches van die Russiese attachés, kol. Stakhovitch en lt.kol. Gurko" in *Christiaan de Wet-Annale*, 3. Pretoria & Bloemfontein: S.A. Akademie vir Wetenskap & Kuns & Oorlogsmuseum, Oct. 1975.

F OTHER WORKS: BOOKS, PAMPHLETS, ARTICLES, UNPUBLISHED PAPERS, DISSERTATIONS AND THESES

Ackermann, P.C.M., "Aardrykskundige invloede in die stryd tussen Brittanje en die Boererepublieke met besondere verwysing na die Tweede Vryheidsoorlog" (Unpublished D.Phil. thesis, Unisa), 1957.
Amery, J., *The Life of Joseph Chamberlain, 1901–1903, IV*. London: MacMillan, 1951.
Amery, L.S. (ed.), *The Times History of the War in South Africa, 1899–1902. I–VII*. London: Sampson Low, Marston, 1900–1909.
——, *Days of Fresh Air, being Reminiscences of Outdoor Life*. London: Jarrolds, 1939.
Anonymous [O. Hintrager], *Steijn, De Wet und die Oranje-Freistaater, Tagebuchblätter aus dem Südafrikanischen Kriege*. Tübingen: H. Laupp, 1902.
Arkin, M., "Samuel Marks" in W.J. de Kock (ed). *DSAB, I.* Pretoria: Human Sciences Research Council. 1968.
Arthur, G., *Life of Lord Kitchener, I–III*. New York: MacMillan, 1920.
——, *General Sir John Maxwell*. London, 1932.
Badenhorst, C.C.J., *Uit den Boeren-oorlog 1899–1902*. Amsterdam: Höveker & Wormser, 1903.
Bakkes, C.M., *Die Britse Deurbraak aan die Benede-Tugela op Majubadag 1900*. Pretoria: Government Printer, 1973.
Barnard, C.J., *Generaal Louis Botha op die Natalse front 1899–1900*. Cape Town: A.A. Balkema, 1970.
——, "Grepe uit die Krygskuns van die Boeregeneraals" in *Historia*, 19(1), May 1974.
Barnard, J.H., "Die Politieke strominge in die Volksraad van die Suid-Afrikaanse Republiek van 1881–1899" (Unpublished MA dissertation, UP), 1944.
Basson, J.L., "Die Slag van Paardeberg" (Unpublished MA dissertation, UP), 1971.
Basson, M.A., "Die Britse invloed in die Transvaalse Onderwys, 1836–1907" in *Archives Yearbook for South African History*, 19(II), Pretoria: Government Printer, 1956.
Batts, H.J., *Pretoria from within during the War, 1899–1900*. London: John F. Shaw, undated.
Baty, T., *International Law in South Africa*. London: Stevens & Haynes, 1900.
Beak, G.B., *The Aftermath of War. An Account of the Repatriation of the Boers and Natives in Orange River Colony, 1902–1904*. London: Edward Arnold, 1906.
Bodenstein, H.D.J., *Was Generaal Botha in 1900 'n Verrader?* Amsterdam: J.H. de Bussy, 1916.
Boldingh, G., *Een Hollandsch officier in Zuid-Afrika: Nagelaten geschriften van luitenant Gerrit Boldingh*. Rotterdam: B. van de Watering, 1903.
Bornman, M.J. (Buurman), *Oorlogswolke oor die Republieke: Die Herinneringe van 'n Boere-offisier*. Johannesburg: Voortrekkerpers, 1944.
Bosman, H.S., *Een Terugblik op kerkelijke en godsdienstige toestanden in de Transvaal*. Cape Town: Van de Sandt de Villiers, 1923.
Botha, B.J., "Mnr. Koos Smit se rol in die Oorlog" in *Die Huisgenoot*, 6 November 1953.
Botha, P.M., *From Boer to Boer and Englishman*. Cape Town: J.C. Juta, 1900.
Bothanicus [B. de Haan], *De Onderhandelingen van Lord Kitchener en Louis Botha, zooals de Commandant-general Botha mij deze Gebeurtenis verteld Heeft*. Rotterdam: J.H. de Bussy, 1901.
Boveri, M., *Treason in the Twentieth century*. London, 1971.
Brandt, J., *Die Kappie Kommando of Boerenvrouwen in Geheime Dienst*. Amsterdam: J.H. de Bussy, 1913.
Breytenbach, J.H. (ed), *Gedenkalbum van die Tweede Vryheidsoorlog*. Cape Town: Nasionale Pers, 1949.
——, *Die Geskiedenis van die Tweede Vryheidsoorlog in Suid-Afrika, 1899–1902, I–III*. Pretoria: Government Printer, 1969–1973.
Brink, J.N., *Oorlog en Ballingskap*. Cape Town: Nasionale Pers, 1940.
Brits, J.P., "Generaal Andries Petrus Johannes Cronjé" (Unpublished manuscript for use in *DSAB, III*).
Bromberger, N., "General Botha and the Conciliation Policy" (Unpublished BA Hons essay, UK), 1957.
Brothers, O.F., *The First Transvaal Parliament*. Johannesburg: Transvaal Leader, 1907.
Burnett, C., *The 18th Hussars in South Africa*. Winchester: Warren & Son, 1905.
Buys, M.H., "Militêre Regering in Transvaal, 1900–1902" (Unpublished D.Phil. thesis, UP), 1972.
Campbell, A., *Guerilas: A History and Analysis*. London: Arthur Baker, 1967.
Changuion, L.J.S., "Die Verhuising van Boere na Oos-Afrika, 1902–1914" (Unpublished MA dissertation, UP), 1975.

Chilvers, H., *Out of the Crucible.* London: Cassell, 1929.
Coates, J.H. & Pellegrin, J.R., *Military Sociology.* New York, 1965.
Coetzee, J.A., *Politieke Groeperinge in die Wording van die Afrikanernasie.* Johannesburg: Voortrekkerpers, 1941.
Conradie, F.D., *Met Cronjé op die Wesfront.* Cape Town: Nasionale Pers, 1946.
Crankshaw, E., *The Forsaken Idea. A Study of Viscount Milner.* London: Longmans, Green, 1952.
Davenport, T.R.H., *The Afrikaner Bond, the History of a South African Political Party, 1880–1911.* Cape Town: Oxford University Press, 1966.
Davitt, M., *The Boer Fight for Freedom.* New York: Funk & Wagnalls, 1902.
De Jongh, C. & Ploeger, J., "Verslae van Neutrale Militêre Waarnemers tydens die Anglo-Boereoorlog (kapt. J. Allum)" in *Militaria*, 4(1), 1973.
Delport, P.J., "Die Rol van generaal Marthinus Prinsloo gedurende die Tweede Vryheidsoorlog" (Unpublished MA dissertation, UOVS), 1972.
Denoon, D.J.N., "Decolonisation of South African History" in *University of East Africa Social Science Conference Papers.* Makerere, 1968.
——, "Participation in the Boer War: People's War, People's Non-War, or Non-People's War?" in B.A. Ogot (ed.), *War and Society in Africa.* London: Frank Cass, 1972.
——, *Southern Africa since 1800.* London: Longman, 1973.
——, *A Grand Illusion: The failure of imperial policy in the Transvaal Colony during the period of reconstruction 1900–1905.* London: Longman, 1973.
De Souza, C.W.L., *No Charge for Delivery.* Cape Town: Books of Africa, 1969.
Despagnet, F., *La Guerre Sud-Africaine au point de vue du Droit International.* Paris: A. Pedone, 1902.
Devitt, N., *The Concentration Camps in South Africa during the Anglo-Boer War of 1899–1902.* Pietermaritzburg: Shuter & Shooter, 1941.
De Villebois-Mareuil, [G.], *War Notes: The diary of Colonel de Villebois-Mareuil from November 24, 1899 to April 7, 1900,* Translated by Frederic Lees. London: Methuen, 1901.
De Villiers, O.T., *Met Steyn en De Wet in het veld.* Amsterdam: Elsevier, 1903.
De Vos, P.J., "'Die Bywoner': 'n Sosiologiese Studie oor die Bywonerskap in sekere Hoë- en Middelvelddistrikte in die Transvaal en Vrystaat" (Unpublished MA dissertation, UP), 1937.
De Wet, C.R., *De Strijd tusschen Boer en Brit.* Eighteenth edition, Amsterdam: Höveker & Wormser, 1903.
De Wet, I.J.C., *Met Generaal de Wet op Kommando.* Johannesburg: Afrikaanse Pers, 1954.
Doyle, A.C., *The Great Boer War: A two years' Record, 1899–1901.* London: Smith, Elder, 1902.
Duff, B., *What is now being done in South Africa.* Westminster: Vacher & Sons, 1901.
Du Plessis, J.S., "Generaal Jacobus Hercules de la Rey" in W.J. De Kock (general ed.). *DSAB, I,* Pretoria: Human Sciences Research Council, 1968.
Du Toit, F.G.M., "Hermanus Stephanus Bosman 1848–1933" (Unpublished D.Th. thesis, UP), 1975.
Encyclopaedia Brittanica, 20.
Engelenburg, F.V., *Genl. Louis Botha.* Pretoria: J.L. van Schaik, 1928.
Engelenburg, F.V. & Preller, G.S., *Onze Krijgs-Officieren.* Pretoria: Volksstem, 1904.
Esterhuizen. S.J., "Die ekonomiese rehabilitasie pogings gedurende en onmiddellik na die Tweede Vryheidsoorlog ter opheffing van die Transvaalse burgers" (Unpublished MA dissertation, UP), 1952.
——, "Die ekonomiese en maatskaplike toestande van die gewese republikeinse burgers in die Transvaal-kolonie, 1900–1910" (Unpublished D.Phil. thesis, UP), 1966.
Farrer, J.A., *Military Manners and Customs: The Laws and Observances of Warfare in Ancient and Modern Times.* London, 1885. Reprinted, 1968.
Fisher, J., *That Miss Hobhouse.* London: Secker & Warburg, 1971.
Fourie, H.W., *An Afrikaner's Appeal to Afrikaners to assist in Bringing about Peace in South Africa.* Cape Town: De Kolonist, 1902.
Fourie, H.W., *Een Afrikaners beroep om te helpen vrede tot stand te brengen in Zuid-Afrika.* Cape Town: Townshend, Taylor & Snashall, 1902.
Fraser, J.G., *Episodes from My Life.* Cape Town: Juta, 1922.
Fuller, J.F.C., *The Last of the Gentleman's Wars.* London: Faber & Faber, 1937.
Gann, L.H., *Guerillas in History.* Stanford, 1971.

Garson, N.G., "'Het Volk': the Botha-Smuts party in the Transvaal, 1904–1911" in *The Historical Journal*, 9(1), 1966.
Geyser, O. & Marais, A.H. (eds), *Die Nasionale Party, I, Agtergrond, Stigting en Konsolidasie*. Pretoria, 1975.
Gibson, G.F., *The Story of the Imperial Light Horse in the South African War, 1899–1902*. London: G.D. & Co., 1937.
Goldmann, C.S., *With General French and the Cavalry in South Africa*. London: MacMillan, 1902.
Gordon, C.T., *The Growth of Boer opposition to Kruger, 1890–1895*. Cape Town: Oxford University Press, 1970.
Grobbelaar, P.W. (ed.), *Die Afrikaner en sy Kultuur, II, Spieëlbeeld Oorlog 1899–1902*. (Compiled by C.J. Scheepers Strydom). Cape Town: Tafelberg, 1974.
——, *Die Afrikaner en sy Kultuur, IV, Afrikaners in die Vreemde*. (Compiled by C.J. Scheepers Strydom). Cape Town: Tafelberg, 1976.
Grobler, F.J., "Die Carolina-kommando in die Tweede Vryheidsoorlog. 1899–1902" (Unpublished MA dissertation, Potch), 1960.
Grobler, M.J., *Met die Vrystaters onder die Wapen*. Bloemfontein: Nasionale Pers, 1937.
Groenewald, W.C., "Bedreiging in die Nag" in *Die Huisgenoot*, 6 May 1938.
Gronum, M.A., *Die Engelse Oorlog 1899–1902: Die gevegsmetodes waarmee die Boererepublieke verower is*. Cape Town: Tafelberg, 1972.
——, *Die Bittereinders, Junie 1901 – Mei 1902*. Cape Town: Tafelberg, 1974.
Grundlingh, A.M., "Die Stigting van Senekal en Ontwikkeling in die dorp en Wyk Onderwittebergen tot 1899" (Unpublished BA Hons essay, UOVS), 1971.
Guest, H.M., *Vicissitudes of a Transvaal dorp*. Klerksdorp: H.M. Guest, 1901.
——, *With Lord Methuen and the First Division*. Klerksdorp: H.M. Guest, 1902.
Gutsche, T., *'n Spoggerige Medalje. Die Verhaal van die Witwatersrandse Landbougenootskap*. Cape Town, 1970.
Hall, W.E., *A treatise on International Law*. Oxford: Clarendon Press, 1924.
Halperin, V., *Lord Milner and the Empire*. London, 1952.
Hancock, W.K., *Smuts, I, The Sanguine Years 1870–1919*. Cambridge: Cambridge University Press, 1962.
Hanekom, T.N., *Ons Nederduits Gereformeerde Kerk: gedenkboek by ons derde eeufees*. Cape Town: N.G. Kerk Publishers, 1952.
Hannah, W.H., *Bobs: Kipling's General. The Life of Field-marshal Earl Roberts of Kandahar, V.C.* London: Leo Cooper, 1972.
Hattingh, J.L., "Die Irenekonsentrasiekamp" in *Archives Yearbook for South African History*, 30(1), 1967.
——, "Die geval van Meyer de Kock en die ontstaan van die Konsentrasiekampe tydens die Anglo-Boereoorlog, 1899–1902" in *Historia*, 18(3), September 1973.
——, "Die Trekke uit die Suid-Afrikaanse Republiek en die Oranje-Vrystaat, 1875–1895" (Unpublished D.Phil. thesis, UP), 1975.
Hillegas, H.C., *With the Boer Forces*. London: Methuen, 1900.
Hobhouse, E., *The Brunt of the War and Where it fell*. London: Methuen, 1902.
——, *War without Glamour*. Bloemfontein: Nasionale Pers, 1924.
Hodder-Williams, R., "Afrikaners in Rhodesia" in *African Social Research*, 18, December 1974.
Hofmeyr, A., *The story of my captivity during the Transvaal War 1899–1900*. London: Edward Arnold, 1900.
Hofmeyr, N., *Zes maanden bij de commando's*. 's-Gravenhage: W.P. van Stockum & Zoon, 1903.
Holt, E., *The Boer War*. London: Putnam, 1958.
Howard, M., *Studies in War and Peace*. London: Temple Smith, 1970.
Iklé, F.C., *Every War Must End*. New York: Columbia University Press, 1971.
Jackson, M.C., *A Soldier's Diary, South Africa 1899–1901*. London: Max Goschen, 1913.
James. D., *Lord Roberts*. London: Hollis & Carter, 1954.
Jamneck, C.P., "Die Milner-regime in Transvaal, 1902–1905" (Unpublished MA dissertation, Unisa), 1947.
Keet. D.J. (ed), *Wonderdade van God: Jubileum Gedenkboek, 1842–1942*. Pretoria: Voortrekkerpers, 1942.
Kemp, J.C.G., *Die pad van die veroweraar: 'n Vervolg op Vir vryheid en vir reg*. Cape Town: Nasionale Pers, 1942.

―――, *Vir vryheid en vir reg.* Cape Town: Nasionale Pers, 1946.
Kestell, J.D., *Met de Boeren-Commando's: Mijne ervaringen als veldprediker.* Amsterdam: Höveker & Wormser, 1902.
―――, *Christiaan de Wet. 'n Lewensbeskrywing.* Cape Town: De Nationale Pers, 1920.
Kirstein, J., "Some Foundations of Afrikaner Nationalism 1902–1910" (Unpublished BA Hons essay, UK), 1956.
Kleynhans, W.A., "Politieke Strominge en Verantwoordelike Bestuur in Transvaal 1905–1909" (Unpublished MA dissertation, UP), 1952.
Knight, E.F., *South Africa after the War. A Narrative of Recent Travel.* London: Longmans, Green, 1903.
Knop [pseudonym for Gustav Preller], *Agt Jaar s'n Politiek: Skoon Geskiedenis van die Suidafr. Nasionale Partij, 1902–1910.* Pretoria: Volkstem, 1910.
Kotzé, J.P., "Die Runderpes in die Transvaal en die onmiddellike gevolge daarvan, 1896–1899" (Unpublished MA dissertation, RAU), 1974.
Kriel, J.D., "Emily Hobhouse en die naweë van die Anglo-Boere Oorlog. 'n Studie in altruïsme en pasifisme" (Unpublished D.Phil. thesis, UOVS), 1957.
Krige, J., *American Sympathy in the Boer War: A Plain tale of Commando Life in the Boer War 1899–1900 and subsequent Adventures in the United States of America.* Johannesburg: Automatic Printing Press, 1933.
Kruger, C.J.H., "Militêre Bewind in die Oranje-Vrystaat, Maart 1900 – Januarie 1901" (Unpublished MA dissertation, UP), 1958.
Krüger, D.W., *Paul Kruger, II, 1883–1904.* Johannesburg: Afrikaanse Pers, 1963.
―――, *Die Ander Oorlog. Die Stryd om die Openbare Mening in Engeland gedurende die Tweede Vryheidsoorlog.* Cape Town: Tafelberg, 1974.
Kruger, R., *Good-bye Dolly Gray: The story of the Boer War.* London: Cassell, 1964.
Kuit, A., *'n Kommandoprediker.* Pretoria: J.H. de Bussy, 1948.
Lagden, G., *The Basutos, II.* London: Hutchinson, 1909.
La Grange Lombard, J.P., *Bang Plekke.* Johannesburg, 1941.
Lamprecht, G.J., "Die Ekonomiese Ontwikkeling van die Vrystaat van 1870 tot 1899" (Unpublished D.Phil. thesis, US), 1954.
Lewis, I.M., *The Modern History of Somaliland.* London: Weidenfeld & Nicholson, 1965.
Le May, G.H.L., *British Supremacy in South Africa, 1899–1907.* Oxford: Clarendon Press, 1965.
Lombard, P.S. (Compiled by A.M. Jackson), *Uit die dagboek van 'n Wildeboer.* Johannesburg: Afrikaanse Pers, 1939.
Macdonald, J.R., *Wat ek in Suid-Afrika gesien het, September en Oktober 1902* (Translated by J. Albert Coetzee). Johannesburg: Voortrekkerpers, 1941.
Magnus, P., *Kitchener, Portrait of an imperialist.* London: John Murray, 1958.
Malan, S.F., "Die Rol van J. Geo. Fraser in die Vrystaat 1863–1927" (Unpublished MA dissertation, UOVS), 1971.
―――, "Die Britse Besetting van Bloemfontein, 13 Maart 1900" in *Historia*, 20(1), May 1975.
Marais, A.H., "Die Ontstaan en Ontwikkeling van Partypolitiek in die Oranjerivierkolonie, 1902–1912" (Unpublished MA dissertation, UOVS), 1967.
Marais, J.S., *The Fall of Kruger's Republic.* Oxford: Clarendon Press, 1961.
Martin, A.C., *The Concentration Camps 1900–1902: Facts, Figures, and Fables.* Cape Town: Howard Timmins, 1957.
Maurice, F. & Grant, M.H., *History of the War in South Africa 1899–1902. Compiled by the Direction of His Majesty's Government, I–IV.* London: Hurst & Blackett Ltd., 1906–1910.
Mawby, A.A., "The Political Behaviour of the British Population of the Transvaal 1902–1907" (Unpublished Ph.D. thesis, UW), 1969.
Maxwell, C.A. (ed.), *Frank Maxwell, Brigadier-general, V.C., C.S.I., D.S.O. A Memoir and some Letters.* London: John Murray, 1921.
Meintjes, J.H., "Die Selati-spoorwegskandaal met besondere verwysing na Regeringskommissaris van Spoorweë J.S. Smit" (Unpublished MA dissertation, UP), 1953.
Methuen, A.M.S., *Peace or War in South Africa.* London: Methuen, 1901.
Miller, M., *A Captain of the Gordons.* London: Sampson Low, Marston, 1914.

Moll, J.C., "Francis William Reitz en die Republiek van die Oranje-Vrystaat" (Unpublished D.Litt. thesis, UOVS), 1968.
Mostert, D., *Slegtkamp van Spioenkop: Oorlogsherinneringe van Kapt. Henri Slegtkamp, Saamgestel uit sy Dagboek.* Cape Town: Nasionale Pers, 1935.
Muller, C.H., *Oorlogsherinneringe.* Cape Town: Nasionale Pers, 1936.
Naudé, J.F., *Vechten en Vluchten van Beyers en Kemp "bôkant" De Wet.* Rotterdam: Nijgh & Van Ditmar, 1903.
Naudé, P., "Boerdery in die Suid-Afrikaanse Republiek, 1858–1899" (Unpublished D.Litt. thesis, Unisa), 1954.
——, "Die Verskynsel van Gebrek aan Grondbesit by die Burger van die Suid-Afrikaanse Republiek" in *Historia,* 1(1), 1956.
Neethling, E. (Mrs Revd H.L.), *Vergeten?* Cape Town: De Nationale Pers, 1917.
Nevinson, H.W., *Changes and chances.* London: Nisbet & Co., 1923.
Oberholster, J.A.S., *Die Gereformeerde Kerke onder die kruis in Suid-Afrika: hul ontstaan en ontwikkeling.* Cape Town: HAUM, 1956.
Oberholster, J.J. & Van Schoor, M.C.E., *Die Nederduitse Gereformeerde Kerk in die Oranje-Vrystaat.* Bloemfontein: N.G. Kerk Publishers, 1963.
Olivier, C.P.H., "Die Geskiedenis van die Scoutkerk in Transvaal" (Unpublished proponent thesis, UP), 1969.
Oosthuizen, J., "Jacobus Herculas de la Rey en die Tweede Vryheidsoorlog" (Unpublished D.Litt. thesis, Potch), 1949.
Oosthuizen, S.P.R., "Die beheer, behandeling en lewe van die Krygsgevangenes gedurende die Anglo-Boereoorlog, 1899–1902" (Unpublished D.Phil. thesis UOVS), 1975.
Oppenheim, L., *International Law. A Treatise.* H. Lauterpacht (ed.), II, *Disputes, War and Neutrality,* Seventh edition, London: Longmans, 1952.
Otto, J.C., *Die Konsentrasiekampe.* Cape Town: Nasionale Pers, 1954.
Pearson, J.D. (ed.), *A Guide to Manuscripts and Documents in the British Isles relating to Africa.* London: Oxford University Press, 1971.
Pelzer, A.N., "Die 'arm-blanke' in die Suid-Afrikaanse Republiek tussen die jare 1882–1899" in *Historiese studies,* II(3–4) and III(1–2), 1941–1942.
Penning, L., *De Oorlog in Zuid-Afrika I–III.* Rotterdam: D.A. Daamen, 1904.
Philips, L., *Transvaal Problems. Some Notes on Current Politics.* London: John Murray, 1905.
Phillips, L.M., *With Rimington.* London: Edward Arnold, 1902.
Pienaar, A.J., "Christiaan Roedolf de Wet in die Anglo-Boereoorlog" (Unpublished MA dissertation, Potch), 1974.
Pienaar, P., *Met Steyn en De Wet.* Middelburg: F.B. den Boer, 1902.
Postma, M.M., *Stemme uit die Vrouekampe gedurende die Tweede Vryheidsoorlog tussen Boer en Brit van 1899–1902.* Potchefstroom, 1925.
Preller, G.S., *Kaptein Hindon: Oorlogsaventure van 'n Baas verkenner.* Pretoria: J.L. van Schaik, 1916.
——, "Die National Scouts" in *Die Burger,* 1 July 1926.
Pretorius, F., "Die Eerste Dryfjag op hoofkmdt. C.R. de Wet" (Unpublished MA dissertation, UP), 1975.
Pyrah, G.B., *Imperial Policy and South Africa 1902–1910.* Oxford: Clarendon Press, 1955.
Reckitt, B.N., *The Lindley Affair: A diary of the Boer War.* Hull: Brown & Sons, 1972.
Reitz, D., *Kommando: 'n Boere-dagboek uit die Engelse Oorlog.* Bloemfontein: A.C. White D. & U., undated.
Richmond, A., *Twenty-Six Years, 1879–1905.* London. 1961.
Rompel, F., *Uit den Tweeden Vrijheidsoorlog: Schetsen en Portretten.* Amsterdam: Van Holkema & Warendorf, undated.
——, *Een Studie in Proclamaties.* Dordrecht: Corns. Morks, 1901.
Roos, J.C., "Johannesburg en die Tweede Vryheidsoorlog, Oktober 1899 – Mei 1900" (Unpublished D.Litt. thesis, UNISA), 1949.
Rousseau, L., *Die Groot Verlange: Die Verhaal van Eugène N. Marais.* Cape Town: Human & Rousseau, 1974.
Sandberg, C.G.S., *Twintig Jaren onder Krugers Boeren in voor en tegenspoed.* Amsterdam: Amsterdamsche Keurkamer, 1943.

Scheepers Strydom, C.J., *Ruitervuur*. Cape Town: Tafelberg, 1970.
Schikkerling, R.W., *Hoe ry die Boere ('n Kommando-dagboek)*. Johannesburg: Afrikaanse Pers, 1964.
Schoeman, J., *Generaal Hendrik Schoeman. Was hy 'n Verraaier?* Broederstroom: Johan Schoeman, 1950.
Scholtz, D.A., "Ds. S.J. du Toit as Kerkman en Kultuurleier" (Unpublished D.Th. thesis, US), 1975.
Scholtz, G.D., *Europa en die Tweede Vryheidsoorlog 1899–1902*. Johannesburg: Voortrekkerpers, 1939.
——, *In Doodsgevaar: Die Oorlogservarings van kapt. J.J. Naudé*. Johannesburg: Voortrekkerpers, 1940.
——, *Generaal Christiaan Frederik Beyers 1869–1914*. Johannesburg: Voortrekkerpers, 1941.
——, *Die Geskiedenis van die Nederduitse Hervormde of Gereformeerde Kerk van Suid-Afrika, 1885–1910, II*. Cape Town: N.G. Kerk Publishers, 1960.
——, "Die Tweede Vryheidsoorlog in Wêreldverband III", in *Historia*, 20(2), September 1975.
Scholtz, W.L. von R., "Die Betrekkinge tussen die Zuid-Afrikaansche Republiek en die Oranje-Vrijstaat, 1899–1902" (Unpublished MA dissertation, RAU), 1971.
——, "Hoofregter Melius De Villiers se Mededeling oor 'Swart Troepe' in die Oorlog" in *Historia*, 21(2), September 1976.
Schoonnees, P.C. et al., *Verklarende Handwoordeboek van die Afrikaanse Taal*. Pretoria, 1970.
Schultz, B.G., "Die slag van Bergendal (Dalmanutha)" (Unpublished MA disertation, UP), 1974.
Smit, J.P., "Die Rol van generaal J.H. de la Rey in die Suid-Afrikaanse Politiek 1902–1914" (Unpublished MA dissertation, RAU), 1974.
Snyman, J.H., "Die Afrikaner in Kaapland, 1899–1902" (Unpublished D.Litt. thesis, Potch), 1973.
Solomon, V.E., "The Hands-Uppers" in *Krygshistoriese Tydskrif*, 3(1), June 1974.
Spaight, J.M., *War Rights on Land*. London, 1911.
Spender, H., *Generaal Botha, The Career and the Man*. London: Constable & Co., Second edition, 1919.
Spies, S.B., "The Hague Convention of 1899 and the Boer Republics" in *Historia*, 15(1), March 1970.
——, "Roberts and Kitchener and Civilians in the Boer Republics, January 1900 – May 1902" (Unpublished Ph.D. thesis, UW), 1973.
Spoelstra, B., "Die Bewindsaanvaarding van die Botha regering oor Transvaal as selfregerende Britse Kolonie in 1907" in *Archives Yearbook for South African History*, 16(II), Pretoria: Government Printer, 1953.
Standertonner [pseudonym], "Die Laaste Slag op die Hoëveld, Boesmanskop, 1 April 1902" in *Die Huisgenoot*, 29 October 1937.
Starke, J.G., *An Introduction to International Law*. London: Butterworths, 1963.
Stead, W.T., *How not to Make Peace*. London: Stop the War Committee, 1900.
——, *Methods of Barbarism*. London: Mowbray House, 1901.
Steinmeyer, J., *Spykers met Koppe*. Cape Town: Nasionale Pers, 1946.
Stemmet, J.F., "Gepubliseerde Outobiografiese Bronne oor die Tweede Vryheidsoorlog" (Unpublished MA dissertation, Potch), 1973.
Steyl, P.J. (ed.), *N.G. Kerk Lindley, 1876–1951*. Bloemfontein: N.G. Sendingpers, 1951.
Streak, M., *Lord Milner's Immigration Policy for the Transvaal 1897–1905. RAU Publications, 1*. Johannesburg: RAU, 1970.
Sundermeier, T. (ed.), *Church and Nationalism in South Africa*. Johannesburg: Ravan, 1975.
Thompson, L.M., *The Unification of South Africa 1902–1910*. Oxford, 1960.
Thomson, S.J., *The Transvaal Burgher Camps, South Africa*. Allahabad: Pioneer Press, 1904.
Trapido, S., "The South African Republic: Class Formation and the State 1850–1900" in *Collected seminar papers on the Societies of Southern Africa in the 19th and 20th Centuries*, 3, 16, University of London, June 1972.
Uys, C.J., *Rouxville (1863–1963)*. Rouxville, 1963.
Van Aardt, J.M.H., "Die Botha-bewind in die Transvaal 1907–1910" (Unpublished D.Litt. thesis, Potch), 1958.
Van Coller, H.P., "Generaal P.A. Cronjé, 'n Lewenskets" (Unpublished D.Phil. thesis, UP), 1945.
Van den Aardweg, M., "The Field of Military Sociology" (Unpublished MA dissertation, UP), 1971.
Van den Heever, C.M., *Generaal J.B.M. Hertzog*. Johannesburg: Afrikaanse Pers, 1944.
Van der Merwe, N.J., *Marthinus Theunis Steyn. 'n Lewensbeskrywing, II*. Cape Town: Nasionale Pers, 1921.
Van der Walt, A.J.H., Wiid, J.A. & Geyer, A.L., verwerk deur Kruger, D.W., *Geskiedenis van Suid-Afrika*. Cape Town: Nasou, 1965.

Van Everdingen, W., *De Oorlog in Zuid-Afrika, I–III*. Delft: J. Waltman Jr., 1902–1915.
Van Loggerenberg, J.H., "Kerklike Opsig en Tug in die Nederduitse Gereformeerde Gemeente Bloemfontein, 1848–1948" (Unpublished M.Th. dissertation, US), 1972.
Van Niekerk. L.E., "Dr. W.J. Leyds as Gesant van die Zuid-Afrikaansche Republiek" (Unpublished D.Phil. thesis, UOVS), 1972.
Van Rensburg, A.P.J., "Die Ekonomiese Herstel van die Afrikaner in die Oranjerivierkolonie 1902–1907" in *Archives Yearbook for South African History*, 30(II), Pretoria: Government Printer, 1967.
——, "Die Skandkol wat nie wou toegroei nie" in *Die Huisgenoot*, 8 August 1969.
——, "Pieter Daniël de Wet" in W.J. de Kock & D.W. Krüger (general eds). *DSAB, II*. Pretoria: Human Sciences Research Council, 1970.
——, & Van Schoor, M.C.E., *Die Geskiedenis van Bethlehem, 1864–1964*. Bethlehem: Bethlehem Municipality, undated.
Van Schoor, M.C.E., Malan, I.S. & Oberholster, J.J., *Christiaan Rudolph de Wet 1854–1922*. Bloemfontein: Nasionale Vrouemonumentekommissie, 1954.
Van Schoor, M.C.E., "Christiaan Rudolph de Wet" in W.J. de Kock (general eds). *DSAB, I*. Pretoria: Human Sciences Research Council, 1968.
——, *De Wet en Sy Verkenners*. Cape Town, 1973.
——, "Boereverraaier se Dagboek" in *Die Volksblad*, 15 November 1974.
Van Vreden, C. de W., "Pretoria en die Tweede Vryheidsoorlog, 11 Oktober 1899 – 5 Junie 1900" (Unpublished MA dissertation, UP), 1955.
Van Warmelo, D.S., *Mijn Commando en Guerilla Commando-Leven*. Amsterdam: W. Versluys, 1901.
Venter, W.H., "Die Geskiedenis van Winburg tot 1902" (Unpublished MA dissertation, UOVS), 1974.
Ver Loren van Themaat, H. *Twee jaren in den Boerenoorlog*. Haarlem: H.D. Tjeenk Willink & Zoon, 1903.
Viljoen, B.J., *Mijne Herinneringen uit den Anglo-Boeren-Oorlog*. Amsterdam: W. Versluys, 1902.
——, *My Reminiscences of the Anglo-Boer War*. Londen 1902. Reprint, Cape Town: Struik, 1973.
Visscher, J., *De Ondergang van Een Wereld: Historisch-economische Studie over de Oorzaken van den Anglo-Boer Oorlog (1899–1902)*. Amsterdam: A.B. Soep, 1903.
Viviers, J.M., "Die Presidentsverkiesing van 1893 in die Zuid-Afrikaansche Republiek" (Unpublished MA dissertation, Potch), 1970.
Walker, E.A., *Lord De Villiers and His Times: South Africa, 1842–1914*. London: Constable, 1925.
Warwick, P., "The African Refugee Problem in the Transvaal and Orange River Colony, 1900–1902" in *Centre for Southern African Studies Collected Seminar Papers*, 2, January 1976.
Weeber, E.J., *Op die Transvaalse Front: 1 Junie 1900 – 31 Oktober 1900*. Bloemfontein: Nasionale Pers, 1942.
Weideman, N.C., "Die Politieke Naweë van die Anglo-Boereoorlog in Transvaal tot 1907" (Unpublished D.Phil. thesis, UP), 1955.
Wells, P., *The American War of Independence*. London, 1971.
West, R., *The meaning of treason*. London: The Reprint Society, 1952.
Wilcocks, R., "Die Arm Blanke" in *Verslag van die Carnegie Kommissie, II*. Stellenbosch, 1932.
Wills, W.H. (ed.), *The Anglo-African Who's Who and Biographical Sketch Book*. London, 1907.
Wood, W.B. & Edmonds, J.E., *The Civil War in the United States with Special Reference to the Campaigns of 1864 and 1865*. London: Methuen, 1937.
Worsfold, W.B., *Lord Milner's Work in South Africa*. London: John Murray, 1906.
——, *The Reconstruction of the New Colonies under Lord Milner, I–II*. London: Kegan, Paul, 1913.
Wrench, J.E., *Alfred Lord Milner: The man of no illusions 1854–1925*. London: Eyre & Spottiswoode, 1958.

Index

Abercrombie, H.R., 85
Abrahamskraal, 25, 325, 338, 346, 349
Adelaide, 158
Adendorf, J., 233
Adendorff, J.H.G., 132
Adendorff, P.J., 132–133
African Agricultural and Finance Corporation Limited, 388
Afrikaner, Die, 466
Afrikaner Bond, 152, 154–155, 386
Agterryer (mounted manservant), 293
Ahrens, H., 60
Alberts, General J.J., 282
Alberts, Commandant S.F. (Sarel), 289
Alcobaça, 77
Aldridge, Lieutenant H.H., 221
Aliwal North, 82
Allegiance, oath of, 30, 52, 77, 118, 143, 203–212, 230, 234–235, 251, 268, 329, 353, 372, 391, 400
Allenby, Lieutenant-colonel (later Field-marshal Lord) E.H.H., 243, 288
Allison, Captain, T.S., 272, 278, 386–387
Allum, Captain J., 23
Amajuba, 323
American Civil War (1861–1865), 212
American War of Independence (1775–1783), 212
Amery, L.S. (Leo), 300, 352
Anderson, Revd C.E., 422
Anderson, Lieutenant-colonel W.C., 283
Anderson, Captain W.P., 95, 267
Apthorp, Major K.P., 43, 84
Ardagh, Major-general Sir John, 15, 118–119
Arundel, 325
Ashburnham, Assistant Commissioner, 80

Badenhorst, General (Chief Commandant, formerly Commandant) C.C.J., 53–59, 233, 332
Badenhorst, A., 128
Baden-Powell, Colonel (later Major-general) R.S.S., 40
Bakenlaagte, 244
Ballot (a National Scout), 413

Balmoral, 418
Bannatyne, Captain W.S., 187
Baptist Church, 88
Barberton, 95, 97, 129–130, 132, 453
Barker, Lieutenant-colonel J.S.S., 238–239
Basutoland (Lesotho), 37, 73–75, 343, 412
Batts, H.J., 88, 96–97
Beak, G.B., 369, 373, 379
Bechuanaland (Botswana), 78–81, 142, 284, 377, 452
Beddy, Captain W.H., 254, 375, 455
Beddy's Scouts, 253–254, 375, 455
Bekker, Mrs H.G., 193–194
Belfast, 120–123, 129, 135, 278–280, 418
Bellevue, *see* Concentration camps
Benade, J., 417
Benadi, J.G.M., 242
Benson, Lieutenant-colonel (formerly Major) G.E., 243–244
Bentinck, Captain W.G., 249–250
Bergendal, 75
Bergh, Captain O.M., 237–239
Bergstedt, T.C.L., 68, 101
Bergstedt, T.C.L. (Winburg), 222
Bermuda, 275–276
Bester, Commandant A.J. (Andries), 397
Bester, Assistant Field-cornet J.R., 95
Bethal, 55, 57, 132, 423–426, 431, 451
Bethlehem, 66, 128, 150, 159, 222, 224, 239, 244, 248, 323–324, 396, 412, 414–416
Bethulie, 38, 42, 53, 242
Beukes, M.J., 147
Beukes, P., 238
Beyers, General (later Assistant Commandant-general) C.F. (Chrisjan), 54–55, 62, 78, 81, 164, 197, 199, 211, 285–287, 296, 349–350, 451–453
Bezuidenhout, B.C., 122
Bezuidenhout, C.F., 314
Bezuidenhout, M.M., 350
Bezuidenhout, P.H., 240
Biddulphsberg, 339
Bierens, de Haan, Dr J.C.J., 243
Bisset, Captain C., 223
Bitterenders, 12–13, 63, 74, 90, 101, 123, 126,

132, 147, 190–191, 207, 212, 228, 276, 297–299, 311, 316, 321, 351–352, 365, 370–387, 390–391, 394–397, 401, 409–422, 427, 446, 448, 450–451, 453–454, 458–462
Blakemore, Captain P.H.J., 281–282, 368, 371, 373
Blesbokfontein (Lindley district), 328
Bloemfontein, 23, 25–26, 29, 35–38, 40–44, 51, 53, 56–60, 64, 72, 74–75, 81, 86–89, 92, 95, 128–129, 132, 138, 142–143, 146–147, 149–159, 162, 164, 166–167, 183, 193, 196, 198, 201, 206, 222–223, 225–226, 230–240, 254, 271–272, 275–276, 281, 285, 292, 313, 321, 323–326, 329, 333–340, 343–344, 346, 349, 366–367, 370–371, 376–377, 392–393, 397, 409–411, 415–417, 422, 455, 459–460, 462
Bloemfontein Post, The, 58–59, 138, 167, 205, 235, 275, 409
Boereverenigings (Boer associations), 450
Boksburg, 122, 240
Bonham, Captain W., 207
Bornman, C.J., 128
Boschmanskop (Springs district), 282–283
Boshof (Free State), 38, 53, 56, 59, 62, 66, 83–84, 149, 233, 346
Boshoff, A., 398
Boshoff, A.J., 123
Boshoff, H.C., 246
Bosman, H.J., 298
Bosman, Revd H.S., 98–99, 122, 141–142, 422–426, 428–429, 432, 437
Bosman, J.L., 128
Boswell (a special commissioner), 235
Botha, (a burgher who was murdered), 293
Botha, (the father-in-law of Broeksma), 412
Botha, Ampie, 238
Botha, Mrs Annie, 138–139
Botha, A.L., 376
Botha, Adv. C.L., 128, 151, 154, 158–159, 161, 163, 191–192
Botha, B.J., 91
Botha, General Chris, 209, 312
Botha, D.H., 128
Botha, H.S., 457
Botha, J. (Cattle Ranger Corps), 254
Botha, J. (Guide in service of Lieutenant-colonel Byng, 243
Botha, Revd J.F., 152
Botha, General (later Commandant-general) L. (Louis)
issues call-up instructions, 20–21, 55, 57–58; outstanding leadership, 22, 62, 123, 384; involved in re-commandeering of surrendered burghers, 55; moves northwards from Hectorspruit, 75; attitude towards peace emissaries and peace committees, 89–92, 97–100, 118, 130, 133, 137–141, 158, 161, 164, 209, 300; sporadic peace initiatives, 94; holds discussions with Kitchener at Middelburg, 146; decision taken at meeting held at Immigratie, 209; opinion of impact on National Scouts, 273, 294, 297; works for a policy of post-war reconciliation towards National Scouts and surrendered burghers, 288, 301–302, 380; regards political opponents in 1915 as National Scouts, 446–450; interpretation of peace treaty, 390–391; and Afrikaner nationalism, 457, 459, 463; and post-war Afrikaner politics, 447–454; military support, 466
Botha, General P.R. (Philip), 20, 54, 147, 346, 451
Botha, M.A., 320
Botha, P. (Beddy's Scouts), 254
Botha, P.M. (Paul), 93
Botha, P.J., 397
Botha, P.M. (Paul), 92–93, 128, 147–150, 222–223, 227
Bothasberg (eastern Transvaal), 289
Bouwer, Commandant (later General) B.D. (Ben), 294, 410
Bouwer, Piet, 294
Boveri, M., 317
Boyd, R., 60
Brabant, Brigadier-general E.Y., 82
Brabant's Horse, 82
Brain, Thomas, 245
Bramley, H., 345
Brand, J.F., 274
Brandfort, 51, 188, 232, 301, 401, 459, 460–461
Brandfort manifesto, 460
Brandt, Johanna, 189, 267, 291, 298, 397
Brandwater Basin, 160, 332, 342–343
Breedt, G.C.J., 128
Bremmer, D., 319
Bremmer, J.G., 319
Bremmer, Jacobus, 319
Bremmer, Martinus, 319
Brereton, Major E.F., 199
Brett, Captain H.M.R., 225, 391
Brett's Scouts, 225
Breyten, 426, 427
Breytenbach, J.H., 19, 95
Breytenbach, Commandant N.J., 278, 423–426, 435–436, 452
Briel, Field-cornet A.Z.A., 23, 278

Briggs, Lieutenant-colonel C.J., 244
Brink, Revd C.J., 425, 436
Brink, J., 448
Brink, Adjutant J.N., 338–340, 344
British Colonial Office, 15, 117–119, 134, 255
British East Africa, 414–415
British military information service (London), 15, 118, 285, 318
British military intelligence service, 55
British South Africa Police (B.S.A.P.), 78–79, 377
Brits, J.P., 13
Britstown, 154
Broadwood, Brigadier-general R.G., 245–246, 328, 338
Brodrick, St John, 136, 138, 208, 255, 270
Broeksma (a surrendered burgher), 412
Bronkhorstspruit, 252
Brugman, J.L., 202
Buitendach, Casper, 246
Bulawayo, 78–79
Buller, General Sir Redvers, 62, 82
Bulmer, A.F., 123
Bultfontein, 39
Burger, General S.W. (Schalk), 94, 123, 136, 138, 152, 210–211, 282, 294, 297, 311, 313–314, 349, 369, 380, 384, 423, 451, 466
Burgher Camp Police (B.C.P.), 198
Burgher corps (in British military service), *see also* National Scouts & Orange River Colony Volunteers
establishment of, 169, 196, 221–231; payment and recruitment of, 226–227, 230, 251–256; number of members, 230–231, 254, 256; legal status of, 235, 369; imprisonment of members by republican forces, 229, 233; difference between various corps, 229–230, 255, 267–268, 277, 315; activities in the Free state, 231, 335, 239; activities in the Transvaal, 249–257
Burgher peace committees, 149, 202, 333–334, 353, 446, 448; lead up to, 101; establishment of, 117–129; pre-war political orientation of members, 123–124; relationship with British military authority, 149–150, 333; concentration camp policy, 125–127; number of pamphlets distributed, 129; activities in the Transvaal, 129–142; punishment inflicted on members, 130–131; activities in the Free State, 127, 142–163, 334; negotiations with the Afrikaner Bond, 152–155; activities in Cape Town, 153–163; influence of, 166–169; possible
promises to, 166; morality of conduct, 166–167; significance of, 163–186; recommend more drastic steps against compatriots, 267–277
Burgher Police, 231–234, *see also* Farmers' Guard
Burgersdorp, 153
Burton, H., 465
Butler, W.J., 91
Buttery J. (John), 97, 117–119
Buys, M.H., 12, 96
Byng, Lieutenant-colonel (formerly Major, later Field-marshal Lord) J.H.G., 243

Caldas da Reinha, 77
Caledon River Burghers, 91
Campbell, Colonel W.P., 243
Candy (Winburg district), 238
Cape Argus, The, 94
Cape Times, The, 208, 311, 320, 421
Cape Town, 37, 94, 148, 154, 156, 158, 160–162, 166, 353, 365, 390
Carliss, W., 388
Carolina (Transvaal), 20, 91, 122, 125, 130, 247, 299, 312, 378, 418, 423, 426
Carolina (USA), 212
Cartwright, A., 165–166, 190
Cattle Ranger Corps, 199, 253–254
Celliers, General J. (Free State), 348
Celliers, Commandant J.G., 159, 271, 278, 281, 283, 286–290, 296, 322, 348–350
Celliers, General J.G. (Lichtenburg), 348
Central Judicial Commission, 394–396, 398, 400
Ceylon, 70, 128, 226, 275–276
Chamberlain, Sir Joseph, 29–30, 119–120, 125, 150, 233–234, 275–276, 335, 374, 378, 380, 383–385, 390–394, 411, 428–429, 434, 447, 459
Chinese labour, 450
Christiana, 122, 346, 412–413
Church Square (Pretoria), 267, 365–366
Clarke, M., 78
Clements, Major-general R.A.P., 37
Cloete, C.J., 128, 150, 224, 414–415
Cloete, C.J. (Bethlehem), 222
Cloete, Commandant F., 38
Cochins, J.C., 242
Coetzee, D., 133
Coetzee, J.C., 233
Coetzee, M.C., 132
Coetzee, N.J., 233
Coetzee, P.B., 131
Coetzee, S.A., 293

Coetzee, W.P., 293
Coetzer, General J., 76
Colenbrander, Lieutenant-colonel J.W., 286–287
Colenso, 24
Colesberg, 327, 345, 349
Colley, General G., 323
Commando
 Boksburg, 92–93, 249; Carolina (Transvaal), 126; Edenburg, 38; Elandsfontein, 92; Ficksburg, 60; Jacobsdal, 23; Ladybrand, 38; Lydenburg, 135; Rouxville, 38; Smithfield, 38; Soutpansberg, 23–24; Wakkerstroom, 297; Waterberg, 80; Wepener, 38
Commission of inquiry, prisoners-of-war, 162, 377
Concentration camps, 57, 65, 87, 91, 125–127, 141, 162–164, 184–187, 191–205, 211, 234, 237, 239, 246–249, 255, 272–275, 279–280, 298, 300, 315–318, 322, 382–383, 417; Aliwal North, 197, 425; Balmoral, 80; Belfast, 272, 466; Bloemfontein, 84, 195–197, 281; Cape Town, 158; Durban, 70; Free State, 197, 200; Heilbron, 195–196; Howick, 194; Irene, 86, 192–199, 239, 316; Johannesburg, 202, 274; Klerksdorp, 193, 198, 348; Kroonstad, 162, 197, 409, 415; Mafeking, 194, 205; Middelburg (Transvaal), 194; Nylstroom, 196, 199, 254; Pietersburg, 197, 200, 275, 286, 316; Pretoria, 120, 127, 272, 275, 296; Simon's Town, 159, 161, 235, 275, 425; Standerton, 194; Transvaal, 79, 193, 272; Vereeniging, 195, 249–250; Volksrust, 195, 198, 201; Winburg, 162, 197
Conradie, F.D., 299
Corbett, J.A., 412
Cornelisse, H.A., 316–317
Covenant, Day of the, 416
Craven, Thomas, 328
Criterion mine, 79
Crocodile River, 81, 122
Cronjé, A.P (father of A.P.J.), 345
Cronjé, A.P. (Andries), 271, 278, 283, 285, 345–348, 371, 378, 385, 389, 392, 447–448, 457–458
Cronjé, General A.P. (Andries), 245
Cronjé, General A.P.J. (Andries), 122, 124, 127, 161, 269, 322, 345
Cronjé, J. (a National scout), 457
Cronjé, Johanna Christina (née Geldenhuys), 345
Cronjé, P.A. (Piet), 24–25

Cronjé, General P.A. (Andries), 128
Cronjé, General P.A. (Piet), 26, 89, 122, 160–162
Cronjé, General P.J. (Piet), 161–162, 285, 325, 338, 345–347
Crowe, F., 77
Crowther, General J., 341
Cruse, G.S., 317, 414

Dalzell, Lieutenant-colonel A.E., 224–225
Dannhauser, Commandant A.B., 189
Dartnell, Brigadier-general Sir J.G., 242, 248
Davel, Commandant H., 453
Davel, Commandant O.A., 245
Davenport, T.R.H., 155
Davidson, W.E., 369, 373
Davitt, Michael, 327, 337, 340
De Beer (a bitterender), 462
De Beer, J.A.B., 246
De Beer, J.F., 90, 122
De Beer, Jan du Plessis, 78, 452
De Beer, Field-cornet J.M., 130
De Beer, Z.C., 196
De Bertodano, Captain F.R., 92, 223, 227
De Bruijn, H.J., 233
De Bruin, P.C., 246
De Clerq, Mrs I.A. Grobler, 199
De Gier, L.C., 122
De Jager, G.J.W., 123
De Jager, Field-cornet H., 289
De Klerk, Mrs J.J., 238
De Kock, Meyer, 120–124, 127, 129, 135–136, 166
De Kock, S.N., 80
De la Rey, General J.H. (Koos), 22, 54–55, 60, 62, 89, 95–98, 123, 202, 211, 269, 283–284, 289, 325, 346, 349, 384, 391, 430, 447, 449, 451–452
De Rust (Senekal district), 337
De Souza, L.F., 89
De Villebois-Mareuil, Colonel (later General) G.H.A.V., 23
De Villiers, General A.J., 339
De Villiers, Judge J.H., 154
De Villiers, M., 202
De Villiers, O.T., 144–145
De Villiers, Rocco, 245
De Villiers, Field-cornet W., 453
De Villiers, Z.J., 448
De Water, Dr T, 152
De Wet, Mrs A.S.M. (Susanna, born Strydom), 323
De Wet, Barend, 324, 332
De Wet, General C.R. (Christiaan), 22–27, 33,

38–42, 51–58, 60, 62, 92, 123, 128, 143–146, 150–153, 158–159, 161, 211, 222–223, 229, 236–239, 244–246, 248–249, 272, 281, 283–84, 289, 292, 298–299, 301–302, 312, 315, 319–320, 323, 326–339, 341–342, 344, 346, 349, 384, 390, 395, 401, 409–410, 446, 455, 459, 461–462
De Wet, Cornelia, 333
De Wet, Gideon, 72
De Wet, H.C., 335
De Wet, H.G., 236, 327, 329, 334
De Wet, I.J.C. (Izak), 144–145, 299
De Wet, J.I., 323
De Wet, General P.D. (Piet)
  chairman of Free State central peace committee, 128, 333–334; request C.R. de Wet to abandon the struggle, 150–151; decides to undertake a peace mission to the Cape Colony, 153–155; work as peace emissary in Cape Colony, 158–159; establishment of ORC Volunteers, 281–282; leader of Heilbron section of ORC Volunteers, 291; pre-war career of, 323–325; personality of, 323–324, 327; attitude when the Anglo-Boer War begins, 324–325; participation in the war until July 1900, 325–326; relationship with C.R de Wet, 325–333; motivation for his voluntary surrender, 327–332; concern for civilian population, 330, 333; on parole to Durban, 334; motivation for fighting on British side, 334–335; assets at the time of the war, 327, 335–336; serves on repatriary board, 370–371; stance on peace terms, 392; opinion on compensation, 336, 383, 392–395, 401; viewpoint of motives of disloyal burghers, 409, 411; appeal for post-war reconciliation in Afrikaner ranks, 446; stand in 1907 election, 463–464
De Wet, Mrs S.M. (Susanna), 323, 331
Delagoa Bay, 75, 117, 320
Delport, P.J., 193
Denny, Lieutenant-colonel H.C., 286
Denoon, D.J.N., 13, 311–312, 396, 434, 455–456
Dercksen, Commandant A.J., 92–95, 122, 452–453
Despagnet, F., 146, 229
Dewetsdorp, 38, 52, 66, 323, 326
Diamond Hill (Donkerhoek), 90
Dieperink, Adv. A., 194
Dinkelman (a National Scout), 319
Donkerhoek (Diamond Hill), 90

Doornberg (between Winburg and Senekal), 238
Doornfontein (Pietersburg district), 350
Doornkop, 26
Douglas, Major-general (formerly Colonel) C.W.H., 98, 246
Drake, L.F., 245
Driefontein (Middelburg district), 242
Drotsky, (of Morley's Scouts), 252
Du Plessis, Revd H.E., 54, 78, 154–157, 191, 411, 415–416, 418, 425, 430–431, 437, 452
Du Plessis, I.M., 132–133
Du Plessis de Beer, J., see De Beer, Jan du Plessis
Du Toit, F., 123
Du Toit, P.J., 184, 243, 320, 333
Du Toit, Revd S.J., 58–59, 392–393, 417, 437
Du Toit, Sarah, 337
Duncan, Patric, 386
Durban, 70, 128, 333–334

East Africa, 414
Edenburg, 37–38, 337
Edwards, Lieutenant-colonel A.H.M., 85
Edwards, W.M., 140–141
Eerste Fabrieken (First Factories), 252
Elandsfontein, 92
Elliot, Major-general E.L., 334
Ellison (brothers, members of ORC Volunteers), 292
Eloff, F., 89, 100
Els, Field-cornet F., 68
Els, J., 134
Els, Jan (Slootkraal), 225
Emmenis, Dolf, 294
Engelenburg, F.V., 139
Erasmus, A., 414
Erasmus, Commandant J.J., 278
Erasmus, J.W., 117–120
Erasmus, Field-cornet P.R., 233
Erasmus, W., 242
Ermelo, 42, 55, 209, 312, 398, 413–414, 418, 423, 426, 452–453, 458
Erwee, G.H., 460
Esselen, E., 451
Esser, Judge J., 88
Eva, J.J., 233
Everett, R.H., 78–79

Fanshawe, Lieutenant-colonel H.D., 282
Farmers' Association, 382, 386
Farmers' Guard, 226, 230, 234–237, 366–367, 377, 412
Farrar, J.A., 166–167

Fauré, P.H., 161
Fauresmith, 37–38, 53, 84, 128
Ferreira, G., 314
Ferreira, J., 199
Ficksburg, 38, 52, 73, 292, 412, 417
Fiddes, G.V., 68–69
Fischer, Mrs M, 194
Floyd, T.B., 466
Forster, Major T.H.B., 70, 205
Fort Edward, 286, 288
Fouché, A.J., 412
Fouché, P., 141
Fouché, Commandant W.D., 197
Fourie, C.E., 130–131
Fourie, Commandant P.J., 53–54
Fouriesburg, 56, 341
Frankfort, 54, 246, 318, 417–418, 461
Franks, Dr K., 250
Fraser, Gordon A., 245
Fraser, J.G., 25–26, 65, 88, 128, 148, 151–152, 197, 352, 446
Fraserburg, 348
French, Lieutenant-general (formerly Major-general, later Field-marshal Lord) J.D.P., 37, 95, 346
Friend, The, 188, 337, 374, 395, 410
Froneman, General C.C., 53, 143–146, 292
Fuller, Lieutenant J.F.C., 225, 332

Garrat, Lieutenant-colonel F.S., 242
Garson, N.G., 449
Gatacre, Major-general (later Lieutenant-general) Sir W.F., 37, 53
Gazaland, 75
Geary, Lieutenant-general H.L., 276
Geerling, W.J., 77
Genootskap van Regte Afrikaners (G.R.A.), 59
Georgia (USA), 212
Gibson, Lieutenant G.F., 245
Glencoe, 21
Globe mine, 79
Goedgevonden (Potchefstroom district), 345
Goold-Adams, Lieutenant-governor H, 21, 72, 195, 205, 313, 366–368, 370, 373, 377, 394, 396, 399– 401, 416, 428, 446, 460–464
Gous, Field-cornet, 133
Gouws, Field-cornet N.P. (Nicholas), 189
Graaff-Reinet, 152
Grady, Hans, 456
Graham, Captain J.M., 132
Gregon, M.J., 123
Gregorowski, Judge R., 88, 99
Grenfell, Lieutenant-colonel H.M., 78

Grey, L., 246, 247
Greylingstad, 41
Griqualand, 142
Griqualand West, 347
Grobbelaar, Field-cornet, 147
Grobbelaar, J.C.P., 131
Grobler, (a guide in Bethlehem district), 222
Grobler, Adjutant Albert, 333
Grobler, General (Chief Commandant) E.R., 151–152, 325
Grobler, J.Z., 456
Grobler, Commandant S.P., 80–81, 142, 424–426, 428, 431–437
Groenewald, P.A., 195
Groesbeek, Field-cornet P., 92, 123
Gruisfontein (Lichtenburg district), 289
Guest, H.M., 60, 316, 317
Guides (burghers in British military service), *see* Burger corps, National Scouts, Orange River Colony Volunteers
Gurko, Lieutenant-colonel V.I., 27

Haarhoff, I., 202–203
Haasbroek, Commandant S.F. (Sarel), 101, 238–239
Hague Convention (1899), 14, 15, 30, 33–34, 60, 63–64, 68, 71, 130, 146, 204, 229, 293
Hamilton, Major-general Bruce, 243–244
Hamilton, Lieutenant-general I.S.M. (Ian), 39, 327
Hammanskraal, 254
Harrismith, 58, 87, 128, 147, 149, 222, 242, 248, 417
Hartebeesfontein, 184, 246, 294
Hasan, Muhammed Abdallah, 377
Hattingh, J.L., 13, 168
Hectorspruit, 75, 93
Hefer, Revd J.C., 417
Heidelberg (Transvaal), 55, 69, 85, 92, 98, 122–123, 132, 226, 294, 323, 377, 382, 418, 426, 450–451, 456
Heidelberg Volunteers, 226
Heilbron, 39, 56, 66, 68, 143, 149, 211, 224–227, 240, 242, 281–282, 291–292, 334, 396, 412
Henderson, Colonel D., 120, 124, 127, 185, 200, 249, 253–254, 285–286, 288, 296, 397
Hendsoppers, 72, 301, 391, 393, 413–414, 430, 447, 454, 466, *see also* surrendered burghers
Henning, J.C., 275
Hertzog, General J.B.M., 53–54, 297, 300, 328, 331, 341–342, 410, 461–463
Hess, L., 388, 394, 449
Heyman, Lieutenant-colonel C., 160

Hindon, Captain O.J. (Jack), 242–243
Hintrager, Oskar, 42, 324, 328, 331
Historiography (on collaboration, Anglo-Boer War), 12–13, 227, 341
Hobhouse, Emily, 72, 197
Hodder-Williams, R., 79
Hofmeyr, Revd J.H., 158
Hollard, Adv. W.E., 88–89, 99
Honey, Mrs C.F., 100
Honiball, 92
Hoopstad, 38–39, 53, 412, 417
Hoskins, Major A., 278
Houtbos Mountains, 286
Hubbel, W.S., 250
Hughes, F.G, 129–130
Hume, Captain A., 195
Hunter, Lieutenant-general Sir Archibald, 40, 342, 346

Immigratie (between Ermelo and Wakkerstroom), 209
Imperial Light Horse, 223, 242, 244–245, 248
Imperial Military Railways, 278
Imperial Yeomanry, 326
India, 275

Jacobsdal, 38, 53, 64, 66
Jacobsz, L.J. (Louis), 135
Jagersfontein, 38, 221
Jameson Raid, 244, 324, 345
Jamieson, Captain M.C., 277–278
Johannesburg, 20, 26, 36, 121, 130, 132, 160, 201–202, 232, 243, 271, 333, 375, 399, 448
Johnson, R., 132
Joiners, *see* Burger corps, National Scouts, Orange Rivier Colony Volunteers
Jones Mrs D., 198
Joubert, C.G., 132
Joubert, C.J., 89, 99
Joubert, D.C., 130
Joubert, Field-cornet G., 289
Joubert, G.F. (Gideon), 136
Joubert, G.J., 145, 331
Joubert, Mrs G.W., 194
Joubert, Field-cornet H.J., 278
Joubert, Mrs Hendrina, 99–100
Joubert, Commandant J.A., 453
Joubert, J.H., 273, 321
Joubert, Mrs M.C., 247
Joubert, Commandant-general P.J. (Piet), 19, 92, 99, 123, 130–131, 136, 321, 323, 453
Junius, H.G., 98
Just, H.W., 255

Kaalspruit (Bloemfontein district), 147
Kaapmuiden, 127
Kaapsche Hoop, 129, 278
Kafferskop (Bethlehem district), 239
Kafferskraal (farm between Senekal and Ficksburg), 292
Karroospruit (Lindley district), 328
Kay, Dr James, 296
Kekewich, Colonel R.G., 284–285
Kellner, B.O., 25
Kelly-Kenny, Lieutenant-general Thomas, 85–87, 333
Kemp, General (formerly Field-cornet and Commandant) J.C.G., 95, 283–284, 289, 380
Kestell, Revd J.D., 187–188, 208, 291, 417
Khama, 81
Kimberley, 89, 346
Kimberley Mounted Corps, 347
Kings's Own Scottish Borders, 79
Kitchener, General Sir (later Field-marshal Lord) H.H., 57, 146, 152, 157–158, 160–166, 199–200, 212, 249, 296, 336; and peace committees, 119–125, 128–131, 134–141, 149, 157–158, 265, 333–334; and origin of concentration camp policy, 57, 125–127, 164, 192; reaction to Meyer de Kock's execution, 136; holds discussions at Middelburg, 140–141; reaction to the death of J.J. Morgendaal, 146; scorched earth policy (campaign of destruction), 183–184, 256; blockhouse lines, 185; banishment proclamation, 188–189, 211; and putting Boer hostages on trains, 202–203; encourages commanding officers to form burgher corps, 226; opinion on British arming of surrendered burghers, 224–225; opinion on burgher corps, 226–227, 231– 235, 239, 250–251, 253–256, 335; and formation of burgher corps in Transvaal, 249–257; his motives regarding National Scouts, 268–270, 272–277; opinion on contribution of National Scouts, 270–275, 285, 288, 290–291, 351, 353, 365–366, 372; viewpoint on motives of disloyal burghers, 318–319
Kitchener, Major-general F.W. (Walter), 246, 284, 378
Klaas (guide), 245
Klerck, W.G., 161
Klerksdorp, 66, 101, 133, 205, 210, 274, 278–279, 283–284, 294, 312, 315, 345, 347, 392, 412, 452, 457
Klerksdorp Mining Record, 60, 316

INDEX

Knight, E.F., 299, 366, 373, 380, 391–393
Knox, Major-general (formerly Colonel) William, 146, 336
Kock, F.W., 201
Koffiefontein, 38
Komati Drift, 90
Komati River, 76
Komatipoort, 75–76, 93
Krause, Commandant L.E. (Lodi), 24, 95, 97
Kriel, D., 122, 124, 127
Krige, J., 349
Kroonstad, 39, 51, 86, 92, 128–129, 142–143, 146, 148, 151, 153, 159, 169, 193, 222–223, 225, 227, 254, 268, 281, 320, 328, 332–334, 417
Kroonstad Burgher Scouts, 225, 227, 229, 257
Krüger, D.W., 89, 208–209
Kruger, J.C., 193
Kruger, President S.J.P. (Paul), 25–26, 29, 35–36, 52, 88–91, 94–95, 118, 123–124, 133, 148, 159, 186, 193, 209–210, 246, 269, 283, 320, 324–325, 329, 412
Krugersdorp, 40, 85, 123, 132, 134, 239, 269, 273, 279, 367, 372, 380, 413, 451
Kruiskerk, 417, 437
Krynauw, A.C., 59–60
Krynauw, Mrs L.F., 59–60

Labuschagne, (a refugee), 78
Ladybrand, 59, 73, 221, 341, 412
Ladysmith, 89, 325
Lagden, Sir G.Y. (Godfrey), 37, 73
Lambert, Captain H., 347
Land en Volk, 368, 410, 426
Land settlement, 382, 416, 448, 454
Lange, J., 244
Lange-Brink, Adv. A., 160–162
Lawley, Sir Arthur, 428, 430–436
Lawley, Lieutenant-colonel R.T., 282
Le Grange, L.J., 36
Le May, G.H.L., 13, 62, 288, 451, 453–454
Le Roux, J., 241
Le Roux, P., 285
Leader, Major (later Lieutenant-colonel) H.P., 289
Lebombo Scouts, 253, 255
Leggett, Major E.M.H., 239, 268, 272, 274, 278–279, 295, 319, 366, 371–377, 379, 381–387, 389, 425, 429–431, 435–436, 455, 457–458
Lemmer, General H.R., 95
Leribe, 74
Lerothodi, 75
Lesotho, *see* Basutoland
Letsikas, 74

Lewis, I., 89
Leyds, Dr W.J. (Willem), 77, 449, 451, 453
Leydsdorp, 93
Lichtenburg, 98, 289, 348, 418, 429, 452
Liebenberg, General P.J., 101, 133, 184, 333
Lindley (Free State), 145, 156, 191, 243, 323–324, 326, 328, 330, 336, 412, 415–416, 425, 462–464
Linton, G., 274
Lloyd, Major A.M., 280
Locke, Lieutenant, 84
Lombard, H.S., 350
Lombard, Isabella Johanna (née Botha), 345
Lombard, J.P. la Grange, 272
Lombard, J.P.L., 410
Lombard, N, 398
Lombard, P.S., 57, 284, 299
London, 117, 415
Lotz, N.J., 317, 457
Louis Trichardt, 466
Lourenço Marques, 77
Louw, Revd A.J., 419
Luckhoff (Free State), 38, 317, 457
Luckhoff, H., 420
Lydenburg, 130, 131, 278, 293, 295, 412, 414, 455
Lydenburg Volunteer Burgher corps, 253–254
Lyon, G., 466–467
Lyon, Major E., 235

Maartins, J., 98
Maas, W.H., 460
Macdonald, P. (Wepener), 222
Macdonald, Ramsay, 379
Macfarlane, R., 446
Macfarlane, R. (Harrismith), 222
Macgregor, J.C., 74
Machado, J., 76
Mackenzie, Colonel C.J., 36
Magato, 345
Magersfontein, 24, 346
Magoeba, 345
Majuba, *see* Amajuba
Malaboch, 314, 345
Malan, Mrs A., 99
Malan, Commandant A.H., 99–101, 184
Malepspoort, 286–287
Manual of Military Law, 52
Manzingama, 79
Mapoch's Gronden (Mapoch's land), 141
Marais, A.H., 459
Marais, Eugène N., 368–369, 410–411, 418, 434–435

525

Marais, H.C., 65, 392
Marais, J.P., 460
Marais, P., 242
Marico, 411, 448
Marks, Sammy, 89, 99–101
Marquard, Revd J.T.T., 101, 158, 292, 428
Marquard, Margaret, 101
Maseru, 73
Massouw, 345
Matthysen, C.J., 60
Maxwell, Captain Frank, 272, 375
Maxwell, Major-general J.G. (John), 36, 71, 82, 95–96, 124–126, 135, 138, 192, 196, 198, 202, 205, 253, 270
McFie, M., 348
McHardy, A., 245
McInnery, Major I.M., 398
McKay, C., 253
McLachlan, R., 60
McQueen, Captain, 286
Meintjeskop, 196, 280–281, 365, 411
Meiring, (an ORC Volunteer), 292, 420
Mels, Willem, 293
Mentz, Commandant F.E., 211
Merriman, John X, 158, 298, 313, 448, 466
Methuen, Lieutenant-general Lord, 284, 327, 329, 346
Meyer, General Lucas, 297
Meyer, Field-cornet N.J., 269–271
Middelburg (Transvaal), 70, 122, 131–133, 139–140, 146, 187, 189, 193, 197, 242–243, 271, 278, 288–289, 293–294, 381, 426, 451
Middel-Liebenbergsvlei (Bethlehem district), 323
Military Compensation Fund, 394
Military service (republican forces), 11–13, 19–21, 34, 41, 51, 54, 57, 64, 72–73, 87, 183, 200, 206–208, 211–212, 221, 227, 229, 221–231, 267, 271, 275, 279, 299, 313, 332, 336, 351–353, 367–368, 389, 394, 409, 460
Miller, Captain M., 241
Milne, Major G.F., 240
Milner, Sir (later Lord) Alfred, 37, 66, 77, 82, 139, 249, 390–391, 418; and British proclamations, 29–30, 42, 71, 204; and annexation of the republics, 35, 39, 42; and refugees in Mozambique, 74–75; and concentration camps, 79–80, 85, 159–161, 185, 197; opinion on sporadic peace initiatives, 88, 91, 118–120; views on peace committees, 122, 125, 138, 149–150, 156, 159–162, 164; opinion of Burgher corps, 222–223, 226, 231; and establishment of protected areas, 230–235; opinion of National Scouts, 271, 274, 276, 321; post-war policy towards National Scouts, 352, 368–370, 373, 375, 379–387, 392, 465; interpretation of peace treaty and legislative council, 390, 393, 400–401; and post-war Afrikaner politics, 428–429, 446–447, 450
Milward, W., 251, 252
Minnaar, Revd D.J., 68
Minnaar, G.F., 128
Mobilisation (republican forces), 19–21, 450, 459, 465
Modder River, 84, 325, 346
Modjadji, 345
Money, Lieutenant-colonel H.C, 159
Morgendaal, J.J., 142–147, 151, 335
Morgendaal, Mrs S.E., 145
Morley, Captain R.W., 250–253, 256, 386
Morley's Scouts, 250–253, 256, 386
Morning Post, The, 299
Morris, Major E.M., 236
Mostert, J.A., 132
Mostertshoek, 53
Mozambique, 75–77
Mphefu, 345
Muller, A.C., 254
Muller, General C.H. (Chris), 249
Muller, G., 417
Muller, G.H., 318
Muller, G.L., 144–145
Muller, P.J., 238
Murray, Revd Andrew, 157–158
Murray, Revd Charles, 152
National Scouts, *see also* Burgher corps; 34, 238, 270; organisation of, 230, 257, 267–268, 278–279; difference between various corps, 230, 257; recruitment of, 271–277; payment to, 273–274, 279; promises to, 274; numbers, 267, 271–273, 275, 277–280; uniform worn by, 277; separate camps for participation in war, 196, 280; reaction of republican forces to reprehensible conduct during the war, 279–280, 293–295; impact on the struggle, 289–203; motives of, 311–351; 466; leaders of, 271, 278, 345, 322–351; participation in war, 282–302; status at peace of Vereeniging, 322, 351–354; participation in celebrations on Church Square, 365; attitude of post-war British civil administration towards, 366–368; post-war political role of, 368–370, 385–386; repatriation assistance to, 374–381; representation on repatriation boards,

371–374; and land settlement, 381–389; compensation to, 390–392, 394–395, 397; post-war attitude to and interaction with bitterenders, 383, 410–414, 418; proposed emigration of, 414–415; and N.H. of G. Kerk, 418–421, 433–434; reaction to church discipline, 421–424; and separate church, 424–427; and legislative council, 447–449, 459; and post-war Afrikaner politics, 427–435, 447, 449–453; pleas for forgiveness, 454–458; terms in subsequent South African politics, 454–458, 409
Naudé, F.P., 128
Nederduitsch Gereformeerde Kerk van Transvaalkolonie, see Scout Church
Nel, Mrs E.L., 196
Nel, H.F., 274
Nel, W.C., 196
Nell, J.C.P., 255
Neser, J.A., 101
Neudecker, 145
Neutrality, oath of, 11, 23, 28, 30–34, 43, 51–53, 55–56, 58–59, 62–65, 68–73, 81–82, 162, 202–204, 399–400, 460
Nicholson, R. Granville, 256, 377
Nicholson's Nek, 324
Nierstrasz, P.A., 237–238
Njabela, 323
Nobelsfontein, 144
North Stafford Regiment, 278
Norvalspont, 325, 326
Nuwejaarsfontein (Dewetsdorp district), 323
Nwapa, 81
Nylstroom, 20, 95–96, 254, 452

Oberholster, J.A.S., 13, 326, 338, 416–420, 424–425, 428, 437
Official History, 23, 248, 284–285, 287
Olifantsnek, 36
Olivier, C.P.H., 13, 419, 424–425, 428, 431–432, 437
Olivier, Henning, 330
Olivier, J., 128
Olivier, General (Chief Commandant, formerly Commandant) J.H., 128, 226, 330–331
Onder-Valsrivier (Kroonstad district), 142
Oosthuizen, J., 338, 409
Oppenheim, L., 30, 33, 36, 130
Orange River, 82, 325
Orange River Colony, 13, 21, 38, 68, 71–72, 75, 118, 121, 124, 149, 162, 201, 227, 271, 292, 314, 369, 371–372, 379–380, 388, 391–392, 396, 398–399, 410, 415, 417–418, 421, 428, 446, 457–464
Orange River Colony Volunteers (ORC Volunteers), see also Burgher corps & National Scouts, origins of, 169, 230–231; difference between various corps, 229–230; numbers, 281–282, 292; role in the war, 282, 291–292; motives of, 281, 297, 313, 322–351; leaders of, 322–351; attitude of post-war British civil administration towards, 366, 368, 371–377; and the N.G. Kerk, 415–417; reconciliation with Bitterenders, 418–419; and Afrikaner nationalism, 455, 457, 463; and land settlement, 383; compensation to, 336; post-war attitude towards bitterenders, 416
Orangia Unie, 460, 463–464
Orsmond, R., 350
Oshoek, 130
Otto, Mrs C., 194, 200, 237

Paardeberg, 24, 29, 41, 44, 122, 160–161, 276, 325, 329, 338, 346
Paardekraal (Free State), 143, 323
Paget, Major-general A.H., 93
Palapye, 80–81
Palmer, J., 128
Palmietfontein (Potchefstroom district), 345
Panstasie, 293
Papenfus, H.F.D., 25, 128
Park, Colonel (formerly Major) C.W., 288–289, 353
Parys, 39, 314, 417
Peace of Vereeniging, 227–228, 237, 351, 370, 391–393, 420, 446, 454
Peniche (Portugal), 77
Pennsylvania (USA), 212
Pentz, E., 242
Pepler, H., 462
Perseverance mine, 85
Petrusburg, 170
Philippolis, 20, 37–38, 53, 151
Phoenix mine, 79
Pickard, Commandant A.B., 278, 389
Pienaar, B.D., 101
Pienaar, Mrs B.D., 101
Pienaar, General F.J., 76–77
Pienaar, P.F. (Philip), 41, 123, 380
Piet Potgietersrus, 36
Piet Retief, 132, 418, 422
Pietersburg (now Polokwane), 22, 24, 36, 95–96, 184, 202, 278–280, 286, 287, 289, 350,

373, 396–397, 413, 418, 423, 450
Pietershoogte, 24
Pilcher, Lieutenant-colonel T.D., 242
Pilkington, Colonel, 376–377
Pistorius, W.P., 122
Plumer, Brigadier-general (formerly Lieutenant-colonel, later Field-marshal Lord) H.C.O., 96
Pohl, A., 36
Pole-Carew, Lieutenant-general R., 37–38, 76
Pontdrif, 78
Poore, Lieutenant-colonel R.M., 142, 152, 187, 196, 200, 206, 240, 267–268, 291
Poplar Grove, 25
Portugal, 77
Potchefstroom, 66, 85, 101, 122, 138, 269–270, 272, 279, 345–346, 348, 378, 419, 452, 457
Potchefstroom-Klerksdorp settlement, 384, 387–389
Potgieter, (a murdered burgher), 238
Potgieter, C., 125
Potgieter, F.C., 255
Potgieter, Commandant F.J. (Wolmaransstad), 285
Potgieter, P., 100
Potgietersrus, 349
Poutsma Dr J.H., 144–146
Preller, G.S. (Gustav), 207–208, 256, 311, 313, 349, 369, 410, 423, 450
Pretoria, 26–27, 32, 36, 40–41, 44, 65–66, 68, 83, 86, 88, 89–91, 93, 95–96, 98–100, 117, 121–124, 128–129, 132, 150, 161, 183, 189, 201–202, 206–207, 240, 248, 250–254, 267, 269, 278–280, 288, 295–296, 317, 324, 326–327, 347, 350, 365, 367, 371–377, 381, 383–385, 392, 399, 410–414, 419–429, 435, 449–452, 456–457
Pretoria News, 423, 425, 449
Pretorius, Captain, 341
Pretorius, J., 243
Pretorius, ex-president M.W., 137–139, 166, 416
Pretyman, Major-general G.T., 36, 43, 65, 70, 223–224, 446
Prinsloo, General Marthinus, 160, 326, 330–333, 342–343
Prisoner-of-war camps, 11, 70, 82, 86, 134, 163, 192; Cape Town, 65–66; Green Point, 159, 161, 193, 196–197, 460; Natal, 205; St Helena, 409
Proclamation Hill (Pretoria), 267
Protected areas, 232, 234, 353
Protected Burgher Fund, 394, 396, 400
Provisional Mounted Police, 221

Queen's Bays (2nd Dragoon Guards), 282
Quinlan, C., 127

Raaff (sheriff), 25
Rademan, J., 58
Rademeyer & De Beer (attorneys), 367
Ram, Captain J.H., 21
Rand Daily Mail, 413, 421, 458
Rattray, J., 184
Raubenheimer, I. van W., 60
Rawlinson, Colonel Sir (later Lord) Henry, 284–285
Rebellion (1914), 332, 465
Reddersburg, 37, 52
Reform Committee, 243
Reitz, (Free State), 146, 245, 341, 416
Reitz, ex-president (state secretary) F.W. (Francis), 52, 89, 99, 239, 244, 246
Reynders, J.D., 252
Rhodes Drift, 78
Rhodes, C.J. (Cecil), 59, 79, 161, 324
Rhodesia, 77–79, 349, 377, 414, 452
Rhodesian Field Force, 78
Richmond (Cape), 152
Richmond, A., 366
Ridley, Captain C., 226, 231
Rimington, Colonel M.F., 240
Roberts, Field-marshal Lord F.S., 27, 53, 75, 96, 119, 151, 333, 339, 347; march to Bloemfontein, 25, 38–39; march to Pretoria, 26; proclamation of, 28–34, 37–44, 51–52, 65–71, 80, 92–93, 163, 327, 331, 340–341, 391–392, 394–395, 398–400, 462; annexations of republics, 27, 35–38, 56, 75, 326, 346; inability to honor promises made to surrendered burghers, 55, 62–63, 69, 72; and refugees in Mozambique, 76–77; and concentration camps, 85–87, 127; view on sporadic peace initiatives, 89–91, 94–95, 98–99, 118, 143; scorched-earth policy, 86–89, 183–184, 211, 256, 300; opinion on British arming of surrendered burghers, 224, 226, 282, 328
Roberts, T.C., 195
Robertson, J., 75
Robertson, T., 75
Roets (a National Scout), 384
Rompel, Frederik, 41
Rood, Karel, 99, 100, 122, 124–125
Rooiwal (Transvaal), 53, 284–285, 288
Roos, Field-cornet S.J., 122
Roos, J.A., 192
Roos, P., 68
Roos, Willem, 246

Roossenekal, 131, 135, 425
Rooth, Edward, 68, 99
Ross, Commandant A., 54
Ross, Captain R.J., 59, 62, 83–84
Rousseau, Leon, 368, 410
Roux, D., 68, 101
Roux, Hennie, 84
Roux, Field-cornet P., 448
Rouxville, 53, 66, 72, 221, 226, 242
Roy, Major C., 283
Rumenyi River, 79
Rundle, Lieutenant-general Sir Leslie, 242
Rustenburg, 40, 43, 66, 131, 246, 269, 271–272, 313, 373, 397–398, 425, 430, 448, 458

Salisbury (Rhodesia), 78–79
Salisbury, Lord, 25
San's Post, 81
Sannaspos, 232, 326, 338–339
Scheepers, Barend, 59–60, 415
Scheepers, Strydom C.J., 348
Schikkerling, R.W., 293, 295, 299
Schoeman, General H.J. (Hendrik), 95–97, 100, 118, 325
Scholtz, Conrad, 141
Scholtz, Dr G.D., 13, 419, 424–425, 427–428, 437, 452
Scholtz, N.J., 196
Scholtz, Dr W.D., 91
Scholtz, Dr W.C., 90
Schutte, P.D., 366
Schweizer, C.A., 153, 418
Schweizer-Reneke, 418
Scots Guards, 37
Scott, Jan, 238, 388
Scott, William, 238
Scout Church, *see* National Scouts
Second War of Independence, 60
Secret Service, 189, 298
Selati railway line, 90
Selborne, Lord, 271, 369–370, 382, 387, 398, 401, 465
Senekal, 39, 91, 238, 281, 292, 337, 339, 341, 463, 464
Settle, Brigadier-general Sir H.H., 64
Sherman, General W.T. (USA), 212
Silkaatsnek, 54
Skeerpoort (Pretoria District), 427
Slegtkamp, Captain H.F. (Henri), 298
Slootkraal, 225
Smaldeel, 51, 233
Smit, J.S., 90–91, 99, 202
Smith, Mrs R., 200
Smitherman, Captain, 93

Smithfield, 38, 43, 53, 66, 84, 91, 149, 161
Smuts, General J.C. (Jan), 27, 34, 36, 38, 40, 54, 72, 95, 184–187, 190–191, 209, 239, 300, 313, 384, 447–448, 451–452, 466
Snyman, C. (peace emissary), 147
Snyman, Field-cornet C., 254
Solomon, V.E., 13, 168, 387–388, 413, 428
Somaliland, 377
South African Constabulary, 187, 226, 231–235, 252, 375, 377, 412, 461
South African Mounted Irregular Forces, 278
South African News, The, 117, 148, 153, 165, 190
South African War medals, 277
Soutpansberg, 78, 90, 202, 271, 348, 372, 450
Spaight, J.M., 30, 33, 228–229, 296, 312
Spain, Lieutenant, 79
Spies, S.B., 12, 69, 86, 138, 185
Spioenkop, 24
Spragge, Lieutenant-colonel B.E., 326
Sprigg, Sir Gordon, 154
Springfontein, 37
Springs, 282
St Helena, 90, 128, 161–162, 275, 409
Standard and Diggers' News, The, 97, 117
Standerton, 122–123, 128, 137, 210, 278–279, 294, 380, 384, 386, 411–412, 416, 423–424, 426, 429–432, 452
Star, The, 185, 205–208, 270, 372, 376, 385, 421, 451–452, 465
Stead, W.T., 184, 190
Steenekamp, J., 245, 246
Steenekamp, Commandant John, 430
Steenkamp, Commandant J.W., 270, 278, 417
Steinaecker, Major F.C.L., 132
Steinaecker's Horse, 132, 286–287
Stellenbosch, 460
Stent, Vere, 425
Steyn, (an ORC Volunteer), 292
Steyn, D.G., 122
Steyn, J.J., 466
Steyn, Mrs J.E.D. (née Steyn), 345
Steyn, President M.T., 25–26, 35, 37, 40, 51–52, 58–59, 82, 87–89, 99, 123, 145, 148, 151–153, 159, 161, 209–210, 212, 228, 233, 245, 272, 281, 314, 320, 324–325, 328–331, 336, 343–344, 347, 351, 412, 416, 451, 466–467
Steyn, Field-cornet P., 245
Steyn, W.J., 122–124, 127, 136, 392–393, 452, 467
Steytler, Revd J.A., 148, 156–157, 167, 353
Stormberg, 24, 226
Strassheim, Revd J.W.G., 458
Stuart, Major A.R., 160–162

Surrendered burghers, *see also* Burgher peace committees
use of the term, 11–13; origins of, 15–16, 19; numbers, 24, 38–40, 54–55, 62, 65, 81, 134, 164–165, 183, 186, 201, 205–208, 272; position of after Roberts's first proclamation, 33–34, 51; motives of, 41–44; recommandeering of by republican forces, 43, 52–59, 62; effect of annexations on, 55–56; treatment of by republican forces, 52–59, 237–238; oath of loyalty, 56; British treatment of republican forces, 61–72, 162–163, 234–235; cross republican borders, 73–81; and refugees in Mozambique, 75–77; and refugees in Rhodesia, 77–79; refugee camp (Bulawayo), 79; and refugees in Botswana, 80–81; British means to protect the, 81–87; accommodated in towns, 82–83; accomodated in camps, 65–66, 68, 83–87, 315–319; sporadic peace initiatives by, 87–101, 129, 139–142, 150–152, 166, 168–169; reasons for laying down arms, 183–192, 322; demoralising, 187, 209–210; food ratio in concentration camps, 192–193; work undertaken in concentration camps, 193; attitude towards women in camps, 194–196, 199–200, 246–247; escape from concentration camps, 196–197, 203–204; acted as camp police, 198–199; impact on war, 200–212, 221–222, 268–275; harassment by Boer patrols, 224; status at Peace of Vereeniging, 229, 351–354; as guides and scouts, 239–241, 248–249; representation on repatriation board, 376–381; compensation to, 389–401, 460, 462; dissatisfaction over compensation, 394–399; relation within Afrikaner ranks, 409; post-war attitude to and interaction with bitterenders, 410, 412, 416; and the *N.H. of G. Kerk*, 418–419, 422; and legislative council, 446–449; and post-war Afrikaner politics, 447, 449, 452–453; and Afrikaner nationalism, 454–463
Swaine, W.H., 130
Swanepoel (from Winburg), 101
Swanepoel (a National Scout from Christiana), 412–413
Swanepoel, D.J.S., 294
Swart, P.L., 320
Swaziland, 75, 132
Sybrandskraal, 93

Sykes, Major H., 85

Tancred, L.A., 71–72
Taute, Field-cornet P., 131
Thaba Nchu, 38, 292
Theron, Captain Danie, 56, 328
Theron, J.S., 128, 147
Theron, T.P., 152–156
Theunissen, Revd, 430
Theunissen, C.L., 269
Theunissen, J.P.D., 60
Thomson, Lieutenant L.W.J.K., 21
Thynne, A., 152
Tierkloofspruit (between Bethlehem and Harrismith), 248–249
Times History, 75, 136, 186, 210–211, 232, 241, 244, 247, 252–256, 267, 274, 287, 289, 296, 300, 312, 327, 351, 368, 370, 454
Times, The, 12, 249, 272–273, 277, 290–291, 296, 371, 381, 384–385, 415, 421, 454
Tomar (previously Thomar), 77
Town Guard, 226
Transvaal Constabulary, 95, 267
Transvaal Critic, The, 388, 394, 395, 449
Trichardt, Captain C.J., 293
Trichardt, J.L.K., 131–132, 467
Trollope (a National Scout), 319
Trollope, A.C., 197
Tromp (an ORC Volunteer), 292
Trompsburg, 38, 292
Tsietasnek, 74
Tucker, W.K., 193, 195–196, 198
Tuli, 78
Tweebosch, 284, 285, 288

Uganda, 80, 414
Umchabez Rivers, 79
Urmston, Lieutenant-colonel E.B., 288
Utrecht, 55, 123, 134, 314, 418
Uys, C.J., 74

Vaal River, 26, 31, 53, 346, 388
Vaalkop (near Arundel), 325
Vallentin, Captain J.M., 85, 92, 98, 226
Valley Forge (Pennsylvania, USA), 212
Van Aswegen, J.P., 91
Van Aswegen, P.J de Wet, 196
Van Biljon, J.A., 145
Van Dal, J., 349
Van den Berg, N., 202
Van den Heever, G.J.S., 238–239, 292, 410, 461
Van der Berg, Commandant, 147, 236
Van der Brugge, H.W.J., 367
Van der Heever, D.J., 255

Van der Lingen, Revd A.A., 87–88
Van der Merwe, A.A., 254
Van der Merwe, C.P., 330
Van der Walt, J.L., 252
Van Dijk, Mrs C.P.M., 246
Van Dijk, J.G., 164
Van Emmenis, Assistant Field-cornet S.A., 199
Van Everdingen, W., 342
Van Graan, G.J., 460
Van Heerden, H.A., 144–145
Van Heerden, J., 252–253
Van Helsdingen, J.G., 131–132
Van Leeuwen, Judge J.A., 88
Van Niekerk, D.J.H., 128, 153–154, 191–192
Van Niekerk, I.J., 188
Van Oudtshoorn (brothers), 413
Van Rensburg, A.P.J., 13, 371, 376, 379, 383, 389, 391, 394–398, 401, 412, 416–417, 446, 459–462
Van Rensburg, H.P.F.J., 122–123, 135, 137, 324, 326, 448
Van Rensburg, J., 413
Van Rensburg, J.F.J., 446
Van Rensburg, J.J., 460
Van Rensburg, J.J.J., 69
Van Rensburg, J.N., 22
Van Rensburg, N.J.J.J., 42
Van Rensburg, R., 417
Van Rooyen, Field-cornet Hans, 341, 344
Van Rooyen family, 319
Van Rooyen, J., 254
Van Schalkwyk, Ampie, 238
Van Schalkwyk, Field-cornet C.T., 237
Van Schoor, General M., 145, 327, 417, 420
Van Tonder, G.J., 128
Van Tondershoek, 137
Van Vuuren, Commandant P.A., 278
Van Vuuren, Commandant P.J.J., 278
Van Warmelo, Hansie, see Brandt, Johanna
Van Wyk, H., 147, 158
Van Wyk, J., 187
Van Wyk, Revd J.H., 158
Van Zyl, Field-cornet (later Commandant, then General) J.A., 347
Van Zyl, J.P., 128
Vandeleur, Captain C.B., 242–243
Ventersburg, 418
Ventersdorp, 426
Vereeniging, 185, 187, 196, 210–211, 250, 257, 279, 297, 300–301, 311, 351–352, 420, 422–428, 432–433, 456–457
Vereeniging Burgher corps, 249–250, 253
Vermaak, N.J., 460

Verschuur, J.A., 466
Victoria, British Queen, 37
Viljoen, Field-cornet A.J., 289
Viljoen, General (formerly Commandant) B.J. (Ben), 20, 61, 75, 91, 135, 138, 209, 294
Viljoen, Revd D.J., 416
Viljoen, H.S., 159, 162, 197, 323
Viljoen, General P.R. (Piet), 253, 282
Viljoen, Commandant W.J. (Wynand), 294, 450
Vilonel, Commandant S.G., 281–282, 292, 322, 337–345, 352, 371, 374, 376, 378, 392–393, 463–464
Vilonel, F.P.J., 337
Vinkfontein (Lindey district), 323
Visscher, J., 461, 463
Visser, C., 128
Vlakfontein, 232, 384
Vlaklaagte (Standerton district), 278, 280, 424, 432
Vlotman, J., 459–462
Volk, Het, 451–453, 457, 463–464
Volksblad, Die, 329
Volksraad, 16, 37, 42, 77, 117–119, 122, 136, 143, 162, 194, 202, 245, 323–324, 420
Volksraad members, 16, 25–26, 42, 68, 101, 128, 143, 147, 150–151, 159, 197, 222, 224, 227, 245, 314, 323, 324, 414, 452
Volksrust, 58, 123, 129, 134, 141, 193, 195, 198, 201, 270, 280, 367, 413, 423
Volksstem, De, 314
Vorster, B.J., 202
Vosloo, Commandant G.L., 278, 294, 381
Voss, J.H., 347, 392
Vrede (Free State), 20, 54, 147, 314, 398, 412, 416, 451, 462, 466
Vredefort, 39, 417
Vriend, De, 398, 416, 457, 459, 461, 463
Vryheid, 189, 422

Wahl, L., 388
Wakkerstroom, 134–135, 209
Walker (a British officer), 240
Walters, Captain, 242
Walton, Captain C., 187
Warmbaths, 452
Washington, George, 212
Wasserman, T.D., 233
Waterberg, 77, 164, 254, 314
Waterval, 210, 294
Wedgewood, J.C., 312
Weeber, E.J., 133, 296, 313, 315
Weeber, O.C., 122, 133
Wellington, 154, 157

Wepener, 53, 66, 149, 222, 380
Wessels, A.B. (Andries), 142–146
Wessels, A.S., 66
Wessels, General J.B., 245
Wessels, J.M., 446
Wessels, Tewie, 101
West Ridgeway, Sir J., 276, 371, 401, 463
Western, Colonel A., 56
White, Major F., 221
Wighley, Colonel C.M., 224–226
Williams, Lieutenant-colonel E.C., 242
Willis (from Vrede), 462
Wilson, H.F., 72, 227, 234, 314, 412
Winburg, 20, 68, 101, 128, 162, 222, 233, 237, 238, 282, 292, 343, 392, 398, 460
Witnek, 93
Wittebergen, 159

Wolhuter Revd J.P., 141, 418, 422
Wolmarans, A.D.W., 117
Wolmarans, J.B., 117–120, 134, 451–453
Wolmaransstad, 40, 60–61, 131, 285
Wood, Captain, 252, 377
Woodlands (Ladybrand district), 59
Woodroffe, Dr G.B., 194
Woolls-Sampson, Colonel (formerly Major) A., 243–244

Ysterspruit, 283–284

Zastron, 53
Zeederberg, Field-cornet P.F., 99, 124, 127
Zeerust, 66, 117, 123, 155, 426–427
Zoutpansberg Wachter, De, 54
Zuid-Afrikaan, De, 56